WAR,
PEACE, AND
INTERNATIONAL
POLITICS

WAR, PEACE, AND INTERNATIONAL POLITICS

Sixth Edition

David W. Ziegler

WESTERN WASHINGTON UNIVERSITY

HarperCollins*CollegePublishers*

Acquisitions Editor: Maria Hartwell
Project Editor: Cynthia Funkhouser
Design Supervisor: Mary Archondes
Cover Design: John Callahan
Text Art: FineLine
Production Manager/Assistant: Willie Lane/Sunaina Sehwani
Compositor: Circle Graphics, Inc.
Printer and Binder: R. R. Donnelley & Sons Company
Cover Printer: The Lehigh Press, Inc.

War, Peace, and International Politics, Sixth Edition

Copyright ©1993 by David Ziegler

Library of Congress Cataloging-in-Publication Data

Ziegler, David W.
    War, peace, and international politics / David W. Ziegler.—6th
ed.
        p.   cm.
    Includes bibliographical references and index.
    ISBN 0-673-52287-3
    1. International relations.   2. War (International law)   3. Peace.
I. Title.
JX1391.Z53   1993
327'.09'04—dc20   92-42865
                                                                        CIP

94 95 96 9 8 7 6 5 4

This book is for
my beloved wife Rena

אֵשֶׁת־חַיִל מִי יִמְצָא

CONTENTS

Preface   *xv*

INTRODUCTION   AMERICA IN THE WORLD   **1**
The United States in the World   1
The National Defense   2
The Economic Threat   3
Responses   5
Consequences of Decline   6
Reasons for Decline: Military Spending   8
Reasons for Decline: Economic Rivals   9
Global Thinking   10
Looking for Answers   12

PART I

SECURITY ISSUES   **15**

CHAPTER 1   WAR IN THE PAST   **17**
The German National Problem   18
Otto von Bismarck and the "Realistic" Analysis   20
The Use of War Against Denmark and Austria   22

The Decisive Role of Technology   24
The Use of War Against France   26
Bismarck as a Political Realist   28

CHAPTER 2   WORLD WAR I AND WORLD WAR II   31
War as "Total War"   32
Technology and the Outbreak of World War I   33
Other Causes of World War I   35
The Role of Technology in Warfare: Poison Gas,
Submarines   37
The Results of World War I: The Versailles Treaty   39
German Reaction to Versailles and the Rise of Hitler   41
Hitler's Foreign Policy and Western Appeasement   43
Escalation into Total War   46
The Role of Technology in Warfare: Airplanes, the Atomic
Bomb   47
The Results of World War II   48

CHAPTER 3   THE COLD WAR AND THE KOREAN WAR   53
Origins of the Cold War   53
Origins of the US–Soviet Rivalry: Iran   54
Turkey, Greece, and the Truman Doctrine   56
The Division of Europe and the Berlin Blockade   59
Bipolarity   60
Hot War in Korea   61
Causes of the Korean War   62
The Course of the Korean War   65
The Practice of Limited War   68
Why It Ended   69
Interpreting the Cold War   71

CHAPTER 4   WARS IN THE MIDDLE EAST   75
Zionism   75
Arab Nationalism   77
Issues Leading to War   79
The 1948 War   80
The 1956 War   80
The 1967 War   83
The 1973 War   85
Israel and Lebanon   88
The Palestinian Uprising   91

CHAPTER 5   RECENT WARS   **95**

Pakistan and the Bengalis   96
India's Preparation for War   99
War Between India and Pakistan   100
The Problem of Cyprus   101
Crisis in 1974: The Coup Against Makarios   103
War Between Turkey and Cyprus   104
The Iraq-Iran War   107
Outbreak of War   108
Initial Phase of the War   109
The Course of the War   110
The Tanker War   111
War Termination and Outcome   112

PART II

**THE THREAT OF WAR IN THE CONTEMPORARY
WORLD**   **115**

CHAPTER 6   THREATS TO PEACE   **117**

All-Out Nuclear War   117
Allies and Extended Deterrence   119
Regional Powers   121
Nuclear Proliferation   122
Low Intensity Conflict   124
Terrorism   125
Terrorism in International Politics   127
Gravity of the Threat   130

**CHAPTER 7   THE PRINCIPLES OF INTERNATIONAL
RELATIONS**   **135**

The Traditional State-Centric View   136
State and Nation   138
Sovereignty   139
Recognition   141
Non-State Actors   144
Implications of International Anarchy   146

CHAPTER 8   CAUSES OF WAR   **151**

Causal Explanation   151
Causation and War   153
Human Nature: Konrad Lorenz   153

"Troublemakers": Power Groups, Merchants of Death, Wicked
States   157
Critique of Troublemakers as the Cause of War   158
Nationalism: Mazzini   161

PART III

ARE ARMS NECESSARY FOR PEACE?   165

CHAPTER 9   ARMAMENTS   167
"If You Want Peace, Prepare for War"   168
Quantitative Arms Races: The Pre–World War I Race and
Worst-Case Estimation   170
Technological Arms Race   172
Arms Races as Action–Reaction   173
Other Sources of Arms Races   175
Arms Races and War   177
Costs and Hazards of Arms Races   178

CHAPTER 10   DISARMAMENT   183
Ways to Disarm   183
A History of Disarmament Agreements: From Rush–Bagot to
General and Complete Disarmament   188
Disarmament: INF and START   191
Obstacles to Disarmament: Inspection   193
Obstacles to Disarmament: Enforcement   195
Obstacles to Disarmament: Agreement   197
New Conditions, New Obstacles   199
The Evolution of Cooperation   201

CHAPTER 11   NUCLEAR WEAPONS   205
The Nature of Nuclear Weapons   205
The Difference That Nuclear Weapons Made   207
Deterrence   210
Minimum Deterrence   211
MAD and Its Critics   213
Finite Deterrence's Logical Extreme: Nuclear Winter   215
Damage Limitation's Logical Extreme: The Strategic Defense
Initiative   217
Nuclear Weapons After the Cold War   220

CHAPTER 12   ARMS CONTROL   223
Accidental and Unauthorized Attacks: The Hot Line,
Reconnaissance   225
Excessive Collateral Damage and Thresholds   230
War Termination and Cost Reduction   231
Difficulties with Arms Control   232
New Issues in Arms Control   234

PART IV

ALTERNATIVES TO ARMS   239

CHAPTER 13   WORLD GOVERNMENT   241
World Government Theory   241
Arguments in Favor of World Government   246
Advocates of World Government   248
Practical Details of the World State   249
Resistance to World Government   253
Consensus Versus Coercion   256
A World Police Force   257

CHAPTER 14   REGIONAL INTEGRATION   261
The Road to World Government: The Example
of Europe   262
The Europe of the Six   263
The Enlargement of the European Community   265
Project 1992   266
A Partial Success   269
Other Examples   269

CHAPTER 15   WORLD LAW   271
What Law Is   271
Examples of International Law   272
Sources of Law   276
Reasons for Observing Treaties   278
Difficulties with International Law   280
Two Revolutions and Their Effects   284
World Peace Through World Law?   286

CHAPTER 16   BALANCE OF POWER   289
The Balance of Power as International System   289
Rules of the Balance of Power   291

Balance of Power and the Control of International
Violence   293
A Return to the Balance of Power?   294
End of Bipolarity   295
The Balance of Power in the Contemporary World   296

CHAPTER 17   COLLECTIVE SECURITY   **301**
What Collective Security Is   301
The Advantages of Collective Security   302
An Attempt to Implement Collective Security: The League of
Nations   304
History of the League   306
Reasons for the Failure of the League   311
The Problems of Collective Security   312
Regional Collective Security   318

CHAPTER 18   DIPLOMACY   **325**
The Structure of Diplomacy   326
Modern Technology and Diplomacy   327
Duties of Diplomats   330
Diplomatic Procedure   333
The Value of Diplomacy   336
The New Diplomacy and Its Problems   339
Limitations of Diplomacy   342

CHAPTER 19   THIRD PARTIES   **345**
The Value of Third Parties   346
Mediation: Cyprus, Indochina, the Middle East   348
Arbitration: The Rann of Cutch, the *Alabama* Claims   351
Adjudication: The "Lobster War," the Corfu Channel   352
An Evaluation: El Chamizal, Spanish Sahara   356

CHAPTER 20   THE UNITED NATIONS   **361**
The United Nations System   361
The United Nations and Collective Security   363
The United Nations and the Korean War   364
The United Nations and Prevention of War   366
Contributions of the United Nations to Peace   370
A Revival of the United Nations   373
A Return to Collective Security?   375
United Nations Peace-Keeping Forces   377
Limitations of Peace-Keeping   380

CHAPTER 21   FUNCTIONALISM   **385**

Functionalism's Three-Pronged Attack   386
Robbers' Cave and Middle East Water   388
A Critique of Functionalism   389

PART V

ECONOMIC ISSUES   **397**

CHAPTER 22   TRADE AND TRADE WARS   **399**

New Economic Conditions   400
Outright Protectionism   402
Restrictive Practices   403
Balance on Protected Trade   405
Virtues   405
Solution: Protectionism?   409
The Case Against Protectionism   409
The Case for Protectionism   411
Solution: Negotiations?   412
Solution: Trade Blocs?   413
Puzzles of Trade   415
Outlook   416

CHAPTER 23   GLOBAL ISSUES   **421**

Population   422
Consequences of Population Growth   424
Food   426
Nonrenewable Resources   428
Environmental Pollution   431
Predicted Consequences for International Politics   435
An Evaluation   437

FINAL CONSIDERATIONS
THE UNITED STATES IN THE WORLD: THE FUTURE   **441**

The Persistence of Sovereignty   442
The World Is a Dangerous Place   443
American Institutions   444
American Policies   446
Conclusion   448

Index   451

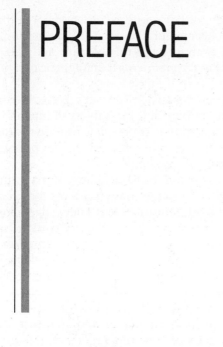

PREFACE

From its inception, this book attempted to provide not so much an encyclopedic collection of facts as to provide a coherent story. For coherence the book was constructed around a theme. In the first five editions the theme was war.

The sixth edition continues that coherence but broadens the theme. In the contemporary world people perceive threats to their well-being not only from war but from economic competition as well. Ross Perot appealed to this perception in a television advertisement in the 1992 campaign, declaring the red flag of communism had been replaced by the red flag of deficit. At another point he stated, "It's World War II in the Pacific all over again; nobody gets killed but armies of people lose their jobs."[1] The two themes are joined by the claim that America performs less well in international economic competition because it has invested so heavily in military competition. These issues are raised in Part I.

For many Americans, the fear of war has receded. Some, with memories of a century dominated by war or preparation for war, find this new attitude naive. They warn, "History will tell you we will not have a peaceful world. . . . "[2] To examine their claims, one must look at history to see what it does "tell" us. Part II examines representative wars from the past. Part III uses these cases to draw out lessons on the causes of war and the continuing threat of war.

Even those who believe we will not have a peaceful world agree that "America cannot afford to be the policeman of the world." In an examination of alternatives to war, Part IV examines the role of arms and Part V examines alternatives to arms, including components that might be part of a "new world order."

Issues of war and peace have been debated for decades. Issues of economics and environment are newer and are still the subject of much disagreement among politicians. The chapters in Part VI seek to introduce some main issues and major arguments on these topics. A final chapter presents some prescriptions for dealing with these problems.

The book is intended as an introduction to the field, a goal that influences its style as well as its contents. Although many students today are intellectually capable, they are often deficient in factual knowledge about major occurrences in the recent past and in the contemporary world. They are capable of grasping even difficult concepts but, as William James once wrote, "No one sees farther into a generalization than his own knowledge of details extends. . . . "[3] Therefore the book tries to provide as much background as is feasible in a limited space.

Most students enroll in international relations courses either to satisfy their curiosity about the world or to meet graduation requirements, not because they expect to become Secretary of State or a professor of international relations. Thus an emphasis on the lastest academic trends is irrelevant to their needs. Questions of methodology and sophisticated tools of analysis are at best of only passing interest. This book draws on recent research only where substantive results are of interest to the nonspecialist (for example, Robert Axelrod's work using game theory).

The book is written in simple and straightforward style. As John Allen Paulos declared in his book *Innumeracy*, "It is almost always possible to present an intellectually honest and engaging account of any field, using a minimum of technical apparatus. This is seldom done, however, since most priesthoods (mathematicians included) are inclined to hide behind a wall of mystery and to commune only with their fellow priests."[4]

I would like to thank people who were helpful to me in writing this book. Patrick Morgan of Washington State University provided me with a model of light style and solid content in his *Theories and Approaches to International Politics*. The following manuscript reviewers were most helpful: Vincent Ferraro, Mount Holyoke College; Joseph Georges, El Camino College; James S. Magee, Eastern Michigan University; Curtis G. Reithel, University of Wisconsin, La Crosse; and Kenneth A. Rodman, Colby College.

I am especially grateful to my wife Rena for the time and energy she took from her own professional life to read and comment on many drafts of the manuscript. I am fortunate to have an alert and intelligent reader without any background in the field of international relations who can tell me when I am being clear and when I am not. For whatever clarity this book may have, she deserves equal credit.

David W. Ziegler

NOTES

1. Cited by Maryann Keller, *Rude Awakening* (New York: Morrow, 1989), p. 186.

2. Sam F. Iacobellis, chief operating officer, Rockwell International, quoted by Louis Uchitelle, "Arms Makers: Rather Fight Than Switch," *The New York Times*, September 20, 1992, p. F6.

3. Gay Wilson Allen, *William James: A Biography* (New York: The Viking Press, 1967), p. 111.

4. New York: Hill & Wang, 1988, p. 80.

AMERICA
IN THE WORLD

In 1941 Henry Luce, the publisher of *Time* and *Life*, declared that the years to come would be the "American Century."[1] Yet before even half a century had passed, the dominant concern of the American people had become their decline. In 1990 fully 75 percent agreed with the statement that "the U.S. is in a state of decline compared with Japan, West Germany, and other leading Asian and European countries."[2] Public opinion polls showed that nine out of ten Americans were disturbed by economic trends; six out of ten viewed these trends with alarm.[3]

It is not surprising that the subject of decline produced a vigorous debate. Some argued that decline was serious; others argued that it existed mostly in the overheated imaginations of a few alarmists. Many people offered explanations; almost as many came forward with remedies. What is of interest to the student of international relations is that much of the debate revolved around the question of the place of the United States in the world. Many central issues in this debate are the issues that make up the core of international politics.

THE UNITED STATES IN THE WORLD

For years we have heard about the shrinking world. Our lives, we are told, are affected in many ways by what happens beyond our borders. Some people use the phrase "global village." Over the last decade even the major rivals in postwar international politics came to accept this view. For years China pursued a policy of economic self-sufficiency. Yet in 1984, Chinese Communist Party leader Deng Xiaoping, addressing the Party Central Committee, said, "no country can now develop by closing its door."[4] For decades the Soviet Union confined its economic activity to its own bloc of "socialist" countries, not participating in world economic organizations such as the World Bank or the International Monetary Fund. Yet in 1989 Soviet leader Mikhail Gorbachev, addressing the United Nations, said, "The world economy is becoming a single entity, outside which no state can develop normally, regardless of its social system or economic level."[5]

But if there is a "global village," it is a big place. The United States is one state among almost 200; the United States' population amounts to less than 5 percent of the total. The states vary widely in present standards of living and trends in growth. Those that are wealthy have made only small efforts to share their wealth; those that are growing rapidly have often done so because they have been successful in their economic competition with others.

The "global village" is not only a place of competition. It is also, in the minds of many, a dangerous place. In this century alone, wars have taken millions of lives and military preparations undertaken to prevent more wars have cost billions of dollars. The intense rivalry of the Cold War had barely died down when Iraq's aggression against its small neighbor Kuwait set off another war.

THE NATIONAL DEFENSE

States have traditionally been held responsible for the security of their inhabitants. In the seventeenth century the political philosopher John Locke held that people join in societies for "the mutual Preservation of their Lives, Liberties and Estates."[6] This concern with security entered into the American Constitution in the phrase in the preamble, "to provide for the Common Defense." Alexander Hamilton, arguing for the new Constitution in 1787 in Federalist Paper No. 23, declared that governmental powers for self-defense "ought to exist without limitation, because it is impossible to foresee or define the extent and variety of national exigencies. . . . The circumstances that endanger the safety of nations are infinite. . . . "

What Hamilton and others had in mind was protection against the threat of foreign invaders. In the eighteenth and early nineteenth centuries the threat was a real one. In 1814 British troops burned the White House. In 1817 Seminoles raided from the territory of Spanish Florida. Over the decades the threat of foreign invasion diminished as the American Republic grew stronger and concluded agreements with its neighbors. Still, defense against invasion is the underlying justification for the large American military establishment, including about two million armed forces personnel and $300 billion in costs in 1990.

Several developments during World War II added a new dimension to security. The long-range bomber and the rocket made attack possible from long distances. Nuclear weapons made even a few attacks potentially devastating. With the first Soviet test in 1949, nuclear weapons became a direct threat to the United States. At first the nuclear threat was seen as a more powerful version of the fears that had troubled Hamilton, a weapon in the hand of an enemy bent on conquest. But as the awesome power of the nuclear weapon was revealed in subsequent years, a second fear was added—fear of the weapons themselves. Merely engaging in a war, quite apart from winning or losing, was seen as a threat to security. Even the winner would suffer terrible casualties—from fallout or from environmental effects such as "nuclear winter." In subsequent decades people began to talk about a third threat to security, one coming from insurgents or guerrillas or terrorists. In a passage typical of the 1960s, one writer wrote:

> Two weapons today threaten freedom in our world. One—the 100-megaton hydrogen bomb—requires vast resources of technology, effort, and money. It is an ultimate weapon of civilized and scientific man. The other—a nail and a piece of wood buried in a rice paddy—is deceptively simple, the weapon of a peasant.[7]

Today one encounters similar rhetoric about terrorists.

THE ECONOMIC THREAT

States are held responsible for more than security. Their citizens want to do more than survive. They want to prosper as well. The United States Constitution adds, after calling for "the Common Defense," as its next purpose to "promote the general welfare."

Throughout history states always pursued both goals. Recently, as the military threat has diminished, the importance of prospering economically has increased. The change was acknowledged in populist political style by Senator Ernest F. Hollings of South Carolina: "Last year, we won the cold war. This year, we won the Gulf War. Now it is time to win the war that really matters for America's future: the trade war—the no-holds-barred struggle among nations for market share and standard of living in a largely zero-sum world marketplace."[8]

The economic threat to which Senator Hollings was referring was two-fold: the deterioration of the American economy and the simultaneous rise of powerful rivals. For many analysts, the deterioration began in the year 1973. In that year the Organization of Petroleum Exporting Countries (OPEC) raised oil prices fourfold, and since that year economic life for average

Americans has not improved. Median family income was $30,820 in 1973 and (allowing for inflation) a virtually unchanged $30,853 in 1987.[9] Even that figure is somewhat deceptive, because family income stayed the same only because more members of families worked. Individual earnings actually have gone down. Adjusted for inflation, in 1970 the average weekly wage was $186.94, in 1980, $172.74, in 1989, $166.52.[10]

Confronted with evidence of economic adversity in their daily lives, people began casting about for explanations. One plausible explanation was the growth of foreign competition. A decade ago the Office of the US Trade Representative documented a shift in the US economy. Using figures from January 1979 through June 1982, they found the results shown in Table I.1.

In other words, in the traditional major industries of America, employment was going down as imports increased. Many people saw a connection. American workers were losing jobs because American consumers preferred goods made elsewhere.

Some people recommended that the United States erect tariff barriers to make foreign goods more expensive. Such a political remedy would not have solved the fundamental economic problem—that American goods were not economically competitive. Furthermore, legislation might keep Americans buying American goods but it could not change the behavior of foreign consumers. Tariffs might make Americans buy Fords and Chevrolets instead of Toyotas and Hondas, but the United States could not impose the same limitation of choice on Thais or Brazilians. The basic issue was expressed in a report from the MIT Commission on Industrial Productivity: "Certain American industries that once dominated world commerce—automobiles and steel come immediately to mind—have lost much of their market share both at home and abroad; in a few industries, such as consumer electronics, the American presence in the market has all but disappeared."[11]

A cautious reader might begin to raise questions at this point. Someone is always raising an alarm, even in the best of times. In 1958, in what now is portrayed as the middle of the "Golden Age," Drew Pearson and Jack

Table I.1   EMPLOYMENT LOSSES AND IMPORT GAINS IN MAJOR AMERICAN INDUSTRIES, JANUARY 1979–JUNE 1982

Industry	Employment	Imports (in constant $)
automobiles/trucks	− 34.2%	+ 9.4%
steel	− 29.6%	+ 25.5%
apparel	− 23.3%	+ 26.4%
footwear	− 23.9%	+ 22.0%

Source: Executive Office of the President, Twenty-Sixth Annual Report of the President of the United States on the Trade Agreements Program, 1981–1982, transmitted to Congress November 1982, Table 7, p. 25.

Anderson published a book titled *U.S.A.—Second Class Power!*[12] Furthermore, a skeptic might point out, statistics are often distorted for political ends. The political party out of office always wants to make the party in office look bad. Democrats, excluded from the White House since 1980, are happy to emphasize unfavorable statistics on the economy. Republicans, as might be expected, cite other statistics that show economic conditions are not so bad.

RESPONSES

Debate on decline examined such issues as trade statistics, manufacturing performance, and education achievement. Those who argued that America was in decline pointed to a continuing imbalance in trade, as American manufacturers sold less abroad than Americans were importing. They pointed to the loss of competitiveness not only in "mature" industries such as automobiles but also in newer industries such as electronics. They pointed to low test scores by American students, particularly in mathematics, compared with students in other countries.

In response, one group of analysts argued that these facts, although true, were not necessarily relevant. The trade balance, they argued, was improving. In certain industries, such as biotechnology, America remained competitive. And test scores unfairly compared the elite of many nations with the average American.[13]

Another group acknowledged that there was a decline, but argued that it was temporary, a result of policies followed by the Reagan Administration. Prominent Democrats were among this group—Senator Daniel Patrick Moynihan of New York and Joseph Nye, an academic who had worked for the Carter Administration.[14] These analysts argued that if only other policies were followed, the decline would be reversed.

But there were others who believed that America's decline was serious. They argued that if anything the economic challenge was not being taken seriously enough. Although some members of Congress referred to economic threats, the perception was not widespread. Much more trivial threats, such as taking hostages, loomed larger in public perceptions because of the nature of the news media. One is more likely to be struck by lightning than die from terrorism, yet some Americans spoke of terrorism as a major threat. On the other hand, the economic challenge posed by rival economies was not given much attention because it does not produce "action news." The media bias toward action was illustrated by the war in the Persian Gulf. Saddam Hussein rose to power in Iraq unnoticed by the major news media. Yet when war broke out television gave the fighting saturation coverage.

Two other factors have kept economic decline from being seen as a major threat. The effects are not felt immediately. Economic leads slip slowly, but American firms continue to sell products. Businesses lay off, but in small batches. In some industries, such as automobile manufacturing, long-time workers are protected by guaranteed annual incomes, so the economic effect is less obvious. The ones affected are young people who will not be hired, but there is less pain in not getting a job in the first place than in being fired. Americans can continue to consume by borrowing and by selling off assets. As those who have gone deeply into personal debt can tell you, at first one hardly notices. It is only over time that the consequences are brought home.

Another factor is that America's main economic rivals, the Japanese, have discovered that they can deflect criticism by calling critics "Japan-bashers." The label works like a magic incantation. Serious analysis is transformed into an emotional tempest. In the most heated debate, critics of Japan are met not with arguments but with accusations of "racism."

In addition, the issue of economic competitiveness is muddied by partisan politics. Democrats tried to use the issue to force Republican administrations into a defensive position. Understandably, Republicans have responded with truculence unjustified by the facts. President Bush told Congress on March 6, 1991, that the recent war in the Persian Gulf proved that America was not falling behind:

> We hear so often about our young people in turmoil, how our children fall short, how our schools fail us, how American products and American workers are second class. Well, don't you believe it. The America we saw in Desert Storm was first class talent. And they did it using America's state-of-the-art technology. We saw the excellence embodied in the Patriot missile and the patriots who made it work.[15]

Bush's statement may have been good politics but it was poor analysis. The Scud missile against which the Patriot missile was targeted was a very early, very primitive missile, dating from the 1950s. Postwar analysis suggested that the Patriot was not as effective as originally thought—and may in fact have increased the amount of damage suffered by the Israeli and Saudi Arabian targets it was supposed to defend. Perhaps most significant was the fact that when the Patriot missile entered development (in the early 1970s), the United States had more than 70 percent of the world's consumer electronics market. By the time Bush gave his speech in 1991, the US share had fallen to 13 percent.[16] One might argue that dominance of over two-thirds of the world's electronics market was not necessary for American prosperity, but a decline to only 13 percent was cause for concern, particularly because it was not clear that the decline would stop at 13 percent.

CONSEQUENCES OF DECLINE

Assume for a minute that economic decline is a problem. One consequence is that the longer it goes on, the harder it is to reverse. Greater indebtedness requires greater sacrifice to end it. People pointed out, for example, that a slowing economy was creating difficulties in financing major research projects. A project for research into basic physics, the "Superconducting Supercollider," was estimated to cost $8 billion; a follow-on project planned for the 1990s was estimated to cost $60 billion. Defenders of such projects argued that they were necessary to produce the fundamental knowledge on which future prosperity depends. Critics did not oppose the expansion of knowledge but argued that funds were scarce and must be more carefully apportioned.

Because they are doing so well, Japanese computer and electronics companies can open laboratories in the United States to do basic research and can hire the best American computer scientists to work for them. The results of their research will benefit Japanese firms, not American ones, making the Japanese even more competitive.[17]

Another consequence of decline is its effect on America's world role. Henry Kissinger, writing in 1968 just before he became President Nixon's national security adviser, worried that a legacy of Vietnam would be a reluctance to risk overseas involvements.[18] It was almost a quarter of a century later that the Persian Gulf War of 1991 put the legacy of Vietnam behind. But by this time the issue was no longer reluctance to act but ability. By the end of the 1980s the United States found itself unable to afford overseas involvement. The United States was unable to offer economic aid to Poland, Czechoslovakia, Panama, Nicaragua—in short, to all the countries whose hearts and minds had finally been won and who had converted to democracy. Even the triumphant Gulf War had been subsidized by allies.

One of the great triumphs of American policy was the Marshall Plan. Under this program the United States gave large amounts of money to the states of Western Europe to help them recover from the devastation of World War II. The program produced quick results and has been held up as a model ever since. The actual Marshall Plan cost $6.05 billion in its first year, 16.5 percent of the total federal budget for that year. Marshall Plan aid, a mixture of generosity and self-interest, was possible because of American economic strength. In 1947, the year the Marshall Plan was conceived, the United States ran a budget surplus of $6.6 billion, 17 percent of total outlays; a comparable surplus in 1989 would have been over $180 billion.

A little more than forty years after Secretary of State Marshall made his original proposal, the states of Eastern Europe broke free of Soviet control. Years of communist domination had devastated their economies, and there were calls for a new Marshall Plan. For the United States an equivalent percentage of its budget would have been $140 billion. Yet instead of the budget surplus of 1947, the United States was grappling with a budget deficit that led to freezes on spending. The United States was not financially capable of helping, even if it had wanted to. In the words of Senator Daniel Patrick

Moynihan, "At the moment in foreign policy we've waited for and worked toward for half a century, we're broke."[19]

REASONS FOR DECLINE: MILITARY SPENDING

The core of the argument is that the American economy is doing less well than it had been and less well than foreign competitors. But even those who agreed on this point found different explanations.

Some people focussed on defense spending. They argued that the pursuit of the goal of security stood in the way of achieving the goal of economic prosperity. The deterioration of the United States' economic position under President Reagan was accompanied by extensive overseas military commitments. A report by the Comptroller General of the United States in 1988 found that the United States had treaties with, or political commitments to, 60 countries. On any given day, according to this report, one-third of US armed forces personnel were outside the United States. Those deployments cost $30 billion a year and took up 10 percent of the defense budget.[20] A Defense Department study found that of the military budget for fiscal year 1985, 58 percent went to defend other members of NATO.[21]

Military spending as a percentage of gross national product is referred to as "the defense burden." In 1986, the defense burden for Japan was 1.0 percent, for West Germany, 3.1 percent; both these countries were doing well in international trade. For the United States, which was running a deficit, the defense burden was 6.7 percent.[22]

Although the effect of military spending on economic performance has not been extensively studied, several economists have advanced the argument that defense spending reduces economic competitiveness. In 1986 three British economists found that the more a country spent on military research, the less competitive it was. (See Table I.2. Competitiveness was measured using a standard economic index, comparing industrial output with domestic absorption. If a country scores 100, it consumes all it produces; if it scores below 100, it has net exports; if it scores above 100, it has net imports.) The two leading exporting countries, Japan and Germany, spent one-tenth of a percent or less of their gross domestic product* for military research. Two countries with chronic problems in world trade, Britain and the United States, devoted around seven times as much to military research.

---

*A measure similar to gross national product preferred by British economists. GDP includes only income generated within a country. GNP adds (or subtracts) earnings (or losses) overseas. Thus a Japanese-owned automobile plant in Ohio would add to the U.S. GNP but subtract from the GDP.

Table I.2   COMPETITIVENESS COMPARED WITH R & D
EXPENDITURES, 1982

	Competitiveness Indicator	Military R & D as % of GDP
Britain	94.3	0.68
United States	99.7	0.72
France	100.2	0.38
Sweden	117.2	0.24
West Germany	128.9	0.11
Japan	138.3	0.01 [1980]

Source: Mary Kaldor, Margaret Sharp, and William Walker, "Industrial Competitiveness and Britain's Defence," *Lloyds Bank Review*, No. 162 (October 1986), p. 32.

Several years later an American economist calculated that each percentage point of gross national product devoted to military spending reduced economic growth by one-half of a percentage point. With the United States at that time devoting 6 percent of GNP to military and Japan only 1 percent, one would expect the Japanese economy to grow at a rate three percentage points higher than the American, which was in fact the case. He argued that this distribution of domestic spending was more important in explaining economic performance than a state's trade policy, its industrial policy, or its national character.[23]

A long-time opponent of military spending, Seymour Melman, pointed out that much more investment went to military purposes in the United States than in the economies of its two big rivals. The ratio of civilian to military capital formation was 100:40 for the United States, but 100:13 for West Germany and 100:3 for Japan. Melman further pointed out that 25 to 30 percent of American engineers and scientists work in military enterprises. With so much money and talent going to the military, he argued, it was not surprising that commercial enterprises did less well.[24]

Even President Kennedy's secretary of defense, Robert McNamara, who held office during a surge of military spending greater than the Reagan buildup, argued before the Senate Budget Committee in 1989 that the United States needed to direct spending from military to economic. Although disagreeing with the implication that the United States is in decline, he agreed that "our position in the world is adversely affected by economic weakness."[25]

REASONS FOR DECLINE: ECONOMIC RIVALS

But while some people were focussing on military spending, others were focussed on rival states. The argument was that other countries don't play fair. Japan was a special target, because the trade deficit with Japan was so high and because of highly publicized Japanese moves. Among other things, the Japanese were accused of pirating American inventions. One of the basic components of the modern electronics industry is a semiconductor designed by Jack S. Kilby in 1958 and patented in the United States by Texas Instruments in 1964. Texas Instruments applied for patent in Japan on its original semiconductor on February 6, 1960. A patent was granted by Japanese Patent Office on October 30, 1989. By this time Japanese chip makers were selling 90 percent of the computer chips bought in Japan and 80 percent of those bought in the United States.[26]

Another charge was that Japan is fiercely protective of its agriculture. Despite the fact that the Japanese consumer must pay 2½ times as much as Americans for rice, the Japanese barred all American imports, even threatening Americans at a trade fair with arrest for exhibiting 10 pounds of American rice.[27]

Japan was not the only country accused of unfair practices. The gradually integrating European Community was also becoming a rival. In the name of preserving "cultural sovereignty," European countries required that a certain percentage of their television programming be produced in Europe, thereby limiting American access to an important market. (In 1988, the United States sold $630 million worth of television programming to Europe, and the market was growing). In Germany, a country with a big trade surplus, toy manufacturers tried to scare customers away from an American self-service toy supermarket with a public relations campaign suggesting that only with the services of a *Fachmann* (expert) could German parents be certain of not buying a toy that would injure their children.[28] In the end the Americans prevailed only because the parent company in the United States was willing to commit hundreds of millions of dollars until the venture succeeded.

GLOBAL THINKING

There is another set of opinions that merits attention. Some people argue that the question is misstated. The very use of terms such as "US decline" and "national competitiveness" is in this view outmoded or "vestigial thinking."

One of the arguments for decline is the trade imbalance. But critics point out that statistics on international trade have become almost meaningless. Corporations are no longer national but global, and their activities take place anywhere in the world that they can make a profit. In 1989 the Honda Accord became the best-selling car in America. Because the Honda is a Japanese car, one might cite this as further evidence of American decline. But is it? Many Hondas are assembled in the United States in a plant in Marysville, Ohio. The workers in the plant are American. Many of their suppliers are American. Several models of the Honda are exported to Taiwan, South Korea, and even Japan itself. In 1991 Honda introduced a station wagon that was in part designed and wholly engineered and tested in America. According to the company, three-quarters of the components of the station wagon came from the United States. At what point does the car cease being Japanese and become American?

A cogent statement of this view is one by Robert B. Reich in *The Work of Nations*.[29] He argues that the globalization of the economy makes these concepts outdated. He acknowledges that there are indeed winners and losers in the changing world economy and that American income really has declined, but for Reich the remedy lies elsewhere than in pure national competitiveness.

Finally, there are those who think that present military and economic problems are less significant than more fundamental global problems. Mikhail Gorbachev articulated this view in a speech to the United Nations, on December 7, 1988:

> . . . the revolution in science and technology has turned economic, food, energy, ecological, information and demographic problems, which only recently were of national or regional character, into global problems. . . . [5]

The list is familiar. The coolants used in refrigerators and the propellants used in hair spray eventually find their way into the stratosphere, depleting the layer of ozone that shields the surface of the earth from the harmful ultraviolet rays of the sun. If too much of the ozone is depleted, the increase in ultraviolet radiation could possibly kill photoplankton, the tiny organisms that live on the surface of the ocean and provide the basis for the food chain for everything else.

The use of wood in cooking fires and gasoline in cars could put so much carbon dioxide into the atmosphere that it would act like a giant greenhouse window, raising the temperature of the earth's surface and creating deserts where farmlands now exist or raising the oceans and flooding coastal cities.

As population continues to grow, the ability of the earth to support life is threatened. Unsettled areas, once called "wastelands," are now seen to have important functions as reservoirs that purify the air, cleanse the water, help dispose of waste, and provide biological diversity. As these areas come to be inhabited, they narrow the margin of safety needed to cope with disasters. Population pressure on the land in Bangladesh is already so great that people settle silt islands barely above sea level, leading to catastrophic loss of life during storms. Population pressure in Haiti has already led to almost complete deforestation and consequent erosion of topsoil; after heavy rains, bulldozers are needed to clear the streets of the capital of mud. Bangladesh and Haiti suggest that unchecked population growth may in the long run be a greater threat than military aggressors or economic competition.

LOOKING FOR ANSWERS

The debate on American decline involves many fields—economics, business and management, education and testing. But some parts of it are of direct interest to students of international politics.

If military spending is a drag on the economy, then one should look carefully at the need for it. Is the world such a dangerous place that countries must cripple their economies to maintain military establishments? Indeed, does the United States or any country in today's world need any forces at all? Exactly what are the dangers that justify military spending?

Even assuming there are dangers to security, are there alternatives to military spending? Must conflicts always be resolved by military means, or is the peaceful resolution of conflict possible? Instead of arms, could we rely on international law or international organizations?

On the other hand, if the root of the problem is that other countries have become economic aggressors, then the danger has shifted from the military to the economic sphere. Having recognized an economic threat, we must analyze it with the same attention that has been applied to the military threat. We must examine alternative policies for dealing with the issue of prosperity. Are protective measures such as tariffs the best solution? Or do countries that have succeeded in world trade provide examples that we should imitate?

Finally, while looking at the traditional problems of military security and economic prosperity, we should be aware that the world is changing. We must consider whether the newly recognized global problems such as depletion of the ozone layer and global warming may be supplanting the older issues of security and prosperity as the greatest threats of all.

NOTES

1. "The American Century," *Life*, February 11, 1941, pp. 61–65.
2. Louis Harris, "Bush Isn't a Shoo-In for '92," *The New York Times*, May 23, 1990, p. Z A17.
3. Ibid.
4. Statement to Third Plenary Session of the 12th Central Committee of the Chinese Communist Party, October 20, 1984. See "Decision of the Central Committee," *Beijing Review*, Vol. 27, No. 44 (October 29, 1984), p. XIII.
5. Speech delivered before the United Nations General Assembly, December 7, 1988, text from Novosti Press Agency, in *Vital Speeches of the Day*, February 1, 1989, p. 229.
6. *Second Treatise of Government*, Chapter IX.
7. T. N. Greene, "Introduction," *The Guerrilla—and How to Fight Him: Selections from the Marine Corps Gazette* (New York: Frederick A. Praeger, 1962), p. v.
8. Ernest F. Hollings, "No More Uncle Sucker," [Op-Ed], *The New York Times*, March 26, 1991, p. Z A15.
9. *The Economist*, July 7, 1990, p. 34.
10. William E. Schmidt, "Hard Work Can't Stop Hard Times," *The New York Times*, November 25, 1990, p. Y1.

11. Michael L. Dertouzos et al., *Made in America* (Cambridge, Mass.: MIT Press, 1989), p. 1.

12. New York: Simon & Schuster, 1958.

13. See, for example, Samuel P. Huntington, "The U.S.—Decline or Renewal?" *Foreign Policy*, Vol. 67, No. 2 (Winter 1988/89), pp. 76–96.

14. Daniel Patrick Moynihan, "Debunking the Myth of Decline," *The New York Times Magazine*, June 19, 1988, pp. 34, 52, 53; Joseph Nye, *Bound to Lead* (New York: Basic Books, 1990).

15. Quoted by Martin Walker, "Dateline Washington: Victory and Delusion," *Foreign Policy*, No. 83 (Summer 1991), p. 161.

16. Ibid., pp. 161–162.

17. Gina Kolata, "Japanese Labs in U.S. Luring America's Computer Experts," *The New York Times*, November 11, 1990, pp. Y1, Y15.

18. Kissinger quotes his own essay in *White House Years* (Boston: Little, Brown, 1979), p. 66.

19. Quoted by Susan F. Rasky, "The Operative Word in America: Deficit," *The New York Times*, August 5, 1990, p. E5.

20. Report by Comptroller General of the United States, Charles A. Bowsher, head of the General Accounting Office, November 21, 1988, cited in Robert Pear, "Reagan Is Leaving Many Costly Domestic Problems, the G.A.O. Tells Bush," *The New York Times*, November 22, 1988, p. Y10.

21. "United States Expenditures in Support of NATO," cited by Richard Halloran, "Two Studies Say Defense of Western Europe Is Biggest U.S. Military Cost," *The New York Times*, July 20, 1984, p. Y4.

22. Figures from *The Economist*, January 17, 1987, p. 40, calculated from International Institute for Strategic Studies and NATO sources.

23. Joshua S. Goldstein, "How Military Might Robs an Economy," *The New York Times*, October 16, 1988, p. F3.

24. Seymour Melman, "What to Do with the Cold War Money," *The New York Times*, December 17, 1989, p. F3.

25. U.S. Senate Committee on the Budget. *After the Thaw: National Security Objectives in the Post–Cold War Era*. Hearing, December 12, 1989, p. 8.

26. Thomas C. Hayes, "U.S. Chip Gets Patent in Japan," *The New York Times*, November 22, 1989, p. Z C1.

27. David E. Sanger, "Japan Shuts U.S. Rice Exhibition," *The New York Times*, March 18, 1991, p. Z C1.

28. Ferdinand Protzman, "Greetings from Fortress Germany," *The New York Times*, August 18, 1991, p. F1.

29. New York: Alfred A. Knopf, 1991.

PART I

SECURITY ISSUES

CHAPTER 1

WAR IN THE PAST

If military spending impairs a state's economic performance, states' leaders should consider carefully how many resources to devote to defense. A major component of that consideration is an evaluation of how dangerous a place the world is.

Historically there have been two schools of thought on the risk of war in international relations. One school believes in an underlying harmony in human relations. According to this view, violence in general, and war in particular, is abnormal. Deep down, it is believed, people don't want to fight. Wars result from accidents, misunderstandings, and other failures that can be corrected.

Adherents to this school are called "idealists." Sometimes their views are the result of carefully thought out arguments. More often they are merely unexamined assumptions. Idealist assumptions appear to have guided the British Prime Minister Neville Chamberlain in the 1930s when he confronted an increasingly aggressive Germany under Adolf Hitler. Chamberlain told a foreign diplomat that "if only we could sit down at a table with the Germans and run through all their complaints and claims with a pencil, this would greatly relieve all tension."[1] Idealist assumptions also seem to have underlain much of President Jimmy Carter's policy. Carter's secretary of state reported that his boss seemed to feel that "if only he could just sit down with the Soviet leadership, he could break through the political, cultural and ideological differences," that "common ground could be found."[2]

The views of idealists are usually contrasted with those of another school, known as "realists," who see war as an inextricable part of the world of international politics. The fundamental premise of realism appears in the ancient Greek historian Thucydides, in words he attributed to a representative of the most powerful Greek city-state, Athens: "You know as well as we do that right, as the world goes, is only in questions between equals in power, while the strong do what they can and the weak suffer what they must."[3]

The realist view on war was given classic expression at the beginning of the nineteenth century by a Prussian military writer, Carl von Clausewitz. "The fact that slaughter is a horrifying spectacle," he wrote, "must make us take war more seriously, but not provide an excuse for gradually blunting our swords in the name of humanity. Sooner or later someone will come along with a sharp sword and hack off our arms."[4]

Both idealists and realists have been making their claims for a long time, and representatives of both schools can be found in contemporary international politics. To help you begin to make some sense of these competing claims, we will look at some historical cases of war.

The first of these wars, the wars of German unification, were widely taken as confirming the realist views of Clausewitz. War, Clausewitz wrote, is "a true political instrument, a continuation of political activity by other means."[5] Half a century after Clausewitz wrote these words the chancellor of Prussia, Otto von Bismarck, was putting them into practice.

Bismarck was pursuing the goal of German unification under Prussian leadership. On three occasions between 1864 and 1870, Prussia resorted to war to achieve this goal. The reason for going to war in those days was self-evident: War enabled a state to get what it wanted. You might say that wars were viewed no differently from the way we view superhighways. Both are used to obtain something desirable. Wars take a toll in human lives; superhighways do the same. We could save lives by abolishing superhighways, but then we would have to do without the benefits that superhighways bring. Wars are the same. To see why wars were viewed as useful instruments of policy, we must turn to historical circumstances in the second half of the nineteenth century.

THE GERMAN NATIONAL PROBLEM

The Europe of 1848 was different in many ways from the Europe of today. Among the countries active in international politics, only England and France were much as we know them now (see Figure 1.1). Russia was much larger, including at that time parts of the lands that are today Finland, Poland, Rumania, and Turkey. Austria was also much larger, including parts of what are today Italy, Yugoslavia, Hungary, and Czechoslovakia. On the other hand, Italy and Germany were not single states at all, but were divided

Figure 1.1   Europe in 1848

into much smaller units. The area called Germany was more like a miniature United Nations—a confederation of thirty-eight states held together in a very loose organization. Some of these thirty-eight states were tiny, no larger than a typical county in the United States; others were good-sized countries, such as Prussia and Austria. The constitution of the German Confederation required unanimity of all thirty-eight states on important matters, guaranteeing only that most of the time it did nothing.

Events in Europe in the nineteenth century had encouraged many Germans to think of creating a single state in which all Germans could be combined. This was the meaning of their national hymn, *Deutschland, Deutschland über alles.* The words seem threatening when translated into English as "Germany, Germany over all," but to those who heard it in the nineteenth century it meant they should put aside their parochial feelings as Bavarians or Saxons or Prussians and think of themselves as Germans above all. There were several reasons for this growth of national feeling. Throughout Europe the idea of nationalism was winning acceptance. More and more people accepted it as right that those who spoke the same language and shared the same customs belonged together in the same state. The example of the Italians, who had developed this feeling some years earlier, was a big influence on the Germans. German nationalism also grew because of the belief that only when the many small German states were united would they be able to keep other countries from pushing them around, both dictating policy to them and using their territory as a battlefield. Napoleon had had an easy time taking over Germany in 1806, running into real trouble only when he reached Russia. The obvious power of a unified French or Russian national state was not lost on the Germans.

If agreement was growing on the need for a German state, disagreement continued on how to go about achieving it. Part of the argument was on leadership—would it be Prussian or Austrian? Prussia had a reputation for being militaristic and rigid. Many smaller German states supported Austrian leadership because they expected that under Austria more local rights would be respected. On the other hand, some Germans (as well as some outsiders such as the English) favored Prussian leadership because they saw that only Prussian leadership would be dynamic enough to fashion a state strong enough to balance the French. But Prussia's conservative leaders were not sure they wanted to lead a national movement. Today we associate nationalism with right-wing conservatives, but in the nineteenth century things were reversed. German nationalists usually were liberals who believed in constitutional government, guaranteed civil liberties, and participation by citizens in government decisions. Prussian conservatives viewed with suspicion a movement that would have given more power to the masses even if it would have increased the size of the Prussian state. They also believed that the conservative principle of monarchic solidarity called for their cooperation with the monarchy of Austria, even if Austria was Prussia's major rival for German leadership.[6]

German liberal nationalists assembled in the city of Frankfurt in 1848 and drew up a petition asking for a new unified German state with the king of Prussia as its head. The king rejected the offer. As a conservative he could not accept an initiative from the people. He said he didn't want a crown offered from the gutter. With the failure of this attempt, the liberals were at a loss as to what to do next and the movement toward German unification under their leadership died out.

OTTO VON BISMARCK AND THE "REALISTIC" ANALYSIS

Bismarck was no liberal. He had been active in 1848 but had spent his time heaping scorn on the liberal efforts. It was because he had a reputation as an outspoken conservative that the king of Prussia named him chancellor in 1862. The king had been trying to get the Prussian Parliament to approve funds for building a bigger army, and the Parliament was trying to return to get some voice in governmental decisions. Bismarck, on becoming chancellor, broke the deadlock by simply instituting the changes in the army and collecting the taxes without parliamentary approval. Before he took this direct approach, he appeared before the Parliament's budget committee and tried to distract the liberal deputies with the prospect of using the enlarged army for foreign conquest. His words, although they failed at that time to win over the liberals, indicate his own philosophy: "It is not by speeches and resolutions that the great questions of the time are decided . . . but by iron and blood."

Bismarck was unquestionably conservative in his aims. It would be more accurate to call him a patriot than a nationalist. He came from a class of aristocrats known as Junkers, and like them his loyalty was to the state and its ruling dynasty, not to German culture. He did want to build up the power of the Prussian state, but not in order to unite all German-speaking people. He wanted only to increase Prussia's security.

But in his choice of methods Bismarck was not doctrinaire. "I am still a Junker," he said, "but I recognize realities." One reality in the 1860s was that, increasingly, a monarch needed popular support. The mid-nineteenth century was a period of growth for the German states, in both population and economics. To cite just one statistic: In 1846 Germany had 1,416 steam engines; in 1861, 10,113. The growth of the economy was accompanied by an increase in the number of groups that crossed the political boundaries of the individual German states. Lawyers, schoolteachers, and booksellers held conventions of their members representing many states, and these conventions increased national sentiment. National festivals, emphasizing German history and culture were held by choral societies, hunting societies, and gymnastic societies. This feeling was so advanced in 1861 that an assassin tried to kill the king of Prussia for not doing enough to bring about German unity. Even though he did not share it, Bismarck recognized that this national sentiment was a source of power and could be used to achieve a unified state.

Bismarck also realized that Austria was the major obstacle to German unification. The problem was that the Austrian monarch ruled many non-German lands—Hungary, Czechoslovakia, and Italy, among others—and could not create a strongly centralized state. For one thing, a German unified state would never be able to agree on a common language. A state in which the Hungarians could be happy would not satisfy the aspirations of the German Nationalists; a state that would satisfy them would drive out the Hungarians. Furthermore, Austria was the only other major power in the German Confederation. A new German state could be shaped and dominated by Prussia only if Austria were excluded. Therefore Bismarck was willing to violate a cardinal principle of Prussian conservatives: solidarity with Austria. His willingness to utilize German nationalism, even though he did not share it, and to forsake conservative solidarity with Austria are the basis for what is called Bismarck's "realism." Feelings and even principles were put aside if they got in the way of achieving a major state goal.

Bismarck's speech to the budget committee of the Prussian Parliament, using the phrase "iron and blood" to describe military power, hinted at another element in his realism: his willingness to make use of the army that Prussia was building up. He believed, as Clausewitz had written, that war is an instrument of state policy. But he saw war as only one of several instruments. He also made use of diplomacy, winning over allies, making promises, trading concessions, and using all the other devices he could think of. It would be accurate to say that Bismarck did not want war if he could achieve his aims without it. But that is no better than saying, as you hold up the corner store with your pistol, "I don't want to use this pistol." The important question is: What if the goal cannot be achieved in any other way? For Bismarck, the answer was that using force was preferable to going without achieving his goal.

THE USE OF WAR AGAINST DENMARK AND AUSTRIA

Historians say that Bismarck fought three wars to achieve his aim. This statement suggests a lot more calculation and planning than he actually engaged in. In each case, war was a continuation of a policy already being pursued by other means. War was chosen because the other means were not working and because an opportunity presented itself in which military force could be useful.

The first of these wars was fought with Denmark in 1864 over the duchies of Schleswig and Holstein (see Figure 1.2). These two duchies, although ruled personally by the Danish king, were not constitutionally a part of Denmark. Complex arrangements such as that were frequent in the nineteenth century. Because large numbers of Germans lived in Holstein and Schleswig, separation of the duchies from Denmark was a passionate issue for German nationalists. Bismarck wanted them separated too, but not, like the liberal nationalists, to be turned into more tiny German states. He wanted to incorporate them into Prussia. They would enlarge Prussia, of course, but more important to Bismarck's long-range plans, they could be used as an issue to separate Austria from political cooperation with the other German states.

Bismarck's chance came when the king of Denmark died without a direct heir and the question arose: Will Schleswig and Holstein go to the new Danish king along with the rest of Denmark, or is another rule available with a better claim to rule these two states? The German nationalists thought there was, in the person of the prince of Augustenburg. Bismarck was willing

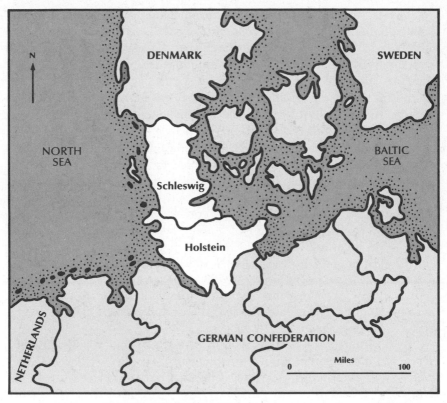

Figure 1.2   Schleswig and Holstein in 1863

,to use the issue as an excuse to go to war, although he had no intention of letting the prince of Augustenburg ever rule the duchies as an independent state. The new Danish king made matters easier for Bismarck by not only claiming the duchies but also annexing the northern one (Schleswig) to the Danish state, a clear violation of an international treaty. Bismarck used this treaty violation as his reason for going to war. By clever diplomacy he got Austria to join with Prussia alone, making the war a joint Austro-Prussian undertaking rather than one of the whole German Confederation. This was his first move in detaching Austria from the other German states. The small states might have followed Austria, as they would not have followed Prussia, but Austria offered no lead. The war was over quickly, the two big German states being more than a match for little Denmark, and after the war Bismarck's diplomatic moves succeeded again. First he got the Austrians to agree to joint sovereignty over the two duchies, instead of turning them into an independent state. Then he got the Austrians to agree to separate administrations for them, with Prussia taking Schleswig and Austria taking Holstein.

All this, we can see now, was designed to maneuver Austria into a more isolated position. But it would be a mistake to believe that Bismarck had a carefully worked out plan for going to war with Austria. War was only one of several possibilities. If he could have accomplished his aims by diplomacy alone he undoubtedly would have done so. The agreement dividing the administration of the duchies merely provided a rich source of friction between the two countries that could be exploited if the occasion arose.

The moment came two years later, but only after Bismarck's diplomacy had isolated Austria internationally. The major European powers he had to worry about were Russia, England, and France. Prussia had won Russia to its side because of a common concern over Polish nationalism, which threatened both states. Prussia had the support of Britain because the British saw Prussia as a potential balance to an enemy they feared more, France. Yet Prussia also had the support of France, both because the French ruler was eager to do anything that would help the Italian nationalists struggling against Austria and because Bismarck hinted to the French ruler that an Austrian defeat just might be followed by some territorial expansion for the French somewhere along the Rhine. Austria made Bismarck's job easier. Because it considered itself militarily superior to Prussia it did not assiduously search for allies.

By the military standards of the time, Austria's smugness was justified. Yet we call the war that Prussia fought against Austria in 1866 the Seven Weeks' War because it took Prussia only that long to defeat Austria. The startling Prussian victory was made possible by a factor that has loomed increasingly large in every war since then—modern industrial technology. In addition to showing the use of war as an instrument of policy, Bismarck's wars marked the entrance of that technology as a decisive factor in international politics. The development that led to the atomic bomb and the intercontinental missile had its beginnings here.

THE DECISIVE ROLE OF TECHNOLOGY

Three major technological developments contributed to the Prussian victory. The most important one may surprise you. It was not some new type of cannon or explosive, but the railroad. This was so important to the Prussian army that the general staff had a special Railway Subsection. The railroad was important in two ways. It made possible rapid mobilization of troops from reserve status to front-line units. Soldiers who were to be used in combat did not have to be kept in a perpetual combat-ready status in fortifications along the frontier. They could be held in reserve at home, even while working at civilian occupations. When war was declared, the railroads could transport them and their equipment rapidly to the front. The railroad also enabled the Prussians, who lacked overall superiority in numbers, to achieve superiority in the one spot where it counted, the battlefield. Rapid transportation meant that the Prussian general staff could achieve the condition that wins battles—concentrated firepower—without leaving other areas of their frontier long exposed to the numerically superior but much slower-moving enemy.

Closely linked to the railroad was a second technological innovation, the telegraph. It enabled mobilization orders to go out rapidly. It enabled the Railway Subsection to control trains. Most important, it enabled one general to control a much larger army than had been possible in the past. Pictures of Napoleon at Waterloo or Lee at Gettysburg show how it used to be done: a general sitting on a horse on high ground, overseeing the entire battlefield. When more men were engaged than could easily be seen from one spot, battles got out of control (as both Napoleon and Lee discovered). The telegraph expanded the commander's control of his troops so much that the Prussian commander, Helmut von Moltke, was able to direct the entire Prussian campaign without leaving Berlin, yet with firmer control over military operations than Napoleon or Lee could have hoped for. The railroad gave the advantage to the smaller Prussian army. The telegraph had the potential, in future wars, of making it advantageous to use much larger armies than ever before.

The third technological innovation was a new kind of rifle, loaded not from the muzzle but from the back. An obvious advantage was that it took less time to feed a shell into the breech of a rifle than it did to ram powder and lead balls down the muzzle. Another was that it enabled Prussian soldiers to fire repeatedly while lying flat. Commanders could concentrate firepower by placing soldiers very close to each other, some standing, some crouching, and some lying flat.[7]

Prussia won the war in seven weeks. As a result, Austria gave up its membership in the German Confederation and its influence among the small German states. Prussia incorporated a few of the small German states, although by no means all. The remaining ones in the northern part of Germany were brought together in a North German Confederation. Unlike the old German Confederation it replaced, no absolute veto was granted to each state. Rather, voting was weighted, with Prussia getting the clear advantage.

Almost as important as what Prussia did after its victory was what it did not do. After defeating the Austrian army at the decisive battle of Sadowa, the Prussian army did not pursue the Austrian army across the Danube River. It did not hold a victory parade through the streets of Vienna, although the king of Prussia would have been happy to get back at Austria in this way for past humiliations. (The principle of conservative solidarity seems to have been forgotten in the heady experience of victory.) Prussia did not annex portions of Austria near its own borders, even though some justification could have been made for incorporation. This policy of restraint was achieved by some effort on Bismarck's part, against the desires of the king and some of his advisers. Bismarck realized, as the king did not, that the work of German unification was not yet completed, and a humiliated and bitter Austria would be a potential ally for the country that now stood in Prussia's way, France.

THE USE OF WAR AGAINST FRANCE

France opposed a takeover of the remaining south German states (those not incorporated into the North German Confederation), and Bismarck saw that only if French power were somehow nullified would German unification be possible. For four years he tried to eliminate French influence and in 1870 he finally had his chance. Mainly because of the erratic policies of its ruler, Napoleon III, France was diplomatically isolated. The French populace, well aware of growing Prussian military and economic strength, was eager to go to war to demonstrate that they were still "number one" in power on the continent. By the simple device of editing a telegram to make a normal diplomatic interview look like an insulting one, Bismarck provoked the French into declaring war on Germany.

The Franco-Prussian War, which began in 1870, consisted of six weeks of fighting, followed by six months of chaos. The German army won so startling a victory that there was no French government left to surrender. Again the new technology was decisive. Two weeks after war was declared, the Germans, by using their railroads, had mobilized and sent to the front 1,180,000 troops. The French in this time had mobilized only 330,000.

The Franco-Prussian War revealed another lesson of modern technology: It was not the mere possession of advanced weapons that was decisive, but the practiced ability to use them and the knowledge to use them well. The French lost the war although they had two weapons superior to those of the Germans. The French version of the breech-loading rifle (the chassepot) was twice as efficient as the German one (the needle-gun), but the French were not as well instructed in using their weapons. Furthermore, the French used a weapon the Germans did not even have, the machine gun. But they used it poorly; they treated machine guns like artillery pieces and deployed them singly in the midst of infantry. The Germans simply concentrated their artillery on a machine gun until it was destroyed, then advanced. Only in World War I did the French learn to group machine guns so that each could defend the others.

Eventually the Germans found someone with whom they could make peace and a peace agreement was signed. But this time Bismarck was not able to exercise the restraint over the king and army that he had after the war with Austria. The euphoria of victory was too much. A new German Empire was proclaimed, which was certainly justifiable, but the site chosen for the proclamation was not. It was not in Germany, as you might expect, but in France, in the palace of the most magnificent of the French kings, the Versailles Palace of Louis XIV. (The French did not forget this humiliation. The Germans had to sign the treaty acknowledging their defeat in 1919 in the Palace of Versailles.) On top of this the Germans held a victory parade through the streets of Paris. The French had to pay an indemnity to Germany of 6 billion French francs, to cover the cost of the war. All these were one-time occurrences that were soon over (although not entirely forgotten). But the Germans went on to create a permanent source of resentment by annexing French territory.

The Germans annexed the French provinces of Alsace and Lorraine (see Figure 1.3). They had some justification for annexing Alsace: Most of its people could speak German; it had belonged to German kings before 1648.

Figure 1.3   Alsace, Lorraine, and the Saar

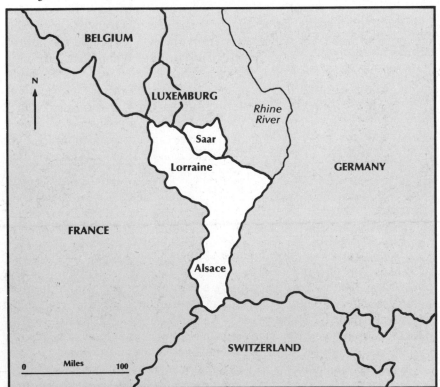

In the case of Lorraine, Germany had no nationalist justification. The people spoke French and wanted to remain part of France. But Lorraine had a major iron and steel industry, as well as some major forts. The Germans annexed it for the contribution it would make to German military strength. Bismarck did successfully oppose some of the more extreme demands the Prussian army made, so that French fortifications were not dismantled and the strength of the French army was not restricted. But what was done was enough. The slogan of the French politicians, contemplating their day of revenge, was, "Never speak of it, always think of it." In 1914, when the fighting began between Germany and France, one of the first gestures of an enthusiastic French population was to remove the mourning crepe that had decked the statue of Lorraine in Paris.

BISMARCK AS A POLITICAL REALIST

Bismarck is a controversial figure for historians, especially for his role in internal German developments. But even among his critics the characteristics of his foreign policy are often held up for admiration. One of these was his ability to keep war limited to achieving specific political goals. Clausewitz, in one of his formulations, wrote that "war is an act of violence to compel an opponent to fulfill our will." Wars are not fought to extend a country's winning streak but to accomplish some purpose. When that purpose is achieved, the war stops. Prussia's war with Austria was not fought to dismantle the Austrian Empire or to gain Austrian territory but simply to exclude Austrian influence from German affairs. The war with Austria lasted only seven weeks because that was long enough to achieve that limited purpose. All three wars were fought to achieve German unification, and once that was accomplished, in 1871, Bismarck engaged in no more wars. Prussia did not embark on a program of conquest, as Napoleon had done earlier and Hitler was to do later. To use modern terminology, Bismarck had a plan for "war termination." Unlike the Japanese after their brilliant tactical victory at Pearl Harbor, he had plans for the war beyond the action on the opening day. War was a coherent part of his policy, not a rash or desperate act.[8]

Bismarck is also admired for his diplomatic flexibility. He recognized the need to prepare diplomatically for any use of force. He was careful to isolate potential opponents before beginning a war. He was also careful to avoid treating a defeated country as a permanent enemy. Austria was treated generously after the Seven Weeks' War, not out of benevolence on Bismarck's part but to encourage Austria to remain neutral in what he already saw would be the coming struggle between France and Prussia.

In choosing allies Bismarck was not motivated by principle or sentiment but by the interest of the state. At one time he refused to side with France in supporting Italian nationalists in the state of Sardinia. Such a refusal might have been expected of him, because he was a conservative and conservatives were hostile to nationalism, but Bismarck's explanation was, "I do not go with France and Sardinia—not because I hold it to be morally wrong, but because I consider it harmful to the interest of our security."[9] This overriding concern with the interests of the state, and particularly with interests defined in terms of power, was the essence of his realism. Realists are usually contrasted with idealists. For the realists the power of armies, railroads, and heavy industry is decisive; the idealists base their policy on ideals and principles, whether monarchic solidarity or democratic nationalism. The success of Bismarck's policies converted many people to realism.

The accomplishments of Bismarck in achieving German unification were not unnoticed by the other states of Europe. The three wars that led to unification provided a number of obvious lessons, which other states dutifully learned and applied to their own policies. As time passed, it turned out that these lessons were wrong, but that did not make them less influential.

First was the lesson that Clausewitz was right, that war is a useful instrument of policy. Bismarck, with his policy of iron and blood, had accomplished what the liberals with their petitions and assemblies had not. To be sure, the wars were destructive, as you see in Table 1.1. Large numbers of soldiers died (although the number was lower if you were on the winning side). But wars were not disruptive because they were so rapid. That was another lesson of these wars. The fighting was measured in mere weeks. Too long a war, people feared, would disrupt the industrial economies of the countries fighting them. This was seen as a barrier to any drawn-out war. Among the demands imposed by war was that armies depended on reservists who had to be drawn away from their civilian jobs for the duration of the war. If they were gone too long industrial strength would decline, and industrial strength was seen as the basis for military prowess. That was the third lesson. The German military victory had depended on the German railroad network, the German steel industry, and all the other advances of the new industrial technology. Technology was considered decisive; not only the possession of modern weapons such as breech-

Table 1.1 BATTLE DEATHS IN WARS FOR GERMAN UNIFICATION

Wars	Total Battle Deaths	Prussian Battle Deaths
War with Denmark, 1864	4,500	1,000
War with Austria, 1866	36,100	10,000
War with France, 1870–71	187,500	40,000

Source: Data from J. David Singer and Melvin Small, *The Wages of War, 1816–1965* (New York: John Wiley, 1972), pp. 62–63.

loading rifles but practice in using them and careful planning long in advance were necessary.

The years following the wars of Bismarck were peaceful ones for Europe. Some wars did occur, but only on the fringes—the Boer War in South Africa, the wars in the Balkans. In the meantime, the military staffs were busily applying the lessons of the Bismarck wars, acquiring new weapons, training soldiers in their use, drawing up detailed mobilization schedules, all in an effort to be among the winners and not the losers of the next rapid war.

NOTES

1. Williamson Murray, *The Change in the European Balance of Power, 1938–1939* (Princeton: Princeton University Press, 1984), p. 58.

2. Cyrus Vance, *Hard Choices* (New York: Simon & Schuster, 1983), p. 138.

3. *The Peloponnesian War*, Book XVII.

4. *On War*, Book IV, Chapter 11, edited and translated by Michael Howard and Peter Paret (Princeton: Princeton University Press, 1976), p. 260.

5. Ibid., Book I, Chapter 1, Part 24 (p. 87).

6. There are a number of standard works on Bismarck and the creation of modern Germany. A very readable one is by Hajo Holborn, *A History of Modern Germany, 1840–1945* (New York: Alfred A. Knopf, 1969).

7. Bernard Brodie and Fawn Brodie, *From Crossbow to H-Bomb* (Bloomington, Ind.: Indiana University Press, 1973), Chapter 6; Richard A. Preston, Sydney F. Wise, and Herman O. Werner, *Men in Arms* (New York: Frederick A. Praeger, 1962), Chapter 15.

8. A general discussion of this problem, although without specific reference to Bismarck, is Fred Charles Iklé, *Every War Must End* (New York: Columbia University Press, 1971).

9. Otto Pflanze, *Bismarck and the Development of Germany* (Princeton: Princeton University Press, 1963), p. 134.

CHAPTER 2

WORLD WAR I AND WORLD WAR II

For the forty years following the wars of Bismarck, the military staffs of all the major European countries based their planning on three lessons learned in those wars. Wars are an inexpensive means of attaining foreign policy goals. Because they are short, they do not disrupt economic and political life back home. The side that strikes first with the latest weapons will win. World War I showed that all these lessons were wrong.

The war that began in August 1914 was a great shock. It came after four decades when major European countries had not been at war with each other; it followed more than a century of no wars at all in the heartland of Europe involving all the major countries. It also cruelly violated the assumption that war was a useful instrument of policy. In the first full month of war, the French demonstrated that they had learned the lessons of rapid mobilization by putting 1,300,000 troops into combat. From that number they suffered in August 1914 alone 600,000 casualties (casualties are troops no longer capable of fighting because they are dead, seriously wounded, captured by the enemy, or missing). On one day alone, July 1, 1916, the British attacked with 140,000 troops and suffered 60,000 casualties. On another occasion it cost the French 160,000 casualties to gain 7,000 yards. At Paschendaele it cost the British 370,000 casualties for no gain at all.

People tend to form their beliefs about social and political conditions on the basis of very little evidence. This was the case in the years before 1914. The peace that Europe had enjoyed in the decades before World War I was not seen as the result of luck (the chance combination of a number of favorable circumstances) but as proof of theories about society. We might call the two most popular views the Myth of Socialist Solidarity and the Myth of Capitalist Solidarity. The socialists, all good followers of Karl Marx, took seriously Marx's statement that "the workingmen have no country."[1] They believed that a German worker, exploited as he was by the German ruling class, would have more sympathy for a French worker than for a German capitalist. Many leaders of the various nationalist parties of socialists believed that a war on a world scale was not possible because the workers would simply refuse to fight. A declaration of war by governments would be met by a declaration of a general strike by socialists, making war impossible. You couldn't run a war without foot soldiers, any more than you could run a factory without workers. The actual outbreak of war quickly shattered this myth—French socialists and German socialists marched off to war against each other, each singing their socialist songs, each convinced that victory by their country would hasten world socialism.

Paralleling the Myth of Socialist Solidarity was the Myth of Capitalist Solidarity, articulated by British writer Norman Angell in his international best seller *The Great Illusion*. Angell argued, convincing millions of readers, that war was not profitable and in fact was harmful to capitalism. Far from making greater profits in time of war, capitalists did much better in peacetime. War interrupted access to international markets and sources of raw materials. A war that lasted any length of time, Angell believed, would destroy the capitalist system. Therefore, there could be no great war—it would be irrational.

WAR AS "TOTAL WAR"

It quickly became apparent that the war that began in August 1914 was not going to be another of the quick, decisive wars of the late nineteenth century. As months passed and no decisive victories were achieved, more and more men were conscripted into the armies. More and more resources were devoted to war production. Civilians far from the front were affected as much as the soldiers by such things as food rationing, mobilization into munitions production, and (later in the war) air raids from dirigibles. The German economy was put under a central direction so pervasive that it was called "war socialism." A German first used the name for this new experience: "total war."

Before all this became apparent, many people in all countries welcomed the coming of the war. Crowds gathered in Paris to cheer the reservists marching off to their units. Germans gathered in a square and sang, "Now Thank We All Our God." A British poet wrote, "Now God be thanked Who has matched us with His hour."[2] The myth of the short, decisive war was even more entrenched than those about Socialist Solidarity or Capitalist Solidarity. Yet it was held on the basis of equally flimsy evidence. True, the three wars Prussia had fought for German unification had been short and decisive. But there had been other wars that did not conform to this model; as with many pieces of evidence that do not fit a hypothesis, they were ignored. The American Civil War (1861–1865) was long and destructive, although in the end decisive. The British began fighting the Dutch settlers (Boers) in South Africa in 1899 and found it difficult to inflict a decisive defeat on them despite Britain's clear industrial superiority. The Russians and Japanese fought each other in 1904 and 1905. Although the decisive engagements took place at sea, the land warfare was a war for position rather than one of movement, dominated by trenches and barbed wire and other features that would become familiar during World War I.

When military observers brought back reports of these wars, their assessments were dismissed with the argument that the experience did not apply to Europe.[3] The planners went ahead trying to create the conditions that would have led to a perfect victory in the wars of the nineteenth century. The problem was that when both sides were prepared, with rapid mobilization using railroads, central direction using the telegraph, and concentrated firepower using breech-loading rifles, neither could win a decisive, sudden victory. The Germans with their Schlieffen Plan intended to pour into France toward the north along the English Channel; the French with their Plan 17 prepared to pour into Germany toward the south near the Swiss Alps. If both plans had succeeded the armies would have passed each other as in a revolving door. In fact, both plans failed, mostly because of a further technological development that nullified the great advantage the offensive side had enjoyed in the Prussian wars. That development was the machine gun, a model improved over the one used unsuccessfully by the French in the Franco-Prussian War and, more important, now correctly deployed. The bold assaults of the French, and to a lesser extent of the Germans, ground to a bloody halt against the concentrated firepower of this new piece of technology. In this transformation in the first weeks of World War I from a war of movement to one of position we see a lesson that was not to be proved false by future wars: Political leaders and military planners cannot fully comprehend the new technology with which they must work. The one consistent winner of modern warfare has been technology; the consistent loser has been humanity.

TECHNOLOGY AND THE OUTBREAK OF WORLD WAR I

Technology, you could argue, was even responsible for the war in the first place. The typical explanation of World War I begins with the assassination of Archduke Franz Ferdinand in Sarajevo on June 28, 1914. But how did this event result in the German invasion of France on August 3, 1914? The connection is not at all obvious and needs to be carefully traced. Archduke Franz Ferdinand was heir to the throne of the Austrian Empire. It was widely believed that when his aging uncle, Emperor Franz Josef, died it would be difficult to keep the diverse nationalities of the empire together. Germans in Austria, Czechs in Bohemia, Magyars in Hungary, Serbs in Bosnia—each would want their own state. The problem in Bosnia, where Franz Ferdinand was visiting when he was shot, was acute because its inhabitants made up only about half of the Serb nation; the rest were in the neighboring independent state of Serbia. To make matters worse, Archduke Franz Ferdinand was visiting the Bosnian capital of Sarajevo on June 28, a day of national importance to the Serbs, commemorating a national defeat centuries before. Sending the archduke to visit on this day was like having the Prince of Wales visit Dublin on Easter Sunday. It is not surprising that young Serb nationalists, with weapons acquired from a semiofficial Serbian organization, sneaked across the border and assassinated him.

The Austrians were aware that this was part of the Serbian nationalist attack on their control of Bosnia and on July 23, 1914, sent an ultimatum to Serbia, demanding that that country curb nationalist agitation for the liberation of the Serbs in Bosnia. An ultimatum is a demand for some kind of behavior coupled with a threat that will be implemented after a set time has elapsed if the demand is not met. Despite a basically conciliatory reply by Serbia, when the time ran out Austria chose to declare war on Serbia. The Serbs had been issued a similar ultimatum in 1909 and had complied fully with it then, but in 1914 they were less willing to be totally subservient because they were receiving more support from Russia. Russia, in the name of Slavic solidarity, encouraged the Serbs to stand up to the Austrians and, to back them up, on July 29 ordered mobilization of the Russian army, which would be held in readiness for possible use against Austria. The Russian tsar showed some hesitation, at first agreeing to mobilization and then canceling it, but the next day (July 30) Russian mobilization went into effect. It was this act that brought in the Germans.

German preparation for war followed the Schlieffen Plan, which rested on several assumptions. One was that any major war in Europe would be for the Germans a two-front war, against Russia in the east and against France (allied to Russia) in the west. Another assumption was that the huge Russian army would be impossible to defeat; the most the Germans could hope to do would be to keep the Russian army from defeating them. The one advantage that the Germans had, the Schlieffen Plan assumed, was technological superiority, particularly the ability to mobilize quickly. They assumed they could mobilize in two weeks; the Russians, with more territory and a less-developed railway network, would need six weeks. Therefore, the Schlieffen Plan called for a major offensive first against France, to knock it out of the war, before turning the German army to the more difficult task of fighting the Russian army. For this reason, the Russian mobilization was greeted with alarm in Berlin. If the Schlieffen Plan were to work (and for all practical purposes it was the only plan the Germans had), then it was essential that the Germans begin mobilizing as soon as the Russians did. Otherwise they would lose the advantage afforded them by their superior technology. Never mind that the Russian mobilization was directed against Austria. The crucial factor, in German eyes, was mobilization.

Thus when the Germans in their turn delivered an ultimatum to Russia on July 31, demanding that they demobilize, it was not so much in defense of Austria as in defense of their own strategic situation. When Russia declined to demobilize, the Germans mobilized. The French, realizing what was coming, did so too. On August 1, Germany declared war on Russia; on August 3, Germany declared war on France. The advance of troops began two weeks later; the first battle of the war was fought within three weeks of its declaration.

The connecting thread, from the assassination in Sarajevo to the German attack on France, was military planning. Yet no one thought anything was wrong with military planning. Because wars were expected to be swift, planning in advance was believed necessary. There would be no time to improvise once war had been declared. Once the best conceivable plan was devised, preparation and practice were geared to it. That war broke out over an event that had not been foreseen, over an issue indirectly related to the major countries fighting, was not important. Each state had expected war to come sooner or later and had prepared for it. Preparations in one country had only increased the suspicions of neighboring countries, leading them to preparation of their own. In such a climate of mutual distrust, a minor incident like the assassination of Franz Ferdinand could trigger a war.

OTHER CAUSES OF WORLD WAR I

No one can deny how important military planning and military preparation were in the outbreak of World War I.[4] Yet scholars have identified other causes as well. The literature on the causes of the war is enormous, with many authors of books and articles working as hard to attack the theories of others as to advance their own. The war is a rich hunting ground for those looking for evidence to prove some theory. Probably the all-time best seller on the causes of World War I is *Imperialism*, by V.I. Lenin.[5] He argued that the capitalist system in general and the leading capitalist countries in particular were responsible for the war. The essence of capitalism, wrote Lenin (drawing on Karl Marx), is constant expansion. Profits must be reinvested to produce more profits or the system collapses. The collapse of capitalism had not come about as rapidly as Marx had predicted, Lenin wrote, because the capitalist countries had found a new outlet for their surplus capital in investments overseas. This newest form of capitalism, in which banks rather than manufacturers took a leading role, Lenin called "imperialism." At first it worked, giving capitalism a respite, but by 1914 all the unclaimed areas of the world had been divided into colonies or spheres of influence. The countries that were left out, particularly Germany (which had no colonies to speak of), wanted to see the world redivided for their benefit. As Lenin put it, the war was to decide whether "the British or German group of financial marauders was to receive the lion's share."[6]

Lenin, who was writing at the time of the war, blamed the whole system as it then existed. But many writers at that time picked out particular states and attributed the war to them. A typical book from the early days of the war is by James Beck, an American political figure, *The Evidence in the Case in the Supreme Court of Civilization as to the Moral Responsibility for the War*, published in 1914.[7] As we would expect of a man who wanted the United States to enter the war on the side of the British, Beck found that Germany and Austria were guilty of starting the war. He accused them "in a time of profound peace" of secretly conspiring "to impose their will upon Europe in a matter affecting the balance of power."[8] Beck believed Austria was guilty of going to war with Serbia, thereby threatening the Russians in the Balkans, and Germany was guilty of not stopping Austria. England, France, Italy, and Russia, on the other hand, were all sincerely working for peace. The crucial event of Russian mobilization, Beck argued, was no justification for Germany's declaration of war because it was *legal*. A sovereign state, Beck declared, has the right to mobilize so long as its troops do not cross the border.

This extremely legalistic view, which dominated much of the writing about the war while it was being fought and in the years immediately following, provoked a reaction among academic historians in the 1920s. Because they were trying to revise the standard view of World War I— Germany crossed the frontier first, therefore Germany was guilty—they called themselves Revisionists. Most prominent among them was Sidney B. Fay, whose book *The Origins of the World War*, published in 1928, was the monument of this school.[9] Fay's primary point was that all the major powers were more or less responsible, but because no one was deliberately working to bring about a general European war, none was guilty.[10] But after making this claim, Fay went on to apportion some blame anyhow. France and Italy were accused of being at least pleased that war did break out because it gave them the chance to acquire territory. That the French territory (Alsace and Lorraine) had been seized by Germany in the last war was not a mitigating factor in Fay's eyes. Serbia was blamed for the assassination of Franz Ferdinand and Russia was blamed for backing up Serbia; the claims of Serbian nationalism got little sympathy from Fay. On the other hand, Austria and

Germany were forgiven for their part in the events of 1914 because Fay believed they were acting in self-defense, Austria from the threat of dismemberment voiced in the nationalist claims of the Serbs and Germany from the threat posed by Russian mobilization.[11]

All this scholarly debate is not very satisfying to the student who wants a clear answer to the question, "What caused World War I?" But there is no agreement on an answer, and for whatever view you prefer, you can find an authority to back you up (although in some places Lenin might not be considered an authority and in other places anyone other than Lenin might not be considered an authority). This lack of agreement on the causes of war goes back to the years of the war itself. It has been argued, in fact, that this is one of the reasons the conflict escalated to total war: No country ever specified exactly what it was fighting for, and in the absence of such information each country assumed the worst of its enemies. The French never said, "We are fighting only to get back Alsace and Lorraine," so the Germans assumed they were trying to turn the clock back past 1870 and split the German Empire into small states again. The Germans never said, "We are fighting only to annex Luxemburg," so the French assumed they were going to annex Luxemburg, Belgium, and a slice of France as well. But whatever the ultimate goals of the war, no one doubted that they had to keep fighting for the immediate goal of not losing.

THE ROLE OF TECHNOLOGY IN WARFARE: POISON GAS, SUBMARINES

The new military technology decisively influenced the outbreak of war in 1914. The Germans attacked when and how they did because their strategy was based on exploiting their industrial superiority. The war failed to develop as preceding wars had because of even newer technology, particularly the machine gun. Technology continued to influence the war throughout its duration. New forms of warfare made their appearance, although they were introduced with little understanding of what they could accomplish or how effective they would be.

One of these technological innovations was poison gas. As industry developed and expanded during the nineteenth century, dangerous industrial chemicals such as chlorine went into widespread use. Before long some planner began thinking about how such chemicals could be applied to warfare. The idea was already so widespread in 1899 that in a conference that year at The Hague, many states agreed to outlaw artillery shells designed to fire poison gas. But sixteen years later, frustrated by seeing their plans fail as mobile warfare turned into war of position, with lines of trenches facing each other from Switzerland to the North Sea, the Germans began to consider whether the use of poison gas might break the stalemate. On April

22, 1915, the Germans used chlorine gas against the French along the front in Belgium, releasing it from canisters in the ground so that technically they did not violate the Hague Gas Declaration. The gas was successful beyond German expectations. French troops fled, leaving a gap 4 miles wide through which the Germans could have marched to Paris. But because the Germans were not expecting any such success, they were not prepared to follow it up. By the time they had completed the necessary preparations and were ready to use gas again, on May 1, 1915, they found the French were equipped with gas masks and able to stop the assault. From then on, both sides began to use gas (and gas masks) in increasing quantities, in artillery shells and grenades as well as in buried canisters, until in the 1918 German offensive, 50 percent of the shells fired carried gas.[12] The initial advantage of surprise on April 22, 1915, was not exploited, and from then on the war was stalemated again, only at a higher level of violence. During World War I, 1.3 million casualties were attributed to gas, 91,000 of them fatalities (although debate has raged over whether this low ratio of those killed to those merely wounded makes it a more or less humane weapon).[13]

The Germans also pioneered another weapon, the submarine. As with poison gas, the weapon was not decisive. Despite the role that German–British naval competition had played in creating tensions between the two countries in the years preceding the war, when the fighting broke out the Germans found that their navy was useless. In any encounter with the larger British navy, it would have been decisively defeated. Therefore the Germans turned to submarines, which could damage the British in an area vital to the British Isles: importation of food, munitions, and other materials needed to fight the war. The submarine proved an effective weapon in sinking ships, but the Germans were limited by international law in how far they could apply this weapon. According to law, attacks on neutral ships were illegal, and it was neutral ships, particularly those under the American flag, that were carrying a large part of the goods. After much debate in German policy-making circles, the general staff convinced the political leaders to agree to "unrestricted" submarine warfare—attacks on all ships going to England, neutral or not.

The German military's justification for this policy illustrates again the difficulty of comprehending the effects of technology even when the utmost care is given to calculation. The German general staff argued that they would be able to sink 600,000 tons of shipping a month and that after six months the British economy would collapse. They also predicted that unrestricted submarine warfare would bring the United States into the war on the side of the British but that it would not matter because America would take a year to mobilize and even then German submarines could sink US troop transport ships before they reached Europe.[14]

The German technical predictions were remarkably accurate. The average amount of shipping sunk during the crucial first five months was 658,000 tons a month, a little over the predicted average. The Germans went wrong in their prediction of what effect these losses would have on British policy. Perhaps if the British had been fighting alone they would have accepted the hopelessness of their position and given up. But the other German prediction—that America would enter the war—came true, and this changed the British calculation. They decided they could hold out until American help arrived. The German technical prediction was correct, but their estimation of the effect of technical factors on political decisions was entirely wrong.[15]

United States entry into the war was one of the factors (although not the only one) that eventually led to victory by the Western Allies. Several times during the war changes in tactics or technical improvements in weapons were introduced that might have made a decisive difference even if the United States had not entered. It is easier to see the effect today, with the benefit of hindsight, than it was then. In 1918, when the German military finally panicked and insisted that their politicians make peace, it was easier to draw a more obvious conclusion, that the United States with its large industrial capacity and its reserve of manpower was the decisive factor in the Western victory.

THE RESULTS OF WORLD WAR I: THE VERSAILLES TREATY

The results of World War I were embodied in the Versailles Peace Treaty of 1919. The treaty was quite long, running to several hundred clauses, but we can summarize its four most important features.

1. *New borders for Germany*. In the west, the provinces of Alsace and Lorraine were returned to France, removing one of the grievances that had made the French eager for war in 1914. But at the same time the French ignored the obvious lesson that this exchange seemed to teach about the price a state pays for detaching territory from another and proceeded to detach territory from Germany for their own benefit. This was the Saar, bordering on Lorraine and like Lorraine a coal and steel producing area, but just as German in its population as Lorraine was French (see Figure 1.3). The French did not go quite as far as the Germans had; they did not annex the Saar but put it under the administration of the new League of Nations, taking over control of its mines and industry.

In the east, new boundaries between Germany and Poland were drawn, but the problem was too complex to be settled so simply. Germans lived among Poles, Polish villages were scattered among German villages, and no border could be totally satisfactory. The 1919 border was no more fair than any other; it differed from the prewar border only by including more Germans under Polish jurisdiction.

2. *New states.* The Versailles Treaty with Germany was only one of several negotiated at the end of the war. The whole package, which we might call the Versailles Settlement, created a number of new states in central and eastern Europe on the principle of national self-determination, replacing the old multinational empire of the Austrian rulers. Under this principle, nationalities or closely related groups of nationalities were given states of their own. The Serbs were united with Bosnia and other Slavic areas to form Yugoslavia or the "South Slavs" state. Slavic peoples in the middle of Europe, the Czechs and the Slovaks, were put together in the state of Czechoslovakia. The states of Poland, Hungary, and Austria were also given borders on the principles of national self-determination. But this principle was not applied to the Germans. First, the state of Austria, although consisting primarily of German-speaking members of the old Austrian empire, was forbidden to unite with Germany. Second, the new state of Czechoslovakia included about 2 million people who spoke German. They lived in the border regions in the Sudeten Mountains and were known as the Sudeten Germans. Before World War I they had been part of the Austrian Empire, but now they were put under a government controlled by Slavs instead of being allowed to join either Germany or Austria. Third, the southern portion of the Austrian province of Tyrol was put under Italian rule, mainly as a reward to the Italians for joining the war on the side of the British and French.

3. *German disarmament.* The Versailles Settlement imposed severe limitations on German armaments, justifying this restriction as the first step toward general European disarmament. Germany would go first, for after all, Germany had lost the war, but the other states would follow. The army was limited to 100,000 men, and each soldier had to serve a minimum of twelve years (to keep the Germans from using the army as a training school for reserves). The navy was limited to 15,000 men and a few ships. An air force was forbidden altogether. Portions of Germany were turned into a demilitarized zone, where no troops could be stationed and no fortifications built. This area extended 50 kilometers on the east bank of the Rhine along the stretch of river that formed the boundary with France and on the entire west bank of the Rhine for the rest of its length (see Figure 2.1).

4. *Reparations.* The issue that probably held the greatest interest for the public was reparations. The Germans had imposed reparations on the French after 1871, to make them pay for the war, and in 1919 a number of French and British politicians were determined to make the Germans pay for this much more expensive war just completed. In the end, the demands were so extravagant, far beyond any reasonable ability on the part of the Germans to pay, that no figure was set and the treaty merely set forth the principle that the Germans would pay. The part of the treaty that laid down this principle,

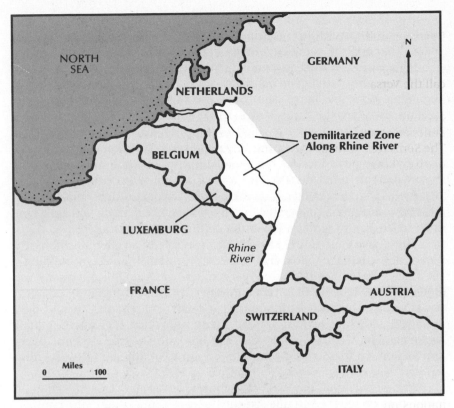

Figure 2.1   The Demilitarized Zone along the Rhine

Clause 231, was similar to an economic liability clause in a commercial contract but became known as the "war guilt" clause. The section on reparations also specified that Germany could be occupied by foreign troops if it failed to meet its payments, as the French in fact did in 1923 when a great inflation led to the collapse of the Germany economy.

GERMAN REACTION TO VERSAILLES AND THE RISE OF HITLER

Imagine that you are a German radical looking for topics for beer hall speeches. What a gold mine you would find in the Versailles Treaty. Alsace and Lorraine are taken away (on the argument that it is wrong to detach territory from another state) at the same time that the Saar is being detached from Germany. New states are being set up everywhere on the principle of national self-determination, but Germans in the Sudetenland, Austria, and South Tyrol are denied this right. Germany must disarm and pay for the war because of "war guilt." You could add that it was a dictated peace—Germany was not invited to participate in the Versailles conference but was instead handed the completed treaty and told to sign within seven days.

It is easy to construct an argument that the Versailles Treaty was responsible for the rise of Hitler and hence for World War II. But this is not the only argument you could make. You could also say the Versailles Treaty was a mistake, assuming the victors had no will to enforce it. If it had been enforced with the same sternness with which it was drawn up, it might have worked. We will never know, because the only part ever to be enforced was the least essential: the provisions for reparations, not those for disarmament. And even when the French occupied the industrial area of the Ruhr in 1923 they discovered that they could not mine coal with bayonets. Right-wing extremists and communists cooperated to resist foreign occupation, and in the end the French had to withdraw without getting any reparations.

The French effort in 1923 failed, yet it was at least an effort to enforce the treaty, more than the victors did to prevent rearmament. It was something of an open secret in Germany that rearmament was going on. Germany was not allowed to have an air force but the government was encouraging "sport flying" clubs. The airline Lufthansa opened six "pilot schools," turning out a hundred pilots a year in a system of education that had many military elements. The Germans set up factories abroad in return for some of the production. In the Soviet Union they set up two airplane factories, three artillery shell factories, and a poison gas factory.[16]

As time went on, the Western democracies became less and less interested in enforcing the Versailles Treaty. Partly it was because of the nature of these societies, which gave priority to pursuit of private happiness over the concerns of state; there was no public support for maintaining a large army of occupation in Germany. Partly it was the result of widespread pacifism, particularly encouraged by left-wing political parties. And partly it was the result of influence exerted by academic historians such as Sidney Fay, who were arguing that no one country (and certainly not Germany) was guilty of starting the war. With no war guilt, the justification for such a harsh treaty was hard to find.

The decline in Western self-confidence was paralleled in Germany by the rise to power of a political leader with total self-confidence, Adolf Hitler. Hitler had first come to world attention in 1923, when, imitating Benito Mussolini, he tried to take over the government in Munich. But unlike Mussolini, whose march on Rome had been successful, Hitler failed and went to jail. While there, he wrote a book he called *Four and a Half Years of Struggle Against Lies, Stupidity, and Cowardice.* (His publisher got him to cut the title down to *My Struggle*—in German, *Mein Kampf.*) Consciously echoing Bismarck he wrote, "We must clearly recognize the fact that the recovery of the lost territories is not won through solemn appeals to the Lord or through pious hopes in a League of Nations, but only by force of arms."[17] By 1933 he was chancellor of Germany.

HITLER'S FOREIGN POLICY AND WESTERN APPEASEMENT

Hitler's own statements and the policies he later followed are grounds for saying that he alone was responsible for World War II. But on closer examination, it is not quite so simple. For one thing, his views on the treatment of Germany after World War I were widely shared. The unwillingness of Western political leaders to make any concessions to Hitler's more moderate predecessors made more plausible his argument that only force of arms would bring change—Germany had not even been admitted to the League of Nations until 1926. For another, had Western political leaders followed different policies once Hitler did take office, he never would have gotten a weak and disarmed Germany into a position from which it could hope to make war against all the other countries of Europe with any chance of success.

Yet without question the story of the outbreak of World War II is in large part the personal story of Hitler and his diplomacy. This diplomacy may, for convenience, be divided into two phases. Phase I begins with Hitler's accession to power in January 1933. His first years were spent consolidating domestic control and he made few foreign policy moves. One thing he did was to take Germany out of the League of Nations in October 1933, on the argument that Germany was being denied equal rights on the question of arms. Germany had disarmed but the other states had not followed. Now, said Hitler, either the others disarm down to our level or we have the right to arm up to theirs. The League, which was sponsoring a disarmament conference at this time, was unable to give an answer and so Germany withdrew. Hitler's next move, in January 1934, was to sign a Non-Aggression Pact with Poland. It was something no moderate German leader would have dared without risking a venomous attack from right-wingers such as the Nazis. But Hitler's patriotism was above criticism and the Nazis by now had eliminated most critics. The treaty with Poland served two purposes: It strengthened Hitler's peace image (and he was later to refer to it as proof of his sincere desire for peace with his neighbors), and it lulled the Poles into thinking they could pursue a policy of independent neutrality and thus made them less willing to cooperate with France against Germany.

In January 1935, Hitler got a kind of foreign policy victory that, had it come five years earlier, might have meant a Hitler never would have come to power. The League of Nations conducted a plebiscite in the Saar to see whether its citizens wanted to return to Germany. (They did, overwhelmingly.) Hitler had little to do with bringing about this vote. A plebiscite had been scheduled for fifteen years after the Saar was detached from

Germany. But Hitler got all the credit for recovering this piece of "lost territory." The final piece of Hitler's policy in Phase I was his announcement, in March 1935, of compulsory universal military service; in other words, his denunciation of the disarmament clauses of the Versailles Treaty.

At any time during Phase I it would have been easy for the Western democracies to move against Hitler. Germany was still disarmed and Hitler's own position in Germany was not totally secure. Yet nothing Hitler did was unequivocally threatening to the Western countries. Rather than make the effort to stop Hitler, it was easier to find a justification for each of his actions. Even denouncing the Versailles Treaty could be justified. Far from fulfilling the pledge of Versailles to disarm down to the German level, France had just doubled the term of service for its soldiers. Hitler himself was careful to keep his announced intentions limited; although he was introducing universal military service he pledged not to rearm the demilitarized zone of the Rhineland. Hitler's tactics are an example of what a contemporary strategist has called, "Give me that last piece of toast or I'll blow my brains out on your new suit!" Of course if you called his bluff, it would hurt him more than it hurt you, but if you calculate rationally you will decide that a piece of toast is less expensive than a dry cleaning bill.[18]

In Phase II Hitler engaged in foreign policy acts that were increasingly threatening to Germany's neighbors. In March 1936, he ordered German troops into the demilitarized zone along the Rhine, even though he had explicitly promised not to do so only a year earlier. In March 1938, he annexed Austria, against both the prescriptions of the Versailles Treaty and the wishes of most of the Austrian people. In September 1938, his threat to go to war against Czechoslovakia led to the surrender of the Sudetenland to Germany. In March 1939, Germany annexed the remaining non-German part of Czechoslovakia.

We might wonder why Hitler was able to get away with these acts. In part it was because Western political leaders were carefully avoiding the conditions that led to World War I. In the postwar analysis everyone agreed that the pre-1914 arms race had been a major source of tension. Spending for arms was therefore kept low after the war. Although the Western democracies were stubbornly refusing to disarm completely, they were also failing to keep up with weapons development, particularly once Germany began open rearmament in 1935. At the time of the Sudetenland crisis in 1938, England had only one operational wing of modern fighter aircraft.[19] The French chief of staff of the air force had been so impressed by his visits to German airplane factories that he warned in August 1938, "If war comes this autumn, as you fear, there will not be one French plane left after fifteen days."[20] As it became ever clearer that Hitler did not keep his promises, France and Britain did begin to rearm, but rearmament with modern weapons is a lengthy process and years were required before new weapons would provide backing for strong diplomatic actions.

Another important cause of World War I was the failure of the major states to conciliate states that had grievances, particularly those caused by national feelings. It was the quarrel over nationalism between the Serbs and the Austrians that set the armies in motion. After World War I Western political leaders listened sympathetically to demands for redressing national grievances. This policy of being conciliatory in the face of justified demands was known as "appeasement," a word that at the time had only favorable connotations. To be against appeasement was to be rigid, inflexible, in favor of the policies that had led to World War I.

The most famous example of appeasement was the Munich conference, at which the Sudentenland was transferred from Czechoslovakia to Germany. Hitler had used a branch of the Nazi Party to stir up trouble in the Sudetenland, telling them always to ask for so much that they could never be satisfied. He then used these incidents as a pretext for demanding that the Sudeten Germans be put under German rule. The Czechs refused to be bullied and mobilized their reserves, but the rest of the world was afraid of war and insisted on an international conference instead. The conference, so eagerly sought as an alternative to war by Western leaders (including the American president), was far from a model of impartiality. It was held in the German city of Munich, site of the Nazi Party's headquarters. It was attended by Britain, France, Italy, and Germany but not by the country most directly threatened, Czechoslovakia. As a result of the conference, the Czechs were ordered to hand over the Sudetenland, including border fortifications and economic resources as well as about 700,000 Czechs who would now go under German rule. Yet Neville Chamberlain, the British prime minister, came back from Munich with his black umbrella in one hand and a piece of paper in the other, saying, "I believe it is peace for our time."[21] The paper was important because Chamberlain had on it Hitler's own promise that this was his last territorial demand in Europe. And it was reasonable to believe him. The German claim to rule Germans in the Sudetenland and Austria was justified by the principle of national self-determination. The issue of Germans in South Tyrol and Germans in the areas along the Polish border remained, but Hitler had concluded treaties with both Italy and Poland.

The Western political leaders quickly discovered that their appeasement policy was mistaken when, only six months later, Hitler took over the rest of Czechoslovakia in clear violation of his pledges at Munich. War had become inevitable. In retrospect most Western policy-makers agreed that they should have gone to war to aid Czechoslovakia. But it was too late for that. The next country to be threatened by Hitler was Poland. Its cause was less just, its regime less compatible with Western ideas of democracy or even human decency, and its terrain a lot harder to defend. It was, in fact, as Hitler calculated, irrational for the French and British to get into a major war with Germany over Poland. Nevertheless, the British and French leaders made that irrational choice and World War II began.

ESCALATION INTO TOTAL WAR

Hitler was aware that military action against Poland was a gamble that could turn into a major war. Like Bismarck before him in 1870 and the German general staff in 1914, he faced the threat of a two-front war. Germany, at the center of Europe, could be attacked simultaneously from east and west. The German general staff had tried to solve the problem in 1914 by careful military planning—a knockout blow to the west, followed by an extended campaign in the east—but the plan had failed. Hitler chose to imitate Bismarck and prevent a two-front war by diplomacy. In August 1939, Germany signed a Non-Aggression Pact with Russia. (Anyone who believed that *Mein Kampf* was a blueprint for Hitler's actions would have been misled here; Hitler had written that he would never ally with the Bolsheviks or, as he put it, use the devil to drive out Beelzebub.)[22]

With the threat of Russian reaction out of the way, Germany went to war against Poland in September 1939, the date we usually give for the opening of World War II. (In one sense the war in the Pacific had begun in 1937 with the fighting between China and Japan; in another sense it did not truly become a world war until the Japanese attacked Pearl Harbor in 1941.) The Germans were staging a victory parade through the streets of Poland's capital long before French and British forces could come to Poland's aid. Hitler hoped that the French and British would see how unreasonable it was to continue in a state of war with Germany once Poland was defeated. After a winter with no fighting, when he was unable to persuade the French and British to make peace, Hitler launched a lightning campaign against France in the spring of 1940. Within six weeks France surrendered. Hitler now seriously undertook to defeat England. As a London news vendor put it, "French sign peace treaty: we're in the finals."[23] But before any invasion could be undertaken, the Germans felt they had to destroy British defenses and so mounted an aerial campaign that became known as the Battle of Britain.

Subduing England from the air was more difficult than many prewar advocates of air power had predicted. Paradoxically, the British had an advantage precisely because they had delayed so long in rearming. If they had heeded the warnings of men such as Winston Churchill and rearmed in 1933, they would have been massively equipped with inferior aircraft. The British won the Battle of Britain in large part because of their superior fighter aircraft, but the prototype of the Hurricane was first flown only in November 1935, the prototype of the Spitfire in March 1936.[24]

The decisive role of technology in the Battle of Britain reinforced the pessimistic conclusions that had emerged from studies of the conduct of World War I, one of which was the increasing importance of technology. Another was the decreasing ability of human beings to manage technology. Britain won the Battle of Britain because of superior airplanes; Germany would have won if it had developed its jet planes a little sooner. But the British succeeded by luck, not careful planning. The crucial question in modern warfare is: When do we stop developing new weaponry and go into production? The Germans were a bit too early. At the other extreme, the French were a bit too late; their aircraft were still on the assembly lines when the Germans attacked. The British got it right, but only by luck.

THE ROLE OF TECHNOLOGY IN WARFARE: AIRPLANES, THE ATOMIC BOMB

Before fighting began in 1939 many predicted how horrible the coming war would be because of the new technology. On the horror of the war the predictions were correct but not on much else. The most popular prewar version was that poison gas would be widely used, most likely dropped from airplanes onto cities. At the time of the Sudeten crisis in 1938, 38 million gas masks were distributed in Britain. Yet during World War II poison gas was not used at all between major belligerents. (The one exception was its limited use in 1941 by the Japanese against the technologically less advanced Chinese.)

The prediction that airplanes would attack cities was correct (although they did it with high-explosive bombs, not gas). But the prediction that these attacks would be decisive was wrong. World War II was eventually won on the ground, not from the air. Airplanes were decisive when used tactically (that is, coordinated with ground action), but not when used strategically. There were a number of reasons for this. One was that antiaircraft defense was more effective than expected; a loss of more than 10 percent in planes for each attack (such as the Germans suffered in the Battle of Britain) was enough to make air raids too costly. British and American raids in 1942 and 1943 often suffered losses much higher than that. Another reason was the gross inaccuracy of bombing. In 1941, the Royal Air Force of Britain determined that fewer than 20 percent of the bombers it sent out had bombed within a circle 75 square miles in area around the designated target area. In heavily defended areas such as industrial targets, only 7 percent were dropping bombs within 75 square miles. News stories of "pinpoint" attacks were nothing more than war propaganda.[25] Still another reason for the failure of strategic bombing was that the United States and Britain did not devise a successful strategy for employing bombers. Only in June 1944 did they finally begin to use them in a way that would be decisive, in a single-minded concentration on destroying petroleum products to deprive the German armed forces of fuel. But by the time this aerial strategy began to take hold the war had already begun to turn against the Germans on the ground.[26]

Predictions of the horror of aerial warfare were finally vindicated on August 6, 1945, when the United States dropped the first atomic bomb on Hiroshima. This was not the most destructive raid of the war—raids on Tokyo and Dresden with high-explosive and incendiary bombs killed more people. But the atomic raid required only one airplane and one bomb; the amount of destruction for the area it covered was much greater than that of conventional bombs. Yet the dropping of the atomic bomb is only a further illustration of human inability to come to terms with modern technology. One question has troubled many people since Hiroshima: Was the use of the atomic bomb necessary at all? It was built, after all, out of fear that the Germans would develop one first. It turned out that the Germans had made managerial mistakes and were nowhere close to having a bomb by the time they surrendered. If the United States had been at war with Japan alone there never would have been an expensive crash program to build an atomic bomb. But once the time and money had been invested, it seemed easiest to go on and use it on Japan.

But why, people ask, did we use it to kill people instead of in a harmless way that would still have demonstrated its destructive power? The answer is that scientists could not think of a convincing technical demonstration. Robert Oppenheimer, scientific director of the project that built the bomb, did not think exploding one of them like a firecracker over the desert would be impressive.[27] Another nuclear scientist, Isador Rabi, said it would have required very detailed instructions to the Japanese, more than were possible during the war. "You would have to tell them what instruments to bring," Rabi said, "and where to stand, and what to measure. Otherwise, it would look like a lot of pyrotechnics. It would take someone who understood the theory to realize what he was seeing."[28] Part of this inability to devise an appropriate demonstration came from gross underestimation of the new weapon's power. General Groves, the top administrator of the atomic project, estimated in December 1944 that the bomb would have a force equivalent to 500 tons of TNT. By May 1945 the heads of the Los Alamos laboratories were predicting 700 to 1,500 tons of TNT. The actual power of the Hiroshima explosion was close to 14,000 tons of TNT, or ten times what scientists were saying in the crucial days when the decision was being made.[29]

THE RESULTS OF WORLD WAR II

The dropping of the first atomic bomb on Japan on August 6, 1945 (and another on Nagasaki three days later) was followed in less than a week by the Japanese decision to surrender. It was convincing proof to much of the world that technology was the decisive winner of World War II. If a scientific breakthrough had given the Germans the bomb first, the outcome of the war would surely have been different. The lesson people drew was that a modern industrial economy and a scientific establishment were the major components of military power. In these the United States excelled. The old term "great power" was replaced by a new one, "superpower," implying that all other states of the world combined could not prevail against such a state armed with the latest weapons.

In another way World War II changed the structures of world politics. It marked the emergence of the United States from self-imposed isolation. It also marked the emergence of the Soviet Union from an externally imposed isolation. Soviet ground forces fighting in eastern Europe had reversed the German tide of fortune in the war. Now, although weakened by losses in the war—10 percent of its population, 25 percent of its industry—Russia was a major world power second only to the United States. Russia's traditional enemies, Japan in Asia and Germany in Europe, had been eliminated as major rivals by defeat in war. The other traditional powers in Europe had been removed as major factors as well. Italy was among the defeated countries. France was a winner in a technical sense only, having been defeated and occupied by the Germans in 1940. Britain was so weakened by the war that it had to give up most of its overseas interests and concentrate on rebuilding at home. In a few years large portions of the overseas possessions of France and Britain were to receive independence and others were to move into positions from which they could demand it.

Germany was treated far more harshly after World War II than after World War I, yet because the Germans were psychologically more prepared to acknowledge defeat, there was almost no resistance. In 1918, Germany had not even been entered by enemy troops; in 1945, Germany was devastated and occupied. Without even the benefit of a peace treaty this time, Germany was divided into three parts (one part was annexed by the Soviet Union and Poland, the other two parts became separate states). All of Germany was put under foreign administration and, in the zones occupied by the Russians and the French, looted of food and industrial equipment. The troublesome border problems with Poland and Czechoslovakia were solved with brutal finality by simply expelling all Germans from areas now governed by Poland and Czechoslovakia. About 10 million Germans became refugees, most eventually finding their way into West Germany where they made up 25 percent of the population. Although it was brutal, it did solve the troubled border issue that had caused friction between Germany and its neighbors after World War I. The Germans accepted this solution and successfully absorbed the huge refugee population. In the years after World War II it was not from the defeated but from the victors that the seeds of the next conflict would come.

The two great wars of the twentieth century seemed to demonstrate that the precepts of Clausewitz and the optimism of the age of Bismarck were no longer valid. Instead of being short, useful instruments of state policy, wars turned out to be long and enormously destructive. Battle deaths in World War I numbered around 9 million, yet the political goals were so unclear that we still are debating the reasons for the war. The reasons for World War II seem clearer, yet the destruction was much greater. In addition to about 15 million battle deaths, large numbers of civilians were killed, so that deaths from World War II were around 60 million, or 3 percent of the world's population.[30] The destructiveness of the two wars convinced many people that war was no longer a useful means of settling disputes between states. The development of nuclear weapons during World War II made the need to find an alternative to war a matter of urgency.

NOTES

1. Karl Marx and Friedrich Engels, *Manifesto of the Communist Party* (first published in 1848), Part II.

2. The British, French, and German reactions are described by Barbara Tuchman in *The Guns of August* (New York: Dell, 1962), pp. 94, 111; the British poet was Rupert Brooke, who wrote "The 1914 Sonnets."

3. A dramatic illustration of the military establishment's reluctance to accept the lessons of the recent wars is provided by Edward L. Katzenback, Jr., "The Horse Cavalry in the Twentieth Century," *Public Policy: A Yearbook of the Graduate School of Public Administration, Harvard University*, ed. Carl J. Friedrich and Seymour E. Harris, 1958.

4. The importance of military planning is the main thesis of Tuchman's book cited above.

5. V. I. Lenin, *Imperialism: The Highest Stage of Capitalism*, first published in 1917 (New York: International Publishers, 1939).

6. Ibid., p. 11.

7. New York: G. P. Putnam's Sons.

8. Beck, p. 198.

9. New York: Macmillan (2 volumes).

10. Fay, Vol. I, pp. 2, 34.

11. Fay, Vol. I, pp. 124, 403; Vol. II, pp. 550–552, 554.

12. Frederick J. Brown, *Chemical Warfare* (Princeton: Princeton University Press, 1968), p. 43.

13. Seymour M. Hersh, *Chemical and Biological Warfare* (Garden City, N.Y.: Anchor Books, 1969), p. 2.

14. Fred Charles Iklé, *Every War Must End* (New York: Columbia University Press, 1971), pp. 42–50.

15. Ibid.

16. S. William Halperin, *Germany Tried Democracy: A Political History of the Reich from 1918 to 1933* (New York: W. W. Norton, 1946), p. 211.

17. Chapter 13. The most accessible edition in English is translated by Ralph Manheim (Boston: Houghton Mifflin, 1943), p. 627.

18. Thomas Schelling, *The Strategy of Conflict* (New York: Oxford University Press, 1963), p. 127.

19. Iain Macleod, *Neville Chamberlain* (New York: Atheneum, 1962), p. 261.

20. William L. Shirer, *The Collapse of the Third Republic* (New York: Simon & Schuster, 1969), p. 352.

21. For a defense of Chamberlain, see Macleod. (See note 19.)

22.   Hitler, Chapter 14 (p. 662 in Houghton Mifflin edition). (See note 17.)

23.   Alistair Horne, *To Lose a Battle* (Boston: Little, Brown, 1969), p. 579.

24.   Winston Churchill, *The Gathering Storm* (Boston: Houghton Mifflin, 1948), p. 128.

25.   Charles Kinsley Webster and Noble Frankland, *The Strategic Air Offensive Against Germany, 1939–1945* (London: H.M. Stationery Office, 1961), Vol. I, p. 247.

26.   Bernard Brodie, *Strategy in the Missile Age* (Princeton: Princeton University Press, 1959), Chapter 4.

27.   Len Giovannitti and Fred Freed, *The Decision to Drop the Bomb* (New York: Coward-McCann, 1965), p, 123.

28.   *The New Yorker*, October 20, 1975, p. 61.

29.   Herbert Feis, *The Atomic Bomb and the End of World War II* (Princeton: Princeton University Press, 1966), p. 29.

30.   Quincy Wright, *A Study of War*, 2nd ed. (Chicago: University of Chicago Press, 1965), p. 1543.

CHAPTER 3

THE COLD WAR AND THE KOREAN WAR

By the end of the 1950s, "Cold War" had become a term of disapproval, often contrasted with "relaxation of tensions" or "détente." Yet when the term was first used, the emphasis was on the adjective "cold," not the noun "war." Cold war was contrasted with "hot war" or "shooting war."

Despite the intense rivalry between the United States and the USSR in the late 1940s and early 1950s, the struggle never did turn into all-out war between them. But the Cold War period did include a highly destructive war in Korea (2 million battle deaths), which was widely viewed at the time as a war between the United States and the USSR (with the North Koreans and the Chinese acting as Soviet proxies). We will look first at the Cold War as a background to understanding how a local dispute in the Korean peninsula became a conflict involving major powers.

ORIGINS OF THE COLD WAR

The search for the origins of the Cold War has been a major scholarly activity. There are vast numbers of books and articles on the subject to choose from, and the new availability of sources from the collapsed Soviet Union will most likely lead to many new ones. Some trace the origins of the war back to 1917 and the Bolshevik victory in Russia. Others see the origin in the policies of one country or another during World War II.[1]

Some points about the Cold War are agreed on. First, historians agree that it was unexpected. The victors of World War II expected postwar harmony.

Second, they agree that it developed gradually. For this reason it is difficult to pinpoint a beginning date. Rather, the conflict grew out of a series of incidents that, as seen by Americans, seemed to demonstrate that the Soviet Union was an expansionist country, differing from Nazi Germany only in ideology.

Third, historians agree in general on what the most important of these incidents were. Conflicts arose over Iran, Turkey, Greece, Berlin, and Korea. Although the specific origins of these conflicts and the goals each country was pursuing continue to be hotly debated by historians, the fact that this handful of events was crucial is generally accepted.

ORIGINS OF THE US–SOVIET RIVALRY: IRAN

As a result of World War II, the Soviet Union acquired (or in some cases reacquired) large amounts of territory in Europe along its eastern borders—parts of Finland; the entire countries of Estonia, Latvia, and Lithuania; parts of Poland, Germany, and Rumania (see Figure 3.1). This acquisition of territory was passively accepted by the Western democracies, in part because they felt Russia deserved something in return for its losses in fighting the Germans and also because the Red Army was firmly in control of these areas and nothing could be done to remove them short of starting World War III. Along its southern border, however, Soviet occupation of foreign territory provoked conflict. In 1941, acting out of fear of losing Iran's oil resources to the Germans because of the pro-German sympathies of the shah of Iran, the Soviet Union and Britain together occupied Iran, removed the shah, and established their own troops in the country, the Russians in the north, the British in the south. They agreed to remove the troops as soon as the war ended.

The British did remove their troops, the Russians did not. Instead they supported the creation of an autonomous Azerbaijani Republic, just over the border from the Soviet republic of Azerbaijan, run by local communists (see Figure 3.2). By 1946, the situation was tense. If the pattern of Europe were to be repeated, then the Red Army would not withdraw but stay to support a puppet regime. In April 1946, after a period of diplomatic maneuvering, the Russians agreed to withdraw in return for promises of reform in Azerbaijan and the establishment of a Soviet–Iranian oil company. By May 1946 the Soviet troops had withdrawn. The Iranian army then occupied the province, executed the leaders of the autonomous republic, and suppressed the communist party. Furthermore, the Iranian

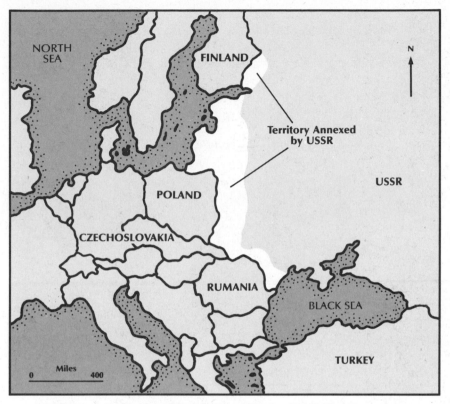

Figure 3.1   Soviet Acquisitions in Euope during World War II

parliament refused to ratify the Soviet–Iranian Oil Company, so the Russians gained nothing at all.

Like other events in the Cold War, the Azerbaijan incident can be cited to prove different contentions. It supports the view that Stalin was not committed to expansion, but it also supports the view that Stalin's expansionist desires could be checked only by vigorous resistance. Various analyses of the episode have given credit for bringing about the Russian withdrawal to the United Nations (then just getting started and still meeting in London), to the British (who sent a note of protest), to the Americans (who talked about extending the draft), to the British and Americans together (who showed their solidarity through Churchill's "Iron Curtain" speech at Fulton, Missouri), or to the skillful diplomacy of the premier of Iran. What is significant for the development of the Cold War is that Soviet policy in Azerbaijan was perceived by President Truman and his advisers as an attempt at Soviet expansion that was repulsed by Western policy. It was taken as a model of how to deal with the Russians.[2]

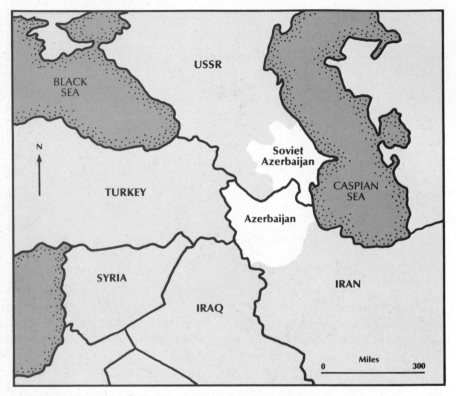

Figure 3.2   Azerbaijan

TURKEY, GREECE, AND THE TRUMAN DOCTRINE

A seemingly parallel situation appeared in two other countries to the south of the Soviet Union, Turkey and Greece. Like many of the other countries bordering on former Russian Empire, Turkey had taken advantage of Russian weakness during the Bolshevik revolution and the civil war that followed it in the 1920s to reclaim some disputed territory, in particular the province of Khars. Following the end of the war in Europe in 1945, the Soviet foreign minister requested that the Turks hand this territory over to the Soviet Union (see Figure 3.3). Soviet diplomacy was accompanied by reports of military maneuvers in the bordering areas of the Soviet Union. The Turks rejected the Soviet request but were uneasy about how far Soviet pressure would go.

In the case of Greece, there was no claim to territory by the Soviet Union or actual occupation of territory by the Red Army. Rather, the Greek government was fighting a civil war against communist guerrillas who, it was assumed, were controlled by Stalin. Both Greece and Turkey had tradi-

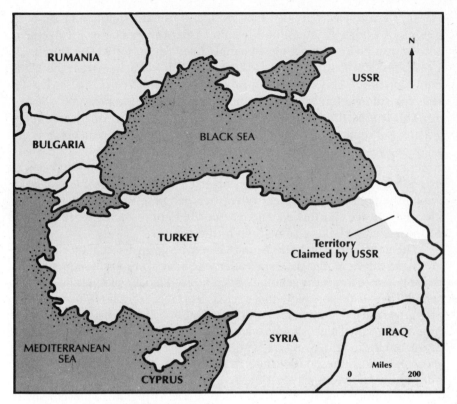

Figure 3.3   Soviet Claims on Turkey

tionally looked to Britain as the great power that supported them against their powerful northern neighbor. But Britain, weakened by the burden of fighting the Germans during the war, was suffering a financial crisis that made it impossible for it to continue to play the role of a great power in this part of the world. The British approached the Americans and asked them if they would consider abandoning their traditional policy of isolation and provide aid to Turkey and Greece.

This British request was followed by weeks of feverish activity in Washington as government officials debated whether the United States should assume the role traditionally played by a great power and whether the American people would accept this departure from the traditional policy of isolation. This second question was much more important in the minds of the officials. Everyone remembered how Woodrow Wilson had failed to win the support of the Congress for his plan for a League of Nations, with the result that the United States made little contribution to world politics in the two decades that led up to World War II. In an effort to avoid repeating

Wilson's error, it was decided that President Truman should address both houses of Congress, outlining the new American policy of involvement abroad and giving the broadest possible justification for it. On March 12, 1947, President Truman made the address that became known as the "Truman Doctrine." This was a US pledge to "support free peoples who are resisting subjugation by armed minorities or by outside pressure."[3]

The Truman Doctrine was clearly a turning point in American foreign policy; as disenchantment with American involvement abroad grew in the following years, critics concentrated on the charter that had led to the rise of American globalism. Even some who agreed at the time with the policy of extending aid to Greece and Turkey objected to the universal language in which the policy was couched. Why "free peoples," they asked. Why not just say "Greece and Turkey" and reserve the right to decide whether other countries will get aid at some time in the future?

The ease with which the Truman Doctrine gained acceptance by Congress and the support it got from leaders of both parties in subsequent years make it easy to forget the genuine fears that troubled the planners in 1947. It seemed a realistic possibility that such a departure from traditional policies might be rejected, on the one hand by traditional isolationists, on the other by a new group of idealists who wanted to rely totally on the United Nations. The Truman Doctrine was widely thought at the time to be a step toward a more mature and responsible foreign policy than the one that America had followed in the years between the two world wars.

The Truman Doctrine, seen by Americans as a program to prevent Soviet interference in Greece and Turkey, was immediately interpreted by the Soviet Union as a "fresh intrusion of the USA into the affairs of other states."[4] This became the typical pattern of Cold War exchanges. Each side interpreted its own moves as defensive and those of its rival as aggressive.

Convinced of Soviet aggressive intentions, the West reacted with defensive measures, first in Azerbaijan, then in Greece and Turkey. The weak condition of the European economies became a cause for concern, not only for humanitarian reasons but also because it was believed that weak economies would make these countries more susceptible to communist takeovers. A few months after President Truman had announced that the United States would give military assistance to Greece and Turkey, his secretary of state, George Marshall, suggested that the United States could make available economic assistance to all the countries of Europe. This offer of aid was open to all, but it seemed likely to the planners in Washington that the Russians would find such aid incompatible with the rigid control and secrecy they were accustomed to exercising over their own economy. The Washington planners were correct. Marshall Plan aid was rejected both by the USSR and by countries under its control.

THE DIVISION OF EUROPE AND THE BERLIN BLOCKADE

Whatever suspicions Stalin had could only be confirmed by these policies. Measures that the West interpreted as defensive were seen from the Russian perspective as preparations for aggression. Whatever Stalin's original intentions for the countries of Eastern Europe, there was no longer any possibility of independent development. Perhaps it had been his intention all along, perhaps Western policy had only speeded up his schedule, perhaps Western policy provoked him into it. Whatever the origin, Stalin now proceeded to eliminate anyone with pro-Western leanings in countries liberated from the Nazis by the Red Army—Bulgaria, Rumania, and Hungary. The countries of Eastern Europe became in effect a Soviet empire. In the words of a recent analyst, Stalin's consolidation of control in Eastern Europe "was tangible evidence of aggressive intent, conjured up memories of the Nazis, and by placing troops on the border (even if they were only imperial occupation troops) enabled alarmists to prove the capability if not the intention to attack the West."[5]

By 1947 it was clear that Poland would be ruled by the Polish Communist Party in a way acceptable to Russia. In February 1948 the government of Czechoslovakia was expunged of its pro-Western parties. In June 1948 the city of Berlin, itself under four-power administration but totally surrounded by the Soviet Zone of Occupation, was cut off from contact with the rest of Germany by a Soviet blockade. The situation in Germany was different from that in Poland, Czechoslovakia, and other East European countries. American forces still occupied Germany, and the United States shared in a four-power military government of the country. The four-power division of the former German capital city was part of the overall four-power government of the country.

The United States wished to react strongly to the Berlin blockade because it believed that its legal right to be in Berlin was unassailable, but it lacked the military means to do much. Only one combat-ready division in the entire US Army was not committed to occupation duty. General Marshall said, "We did not have enough to defend the airstrip at Fairbanks."[6] President Truman decided to airlift supplies into Berlin, but it took all the available transport aircraft in the Air Force to accomplish that. As a gesture to show US firmness, President Truman made one of the few moves available to him and sent a number of B-29 bombers to Britain. This was the first time since the end of the war that bombers (ones capable of carrying the atomic bomb) had been stationed outside the United States. The move was followed by discussion within the government of assistance to a rearmed Europe, eventually including Germany. In June 1948 the United States Senate passed a bipartisan resolution supporting collective defense in Western Europe, and in April 1949 the North Atlantic Treaty was signed, by which "the Parties agree that an armed attack against one or more of them in Europe or North America shall be considered an attack against them all." From this treaty developed the North Atlantic Treaty Organization, or NATO.

BIPOLARITY

Whatever date one picks for the beginning of the Cold War, by 1949, when the North Atlantic Treaty was signed, the two major powers were clearly deeply involved in it. A number of features set this period off from times of peace. One was a high level of hostility between East and West, as manifested in public statements and propaganda as well as large defense budgets and military conscription. Another was recurring international crises provoked by incidents of violence, such as the shooting down of US airplanes flying near the border of the Soviet Union. Still another feature was the spread of US–Soviet rivalry into nearly every area of life. Anything that hurt the United States helped the Soviet Union and vice versa. For example, in 1954 Richard Nixon, then vice president, welcomed the Supreme Court decision outlawing school segregation not because it was a triumph for justice but because it would improve America's image abroad; he called it "our greatest victory in the Cold War."[7]

As more and more areas of life were affected by the rivalry between the United States and the USSR, a new form of international politics took shape, quite different from the system of the nineteenth or first half of the twentieth centuries. Instead of several major states, there were only two, and these so exceeded in power all others that they were known as superpowers. Each acted as a pole around which other countries in the world aligned themselves, giving this form of international politics its name, bipolarity. Each superpower and its surrounding client states were known as a "bloc"—the Soviet bloc or the Western bloc. These blocs were held together by military alliances (NATO in the West, the Warsaw Pact in the East), by economic organizations (the Organization for European Economic Cooperation in the West, the Council for Mutual Economic Assistance in the East), and by political values shared by the political leaders. States not part of either bloc were of two types—one group that was explicitly neutral by choice or imposition (Sweden, Switzerland, and Austria, for example), and a group of "nonaligned" states in Africa, Asia, and Latin America that became known as the Third World.

In the early days of the Cold War, both superpowers looked on nonalignment as immoral. Stalin, speaking for the Soviet Union, said he saw no difference in India after the British departed in 1947. If a country was not with the socialist camp, then it was against them. The Soviet attitude toward the Third World began to shift around the time of the death of Stalin in 1953.

From then on, third world countries were wooed by the communists, but the United States persisted for several years more in condemning neutralism. John Foster Dulles, secretary of state under President Eisenhower, called nonalignment "an immoral and shortsighted conception."[8] Only under President Kennedy did the United States move toward the same policy as the Soviet Union and show more tolerance of neutralism.

The Cold War was a period of intense rivalry stopping short of all-out war. Preparations for war were made and the enemy in a potential war was clearly identified, but the weapons were not used. Each side engaged in propaganda warfare in such forums as the United Nations and radio broadcasts. Each side practiced subversion—that is, contacts with citizens of other countries, without the approval of their government, to encourage those citizens to engage in hostile actions against their governments. Each side maintained sizable armed forces; the United States for the first time continued the draft into peacetime. But US troops never went into combat against Soviet troops.

HOT WAR IN KOREA

One characteristic of the Cold War was that events in distant areas of the world were frequently seen as part of the US–USSR rivalry. Thus, when fighting broke out in Korea in June 1950, Americans saw it as a new episode in the Cold War. Because the Russians, though not themselves fighting, were supplying material and advisers to the North Koreans, Americans often referred to the conflict as "war by proxy." For its part, however, the United States did not leave all the fighting to its South Korean proxy but sent its own troops, ultimately committing about 250,000 soldiers. Yet, despite this outbreak of a shooting war, the conflict remained limited and did not escalate into World War III, as everyone feared it would.

Korea had been under Japanese control ever since the Russo-Japanese War ended in 1905. After Japan's defeat in 1945, Korea was divided in the middle, at the 38th parallel, primarily to facilitate the Japanese surrender. The Russians (who had been fighting the Japanese north of Korea in Manchuria) occupied the northern half; the Americans occupied the southern. Koreans in both parts of the country made clear that they wanted reunification, but an American–Soviet commission was unable to agree on means for achieving it. In 1947 a UN resolution called for countrywide elections to a single Korean parliament, which was then to set up a provisional government. The Russians refused entry to the UN commission that was to supervise these elections, and in May 1948 elections were held by the UN in the South alone. Three months later Soviet-style elections were conducted by the Russians in the North.

With the Korean Communist Party firmly in control in the North, the Russians announced the withdrawal of their occupation forces, which was completed by January 1949. This move increased pressure on the Americans to withdraw from the South, a move that was already under consideration for other reasons. One of these reasons was the hostility of the Koreans to foreign occupation: US military leaders anticipated demonstrations, riots, and other acts of violence that would make continued occupation difficult. Another reason was budgetary pressure from domestic sources to cut back all military spending. Military leaders did not see any great need for retaining troops in Korea. They considered the peninsula to be a liability in any future war, which they were convinced would be fought globally with nuclear weapons. Therefore, in June 1949, the United States withdrew its troops, leaving behind (as the Russians had in the North) military advisers— a total of 500 for the army of 60,000. But to keep the South from going to war and reunifying the country by force, the United States took with its departing forces all weapons that could be used offensively—airplanes, tanks, and heavy artillery.

CAUSES OF THE KOREAN WAR

A year after the US withdrawal, on June 25, 1950, the North Koreans launched a massive attack on the South. It was not the low-level violence that had characterized past episodes in the Cold War, such as guerrilla warfare in Greece or harassment of planes airlifting supplies to Berlin during the blockade, but conventional warfare—armed troops in tanks crossing a well-demarcated frontier. The attack was obviously carefully planned, and because there were 3,000 Russian advisers with the North Korean army (and because supplies such as gasoline were coming from Russia), it was assumed that the Russians were responsible for the attack.[9]

But the reason behind the attack was a subject of debate in Washington. A number of interpretations were offered at the time.[10] The most popular was the belief that the Korean attack was a feint, a diversionary move to weaken the defense of Europe. The rearmament of Europe was just getting under way, and American attention was concentrated there. Even General Charles de Gaulle of France, not noted for being pro-American or anti-Russian, expected a Russian attack in Europe. The analogy between divided Korea and divided Germany was compelling. In each case the section of the country occupied by the Russians had built up military forces and was issuing belligerent statements, while the section occupied by the West was still weak, underarmed, and inadequately protected.

Another popular explanation for the attack was that it was a Soviet probe for soft spots. After all, Secretary of State Dean Acheson just six months before had declared that the United States would not defend Korea.

He had defined a "defensive perimeter" for the United States in the Pacific, running from the Aleutian Islands through Japan and then the Ryukyu Islands (Okinawa) and the Philippines (see Figure 3.4). Outside the perimeter were the islands of Formosa, where the Nationalist Chinese were holding out against the Communists, and Korea. "It must be clear," Acheson said, "that no person can guarantee these areas against attack."[11] One could explain the Korean War by saying the North Koreans were simply taking Acheson at his word. When you draw a line in the dirt and warn the other guy not to cross it, you expect at the least that he will step up to the line.

Although some Americans interpreted the attack in this way, others held the contradictory view that the Russians were testing the West's resolve, just as Hitler had done at Munich. President Truman said we had been tough in Iran, Berlin, and Greece, and we must show the same toughness in Asia. Chairman of the Joint Chiefs of Staff Omar Bradley said, "We have to draw the line somewhere."[12] Evidently Bradley and Truman forgot that Acheson had drawn a line only six months before.

Figure 3.4   Secretary of State Acheson's Defensive Perimeter

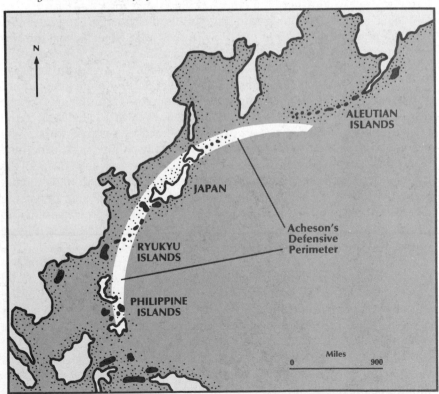

Some of the president's advisers interpreted this attack as something more serious, the opening of a Soviet move for world conquest. General Douglas MacArthur, head of US occupation forces in Japan, wrote that "here in Asia is where the Communist conspirators have elected to make their play for global conquest."[13] John Foster Dulles, a Republican then working for the Truman Administration to prepare a peace treaty with Japan, saw the Korean attack as a move to head off a Pacific version of NATO. Russia already owned Sakhalin Island and the Kurile Islands to the north of Japan. A communist Korea, Dulles believed, would threaten Japan from the south, so Russia's strategic move would place Japan "between the upper and lower jaws of the Russian bear."[14] From such a dominating position Russia could exert diplomatic pressure to keep Japan, at the very least, neutral between East and West.

No one in 1950 seems to have considered a theory for the start of the war that has come to seem more plausible: The simple desire by the North Koreans for reunification. Stalin's power and position in relation to North Korea makes it unlikely that the North Koreans could have started the war without his permission, but it is possible that the North Korean leader Kim Il Sung was able to convince Stalin that he could win a quick and easy victory, and Stalin agreed to go along with him. In this interpretation, responsibility for beginning the war rests primarily with the North Koreans, and the war seems less closely related to the global Cold War.

Despite Acheson's speech putting Korea outside the American defensive perimeter, the United States did go to the aid of South Korea, first with air and naval units, then with ground troops brought over from Japan.[15] As the decision to aid South Korea was being made, it was also decided to go to the United Nations and request Security Council action. Because Russia was then boycotting the Security Council to protest its failure to seat the new communist regime in China, it was not present to use its veto, and the Council supported the US position. Thus, US military action in Korea became UN military action, although the United States provided by far the largest contingent of UN forces and all UN forces were under US command. United Nations involvement further broadened the war and placed it more firmly in the context of global rivalry between East and West.

From the perspective of thirty years we might say that nationalism and the nationalist desire to have a unified country were the basic causes of the Korean War. But what leaders believed at the time about the causes of the war was what determined policy. Because events in Korea were seen as part of the Cold War, the United States made some changes in its policies in Asia—changes that were to have consequences lasting for decades. The United States reversed itself on the issue of Formosa (or Taiwan, as we have come to call it), putting that island and the Nationalist Chinese on it inside the American defensive perimeter by sending the Seventh Fleet to patrol the

Straits of Formosa. The United States also abandoned its opposition to colonial regimes and increased American aid to the French, who were fighting a Vietnamese Communist–Nationalist movement in Indochina. Aid to the French had begun in early 1950, and because of the Korean War the program was enlarged and intensified. By 1951 it had the second highest priority, just behind the Korean War program itself.[16]

THE COURSE OF THE KOREAN WAR

Lacking substantial weapons, the South Koreans were unable to resist the North Korean army and fell back to the south, almost before US troops arrived. But the United States was able to maintain a toehold on the Korean peninsula inside a small perimeter around the port of Pusan (see Figure 3.5). Then on September 15, 1950, in a bold and risky move, General MacArthur staged an amphibious landing in the center of the west coast of Korea at Inchon. The landing was a success, and the United States and its allies were

Figure 3.5   Korea in 1950

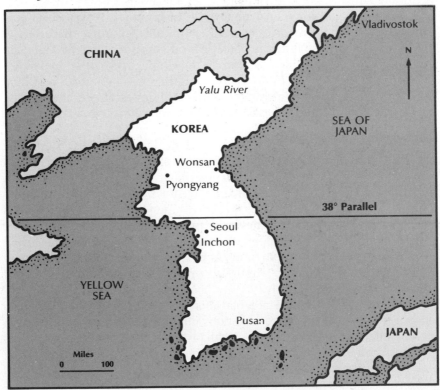

able to drive in from Inchon toward the capital, Seoul, trapping North Korean forces as reinforced UN troops broke out of the Pusan perimeter. The success of this move reversed the fortunes of the war and encouraged US leaders to consider a more ambitious aim than the one they had started with (which was merely the expulsion of the North Koreans from the South). The United States now decided to push on across the 38th parallel and reunite the entire country by force.

The major objection to this move within the Truman Administration was that it might provoke China to intervene in the war. China had signaled its concern about the course of events in Korea, and the United States gave serious consideration to the possibility of Chinese intervention. In November 1950 the Chinese did intervene massively, inflicting a grave defeat on US forces, provoking an increased US commitment, and prolonging the war for almost three more years. As observers at the time recognized, Chinese entry created an entirely new and avoidable war.

The second part of the Korean conflict appears to have been a case where nobody wanted war—at least not the specific kind of war that developed between American and Chinese troops. The United States certainly did not. Reuniting Korea was indeed a foreign policy goal of the Truman Administration, but it was far down on Truman's list of priorities. It was not a goal important enough to be worth committing the kind of resources necessary to defeat a large Chinese army in Korea. And it was not a goal of American foreign policy to fight China or to undo the Chinese revolution by force.[17]

For the Chinese, war in Korea risked escalation to an attack on China itself, possibly with atomic weapons. Even without escalation the fighting was highly costly to the Chinese. More important, Chinese goals could have been achieved without actual fighting.

China's goals have been a topic of debate since 1950. For a time the accepted interpretation was that the Chinese Communists desired to keep in being the communist regime on Korean soil. But recently it has been persuasively argued that an equally important if not overriding goal for the Chinese was simply national security. The Chinese had seen alarming shifts in US policy—from Acheson's defensive perimeter to engagement in Korea, from a hands-off policy to support of the nationalist regime on Formosa, and from limited goals in Korea to more ambitious ones. According to the new interpretation, the Chinese wanted to prevent further shifts that would threaten China more directly.[18]

Undeniably the United States had allowed its success on the battlefield to encourage it to pursue more ambitious aims. Troops were sent to South Korea initially to repel the North Korean invaders. But with the easy success of the Inchon landing the goal shifted to reunification. United States policy had shifted from containment of communism to rollback of the Iron Curtain. Who was to say that, once reunification was accomplished, American troops wouldn't keep going right into Manchuria and try to undo the Chinese Communist revolution? Perhaps, as the French proverb puts it, the appetite comes with eating.

In fact the United States had no intention of invading China. The conflict resulted from failures to signal intentions and read signals properly. President Truman's limited aims in Korea were undermined by belligerent statements by members of his Administration, including General MacArthur himself (statements that ultimately led to the general's dismissal in April 1951). The Chinese had trouble deciding who really did speak for the United States.

The Chinese suffered from lack of direct contact with the United States. They had no diplomats and no permanent representatives at the United Nations. When they did issue an explicit warning to the United States not to allow American troops to cross the 38th parallel, they sent it through the Indian ambassador, K. M. Pannikar. But because Pannikar and other Indians had shown sympathy for the Chinese Communists in the past, the American decision-makers dismissed the warnings. In any case, the Chinese warning did not come until the eve of the UN vote on a resolution to approve the expansion of the war, and US effort was concentrated on getting the resolution approved. American leaders did not have time or energy to listen to a signal that would have made them reassess their entire policy.

The United States greatly underestimated China's military capability and willingness to take risks. In part this was because the Chinese had prepared for military entry into the war with great secrecy, moving great numbers of men at night and keeping them carefully hidden from US reconnaissance aircraft during the day. The movement of large numbers of Chinese troops into Korea in an open way before US troops crossed the 38th parallel could have prevented escalation of the war. MacArthur had authority to conduct operations in North Korea only as long as there was "no entry into North Korea by major Soviet or Chinese Communist forces, no announcement of an intended entry, and no threat by Russian or Chinese Communists to counter our military operations militarily in North Korea."[19] By keeping the entry of their forces secret, the Chinese were able to win a great tactical victory. If they had entered Korea openly, they might have been able to achieve their strategic goals by avoiding fighting altogether.[20]

Even so, the Chinese gave the Americans one last chance. On October 26 and November 2, Chinese forces in Korea met US and South Korean forces in several sharp engagements but then disengaged on November 8. Very likely this was intended as a signal that, although they wished to avoid full-fledged war, they were willing to fight to keep US forces away from China. The United States interpreted China's action as a symbolic objection and pressed on to the Yalu River. On November 26, Chinese forces numbering over 240,000 (over four times the number United States intelligence had estimated) launched an all-out attack that drove the UN forces back south of the 38th parallel.[21]

Once US prestige was involved in this way, it was unlikely that the Americans would quit (any more than that they would have capitulated to Japan after the Japanese victory at Pearl Harbor). If the United States had carried the war into China, as some American leaders were advocating, the results would have been disastrous for China. Even as it was, the Chinese suffered severely from the fighting in Korea.[22]

But the worst did not come to pass. The war remained limited. China's entry resulted in a US retreat to the south, then a counterattack north that resulted in a stabilized line in about the middle of the peninsula. Armistice talks began in 1951; they were completed in July 1953, when an armistice line similar to the one achieved in 1951 was agreed on.

THE PRACTICE OF LIMITED WAR

During all this time the war remained limited in a number of important ways.[23] Of foremost importance was the limitation on weapons: No type of atomic weapon was used. At the time the Korean War broke out, both sides had the potential to use these weapons, although not to the extent they would later. The Russians had only recently acquired a nuclear capability: President Truman announced in September 1949 that they had exploded an atomic device. The United States had, of course, exploded its first atomic devices in 1945, but since that time had been building weapons very slowly without any sense of urgency. The conviction of many military leaders that the Korean action was only a feint led them to recommend saving the relatively scarce atomic bombs for use where greater US interests were at stake, in a potential European war.[24] Thus one could say that, because it is not certain that either side was in a position to use them, the limitation on weapons in Korea was not clear proof that wars could be kept limited. But other limitations were significant, for they were observed despite advantages to one side or the other in ignoring them. The war was limited geographically to the Korean peninsula. The United States did not bomb across the Yalu River into China or even pursue aircraft over it into Chinese territory. Nor did it extend the war to the part of the Soviet Union that borders a tiny strip of Korea in the northeast. The Communist forces, for their part, did not broaden the war to include Japan, which the United States was using as its supply base and staging area.

Another limitation, treated as frivolous at the time, seems from our viewpoint to have greater significance, and that was the legal limitation. The participants in the Korean War did not declare war on each other (although there was a report of a declaration of war by radio by North Korea on the first day). The United States preferred to call it a "military police action." The

Chinese claimed they were sending not their regular army but "volunteers." By itself this restraint of language would not have meant much, but given the real limitations in geography and weapons, the legal restraints can be seen as recognizing and reinforcing other restraints.

It is clear why the United States wanted to keep the war limited. As the chairman of the Joint Chiefs of Staff said, a wider war would be "at the wrong place, at the wrong time, and with the wrong enemy."[25] There was a widespread feeling that getting bogged down in a land war in Asia impaired American ability to help Europe withstand a Russian invasion. For the same reason the small stockpile of atomic bombs was hoarded for use against targets more substantial than peasant huts and dirt roads. The United States was also restrained by fighting in a coalition with other UN members. Even though their numbers were not significant (in June 1951, in addition to 250,000 Americans and 275,000 South Koreans, there were only 28,000 others, and they came from 15 countries), the United States was concerned about their opinion on our policy.

It is harder to understand why the Communist forces observed these limits. After all, they had started the fighting. On reflection it appears that they assumed there would be at the most only token resistance. They expected to achieve a quick, decisive takeover of all of Korea, or what we call a *fait accompli*. Once they had control of Korea, the West would have found it extremely difficult to retake the peninsula, by, say, an amphibious invasion, and the rest of the world in all likelihood would have accepted the takeover. That is the advantage of the technique of the fait accompli: If you can achieve your ends quickly, before the other side can organize to stop you, chances are they won't want to go to the trouble of undoing what you have done. Putting the other side in the position where the next move is up to them always gives your side an advantage. Having failed to achieve a fait accompli in Korea, the Communists were willing to accept a stalemate.

WHY IT ENDED

The Cold War continued after the armistice in Korea, although never at such a level of violence and punctuated by "thaws" of varying lengths that often accompanied summit meetings. Thus journalists wrote of "the spirit of Geneva" of 1955 and the "spirit of Camp David" of 1959. Some saw the end of the Cold War in the successful resolution of the Cuban missile crisis of 1962, although nuclear arsenals grew to unprecedented levels in the years following.

But for others the Cold War continued until the Soviet withdrawal from the countries in Eastern Europe it occupied after World War II. As late as 1989, one analyst could write, "The core of the cold war in Europe is Soviet domination of Eastern Europe." He went on to argue that because "Moscow has imposed unwanted and illegitimate communist regimes on countries that, if free to choose, would have governments much more like those in Western Europe," only the ending of those regimes could end the Cold War.[26] Thus the opening of the Berlin Wall in November of 1989 provides a good symbolic end to the Cold War. It was only a year later that the President of the United States finally said, "The Cold War is over."[27]

But whatever final date one picks, it was clear that the intensity was diminishing over time. Coral Bell, writing in 1986, attributed the moderation of the Cold War to a gradual learning process plus "prudent crisis management."[28] Over time, she argued, the two superpowers learned to manage their relationship. Both sides developed a less frivolous attitude toward nuclear weapons, paying more attention to the command and control of their own systems and to communication with each other in times of crisis.

As the rivalry grew less intense, specific episodes of conflict became less significant. Bell says that the United States and the Soviet Union learned to "win a few, lose a few." Thus the United States backed down after the abortive Bay of Pigs invasion in 1961, eventually pulled out of Vietnam in 1973, and withdrew from Lebanon after a much shorter engagement in 1983; the USSR backed down in the Cuban missile crisis in 1962, let its troops be ejected from Egypt in 1972, and accepted exclusion from the Middle East peacemaking that followed the war in 1973.

Over time, disputes in distant parts of the world were no longer automatically drawn into the US–Soviet rivalry—they were "decoupled" from the Cold War. In 1950 the conflict in Korea drew both sides in; in 1980 the conflict between Iran and Iraq did not.

Several basic structural factors contributed to the moderation of the conflict. John Lewis Gaddis pointed out that the two countries really had little to fight about, in part because they were quite independent of each other.[29] Unlike rivals earlier in the century such as Germany and France they had no ongoing border dispute or claims of stolen land. They lacked the frictions that economic interdependence can often bring.

The fact that there were only two major powers increased stability. Many analysts have argued that a bipolar system is inherently more stable than one with many powers. In a multipower system, war can start from any number of quarrels; in a bipolar system, major wars can start only if the one of the two superpowers allows it to. During the Cold War, nuclear weapons gave both superpowers an incentive to avoid war.

Bell argues that "if the endemic crises of a relationship are managed successfully from year to year over a reasonable period, the relationship itself tends to lose its head of steam . . . so that in time, policy-makers begin to ask why the conflict ever seemed to warrant contemplation of war."[30]

INTERPRETING THE COLD WAR

The origin of the Cold War has been examined even more extensively than its ending. Some of the first historians had participated in foreign policy and wrote accounts that reflected their experience.[31] They tended to attribute expansionist goals to the Soviet Union and interpreted US policies as a reaction to Soviet initiatives. Historians who began to publish in the 1960s wanted to "revise" this standard view and tried to share the blame.[32] Often these revisionist historians went so far as to put the primary blame on the United States. For example, the Soviet blockade of Berlin, seen at the time by most Americans as an attempt to bring troublesome Berliners under control, was interpreted by the revisionists primarily as a defensive reaction by the Soviets to the introduction of a new currency system in the Western zones of occupation.

Historians tend to focus on specific details that make events unique; political scientists try to detect larger patterns in events. Many political scientists were attracted to systems theory. This form of analysis puts most emphasis on the configuration international system, for example, number of states and their relative power. Because World War II effectively destroyed the power of all but two of the winners, it was inevitable, in their view, that a bipolar system should develop, with rivalry between the two powers.[33]

Most recently, it has become fashionable to view the Cold War not as "war" at all but as a "long peace." John Lewis Gaddis, who originated the term, compares the postwar period to periods in the nineteenth century that we have come to look at with nostalgia—the "Concert of Europe" following the demise of Napoleon, or the era of Bismarck. One political scientist has gone so far as to predict that the world will come to regret its the passing of the Cold War. He fears that the stability brought on by bipolarity and nuclear weapons will disappear in a world of many power centers.[34]

Their views are worth considering. It is also worth considering that during the last decade of the Cold War, the two major rivals possessed extensive armaments (including 40,000 nuclear weapons), immense armies (over 5 million Soviet troops, over 2 million American), and enormous expenditures for arms. Although the Cold War period saw only a few isolated cases where Soviet and American troops fired on each other, it did include several major wars that were unlikely, if not unthinkable, in the absence of the intense US–USSR rivalry. It is difficult to imagine that the United States would have fought for twelve years in Vietnam, with losses of its own of 56,000 and over-all battle deaths of over 1 million, had it not seen Vietnam as an arena the struggle with communist expansion. Although we can be less certain, it appears that the Soviet move into Afghanistan in 1980, leading to a war that produced more than 1 million battle deaths, was motivated by the desire of Soviet leaders to secure their southern flank. And it seems highly unlikely than conflict over the reunification of the two parts of Korea would have lasted for three years and produced 2 million battle deaths had it not been viewed as part of the struggle between the Soviet Union and the United States.

NOTES

1. A staggering number of books have been published on the Cold War. Among the most readable of the earlier interpretations is Adam Ulam, *The Rivals* (New York: Viking Press, 1971). One of the more widely read of the revisionist histories is Daniel Yergin, *The Shattered Peace* (Boston: Houghton Mifflin, 1978).
2. One account of events in Azerbaijan is Joseph Marion Jones, *The Fifteen Weeks* (New York: Viking Press, 1955), pp. 48–58.
3. The entire speech is printed as an appendix in Jones's book, pp. 269–274. (See note 2.)
4. *Izvestia* (March 13, 1947), quoted in Alvin Z. Rubinstein, ed., *The Foreign Policy of the Soviet Union*, 2nd ed. (New York: Random House, 1966), p. 231.
5. Seweryn Bialer "'New Thinking' and Soviet Foreign Policy" *Survival* Vol. 30, No. 4 (July/August 1988) pp. 291–309.
6. Quoted in John C. Sparrow, *History of Personnel Demobilization in the United States Army* (Washington, D.C.: Office of the Chief of Military History, Department of the Army, 1951), p. 380.
7. Cited by Kenneth Waltz, "The Stability of a Bipolar World," *Daedalus*, Vol. 93, No. 3 (Summer 1964), p. 883.
8. Commencement address at Iowa State College, Ames, Iowa, June 9, 1956, in *Department of State Bulletin*, Vol. 34, No. 886 (June 18, 1956), pp. 99–100.
9. David Rees, *Korea: The Limited War* (New York: St. Martin's Press, 1964), pp. 19–20.
10. Contemporary interpretations are described by Alexander L. George in "American Policy-Making and the North Korean Aggression," *World Politics*, Vol. 7, No. 2 (January 1955), pp. 209–232.
11. The speech was published in *Department of State Bulletin*, Vol. 22, No. 551 (January 23, 1950), pp. 111–118. For Acheson's justification of his speech, see his *Present at the Creation* (New York: Signet Books, 1969), p. 467.
12. Harry Truman, *Memoirs*, Vol. 2: *Years of Trial and Hope* (Garden City, N.Y.: Doubleday, 1956), p. 335.
13. Ibid., p. 445.
14. John Spanier, *The Truman–MacArthur Controversy and the Korean War* (Cambridge, Mass.: Harvard University Press, 1959), p. 25.
15. For an explanation of why the United States responded in spite of its declared policy not to, see Ernest May, "The Nature of Foreign Policy: The Calculated versus the Axiomatic," *Daedalus*, Vol. 91, No. 4 (Fall 1962), pp. 633–667.
16. *The Pentagon Papers* (Senator Gravel Edition), Vol. I (Boston: Beacon Press, 1971), p. 83.
17. Richard Neustadt, *Presidential Power* (New York: Signet Books, 1964), especially p. 131.
18. Allen S. Whiting, *China Crosses the Yalu* (Stanford: Stanford University Press, 1960), p. 155; Edward Friedman, "Problems in Dealing with an Irrational Power: America Declares War on China," in *America's Asia: Dissenting Essays on Asian-American Relations*, ed. Edward Friedman and Mark Selden (New York: Pantheon Books, 1969), pp. 207–252.
19. Truman, Vol. 2, p. 360. (See note 12.)
20. Thomas C. Schelling, *Arms and Influence* (New Haven: Yale University Press, 1966), p. 55 n.
21. Friedman, pp. 228–238. (See note 18.)
22. Frank E. Armbruster, "China's Conventional Military Capability," in Frank E. Armbruster et al., *China Briefing* (Chicago: University of Chicago Center for Policy Study 1968), pp. 59–60.

23.   For a thorough discussion of this point, see Morton H. Halperin, *Limited War in the Nuclear Age* (New York: John Wiley, 1963), Chapter 3.

24.   Bernard Brodie, *Strategy in the Missile Age* (Princeton: Princeton University Press, 1959), pp. 319–321.

25.   Testimony at the "MacArthur Hearings," published as *Military Situation in the Far East*, quoted by Rees, p. 274. (See note 9.)

26.   Michael Mandelbaum, "Ending the Cold War," *Foreign Affairs* Vol. 68, No. 2 (Spring 1989) p. 21.

27.   R. W. Apple, Jr., "34 Lands Proclaim a United Europe in Paris Charter," *The New York Times*, November 22, 1990, pp. A1, A4.

28.   Coral Bell, "Managing to Survive," *The National Interest*, No. 2 (Winter 1986), pp. 36–45.

29.   John Lewis Gaddis, "The Long Peace," *International Security*, Vol. 10, No. 4 (Spring 1986), pp. 99–142.

30.   Bell, p. 42. (See note 28.)

31.   For example, Herbert Feis, *From Trust to Terror* (New York: Norton, 1970); also, Jones. (See note 2.)

32.   One of the first was Gar Alperovitz, *Atomic Diplomacy* (New York: Simon & Schuster, 1965). A representative book is Gabriel Kolko and Joyce Kolko, *The Limits of Power* (New York: Harper & Row, 1972).

33.   Morton Kaplan, *System and Process in International Politics* (New York: John Wiley, 1957).

34.   John Mearsheimer, "Back to the Future: Instability in Europe After the Cold War," *International Security*, Vol. 15, No. 1, pp. 5–56.

CHAPTER 4

WARS IN THE MIDDLE EAST

The Middle East has had more than its share of tension and conflict among states. The conflict that is most serious both in the casualties it has produced and in the threat it poses to world peace is the ongoing one between Israel and the Arab states. The basic issue is simple: Two separate groups of people want to build a state on the same piece of land. The complexity of the problem emerges when we examine how both Jews and Arabs happened to claim the same land.

ZIONISM

Through centuries when nations appeared, merged, and disappeared, the Jews distinguished themselves by maintaining a separate identity. In part their separateness was forced on them by persecution, especially by the Christian church. But it was reinforced by the basic tenets of their religion, which stressed codes of behavior. Various dietary laws—for example, no mixing of milk and meat—made it simpler for Jews to avoid eating with non-Jews and thus cut off one common avenue of social interchange.

Judaism also stressed membership in a community, belonging to a people. The sacred writings of Judaism were as much the history of the Jews as anything else, and that history took place on a particular piece of land, which the Jews called the land of Israel and we today know as Palestine. Even though most Jews had been expelled from their historic homeland by the Romans, over the centuries Jews everywhere kept alive their ties to the land by religious practices. Many of their religious holidays were intimately connected with the seasons in Palestine. The spring holiday of Shavuot, for example, was basically a harvest festival. For Jews celebrating Shavuot in the cold, wet spring of Poland and Russia, the holiday made sense only if they remembered the spring harvest of grain in the land of Israel.

Ties to the historic homeland of the Jews—sometimes poetically called Zion—were thus kept alive in a form we call religious Zionism. It had few practical consequences. Pious Jews wished to be buried in the land of Israel and hoped that someday a Messiah would come to restore the glories of the ancient kingdom of David.

For centuries the Jews were the victims of anti-Semitism, or prejudice, because of their religion. They were disliked because of their beliefs. If they changed their beliefs and converted to Christianity, they were accepted. Attitudes toward Jews changed in the nineteenth century, and the changes brought changes to Zionism. In the nineteenth century, anti-Semitism came to be based on race. Jews were disliked because of what they were, and no change could make them acceptable. Racial anti-Semitism accompanied the rise of extreme nationalism. Russian nationalists reemphasized the Slavic language and race. The French emphasized their origins in ancient Gaul. Outsiders, even converted and assimilated Jews, could never hope to become members of these nations.

With people around them emphasizing their own historic origins, Jews too began thinking about their roots. When their neighbors began telling them they were outsiders, they began to look for a part of the world they could call home. Religious Zionism provided the answer. By the end of the nineteenth century, young Jews began forming societies to encourage a return to their historic homeland. The first such groups appeared in Russia around 1880. Zionism became an international political movement after the publication in 1896 of a pamphlet called *The Jewish State* by an Austrian Jew, Theodore Herzl. The following year Herzl organized the first World Zionist Congress to provide an organizational structure for the movement.

A small number of Jews left Europe to escape anti-Semitic persecution and set up the beginnings of their own state. They were able to establish colonies in Palestine because national currents had not yet reached the people living in that part of the world (a condition that was to make possible their initial success but lay the foundation for later tragedy). To the Arabs living in Palestine, Europeans arriving to set up settlements were objects of curiosity but not alarm. Although not empty, the land was not nearly as populous as it would become later. Maladministration by the Turks, who had ruled the area for centuries, had not encouraged population growth. In the late nineteenth century, Palestine was a home for many utopian schemers, including Russian Orthodox pilgrims and German Pietists. Zionists were just one more group.[1]

ARAB NATIONALISM

The same national stirrings that hit the European Jews in the late nineteenth century affected the Arabs about twenty-five years later. Some of the first writings about an Arab state appeared in the first years of the twentieth century.[2] But the major impetus came from World War I. The Turks had joined the war on the side of the Germans, and the British were fearful for their possessions in the Middle East, particularly the Suez Canal. Hoping to protect their holdings by exploiting Arab resentment against the Turks, who were still the nominal rulers, the British promoted an Arab revolt. In return for British military support and the promise of an Arab state after the war, the Arabs were to rise up against the Turks.

Sherif Hussein of Mecca, the great-great-grandfather of King Hussein, the current ruler of Jordan, led the revolt. He expected that after the war he would head an Arab state centered in Damascus and including the area today known as Syria, Lebanon, Israel, and Jordan. But the Arab revolt did not proceed fast enough for the Arabs to be firmly in control of this territory by the time the war was ended. The Arabs then discovered that the British, in addition to promising this land to them, had promised a portion of the area to the Jews (in the Balfour Declaration of 1917) and another portion to the French (in the Sykes–Picot agreement of 1916).

The Arab forces were no match for the French and British troops, and by 1922 the European powers had a new system firmly in place, sanctioned by the new League of Nations as mandates that were to train the natives for self-government. The dividing line between the French and British mandates separated what has become Syria from what has become Jordan. Within each mandate, the European powers made further divisions. The French divided the Christian area of Lebanon from Syria; the British divided the strictly Arab area of Trans-Jordan from the area of Palestine, where Jews were allowed to settle (see Figure 4.1).

Arab nationalists were left with many grievances. In addition to a betrayal of promises and foreign domination, they saw European rulers allowing European Jews to settle on Arab land. Such settlement was in conflict with the widespread belief that nations must have exclusive control of a state. Indeed, it was just this belief that made the Jews insist on creating a state entirely under their own control. The most persistent demand of Arab nationalists during the 1920s and 1930s was a halt to Jewish immigration and land sales.

When the British established their mandate in Palestine, the conflict between Arabs and Jews was not yet acute. Total Zionist immigration to that

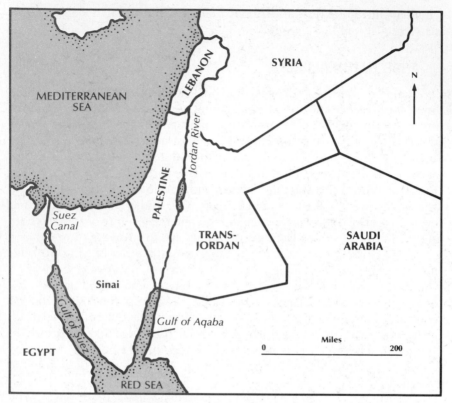

Figure 4.1   The Middle East, 1947

time numbered only 90,000. The Zionists had paid for all the land they bought, and they were improving the economic life of the country, providing employment and improving standards of living.

But life in Palestine was hard, and most European Jews were not Zionists. Far more wanted to emigrate to America. In the period when fewer than 100,000 were leaving for Palestine, over a million and a half left Russia for America. The Zionist settlement of Palestine might have become no more than a footnote in history had it not been for two major events, both external to the Middle East. First, Britain and then America severely restricted immigration from Russia and Eastern Europe (meaning, above all, Jewish immigration). Second, the rise to power of the Nazis made the need to emigrate all the more urgent. Despite obstacles created by the Nazis and immigration restrictions imposed by the British Mandate authorities, over 350,000 Jews moved to Palestine during the Nazi era. Palestine, with a population that was 30 percent Jewish, had the densest concentration of Jews in the world.

ISSUES LEADING TO WAR

The stake in the conflict was clear. Two peoples wanted to set up a state on the same piece of land. For the Zionists, the justification was that Jews everywhere were being told that they were not welcome because they were outsiders. In effect, hostile governments were saying to them, "Why don't you go back where you came from?" Where they came from was Palestine or, as they called it, the land of Israel, and to there they had returned in significant numbers. No place on earth had a higher proportion of Jews in its population. No other place was better qualified as a site for a Jewish state, and recent events in Europe had demonstrated that without a state of their own they were doomed. As the Zionist leader David Ben-Gurion put it, "If we have the choice between riots in Germany, Poland or any other country, and riots in Palestine, we prefer riots in Palestine." For the Arabs, the justification was much simpler. They wanted a state in Palestine because that is where they were living, and, despite the large number of Jewish immigrants, still formed the majority.

Underlying this desire for a state were several basic ideas of modern political thought. Both sides believed they needed an exclusive state. Only a small minority among Jews and Arabs were willing to try other arrangements, such as a confederation of provinces or a dual-nationality state. The Jews had experienced centuries of insecurity as a minority. They knew too well that the firmest constitutional guarantees could be terminated overnight by a ruler such as Hitler. The Arabs had suffered centuries of misrule as a province of the Turks in the Ottoman Empire. For them foreign rule had meant exploitation. According to modern notions of national self-determination held by Jews and Arabs alike, it was no longer feasible for two separate peoples to live side by side within one nation as they had in many cases in the past.

A final factor leading to war in 1948 was involvement of the great powers. The Zionists had powerful support in the United States, especially from Congress and the president. The Arabs found support with the British, who valued their good relations with the Arabs and wanted to protect their economic interests, including oil, in the several Arab states. In the UN debate about what to do with Palestine, the Americans were backed by the Soviet Union, not because Stalin had any concern for the plight of the Jews but because he saw the issue as a wedge that could be driven between his two most powerful capitalist enemies. Thus, in November 1947 the UN General Assembly passed a resolution, jointly sponsored by the United States and the Soviet Union, calling for the establishment of two states in the British Mandate of Palestine, a Jewish state and an Arab one.

THE 1948 WAR

On May 14, 1948, Zionist leaders declared independence for their new state, naming it Israel. The Arabs, who had bitterly opposed the UN vote, had no intention of letting a Jewish state come into existence in their midst. On May 15, Arab armies attacked.

Because the issues were so clear, war had been expected. The Israelis were fighting for the survival of their state and, most of them believed, for their physical survival as well. The Arab states opposing Israel were united in their goal of preventing such a state from coming into existence. Beyond that negative goal, however, the Arabs did not agree, and their lack of agreement was the fundamental cause of their defeat.

The strongest Arab force was the Arab Legion of Trans-Jordan (now Jordan). But the king of Trans-Jordan, Abdullah, was not fighting on behalf of a Palestinian state. He intended to annex the area to his own kingdom. It was primarily to keep this from happening that Egypt entered the war. All the Arabs assumed the Israelis would be easy to defeat. Egypt's primary concern in deploying its armies was to keep the Arab Legion from gaining control over the entire territory. Egypt favored a separate Palestinian state because it believed such a state would be weak and would quickly become an Egyptian client. Syria and Lebanon also participated, partly out of feelings of solidarity, partly in the hope of adding to their own territory. Iraq sent some troops as well. The weakest contingents of all were the armed bands of Arabs from Palestine itself.

By skillful fighting and skillful diplomacy, taking advantage of Arab divisions, the Israelis were able to prevail. The war consisted of short periods of violent fighting, each lasting a few weeks, interspersed with truces. The Israelis were able to get their foes to break the truces; then they defeated them one by one in short, well-planned campaigns. Because of Arab distrust, the Arab Legion stood aside while the Israelis defeated the Egyptians in the south; then the Egyptians stood aside while the Israelis defeated the Arab Legion. Finally, in early 1949, Egypt concluded an armistice with Israel. In the next few months the other Arab belligerents followed except for Iraq, which had no borders in common with Israel and thus needed no formal agreement.

THE 1956 WAR

For Israel, the 1948 war was a tentative success, a first step toward security. But the victory was not complete. Israel had no internationally recognized boundaries, only armistice lines. Arab neighbors still considered themselves in a state of war. All the states of the Middle East felt that the basic issue of the existence of a Jewish state was not yet resolved. Another armed clash would come; the only question was when.

Partly as a result of their defeat in the 1948 war, a group of Egyptian army officers in 1952 deposed their king, whom they blamed for the corruption and inefficiency in their society. The most important of these officers was Gamal Abdel Nasser, who became president in 1954. The elimination of the state of Israel was always a goal of Nasser's foreign policy. As he was to put it, the very existence of the state of Israel was an act of aggression.[3] What determines a state's actual policy, however, is not what its leaders wish but how much they are willing to sacrifice to see their wishes realized. In the first years of Nasser's rule, he seemed content to give only lip service to the goal of eliminating Israel, concentrating instead on strengthening Egypt's political system and economy.

Nasser's policies changed after February 1955, when Israeli troops crossed the armistice line into the Gaza Strip (a section of Palestine under Egyptian control) in retaliation for a terrorist attack. Arab attacks across the armistice line into Israel were common, but before February 1955 they were individual efforts not sponsored by any Arab government. After the Gaza Strip raid, however, Nasser set up an organization to conduct raids into Israel. The existence of terrorist bases in territory controlled by Egypt became a serious concern to Israel, serious enough that it was willing to contemplate war to see them eliminated.

A second reason for Israel to contemplate war was Nasser's restrictions on Israeli shipping. When Britain gave control of the Suez Canal to Egypt in a treaty signed in October 1954, all cargo destined for or coming from Israel, even in non-Israeli ships, was prohibited by Egypt from going through the canal. This meant that if Israel wished to trade with countries around the Indian Ocean or in the Pacific, it had to use the long route around the southern tip of Africa. The only other possibility was to use the Israeli port of Elat and travel through the Gulf of Aqaba out into the Red Sea. But Egypt controlled the strategic heights of Sharm el Sheik, which overlooked the Strait of Tiran, the exit from the Gulf of Aqaba into the Red Sea. Thus Egypt was able to prevent Israeli shipping from using that route as well. In September 1955, in response to another Israeli retaliatory raid, Nasser announced that even air travel over the Gulf of Aqaba was prohibited.

Meanwhile, quite independent of the conflict between Egypt and Israel, British troops were withdrawing from the Suez Canal zone under the terms of the October 1954 treaty. Even though the British were not friendly toward Israel, the presence of their troops had provided a buffer between Egyptian forces and Israel. With the British withdrawal, the Israelis felt less secure, but so did Nasser. He had insisted that the British leave in order to remove the last vestige of colonialism, but he was not sure the Egyptian army was strong enough to face the Israelis. He set about to modernize his forces and, after being rebuffed by the United States, turned to the Soviet Union. In September 1955, he announced an arms deal with the Soviet bloc.

The arms deal was one of several issues that soured relations between the United States and Egypt in 1955 and 1956 and made it politically difficult for President Eisenhower to go ahead with a proposed loan for a major economic project in Egypt, a new high dam on the Nile at Aswan. In July 1956, Secretary of State John Foster Dulles abruptly withdrew support for such a loan. The news came as a surprise and shock to Nasser. Within a week he announced he was nationalizing the private international company that ran the Suez Canal. Because the company's stockholders were mainly British and French, Nasser's action most disturbed Britain and France.

The French already disliked Nasser because of the support he was giving to an Arab insurrection in their territory of Algeria. Many believed that action to stop the rebellion at its source in Egypt would be more effective than sending more troops to Algeria, but they lacked the physical means to conduct operations against Egypt. When Nasser nationalized the canal company, he provided the French with both an ally for action and an excuse for acting.

The French military staff (later joined by the British) worked out a plan with Israel (later joined by Britain). Israel would attack Egypt to achieve its main objectives—elimination of terrorist bases and the opening of passages through the Strait of Tiran. France and England would secretly provide air cover for Israel during this attack, but they would pretend to be surprised by it and would demand an immediate cease-fire and pullback of troops to protect the Suez Canal from damage. If Nasser did not comply (and they did not believe he would), they would land troops in the canal zone in order to protect it.

The Israeli part of the plan worked very well. On the night of October 29, 1956, Israeli forces attacked Egypt. By November 5 they had reached the canal. The British and French part failed. Because of extreme caution they did not even begin to land troops until November 6. By then, pressure from other countries for a cease-fire was irresistible. Most surprising was pressure from the United States. Britain and France had calculated that the United States would remain neutral, but they were wrong. Partly out of anger at not being informed in advance, partly to preserve Eisenhower's image as a man of peace during a presidential election, partly to avoid any recrimination that would detract from US condemnation of the Soviet suppression of a rebellion simultaneously occurring in Hungary, the United States took the lead at the UN in condemning the invasion. The United States backed its condemnation with economic moves (such as restricting the flow of oil to Britain) designed to force capitulation.

The British and French were forced to withdraw and make way for a UN peace-keeping force, an operation that took only a few days. The Israelis fared slightly better, remaining in possession of the Sinai Peninsula until March 1957, when US pressure forced them to retreat in favor of a UN force as well. The Suez Canal remained in Egyptian control. Nevertheless, the war achieved what Israel wanted. The presence of the UN force in Sinai inhibited terrorist attacks from Egyptian territory and guaranteed free passage through the Strait of Tiran. At a cost of only 189 battle deaths, Israel had achieved some important foreign policy goals.

THE 1967 WAR

The Sinai campaign brought Israel the longest period of peace in its history—from 1956 to 1967. During that time the state and economy of Israel grew stronger, as did its military power. Outside observers considered war unlikely because the Arab armies were no match for Israel. Despite these expectations, however, in the spring of 1967 a crisis developed and turned into a war in a matter of weeks. On June 5, Israeli forces attacked Egypt; within days they had defeated Jordan and Syria as well. The prewar calculation of Israeli superiority was thus proved correct. Yet, because that calculation had not been convincing to all sides, war had occurred.

The most serious miscalculation was made by President Nasser. He had resigned himself to tolerate Israel's existence until three conditions changed: the Arabs acquired military superiority, Israel was diplomatically isolated, and the Arabs were united. Within a few weeks, in May 1967, Nasser deceived himself into thinking that these conditions had been met.[4]

Nasser's belief that the Arabs had achieved military superiority resulted from his confusing the possession of military equipment with its actual assimilation by his troops. The Soviet Union had supplied substantial amounts of equipment, but Egyptian soldiers were still far from proficient in its use. Evidence of their lack of combat readiness was soon apparent. When the Israelis overran the Sinai Peninsula in the course of the 1967 war, they did not find a single tank-repair shop. They did find plans for an Egyptian air strike on Israel similar to the strike that Israel had launched to begin the war on Egypt. But whereas the Israelis had needed only seven and one-half minutes to rearm and refuel planes between missions, the Egyptians had planned to allow from thirty to forty minutes.[5] Furthermore, the best Egyptian troops—40,000 of them—were at the southern tip of the Arabian peninsula fighting a war in Yemen, and they could not be withdrawn in time to make a difference.

Nasser's belief in Israel's diplomatic isolation was a misperception, based in part on false information, fed to him by the Soviets, that Israel was mobilizing troops on its northern frontier to attack Syria. If Israel launched such an attack, Nasser believed, no country would support it. Israel offered to allow foreign diplomats to tour its northern region to see that no such mobilization was taking place, and UN observers subsequently confirmed the Israeli claim, but Nasser persisted in his belief in Israeli aggressive designs until too late. As the focus of the crisis shifted from Syria to Egypt, Nasser persisted in his policy of tempting Israel to strike first in order to ensure its diplomatic isolation. But when war did break out, it was seen by most countries (most important, by the United States) not as Israeli aggression but as an Israeli response to provocations by Nasser. Thus, unlike in 1956, Israel did not find itself condemned by the United States and under heavy pressure to relinquish its conquests.

Even more serious for Nasser were the military consequences of allowing Israel to strike first. He even predicted that Israel would launch an air strike on June 5, the very date it occurred. But he erred in predicting a loss to Egypt of only 20 percent of its planes; the actual loss was a crippling 60 percent, not to mention damage to all radar stations and air fields.[6]

His final miscalculation was a belief that he had achieved Arab unity. Verbal support, amounting to war fever in the Arab countries, misled Nasser into believing that his persistent but elusive goal had been achieved. A joint command structure of the armies of Egypt, Jordan, and Syria existed on paper, suggesting that in this war, unlike the previous ones, all Arab belligerents would follow a unified and coherent strategy. But during the actual fighting, Israel again triumphed because it was able to deal with its opponents one by one, just as in the 1948 war.

Not all the miscalculations were on the Egyptian side, however. Nasser had set events in motion by ordering Egyptian troops into the Sinai Peninsula on May 14. Such a move set the stage for war, for Egypt usually held the Sinai with only a small garrison force. The move was not legally an act of aggression, because the Sinai was acknowledged Egyptian territory. Nevertheless, Nasser expected a firm Israeli reaction such as mobilization. Encountering no such reaction, Nasser proceeded on May 18 to the next step, ordering the withdrawal of the UN buffer force from Egyptian territory. This move was more serious, undoing one of the accomplishments of the 1956 war, but again Nasser provoked no threatening military reaction from the Israelis.[7] The Israeli government was divided and headed by a cautious prime minister, Levi Eshkol. Moreover, the Israelis recalled that Nasser had moved troops into the Sinai in 1960, provoking a brief war scare at that time, but nothing had come of it. Thus Israel did not feel threatened by these most recent moves.

Israel was not alone in its failure to react strongly. The US response to Nasser's actions was very mild as well. The United States wanted very much to avoid a war in the Middle East because of the risk of involving American troops there when US forces were strained by the war in Vietnam. Initially American diplomatic notes to Israel were much harsher, urging restraint in response to Nasser's moves.[8]

Emboldened by the caution of his opponent, Nasser pushed on. On May 22 he announced the closure of the Strait of Tiran to Israeli shipping, thereby undoing the other major accomplishment of the 1956 war. Despite the Israeli position that such an action would be treated as a *casus belli*, or action justifying war, the Israeli prime minister reacted again with a mild speech. His concluding line was not a dramatic threat but the prosaic comment that Nasser's action would "be a dangerous precedent."[9]

Nasser's belief that his three conditions had been fulfilled was reinforced by Israel's caution. Believing that time was on his side, Nasser continued to apply pressure. Egyptian troops that had been fighting in a civil war in Yemen were recalled home. An airlift of Egyptian troops into Jordan began. As the pressure for Israel to strike the first blow increased, Egypt's own military strength to withstand such a blow increased, or so Nasser believed.

But, having made war more likely by its caution and delay, Israel was now organizing itself to act. A new Cabinet was formed, including members of all Israel's political parties except the Communists. The general who had organized the 1956 Sinai campaign, Moshe Dayan, was named minister of defense. Israeli military leaders prepared to implement their plan for a first strike designed to eliminate the Egyptian air force. The strike was carried out successfully on June 5.

As in 1956, Israeli forces quickly occupied the Sinai Peninsula. But unlike in 1956, they did not subsequently withdraw. The speedy withdrawal of the UN buffer force when it was ordered out by Nasser had weakened arguments in favor of relying on such a force a second time.

In 1967 Israel fought against Jordan and Syria as well as Egypt. From Jordan the Israelis took all the territory on the west bank of the Jordan River, including parts of the city of Jerusalem that had been under Jordanian control since 1948. From Syria they captured the strategic territory of the Golan Heights, which overlooks Israeli settlements around the Sea of Galilee.

The war turned out badly for Nasser, who had set in motion the events that led to the fighting. In addition to a humiliating military defeat, Egypt lost the Sinai Peninsula and the revenues from the Suez Canal, which was blocked by Nasser when the war began and subsequently served as the cease-fire line between Israeli and Egyptian troops. For the Israelis, who struck the first blow, the war turned out well. Not only was the security of the state enhanced, as it had been by the wars of 1948 and 1956, but Israel now possessed territory that it hoped it could trade for a permanent peace settlement. War appeared to have produced results unachievable by the peaceful means of diplomacy.

THE 1973 WAR

Neither the 1948 war nor the 1956 war had begun entirely at the initiative of the Arabs. In 1948 the Arabs could have chosen to accept the new state of Israel. When they decided against acceptance, the timing of the war was determined by the departure of the British and the Israeli declaration of independence. In 1956 the war clearly originated with the British, French, and Israelis. In 1967, however, despite the fact that Israel struck the first blow, the war resulted from Nasser's initiatives but failed to achieve the results he had hoped for. War for him was an extension of diplomacy by other means, although in this case the other means were as unsuccessful as diplomacy had been. In 1973 Egypt again resorted to war to achieve its goals.

President Nasser died in 1970, having failed to undo the results of the 1967 war. His successor, Anwar Sadat, had some advantages in conducting foreign policy that Nassar had lacked. Because Sadat was less flamboyant, he could dissociate himself from some of the more extreme policies of his predecessor, especially the claims to a pan-Arab state under Egyptian leadership, which threatened the stability of all the other Arab governments. Sadat's moderation won him the support of conservative Arab states such as Saudi Arabia but still did not win the support of the United States. Even Sadat's dramatic gesture of expelling all Russian advisers in 1972 did not win him American support. Nevertheless, Sadat's basic understanding of the situation was correct. Only the United States was in a position to deliver what Egypt wanted most, the restoration of the Sinai Peninsula and its accompanying economic advantages—oil from its oil fields and revenue from the Suez Canal, which could be reopened if it no longer served as a cease-fire line. As long as Israel was sure of American diplomatic and military support, Israel could dictate the terms under which the Sinai would be returned. For Sadat these terms were too high a price to pay. Only if the Americans found it in their interest to give less than total support to Israel could the deadlock be broken.

Sadat continued his diplomatic efforts into 1973, dispatching his national security adviser to consult once again with the Americans. At the same time he prepared to resort to force if his diplomacy failed. His aim was concrete and limited—the establishment of a small area under Egyptian control on the east bank of the Suez Canal. Strategically such a goal made sense because of the dilemma Israel found itself in. It could guard the canal heavily only at the great cost to its economy of maintaining a force 200 miles from its own territory. But failure to guard the canal heavily would open it to precisely the kind of move Sadat had in mind. Because the west bank of the canal was so close to the heart of Egypt, it was easy for Sadat to keep troops in a threatening posture. Furthermore, Egypt's larger population enabled it to maintain a larger standing army. Israel's civilian army rapidly mobilized in time of war could match Egypt in short periods of combat, but Israel could not keep its army mobilized for any great length of time without crippling its economy.

The Egyptian military planners had learned a few lessons from the defeat in 1967. Recognizing that their soldiers had less technological proficiency than the Israelis, in 1973 they made less ambitious plans. They intended merely to cross the canal, establish themselves on a few miles of territory, and dig in. Soldiers practiced the necessary operations, such as unloading bridging equipment from trucks, again and again, day after day. The initiative and improvisation characteristic of the Israeli forces would give the Israelis little advantage in the kind of operation that the Egyptians were planning.[10]

In the spring of 1973, Egypt moved a large force into the canal area. Perhaps they were only engaging in maneuvers; perhaps they were preparing for an attack. The Israelis noticed and mobilized their army. Egypt proceeded with military maneuvers but did not attack. Israel demobilized. After a summer of further diplomacy, Egypt again moved large forces into the canal zone in the fall. Again Israel noticed, but now decided not to undergo the expense of mobilization. This time Egypt attacked.

The Egyptian attack was coordinated with a Syrian attack in the Golan Heights, a level of coordination the Arabs had not achieved in previous wars. Because of the coordination and the surprise, the Arab armies did quite well.

Despite the fact that the war began with an unambiguous Arab attack, the United States was slow in coming to the aid of Israel. In the mind of the American secretary of state, Henry Kissinger, Israel's overwhelming victory in 1967 had actually hindered movement toward peace. The Israelis were so confident that they felt no pressure to make concessions. The Arabs had been so humiliated that only after they had redeemed themselves in battle could they consider making peace as equals. Thus Kissinger did not want a repetition of the 1967 war.

Events outran Kissinger's policy. Working with the advantages of surprise and initiative, the Arab armies fought well. The Israelis, suffering from confusion and carelessness engendered by overconfidence, were not able to make a decisive counterattack. In the north they were able to halt the Syrian attack, but their counterattacks failed. Along the Suez Canal they could not dislodge the Egyptians.

Both sides were using munitions at a prodigious rate. The war had begun on October 5. By October 10 the Soviets began resupplying the Egyptians and Syrians. Israel began pressing the United States for new supplies. In the years since 1948, military technology had grown increasingly complex. Wars of even short duration became intense. More tanks faced each other in the Sinai than in the major tank battles of World War II. The complexity of weapons as well as the rapid rate at which they used up ammunition increased the dependence of the combatants on their suppliers. This dependency created the danger of the war's escalating by drawing in the suppliers, but it also gave the suppliers increased opportunities for influencing the outcome.

On October 14 the Israelis began to reverse the course of the war by crossing the Suez Canal to the Egyptian side, spreading out and threatening to trap the Egyptian armies already on the west side. This move would have created a military victory as spectacular as the one of 1967, precisely the outcome the Americans did not want. Because of the total dependence of Israel on the United States for supplies, the United States was able to force Israel to agree to a cease-fire before it had entirely trapped the Egyptian armies. To the complaints of Israeli officers who felt they were being denied the victory they deserved, the minister of defense, Moshe Dayan, replied, "Shells they are firing today were not in their possession a week ago."[11]

The 1973 war ended with each side able to claim some victories. The Arab states had mounted a successful attack and, in the south, maintained a foothold in territory that had been occupied by Israel after 1967. The Israelis had recovered from the shock of surprise, held their own lines in the north, and, in the south, mounted a counterattack that put them in control of Egyptian territory on the west bank of the Suez Canal.

Kissinger's analysis was proved correct. The somewhat ambiguous results of the 1973 war paved the way for a peace treaty between Israel and Egypt signed in 1979. For Egypt the war and the resulting agreements accomplished major foreign policy objectives—a restoration of honor, a return to the Sinai Peninsula, economic gains from oil fields and the re-opened Suez Canal, and the beginnings of a reduced defense burden.

For Israel, the results were less satisfactory. Recognition by one of its Arab neighbors and the conclusion of peace with it was the major gain. But Israel remained under attack from the other Arab states. The loss of the oil fields in the Sinai made Israel even more dependent on outsiders—particularly the United States, which had guaranteed to supply oil in the last resort. It is unlikely that Israel would have paid the price it did if Egypt had not gone to war.

ISRAEL AND LEBANON

In June 1982 the Middle East experienced yet another major war, this time on Israel's initiative. The war, much to the shock of some Israelis,[12] was less to repulse a clear threat to their security than to accomplish more abstract political ends. One could say that the 1956 war was not primarily defensive either; at least one could question the seriousness of the threat to Israel posed then by the terrorists operating from the Gaza Strip and the potential threat posed by the Egyptian acquisition of Russian arms. In 1982 the same two issues reappeared.

After a civil war in Jordan in 1970 between the forces of King Hussein and the forces of the various Palestinian guerrilla groups, the Palestinians were forced to relocate their political and military activities to Lebanon. The

Lebanese state was too weak and divided by its own sectarian differences to impose any serious limits on their actions. As a result, the Palestinians, under the umbrella organization of the Palestinian Liberation Organization (PLO), increased in power, establishing themselves as virtual rulers in several areas of Lebanon, mounting terrorist attacks into Israel, and building up arsenals that by 1981 began to include heavy weapons—artillery, rocket launchers, and tanks. This increase in military power was accompanied by increasing international recognition, such as the invitation extended in 1974 to the head of the PLO, Yasir Arafat, to address the General Assembly of the United Nations with the same honors accorded to a head of state.

As the international stature of the PLO grew, its forays into Israel diminished, partly because of PLO policy, partly because of better Israeli security, and partly because of agreements worked out by the United States. Nevertheless, Israel expressed alarm at the growth in military potential as the PLO acquired long-range weapons such as rockets and artillery, which would endanger Israel if the cease-fire on its northern border ever broke down. Perhaps more alarming, although not emphasized publicly by Israeli leaders, was the growth in political power of the PLO. In Western Europe and in the United States, more groups and even governments called for some form of recognition and statehood for the Palestinians.

Since 1977 Israel had been governed (for the first time in its history) by a right-wing coalition, headed by Menachem Begin. Prominent among his cabinet ministers was Ariel Sharon, who earlier as military governor of the Gaza Strip had demonstrated his belief in the usefulness of force. Both men were committed to the annexation of the West Bank of the Jordan River— territory captured by Israel in the 1967 war—as land to which Israel had a historic claim. Both were opposed to the creation of a Palestinian state on land claimed by Israel—or anywhere if such a state were to present a military threat to Israel.

In June 1982 a gunman shot the Israeli ambassador to Britain; immediately Israeli forces in large numbers moved north into Lebanon in an obviously well-planned operation. The ineffectual Lebanese army was in no position to offer resistance. The real opponents were the forces of the PLO and the troops of Syria, who had been stationed in Lebanon since 1976 in an effort to end fighting among various factions inside Lebanon. Despite emphasis by Prime Minister Begin on the security threat to Israel posed by PLO forces in southern Lebanon, it became clear that the real target was the PLO as a political force. Israeli troops advanced to the capital, Beirut, then paused as straightforward military missions were complicated by political problems. The Syrians offered little resistance to the Israelis, withdrawing toward their own border to protect their homeland. But at the same time they did not pressure the Palestinians to surrender or evacuate. Israel could have mounted a direct military assault on Palestinian strongholds in Beirut, but only at high cost to its own troops (a move unpopular at home) and to civilians in Beirut (a move unpopular abroad, especially in the United States).

The ensuing dilemma meant that instead of a war measured in days, Israel was engaged in weeks of siege warfare, attacking Beirut by airplane and artillery while suffering small but steady losses in its own forces. The siege ended with a negotiated withdrawal of PLO forces from Beirut, ostensibly to distant Arab states such as Tunisia. Yet many of these forces quickly returned to Lebanon by way of Syria. The PLO suffered a political setback but was not eliminated as a political force. Syrian forces remained in control of much of Lebanon, and to counterbalance them many Israelis remained as occupation troops.

President Sadat initiated war against Israel in 1973 with a clear political goal. From a purely military standpoint the war appeared to go badly for Egypt, with Israeli troops ending in possession of territory on both banks of the Suez Canal. Yet the diplomacy and military pressure of the following years did lead to a peace settlement, completed in 1982 by the final Israeli withdrawal from land in the Sinai captured in 1967.

The 1982 invasion of Lebanon by Israel appears to have had a similarly clear political goal. But willingness to pursue politics "by other means" (to use Clausewitz's description of war) is no guarantee of success. The Israelis did achieve some of their goals. They forced the PLO to give up its headquarters in Beirut and the quasi-sovereign status it enjoyed in some parts of Lebanon. Instead of operating from one central stronghold, it would henceforward be scattered among several countries. The more realistic Palestinians recognized their defeat almost immediately. Commenting on a meeting of the Palestine National Council in Algiers the next year (1983), one PLO official said:

> It was outrageous that all of the secretaries general of the different PLO organizations painted a picture of Lebanon as a glowing victory. Lebanon was a disaster. I bow my head to the courage of the people who fought there. But if Beirut was such a great victory, then all we need is a series of such victories and we will be holding our next national council meeting in Fiji.[13]

Within five years even Arab historians began to refer to "the defeat in Beirut."[14] More significant, Chairman Yasir Arafat and his colleagues were telling journalists that they had abandoned the hope of defeating Israel either by the force of their own guerrillas or by persuading other Arab states to fight for them.[15]

But in weakening one of its enemies, Israel had created a new one. Many of the people living in southern Lebanon were Shiite Muslims. In the preceding decades they had not played a direct role in the clashes between Palestinians and Israelis along the border. But the prolonged Israeli occupation of their territory now drew them into the conflict. Repeated attacks on the Israeli occupation forces, often in the form of car bombs driven by suicide drivers, eventually forced the Israelis to withdraw. In June of 1985, by which time their total deaths in Lebanon had reached 654, they pulled out from all but a small strip they declared a "security zone" on the Lebanese side of the border, which they patrolled with the assistance of Lebanese allies. Many Israelis were disenchanted with the inconclusive results of their resort to arms.

THE PALESTINIAN UPRISING

Furthermore, the invasion failed to achieve the equally important goal of subduing Arab nationalism in the occupied territories. According to an Israeli analysis, in the 5 years preceding the invasions (1977 to 1982), there were about 500 violent demonstrations a year by Palestinians. After the invasion in 1982, the number of violent demonstrations rose to about 3,000 a year.[16] In December 1987, the demonstrations became so numerous and openly defiant that the Palestinians referred to them as the *intifada*, literally "the casting off" or uprising. An underground committee, operating within the occupied territories, coordinated demonstrations and ordered periodic strikes of Palestinian workers and closing hours for Palestinian stores. Israeli repressive measures were unable to stop them.

Yet because the intifada originated within the occupied territories, it represented a further loss of power by the PLO leadership, now located in Tunisia. On top of these losses, additional impetus for new initiatives to recapture the leadership of the Palestinians came from a dramatic act by King Hussein of Jordan. As far back as 1974, the Arab League had designated the PLO as "the sole legitimate representative of the Palestinian people." Despite this declaration, the state of Jordan, with Israeli compliance, continued to exert influence in its former territories—for example, paying salaries of some officials. In the summer of 1988 King Hussein announced he was severing all ties with the West Bank of the Jordan, thereby depriving the Palestinians of what governmental services they had that were not totally under Israeli control. In effect, Hussein was daring the PLO to prove that it could provide for the welfare of its own people.

After a delay to build consensus, the Palestinians convened a meeting of their National Council in Algiers in November 1988. In a major departure from past policy, the Council agreed to accept UN Resolution 242, which implied recognition of Israel and hence acceptance forty years after the event of the partition of Palestine. As a journalist present at the Council reported, "Despite ambiguities in the wording . . . , everyone in the hall knew that Palestinians were at last bidding farewell to the long-cherished dream that they would one day reclaim all their ancestral lands."[17]

Acceptance of Resolution 242 was one condition the United States had laid down for accepting the PLO as a party to negotiations. The United States had laid down another condition, and the Council met it by a renunciation of terrorism. These radical departures from past PLO policy were overshadowed in the media by news of the declaration of an independent Palestinian state. In fact, because the PLO leadership had no access to Palestinian territory, which remained firmly under Israeli military occupation, the declaration was mainly a symbolic gesture. Radical Palestinians, such as George Habash of the Popular Front for the Liberation of Palestine, realized that the declaration of statehood was being used as a cover for a fundamental change away from conflict and toward negotiation and compromise. They refused to vote for the resolution, although they agreed not to oppose Arafat for the time being.

The Israelis were not happy with these events. Now that the PLO had met the American conditions for dialogue, the Israelis feared that their closest ally would begin to push them toward compromise. In the two decades since they had acquired the occupied territories, Israeli attitudes had shifted to a more uncompromising position. In 1967 a majority would have traded land for peace; by 1988 many Israeli settlements had been established and a strong movement favored retaining the land as part of the historic land of Israel. Acceptance of partition had become as difficult for the Israelis as for the Palestinians.

Yet for all the remaining difficulties, the 1982 war in Lebanon seemed to repeat the pattern of the militarily indecisive war of 1973. Setbacks for both sides made resort to force less attractive and prepared the way for a diplomatic settlement.

NOTES

1. Amos Elon, *The Israelis: Founders and Sons* (New York: Holt, Rinehart and Winston, 1971), pp. 119–123.

2. Negib Azouri, *Reveil de la nation Arabe dans l'Asie Turque* (1905), in *The Israel–Arab Reader*, 2nd ed., ed. Walter Laqueur (New York: Bantam Books, 1971), p. 5.

3. "Speech to National Assembly Members, 29 May 1967," Appendix 7 in Walter Laqueur, *The Road to Jerusalem* (New York: Macmillan, 1968), pp. 316–319.

4. Nadav Safran, *Israel: The Embattled Ally* (Cambridge, Mass.: Harvard University Press, 1978), pp. 397–399.

5. Nadav Safran, *From War to War* (New York: Pegasus, 1969), pp. 325–327, 353.

6. Safran, *Israel*, p. 241. (See note 4.)

7. William B. Quandt, *Decade of Decisions: American Policy Toward the Arab–Israeli Conflict, 1967–1976* (Berkeley: University of California Press, 1977), pp. 37–43.

8. Ibid., pp. 39, 42.

9. Safran, *Israel*, p. 398. (See note 4.)

10. Chaim Herzog, *The War of Atonement* (Boston: Little, Brown, 1975), pp. 34–35.

11. "Dayan Says U.S. Threat Forced Relief Convoys," *The New York Times*, October 31, 1973, p. 16.

12. Jacobo Timerman, *The Longest War* (New York: Random House, 1982).

13. The official was Issam Sertawi, who was later assassinated by other Palestinians, presumably for being too moderate. *The New York Times*, February 21, 1983, p. Y4.

14. Thomas L. Friedman, "Arab Talks: Topic Is Iran," *The New York Times*, November 10, 1987, p. Y7.

15. For example, Marie Colvin, "The Ambiguous Yasir Arafat," *The New York Times Magazine*, December 18, 1988, p. 34.

16. Data from Meron Benvenisti's West Bank Data Project, cited by Thomas L. Friedman, "How Long Can Israel Deny Its Civil War?" *The New York Times*, December 27, 1987, p. E3.

17. Colvin, p. 63. (See note 15.)

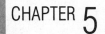

CHAPTER 5

RECENT WARS

Cold War tensions between the United States and the Soviet Union, accompanied by their growing nuclear arsenals, have often distracted attention from the behavior of smaller states. Mikhail Gorbachev, in his book *Perestroika*, declares:

> . . . Clausewitz's dictum that war is the continuation of policy only by different means, which was classic in his time, has grown hopelessly out of date. It now belongs to the libraries.[1]

Twenty-five years earlier, the British Foreign Secretary Douglas Home had expressed the same ideas to the United Nations General Assembly:

> . . . the lesson of the twentieth century and the nuclear age is this—and it is the same for African and Asian and European—that force solves nothing.[2]

Before we accept this judgment on authority, even authority that ranges from the British Foreign Secretary to the Soviet General Secretary, we must look at the evidence. One thing is clear: War has not been rendered obsolete by nuclear weapons. We have already described the war in Korea and five wars between Israel and its Arab neighbors. Since World War II there have been at least fourteen other major wars between states (see Table 5.1).

An exhaustive examination of all these wars would be the best way to test the generalizations made by Gorbachev and Home. But even with a look

Table 5.1 MAJOR WARS SINCE WORLD WAR II

Wars	Years
Soviet Union–Hungary	1956
India–China	1962
Vietnam	1965–1975
Pakistan–India (Kashmir)	1965
El Salvador–Honduras (the Football War)	1969
India–Pakistan (Bangladesh)	1971
Turkey–Cyprus	1974
Vietnam–Cambodia	1978–1989
Tanzania–Uganda	1978–1979
China–Vietnam	1979
USSR–Afghanistan	1980–1989
Iraq–Iran (the Gulf War)	1980–1988
United Kingdom–Argentina (the Falklands War)	1982
Iraq–US-led coalition	1991

at only a few of them we can begin to construct a case. The three wars that follow—the war for Bangladesh (1971), the Turkey–Cyprus war (1974), and the Persian Gulf War (1980–1988)—offer enough variety to show how difficult simple generalizations can be.

PAKISTAN AND THE BENGALIS

The British granted independence to their colonial possessions in India in 1947. For the most part the British had ruled directly through native princes. In 1947 each of them was given the choice of joining a new secular and democratic republic to be called India or a Muslim religious state to be called Pakistan. Most chose to join India; a few in the northeast and north-west chose Pakistan. The status of a large area in the central northern region, the state of Kashmir, was disputed because the ruler (who was Hindu) chose to join India and the population (mostly Muslim) preferred Pakistan; in the end India occupied about two-thirds, Pakistan one-third. What emerged was a Pakistan divided into two parts separated by 1,000 miles. It has been described as two wings without a bird (see Figure 5.1).[3] The only important tie between the two parts of the country was religion; working against it were many differences. Most of the people in the eastern part of Pakistan spoke Bengali; the majority in the western part spoke Urdu. The Bengalis of East Pakistan were racially different from the peoples of West Pakistan. The typical image of a Bengali was someone short in stature, dark in complexion, and energetic in disposition. The typical image of a Punjabi (or a member of a related group in West Pakistan) was someone tall, light, and impassive.

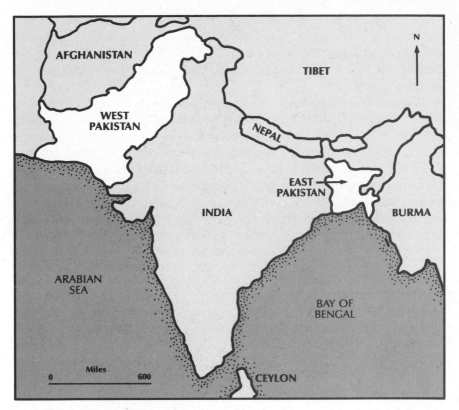

Figure 5.1   Pakistan in 1947–1971

Bengali culture traditionally respected traders and intellectuals; Punjabi culture respected warriors.

The Bengalis accused the West Pakistanis of exploitation. The capital of the country was in the western part. Most government officials came from the West. The army was made up of West Pakistanis. Yet a majority of Pakistanis (55 percent) lived in the East. The Bengalis also pointed to economic exploitation by the West. Most of the foreign exchange of the country was generated by jute and other agricultural products grown in East Pakistan, but the money was invested in the industrialization of the West. The result was that the West Pakistanis were more prosperous than Pakistanis in the East.

Even the religious tie was not too strong. The East had become Muslim much later, by conquest. Not all the East Pakistanis were Muslim; about 10 million (of 80 million) were Hindu. To some extent the two parts of Pakistan were held together by a common fear of India. But this fear was not so great in the East. The Bengalis were less obsessed with the Kashmir issue; they seemed more willing to seek a peaceful settlement with India. In part Bengalis felt this way because large numbers of ethnically similar Indian citizens lived across the border from East Pakistan in the Indian state of Bengal. Sharing language and culture, they found it hard to see each other as permanent enemies.

Despite these differences, the fragile union continued until 1969, when the military government of general Ayub Khan collapsed as a result of public indignation over corruption. The caretaker government that took over Pakistan from Ayub Khan scheduled new elections for December 1970. In these elections the Awami League, led by Sheikh Mujibur Rahman, won 75 percent of the vote in East Pakistan (giving them 167 of the 169 seats allotted to East Pakistan). The Awami League drew its strength from Bengalis who felt exploited by the westerners and were asking for greater autonomy in a federal system. In reaction the federal government, situated in the West and dominated by military men recruited from the West, banned the Awami League. This led the Awami League to escalate its demands to full independence for East Pakistan. They declared the independence of a separate state, which they called "Bengal Nation" or Bangladesh.

The Pakistan government responded by arresting Sheikh Mujib, along with the rest of the Awami League leadership, in March 1971, and jailing them in West Pakistan. The Pakistan army was sent in to suppress rioting by the Bengalis and treated East Pakistan like an enemy country. Reasonable estimates of the number of people massacred range from 300,000 to 1,500,000. A team sent out by the World Bank to evaluate economic development projects for the eastern part of Pakistan reported that the devastation wrought by the Pakistani army resembled that in Europe after World War II.[4]

As might be expected, many East Pakistanis tried to escape the Pakistan army. Millions of refugees, about 90 percent of them from the Hindu minority, crossed the border into India. About 6 million were settled in government-run camps; an estimated 4 million more were refugees outside the camps. It was this large influx of refugees that drew India into the civil conflict and led to the war. India could not very well have stopped the flow of refugees across its borders even if it had wanted to, for political as well as sheer physical reasons. Hindus in India would have opposed a policy of denying refuge to Hindus; Bengalis would have opposed denying refuge to Bengalis. But the cost to the Indian government of maintaining these refugees was enormous. The World Bank estimated that it would run at about $1.2 billion for a full year. The refugees would also use up India's food reserves, which were being accumulated for the first time as the result of India's "green revolution" in agriculture. India's prospects for economic growth were looking good as never before in its history as an independent state, and now resources and administrative talent would have to be diverted to caring for a sudden addition of 10 million people.

INDIA'S PREPARATION FOR WAR

Facing this situation, the most desirable foreign policy goal for India was to create a separate state in East Pakistan. Such a state would be able to take back the millions of refugees, relieving the economic and administrative burden they imposed on India. It would provide guarantees against continued exploitation, persecution, and massacre of the Bengalis. Such a state would have the additional benefit for India of reducing Pakistan's power and thus its ability to threaten Kashmir.

The goal of a new state of Bangladesh could be achieved in a number of ways. The Pakistani government itself could grant East Pakistan independence out of enlightened self-interest. Failing this, the Indian government could apply diplomatic pressure. If diplomatic initiatives failed the Indians could resort to military action. War was by no means an unthinkable or irrational policy option for India. The only constraints were those imposed by the great powers and the United Nations. With proper preparation the Indians could avoid great-power interference. If the war was swift and decisive, the UN would not have time to act.

India began a series of diplomatic and military moves that by themselves might have persuaded the Pakistanis to allow Bangladesh its independence, but, if not, would also serve as preparations for a war against Pakistan to accomplish the same goal. India improved its ties with the Soviet Union, going so far as to sign a "friendship treaty" in August 1971. As Pakistan had ties with both the United States and China, it was logical that India should go to the other great power to counteract their influence. Then Prime Minister Indira Gandhi set off on a world tour to get countries to cut off or reduce aid to Pakistan. By presenting the case against Pakistan on the issue of the Bengalis, she could make it easier for these countries to remain neutral if not actually to support India in the event of war. Indians also encouraged rumors that China had already accepted as inevitable the breakup of the Pakistan state and was making overtures to India. True or not, these introduced an element of doubt into the calculations of other states, including Pakistan.

India also began military preparations, some of which could be interpreted as more severe forms of "diplomatic pressure," but others of which, because they were kept secret, were obviously serious preparation for war. The visible preparations included air raid drills and a call-up of doctors into the armed forces. The Indians also banned flights over Indian territory from West to East Pakistan, necessitating a long detour over the ocean for Pakistani reinforcements. At the same time, India began covert aid to guerrilla forces in East Pakistan. They supplied arms and training as well as sanctuary to a force of 6,000 or 7,000 guerrillas known as Mukti Bahini. This support was kept hidden from foreign observers, including UN observers, and its full extent is still not clearly known. The guerrilla raids provided provocations to which the Pakistani army occasionally responded, furnishing the Indian army with excuses for "probes" and "incursions" and "protective reactions" across the border into Pakistan.

WAR BETWEEN INDIA AND PAKISTAN

The Indian main attack evidently was deliberately delayed until late fall, when preparations were completed and the winter snows had closed the Himalayan passes, preventing any Chinese assistance to Pakistanis. On October 27, 1971, the Indians made their first crossing in force. On November 10 they occupied a salient that stuck out into India. The war itself began in December and lasted two weeks, until the cease-fire on December 17, 1971. The war was kept limited to the single goal of creating a new state in East Pakistan. Indian attacks were intended only to defeat the Pakistani army: Destruction to the countryside was kept at a minimum, cities were not extensively bombed, and offensive operations were confined to East Pakistan. The Indian army, however, was prepared to take the offensive in Kashmir and West Pakistan if Pakistan decided to widen the war.

The war brought complete success for India. As a means of attaining foreign policy goals, military force had not lost its utility. Indian domestic reaction was overwhelming support; the 10,000 casualties suffered by India (including 8,000 missing or killed) was a price the population seemed willing to pay. The success came from careful preparation, both diplomatic and military, and favorable circumstances. India was better armed, getting weapons both from Russia and from its own industry. Pakistan suffered from a US embargo on arms that had been imposed against both India and Pakistan after their last war in 1965 (that time over Kashmir). Pakistan was getting only limited arms from China, France, and the Soviet Union. (Soviet aid, you notice, was going to both sides. The Soviet Union was paying the price for trying to settle the war between the two sides in 1965, a position similar to the one in which the United States found itself in the Middle East after the 1973 war there.)

Pakistan fought from a disadvantageous strategic position. Forces in East Pakistan were cut off and could not be reinforced. The Indians outnumbered the Pakistanis in the East, 160,000 to 93,000. The Pakistanis also had to fight in the midst of a hostile population, including by this time as many as 50,000 Mukti Bahini.

When the fighting began, the United Nations General Assembly had condemned India by a vote of 104 to 11, with 10 abstentions.[5] But as the result of Indian success, world opinion rapidly shifted. No more resolutions were brought before the Assembly condemning India or asking it to stop. In fact, by December 19 the United States was in a lonely minority, condemned by almost all states for giving support to Pakistan, the country that was technically the victim of aggression.[6] India not only won the war but won the support of the world for its policy by doing so.

THE PROBLEM OF CYPRUS

In July 1974, fighting broke out in the island of Cyprus. The main issue was the same as that in Pakistan in 1971—mistreatment of one national group (a Turkish minority) by another (a Greek majority). The size of the Turkish minority on Cyprus made the problem difficult. About 120,000 of 640,000 inhabitants, or 18 percent, were Turks. If the number had been smaller, say 10 percent or less, they would not have attracted much attention and would probably have been tolerated as small minorities are elsewhere. If the number had been larger, say 35 percent, demands for a separate state would have found more supporters. But at 18 percent the Turks were numerous enough to cause problems, yet not numerous enough to justify a drastic solution. Furthermore, they were not concentrated in one part of the island but scattered in enclaves throughout.[7]

The Cyprus problem was complicated by three other factors. One was the proximity of Turkey, only 40 miles away; the mainland of Greece, to which the majority of Cypriots felt allegiance, was 500 miles away (see Figure 5.2). A second complication was the strategic importance of Cyprus to the countries with interests in the eastern end of the Mediterranean: Turkey; Turkey's partners in NATO (especially Britain, which has bases on Cyprus); and the traditional rival of both Turkey and NATO, Russia. Finally, the Cyprus problem was complicated by a history of animosity between Greeks and Turks on many issues other than Cyprus. One important event in this history was the massacre of Greeks by the Turks in the 1920s as the Turks set out to create a purely Turkish national state. Throughout history Greeks had been living along the edges of the Aegean Sea, but in 1923 the Turks expelled them, claiming that the eastern edge of that sea was Turkish territory. Those who did not flee soon enough were killed. This old conflict over territory appeared in new form in the 1970s when oil companies wanted to search for oil beneath the Aegean Sea. Greece claimed the right to grant exploration rights off the shore of islands inhabited by Greeks. Turkey granted exploration rights to the same area, claiming that this area was part of the Turkish continental shelf. Before the war on Cyprus broke out, this quarrel had escalated so far that Turkey had sent planes to practice their bombing in the disputed waters.

The hostility between Greeks and Turks on Cyprus is part of the historic quarrel between the two peoples. Its most recent phase began in 1960, when

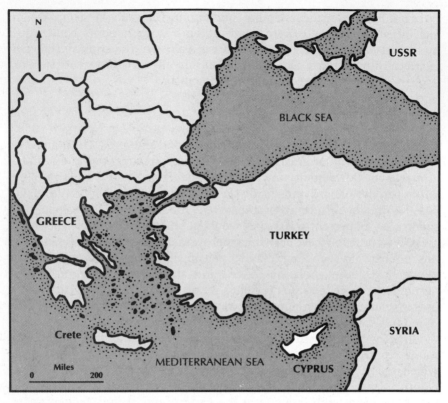

Figure 5.2   Cyprus

Cyprus became an independent country. At that time, the representatives of the Greek Cypriot community agreed to give up demands for union with Greece (although most Greek Cypriots preferred it) in favor of an independent state, and the Turks agreed to give up their demands for partition of the island in return for a guaranteed share of governmental powers. The arrangement lasted only three years. The Greek Cypriots claimed that the arrangement was unworkable because the Turks, with only 18 percent of the population, could veto any important government action. The Turkish Cypriots, on the other hand, claimed that the Greeks were forcing them into subordinate positions. Violent conflict broke out twice, in 1964 and 1967, each time with Greece and Turkey threatening to go to war to help their fellow nationals.

By 1974 the situation was stalemated. Negotiations between the two communities, started after the near war in 1967, were making no progress. The Turks wanted "functional federalism," meaning that Turkish villages were to be patrolled by Turkish police, cleaned up by Turkish garbage collectors, and so on. The Greeks wanted a unitary state. There was little intermingling between the two communities. Cyprus never bothered to acquire a national anthem. Cyprus had its own flag but it was seldom used—citizens flew the flag of Greece or Turkey instead. Each community had its own school system. There was no university on Cyprus—students went to Greece or Turkey instead.

The Turks were in a subordinate position. They had lower-paying jobs and lived in poorer housing. Greek village mayors drove cars, Turkish village mayors rode bicycles.[8] The Greeks admitted that they produced 90 percent of the wealth on Cyprus but argued that they did so because they were a more dynamic people. Some people suspected the president of Cyprus (a representative of the Greek community), Archbishop Makarios, of following a strategy of slowly strangling the Turks economically, forcing them out of productive activity and government jobs until they would no longer be able to resist Greek control. If this was his strategy, it was being frustrated by the Turkish government, which was subsidizing the Turkish community on Cyprus at a rate of about $30 million a year.

CRISIS IN 1974: THE COUP AGAINST MAKARIOS

Under the original agreements giving Cyprus its independence, both Greece and Turkey were allowed to station small contingents of troops on Cyprus. In 1974, 650 Greek army officers were with the Cypriot National Guard. In June 1974 the United States received word that this Greek contingent planned to overthrow President Makarios in a military coup, presumably because he did not advocate immediate union with Greece. The United States passed the warning on to Makarios, who replied that he did not expect such a move until he tried to expel these officers. Makarios was too optimistic. On July 15, 1974, the National Guard did carry out a coup; Makarios was lucky to escape with his life. The new military leaders named as president Nikos Giorgiades Sampson, known not only as a notorious enemy of the Turks but as a pathological killer as well. During the struggle against the British before 1960 he had boasted of how many British soldiers he had personally killed. Sampson's appointment seemed clear confirmation of what everyone already believed about the coup, that it was to prepare the way for union with Greece.

Under the treaties that gave Cyprus its independence, Greece, Turkey, and Britain (as the former colonial power) all had the right to intervene in the internal affairs of Cyprus to preserve its independence. The Turks now asked the British to help them prevent a union of Cyprus with Greece. The British were reluctant to act. They advanced a number of reasons: They wanted to avert a war between NATO allies; their bases on Cyprus depended on the good will of the Greek Cypriot majority; the thousands of British tourists and residents of Cyprus would be subject to harassment by Greek Cypriots.

Britain did try to avert a war by diplomacy. It requested that Greece recall the Greek officers serving with the Cypriot National Guard who had evidently been behind the coup. It also asked the Greeks to come to London for negotiations with the Turks. Greece, ruled at this time by an ultranationalist military junta, denied all responsibility for the coup. It did agree to replace its officers in Cyprus but would not send a representative to negotiate in London.

The Turks believed, not unreasonably, that the Turkish community on Cyprus was in some danger. They asked the British to cooperate with them in an intervention to guarantee the rights of the Turkish minority. When the British refused, they requested that the British at least let them use the British bases as areas in which they could land troops. When the British refused this as well, the Turks launched an amphibious invasion against the northern coast of Cyprus.

WAR BETWEEN TURKEY AND CYPRUS

Even with assistance from the Greek armed forces, the Cypriot National Guard would have been militarily inferior to the Turks. As it was, the Cypriots were fighting the Turks by themselves. Even so, the Turkish attack, beginning on July 20 and continuing until a cease-fire on July 22, was not a complete success. Turkish troops took longer to get ashore and advance than they had planned. They did not take the important airport outside Nicosia, the capital of Cyprus. In the confusion they even sank one of their own ships. When they halted, they controlled a number of Turkish Cypriot villages, but 60,000 Turkish Cypriots still were in areas outside their control.

The government of Greece ordered mobilization, preparatory to an attack on Turkey, but on July 23 the ultranationalist military junta was no longer able to assert its authority. The generals who had been running the government handed power over to generals who had remained out of politics in the regular army, who then recalled the last civilian prime minister, Constantine Caramanlis, from exile. On the same day, Nikos Sampson was replaced as head of Cyprus by the civilian vice-president under Makarios, Glafkos Clerides.

The position of the Turks on Cyprus thus improved somewhat, but these changes did not fulfill all the foreign policy aims of Turkey. They still had no indication from within the Greek Cypriot government that the rights of the Turkish minority would be secure. The Turkish army began landing more troops on the northern coast of Cyprus and then broke the cease-fire by moving out from the enclave it had established there. A second cease-fire on

July 30 halted their advance temporarily. An attempt to start talks at Geneva on a settlement quickly proved unsuccessful and the Turkish army moved once again, until by the time of a third and final cease-fire on August 16, it controlled 40 percent of the territory of Cyprus (see Figure 5.3).

One of the factors that made the Cyprus problem so difficult was that the Turkish minority was not concentrated in one part of the island. When the Turkish army occupied the northern portion, it took control of a number of Greek as well as Turkish villages. Many of the Greeks fled, either out of fear of being involved in the fighting or because of a Turkish policy of expelling them. More than 180,000 Greek Cypriot refugees fled into the Greek-controlled part of the island. The Greek Cypriots in the south, however, wanted to keep the Turks in their midst from fleeing to the north. Many of them were locked up, virtual hostages, in public buildings and sports stadiums. Other Turks fled into nearby British military bases. After some hesitation, the British allowed them to be airlifted out to Turkish soil in January 1975. Many were promptly returned by the Turkish government to

Figure 5.3   Turkish Conquest of Cyprus in 1974

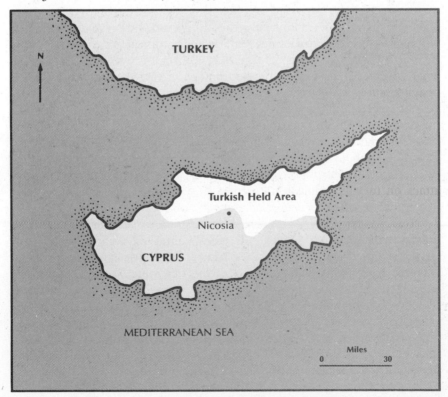

the northern part of Cyprus, an event that precipitated Greek Cypriot riots against the British. By February 1975, only 10,000 Turkish Cypriots were left in Greek Cypriot territory. On February 13, 1975, the Turkish Cypriot leaders proclaimed a separate state in the northern part of Cyprus, with an offer to the Greek Cypriot community to confederate with them in a single state, provided all authority was shared equally.

The Greeks rejected the Turkish offer. Despite military success and a de facto partition of the island into Greek and Turkish sections, the Turks were not able to enjoy the final satisfaction of a solution sanctioned by a treaty with the Greek Cypriots. Although the Turks were able to move unhindered to convert the northern part of Cyprus into a purely Turkish area, painting out all Greek signs, taking over Greek houses and giving them to Turks, and converting churches into mosques, they were unable to get international recognition of the changes they had brought about. The US Congress, responding to pressure from constituents of Greek descent, cut off US military aid in February 1975.

The United States had not found it possible to prevent this war, as it had potential wars between Turkey and Greece in 1964 and 1967; the United States also found it impossible to mediate a negotiated end to it. The major obstacle was weakness of the governments in both Turkey and Greece. The Greeks had just recalled a former prime minister, Constantine Caramanlis, to serve as acting prime minister in July 1974. Elections were set for November 1974 and no Greek politician could hope to make a conciliatory gesture toward the Turks and survive the election. Turkey also suffered from a weak government. The prime minister during the invasion, Bulent Ecevit, was a member of a minority party in a coalition government, and his coalition partners did not want him to profit from the euphoria of the military success. Ecevit very much wanted to call an election, hoping for an electoral windfall, but the Turkish constitution makes it impossible for a prime minister to do so alone. Ecevit was unable to strengthen his power base at home so he could make concessions.

Turkey was to experience a decade of frustration in its attempts to turn its military success into a political one. Finally, in 1984, Turkey declared the northern part of the island to be the "Turkish Republic of Northern Cyprus." But only Turkey extended recognition to this new state. The rest of the world still regarded it as occupied territory, and sporadic negotiations with the Greek-dominated republic of Cyprus produced no results. Still, despite the limited achievement of objectives, it would have been hard to find a Turk who would argue that the use of military force in the summer of 1974 had not been a useful instrument of foreign policy. The Cyprus problem, and particularly the welfare of Cypriots of Turkish descent, which had been a major concern for Turkey since 1960, now receded in importance.

THE IRAQ–IRAN WAR

Studying a third war will give us a more balanced picture. This is the war fought between two countries bordering on the Persian (or Arabian) Gulf—Iran and Iraq (see Figure 5.4). The eight years that passed between the first major offensive in 1980 to the cease-fire in 1988 make it one of the longest wars in recent times. Although casualty figures are imprecise, it was arguably one of the bloodiest, costing probably a million lives.

The Persians who rule Iran and the Arabs who rule Iraq have long been rivals. They both remember and refer to a battle fought between their ancestors in 637, over 1,000 years ago. It is not unusual for two neighbors to have a long-standing rivalry. The question is why it turned into a major war in 1980.

Figure 5.4   Iran and Iraq—the Gulf War Zone

One specific issue was their disagreement over a part of their common border. An important segment of the border is a body of water called the Shatt al Arab, originating where the Tigris and Euphrates rivers flow together and running 100 miles to the Persian Gulf. A look at the map shows that the Shatt supplies Iraq's only useful outlet to the sea. Iran has a long coastline and several ports, but Iraq must depend on this narrow estuary for sending oil by tanker. For years Iraq had claimed rights over the entire Shatt but in 1975 relinquished them under pressure from fellow oil-producing states in the Organization of Petroleum Exporting Countries (OPEC). In a treaty Iraq agreed to divide the Shatt along the middle of the navigable channel; in exchange Iran promised to return other small bits of territory. Iraq was not happy with this arrangement, feeling vulnerable because the Iranians now shared control of the Iraqi lifeline.

With the overthrow of the shah of Iran in 1979 and the assumption of power by Islamic religious leaders, Iraq felt a new cause for alarm. The government of Iran, directed now by the religious leader Ayatollah Ruhollah Khomeini, challenged the legitimacy of the secular governments, an attack that seemed directed particularly at the neighboring secular government of Saddam Hussein in Iraq. Furthermore, the Ayatollah came from the Shiite branch of Islam and had a strong appeal to Shiites in neighboring states. This appeal troubled Iraq because although the ruling circles came from the Sunni branch of Islam, Shiites actually made up a majority of the population in Iraq, perhaps 55 or 60 percent. Furthermore, of the remaining Sunnis, as many as half were ethnically distinct Kurds. Thus the small ruling group of Sunnis had ample reason to be nervous. The appeal by Ayatollah Khomeini to the Shiites was cited by Saddam Hussein in a speech at the beginning of the war as a basic cause for his decision to attack.[9] In the words of one expert, he feared that the fabric of his state might tear under the continued strain of Iranian propaganda.[10]

The regional tensions created by the Islamic revolution in Iran produced a series of escalating incidents in 1980. In response to Iranian calls for Iraqi Shiites to "liberate Iraq," the Iraqis executed some Iraqi Shiites, including a major religious leader. In response, Iran declared three days of national mourning, while Iranian Revolutionary Guards seized the Iraqi embassy. Iran also shelled Iraqi cities and oil installations.

OUTBREAK OF WAR

But the Islamic revolution had also created a window of opportunity for Iraq. The rivalry between the two countries had been held in check in recent decades by British hegemony in the Persian Gulf. This hegemony came to an end in 1971 when Britain abandoned its commitments east of the Suez canal. In the wake of the British departure, both Iraq and Iran increased their arms, Iraq buying from the Soviet Union and Iran from the United States. This competition created a rough balance in armaments and led to a decade of relative stability.

The balance was apparently ended by the Iranian revolution. Iran suffered the turmoil that accompanies all revolutions, aggravated in their case by the attempts of ethnic minorities, such as the Iranian branch of the Kurds, to win more autonomy. On top of this revolutionary chaos, one of Khomeini's first acts after taking power in early 1979 was to dismantle the Iranian army. It was cut in size from 285,000 to 150,000, with severe purges of the officer corps. Over half of the officers in the middle ranks were dismissed; the air force lost half of its pilots.[11] Khomeini turned on the Army because it was so closely associated with the previous ruler, both as a pillar of his regime and a symbol of his profligacy. Statements and publications suggested that revolutionary Iran intended to rely on "people's war" instead.

As the Iraqi regime watched the turmoil in Iran, it came to believe it could win a quick war. Under the shah, Iran with 285,000 soldiers had outnumbered Iraq's 200,000. Now, with only 150,000, it was the smaller of the two. Moreover, the world situation favored Iraq. Iranians had seized American diplomats in November 1979, and when Iraq made the decision to attack in September 1980 the Iranians were still holding them. The animosity created by the incident, the Iraqis reasoned, would make it difficult for Iran to get spare parts or replacements for its largely American-equipped army. For its part, Iraq had by now diversified its arms suppliers, making it impossible for any one country to exercise a veto.

Given the level of tension in the Persian Gulf region, the regime of Saddam Hussein may well have calculated that a war was inevitable. If so, he could have reasoned that it would be better to fight Iran in 1980, when conditions appeared favorable.[12] In the past, such a war was called a "preventive war."

INITIAL PHASE OF THE WAR

The initial Iraqi attack on September 22, 1980, carried the invading force well into Iranian territory. Striking first is a military advantage and attackers usually take territory. But Iraq did not win the easy victory it and outside military observers expected. In part this was because it ignored some traditional military wisdom.

One maxim is the importance of clearly defined objectives. Yet even the Iraqi government admitted it did not communicate clear goals to commanders in the field.[13] Of the military objectives one can choose, it is considered more important to destroy the enemy's forces as effective fighting units than to capture territory. But Iraq was content to seize ground, then halt its advance and announce its willingness to negotiate. Perhaps Saddam Hussein was hoping to duplicate the experience of Egypt's Anwar Sadat in 1973. But Iran was not pressured, as Israel had been in 1973, and the pause merely gave Iran time to regroup.[14]

Despite being materially worse off, Iran was able to use the revolutionary zeal to recruit large numbers of "martyrs." Iran sent large numbers of them, mostly untrained, lightly armed teenagers, in "human wave" attacks. Casualty ratios favored the Iraqis, but with its larger population Iran was willing to take losses. In this sense, the Iranians were right and the Iraqis wrong in their estimate of the importance of the revolution. But in another sense, revolutionary zeal was exaggerated. Despite pleas from Iran, the Shiites of Iraq did not rally to Iran. Religion was not able to overcome nationalism and state control. On the other side, the ethnic Arabs living in the areas of Iran adjacent to Iraq did not rally to the Iraqi cause. Ethnic identity, like religion, proved weaker than nationalism and state police control.

THE COURSE OF THE WAR

Iraq won the initial victories but did not destroy the Iranian armed forces. Iran recovered, then counterattacked, drove the Iraqi forces out of Iraq, and in less than two years—by July 1982—had carried the war into Iraq. Faced with an army that could draw from a much larger population (45 million Iranians versus 15 million Iraqis) and was willing to take bigger risks because of revolutionary zeal, the Iraqi government soon realized it could not win on the battlefield. Iran, once in the war, had declared the removal of the government of Saddam Hussein as its unnegotiable war aim, so the Iraqi leadership could not hope to extract itself by negotiations. Faced with defeat on the ground, it chose to expand the war. Using its air superiority, it attacked industrial targets in Iran, concentrating on oil fields, pumping stations, and ports. For the first time since World War II, the major strategy of a belligerent became the reduction of its enemy's capacity to make war.

As the war continued, attacks on industry were accompanied by, or even replaced by, direct attacks on civilians in what became known as "the war of the cities." In May 1984, the Iraqis began attacking Tehran and other population centers in Iran. Iraq had obtained a relatively large surface-to-surface ballistic missile, the Scud, from the Soviet Union and then modified it so that it could travel further, bringing the Iranian capital in range. For a period of about 6 weeks in early 1987, the Iraqis fired about 180 Scuds into Tehran and other cities. The missiles were not very accurate, and their 600 pounds of TNT demolished city blocks at random. Their purpose was only to demoralize the civilian population. In World War II this was called terror bombing. In examining reasons why the Iranians eventually agreed to a cease-fire, even though they had not achieved their unnegotiable aims, most analysts mentioned the effect of Iraqi missiles in the war of the cities.

If deliberate attacks on civilians were a reversion to the more barbarous practices of World War II, in another way the Iran–Iraq war was also a reversion to World War I. Faced with Iranian human wave attacks by large numbers of lightly armed but fanatic teenagers, the outnumbered Iraqis began to use lethal chemical agents in 1984. Although the main agent used, known as mustard, is in fact a liquid at normal temperatures, this chemical agent is commonly known as poison gas, and Iraqi use constituted the first consistent use of the gas by a major combatant in a war since World War I. The use of poison gas was unambiguously verified and condemned by the UN, yet the Iraqis were not deterred. Faced with a choice of losing the war or facing the condemnation of the world, they chose condemnation as the lesser evil. As events turned out, they discovered that poison gas was militarily effective, but the effects of world condemnation negligible.

Some of the failure on the part of major states to punish Iraq for violating the Geneva Gas Protocol (for example, by refusing to sell arms) was motivated by a fear that perhaps Iran might win. These states could rationalize overlooking a gross violation of international law by pointing out that Iraqi initial use was, after all, defensive, on their own soil, against human wave attacks. But by the end of the war, the Iraqis were using gas in offensive operations as well, and after the cease-fire, Iraq went on using poison gas in counterinsurgency operations against its own Kurdish minority. In each case, Iraq achieved its goals at almost no cost in world sanctions.

THE TANKER WAR

In the end, it was neither missiles nor poison gas that was decisive, but what by 1984 had become known as "the tanker war"—Iraqi attacks on neutral shipping attempting to carry oil from Iran. Using its superiority in the air, where it outnumbered the Iranians by about 400 fighter aircraft to 70, Iraq used bombs and French-made Exocet missiles against tankers moving up the northern side of the Persian Gulf to Iranian ports. The missiles did not always hit, and when they did they did not always cause great damage, but the cumulative effect eventually turned the war to Iraq's favor.

At the very beginning of the war, Iraq's economy had declined sharply. Oil production fell from 1,500,000 barrels a day to 700,000. Not only was the Shatt al Arab closed to Iraqi shipping, but Iraq's neighbor and rival, Syria, shut down pipelines carrying Iraqi oil over its territory. On the other hand, Iran was able to increase its oil production to 3 million barrels a day. In 1980, oil was selling for around $30 a barrel, so even though oil was Iran's only important export, Iran had no trouble financing the war.

By the end of the war, however, Iraqi attacks on oil fields and tankers had deprived Iran of its economic edge. Iranian production had dropped to 1,500,000 barrels per day or perhaps even much less.[15] Iran also suffered from the world glut in oil, which had depressed prices to $17 a barrel. Because of the hazards of shipping through the Persian Gulf, Iran had to discount its oil even below world price. Thus Iran was selling fewer barrels and getting less for each one. This drastic reduction of its single source of foreign funds was causing Iran severe economic strains—a great fall in gross national product, an inflation rate of 30 percent, and unemployment of 30 percent.[16] One expert has written that the Iran–Iraq war provides "perhaps the sole example in history of a successful economic blockade essentially carried out by air power alone."[17]

It was estimated that since 1980 the war with Iraq had cost Iran $70 billion in direct costs (weapons, ammunition), or $140 billion, if indirect costs such as lost production were counted.[18] By 1988 war-weariness had set in. Visitors reported protests and demonstrations.[19] The annual Iranian recruitment drive, which in past years had produced the "martyrs" for human wave attacks, went badly in 1988. Iranian energy was giving out. In these circumstances, Khomeini decided to reverse himself and accept a cease-fire even without his conditions in order to save his regime.

WAR TERMINATION AND OUTCOME

In addition to his often quoted definition of war, Clausewitz offered another one: "War is an act of force to compel our enemy to do our will."[20] War is thus a two-sided equation: force on the one side, our will (or demands) on the other. One can try to end a war by one of two means—increasing force or reducing demands. Through the war of the cities and the tanker war, Iraq applied more force. Eventually Iran responded, not by also increasing force, but by reducing its demands. (Iraq had already abandoned its original goal and considered itself fortunate to end the war with a return to the status quo ante.)

Although it is generally agreed that Iraq committed the first major overt act of aggression, Iran's provocative behavior contributed to the initiation of the war. Both countries started the war and both countries lost.

For Iran, the losses were physical and psychological. Physically, Iran had large numbers of soldiers killed—500,000 or more—and many economic resources destroyed, particularly in oil production. Psychologically, Khomeini had to reverse his position that Iran would fight to the last drop of blood until his demands were met. As the war wore on, it became clear that the Iranian revolution would not be exported, at least not in the near future. Indeed, the strain of the war contributed to the chaos in Iran that undermined the revolution, making it a less attractive model to others in the region.

For Iraq, the losses of life were great, possibly 300,000 or 400,000 soldiers—fewer than Iran lost, but from a much smaller population. The economy, just beginning to develop in 1980, had contracted and now owed $40 billion debt.[21] Even the immense amount of aid from fellow Arab countries had gone toward nonproductive assets, such as arms and ammunition.

Rebuilding would take the money and energy of both countries for years to come. The cost of rebuilding just oil installations was estimated at $25 billion.[22]

We can return now to the question posed at the beginning of the chapter: Is Clausewitz still valid, or must we, as Gorbachev writes, confine him to the libraries?

Our earlier case of the India–Pakistan war must be set side by side with the Iran–Iraq war. The earlier war was perceived, especially by the winner, as a success, achieving India's policy goals amid popular acclaim by the Indian population. The later war was seen by all sides as futile and wasteful. The contrast is similar to that between the wars for German unification and World War I.

War is not always a useful instrument of policy. Sometimes it is a disaster, as World War I, the Korean War, and the Gulf War illustrate. But these disasters must be contrasted with Bismarck's success in 1871, Indira Gandhi's in 1971, or Anwar Sadat's in 1973. Unfortunately, Foreign Secretary Home was wrong when he stated that force can never solve anything. Enough examples of useful wars exist to tempt leaders into trying, hoping that their roll of the iron dice will be lucky.

NOTES

1.   (New York: Harper & Row, 1987), p. 141.
2.   "Communism and Peaceful Coexistence," address to the United Nations General Assembly, New York, October 1, 1963, in *Vital Speeches of the Day*, October 15, 1963, p. 6.
3.   A good summary of events in *Strategic Survey 1971*, published by the International Institute for Strategic Studies (London, 1972).
4.   A graphic description of the destruction is provided by Robert Shaplen, "The Birth of Bangladesh," Parts 1 and 2, *The New Yorker*, February 12 and 19, 1972.
5.   "They Called Each Other Mister," *The Economist*, December 11, 1971, p. 25.
6.   Henry Tanner, "Outgrowth of War: Major Loss Is Seen for U.S. Influence," *The New York Times*, December 20, 1971, p. 1.
7.   A good summary of events is in *Strategic Survey 1974*, published by the International Institute for Strategic Studies (London, 1975). An interesting background report is a survey by Ken Mackenzie, "A State, but Not a Nation," *The Economist*, July 20, 1974.
8.   This as well as other examples of life before the crisis comes from Steven V. Roberts, "In a Cyprus Village, Amity and Antipathy," *The New York Times*, June 15, 1974, p. 2.
9.   Adeed I. Dawisha, "Iraq: The West's Opportunity," *Foreign Policy*, No. 41 (Winter 1986/87), p. 146.

10. Ralph King, "The Iran–Iraq War: The Political Implications," *Adelphi Paper 219* (London: International Institute for Strategic Studies, Spring 1987) p. 14.

11. Efraim Karsh, "The Iran–Iraq War: A Military Analysis," *Adelphi Paper 220* (London: International Institute for Strategic Studies, Spring 1987), p. 14.

12. Shahran Chubin, "Reflections on the Gulf War," *Survival*, Vol. 28, No. 4 (July/August 1986), p. 310.

13. Milton Viorst, "Iraq at War," *Foreign Affairs*, Vol. 65, No. 2 (Winter 1986/87), p. 351.

14. "The Course of the Iran–Iraq War," *Strategic Survey 1985–86* (London: International Institute for Strategic Studies, 1986), pp. 123–124.

15. David Segal, "The Iran–Iraq War: A Military Analysis," *Foreign Affairs*, Vol. 66, No. 5 (Summer 1988), pp. 959–960.

16. State Department official, quoted in Robert Pear, "Iran Action Linked to Anti-War Mood," *The New York Times*, July 22, 1988, p. Y4.

17. Segal, p. 960.

18. Anthony H. Cordesman, quoted in Pear. (See note 16.)

19. Robin Wright of Carnegie Endowment and anonymous State Department official, quoted in Pear. (See note 16.)

20. In Book I Chapter 1 of *On War*, edited and translated by Michael Howard and Peter Paret (Princeton: Princeton University Press, 1976), p. 75.

21. Youssef M. Ibrahim, "Bitter Defeat for Ayatollah," *The New York Times*, July 21, 1988, p. Y6.

22. *The Economist*, August 13, 1988, p. 33.

THE THREAT OF WAR IN THE CONTEMPORARY WORLD

CHAPTER 6

THREATS TO PEACE

The history of the past one hundred and some years suggests that the world has been a dangerous place. The history of those years is not one of constant war, but war occurred frequently enough to make it prudent for states' leaders to assume it was always possible and to prepare themselves accordingly. Several of the wars that occurred were so devastating that even if war was rare, it still posed a major threat to human welfare. But history tells us only what happened in the past. It does not tell us with any certainty what will happen in the future. At best, it can be an aid in an analysis of the likelihood of war in the world today. If we turn from the historical record to the present day, we encounter a variety of possible threats to national security, ranging from nuclear war to terrorism.

ALL-OUT NUCLEAR WAR

Much thought over the past decades was devoted to the possibility of a major war between the United States and the Soviet Union. A large portion of American and Soviet defense spending went into preparing for that possibility. As years passed without war occurring, many people concluded that war between the United States and the Soviet Union had never been very likely in the first place. Analysts found it difficult to construct a plausible description of how a war would begin. Even creators of popular fiction had trouble devising a convincing scenario. One of the more sensational fantasies about nuclear war, the 1983 ABC movie *The Day After*, obscured the issue of causation by allowing the viewers only overheard snatches of radio news at the grocery store checkout. A serious academic attempt to deal with the same problem, the "Avoiding Nuclear War Project" of the Kennedy School of Government at Harvard, had the same difficulty.[1]

In the early years of the Cold War, many leaders remembered the traumatic experience of the Japanese surprise attack on Pearl Harbor in 1941 and visualized a war beginning by a surprise military attack. Typical of this thinking was the consensus of an American delegation preparing for a disarmament conference in Geneva in 1958. For them, the "greatest challenge to peace was the danger of a bolt-from-the-blue, disarming nuclear first strike, and therefore the principal aim of arms control should be to diminish, and if possible eliminate, that danger."[2]

As the years passed, the power of the Pearl Harbor image faded. Today experts argue that "the probability of preventive nuclear attack has been close to zero, as far as we can know from available evidence, since the end of World War II."[3] Passing years have pushed the probability even closer to zero, as arms control agreements have multiplied and tensions have decreased. The fear of a nuclear Pearl Harbor has almost vanished.

Another fear, although more common in the minds of fiction writers than with military or political analysts, was accidental war. Accidental war was a popular subject for novels and films, but their plots relied on accidents that experts found implausible with consequences they thought were unrealistic. Instead of the delicately balanced "hair trigger" that would set off war at the slightest tremor, experts said both superpowers had very stiff triggers; if something unexpected happened, the systems for initiating war would most likely shut down precisely to avoid using them.[4]

It is hard for nonexperts to evaluate this claim, but we might consider two pieces of evidence. First, there have been innumerable accidents, including repeated computer failures that flashed warnings of impending attack, but in no case did the United States even think about preparing for war. The reaction to the false warnings was to examine the warning devices for malfunction. Second, we might consider what happened in September 1983 when the Soviet Union mistook a Korean airliner for an American spy plane and shot it down. In the first hours, the United States and its allies were slow to realize what had happened. One of the things that emerged in later investigations was that American spy planes had indeed been in the air in the same area at the same time. What is significant is how the United States finally reacted to the news that the Korean plane was lost: It grounded all its spy planes. In other words, the reaction of one superpower to a situation of heightened tension was to reduce risky behavior. Considered from the viewpoint of national security, it was an illogical move, for grounding spy planes increased the risk of surprise. Yet caution was the first reaction. Today, in a period of reduced tension, one can expect even greater caution in reacting to unexpected events.

ALLIES AND EXTENDED DETERRENCE

A more likely route to war might have been the escalation of small-scale conflicts. From the Soviet point of view at least, war might have seemed likely had events taken an unfavorable turn in East Europe. For example, the Poles might have organized an effective and popular revolt against Soviet domination (as they in fact did in the Solidarity movement in 1979 and 1980). Then the Poles, encouraged by outsiders (including a Polish pope) might have tried (as in fact they did not) to expel Soviet troops by force. In 1956 Hungarians had tried to expel the Soviets and were put down with Soviet tanks, at a cost of 14,000 lives. In 1956 the West did not intervene, but in the 1980s things might have gone differently. Live coverage by mini-camcorders and satellite dishes might have made Soviet repression intolerable to Western audiences. The Soviets at this point, anticipating some sort of NATO interference, might have taken preliminary defensive steps, such as putting forces on alert, that would have made a war more likely.

The scenario could have taken many possible turns, but by the end of the 1980s it disappeared into the realm of historical fiction. With the Soviets' voluntary and peaceful relinquishing of control over Eastern Europe, the possibility that a conflict in Europe could provoke a major war disappeared.

Next to a revolt in Eastern Europe, the most likely scenario was the escalation of a regional war, possibly in the Middle East or in Asia, that initially involved neither the Soviet Union nor the United States. War would spread because of what was known as "extended deterrence."

In a simple form of deterrence, the United States prevents attacks on itself by threatening to retaliate against attackers. The threat to retaliate is believed and attacks do not occur. When deterrence is extended to allies, it becomes less believable. For example, in 1939 Britain said it would defend Poland if Germany attacked. Hitler did not believe that Britain would risk war for the sake of the Poles and attacked anyhow, setting off World War II.

The contemporary world has seen many examples of extended deterrence. These have followed from the many alliances that the United States and the Soviet Union concluded during the Cold War. And although the United States and the Soviet Union have not gone to war against each other, countries to which they were tied have. In 1950, North Korea attacked South Korea, drawing in American troops directly and some Soviet combat forces at least indirectly. In 1973, Syria and Egypt, closely tied to the Soviet Union, attacked Israel, closely tied to the United States. For a brief moment, both superpowers put forces on alert as if preparing to intervene in that war.

The danger from extended deterrence seems to be receding. The war between Iraq and Iran continued for eight years without drawing in the superpowers, even though Iran had originally been armed by the United States and Iraq by the Soviet Union. Two years after the Iraq–Iran war ended, the United States and the Soviet Union cooperated against Iraq to the extent of voting on the same side in the United Nations.

Because the world is no longer bipolar, countries no longer automatically belong to one side or the other and disputes are no longer interpreted as "we" versus "they." But in one sense, the disappearance of extended deterrence may increase the likelihood of war. Although direct confrontation between superpowers growing out of regional conflicts may be less likely, other kinds of violence in the world may be more likely. Without a superpower rival to inhibit it, the United States may more often get involved in conflicts. In 1979 the United States was deeply disturbed by the Iranian seizure of American diplomats as hostages, yet it refrained from taking military action against Iran, in part because some people feared that harsh measures would drive Iran into the arms of the Soviet Union. With the disappearance of its major rival, the United States may feel emboldened to take military steps if it feels its interests are threatened. Even when the Soviet Union was intact, the United States demonstrated a willingness to act in the Caribbean region, where Soviet reaction was not likely—landing troops in Grenada in 1983 and Panama in 1989. Operations in other areas of the world could come to seem equally free of risk. The end of the Cold War certainly reduces the risk of getting drawn into major war accidentally but may increase the occurrence of deliberate small-scale military adventures.

Some analysts see the very decline of Soviet power as a source of threat. US Army Chief of Staff Carl Vuono writes of the "potential for violence as the collapsing Soviet empire struggles with cataclysmic change."[5] National animosities, he suggests "could ignite armed conflict within and among European nations and directly jeopardize U.S. or allied interests."[6]

Past experience with the fate of multinational empires suggests that disintegration is likely and that it is likely to be violent. The disintegration of the Habsburg Empire in the early twentieth century included violence in the Balkans, which spread to World War I. The British departure from the Indian subcontinent after World War II was accompanied by violence between Hindus and Moslems that killed two million people. Such violence is tragic for the people who must live through it but does not pose much of a military threat to neighboring areas. Europeans did not feel threatened by the American Civil War. Americans suffered at most some minor annoyance when the Mexican revolution spilled over its borders between 1910 and 1920. In the 1990s Europeans tried to stop the disintegration of Yugoslavia, but not because it threatened them militarily.

REGIONAL POWERS

Many people saw the opening of the Berlin Wall in 1989 as the symbolic event marking the end of the Cold War. The war came to an end remarkably peacefully. Even the collapse of the Soviet empire in Eastern Europe was remarkably peaceful, compared with the anticolonial struggle that marked the end of the Dutch, British, French, and Portuguese empires. Czechoslovaks appropriately called their expulsion of Soviet troops and pro-Soviet leaders "the velvet revolution."

Yet nine months later the world was again obsessed with military threats, this time from Iraq. On August 2, 1990, Iraq took over the neighboring country of Kuwait. The United States mobilized resources, moved them to the Middle East, and in early 1991 launched a major offensive against Iraq to restore sovereignty to Kuwait.

Despite the drama of a war fought on cable television, with live broadcasts of American bombing raids on Iraq and Scud missile attacks on Israel, a more sober analysis suggests that the threat posed by Iraq to the security of most countries was not great. The Defense Department shared this assessment, continuing to cut its regular forces even while activating reserves for temporary duty in Operation Desert Shield.

Saddam Hussein was a threat, certainly to Iraq's neighboring states and, because of the oil riches of the region, indirectly to other states as well. But the combination of a leader with Saddam Hussein's mentality and a state with Iraq's power are rare. One would be hard-pressed to come up with another threat. Military leaders are famous for making worst-case estimations. In 1877 a British statesman wrote to a friend, "If you believe the doctors, nothing is wholesome; if you believe the theologians, nothing is innocent; if you believe the soldiers, nothing is safe."[7] Yet in 1991 the American Chairman of the Joint Chiefs Colin Powell had to confess, "I'm running out of demons. . . . I'm down to Castro and Kim Il Sung."[8]

Although Saddam Hussein did pose some threat to the security of more than just his small weak neighbors, in doing so he seriously overextended himself. Many people thought at the time that he had seriously miscalculated and events proved them right. Hitler's successes in the 1930s encouraged others; Saddam Hussein's failure is likely to discourage imitators. Regional conflicts will continue, but the problem will be to contain and resolve them, not to defend against them. Peace-keeping mechanisms, not military prowess, are what will be called for.

In some ways, the existence of two superpowers made some states artificially strong. Some states were able to play the superpower rivals off against each other to acquire modern arms at prices they could afford. Iran under the shah built up a modern arsenal, in large part from the United States. Its regional rival Iraq acquired a large arsenal from the Soviet Union.

During the Gulf War following Iraq's seizure of Kuwait, it was with Soviet weapons that Iraq did much of its fighting. Iraq would not have been able to produce a comparable arsenal on its own.

With the ending of the Cold War, we can expect some of this competitive arming of client states to diminish. Furthermore, states will feel less able to strike challenging poses. President Nasser of Egypt defied the British and French in 1956, in part because the presence of the Soviet Union counter-balanced them. President Saddam Hussein of Iraq discovered in 1990 that such defiance did not work when all the major countries were on the same side.

NUCLEAR PROLIFERATION

Yet in some ways medium-level states have grown in power. In part this has been due to the proliferation of advanced weapons, particularly nuclear ones. Experts have identified nuclear programs in several states—Israel, South Africa, and Pakistan are considered to have or be near a capability. Programs have been identified in South Korea, North Korea, Taiwan, and Iraq, although they have been arrested through various types of international pressure. In general, nuclear programs are associated with "pariah" or outcast states that feel isolated from regional neighbors (Israel, South Africa, Taiwan) or states that are engaged in intense rivalries with neighbors (India with Pakistan, South Korea with North Korea, and, earlier, Argentina with Brazil).

Recent experience has not been encouraging. The fighting between Iraq and Iran escalated to terror attacks on civilians and use of chemical weapons. Iraq fired Scud missiles into Israeli population centers during the Gulf War even though Israel was not a party to the war. In another round of war between India and Pakistan or between Israel and its Arab neighbors, one can imagine the losing side resorting to nuclear weapons in desperation.

The problem of nuclear proliferation has been compounded by the spread of two other types of military technology—medium-range missiles and chemical weapons. Missiles with ranges of at least 1,000 miles are planned or being built by countries as diverse as India, Egypt, and Brazil. In 1988, toward the end of the Iraq–Iran War, China was reported to have sold missiles of such range to Saudi Arabia. During the 1991 Gulf War Saddam Hussein fired antiquated Scuds, causing damage in Israel and loss of life in Saudi Arabia. Scuds were old. New ones would be more destructive.

These delivery systems add a new dimension to the problem of nuclear proliferation. The threat of nuclear weapons in the hands of countries such as Pakistan and Argentina did not seem particularly threatening to any but their immediate neighbors so long as their means of delivery were short-range. But as more and more countries come within range, unease among even distant countries is bound to grow.

To worries about "delivery system proliferation" must be added worries about "chemical-biological warfare proliferation." In the years following Iraq's successful and unpunished usage of chemical weapons in the Gulf War, other third world states began to show an interest in chemical agent production facilities. Reports circulated that states such as Libya and Iran were trying to acquire the ability to make such weapons. Iraq's president Saddam Hussein boasted that he had chemical weapons and that he would use them against Israel. Alarm was compounded by the proliferation of missiles, for chemical weapons could replace nuclear ones as the warheads on such missiles. And because the chemical warfare threshold has already been crossed, it seemed more likely that such weapons might be used. Even if they were not used, their very existence would, like that of nuclear weapons, increase the potential for violence in the Third World.

The proliferation of nuclear and chemical weapons and associated delivery systems worries experts because the new nuclear states lack the very things that are believed to have kept the old nuclear states from using their weapons. The United States and the Soviet Union had vast arsenals. They did not have to worry about losing a handful of weapons in a preventive attack. They had elaborate control procedures to prevent unauthorized use. Their rivalry, while at times fierce, was not based on long years of primitive hatred based on nationality or religion. In the newly proliferated states, the opposite conditions prevail.

Furthermore, one cannot be sure that states' leaders will behave rationally. Granted, irrationality can strike anywhere. But countries with long traditions of political rule and diffused political power are less likely to be thrown off balance by the insanity of a single leader. As the Watergate scandal appeared likely to drive Nixon from office, some of his aides quietly took steps to prevent him from initiating a warlike act, even though as commander in chief of the armed forces it was still within his constitutional authority. Countries ruled by the whims of a single ruler—Uganda under Idi Amin, Iraq under Saddam Hussein—would lack such institutional barriers against the untoward consequences of emotionally disturbed leaders.

States that behave in self-defeating ways are sometimes referred to as "crazy" states.[9] Or one might call them states with leaders willing to take extraordinary risks. Iraq under Saddam Hussein is an example. There was general agreement that at many points during the crisis over Kuwait he could have made major gains with minor concessions. Initially the United States appeared ready to tolerate a minor adjustment of the frontier. Even Iraqi control over some of Kuwait's oil fields would not have led to a major war. Even after US forces began to pour into the area, there was agreement that a conciliatory gesture, even a partial withdrawal, would have thrown the coalition into disarray and likely inhibited moves against him. On the other hand, any rational assessment of forces should have told Saddam Hussein that a military conflict would go hopelessly against him. Nevertheless, he persisted in a belligerent course of action.

LOW INTENSITY CONFLICT

As the threats of both nuclear and conventional warfare appeared to be fading, the Defense Department began to talk of a new threat. In 1987 in his annual report to Congress, Reagan's secretary of defense, Caspar Weinberger, reported that "there seems to be no shortage of adversaries who seek to undermine our security by persistently nibbling away at our interests through these shadow wars carried on by guerrillas, assassins, terrorists, and subversives."[10] He called "these forms of aggression . . . the most likely and the most enduring threats to our security."[11] Three years later, in the process of trying to redefine its role in light of a rapidly receding Soviet threat, the US Army paper made public a paper, "A Strategic Force for the 1990's and Beyond." In it, the Army proposed a restructuring to deal with what it called three threats in the future: regional instability, terrorism, and drug trafficking.[12]

These three threats are often lumped together under the label "low intensity conflict."[13] But sometimes new labels are not helpful, and critics made a good case that this one was not. Instead of clarifying, it confused, merely bringing together three activities that shared little beyond appearing frequently in the news. Some critics accused the Army of engaging in "threat inflation" to keep its share of the budget.

Of the three activities identified in the Army paper, the one identified as "regional instability" fell most clearly within the traditional mandate of the armed forces. This term appeared to be the now favored name for what used to called "insurgency." Examples cited by the Army paper were El Salvador and the Philippines, countries where armed groups were seeking to overthrow the government. One might also put the Kurdish rebellion against Iraqi, Turkish, and Iranian governments, or the Palestinian conflict with Israel (and, to a lesser degree, with Lebanon and Jordan), in the same category.

One could make a case that insurgency or regional instability poses some threat to US interests. Air travel in certain regions might be unsafe for American citizens. American investments in certain countries might be confiscated. But the fundamental question citizens of a country must ask themselves is if the costs of intervening might outweigh any possible benefit. After decades of attempts to deal with insurgencies, governments have reason to be cautious.

For one thing, effective intervention in internal disputes may be beyond the means even of a great power. The experiences of the United States in Vietnam and of the Soviet Union in Afghanistan were equally sobering. In addition to the human cost—56,000 dead for the Americans, 16,000 for the Soviets—both countries' armed forces suffered severe damage to morale when they were unable to prevail. More recently India sent 50,000 troops to Sri Lanka to help control an insurrection by the Tamil minority. The intervention lasted almost three years and cost the Indians 1,200 dead, yet it produced only a loss of prestige for India.

Even limited intervention incurs heavy debts. The United States concerned itself with the internal situations in both Panama and Nicaragua, then found itself with obligations to provide financial support when its intervention succeeded in removing from power the rulers it opposed.

On the other hand, governments have discovered that negotiated settlements to internal disputes may be both possible and preferable to any other solution. A long dispute between the Marxist government of Angola and an insurgency supported at times by groups as varied as South Africa and China finally ended when the United States took a major role in mediation. Negotiated settlements were once distrusted because of the belief that once in power, communist guerrillas never relinquish their control. That belief was undermined by the results of a free election in Nicaragua in which the ruling Sandinistas, a group with distinct sympathies with Marxist regimes in Cuba and East Europe, voluntarily relinquished power.

Although those who see a threat in "low intensity conflict" usually draw their illustrations from insurgencies in countries allied to the United States, the label would fit groups such as the Kurds and the Palestinians just as well. It is useful to think about these groups, for they have been engaged in low intensity conflicts at least since the end of World War II. Yet, as their tragic failures illustrate, other states in the world can ignore regional instability with no great cost to themselves. No one has argued that the United States needs a large military establishment to deal with threats posed by the Kurds or the Palestinians. Despite their grievances, these groups have not had at their disposal enough military power to do more than cause discomfort beyond the regions in which they live.

TERRORISM

The discomfort they cause is usually in the form of terrorism. In his assessment of threats after the war with Iraq, Army Chief of Staff Vuono listed international terrorism as an example of low intensity conflict.[14] But a good case can be made that they are not international threats of the type met by the uniformed military but domestic problems more properly handled by police. In general the military have been reluctant to get involved in the police functions associated with drug wars. Military activity is traditionally heroic. It is the defense of society against open and identified enemies in uniform. Drug campaigns, by contrast, are directed against one's fellow citizens. Anyone may be the enemy. The military maxims of "finding, fixing, and fighting" the enemy are not as helpful as traditional police maxims. Those of us who are not involved in drug trafficking feel more comfortable with the civil liberties traditionally guaranteed by domestic law than with the restrictions on those liberties suggested by the phrase "martial law."

But the military is not alone in seeing terrorism as a threat. In the early 1980s some scholars were willing to make even more extravagant claims. One argued, "The principal security problem of this decade is low-intensity warfare, especially terrorism."[15]

In order to assess this claim, it is important to define what we are talking about. "Terrorist" is a convenient label to attach to someone you dislike: If you get others to accept that label, you have won a substantial victory in the struggle by getting others to adopt your value system.[16] A widely circulated cartoon in the early 1980s showed two identically equipped guerrilla fighters, one in El Salvador, the other in Nicaragua. The cartoon identified one as a "terrorist," the other as a "freedom fighter." The point was to make fun of the political rhetoric that made the definition wholly dependent on whether a guerrilla was on our side or theirs.[17] In the rhetorical struggle, the term was expanded to apply to governments as well. Thus raids by Israel, in retaliation for what it called "terrorist attacks" against its citizens, were routinely labelled "state terrorism" by Israel's enemies.

With its rhetorical usefulness as a nasty label, "terrorism" rapidly degenerates from a useful term to a synonym for "violence that I disapprove of." When Greenpeace activists interfered with illegal whaling by the Japanese, a Japanese official called their actions "terrorism."[18] When Earth First activists vandalized equipment used to clearcut old growth forests, the logging companies called them "terrorists."[19] Such loose usage only impedes level-headed analysis. When we talk about threats to world peace, we do not mean harassing whaling boats and pouring sugar into gas tanks.

Some of the most careful—and nonpartisan—studies of terrorism have been conducted at the Rand Corporation under the direction of Brian Jenkins, and the definition he has offered is free of the political bias of many others. Terrorism, according to Jenkins, is an act or threat of violence calculated to create an atmosphere of fear and alarm. These acts or threats must be ones that would normally be considered criminal, both under domestic law (murder, kidnapping, arson) and under the laws of war (attacking civilians, taking hostages, harming captives).[20] They are usually carried out by organized groups who not only take credit for what they do but seek the widest possible publicity.

It is not the act alone but also the intentions behind it that make it a terrorist act. Assassination alone is not terrorism. John Hinckley attempted to shoot President Reagan in March 1981, but no one considered it an act of terrorism. On the other hand, when the President of Lebanon was blown up by a bomb in September 1982, it was considered to have the wider political purpose of undermining Christian Maronite dominance in Lebanon. In April 1988 the PLO leader Khalil Wazir "Abu Jihad" was assassinated in Tunis by a team of Israeli commandos, a move widely interpreted as intended to weaken the Palestinian uprising. The British Ambassador to the United Nations called it a "senseless act of terrorism,"[21] but he was wrong. If it was senseless, it was not terrorism.

Destruction of property alone is not terrorism. The bomb that blew up Pan Am flight 103 over Lockerbie Scotland appears to have been revenge for the accidental destruction of an Iranian airbus over the Persian Gulf by American ships in 1988. But because no one claimed credit for it and no one coupled any demands with it, it is not clear why it should be classified as an act of terrorism. Perhaps in some one's mind that act of retribution was necessary to settle accounts, but because the Persian Gulf War was over and US naval vessels withdrawn, the destruction of the airliner could not have served the political purpose of deterring future attacks on Iran aircraft.

The purpose of terrorist acts is not the physical damage they cause but the psychological terror they create. One of the definitions gets at this point: "the deliberate and systematic murder, maiming and menacing of the innocent to inspire fear in order to gain political ends."[22] Thus if a Palestinian shopkeeper on the West Bank does not obey the curfew imposed by the leaders of the Palestinian uprising (intifada) and is shot, others take heed. The purpose is only incidentally to punish the shopkeeper. Its broader purpose is to achieve the political end of maintaining a general strike. Likewise, when in October 1983, the Islamic Jihad blew up Marines in barracks, the purpose was only incidentally to kill Marines. The larger political purpose was to drive the United States out of playing an active role in Lebanese politics. The role of publicity is key:

> "If someone mounts a suicide operation and there is no story about it in the West, then it is as though it never happened, no matter how much damage it does," said a senior Israeli official. "You don't do terrorism to kill people," he said. "You do it to create an echo that makes you larger than life. No echo, no success."[23]

TERRORISM IN INTERNATIONAL POLITICS

Terrorist tactics are used by two or perhaps three kinds of groups. One type is the politically motivated domestic opposition group seeking a radical transformation of a domestic regime, such as the Red Army Faction in Germany and the Red Brigades in Italy. Guerrillas seeking to overthrow the governments of several Latin American countries, particularly Colombia and Peru, have been accused of making common cause with organizations that grow, process, and ship cocaine. Their reinforcing efforts have been labelled "narco-terrorism." Such groups tend to confine their activities to their own country and do not present a major problem for international politics except when their activities spill over their borders.

Second are nationalist groups with aspirations to statehood. Their activities are directed against the state or states that thwart their aspirations. Prominent examples are the ETA, a Basque organization that seeks some measure of autonomy from Spain; the IRA, which seeks unification of the British territory of Northern Ireland with the Irish Republic; and various Palestinian groups, united in the umbrella organization of the PLO.

Because they see themselves as states-in-waiting, they tend to play a bigger part in international politics. Often they seek some form of international recognition. The PLO has observer status at the UN and full-fledged membership in some international organizations.

Sometimes nationalist groups may cooperate with each other or with radical domestic groups in procuring weapons, training, and support for operations. Such cooperation gave rise to speculation about an international network of terrorists, reflected in the claim by Attorney General Edwin Meese that Nicaragua had become a "country club" for terrorists, offering refuge to members of the PLO, ETA, IRA, and Red Brigades.[24] Little beyond opportunistic cooperation has been documented: Groups lend help to each other, but no evidence of central planning or coordinating bodies has been uncovered.

This is not to say that groups are not aware of each other. A newspaper columnist visited the headquarters of the political front for the IRA in the Catholic part of Belfast and found displayed there the emblems and posters of other self-styled radical groups; she then crossed town to the equivalent Protestant group and found there posters from the contras in Nicaragua, UNITA in Angola, and other groups supported by conservatives.[25] If anything, what has emerged is not one but two terrorist networks. But in fact the second network, of "conservative terrorists," has shown no more coherence than its radical counterpart. An attempt in 1985 by a conservative American politician to bring four anti-Soviet groups together in what he wanted to call a "Democratic International" produced very little in the way of concrete results.[26] The case that terrorist networks are significant non-state actors in world politics remains unproved.

Some writers refer to a third kind of group they call the "state-sponsored" terrorists. Such groups presumably would not be actors in their own right but mere extensions of other more traditional actors, recognized and sovereign states. At this point we might usefully distinguish among three kinds of state involvement: state-*sponsored* terrorism, state-*supported* terrorism, and state-*tolerated* terrorism.

In the first case, the group would not exist without the active recruitment, supply, and direction of a state. One group that at least in its initial days met this definition was "Renamo" or the Mozambique National Resistance. Mozambique ceased to be a Portuguese colony in 1975. It allowed its areas bordering on Rhodesia to be used as a sanctuary for black guerrillas operating against the white minority government there. In 1976 the Rhodesian intelligence service set up Renamo both to monitor the guerrillas and to put pressure on the Mozambique government. The Rhodesians recruited Renamo from former members of the Portuguese secret police, army deserters, and petty criminals. The first leader of Renamo had been dismissed from the Mozambique army on charges of theft.[27] Despite the Rhodesian effort, the black guerrillas won. When they took power in Rhodesia (changing the name to Zimbabwe), sponsorship of Renamo passed to South Africa, who like Renamo's original sponsors wanted to continue to deter the Mozambique government from providing support to guerrillas. Several years later the government of F. W. de Klerk moved toward accommodation with the black nationalist movement, but by this time Renamo had become a self-sufficient organization that could survive in Mozambique without sponsorship.

The key element of state-*sponsored* terrorism is that the group would not exist independently of the sponsoring government. State-*supported* terrorism, by contrast, would exist independently of outside aid. In 1959 a group of Palestinians, lacking a state of their own, set up a guerrilla organization they called al Fatah, which ten years later became the core group of the Palestine Liberation Organization. Although independent in its origins, the PLO has received a variety of support from many governments. The former communist government of Rumania, for example, provided passports for use by PLO officials. Such support undoubtedly contributes to the effectiveness of such organizations but may not be crucial to their existence. More important, the ability of governments to turn such groups toward their own specific national ends is limited.

Finally, some groups may be merely state-*tolerated* terrorist groups. Some of the more radical groups opposing Castro in Cuba, such as Alpha-77, were not set up by the United States nor were they actively supplied by the United States with weapons, training, or other assistance. Yet because their aims on occasion at least partially coincided with US aims, the United States was not as vigorous in prosecuting them as it might have been.

What is most important about all three types of terrorists is that they are difficult to eradicate because one or more states give them sanctuary from their pursuers. The United States made much of Libya's support for international terrorism, even mounting a bombing raid on Libya in April 1986 in retaliation for an alleged Libyan-sponsored attack on American servicemen in Germany. Yet the actual degree of guilt of Libya for such attacks is not as crucial as the problem that as long as Libya allows such groups the freedom to move about, they are safe from international retaliation. Of course, some terrorists have survived within a country even when the government pursues a vigorous campaign to eradicate them. Despite efforts of the German police, prominent German bankers and industrialists are killed by bomb attacks for which radical groups claim responsibility. But other groups are protected not so much by their own secretiveness as by the international respect for sovereignty which keeps them from being pursued into states which harbor them.

How useful these groups are in serving the ends of states is debatable. The anti-Cuban groups tolerated by the United States annoyed Castro but did not topple him. Groups drawing support from Syria or Libya or Iran have staged kidnappings and generated media coverage of "hostages" but in general have very little to show for it. Despite the publicity given to terrorist attacks, the total number as well as the impact is quite small.

GRAVITY OF THE THREAT

Statistics can be misleading in many ways. Consider crime. Certain crimes may be underreported. Fear and shame have kept many cases of rape from being reported. If the police announce an increase in incidents of rape, it may be that the crime is increasing, or it may be that the crime is being reported more frequently. Another problem is definition. If state laws define rape in such a way that a married person cannot be legally be guilty of raping a spouse, many cases of what ordinarily people think of as rape (for example, involving people legally separated although still married) do not get reported.

Terrorism suffers from the same problem. Although US government statistics are often cited, they suffer serious definitional problems. In 1988, when the government reported a peak of 856 international terrorist incidents (see Table 6.1), it defined terrorism in such a way that violence directed against the Afghan guerrilla movement (which the United States government supported) was considered terrorism but violence against the govern-

Table 6.1 INTERNATIONAL TERRORISM

	Incidents	Killed	Wounded	US Citizens Killed
1985	785	825	1,217	38
1986	774	450	1,125	12
1987	832	295	770	7
1988	856	638	1,125	192
1989	533	407	427	16
1990	455	193	675	10

Source: Complied from U.S. Department of State, *Patterns of Global Terrorism*, issued yearly.

ment of Nicaragua (which the United States government opposed) was not. Likewise, when a bomb blew up an airliner with 169 aboard, that was counted as 169 incidents of violence against Americans, even though it was a single attack.

Nevertheless, even using government figures, it can be seen that the terrorism threat is not grave. The total of 192 Americans killed in 1988 (a figure inflated by a single airplane bomb) dropped to 16 killed in 1989 and 10 in 1990. An American's chances of dying by lightning are almost ten times higher.

An even more significant indicator is what happened during the Persian Gulf War of 1991. Saddam Hussein, accused among other things of sponsoring terrorism, threatened to unleash terrorism as a weapon. Yet during the time of the war (January 16—March 16), there were only 172 incidents worldwide. These were mostly bombings of banks in third world countries, events hardly even perceived by Americans, much less serious enough to make them change their policy. The terrorist threat, it is agreed, was easily defeated by police measures. Spectators at the Super Bowl had to undergo tighter security checks, people leaving unattended cars at airports found them quickly towed, but the inconvenience was minor.

The failure of Iraq to succeed with an announced policy of state-sponsored terrorism illustrates a major point about terrorism. However serious the threat may be, it is primarily a police problem, to be handled by domestic jurisdiction. The only international dimension is the problem of sanctuaries. Terrorists have found it easier to operate when they have had countries to which they could flee. With the collapse of communist regimes in eastern Europe and the realignment of power in the Middle East, these sanctuaries have become rare. Neither the changes in eastern Europe nor those in the Middle East were undertaken to curtail terrorism, but they had that effect.

There are several responses by those who portray terrorism as a serious threat. All agree that even a few incidents can have an greatly amplified effect. Therefore, the effect of terrorism is not reasonably measured by number of incidents but by their effect. In 1986 there was a wave of bombings in Paris, attributed at first to "Arab terrorists" and later more specifically to a group of Lebanese. Yet the attacks affected people's behavior, leading a drop in retail sales and a reduction in cinema attendance as people stayed home more. The attacks generated anti-Arab feeling, but at the same time led the government to make concessions to the Arabs. Nevertheless, the attacks left only 13 dead and 250 injured—probably no more than a week of automobile accidents.[28]

Without question, a government faced with highly publicized if minuscule threats has a problem. But the problem stems mostly from public perceptions. The expenditure of vast resources to eliminate the threat might be less wise than policies designed to put the threat in rational perspective, including severe curbs on sensationalist reporting.

Another argument is that although terrorist attacks have temporarily abated, more might break out at any time. People who argue this way point to the vulnerabilities of modern industrial society—dependence on a few, unguarded natural gas pipelines or electric transmission lines. AT&T depends on just 14 long-distance switching centers.[29] This is coupled with the argument that new technologies favor terrorists.

It is also true that technological advances have produced powerful yet compact explosives. The bomb that blew up the Marine barracks in Beirut in 1983 was judged to have the force of six tons of the traditional explosive TNT, yet it fit in a small pickup truck barely capable of carrying one-tenth that much weight. The bomb that caused a jumbo jet to disintegrate over Lockerbie was small enough to fit inside a tape cassette player-recorder.

Modern warfare has produced precision-guided munitions such as hand-held missiles to shoot down aircraft. One of the earliest and most primitive of these, the Soviet SA-7, was used in August 1986 to shoot down a Sudanese airliner. There have been relatively few other cases of their use against civilian aircraft, but alarmists worry about the large numbers of the more advanced American Stingers distributed by the United States to guerrillas it supported in Afghanistan, southern Africa, and Central America. It seems reasonable to assume that some of these Stingers made their way into the black market in arms. Less likely but more serious is the possibility that chemical or nuclear weapons could fall into the hands of terrorists.

The arguments are worthy of consideration. But the question this book is examining is the use of the traditional means of dealing with military threats from other states. Terrorism may be a problem, but is a standing army the answer? Modern society could be disrupted by terrorists cutting telephone cables. It could also be disrupted by an earthquake. Preparations should be made for dealing with earthquakes, just as they should be made for dealing with terrorists. But not all problems that disrupt societies are problems of international politics, to be solved by the traditional means of international politics. Terrorism is more reasonably treated as a police problem. A reasonable antiterrorist policy is less likely to use high-performance jet fighters and attack submarines than well-trained security guards and alert baggage inspectors.

Looking at the present world, it would be fair to say that threats to national security have diminished, but it would be extreme to say they no longer exist. Even if terrorism can be dealt with by domestic means, aggression by states cannot. As long as sovereign states remain in existence, possessing armaments, the possibility of war remains. The problem facing students of international relations is to devise ways to reduce the possibility of war by dealing with its fundamental causes.

NOTES

1. See their findings in Graham T. Allison et al. eds., *Hawks, Doves, & Owls* (New York: W. W. Norton, 1985).

2. Strobe Talbott, *Master of the Game* (New York: Alfred A. Knopf, 1988), p. 73.

3. Richard Betts, "Surprise Attack and Preemption" in *Hawks, Doves, & Owls*, p. 57.

4. Paul Bracken, *The Command and Control of Nuclear Weapons*, (New Haven: Yale University Press, 1983).

5. Carl E. Vuono, "Desert Storm and Conventional Forces," *Foreign Affairs*, Vol. 70, No. 2 (Spring 1991), p. 53.

6. Ibid.

7. Lord Salisbury, 1877 (letter to Lord Lytton).

8. Quoted in Carl Kaysen, Robert S. McNamara, and George W. Rathjens, "Nuclear Weapons After the Cold War," *Foreign Affairs*, Vol. 70, No. 4 (Fall 1991), p. 96.

9. Yehezkel Dror, *Crazy States* (Lexington, Mass.: Lexington Books, 1971).

10. *Report of the Secretary of Defense Caspar W. Weinberger to the Congress on the FY 1988/FY 1989 Budget* (Washington D.C.: January 12, 1987), p. 57.

11. Ibid., p. 62.

12. Michael R. Gordon with Bernard E. Trainor, "Army, Facing Cuts, Reported Seeking to Reshape Itself," *The New York Times*, December 12, 1989, p. Z A1.

13. See for example, Michael T. Klare and Peter Kornbluh, eds., *Low Intensity Warfare* (New York: Pantheon, 1988), esp. Chapter 1.

14. Vuono, p. 54. (See note 5.)

15. Robert H. Kupperman, "Coping with Terrorism," *The New York Times*, March 18, 1981, p. 23.

16. Brian Jenkins, "Statements about Terrorism," *Annals of the American Academy of Political and Social Science*, Vol. 463 (September 1982), p. 12.

17. *Editorials on File*, Vol. 14, No. 8 (April 16–30, 1983), p. 428.

18. David E. Sanger, "Japanese Whaling Trip Rekindles Old Conflicts," *The New York Times*, February 5, 1989, p. Y12.

19. David Sayre of the Trillium Corporation, *The Bellingham Herald* January 22, 1989, p. B1.

20. Jenkins, p. 12. (See note 16.)

21. Ambassador Crispin Tickell at the Security Council. "Security Council Condemns Assassination of P.L.O. Chief," *The New York Times*, April 26, 1988, p. Y6.

22. Benjamin Netanyahu, *Terrorism: How the West Can Win* (New York: Farrar, Straus & Giroux, 1986), p. 50.

23. *The New York Times* February 16, 1986, p. Y10.

24. Speech to jurists in Washington, D.C., September 14, 1985, reported in *The New York Times*, September 15, 1985, p. Y3.

25. Flora Lewis, "Which Terrorists to Punish?" *The New York Times*, November 15, 1985, p. Y27.

26. Lewis E. Lehrman, acting for "Citizens for America," organized a conference in Angola attended by representatives from Angola, Afghanistan, Laos, and Nicaragua. See Alan Cowell, "4 Rebel Units Sign Anti-Soviet Pact," *The New York Times*, June 6, 1985, p. A16.

27. James Brooke, "Rebels Leave Mozambique a Bloodied and Fallow Land," *The New York Times*, May 11, 1988, p. Y6.

28. *The Economist*, February 9, 1991, p. 50.

29. *The New York Times*, May 26, 1988, p. Y32.

CHAPTER 7

THE PRINCIPLES OF INTERNATIONAL RELATIONS

When we sit down to list causes of all the wars we have looked at, from Prussia and Denmark in 1864 to Iraq and Iran in 1980, we discover not one but a multiplicity of causes. We find that World War I was caused by an arms race (which increased tensions and hostility) and by tension and hostility (which led to the arms race in the first place). We find World War I was also caused by the failure of the major powers to appease national groups that had just grievances (the Austrians failed to allow the Serbs in Bosnia to join themselves to the neighboring state of Serbia and the Germans would not allow Alsace and Lorraine to rejoin France).

Yet when we come to World War II, we find exactly the opposite causes. Hitler could get away with his aggressive moves for so long because the British and the French had so little confidence in their own armed strength. In other words, it was the failure of the British and French to keep up an arms race with Germany that led to war. At the same time, Britain and France were too willing to appease Hitler when he advanced claims based on nationalism. Although World War I was caused by an arms race and lack of appeasement, World War II was brought on by appeasement and lack of an arms race.

Despite these confusing discoveries, we can safely say some things about the cause of *all* wars. One is that wars occur because nothing exists to stop them. No world authority or world force makes war an unacceptable means of settling disputes. As a result, war has become a customary way of settling disputes. We can even go so far as to claim that war is sanctioned by the traditional principles of international politics as they have been understood for the last 300 years. We will examine some of the definitions, concepts, and practices that make up these principles and show how they permit wars to take place.

THE TRADITIONAL STATE-CENTRIC VIEW

We generally say that the present system of international politics goes back 300 years because we often take the date 1648 as the beginning of the modern state system. In 1648 the Peace of Westphalia was signed, ending the Thirty Years' War that had involved most European states and caused great loss of life (perhaps as much as 30 percent of the population in parts of Germany where it was fought). The Thirty Years' War was a war of religion, Catholics against Protestants. The central part of Europe had been ruled (although loosely) as one unit called the Holy Roman Empire (though it had only the vaguest connection with the ancient Roman Empire). The emperor was the ruler of Austria, with power concentrated around Vienna. As years passed, the local rulers—kings and princes—became more powerful and the Holy Roman emperor could exercise less and less control. This erosion of imperial authority became clear during the Protestant Revolution of the sixteenth century when many kings and princes in northern Europe became Protestants in defiance of the Catholic emperor.

The Peace of Westphalia used a formula for making peace that acknowledged the end of the emperor's authority. The formula was poetic in Latin, *cuius regio eius religio,* ''whose the region, his the religion''—that is, the religion of a region would be determined by the religion of the ruler. This doctrine elevated the individual states of Europe above the Holy Roman emperor and the Roman Catholic Church and even above the private rights of the individual. The Peace of Westphalia made the state the most important political unit in the lives of the inhabitants of Europe. The year 1648 marks an important step toward transforming the state into the most important object of people's loyalties. It is remarkable how close we have remained to this principle. We think of ourselves, by and large, first as Americans (or Mexicans, or Canadians). We may quarrel with our individual tax bills but we seldom question the fundamental right of the state to tax us. Despite the objections raised during the Vietnam War to what many saw as a foreign adventure unrelated to US security, most Americans still think it shameful to refuse to die or at least risk one's life in a clear-cut case of defending the country. Few Americans hesitate to stand up and pledge their allegiance to a flag. Is there any other institution for which we would do these things? Would so many people let a church tax them or risk their lives for a trade union, or pledge allegiance to their employer's company banner?

Before we go further, we should stop to look at a definition of the state. Occasionally the question of statehood comes up for some unconventional group—a family living on an abandoned oil rig outside territorial waters, or descendants of an aboriginal group dispossessed by colonial settlers and living on a reservation. To qualify as a state, such an entity must meet three criteria. First, it must be an association of people. Antarctica, which has no permanent human population, is not a state.

Second, these people must be politically organized. They must be capable of acting collectively. When we say, "Ohio State won the Rose Bowl," we mean more than that eleven individuals who just happened to attend Ohio State and just happened to show up on the football field that day won the game. We mean by "Ohio State" the recruiting, training, financing, emotional support, and all the other institutional contributions to the victory. Likewise, an expression such as "Sweden" is not just a metaphor for a collection of individuals. It is a term that expresses the idea that people acting together can do things that people acting individually cannot do, such as raise money by taxation and then make it available in the form of foreign aid to repair war damage in North Vietnam. A "government" is the name we give to the apparatus of decision and execution that enables an association of people to act collectively.

Third, a state is located on a definite territory. This is a very important criterion, because it excludes from treatment as states widely scattered associations of people (such as Gypsies), nomadic tribes, and guerrillas. To put it another way, a state has borders. Along with these borders goes the presumed right to exclude outsiders; there is no accepted right to emigrate to any country you please. Jurisdiction is assumed to be territorial. If I visit Mexico and commit a murder, I will be tried by the laws of Mexico, not by the laws of the United States, even though I am an American citizen.

Governments began to have a real ability to maintain borders for the first time about 1648, which is one of the reasons the Peace of Westphalia gave to states the authority it did. Developments such as gunpowder and conscript armies enabled kings to break the monopoly of force held before by independent noblemen and their knightly retainers. These developments also enabled the king to exclude outside forces, such as the armies of the emperor. Protection of subjects (whether Protestants threatened by Catholics or vice versa) was now possible.

At about the same time (1651 to be precise), an Englishman named Thomas Hobbes published a book titled *Leviathan*. This was a theoretical justification for the new state and its power. Hobbes advanced an idea that is closely associated with the idea of a state: the social contract. According to this idea, a citizen gives loyalty to the state and in return the state protects the citizen from internal disorder and foreign invasion. A citizen who does not give this loyalty has no right to protection. (This is the familiar argument used to justify military service.) The state that cannot provide order at home and protection from foreign enemies does not deserve the loyalty of its citizens (the premise of the terrorist trying to overthrow a government). It is because the state has been (at least until now) so successful in providing security to its citizens that it has been the major actor in the world system.

STATE AND NATION

The belief that states have obligations toward their citizens, as expressed in the idea of the social contract, has been reinforced by another idea, that of nationhood. The words "nation" and "state" are often used interchangeably but the concepts to which the words refer are different and we should distinguish between them. Even though 1648 marks the beginning of the modern state, states then were in at least one way very different from states today. States were then considered the property of the ruler; they could be bought, sold, traded, or used as security for loans. In the eighteenth century the Austrian ruling family mortgaged the province of Silesia to the English and Dutch in return for a loan. A major change in this attitude toward states came with the French Revolution in 1789. Both in France and the countries conquered by France, many people became aware for the first time of a national identity.

A nation is somewhat harder to define than a state. It is a group of people who have some things in common, although precisely what they share may vary. Usually they have a common language, common customs, and a common tradition. To the extent that one of these is absent (for example, Jewish immigrants to Israel have spoken many languages), the other ties will be all the stronger. We say that people develop a national consciousness when they become aware of having these things in common and begin to place a positive value on them. The awareness of a common tradition in the past leads to an awareness of a common fate in the future and gives rise to the basic tenet of nationalism, that nation and state should coincide. Each nation should have its own state, each state should comprise one and only one nation.

The nation-state is only the *ideal* unit of international politics. In fact, not many components of international politics today resemble the ideal. Some states are multinational and seem likely to remain that way for some time—Canada and Switzerland, for example. Some nationalities, such as the Koreans and Germans, have been spread over several states. Other participants in international politics are not states at all—organizations such as the United Nations, for example. You may notice some inconsistency in the use of terms. According to our definitions, the United Nations is not the United "Nations" at all but rather the United "States." International politics could more properly be called "interstate" politics. Nevertheless we accept terms such as "United Nations" and "international" because their usage is well established. The tendency to substitute "nation" for "state" only emphasizes that it is considered the ideal that each state should represent one and only one nation.

Let us summarize our definition of a state by returning to the group that comes forward and asks to join an association of states such as the United Nations. To gain acceptance as a state, we expect it to meet the three basic criteria of statehood: a group of people (who are most likely to be referred to as a nation), controlled by an effective government (which will claim to be acting in the best interests of the nation), in undisputed control of a clearly defined piece of territory. If the group's claim is recognized by other states, we say that the new state is recognized as sovereign.

SOVEREIGNTY

Political, social, economic, and technological developments during the seventeenth century elevated the state to the central role in international politics, signified by the Peace of Westphalia in 1648. From this basic fact of international life evolved a legal doctrine to go with it: state sovereignty.

Sovereignty was invented in 1576 by Jean Bodin. That may sound a bit strange. We normally reserve the word "invent" for mechanical devices such as the telephone, but there is no reason why the word can't be applied to intellectual concepts as well. No idea is entirely original, of course, but no mechanical device is either. For either, one person is usually given credit for successfully combining previous discoveries in a new way and then publicizing this invention. Jean Bodin was really inventing an intellectual weapon for use in the struggle between the church and state. Authority in the medieval state was divided between the two—questions of marriage, divorce, and other personal matters were controlled by the church; business and political affairs were regulated by the state (although often within guidelines laid down by the church—no business on Sunday, no interest rates for loans). One consequence of the increasing power of the rulers of the states was that they wanted less interference from church officials. Because all these rulers claimed to be good Christians, it was hard for them to ignore the arguments of bishops for a role in governing the lives of their citizens. Then Jean Bodin offered an argument that strengthened the king's hand.

Bodin defined sovereignty as "supreme power over citizens and subjects, unrestrained by law."[1] He argued that anything that can be called a state must have a sovereign somewhere—an authority that gives the laws, judges criminals, passes sentences. The important point of his argument was that there could be only one sovereign. If this power was shared it would no longer be sovereign. This argument gave the king an advantage in the quarrel with the church, because only the king had claimed total authority; the church had relied on an older argument of dual authority, a spiritual versus a temporal realm. Bodin's definition reflected the growing power of the state and gave the king arguments to use against the church.

How this internal contest between the church and state developed need not concern us further. What is important is that this doctrine of sovereignty—supreme power unrestricted by law—came to be applied to states in their external dealings as well. One of the first uses of sovereignty in the discussion of relations between states was in a book by a Dutch jurist, Hugo Grotius, *On the Law of War and Peace*. This is often called the first textbook on international relations. He published it in 1625, about the time that the Peace of Westphalia was laying the foundation for modern international politics. Grotius recognized that a state, if sovereign, could not be subject to legal control by another state. But his main interest was in finding a common natural law on which even sovereign states could agree. Not until the next century were the full implications of sovereignty in international relations recognized by a Swiss jurist, Emerich de Vattel. His *Law of Nations*, published in 1758, was the basic text on international relations at the time of the American Revolution. He wrote that states could be restrained neither by other states nor by any law.

Sovereignty in its internal and external applications might be illustrated in this way: It is universally agreed that taking human life is wrong. Legal codes only reinforce a more basic moral code on this point. Yet the sovereign (whether in the form of a king or a congress) may provide for the execution of criminals. Nothing restrains it from prescribing this form of killing, not even the moral code. In external relations, the taking of human life is treated not as a crime but as an act of valor, if done when one sovereign has declared war on another. In 1969 the Swiss courts tried a case of Arab hijackers who had killed Israeli airline passengers. The defense argued that because these Arabs were in a state of war with Israel, the killings were not murders but justifiable acts of war.[2]

Until recently, a handful of states such as Monaco and Liechtenstein claimed internal sovereignty only, giving up external sovereignty by placing their foreign affairs in the hands of larger neighbors (France for Monaco, Switzerland for Liechtenstein). But this practice is disappearing. Liechtenstein recently became a full member of the United Nations, thereby joining the vast majority of states that claim external as well as internal sovereignty. It follows that if all states claim to be sovereign on their own territories, there can be no single world sovereign—no world government, no world law, no restraint of any kind. The sovereign right to act unrestrained by law applies equally to the United States of America and to the Caribbean state of Dominica. Dominica listed its population in 1981 as 47,859, its area as 290 square miles. Its published trade figures for its major exports (bananas, coconuts, and fruit juices) showed earnings of $47 million (although it was estimated that it earned half as much again from illegal trade in marijuana). Its government budget of 4.4 million dollars enabled it to support an army of ninety-nine soldiers—a force so weak that ten mercenaries planned to embark from New Orleans and seize the government. (They were stopped— by the American FBI, not the Dominican armed forces.)[3]

Yet even a state so weak that a handful of mercenaries contemplate taking it over is nonetheless a sovereign and as such the legal equal of the United States. Both states have one vote in the United Nations. Neither can legitimately dictate policy to the other. Even more extreme is the case of the Pacific island of Nauru—8 square miles of guano (bird droppings). Despite its tiny size, the 8,000 inhabitants of Nauru claim the same sovereign rights for their country that the United States enjoys.

If the doctrine of sovereignty leads us to equate Nauru with the United States, then there is a flaw in it, or so thinkers have argued through the centuries since the doctrine first appeared. Gottfried Wilhelm Leibniz, a seventeenth-century writer, argued that external sovereignty should be judged by a state's ability to survive in peace or war, by diplomacy or strategy.[4] During the nineteenth century, sovereignty in practice came close to this meaning. Only a relatively small number of major countries were considered truly sovereign. Other parts of the world were treated as colonies or dependencies or simply unclaimed territory. Nauru was a possession of Germany.

But the twentieth century has seen a turn toward a more legalistic interpretation of sovereignty. National liberation movements, representing the populations of former colonies and dependencies, have found it useful to stress the idea of equality implicit in the doctrine of sovereignty. It is a useful symbol of independence and a tool in pressing for advantages. A small country can extend its fishing rights far beyond the traditional limits of 3 miles or 12 miles and claim that in doing so it is only exercising its sovereignty. A major state might have the military force to resist such an expansion but would hesitate to be accused of violating another state's sovereignty.

RECOGNITION

Once acquired, sovereign status is used to press for advantage. The process by which it is acquired is called *recognition*. We often come across the term, as in the statement, "For thirty years the United States did not recognize China." This does not mean that for thirty years the United States claimed that there was a vacancy on the globe at that spot. It means that the United States did not recognize the sovereignty of the regime governing China.

Recognition is a political act with legal consequences.[5] It is the official way in which one state indicates that it considers another state to exist as a responsible legal entity. By recognizing another state, a state signals that it is ready to do business with that other state, make treaties with it, extend credit, send aid, and engage in other kinds of international contact. Usually recognition is accompanied by establishment of diplomatic relations and exchange of ambassadors, although strictly speaking this step is not necessary.

Recognition is granted by a state that is already recognized. In this way it resembles the social register of high society or the exchange of Alice in *Through the Looking Glass*. Alice encounters a unicorn, who promptly exclaims, "A child! I always thought they were fabulous monsters!" Alice replies, "Do you know, I always thought unicorns were fabulous monsters, too?" The unicorn suggests diplomatically, "Well, now that we have seen each other, if you'll believe in me, I'll believe in you."[6]

Even as late as the Versailles Conference of 1919, recognition meant recognition by the great powers. With the emphasis today on sovereign equality, one state's recognition is no better than another's. There are occasional disagreements about when regimes should be recognized. In the end each state decides for itself and conducts business with only those states it does recognize. The closest we have to an international form of recognition is membership in the United Nations, but even in the UN there are states that do not recognize each other.

One problem is who does the recognizing; another is what is recognized. New states that come into existence as the result of treaties ending wars (Czechoslovakia, created by the Versailles Treaty) or because of successful civil wars (Bangladesh) require recognition. What is recognized is both the state and the political regime that controls it. When Bangladesh was created in 1971, a new regime was created at the same time and both were recognized. Sometimes, however, regimes change without any change in the territorial boundaries of the state. We are not talking here about changes in administrations (what Europeans call governments) but changes in the constitutional order. The United States has not had a change in regime since the Constitution was adopted in 1789. France, by contrast, has had a number of regimes in the same period, the most recent being the Fifth Republic. When a regime comes to power by orderly, constitutional means, the new regime is automatically recognized. When the French people approved the proposed constitution of the Fifth Republic, all countries of the world recognized the new regime and the government headed by General Charles de Gaulle. When the regime is changed by nonconstitutional means, however, the question of recognition arises.

In January 1971, the Ugandan government of President Milton Obote was overthrown by a military officer, Idi Amin. For months Uganda's East African neighbors did not recognize this new government. Practically, this nonrecognition meant they acted as if no one was in charge of the country— they did not meet with the new ruler, sign agreements with him, exchange diplomatic notes, or engage in any business. Recognition of Amin's regime was finally signaled in October 1971 when other countries agreed to attend a conference of the East African Common Market with representatives of the new regime. Treating them as though they were the rulers constituted recognition of the new regime.

When a new state comes into existence or when diplomatic relations have been ruptured for a long time, something more formal than common attendance at a conference is required. We sometimes refer to formal recognition as *de jure* recognition, a declaration by one state that it is extending recognition to another. When we say, "The United States did not recognize China until 1979," we mean the United States had not extended de jure recognition to China. Certainly by 1972 the United States was treating the leaders of the People's Republic of China as though they did govern China—from allowing mail to be sent to sitting on the UN Security Council with them. Treating a regime as though it is the responsible government of a state is sometimes called *de facto* recognition. Obviously de facto recognition can grow so much that the distinction between de facto and de jure no longer has much meaning.

The United States' failure to recognize the Chinese Communist regime for so long is an example of two contending theories on when recognition should be granted. One of these theories, the more traditional or orthodox one, exemplified by the practice of the British government, is that recognition is automatically accorded to the regime in power. If there are contenders for recognition, they must fight it out. The winner is recognized when it controls a governmental apparatus and at least some territory. With a government and territory, the presumption is that a regime will be able to make commitments and carry them out. Following this theory, the British recognized the Chinese Communist government in January 1950.

The other approach to recognition is a political one. It acknowledges that recognition is a political tool that can be used for helping friends and hindering enemies. The United States' refusal to recognize China is one example. The refusal of the Soviet Union to recognize the regime of Francisco Franco in Spain for all of its forty years is another. Both countries were withholding recognition to show disapproval.

The United States has been criticized for its delay in recognizing the communist regime in China. But it has also been criticized for its prompt recognition of regimes that come to power in military coups. If the United States does not recognize a secessionist movement early in its struggle, the movement may be hostile to the United States once it comes to power. But if the United States recognizes a movement that then is defeated, the state that defeated it will be hostile to the United States. Facing these conflicting demands on how to use recognition, a state is safest if it follows the British in a strictly consistent application of the doctrine of control. Another way of describing this approach is to say that if a state can be held responsible for its acts, it should be recognized. By this theory the United States should have extended de jure recognition to North Korea, because when the North Koreans seized the *Pueblo* in January 1968, the United States held North Korea responsible. On the other hand, when the Popular Front for the Liberation of Palestine hijacked a number of airliners in September 1970 and flew them to Jordanian territory, the United States did not hold a Palestinian state responsible. Although the PFLP may have represented some of the Palestinian people, it did not function as a government and was not in control of a clearly defined territory. Even after the declaration of statehood by the PLO in 1988, Palestine did not meet the traditional criteria of international politics. The declaration was made in Algeria, not Palestine. Some states extended "recognition" nevertheless, but that recognition in practice was different from traditional recognition. Such use of recognition as a means of showing political support is not new. There was, for instance, a time when the government of Algeria recognized the Black Panther party as the government of the United States, but that political gesture did little to change the realities of international relations.

NON-STATE ACTORS

Despite the failure of the Palestinians to meet the criteria for statehood, they play a part in international politics, debating in the United Nations as well as hijacking airplanes. This points out one of the inadequacies of the traditional principles of international politics: The sovereign nation-state is not the only actor in the international system. The Palestinian case does not totally invalidate the claim that the nation-state is the ideal actor because the Palestinians clearly aspire to be a state. Once they have a recognized government on a demarcated territory they will presumably claim the traditional privileges of sovereignty. But until they do, they show that groups can influence international politics without constituting themselves states.

Some of these groups are not "states-in-waiting" like the Palestinians. One important type of non-state actor is the intergovernmental organization (IGO). These run all the way from the United Nations to the Permanent International Committee on Canned Food. Often we try to force the more important IGO's into the mold of the sovereign state. We call our representatives to them "ambassadors"; we grant diplomatic immunity to their officers and premises. But it is obvious that in many important ways IGO's are different from states. Nor can we say IGO's are equal to the sum of their parts or that positions taken by IGO's are only the sum of the positions taken by all the member states. Organizations such as the United Nations and the European Economic Community (EEC or Common Market) are important in their own right.

The number of IGO's has grown from only a handful a century ago to more than 350 today.[7] Growth of nongovernmental organizations (NGO's) has been even more spectacular. These are sometimes called transnational organizations (although "trans-state" would be more precise) because members communicate directly with each other, bypassing their state governments. A good example of an NGO is the Roman Catholic Church, which of course is even older than the state system that evolved in 1648. Today the number of NGO's has grown to more than 13,000, including such organizations as the International Olympic Committee, the International Air Transport Association, and the Experiment in International Living.[8] Even the Roman Catholic Church is thought of today not as one but rather as a collection of nongovernmental organizations, from the Society of Jesus to the International Conference of Catholic Scouting.

As interest in non-state actors grows, scholars refine their categories to include such new institutions as multinational business corporations and transnational political groups. Today there is considerable debate among scholars about the importance of these non-state actors. One study found that about 40 percent of the conflict in three regions of the world (the Middle East, Western Europe, and Latin America) resulted from the activities of non-state actors, but other studies play down their importance.[9]

Two facts are indisputably clear: (1) the nation-state has been for the last 300 years and continues to be today the most important unit in international politics; (2) the nation-state has never been the only participant in international politics and at present the world seems to be more than ever crowded by non-state actors. Still, there is much to be said for using the nation-state as the basic unit for analysis. States still control most of the armed force in the world. It is still primarily states that decide to go to war. Most of the non-state actors that resort to violence do so as part of their effort to become states; most of them could not succeed if they did not have the connivance or assistance of already established states.

Nongovernmental organizations and other transnational actors are important but much of their importance comes from the way in which they influence state governments. Multinational oil companies are important actors, but one of the most important things they try to do is to influence state behavior. Sometimes they succeed but sometimes states are able to resist them and they fail. Transnational actors have had much less influence in states such as the Soviet Union, and there is no reason to think that states of this type are on the verge of extinction. Some scholars have suggested that current predictions of increasing importance for transnational actors are based on nothing more than extrapolation of trends in recent years. They argue that these trends developed because of specific conditions that are not likely to continue in the future.[10] For our purposes it seems most sensible to focus on the state and discuss how transnational actors influence it and not vice versa.

IMPLICATIONS OF INTERNATIONAL ANARCHY

One reason why war occurs is that for the last three centuries the state system has not been well organized to prevent it. In fact the most important principle of the state system, that of sovereignty, seems to facilitate it. We can describe international politics as a system of anarchy. Because some nine-teenth-century bomb-throwers called themselves anarchists, a common impression is that anarchy is the equivalent of chaos and violence. But anarchy is simply the absence of a superior authority, and clearly, in interna-tional politics, there is no authority superior to the state.

For this reason international politics differs in many ways from the kind of politics we are familiar with in our own country. All politics is a mixture of conflict and cooperation, but international politics has less cooperation and more conflict than national politics. The level of distrust is higher; there is a feeling that mistakes are more likely to be irreversible.

In national politics we are used to putting the good of the whole over the good of the parts. Even when we favor a selfish interest, we try to do it in a way that denies its selfishness. The head of General Motors, about to become secretary of defense, could justify his interest in the continuing good fortune of that company by stating, "What is good for our country is good for General Motors, and vice versa."[11] But in international politics it is unusual to hear the argument that the good of the whole world is superior to the good of our part of it. Restrictive tariffs are regularly introduced to benefit our own workers, with little feeling about how these tariffs will affect workers in other countries. In 1972 the United States restricted the export of food such as soybeans to keep domestic prices down, even though this meant hardship for the Japanese who depended on American soybeans for protein. In fact, a state can be criticized for not acting in a selfish way. China was criticized in the late 1950s for exporting food to win friends abroad even though there was famine in some parts of China.

The state of affairs in international politics is illustrated in a fable by an eighteenth-century political philosopher, Jean Jacques Rousseau. He de-scribes five hunters who join to hunt a stag. They must cooperate to sur-round the stag. Upon killing it, they will share equally and each will receive enough to feed his family. But then one of the five breaks the ring to pursue a rabbit, which will provide enough food for his own family. The stag escapes and the other four go hungry.[12] Placing personal needs over group needs is not considered immoral in international politics. Indeed, if the hunter were treated as a state would be, he might be criticized if he failed to pursue the rabbit and thus neglected the first chance he had to feed his family, no matter how shortsighted this policy might be.

This widely shared value of national selfishness makes a virtue of the policy of isolation. The idea was expressed clearly by British Prime Minister Neville Chamberlain at the time of the Czechoslovakia crisis in 1938: "How horrible, fantastic, incredible, it is that we should be digging trenches and trying on gas-masks here because of a quarrel in a faraway country between people of whom we know nothing!"[13] Much of contemporary American political opinion finds that those who argue against American involvement in Southeast Asia, Africa, or the Middle East are more moral than those who favor it. It is common to hear such issues debated not on the justice or injustice of the cause, nor for the suffering or lack of suffering that will result from our refusal to intervene, but solely on how much it will cost our country. A good example of such an argument is the widely quoted comment of John Kenneth Galbraith that we should let Vietnam, "return to the obscurity it so richly deserves."

States regularly make distinctions between their own citizens and all others. According to an American newspaper correspondent in Europe, an accident was worth reporting if it involved the death of one American, five Englishmen, or ten Europeans.[14] The war in Vietnam became intolerable to many Americans not because Vietnamese weekly casualties were running in the thousands but because American weekly casualties were running in the hundreds.

Among other things, the special obligation a state feels toward its own citizens means it can never guarantee the security of others as credibly as it can that of its own. This is a fundamental weakness of all alliances and international organizations. The British guaranteed the neutrality of Belgium throughout the nineteenth century and proclaimed that this was a solemn treaty obligation, yet some doubt arose when World War I began whether the British would indeed go to war when Germany invaded Belgium; if the Germans had landed in Scotland, there would have been no question.

This primary concern with one's own affairs is reinforced by a principle derived from the doctrine of sovereignty—noninterference in the internal affairs of another country. In theory any kind of external influence may be rightfully excluded from a country by its government—foreign businesses, tourists, even radio and television broadcasts. Among the staunchest defenders of the most conservative interpretation of the principles of international politics has been the Soviet Union, which has argued that satellite transmission of television programs is an interference in internal affairs. All states have a point at which they react; the Soviet Union has traditionally reacted more quickly than most. But most states have made the claim at one time or another. Brazil called international attempts to control the sale of nuclear materials interference in internal affairs. In 1967, following a military takeover of the government of Greece, opponents of the coup called continued US involvement interference, while supporters of the colonels said cutting off aid would be intervention.

The principle of noninterference is only that—a principle—generally shared as an ideal, usually but by no means always followed in practice. Another way of stating the principle of noninterference is to say that a state's borders are inviolable. The violation of a border—unauthorized entry by the forces of another state—is called "aggression." Even though it is clearly contrary to the principles of international politics, aggression occurs. When it does, the state that is the victim is on its own. There is no higher authority for it to appeal to. The German army's crossing of the French frontier in 1870, followed by Germany's annexation of Alsace and Lorraine, was recognized by all as a clear violation of France's sovereignty, yet there was no world ruler to which France could turn for redress. The implication of sovereignty, that each state has a right to pursue a policy of isolation, meant that France could not expect other European countries to come to its aid. The only redress available to France was what political philosophers used to call "self-help," or resort to violence. In the absence of world government, France had to take the law into its own hands.

The Germans in 1870 could also have argued that they were in the right. In effect France was vetoing the right of the small German states to join with Prussia in a larger nation-state. Lacking an international authority to appeal to for redress of this grievance, Prussia had to resort to self-help, taking the law into its own hands to correct this injustice. With no world tribunal to pass on the justice of these conflicting claims, one claim is as legally valid as the other.

Recourse to self-help is frequent in international politics. According to one comprehensive study, 222 wars were fought between 1648 and 1964, or one war for every one and four-tenths years of the modern nation-state system.[15] Because war has been resorted to so frequently, it has acquired some legitimacy. It is a clearly recognized relationship between states, signified at least in theory by a declaration at the beginning and a treaty at the end. Within a society, the condition of being at war may mean internal changes, such as declaring a national state of emergency or martial law. The people who have been designated to carry out warfare are identified by warpaint or, more recently, uniforms and medals. The conduct of the war itself is subject to regulation by international codes of conduct. Soldiers may not wear the uniforms of the enemy; attacks on civilians are to be avoided; some types of weapons (such as expanding or "dum-dum" bullets) are outlawed.[16]

Despite legal restrictions on certain ways of conducting war, for long periods in modern history the mere act of going to war was not considered illegal. In the twentieth century ideas began to change. In 1920 the League of Nations Covenant declared war illegal if it violated various clauses of the Covenant. But this provision still permitted war once attempts to settle disputes peacefully were exhausted. In 1928 many states signed the Pact of Paris for the Renunciation of War, but despite the pledge implied by the title, states did not abandon their weapons and the treaty remained "a moral preachment."[17] In 1945 the United Nations Charter outlawed all wars of aggression but included the loophole that states could fight in their own defense until the international organization came to their aid. Thus Iran and Iraq could go to war in 1980, each claiming it was fighting in self-defense, and, because the United Nations never acted, neither believed itself in violation of the Charter. As we approach the end of the twentieth century, changes in attitude toward war have not yet progressed to the point at which war in all its forms is clearly contrary to the principles of international politics.

No one will claim that international politics is nothing but war. But resort to war is always possible in relations between states. This shadow lurking in the background means that states are only being prudent when they take measures for defense in the event of war. But each state's defensive preparations are viewed with suspicion by other states, so that they too take up defensive measures. Ultimately states end up less secure than they were before the process of arming began. This condition has been called the "security dilemma."[18] If a state remains unarmed, it may be preyed on by an armed neighbor, but if it arms it may only provoke its neighbor to arm more.

Because states are aware of the possibility of war and because they have at least minimal armed forces to fight with, even peaceful relations between states are not free of military elements. We refer to "diplomatic relations" between states at peace with each other, but the expression "strong diplomatic pressures" may refer to very martial behavior. In 1945, the Soviet government handed a note to the Turkish government, asking for the return of some provinces then under Turkish control but controlled before 1917 by the Russian tsars. This diplomatic move was accompanied by "routine military maneuvers" by Soviet forces just across the border from the contested provinces. The Turks turned to the United States for diplomatic support. By chance, the Turkish ambassador to the United States had died of natural causes while at his post, and the United States returned the body to Turkey on a ship that just happened to be available, the battleship *Missouri*.

For 300 years the state system has been loosely organized according to certain principles, foremost among them the legal doctrine of sovereignty. The fundamental problem of world politics is that these principles work imperfectly. The principle of sovereignty is not so scrupulously respected that a state can be confident that its borders will never be violated or its political independence subverted. Yet sovereignty is regularly invoked by states when attempts are made to impose some order on international politics through a higher authority. The ideal of the sovereign nation-state is being challenged today both by attempts to control state behavior through international organizations and by the appearance of new, non-state actors. But the doctrine of sovereignty, until now at least, has been strong enough to frustrate attempts to prevent the resort to violence among states. We must conclude that one of the reasons wars occur is that the principles of international relations stand in the way of attempts to prevent them.

NOTES

1. Bodin's work *Six Books of the Republic,* is summarized in George H. Sabine, *A History of Political Theory,* 4th ed., revised by Thomas Landon Thorson (Hinsdale, Ill.: Dryden Press, 1973), Chapter 21.

2. "Swiss Convict Three Arabs in Attack on Jet," *The New York Times,* December 23, 1969.

3. Statistics on Dominica from *The States-Man's Yearbook 1985–1986* (New York: St. Martin's Press, 1985), p. 418. On the attempted coup, see Jo Thomas, "Life Remains Unsettled in Dominica after Invasion Aborted in New Orleans," *The New York Times,* June 7, 1981, p. Y16.

4. John Herz, *International Politics in the Atomic Age* (New York: Columbia University Press, 1959), pp. 52–61.

5. Gerhard von Glahn, *Law Among Nations,* 2nd ed. (London: Macmillan, 1970), p. 91.

6. First published in 1871, Chapter 7.

7. *Yearbook of International Organization* (Munich: K. G. Saur, 1983), Vol. 1, p. 904.

8. Ibid.

9. Richard W. Mansbach, Yale H. Ferguson, Donald E. Lampert, *The Web of World Politics* (Englewood Cliffs, N.J.: Prentice-Hall, 1976), p. 281. See also Robert O. Keohane and Joseph S. Nye, Jr., *Transnational Relations and World Politics* (Cambridge, Mass. Harvard University Press, 1970).

10. Gregory Schmid, "Interdependence Has Its Limits," *Foreign Policy,* No. 21 (Winter 1975–1976), pp. 188–197; Robert W. Cox, "On Thinking About Future World Order," *World Politics,* Vol. 28, No. 2 (January 1976), pp. 189–192.

11. *Hearings Before the Committee on Armed Services, U.S. Senate, 83rd Congress, 1st Session, January 15–16, 1953,* p. 15.

12. "A Discourse on the Origin of Inequality," in Jean Jacques Rousseau, *The Social Contract and Discourses,* trans. G. D. H. Cole (New York: E.P. Dutton, 1950), p. 238.

13. Broadcast to the nation, September 27, 1938, quoted in Winston S. Churchill, *The Gathering Storm* (Boston: Houghton Mifflin, 1948), p. 315.

14. E. H. Carr, *The Twenty Years' Crisis* (London: Macmillan, 1946), p. 164.

15. Quincy Wright, *A Study of War,* 2nd ed. (Chicago: University of Chicago Press, 1965), information from tables 34–42 and Appendix C.

16. *Regulations Respecting the Laws and Customs of Wars on Land,* signed at The Hague, October 18, 1907, in *Treaties and Other International Agreements of the United States of America, 1776–1949,* Vol. 1 (Washington, D.C.: Department of State, 1968–1976).

17. Von Glahn, p. 521. (See note 5.)

18. Herz, p. 231. (See note 4.)

CHAPTER 8

CAUSES OF WAR

We have looked at some of the generally accepted principles of international politics, especially those that have a bearing on the problem of war. One way of summarizing Chapter 7 is to say that wars occur because they have always occurred. They have become habitual ways of settling disputes.

All this is true but not very satisfying. It does not explain how war got started in the first place or, more important, why states continue to use such destructive means to attain their ends when other means are available, at least to the imagination.

CAUSAL EXPLANATION

Poll your acquaintances on the cause of war and you will get a wide variety of answers. Advocates of a weapons freeze will tell you armaments cause war. Born-again Christians will tell you that human nature is the cause. Marxists will say the capitalist system. Before we examine any of these claims, we should take a look at the concept of causation itself.

One thing that becomes quickly obvious is that we attribute almost nothing to just one cause. We identify some thing or event as a "result" or "effect" and talk about all the conditions necessary before that effect could occur as the "causes." Any one of the conditions could be called a cause, but there are always many.

Imagine me opening a matchbook, taking out a match, and striking it on the cover—a flame appears. The flame is the effect—what is the cause? If I performed the same act on the moon, no flame would appear. So one condition is oxygen. If I struck so hard that the match head flew off, it might produce a flash but no flame. So another condition is the fuel provided by the paper match stem. And if I did not apply my energy to striking the head against the cover, no flame would appear, because the match would not be hot enough to ignite. Heat plus fuel plus oxygen are conditions that produce a flame. Take away any one and we have no fire.

Compared to human behavior, such as the transformation of a peaceful assembly into a lynch mob, simple chemical reactions such as flaming matches are easy to explain. Yet even the explanation for the appearance of the flame is more complex than we need for most purposes. Consider one variety of fire, the forest fire. Like all fires, forest fires are caused by oxygen plus fuel plus heat. Yet if our purpose is to prevent forest fires, we ignore two of the three conditions and concentrate entirely on the third.

A list prepared by the Forest Service on causes of forest fires in the United States is shown in Table 8.1. This list does not mention anything related to oxygen or fuel. Logically, of course, we could prevent forest fires by removing all oxygen—perhaps constructing huge plastic domes filled only with carbon dioxide. But because such plans are probably not feasible and certainly not economical we never even consider them. Likewise, logically, we could prevent forest fires by removing all the fuel—cutting down all the trees. Again, we don't waste time considering such a plan. We concentrate instead on the third condition—heat.

The example of forest fires provides two more insights on causation. Smokey the Bear is wrong when he says, "Only you can prevent forest fires." The second most frequent cause of forest fires is lightning, and lightning is quite beyond our capabilities to prevent. Having divided the causes of fire

Table 8.1 CAUSES OF FOREST FIRES IN THE UNITED STATES

Cause	Percent
Incendiary	34
Lightning	21
Debris burning	16
Equipment use	8
Smoking	6
Railroads	3
Campfires	2
Children	2
Miscellaneous	8

Source: U.S. Department of Agriculture, Forest Service, *Wildfire Statistics* (April 1980).

into three groups—oxygen, fuel, and heat—we must now subdivide one group further into conditions that result from human actions and conditions that don't.

The most common cause of forest fires is listed as "incendiary," meaning fires deliberately set, and here we must add an additional element, a purpose or intention. The exact means of applying heat—match or blowtorch—is less significant than the motivation in the minds of the persons applying the heat.

CAUSATION AND WAR

As the example of forest fires demonstrates, we can identify multiple causes for any given effect and, further, we can group these causes. Centuries ago the first political scientist, Aristotle, suggested grouping causes into four categories, which he called material, efficient, formal, and final.[1] If we try to explain the origin of a piece of sculpture, we can say the marble was the material cause, the sculptor was the efficient cause, the sculptor's artistic vision was the formal cause, and the money or desire for fame was the final cause. Without copying Aristotle exactly, we can still make use of his approach to help bring some sense to a discussion of the causes of war.

Some causes, such as the sculptor's marble, or the fuel and oxygen consumed in a fire, are always available (at least somewhere in the world), yet by themselves produce no further results. We can identify similar conditions that precede war, conditions that are always present yet do not always lead to war. We may label them material causes or permissive causes, because they permit war to occur. An example might be human nature.

HUMAN NATURE: KONRAD LORENZ

If you asked your acquaintances, you would probably find the theory most of them hold is that causes of war are to be found in human nature. Perhaps the popularity of this theory is a legacy of the Christian tradition, for it has been the orthodox Christian view. Christian teachers have held that human nature is not basically good or even (by itself) capable of becoming good. One practical way in which human nature manifests itself is the inability of human beings to live in harmony with one another. According to Christian teaching, every person has inherent evil desires, sometimes called "original sin," a metaphor derived from the Biblical story of Adam's fall from grace. These desires make people want what they have no business wanting and prompt them to use violence if that is necessary to fulfill these desires. Collective violence, carried out by states against each other, is in the Christian view only a manifestation of this basic individual nature, because states are composed of individuals. Only when the individuals change will states change.[2]

This pessimistic view of human nature is by no means confined to Christians. Hans Morgenthau, author of the first major American textbook on international politics, begins his book with the assertion, "The drives to live, to propagate, and to dominate are common to all men." He calls this "an undeniable fact of experience."[3] Many people agree with these statements, but they do so more as a result of faith than of study of scientific evidence. The Christian religion relies explicitly on faith; Morgenthau's claim does too, although he does add a footnote indicating that chickens also dominate each other. In recent years, however, this view has received scientific support from the work of biologists, especially those who specialize in the branch of biology known as "ethology" or the study of animal behavior. One of the ethologists who has done much to popularize findings in this field is Konrad Lorenz, who in 1962 published *On Aggression*.[4] Although he is not the only or the most recent writer on the subject, his views are among the best-known, and for that reason we will examine them here.

Lorenz begins by arguing that human beings, like other animals, have instincts. Instincts are inherited (as opposed to learned) behavior patterns. Their presence has been convincingly demonstrated in animals; a bird raised in total isolation from other birds will still try to fly south in the autumn. Among the instincts Lorenz finds in human beings is the aggressive instinct. This means that one human being when challenged by another will react with anger and stand to fight (rather than turn and flee in terror). One bit of evidence for the argument that this behavior is inherited and not learned is that many kinds of measurable physiological changes take place when one becomes angry—among them an increase in pulse rate and blood pressure and a rise in the level of blood sugar—and these changes are the same in all human beings and indeed in all animals.[5]

Lorenz further argues that this aggressive instinct, like everything else about the human organism, is the product of evolution. Traits that survive from generation to generation do so because they are "functional"; that is, they enhance the ability of organisms possessing them to survive. Once we accept this assumption, we can make reasonable guesses about the function (or survival value) of any trait. In the case of the aggressive instinct, it seems to serve three functions. First, it distributes members of a species evenly over territory, thus guaranteeing to each one (or at least to each strong one) enough territory to sustain life. This view is supported by the observation that the aggressive instinct manifests itself more strongly in the center of an animal's home territory and grows weaker as the animal moves away from that center. Second, aggression makes it more likely that the strongest members of the species will breed and produce offspring. Third, it makes it more likely that parents will be able to protect their offspring while they are still young and helpless. If animals always fled rather than fought, they would desert their young whenever danger threatened.

During his observations Lorenz came to distinguish two kinds of mammals: those that are not particularly dangerous to each other physically (rabbits, for example) and those that, because they are equipped with fangs and claws, are dangerous to each other (such as wolves). Rabbits display as much aggression as wolves but there is no danger that fighting will have fatal consequences. The natural defense of the rabbit against all danger is to run away, and in fights between rabbits the weaker rabbit runs away from the stronger. (However, if rabbits are confined in an unnatural way, say in cages, they will tear each other to pieces.)[6] When wolves fight, the possibility of fatalities is there, yet they rarely occur. Wolves show aggression but do not kill each other any more often than rabbits do. The reason, according to Lorenz, is that along with its aggressive instinct the wolf has evolved an inhibiting mechanism that checks the aggressive instinct at the crucial moment. The inhibiting mechanism is triggered by a movement that Lorenz calls an appeasement gesture—the losing wolf turns over on its back, exposing its throat in such a way that it would be easy for the winner to kill it. The appeasement gesture is a sign that the loser accepts an inferior status and by doing so saves its own life.

Human beings, Lorenz finds, belong in the category of animals that are harmless to each other. Like monkeys in the zoo, they may pelt each other with rotten fruit, but their natural equipment of short, blunt teeth and stubby, brittle fingernails keeps them from ever being dangerous to each other. Thus human beings have not evolved the inhibiting instinct as have the wolves; it was not necessary. Then, at some time in human development, one human picked up a rock and at that moment became as dangerous to other humans as one wolf to another. From that point, progress from sharp rock to firearms was extraordinarily short (as evolutionary development goes). Human beings are now far more dangerous to each other than wolves are to each other, but they have not yet evolved the mechanism to inhibit aggression. The problem is not, as in the often quoted words of Roman playwright Platus, that "humans are like wolves to other humans" but that humans are not wolflike enough.

We should note carefully what Lorenz is saying. The problem is not aggression—that is, that human beings fight. After all, wolves do too. The problem is that human beings fight to the death. They kill members of their species and wolves do not. It is not our lack of "humanity" but our lack of "animality" that causes our troubles. There are two sides to this feature of human nature. As victors, human beings have the ability to kill helpless victims. As losers, they have the ability not to give up even when defeated. Human beings can die for abstract causes—wolves could never fight a Battle of the Alamo.

Lorenz did not see the human situation as hopeless. Just as an inhibiting mechanism has evolved among wolves, so too could one evolve among human beings. The only difficulty—and it is a serious one—is that the evolutionary process requires a great deal of time, time measured in thousands of years.

Since Lorenz did his work, more recent studies of animal behavior have found many examples of intraspecies killing, suggesting that Lorenz had too benevolent a view of "animality." Subordinate elephant seals have been observed ganging up on a dominant male. Gangs of chimpanzees have been observed killing lone males from bands other than their own. A gorilla was observed killing an older female from his own troop.[7] Many of these examples come from the so-called "higher animals," primates that resemble human beings in many ways. It is possible that another trait they share with human beings is that they too have not yet evolved mechanisms to inhibit aggression.

Even Lorenz's notion of ritualized, nonfatal combat between two males for dominance has been challenged. For some animals, at least, such duels appear to end in death. But in the debate among biologists, the core idea of Lorenz's theory still appears valid—that animals such as wolves that are losing a fight can and do signal defeat and thus inhibit the victor from killing them. The manner in which wolves fight for dominance still appears to be less destructive than the manner in which human beings do.

Even if human nature turns out to be not so different from animal nature, the ability to kill members of our own species must be considered a cause of war, in the sense that it permits wars to happen. If we could change this characteristic of human nature, we could eliminate war. Indeed, using modern techniques of behavior modification and "brainwashing," we might be able to make such changes. What is lacking is the power to force 5 billion people to submit to our treatment; that, of course, is an enormous lack. Surely if we had that much power, we could solve the problem of war much more simply. It is doubtful that techniques for changing human nature, other than drastic ones requiring total control of a person's environment, will work. Preachers and teachers have tried to change human nature by exhortation for more than 4,000 years, with little result. Obviously, if we all became good Christians, wars would cease. They would also cease if we all became good Buddhists or Taoists or just plain good. But the historical record of this approach to peace is not encouraging. The expectation of a messianic age remains a matter of faith.

"TROUBLEMAKERS": POWER GROUPS, MERCHANTS OF DEATH, WICKED STATES

Another permissive cause of war was the theme of Chapter 7: the international system. Wars occur because no sovereign exists that can stop them. If we constructed a scale of human complexity, from the individual through families, clans, nations, and alliances up to the world system, these two permissive causes would fall at opposite ends. Yet they are similar in that they are always present, not stopping war from occurring yet not by themselves enough to set one off. Both human nature and international anarchy in some sense caused the great war of 1914, yet both were present in exactly the same form in the peaceful year of 1913.

Obviously something more is needed to produce war, just as something more than marble is needed to produce a statue. Aristotle identified an agent, which he called an "efficient cause." Similarly in international politics we can identify agents that contribute to the origins of war. We might call these individuals "troublemakers." Eliminate these troublemakers, the theory goes, and you eliminate war.

An example of this approach is found in many of the histories of World War II. Most put the responsibility for the war on Adolf Hitler and his initiatives in foreign policy. Alan Bullock, author of one of the most read biographies of Hitler, titled one of his chapters, "Hitler's War, 1939."[8]

In an attempt to apply this approach to all wars, a psychologist, Theodore Abel, wrote, "Throughout recorded human history, the initiators of war were individuals and groups who held power. . . . "[9] In his own study of twenty-five wars, he identified a power group responsible for each war. World War I he attributed to the Austrian power group, composed of the prime minister, the foreign minister, and the chief of staff. He claims that they had decided to wage war against Serbia as early as 1909 and were only waiting for an occasion, such as the one provided by the assassination of the Austrian heir to the throne.

In the 1930s many in the United States accepted the idea that a small group of arms manufacturers were responsible for United States participation in World War I. They were popularly known as "the merchants of death" and were the subject of books, magazines, and congressional hearings held by Senator Gerald Nye of North Dakota.[10] Actually Senator Nye, as an isolationist, was less interested in an answer to a scholarly problem and more interested in creating support for his policy of keeping America out of the world political crisis of the 1930s. The political impact of the Nye Committee was so great that the head of the du Pont company took his firm out of the business of manufacturing ammunition so that it would not be blamed for any subsequent wars.[11] Unfortunately for Senator Nye's theory, America got into World War II anyhow. Ironically, American business leaders were reluctant to make a full-scale conversion to war production at the beginning of World War II because they remembered that during World War I most American arms had been produced not by private industry but by federal arsenals.[12]

Sometimes the troublemaker is identified as an entire state (although "state" is often only shorthand for the leaders of a state). In 1942, Joseph Grew, former US ambassador to Japan, stated: "Once Japan is destroyed as an aggressive force, we know of no other challenging power that can appear in the Pacific. . . . Japan is the one enemy, and the only enemy, of the peaceful peoples whose shores overlook the Pacific Ocean."[13]

Japan was destroyed as an aggressive force, but the threat of war in the Pacific did not disappear. A new troublemaker was then identified. Richard Nixon, then vice-president, said in 1953, "If it were not for the Communist threat, the free world could live in peace."[14] Nixon was thinking particularly of the conventional military threat of the Sino-Soviet bloc. But even after this threat had been met by a United Nations force in Korea and by NATO in Europe, the threat to world peace reappeared in a new form, Communist-sponsored wars of liberation. In 1968, Secretary of State Dean Rusk said, "Once we remove this kind of aggression, as we are trying to do in Vietnam, the human race can perhaps look forward to peace, to the solutions of lesser problems, and to the benefits deriving from the conquests of science."[15]

CRITIQUE OF TROUBLEMAKERS AS THE CAUSE OF WAR

The regularity with which one troublemaker is eliminated only to be replaced by another should make us suspicious. These claims to have found the cause of war appear to be less analyses of the cause of all war than rationalizations for fighting in particular ones. "Help us fight just one last war," these polemicists seem to say, "and then we will have peace."

In fact none of these theories applies very broadly; once we move away from the one or two wars they were originally applied to, they no longer fit. If World War II can be attributed to an individual such as Hitler, then we cannot very well claim that all wars are started by merchants of death. Eliminating the private manufacture of armaments, which was the remedy proposed after World War I, is then no guarantee that war will be eliminated. But we cannot identify an individual such as Hitler to blame for every war. World War I was distinguished by its lack of individual villains. In the recent wars in Bangladesh and Cyprus, it is difficult to identify individuals or groups who were responsible for starting them. On the other hand, in these wars it is easy to identify political and social issues, such as persecution of ethnic minorities, that led to the conflict. The wars in Bangladesh and Cyprus seem to have been genuinely popular in the countries that initiated them. No power-hungry premier dragged reluctant Indians or Turks into wars against their will.

These exceptions suggest another problem with the individual trouble-maker theory. A leader cannot be effective without followers. Hitler may have made decisions that led to World War II, but if others had not implemented these decisions, nothing would have happened. If Adolf Hitler were to reappear today, he would be ignored as a political crackpot if not subjected to psychiatric care.

These obvious deficiencies with troublemaker theories have led scholars to hunt for more general explanations that will cover all wars. They have looked for patterns that seem likely either to generate grievances or to lead states to warlike ways of resolving grievances. A number of these theories have won wide followings at one time or another.

One of the most important nineteenth-century theorists was Karl Marx. Despite the connotations of political activism that the name "Marxist" has today, Karl Marx himself spent most of his time in the library, not on the barricades. His theories, in spite of the practical uses to which they have been put, were scholarly attempts to take into account all the evidence. For Marx, war was caused mainly by the feudal class, a class whose prime function was fighting. War was common in the Middle Ages, when the feudal class, represented by knights on horseback, was dominant. But Marx expected war to die out with feudalism. Remnants of the feudal class survived the bourgeois revolution in England and France, most of them in the officer corps of the army, but Marx expected them to gradually lose their influence. Capitalism, Marx thought, was essentially peaceful. It transcended national boundaries and worked to create a single world state. War was bad for business. This view is not that of many people who call themselves "Marxists" today, but it is clearly evident in Marx's writings.[16]

Marx was soon proved wrong. Prussia, which was a capitalist society, fought a number of wars in the nineteenth century. Worse for Marx's theory, Prussia seemed to become more, not less, militaristic as its economy developed. When the most advanced capitalist societies of the day (England, Germany, and France) went to war in 1914, it was clear that Marx's views needed correction. One of the best-known updatings of Marx was provided by a Russian follower, Lenin, and because today many political activists come to Marx by way of Lenin, they accept the Leninist version as "Marxist." In a way Marx and Lenin were similar. They both saw wars as caused by a specific economic class. But Lenin identified a different culprit, the capitalist class, and particularly the new type of capitalist who had appeared in the later stages of capitalism, the finance capitalist or banker. We have looked at Lenin's theory when examining explanations for World War I.[17] Though not fundamentally different from Senator Gerald Nye's "merchants of death" theory, it is more complex, blaming not just a handful of private manufacturers of arms but a whole network of bankers, industrialists, and government officials. A good way of seeing whether you have grasped someone's theory on what causes war is to ask, "What would have to be eliminated from social and political life in order to eliminate war?" The remedy proposed by Lenin was more radical than that of Nye—not just prohibiting arms manufacturing by private individuals but completely reordering society to eliminate any private ownership of property. Only when capitalism is replaced by socialism, Lenin argued, will war be eliminated.

Lenin's theory has not held up much better than Marx's. In 1917, followers of Marx and Lenin took over the government of Russia; in 1949 followers of Marx and Lenin took over the government of China. In 1969 the two governments engaged in warlike behavior against each other. Neither society had private ownership of industrial enterprises. Neither had a class of finance capitalists. Yet large armies faced each other across the Ussuri River, shots were exchanged, and soldiers were killed.

One of Lenin's contemporaries was American President Woodrow Wilson. Wilson's analysis was in some ways not very different from Lenin's. Lenin identified a class—finance capitalists—and the states they controlled as the cause of war. Wilson also identified a class—the small ruling class of undemocratic countries unanswerable to the public at large. The states controlled by such small groups are called autocracies. Wilson contrasted autocracies unfavorably with democracies. The common people are the ones who have to fight wars, and these common people, Wilson believed, would not voluntarily send their sons off to fight, particularly in wars of conquest. Furthermore, democracies would put an end to secret diplomacy and secret treaties and thus to the suspicions that had a part in starting World War I. The connection of autocracy with war is indicated by two slogans used during World War I: "The War To End All Wars" and "The War To Make the World Safe for Democracy." The two slogans were logically connected. Once the states of the world were democratic, wars would end.

Subsequent events make us skeptical of the claim that increased popular participation reduces the likelihood of war. Even while President Wilson was promoting his views there was some evidence that should have given him pause. The United States, by no means the most autocratic country in the world at the time, had occupied the Philippines in 1899 and 1900 despite fierce opposition from the inhabitants. The resistance was so fierce that U.S. Army "pacification" programs resulted in the massacre of hundreds of Filipinos. It is hard to see how this could have been interpreted as anything but a war of conquest being conducted by a democracy.

Some forest fires are started by accident, some on purpose. Wars, by contrast, are always begun for a purpose (or almost always—a purely accidental war, especially in the computer age, is at least conceivable). Aristotle referred to purpose as the "final cause." We might find it more in keeping with modern usage to refer to issues.

NATIONALISM: MAZZINI

Looking for some common theme in the seven wars described in earlier chapters, we are struck by the frequency with which issues of nationalism play a part in the origin of wars. The wars of Bismarck were fought to create a national state. In 1914 the Austrians went to war with Serbia because of Serbian nationalist claims; France went to war eagerly to reclaim the provinces of Alsace and Lorraine. In the 1930s Hitler based many of his claims on the right of Germans to live together in one state. The wars in Korea, the Middle East, Bangladesh, and Cyprus had strong national components.

One of the earliest theorists on the role of nationalism in international politics was an Italian, Giuseppe Mazzini.[18] In the middle of the nineteenth century he argued for national independence for the Italians, not just for the benefit of Italians but as a way of promoting international peace. If each nation had its own state, free from control by foreigners, there would be peace. The many conflicts that arise from national differences would be eliminated. Subjects would accept willingly demands from a government of their fellow nationals that they would resist coming from outsiders.

Mazzini's views are discussed today mainly in classes on the history of political thought, not in contemporary political debate. Perhaps it is because his ideas are so widely accepted that there is no need for discussion. The underlying premise of contemporary anticolonialism and national liberation movements is the one put forward by Mazzini. It is seen as "only natural" for people to want to be ruled by members of their own nation, no matter how incompetent or tyrannical, not by colonialists. General Idi Amin may have murdered 200,000 of his fellow Ugandans, but no Ugandan suggested that the remedy was a return to British colonial rule.

Still, the Mazzinian theory is not totally satisfying. First, one can ask, where does the process of granting national self-rule end? The Nigerians may have asked for an end to British colonial rule in 1960 in the name of national liberation, but within seven years one of the major tribal groupings of the Nigerian nation, the Ibos, were proclaiming the right to secede and form a smaller state, which they wanted to call Biafra. Had the Ibos succeeded, there was no guarantee that even smaller tribes among the Ibos, such as the Ibibio and the Ijaw, would not have asked for similar national liberation.

Second, some national problems have not led to war. For the 45 years following the end of World War II, the Germans were divided much as they had been in the time of Bismarck. In addition to the separate states of East and West Germany and Austria, there were German-speaking populations in Switzerland, Italy, and other parts of Europe. We could reasonably have expected an even stronger national resentment than in 1870 because people generally feel more strongly about something they have enjoyed and been deprived of than they do about something they have never enjoyed. Yet the division of Germany was not a cause of war and the reunification of East and West Germany in 1990 was remarkably peaceful. The German-speaking population of Switzerland has not become a source of conflict. For several hundred years they have lived with French- and Italian-speaking Swiss in a state distinguished by its total freedom from any kind of war.

There is a third difficulty in attributing all wars to national quarrels. The major threat to peace during the past four decades, at least as measured by the amount of money spent for armaments, came not from a national dispute but from tension between the Soviet Union and the United States. An unfilled desire for national liberation or persecution of national minorities had almost nothing to do with the core conflict between the two super-powers.

Nationalism is often the basis for a group's feelings that it is being wronged or that it has a grievance. Other types of grievances may also provide issues for wars: violations of territory or national honor, for example. But states can also desire war not because they feel in the wrong but simply because they desire what someone else has. We might call such desires "greed." Of course one's interpretation may depend on one's vested interest. In the 1930s what looked to Poland and Czechoslovakia like Germany's greed was presented to the world by Hitler as rectification of grievances against the German people.

This examination of causes is meant to be illustrative, not exhaustive. The alert reader will amplify and elaborate on the list. Several more need brief mention:

Wars occur because states' leaders have at their disposal instruments of violence—armaments and armed forces. Without arms there could be no war. One might imagine some unpleasantness if Canadians threw rocks at Americans visiting Niagara Falls, but we would hardly label it war.

Wars occur because states' leaders choose not to use alternative means to settle their grievances or satisfy their greed. Without the decision to resort to war there would be no war. At times almost no alternatives exist—the position the world found itself in in 1914 when there was no League of Nations or United Nations. At other times, alternatives exist but states believe that they will not work or will not produce the result desired.

Wars occur because states' leaders believe there is a reasonable prospect of victory. There are far more issues about which states could fight than there are actual wars. The nationalist feelings of people in both North and South Korea were strong before 1950 and remained strong after 1953. Both sides remained armed, and neither could agree on peaceful means of settling their dispute. But neither could see a reasonable prospect of victory, and war on the Korean Peninsula came to an end.

Finally, wars occur because one or more states choose to use force and the victim or victims choose to resist. In 1914 German troops sought to march through Belgium on their way to France, and the Belgians put up armed resistance. In 1940 German troops sought to occupy Denmark, and the Danes decided not to resist. Wars would not occur if the victims of aggression cooperated with the aggressors.

One could approach the problem of war by eliminating any of its many causes—just as one could with forest fires. But as with forest fires, some causes seem easier for us to deal with than do others. Over decades, some approaches to peace have developed that seek to eliminate one or another of the many causes of war. These approaches have dealt with the causes that seemed most amenable to human control, at least within a time span short enough to yield results we could live to benefit from. Transforming human nature would undoubtedly work, yet limiting international anarchy, controlling armaments, influencing leaders' decisions to go to war, and eliminating grievances seem to hold more promise.

NOTES

1. Aristotle, *Physics*, Book 2, Chapter 3. One source is Richard McKeon, ed., *The Basic Works of Aristotle* (New York: Random House, 1941), pp. 240–241.
2. Literature distributed on college campuses in 1972 and 1973 by the Campus Crusade for Christ shows that, among some Christians at least, this view is still widely held.
3. *Politics Among Nations*, 4th ed. (New York: Alfred A. Knopf, 1967), p. 31.
4. The English translation was published in New York by Harcourt, Brace & World in 1966. For a more recent survey on the topic see Peter A. Corning, "The Biological Bases of Behavior and Some Implications for Political Science," *World Politics*, Vol. 23, No. 3 (April 1971), pp. 321–370.
5. Anthony Storr, in his *Human Aggression* (New York: Bantam Books, 1970), refers to the work of W. B. Cannon, *Bodily Changes in Pain, Hunger, Fear and Rage*, first published in 1915.
6. Lorenz gives this and other illustrations in *King Solomon's Ring* (London: Methuen, 1961), pp. 181–185.
7. Natalie Angier, "Mother Nature's Murderers," *Discover* (October 1983), pp. 79–82.
8. *Hitler: A Study in Tyranny*, rev. ed. (New York: Harper & Row, 1962), Chapter 9.
9. "The Element of Decision in the Pattern of War," *American Sociological Review* Vol. 6, No. 6 (December 1941), pp. 853–859.
10. For example, H. C. Engelbrecht and F. C. Hanighen, *Merchants of Death* (New York: Dodd, Mead, 1934).
11. Bernard Brodie, *War and Politics* (New York: Macmillan, 1973), p. 289.
12. Richard J. Barnet, *Roots of War* (New York: Atheneum, 1972), p. 36.
13. Published as *Report from Tokyo* (New York: Simon & Schuster, 1942), pp. 69–70.
14. *The New York Times*, November 19, 1953, quoted by Kenneth N. Waltz in *Man, the State, and War* (New York: Columbia University Press, 1959), p. 157.
15. Quoted by Gary Porter in *The Viet-Nam Reader*, ed. Marcus G. Raskin and Bernard B. Fall (New York: Random House Vintage Books, 1965), p. 324.
16. See, for example, Part I of the *Communist Manifesto*. This point on Marx's theory is made by Adam Ulam in *Expansion and Coexistence* (New York: Frederick A. Praeger, 1968), p. 14.
17. Ibid., p. 26.
18. Mazzini's views are presented by Waltz, p. 143. (See note 14.)

PART III

ARE ARMS NECESSARY FOR PEACE?

CHAPTER 9

ARMAMENTS

War, however mistaken, was a component of international politics in the past. Military spending, however burdensome, was seen as necessary to survival.

Some would argue that military strength was ultimately responsible for the end of the Cold War. President Reagan told the graduating class at the Naval Academy in 1985, when changes in the Soviet Union were first beginning:

> Since the end of the Second World War, American military might has become an immensely positive force in the world. It doesn't take much imagination to know how different things would be had the Soviet Union, not the United States, militarily and economically dominated the world after 1945.[1]

Others argue that, because the danger of war was never great, the massive expenditure on arms was unnecessary. But both sides agree that the Cold War is over and we can move to redirect our resources toward other purposes.

The question remains of how much to direct away from arms. If arms races contribute to peace, states will want to retain some, even if at a reduced level. On the other hand, if they cause war, states should try to get rid of them altogether. The following chapter examines some of the issues.

"IF YOU WANT PEACE, PREPARE FOR WAR"

If we go by what states *do* rather than by what they *say*, then the most widely accepted theory on how to prevent war is to arm. Almost every state spends much more for arms than for its contributions to the United Nations and regional organizations. Iceland and Costa Rica are the only countries with no budget for regular armed forces, but even so Iceland had enough force in the form of coast guard vessels to keep British fishing boats out of waters over which it claimed jurisdiction.[2] Even Sweden and Switzerland, countries with a traditional, explicit policy of neutrality, spend substantial amounts for arms.

All states today refer to these expenditures as "defense spending," and, for the most part, even a cynic wouldn't question that designation. Most arms are not for conquest; they genuinely reflect states' judgments about how best to preserve their security. "Peace Is Our Profession" was the slogan chosen by the United States Strategic Air Command, and it was more than a public relations gimmick. The slogan has a venerable ancestor in Latin, *si vis pacem para bellum*, "If you want peace, prepare for war." It is an idea that seems to make sense. Certainly we see examples of it in everyday life. Police officers on duty are not mugged nearly so often as fragile old women on their way home from cashing their Social Security checks.

But how much preparation for war is needed to secure peace? The ideal would be enough arms to prevent any conceivable enemy from even trying to test your strength. Sir John Fisher, the head of the British navy before World War I, was given to colorful language:

> My sole objective is PEACE in doing all this! Because if you rub it in both at home and abroad that you are ready for instant war with every unit of your strength in the first line and intend to be "first in" and hit your enemy in the belly and kick him when he's down and boil your prisoners in oil (if you take any!) and torture his women and children, then people will keep clear of you.[3]

Many decades have passed since Lord Fisher wrote that, and contemporary writers generally bring up the arms race only to condemn it. But let us pause to ask the questions: Could military expenditure prevent war? Might not all these governments be correct when they spend large amounts for weapons? Could not a sincere proponent of world peace advocate, under some circumstances, *increased* spending for military forces?

We should seriously consider the possibility that these arguments might be correct. Most of the time most states are not at war with each other, and most of the time most have armaments. Is there a connection? Advocates of military spending like to point to the period before World War II, when Western European countries did ignore defense spending and allowed Hitler to achieve the superiority in new weapons that led to the swift German victories in 1939 and 1940. The French planes being built to match the Luftwaffe were still on the assembly lines when the Germans overran the French factories.

We often hear of the dangers of an arms race, but a situation in which only *one* country is arming seems even more dangerous. Even if it were our country alone that had weapons, we might doubt that this was the best road to peace. The distinction between defense uses and other uses (such as conquest) might gradually be erased. There are some psychological experiments showing that if people have a weapon they tend to use it, even if its use doesn't make a lot of sense.[4] Resort to arms by a country with superior weapons might present itself as the simple solution to a foreign policy problem, even if leaders realized it was not the best solution. Or a state might use its weapons to justify both to the leaders and to the taxpayers why it had spent all the money to acquire them. (This was one reason the atomic bomb was dropped on Japan, even though it had been built in a secret race with Germany.)

We find then no serious advocate of unilateral armament—that is, armament by one country to the point of superiority. But in the world today there is no danger that one country alone would arm and others not try to keep up. Realistically, if we are talking about *si vis pacem para bellum*, we mean an armaments race.

Do arms races prevent war? If we use a very narrow definition, we may end up with a biased selection of cases. Lewis F. Richardson, a Quaker who used mathematics to study arms races, wrote, "There have been only three great arms-races. The first two of them ended in wars in 1914 and 1939; the third is still going on."[5] It is easy to see his answer to the question, "Do arms races cause war?" but we may suspect that Richardson already knew what his answer would be before he selected his definition.

On the other hand, a broad definition is equally useless. If we equate arms races with *any* acquisition of armaments by states, then obviously arms races do not prevent but instead cause war; without weapons, no state could fight what we call a war. But with such a broad definition we are really saying, "Armaments cause war," which is as helpful as the statement. "Combustible materials cause fire" would be in a fire marshal's investigation.

We need a definition that will enable us to identify the times when states are not simply arming but are arming *in competition*. Following the suggestions of one scholar, we might confine our use of the label "arms race" to those occasions when two or more countries see themselves as rivals and increase or improve their armaments at a rapid rate, making these increases or improvements with attention to the armaments possessed by their rivals.[6] Agreeing on a definition of "at a rapid rate" would pose some problems, but not serious ones; public health officers are able to make similar judgments about how rapidly a disease must spread to be called an epidemic. A more serious problem is that we might try to measure an arms race by increases in military spending, yet be misled by the results. In the 1860s the British replaced their wooden ships with ironclad ships in response to French innovations; yet the British spent less on their navy in those years than they had in preceding ones, despite the fact they were in an arms race with France.[7]

Even when arms budgets are increasing, the published data are not always reliable, and only limited data are available. Items that are included (such as basic research) change from time to time. The unit of measurement—usually the fiscal year—may be too long to provide frequent enough observations to measure change.[8] With all these problems, it is not surprising that there is no universally accepted list of arms races. Most lists would include the British–German naval race from 1898 to 1914 and the French–German army race from 1911 to 1914, but there is disagreement about the recent relationship between the United States and the Soviet Union. According to some critics, for years the United States was increasing neither the quantity nor the quality of its strategic weapons and in fact was allowing its military spending in this category to drop. It was not an arms race, they say, but at best an "arms crawl."[9] Despite these objections, we will include the recent United States–Soviet rivalry in our list of arms races and look now at what generalizations we can safely make about such races.

QUANTITATIVE ARMS RACES: THE PRE–WORLD WAR I RACE AND WORST-CASE ESTIMATION

We can divide arms races into two types: quantitative and technological. In quantitative races the basic weapons remain the same, and countries compete to see which can acquire the most.[10] An example of a quantitative arms race occurred between France and Germany before World War I. The principal weapon was the foot soldier armed with a rifle. Both the French and the Germans started with armies as prescribed in their constitutions—a minimum of 1 percent of the population. In 1912, after several crises in the Mediterranean area, the German general staff asked for an increase. They estimated that their army would grow in this way:[11]

1912	595,000
1913	694,000
1914	761,000

The French followed events in Germany very closely. They knew the Germans were going to increase the size of their army, but they weren't sure by how much. What mattered from the military point of view was not the number of soldiers in uniform but the number of effectives—soldiers who actually fired their rifles in combat. It wasn't always easy to tell by looking at tables of organization how many effectives the Germans had. Should the French count cooks, telegraph operators, tuba players in military bands? Only the German general staff's secret plans would tell exactly how many men could be thrown into combat. To be on the safe side, the French military did its own estimating and came up with a figure of 870,000 for the German army, more than 100,000 above the Germans' own figure.

France wanted to expand its army. Having a smaller population to draw from than Germany (39 million as opposed to 65 million Germans), it extended the term of military service to three years, giving the army an effective increase of 160,000 troops. The French estimated the size of their army by 1914 would be 736,000. But the German general staff was just as prudent as the French military leaders; and when they counted the number of French soldiers, they arrived at the figure of 882,500. Let's look at these estimates:

> *German estimates*
> French strength in 1914   882,500
> German strength in 1914   <u>761,000</u>
> French superiority   121,500 or 16%
>
> *French estimates*
> German strength in 1914   870,000
> French strength in 1914   <u>736,000</u>
> German superiority   134,000 or 18%
>
> *Actual strength*
> German strength in 1914   761,000 (German estimate)
> French strength in 1914   <u>736,000</u> (French estimate)
> German superiority   25,000 or 3%

The process of assuming the greatest possible strength for an opponent is called *worst-case estimation*. Each side is only being prudent, but the worst-case estimates by both sides speed up an arms race.

Another factor in the 1914 arms race was that each country had allies. Austria had about 450,000 troops, and the French added that number to the German total. France was allied to Russia, which had a large population and a large army. In 1906 the Russian army numbered 1,500,000 troops. It was being reorganized and expanded with French help and was expected to number 2,000,000 troops by 1917.[12] When the Germans compared themselves with the Russians, they felt as the French had felt when they compared themselves with the Germans: They could never catch up. Their rival had too large a population to draw from. The worst-case estimation and the German fear that the Russian army would soon be too large to fight figured prominently in the deliberation of German leaders in the summer of 1914.[13]

TECHNOLOGICAL ARMS RACE

A technological (or qualitative) race differs from a quantitative arms race in that each side tries to introduce new and superior weapons. The emphasis is not on *more* but on *better*. Technological competition first became important during the Industrial Revolution of the mid-nineteenth century. Before that, weapons had remained pretty much the same for long periods. The sailing ship of 1850 was not fundamentally different from that of 1650; the naval gun on that ship was not much different from the gun of 1560.[14] It is hard to imagine a major weapon today remaining in use for 200 years; the arms race we are familiar with is clearly technological.

Technological races differ in some important ways from quantitative ones. In quantitative races, one country would get ahead and stay ahead because of superior resources or greater willingness to make sacrifices. The German army was larger than the French army because there were 20 million more Germans to recruit it from. The British navy stayed larger than any other because of the British conviction that a superior navy was vital to their security. Before the age of rapid technological change, states found it difficult to change their relative power position by internal efforts and so turned to external sources of power in the form of allies. As technology grew more important, the search for allies (the balance of power system) became less important.

In technological races there is always the chance that a new discovery, a technological breakthrough, will suddenly render all existing weapons obsolete and wipe out whatever advantage the leading power might have. In effect, the new discovery starts the race all over again with the states equal. One technological breakthrough was a new type of battleship, capable of high speed and of mounting all big guns. The first one, launched by the British in 1906, was the *Dreadnought*, whose name was later applied to similar battleships. Because the *Dreadnought* could destroy any existing battleship, the navies of the world (including the British navy) suddenly found they had a lot of obsolete ships on their hands. Before 1906, the British had sixty-three battleships, the Germans twenty-six. Overnight this British margin of superiority had been wiped out. If the Germans began to build *Dreadnoughts* at the same rate as the British did, the naval power of the two countries would be nearly equal. (Sir John Fisher, who was responsible for the building of the *Dreadnought*, was criticized for introducing a ship that rendered the British navy obsolete. His defense was that the Germans were about to build a similar ship in any case.)[15]

Another characteristic of a technological race is the difficulty in figuring out who is ahead. Because neither side can be sure how well its own offensive weapons will perform, or how well its opponent's defensive weapons will perform, each side has a strong reason to exercise caution. This caution may be one reason why the competition in strategic arms between the United States and the Soviet Union never turned into actual warfare. Calculations about "who's ahead" were so complex that the question was endlessly debated without a satisfying answer.

Each side relied on three types of nuclear delivery systems—airplanes, land-based intercontinental ballistic missiles (ICBM's), and submarine-launched ballistic missiles (SLBM's). But each side had different proportions of weapons. The United States relied more heavily on SLBM's, the Soviet Union on ICBM's. Each delivery system was capable of delivering different numbers of nuclear weapons—generally called warheads. The warheads themselves were in different sizes. In the 1970s, one widely deployed version of an American SLBM could deliver 14 small warheads at a time when many Soviet ICBM's would deliver just one very big warhead. With these and many other factors as well entering into calculations, it was difficult for specialists to agree on which side would prevail and almost impossible to convince political leaders.

ARMS RACES AS ACTION–REACTION

The kind of technology available can affect arms races, either accelerating or slowing them. A race that keeps escalating is said to be "self-aggravating"; one that eventually slows down is known as a "damped" race. What is crucial is the relative cost and effectiveness of offense as compared with defense. When offensive weapons are cheaper or more effective than defensive ones, races are self-aggravating; when defensive weapons are cheaper or more effective, races are damped. In conventional twentieth-century land warfare, we use a rule of thumb that the attacking side needs 3-to-1 superiority to be successful. A country that intends only to defend itself need build up an army only a third (or slightly more) the size of a potential attacker. The attacker need not fear this build-up, because the defense forces would not be large enough to be used for a successful attack.

On the other hand, if the weapons give a great advantage to the attacker, the race could become self-aggravating. One weapon often cited as a destabilizing weapon was a missile warhead known as MIRV—multiple, independently targetable re-entry vehicle. Imagine two rival countries, each with one hundred missiles and each missile with ten MIRV's. That is a total of one thousand warheads or aiming points. If one side decides to shoot first and wipe out its rival's missiles, it has only one hundred targets to shoot at. It can aim two, three, four, or more warheads per enemy missile and still have hundreds left over to threaten enemy cities once the enemy's missile force is wiped out. Such a race would quickly accelerate as each side tried to acquire more missiles than its rival had warheads.[16]

Such a race would assume that each country builds its weapons in response to the acquisition of weapons by the other. This is known as the *action–reaction phenomenon*. Some people claim that it fuels the arms race today, particularly because of two factors. One is that with present weapons, defense has no clear advantage over offense. In fact, MIRV's, as we have just seen, give an advantage to the side that fires first, and MIRV's are becoming more common. The other factor is worst-case estimation. The claim is made that the United States Department of Defense "invariably exaggerated the Soviet claim to obtain public and congressional support for weapons that will undermine the Soviet deterrent."[17]

Here is how the action–reaction phenomenon works. In the 1960s US intelligence sources noticed a line of radars being built along the western edge of the Soviet Union. Because the line ran through the Baltic city of Tallinn, it was called the Tallinn Line. This was interpreted as the first stage of an antiballistic missile system (ABM), presumably to counter the submarine-launched Polaris missiles. Anticipating this development before the Soviets had even demonstrated that their Tallinn Line would work, the United States took steps to overcome it, substituting a new, bigger submarine-launched missile, the Poseidon, for the Polaris. With bigger missiles American submarines could move farther out into the oceans and launch their missiles from other directions, avoiding the defense of the Tallinn Line.

In the mid-1970s there was still debate about what the Tallinn Line really was, but it never did develop into an ABM system. In fact, the best guess is that it was a Soviet antiaircraft system, built in anticipation of the US deployment of a new bomber, the B-70. The United States never built that bomber, but the Soviets went ahead with their preparations, assuming the worst, that the United States would build it. Meanwhile, US planners, also assuming the worst (that the Tallinn Line was an ABM system) went ahead with their planning. When the error was discovered, the United States did not say, "Oh, we made a mistake," and tear out the more powerful Poseidon missiles. The United States said, in effect, "As long as we have these improved missiles, we might as well keep them." This gave Soviet planners something new to react to.[18]

The action–reaction dynamic provided some but not all of the explanation for the arms competition between the United States and the Soviet Union. One analyst, Albert Wohlstetter, argued that the United States did not invariably overestimate the number of Soviet ICBM's. In fact, in the period from 1962 to 1971, the United States more often underestimated Soviet forces. Of the fifty-one predictions made by the secretary of defense in his annual statement, only nine overestimated what the Soviets subsequently did; in the other forty-two cases, the Soviets actually built more weapons than even the highest estimates by the secretary.

Wohlstetter also argued that the United States did not invariably react by building more weapons. In fact, in at least one case the United States decided not to react. In 1967, Secretary of Defense McNamara argued that the United

States should not build an ABM system because the Soviet ICBM force was so large that antiballistic missile defense would be futile.[19]

A later study by two political scientists, covering a slightly longer period—1952 through 1976—reached the same conclusion. "We conclude," they wrote, "that no arms race was waged, that the two nations were scarcely competing."[20]

OTHER SOURCES OF ARMS RACES

In short, these authors reject the action–reaction explanation of the arms race as a "closed cycle of tightly coupled interaction between US and Soviet processes of decision to acquire weapons."[21] They reach the same conclusion about the recent race that other analysts have reached about arms races in general: Arms are purchased for many reasons. The action–reaction hypothesis assumes that states base their decisions solely on the belief *si vis pacem para bellum*, or that build-ups occur only for the purpose of deterrence. But this is not always so. Any arms build-up is the result of a number of factors. Perhaps one or two motives predominate, but other considerations are usually present as well.[22]

Arms have been purchased primarily to increase the diplomatic weight of a country. This seems to have been the main reason for Germany's decision to build a fleet in 1898. In the late nineteenth century a fleet was a symbol of world influence, reflecting industrial as well as military power and influencing policy in distant parts. (In 1902 German ships participated in the blockade of Venezuelan ports to force that country to pay debts owed to German citizens.) Possibly some Germans believed that Germany needed security on the sea as well as on land. Most German military thinkers, however, agreed that Germany was a land power and its major enemies were also land powers. Therefore a fleet was not needed for national security. The British seem to have misinterpreted German intentions (understandably, because the Germans with all their anti-British talk made their intentions obscure). The British considered naval superiority vital to Britain's well-being, both to defend its island territory and to keep its sea lanes open. For Germany, the British thought, a fleet serves no defensive purpose; it is a waste of money unless they really intend to attack us.

The rather vague goal of increasing diplomatic weight seems to be motivating many states today to try to acquire their own nuclear weapons. In 1975 an Argentine legislator introduced a bill calling on the Argentine government to build its own nuclear bomb. He argued that "recent events have demonstrated that nations gain increasing recognition in the international arena in accordance with their power" and cited China as a state that had been ignored by major powers until it exploded its own nuclear weapons.[23] Whatever the intellectual merits of such arguments, if such legislation succeeded, it would certainly stimulate Argentina's neighbors, Brazil and Chile, to consider acquiring nuclear weapons.

Another reason states build weapons is sometimes called the "ripening plum argument." Just as we pick ripe fruit whether we are hungry or not, so states order new technologies whether they need them or not. To return to the case of the Poseidon submarine missile: Although intended to overcome a possible Soviet ABM system with its greater range, it also had greater accuracy, which could threaten to destroy Soviet missiles in their silos and thus make it possible for the United States to consider striking first in a nuclear war. This greater accuracy was not needed to fulfill the basic mission of Poseidon, which was simply to deter a Soviet strike, but, as one expert testified, "The technology is available—why not use it?"[24]

Domestic politics also affect decisions about weapons. There are always profits to be made by building weapons and careers to be advanced by deploying them. Domestic politics stimulated the German–British naval race. The Kaiser himself took the kind of interest in ships that an adolescent might take in high-performance automobiles. Admiral Tirpitz, head of the German navy, was eager to have his branch of the service get a larger share of the budget. A pressure group, the Navy League, helped the German navy get the government to increase spending on ships.

One political scientist, James Kurth, advanced a more sophisticated version of this argument in what he called "the follow-on imperative." According to Kurth, the production lines for modern weapons are viewed by government planners as a national resource. It takes years to assemble the thousands of scientists, engineers, and skilled workers needed to run Boeing or Lockheed; it takes more time for the team to learn to work together efficiently. If these companies were closed, even temporarily, for lack of contracts, it would take years to reassemble them. Therefore, according to Kurth's argument, a new contract is awarded to a firm whenever a previous contract is about to run out. The new contract is structurally similar to the old one (missiles replacing missiles, for example) and is awarded not to the firm best qualified but to the one with empty production lines. According to Kurth's research, the follow-on imperative explains eleven out of twelve decisions to build major weapons from 1960 to 1972.[25]

But domestic politics, whether in the form of a military–industrial complex or a follow-on imperative, is not a total explanation for arms races. Not all pleas from vested interests are heeded. The United States has canceled some weapons (the B-70 bomber and the B-1A bomber) and has agreed to terminate others (the ABM system), despite military and industrial interest in continuing them.[26] Nor should we neglect the ability of domestic pressure groups to prevent a government from spending on armaments. The British and French governments in the 1930s were slow to engage in an arms race with the Germans because of widespread pacifism among their citizens.

Disillusionment with military spending in the wake of the Vietnam War generated pressures that contributed to President Carter's decision to cancel the B-1 bomber in 1977.

ARMS RACES AND WAR

States may engage in arms races for reasons that have little to do with the objective of preventing war, but it is the effectiveness of these arms races in preventing war that is of primary interest to us. Unfortunately it is difficult to answer the question, "Do arms races make war less or more likely?" because no definitive study on arms races has been carried out. At best we have only fragmentary or preliminary findings.[27] One scholar claims (but without much evidence) that of eighty-four wars ending between 1820 and 1929, only ten were preceded by arms races that someone has asserted were a cause.[28] This suggests that arms races are not the only cause (or even a frequent cause) of wars.

On the other hand, an investigation of serious international disputes between the major powers from 1815 to 1966 found that in those cases in which the dispute was accompanied by an arms race (27 cases), war resulted 23 times. In those cases in which the dispute was not accompanied by an arms race (75 cases), war resulted only 8 times.[29] This research suggests that arms races are not likely to prevent war; indeed, they are more likely to promote it. Yet the author himself cautions that he has discovered only a correlation, not causation. We would not be justified in claiming that arms races invariably end in war. Samuel Huntington listed at least six cases in the last hundred years when arms races ended by peaceful agreement rather than war,[30] and one should add the Soviet–American rivalry (as well as that of NATO and Warsaw Pact allies) to that list.

At the same time, one must keep in mind well-known cases in which the absence of an arms race is widely held to be a major cause of war. In the 1930s, Britain and France did not arm while Germany and Italy did. According to one source, Germany was devoting thirty percent of its gross national product to military purposes while Britain was devoting only seven.[31] As a result, Hitler was emboldened to pursue the policies that led to World War II. In the 1970s, the Persian Gulf area was free from war but experienced a competition in arms between the two largest states. Iran received billions of dollars worth of arms from the United States, Iraq received large quantities from the Soviet Union. In 1979 revolutionary events in Iran led to a collapse of the Iranian military forces and encouraged Iraq's leader to think he could achieve a quick and easy victory. In both cases, an imbalance of arms was followed by war.

Huntington goes on to offer an interesting thesis on the relation of arms races to war. Using the distinction between quantitative races and technological ones, he argues that because quantitative races put progressively greater strains on society, they are more likely to come to a definite end, either in a peace agreement or in war. With more and more soldiers drafted into the army and more and more resources diverted into manufacturing weapons, the time comes when a state's leaders say, "It can't go on like this anymore." A quantitative race that ended in a peace agreement was the race between Chile and Argentina, which began in 1890 and ended with a treaty in 1902. A quantitative race that ended in war was the race preceding World War I.

The qualitative race, Huntington argues, is different. It puts less pressure on society. Scientists and engineers work on new forms of weapons, but not many of their inventions actually go into production. Those that are produced are not produced for long, because soon a new weapon comes along and the process starts all over. Each state can hope that luck will give it the technological breakthrough needed to put it ahead, even if only temporarily. The result is that technological races tend to go on and on. No great pressure is felt to bring them to a definitive end, either by fighting or by agreement.[32]

Huntington's ideas must be regarded as hypotheses rather than as accepted theories; he offers little systematic proof. Because he does not give a precise definition of "technological race," it is hard to know which races fit that category. Even with qualitative change, a state needs a specific quantity of weapons before it gains the upper hand. Still, Huntington's ideas offer a plausible explanation of events in recent years. The United States–Soviet race was primarily technological, and it went on without great pressure for either war or agreement.

COSTS AND HAZARDS OF ARMS RACES

Even if arms races do not inevitably lead to war, they are undesirable in other ways. One of them is cost. Resources diverted to weapons cannot be used to make life more enjoyable. Metal and machinery used for an intercontinental missile ends up sitting inert in a concrete-lined hole in the ground. Metal and machinery used for refrigerators and stoves keeps your beer cold and your pizza warm. More missiles means fewer refrigerators and stoves.

The cost of the arms competition with the Soviet Union was evident even in its early days. In a speech early in his administration, April 16, 1953, President Eisenhower pointed out that for the price of single bomber the nation could build thirty brick schoolhouses. The problem grew much worse in the following years. The most recent American bomber, the B-2, unveiled in 1988, was estimated by the military itself to cost in excess of $500 million. Using Eisenhower's terms, a single bomber could now build 150 modern elementary schools.

By the 1980s, the cost of weapons had escalated so much that even with greatly increased spending the military was able to buy fewer items. During that decade the Navy replaced its F-4 Phantom jet fighter with the new F-14 Tomcat. But the Tomcat cost more than seven times as much as the Phantom.[33] At the beginning of the 1990s, the Air Force came forward with a proposal for a new fighter that was estimated to cost five times more than the F-14.

Despite the greatly increased military spending under President Reagan, the Air Force actually was able to afford fewer planes than it bought under the Carter Administration.[34] One aerospace executive pointed out that if costs continued to escalate at the same rate, by "the year 2054, the entire defense budget will purchase just one tactical aircraft. This aircraft will have to be shared between Air Force and Navy, three and a half days each per week."[35]

President Reagan, in a commencement address at the Naval Academy in 1985, repeated the traditional argument for acquiring arms:

> You will hear during your career that maintaining the military at peak readiness, keeping our forces trained and supplied with the best weapons and equipment is too costly. I say it is too costly for America not to be prepared.
>
> Today, as through our history, it is strength, not weakness, resolve, not vacillation that will keep the peace. . . . The way to prevent war is to be prepared for it.[36]

But even those who agree with this statement must answer the difficult question of what war to prepare for. Armaments are acquired with an eye to potential adversaries. A former official in the Defense Department in charge of weapons acquisition argued after the Gulf War that it will be "crucial to maintain the research and development strategy that contributed to the advantage U.S. forces enjoy today." He called for "a continuing exploration of new military technology" and "a vigorous program to build and test prototypes."[37] Yet with the enormous costs of modern weapons, even a modest program limited only to research and development would impose a large burden on the nation's economy. Pursuit of plums just because they are ripening will become increasingly difficult in the absence of a clearly defined threat.

President Nixon said, "The adversaries in the world are not in conflict because they are armed. They are armed because they are in conflict and have not yet learned peaceful ways to resolve their conflicting national interests."[38] The evaporation of the arms race following changes in the Soviet Union suggests that Nixon was right.

Yet if conflict with the Soviet Union has abated, other conflicts have not. The states of the world have not as yet all learned peaceful ways to resolve their conflicts. It may not be enough simply to wait for these conflicts to do away. Arms races may make the solutions of conflict more difficult. At times they may turn into wars, intentionally or not. The issue of disarmament is still important.

NOTES

1. *The New York Times*, May 23, 1985, p. Y14.
2. Iceland and Costa Rica are the only two traditional states of significant size with no military budget. A number of new microstates also report no military spending. See *World Military Expenditures and Arms Transfers, 1968–1977* (Washington, D.C.: U.S. Arms Control and Disarmament Agency, October, 1979).
3. Quoted by Leonard Wainstein in "The Dreadnought Gap," *United States Naval Institute Proceedings* (September 1966), reprinted in Robert J. Art and Kenneth Waltz, *The Use of Force* (Boston: Little, Brown, 1971), p. 168.
4. See the experiment described by Morton Deutsch and Robert M. Krauss, "Studies of Interpersonal Bargaining," *The Journal of Conflict Resolution*, Vol. 6, No. 1 (March 1962), pp. 52–76.
5. Lewis F. Richardson, "Could an Arms Race End Without Fighting?" *Nature*, Vol. 168 (September 29, 1951), pp. 567–568.
6. Colin S. Gray, "The Arms Race Phenomenon," *World Politics*, Vol. 24, No. 1 (October 1971), p. 40.
7. Samuel P. Huntington, "Arms Races: Prerequisites and Results," in *Public Policy*, ed. Carl Friedrich and Seymour Harris (Cambridge, Mass.: Harvard University, Graduate School of Public Administration, 1958), p. 76.
8. Bruce M. Russet, *What Price Vigilance?* (New Haven: Yale University Press, 1970), pp. 8–9.
9. Albert Wohlstetter, "Racing Forward? or Ambling Back?" *Survey*, Vol. 22, Nos. 3 and 4 (Summer–Autumn 1976), pp. 163–217.
10. Huntington, p. 65. (See note 7.)
11. Bernadotte E. Schmitt, *The Coming of the War, 1914* Vol. 1 (New York: Charles Scribner's Sons, 1930), p. 54 fn.
12. Fritz Fischer, *Germany's Aims in the First World War* (New York: W. W. Norton, 1967), p. 36.
13. Barbara Tuchman, *The Guns of August* (New York: Dell, 1962), pp. 43–44.
14. Huntington, p. 48. (See note 7.)
15. Arthur J. Marder, *From Dreadnought to Scapa Flow*, Vol. 1: *The Road to War, 1904–1914* (London: Oxford University Press, 1961), p. 57.
16. Malcolm W. Hoag, "On Stability in Deterrent Races," in *The Revolution in World Politics*, ed. Morton A. Kaplan (New York: John Wiley, 1962), pp. 338–410.
17. Remarks by Jeremy J. Stone at the Congressional Conference on the Military Budget and National Priorities, Washington, D.C., March 28–29, quoted in *American Militarism, 1970*, ed. Erwin Knoll and Judith Nies McFadden (New York: Viking Press, 1969), p. 71.
18. George Rathjens, "The Dynamics of the Arms Race," *Scientific American*, Vol. 220, No. 4 (April 1969), pp. 15–25.
19. Albert Wohlstetter, "Is There a Strategic Arms Race?" *Foreign Policy*, No. 15 (Summer 1974), pp. 3–20; Albert Wohlstetter, "Rivals, But No 'Race,' " *Foreign Policy*, No. 16 (Fall 1974), pp. 48–81.
20. A. F. K. Organski and Jacek Kugler, *The War Ledger* (Chicago: University of Chicago Press, 1980), p. 192.
21. Ibid., p. 80.
22. Colin Gray, "The Urge to Compete: Rationales for Arms Racing," *World Politics*, Vol. 26, No. 2 (January 1974), pp. 207–233.
23. Jonathan Kandell, "Argentines Assay Their Atom Potential," *The New York Times*, April 2, 1975, p. 2.
24. Charles Schultze in testimony before the Subcommittee on Economy in Government of the Joint Economic Committee, "The Military Budget and National Economic Priorities (Part I)," 91st Cong., 1st sess., June 1969, p. 51.

25.   James Kurth, "Aerospace Production Lines and American Defense Spending," in *Testing the Theory of the Military Industrial Complex*, ed. Steven Rosen (Lexington, Mass.: Lexington Books, 1973), pp. 135–156.

26.   Wohlstetter, "Rivals, But No 'Race,' " p. 73. (See note 19.)

27.   This point is emphasized in the writings of Colin Gray. See the two articles cited in notes 5 and 28.

28.   Michael Nicholson, *Conflict Analysis* (New York: Barnes & Noble, 1971), pp. 133–136.

29.   Michael D. Wallace, "Racing Redux: The Arms Race–Escalation Debate Revisited," in Charles S. Gochman and Alan Ned Sabrosky, eds. *Prisoners of War?* (Lexington Mass.: Lexington Books, 1990), p. 119.

30.   Huntington, pp. 64–65. (See note 7.)

31.   Organski and Kugler, p. 218. (See note 20.)

32.   Huntington, p. 76. (See note 7.)

33.   Drew Middleton, "Rising Plane Costs Stir Air-Tactics Debate," *The New York Times*, December 1, 1974.

34.   Testimony by Franklin C. Spinney to the President's Blue Ribbon Commission on Defense Management, *The New York Times*, December 13, 1985, p. Y11.

35.   Quoted by James Fallows, *National Defense* (New York: Random House, 1981), p. 38.

36.   *The New York Times*, May 23, 1985, p. Y14.

37.   William Perry, "Desert Storm and Deterrence," *Foreign Affairs*, Vol. 70, No. 4 (Fall 1991), p. 80.

38.   Commencement address at the Air Force Academy, quoted in *The New York Times*, June 5, 1969.

CHAPTER 10

DISARMAMENT

What seems to be one of the simplest proposals for preventing war turns out on closer examination to be one of the most complex. Defining *disarmament* is not hard; it means the reduction or elimination of weapons. As a means of preventing war it is logically unassailable. Without the means to fight, you cannot have a war, any more than you can have highway accidents without vehicles. The problem comes when you try to describe precisely what weapons you want states to eliminate.

WAYS TO DISARM

Suppose that governments say they are willing to disarm. What should we recommend? There are at least seven distinct possibilities.

1. *Total disarmament*. This would mean the elimination of all weapons (a "weapon" being defined as any device that could be used to kill or injure). A critic could argue that because you can strangle someone with a shoelace, shoelaces must be prohibited. Such a criticism is a frivolous version of a much more serious objection, that many devices common in modern industrial societies can be used as weapons. Dynamite, for example, has many commercial uses—in logging, mining, and construction. But chemically it is the same substance that is packed into bombs and artillery shells. Commercial jetliners are widely used to transport people, messages, and goods. But if

you load a Boeing 727 with a coal mine's supply of dynamite, you have a bomber more potent than any used in World War II. Total disarmament would mean the elimination of these and many other components of modern industrial life, in effect forcing all humanity into a primitive and frugal existence.

Even if we got rid of all weapons and all potential weapons, we could not do away with the knowledge of how to build them. Even if we get rid of nuclear weapons, we would have to perform lobotomies on all people with advanced degrees in physics to be sure that in times of international crisis someone would not start up their production. The study of physics, engineering, and any other science would have to be strictly prohibited.

Of course we would find no support for any proposal that would lead to the eradication of the pursuit of knowledge or of modern industrial technology built on this knowledge. We would probably not even find support for the elimination of hunting rifles. And with firearms still in private possession there would be a demand for equipping law enforcement officers with firearms as well.

2. *Disarmament to the lowest point consistent with domestic safety.* No government leader has ever advocated disarmament that eliminated even the domestic police force. The most radical proposal seriously advanced was Point Four of Woodrow Wilson's Fourteen Points, "that national armaments will be reduced to the lowest point consistent with domestic safety." But even this proposal was too radical for states to consider. One reason is the great disparity in size among the states. A minimal police force for a large state such as Germany could threaten the security of one of its tiny neighbors such as Luxemburg and would probably make its more sizable neighbor Belgium nervous. Another reason is that states have widely varied opinions about how much domestic safety they need. England in the last century and a half has had a tradition of police armed with no more than a nightstick. France, by contrast, has had a paramilitary force, the Republican Security Companies, living in barracks, equipped with armored vehicles, and carrying firearms, including light machine guns. The French government maintains its Republic Security Companies as a riot control force, but in a totally disarmed world they would serve as an effective invading army against an England defended only by London bobbies and village constables.

3. *Disarmament to the lowest point consistent with national safety.* President Woodrow Wilson's Point Four was reworded at the Versailles Conference so that Article 8 of the Versailles Treaty read, "The maintenance of peace requires the reduction of national armaments to the lowest point consistent with national safety." By changing "domestic safety" to "national safety," a much wider latitude was permitted to states. Regular armies would be allowed, although only for self-defense. This goal has two problems, an old one and a new one. The old one is the question of how much force is needed

for legitimate self-defense. Almost any force could be justified by that lan-guage. Do we set a basic number of 100,000 troops for each country? By those standards Luxemburg would be armed to the teeth. Do some states get larger forces because of special problems such as terrain? Poland, being flat, would need more than Switzerland with its mountains. But don't we then have to account for intentions? In recent European history the Swiss have seemed more trustworthy than the Poles.

As if these old problems weren't staggering enough, we have new ones related to modern weapons. Highly destructive nuclear weapons delivered by planes and missiles differ in fundamental ways from weapons used in the past. They are not very useful as weapons of offense (that is, to seize and hold territory) nor are they very useful as weapons of defense (that is, to expel or hold back invaders). Most states view them as useful mainly to deter other states from using them. This view was reflected in a French statement of disarmament goals in 1991, when it finally agreed to adhere to the treaty limiting the spread of nuclear weapons. "Nuclear arsenals," the French government declared, "should be brought down to the lowest possible levels compatible with dissuasion."

But the same intercontinental missile with a nuclear warhead that dissuades another country from attacking could also be used in a disarming first strike. The bare minimum needed to deal a devastating retaliatory blow could suffice to launch a crippling first strike. How the weapons will be used depends entirely on the intentions of a state's leaders, and those intentions could change quickly, particularly if a coup or revolution brought to power a new group with aggressive intentions.

4. *Qualitative disarmament.* Because of difficulties with the general con-cept of national defense, proponents of disarmament have often turned to more technical discussions of types of weapons. They try to identify some weapons as offensive and eliminate them. This was attempted at the unsuc-cessful Geneva Disarmament Conference of 1932, which found it impossible to separate offensive from defensive weapons because modern weapons can be used for both offense and defense. Recently the United States tried to make the same distinction and failed. When the US occupation of South Korea ended in 1949, the United States took along with its withdrawing forces its tanks and airplanes, to keep South Korea from mounting an offensive against the North. But, as the South Koreans discovered in June 1950, without tanks and airplanes a country cannot conduct a successful defense either. Even something so obviously defensive as fortification (which cannot be moved into an enemy's country) can be part of an overall offensive plan. In 1939, Germany built a defensive line along its border with France to keep France from coming to the aid of East European allies when Germany attacked them.

One promising area for qualitative disarmament has been obnoxious weapons. The first true disarmament agreement to be reached after World War II (that is, one calling for the physical destruction of weapons) was the 1972 treaty outlawing biological weapons. By this treaty signatories agreed not only not to use such weapons in war but also to destroy existing cultures of various disease-causing organisms that could be loaded into shells and bombs. Biological weapons were easy to agree on because their military usefulness has never been demonstrated and is not believed to be great. Part of the reason is that it may take a long time for enemy troops to develop symptoms of a disease, long enough to allow them to continue to mount an offensive, for example. Another reason their use has not been attempted, at least on a large scale, is that biological agents are difficult to deliver on target. Despite science fiction fantasies, it is difficult to make people sick at a distance. The best and perhaps the only way would be a slow-flying airplane, flying over enemy troop concentrations, spraying a cloud of disease germs. Even then it is not clear how many organisms would survive the brief trip to the ground. In any case, any military force that had the ability to fly low and slow over enemy troops would already be in a position to win the war by more conventional means.

Chemical weapons are another obnoxious weapon, but the world did not follow the biological weapons treaty with a similar one to ban them. Unlike biological weapons, chemical ones have demonstrated their usefulness, most recently in the 1980s in the Gulf War between Iraq and Iran. Also, it is difficult to assure compliance with a ban. Even if stocks of chemical weapons are destroyed, new ones can easily be manufactured with equipment and plants used for similar chemicals, such as insecticides or pharmaceuticals.

The most obvious candidate for qualitative disarmament is the nuclear weapon, because more than anything else it has made international politics a serious concern for so many people. In the early 1960s the "ban the bomb" movement was active, contributing the superimposed semaphore signals for *N* and *D* (standing for nuclear disarmament), which have become the emblem of the peace movement. But during the decades of the Cold War, some of the more thoughtful peace activists turned their attention away from the issue of immediate nuclear disarmament. For example, Seymour Melman, a professor of engineering who wrote many thoughtful articles on the arms race, proposed reducing nuclear warheads to the number necessary to destroy all US and Soviet cities with more than 100,000 people (a total of 150 in the United States, 175 in the USSR). Melman claimed that leaders "who would not be deterred from nuclear military initiative by the prospect of destruction of these 150 cities would be too insane to be deterred by anything."[1] He was probably correct, but he was implicitly accepting the continued existence of nuclear weapons. Only with the demise of the Soviet

Union did qualitative proposals for nuclear disarmament, such as "zero ballistic missiles," begin to make their appearance.[2]

5. *Quantitative disarmament.* Instead of seeking to eliminate one type of weapon, as the qualitative approach recommends, states could agree to cut back numbers of one or more types of weapons, or they could agree to preserve a ratio of forces. This attention to numbers of weapons, or a quantitative approach, was used successfully in 1922 at the Washington Naval Conference. The five major powers agreed to reduce the number of battleships each had and to preserve the same ratio when they built new ships to replace old ones. The ratio was 5 : 5 : 3 : 1.67 : 1.67. The United States and Britain had the largest number; Japan was in the middle; and France and Italy had the smallest number.

The agreement, though successful, had two undesirable effects. One was to channel competition into nonregulated fields. The following years saw the states turn to building submarines and cruisers instead of battleships. The other effect was to preserve the status quo. Japan, relegated to a secondary place (only three battleships for every five the United States had), was unhappy and in 1934 demanded that the ratio be changed to allow Japan to build more battleships. When the other powers refused, Japan gave notice that it would refuse to renew the pact.

6. *Budgetary limitation.* Frustrated by the difficulties of either qualitative or quantitative limitations on weapons, states have from time to time turned to an indirect approach: limiting the amount of money states can spend on weapons. At the Hague Conference of 1899, Russia proposed a five-year freeze on all military budgets. The Germans were quick to object. Russia, they pointed out, already had superiority in numbers of soldiers. Russia could use the money saved from military budgets to build more railroads, which, although technically nonmilitary, could be used to transport Russian soldiers more quickly to the front in the event of war.[3]

At the Geneva Disarmament Conference of 1932 the issue of budgetary limitation again came up. In preparation for the conference, a commission compiled statistics on military spending around the world. But the conference never got to make use of them. Again, it was Germany that objected, although this time for different reasons. German armaments already were limited in quantity by the Versailles Treaty; Germany hoped to make up for numerical inferiority in improved quality, which would require more expenditure.[4]

The idea of budgetary limitation has been advanced from time to time since World War II. In 1973 the Soviet Foreign Minister proposed that the major states of the world cut their military budgets by 10 percent and that 10 percent of these savings be donated to developing countries.[5] Yet, as the Soviet Union later admitted, their published budget figure showed only a fraction of their true military spending. It included only personnel, maintenance, and construction, while omitting research, development, and procurement of new weapons.[6] Even in the relatively open society of the United States, Congress sometimes has been slow to discover that agencies in the executive branch have been violating financial limits Congress has tried to impose.[7] It was estimated that the Reagan Administration at one time had as much as 10 percent of military spending in "black" or secret programs.[8]

7. *Regional disarmament*. Finding general disarmament too difficult, states have occasionally tried regional disarmament. Some agreements of this type are in effect right now. They affect Antarctica, outer space, and the seabed. These were easy cases. Very little armament was going on anyway in those areas, and they were not inhabited by people who could claim they needed arms for self-defense. There have been proposals to extend the concept of disarmament by geographic area to other regions—the Indian subcontinent, Latin America, central Europe, Africa. None of them has yet shown any success, though some Latin American states have taken a first step in this direction.

In February 1975, eight Latin American countries signed the Ayacucho Pact, agreeing to limit their acquisition of offensive weapons. But since the signing of the pact there has been no follow-up meeting. Peru, which initiated the agreement, continued to order weapons, including armored personnel carriers, tanks, and submarines. Within three years, Argentina had doubled its military budget. Neither the similarities among these countries nor their common interest in insulating their region from outside pressures was strong enough to overcome the traditional problems in implementing a disarmament agreement.[9]

A HISTORY OF DISARMAMENT AGREEMENTS: FROM RUSH–BAGOT TO GENERAL AND COMPLETE DISARMAMENT

Disarmament proposals are relatively recent additions to the history of the search for peace. Only in recent times have weapons become so specialized that they are clearly distinguishable from the tools of everyday life. The Bible talks of beating swords into plowshares and plowshares back into swords.[10] In Biblical times rearmament could be accomplished overnight. The complexity of modern weapons makes this no longer possible. The disarmament movement came into being only after the Industrial Revolution had created weapons whose complexity gave rise to talk about abolishing weapons.

The late nineteenth century saw a number of organized attempts to get states to reduce their arms, culminating in the conferences at The Hague in 1899 and 1907.[11] The Hague Conferences did provide for laws regulating the conduct of war but did not achieve any reduction or elimination of arms. What is often described as the only successful disarmament agreement of the nineteenth century goes back much earlier. This was the Rush–Bagot Agreement of 1817 between the United States and Britain.

The Rush–Bagot Agreement provided for disarmament on the Great Lakes. Each country agreed to have only three ships, of equal size and armament. Contrary to what many schoolbooks say, the agreement was violated repeatedly. The worst violations occurred in the late 1830s, when the British sent armed ships into the Great Lakes to mount retaliatory raids against American sanctuaries for guerrilla parties who were raiding Canada. Land fortifications were maintained until 1871, when the United States signed a treaty with Britain settling claims arising from the Civil War. Only then was disarmament extended gradually and without formal agreement to the long land border. Not until the twentieth century, when the possibility of war between Canada and the United States finally disappeared from the minds of policy-planners, did violation cease.

The Rush–Bagot Agreement is sometimes cited to prove that disarmament agreement leads to peaceful relations between states. A close examination of the historical record seems to support the opposite view: Only when there are already peaceful relations among states is a disarmament agreement workable. An agreement may exist on paper, such as the Rush–Bagot Agreement did, but it is in danger of violation at any crisis.[12]

The period after World War I saw two kinds of disarmament. One was the disarmament forced on the losing countries by the winners. This was justified as the first step toward general disarmament by all European states. But as the years passed it became clear that the victors did not intend to disarm down to the levels they had imposed on Germany. As a result, the Germans began to insist on the right to arm up to their level. In the end, disarmament only exacerbated the tensions that brought about World War II.

The other kind of disarmament was voluntary, and it met with some success, at least in the beginning. One consequence of World War I was that the United States developed its military potential. Despite the fact that the US was an ally of Britain's, the British looked upon increased US naval power as they did upon increases by any country: with grave suspicion. Partly because of this budding conflict, a naval conference was convened in Washington in 1922. It resulted in the agreement mentioned earlier on reducing the number of battleships.

It is hard to decide what lesson to draw from the 1922 agreement. Some have argued that it proves disarmament possible.[13] Others have used it to illustrate the point that disarmament can be limited to a region or to a type of weapon but cannot be both general (applying to all countries) and complete (covering all weapons).[14] The most pessimistic observers have mentioned that the battleship was already considered obsolescent by the time the conference convened, and the participants had no plans to build more ships in any case.[15] Even by this interpretation, the Washington Naval Treaty did contribute something: At least states did not hang on to outdated weapons just because all other states did. But that contribution was minute.

Even this type of modest contribution was no longer possible by the time of the Geneva Disarmament Conference of 1932. The Geneva Conference was the long-delayed fulfillment of the promise of the Versailles settlement that German disarmament would be the first step toward general disarmament. By the time the conference convened, it was too late for that. The conference failed for both technical and political reasons. Technically, it proved impossible to agree on the questions raised by new weapons. How were tanks and airplanes to be treated? As offensive weapons or as defensive ones? Politically, the conflict between France and Germany was too severe. Germany insisted on equality of armaments with France; France insisted on security from attack by Germany. Any slim hope of compromise was ended by the accession to power of the Nazis in January 1933.

The period after World War II again saw two kinds of disarmament, forced and voluntary. Germany and Japan were forcibly disarmed in consequence of their losing the war. But events in international politics led to very different outcomes this time. The United States' perception of a Soviet threat led it to take the initiative in urging rearmament of both these countries within less than ten years. The most dramatic shift in policy was toward Japan. As part of the American occupation, the Japanese had been given a new constitution that was in effect dictated by the head of the occupation, General Douglas MacArthur. MacArthur had insisted on including Article IX, that "the Japanese people forever renounce war as a sovereign right of the nation and the threat or use of force as a means of settling international disputes." To accomplish this, the article states, "land, sea, and air forces, as well as other war potential, will never be maintained." But in 1950 all four US occupation divisions in Japan were transferred to fight in Korea, and General MacArthur insisted that the Japanese form a National Police Reserve Force of 75,000 men, equipped with tanks, mortars, and machine guns. In 1954 this became the Self-Defense Force. Today, with 250,000 men, it is larger than the defense forces of most other states.[16]

Voluntary attempts to reduce or abolish arms met with failure in the years following World War II. A number of plans were advanced, but none was even accepted as a talking point. The failure of disarmament as an approach to peace during these decades is best illustrated by the official positions of both the United States and the Soviet Union. Both claimed to favor a utopian goal of "general and complete disarmament" (meaning all kinds of weapons and all countries). In a draft treaty submitted to the United Nations in 1962, the United States specified what it meant: elimination of all weapons of mass destruction (nuclear, chemical, and biological); elimination of all nonnuclear forces except (1) those needed for internal security, and (2) agreed personnel for a UN peace force.[17]

A turn toward serious negotiations on disarmament in the 1980s was signaled by the abandonment of such grandiose proposals and their replacement by more limited goals. In January of 1986, General Secretary Gorbachev proposed that within next 5 to 8 years, the USSR and the United States each reduce by half the number of its nuclear weapons that could reach the other's territory. The United States accepted this goal of a 50 percent cut[18] and it became the basis for agreement in the ongoing Strategic Arms Reduction Talks (START) carried out during the Reagan and Bush Administrations.

DISARMAMENT: INF AND START

Even before the START treaty was concluded it was possible for the United States and the Soviet Union to conclude a treaty that led, for the first time since nuclear weapons were introduced, to the physical elimination of one category of such weapons. These were ballistic missiles of intermediate range—too short to reach from continent to continent but too long to be of battlefield use. Most were stationed in Europe, and the Europeans would have suffered most had they ever been used.

The Intermediate Nuclear Forces (INF) Treaty was signed at the Washington Summit meeting of Reagan and Gorbachev in December 1987, with the Senate approving ratification overwhelmingly the next May. It called for the destruction of all missiles with ranges between 500 kilometers (311 miles) and 5,500 kilometers (3,418 miles) within 3 years at the latest. Only the missiles themselves (or the "delivery systems" as they were called) were to be destroyed; the nuclear warheads were first to be removed. Nuclear warheads without means of delivery are not very useful, and in any case the fissile material decays over time, some of it quite rapidly.

The only other agreement since 1945 to call for actual physical destruction of weapons, the Biological Weapons Treaty of 1972, did not call for physical inspection and was followed by accusations of cheating. In the case of the INF treaty, both sides accepted mandatory, on-site verification. Each country opened its bases and manufacturing sites to inspections from the other country and allowed observers to watch the missiles being destroyed. Each side was given the right to conduct inspections on very short notice, or, in other words, to make spot checks. Such monitoring is sometimes called "intrusive" because it allows rivals access to normally secret facilities. For years, failure to agree on on-site inspection was a major stumbling block, and its acceptance as part of the INF marks a major breakthrough.

The Soviet Union's acceptance of such inspection was only one of several major concessions. Another was the agreement to destroy more Soviet weapons, 1,752 missiles versus 859 for the Americans. Still another was not to insist that French and British nuclear weapons be included in the agreement.

The INF Treaty was followed by the START treaty, signed on July 31, 1991, which called for the destruction of some of the long-range nuclear weapons possessed by each side. President Gorbachev took the occasion to declare the arms race ended, saying, "Thank God, as we say in Russian, we stopped this."[19] But START illustrates some of the difficulties with disarmament by formal agreement. The talks themselves dragged on for almost ten years. Although the outlines were essentially agreed to at the Reykjavik summit between Reagan and Gorbachev in 1986, working out the details took another five years. The treaty itself was a 700-page document, much of it taken up with what were called "counting rules." Because the treaty called for only equivalent cuts, not complete disarmament, guidelines were necessary for determining what counted as equivalent weapons. In an effort to account for the differences between the Soviet and American arsenals, the negotiators came up with such complex decisions as the one that a bomber carrying twenty cruise missiles would be counted as if it had ten warheads but a bomber carrying old-fashioned gravity bombs would count as if it had only one.

The delay and complexity occurred despite the obvious interests of both sides—economic and political as well as military—in curbing the arms race. One cause of delay was that both sides had to deal with vested interests— most important, military forces that did not want to be deprived of weapons. Another was habits of caution engendered by years of rivalry. And in the back of the minds of leaders on both sides was the question fundamental to international anarchy: What if this agreement does not hold? What if we revert to our bad old ways?

It was this caution that produced only proportional cuts, not complete disarmament. Under START, the Soviet Union would drop from about 11,000 to 7,000 long-range nuclear weapons, the United States from 12,000 to 9,000. Both sides were left with arsenals that were enormous by the standards of the 1950s and 1960s.

Despite the very limited nature of the disarmament brought about by START, both sides expressed the view that further disarmament by means of a treaty was not likely. The effort to negotiate START had been exhausting for those government officials involved. On the Soviet side, radical changes within the Soviet Union were taking up too much attention. Popular pressure for disarmament, such as had been seen during the nuclear freeze movement during the early 1980s, abated. The changed political conditions that had made agreement possible made the issue of nuclear war less urgent.

In fact, during the 1970s and 1980s conventional weapons were of more concern to Western governments because of a generally acknowledged Soviet superiority in Europe. Assessments based purely on numbers of weapons each side has, sometimes contemptuously called "bean counts," are probably not very accurate predictions of how wars would turn out. In one famous case where the "bean count" was misleading, it was the inferior German tank forces in 1940 that overran France in a few weeks.[20] Still, the raw numbers of Soviet compared with NATO weapons gave pause even to the most optimistic—for example, 67,600 tanks to 31,527, or 44,000 artillery pieces to 18,500.[21] Public opinion polls found that, by a margin of 5 to 3, Americans thought that if nuclear weapons were eliminated, then the Soviet Union would have a "large advantage in non-nuclear forces such as tanks and soldiers."[22]

Back in 1972, after the SALT I agreements, there had been great hopes for the momentum to carry over to conventional force reductions, but talks for "Mutual and Balanced Force Reductions" in Europe stalled for 15 years. Following the accession to power by Gorbachev, a new forum for negotiation on conventional forces in Europe was set up. This time economic pressure in the form of budget deficits was driving both the United States and the USSR. In a radical departure from the hard bargaining so characteristic of the Soviet Union in the past, Gorbachev began making major concessions even before the talks began. He assured the West that cuts would indeed be made and that they would be asymmetrical. In his book *Perestroika*, published in 1987 and directed at American audiences, Gorbachev wrote: "In the West they talk about inequalities and imbalances. That's right, there are imbalances and asymmetries in some kinds of armaments and armed forces on both sides in Europe, caused by historical, geographical and other factors. We stand for eliminating the inequality existing in some areas, but not through a build-up by those who lag behind but through a reduction by those who are ahead."[23] In December 1988, before negotiations had begun, he announced plans to cut 500,000 soldiers from the Red Army (or about 10 percent) and eliminate 10,000 tanks, including specifically some of those facing NATO in Europe.

Despite these unilateral initiatives, the negotiations continued for another two years. It was only on December 19, 1990, at a summit conference of 34 states in Paris, that the Treaty on Conventional Forces in Europe was signed. Put simply, the treaty required the Soviet Union and its allies to destroy weapons down to the level of the United States and its allies. The ceiling on tanks, for example, was fixed at 20,000 for each side, compared to the original NATO number of 22,000 and the Warsaw Pact number of 41,000.

OBSTACLES TO DISARMAMENT: INSPECTION

Much of the post–World War II negotiation between the United States and the USSR stumbled over the issue of inspection to ensure compliance with agreements. The inspection issue has been a troublesome one since people first proposed disarmament. States arm because they distrust each other. Once they begin to disarm, this distrust continues, at least until some evidence to the contrary has been accumulated. Any state that distrusts its rivals enough to arm against them will distrust them enough to require more than their word that they are disarming.

Inspection for disarmament is exceedingly difficult. It requires something almost impossible to provide: positive evidence of nonactivity. Positive evidence of activity is a lot easier to acquire. The part of disarmament that calls for destroying existing weapons is fairly easy. You build a big bonfire, invite your enemies in, and throw your bombers on it. The hard part is to prove that no new weapons are being built and that no existing weapons were hidden to escape the original census that indicated how many each country had. You could have a number of sources of information—tourists, military attachés, airplane flights once a month—and still find nothing. That would not prove that hidden arsenals did not exist, only that you hadn't found any. The problem is more troubling today because of the destructive power modern weapons have. It would not matter if a country hid a couple of dozen tanks under haystacks. They would not be a big threat. A couple of dozen ICBM's with megaton warheads would be an entirely different matter.

We can expect that noncompliance with a disarmament agreement will be accompanied by deception to make discovery more difficult. When the Germans were secretly rearming after World War I, they used a number of devices. One was to build ammunitions factories in Russia in return for some of the output. Another was to develop sport flying clubs and commercial airline pilot schools to train young men for the then-forbidden air force.

One of the most ingenious (and discouraging) examples of deception occurred during the Italian war against Ethiopia in 1935 and 1936. The Italians, contrary to international law, were using poison gas. Foreign journalists discovered what the Italians were doing and photographed victims of the gas attacks. The Italian military censor, instead of forbidding the dispatch of all photographs, substituted pictures showing leprosy victims. The world press printed the substituted pictures with the original captions stating that the pictures showed gas victims. Prominent medical authorities came forward to state that the people shown in the photographs were not gas victims at all but suffered from leprosy. Not only was the truth about what the Italians were doing obscured but subsequent reports were treated with skepticism.[24]

A similar problem developed for the Czechs in 1938, when Hitler began making threats over the issue of the Sudeten Germans. The alarmed Czechs accused the Germans of mobilizing against them. At that time the accusation was false, and Hitler seized the opportunity to invite French and British representatives to tour the border area. They found no signs of mobilization, and as a result French and British faith in the judgment and even in the motives of the Czechs was weakened. It became harder for the Czechs to argue their case in the following months, although we now know that Hitler had his general staff prepare plans for an invasion of Czechoslovakia in 1937.[25]

With all the opportunities the violator has for manipulating inspectors, it is easy to see why inspection has been a stumbling block. The issue was an even more solid obstacle with the Soviet Union because of Soviet secrecy in all things. Exchanges between foreign visitors and Soviet citizens were discouraged. Travel abroad was just about impossible for Soviet citizens. Radio broadcasts from abroad were sometimes jammed. American space flights were televised live from the beginning, but for a long time Soviet flights were not announced until after they were successfully under way. This asymmetry in freedom of information made any inspection proposal seem to the Russians a serious encroachment on their security. Topographic maps of the kind available at an American stationery store were treated in Russia like military documents. Even school atlases were made deliberately inaccurate, as though they otherwise might be of some value to foreign military planners.[26] When President Eisenhower in 1955 proposed "open skies," allowing Soviet planes to make regular inspection flights over the United States and American planes to make similar flights over the USSR, the Russians felt the flights would add little to their knowledge of the United States but would add a great deal to Americans' knowledge of the USSR. They rejected the proposal.

Revelations after the Gulf War showed that Iraq had manipulated inspections of its nuclear facilities. UN inspection teams were surprised to discover a much greater capacity than had been acknowledged. And even with legal access, they were not sure they had discovered all of it.

OBSTACLES TO DISARMAMENT: ENFORCEMENT

Inspection is such a difficult issue that negotiations have often not moved beyond it. When they do, they are confronted by a second obstacle— enforcement. What if inspection reveals a violation? Most of the time, the only remedy acceptable in international relations has been to imitate the violator. In 1922 states meeting at the Washington Naval Conference voluntarily imposed limitations on the number of battleships they would possess. In 1934 the Japanese informed the other parties to the treaty that if Japan were not allowed equality, it would withdraw from the treaty. In the absence of a world government and a world police force, no penalty could be applied to Japan short of going to war. States could respond only by building additional ships of their own.

After World War II the situation was different. Disarmament of Japan (along with Germany) was not voluntary but imposed by the victors. Disarmament was facilitated in both cases by the total discrediting of their military establishments, the total destruction of their economies, and the physical occupation of their territory by troops. The populations themselves accepted their disarmament, and when later the United States wanted the countries to make some contribution against the Soviet threat, they resisted. Even a half-century later, neither Japan nor Germany have nuclear weapons, chemical weapons, missiles, or high-technology weapons of the latest type. Both have restraints on arms exports and on the deployment of what armed forces they have; both refused to contribute troops to the allied coalition against Saddam Hussein.

After the Persian Gulf War, in 1991 Iraq too agreed to disarm, but under conditions closer to those that prevailed after World War I than World War II. Iraq was defeated, but its territory was not occupied and its government not discredited. The international community was able to impose its will—as had happened to Germany in 1919. According to Resolution 687, 3 April 1991, within 45 days (May 18), the UN Secretary General submitted a plan to the Security Council for creation of a Special Commission, which within the next 45 days developed a plan for inspecting all of Iraq's weapons of mass destruction, taking charge of them, and destroying them. By accepting the resolution, Iraq agreed never again to try to develop biological, chemical, or nuclear weapons.[27]

But paper agreement is one thing and actual compliance another. Despite its defeat and its declared adherence to United Nations conditions, Iraq cheated. In the months after the cease-fire, a series of revelations, made grudgingly under threat of renewed military action, revealed the following: a continuing capacity to build nuclear weapons including a stockpile of weapons-grade fissile material, half the prewar chemical stocks, a germ warfare program, and some undestroyed Scud missiles—perhaps as many as 100. Iraq promised to reveal its chemical arsenal and claimed it had fewer than 11,000 shells. Inspectors discovered 46,000.[28]

The case of Iraq involved just the disarmament of just one country. Other countries remained armed and were not panicked by revelations of Iraq's cheating. In the event of general disarmament, a violation by one country might well lead to rearmament by rivals, and however unstable an arms race might be, a rearmament race would be even more unstable. The recent technological arms race was full of uncertainties about what weapons could be built, how well they might work, and what countermeasures the enemy might have. But in a rearmament race, none of these certainties would exist. States would know how to reproduce the weapons they earlier had destroyed, and the first state to rebuild those weapons would be tempted to use them before other states could catch up.

OBSTACLES TO DISARMAMENT: AGREEMENT

Another aspect of the enforcement question is the refusal of some countries to go along with a disarmament agreement. One solution would be to include them by force, going to war if necessary to disarm them. If the countries that refuse to agree are major powers, this course might be unwise. For decades both France and China refused to sign the partial test ban on nuclear weapons. No attempt was made to force them into compliance. Had French or Chinese testing programs ever threatened the security of countries that had signed the treaty, the most likely course would have been for them to break the treaty and resume testing themselves.

Even when the countries that refuse to go along are minor powers, adherence is almost never enforced. The only exceptions occur after a defeat in war. Germany was required to abandon chemical weapons after World War I; Iraq was required to abandon chemical, biological, and nuclear weapons after the Gulf War of 1991.

Otherwise, small states in the exercise of their sovereignty can refuse to go along. Despite alarm about the spread of nuclear weapons, small states such as India, Pakistan, Israel, and South Africa refused to sign the Nuclear Non-Proliferation Treaty of 1968. Often states will argue that such agreements are unfair, because they tend to support the status quo. An Indian diplomat, noting that the Non-Proliferation Treaty did not require the major powers to give up their nuclear weapons, called it an agreement on prohibition dictated by alcoholics.[29] India not only refused to sign it but went ahead and developed its own nuclear explosive device, which it exploded in 1974.

The problem is not a new one. Disarmament proposals in the nineteenth century ran into the same difficulty. Prussia under Bismarck, a country that wanted to change the status quo in the 1870s, resisted the appeals of various disarmament groups most vigorously.[30] Furthermore, even if some of the nineteenth-century proposals had been adopted, they would have permitted colonial wars in the name of maintaining "internal order."[31]

The entrance of former colonial possessions into world politics has compounded the problem of arriving at disarmament agreements. Not all these countries put the avoidance of war at the top of their priorities. Saddam Hussein took Iraq into war against Iran in 1980 and against Kuwait in 1990. Cuba's Che Guevara said in 1962, "We must proceed along the path of liberation, even if that costs millions of atomic victims."[32] Horrifying as that statement might be to Americans, whose own resort to arms for liberation occurred over two centuries ago, it is a reminder that disarmament proposals freezing the status quo will not find universal acceptance.

Because an inferior side is reluctant to make its inferiority permanent, we might expect disarmament to be easiest when two sides approach equality. Unfortunately even this does not always work. The distrust that permeates international relations sometimes makes agreements impossible under the best of circumstances. In 1907 the British were leading in the *Dreadnought* competition, having demonstrated their resolve not to let the Germans or anyone else threaten their naval supremacy. Having made their point, the British offered to cut back on *Dreadnoughts* if other countries would follow. For the Germans this cutback would have been a sensible move because Germany was basically a land power, facing its principal danger from enemies on the continent. But the proponents of the German navy seized on this British initiative to argue their case more fervently. "The British economy must be hurting," they cried. "Now is the time to push harder."[33] Equality or near equality can be as much a spur to increased effort as an incentive to agree.

A greater gap separated the Americans from the rest of the world in 1945, when they alone had atomic weapons. It was thus natural that they viewed their proposal to submit this weapon to international control as a generous move. The US plan, drawn up by Dean Acheson and David Lilienthal but often called the "Baruch Plan" after the man who submitted it, called for establishing an international authority with the right to inspect production facilities around the world. After this authority was in operation, the United States would destroy its atomic weapons. The Russians rejected the Baruch Plan and offered a counterproposal: The United States would destroy its atomic weapons first, and then inspection would be permitted.[34] In each case the proposal was framed in such a way that the other side would have to make the first move in giving up whatever gave it an advantage.

This pattern has been repeated often enough to lead some observers to conclude that disarmament proposals have more often than not simply been moves in the armament game.[35] Eisenhower's "open skies" proposal was one example. The Soviet and American draft treaties on "general and complete disarmament" were another. In the latter case, both countries appeared to be pursuing the same final goal, but the Soviet draft emphasized as a first step eliminating overseas bases (which only the United States had) and the United States draft emphasized inspection (secrecy being more important to the Russians). The problem was often illustrated during the Cold War years by a modern animal fable. The members of the animal kingdom gathered for a disarmament conference. The eagle asked for the abolition of fangs. The lion asked for the abolition of beaks and tusks. The elephant asked for the abolition of talons and teeth. Finally, the bear in tones of sweet reasonableness asked for the abolition of all weapons. Quarrels, he said, should be settled by hugging.[36]

NEW CONDITIONS, NEW OBSTACLES

The record throughout the Cold War years has not been good. With the end of the Cold War, some old obstacles have disappeared but new ones have appeared.

Disarmament comes most easily when driven by market conditions, that is, when states disarm for other reasons, particularly economic ones. Given recent events, suggests John Mueller, states should abandon formal negotiations and let events take their course.[37] For one thing, the process of negotiating formal agreements is very slow. The Non-Proliferation Treaty took six years, the START treaty over nine. For another, the process may even be counterproductive. The existence of negotiations can be used as an argument against reductions. Mueller points out that the United States Congress was seriously considering making unilateral cuts in its troop deployments in Europe in 1973, yet was talked out of it by the argument that it would weaken the US position in the ongoing negotiations. In fact, the argument of negotiations may even be invoked to persuade legislatures to add unnecessary weapons to the arsenal as "bargaining chips." These are weapons built only to be traded away. At least some people have seen the various missile defense programs—ABM, SDI—primarily as bargaining chips.

Furthermore, Mueller argues, arms control and disarmament agreements are not necessarily the optimal solution to the problem of arms. They are a type of centralized regulation, and like all centralized regulations, they are unable to make subtle adjustments to unanticipated changes. The United States, under provisions of the INF treaty, eliminated all its land-based cruise missiles and thus did not have any to use in the Gulf War. The spectacular performance of the sea-based missiles was credited with making the war as short as it was. The absence of land-based cruise missiles was a handicap.

Finally, Mueller argues, history suggests that formal agreements may not be necessary. He cites the history of the United States and Canada. The Rush–Bagot agreement of 1817 was the last agreement to be signed, and it did not end hostilities. Finally, beginning about 1870, Canada and the United States began to demilitarize their border without an agreement.

Even as Mueller was writing, states were beginning to make unilateral cuts. The United States Department of Energy closed one of its weapons fabrication plants for safety reasons. This meant that the new Trident submarines would go to sea with less than a full complement of their missiles. Although arms agreements would permit them to carry 192 warheads, for purely domestic reasons they would carry fewer.[38] The United States Navy had already begun to phase out some of its nuclear-armed antiaircraft and antisubmarine weapons.

Implicitly other states were following the same path in some regards. The Treaty on Conventional Forces in Europe called only for cuts in weapons and equipment, not in personnel. But the numbers of personnel were simultaneously being reduced spontaneously and unilaterally by members of NATO and former members of the Warsaw Pact (which had itself been disbanded in March of 1991).

President Bush moved from implicit to explicit unilateral disarmament by announcing in September of 1991 that the United States would take strategic bombers off alert status and retire many categories of tactical nuclear weapons. The reasons given by the White House were in line with Mueller's thinking—that negotiations would only delay the process, that the Soviet Union had already signaled that it wanted this step and would be sure to respond in kind. The Bush Administration kept its announcement secret until the last minute, to keep opponents within the US government from mobilizing to oppose the unilateral cuts.

The rapid progress in disarmament illustrated a fundamental truth about international politics. When conditions are not ripe, there is not much point in putting effort into crafting the perfect disarmament proposal. Proposals fail not because of specific provisions but in the political conditions of world politics.

The changed conditions in world politics changed some states' definitions of their interests. One of the major problems with arms races is accelerating costs. Nowhere is this more apparent than in the cost of aircraft. In wrestling with its military budget, the United States tried to deal with several programs for "the next generation" of fighters. The Air Force's advanced fighter aircraft program, the F-22, would cost $95 billion for 650 planes, or $146 million apiece.

Advanced fighter aircraft seem like a good candidate for an arms control agreement. All countries could agree not to pursue such expensive programs, thereby saving everybody a lot of money. The traditional argument of a Soviet threat no longer is convincing. But as the old argument for buying such weapons disappeared, a new one appeared. It was precisely such high-performance aircraft that allowed the United States to triumph so easily over Saddam Hussein. Without continued development in this area, eventually that advantage would fade. Continuing to arm thus seems like a better guarantee of keeping the peace than disarmament. Furthermore, American weapons are superior and highly sought after in world markets. From 1974 to 1989, the oil-producing countries of the Middle East purchased $220 to $250 billion worth of weapons.[39] By agreeing not to develop an advanced fighter, the United States would be denying itself a much needed commercial advantage.

Even if several countries agreed, countries would be tempted to defect. The situation would resemble Rousseau's stag hunt. The profits from cheating would be great, and if cheating occurred, eventually another ruler like Saddam Hussein might confront the United States with superior weapons. Thus the same logic that leads states to arm against each other can be used even in time of peace to justify continued arms expenditure.

THE EVOLUTION OF COOPERATION

Although an advocate of disarmament might be encouraged by the sudden burst of progress in disarmament agreements between the United States and its major rival, a skeptic might instead point to the long time it took them to make progress. Even as the two major world rivals were beginning to reduce their arms, other countries continued to compete in arms. Furthermore, a skeptic might argue, it would be rash to assume that the United States will never again face a military rival, or that Russia has permanently disappeared from the ranks of the major powers. Those who are cautious about declaring the arms race permanently over point out that Germany went from a divided and economically ruined country in the 1920s to a military power by the end of the 1930s.

If the world returns to an arms race between superpowers, recent treaties and agreements will be held up as examples that disarmament is possible. Further buttressing this recent historical experience is experimental evidence that suggests that rivals still in the middle of competition may learn to cooperate.[40] The experiments involved not people but computer programs. They were all designed to play a game commonly used in simulations called "Prisoner's Dilemma." The name derives from a supposed bargain a jailer once made separately with each of two male prisoners held for jointly committing a crime. To each the jailer said, "If you confess before your accomplice does, I'll give you one thousand dollars (your accomplice will hang); if you confess at the same time as your accomplice does, you'll both go to jail; if neither of you confesses, you'll both go free." The prisoner understood that the same bargain would be offered to the other, so if he failed to confess but his accomplice did, he would hang and his accomplice would get the reward.

The game is intriguing because a rational decision by each prisoner leads to an irrational choice for both. The first prisoner calculates: "What if the other prisoner holds out? Then if I confess, I get one thousand dollars. If I hold out, I go free." Clearly $1,000 is better than just going free, so in this case, confessing is better. The first prisoner calculates: "What if the other prisoner confesses? Then if I confess I go to jail. If I hold out, I hang." Clearly going to jail is better than hanging, so in this case as well, confessing is better. No matter what the other prisoner does, confessing is better. The other prisoner calculates the same way, both confess and both go to jail—which is clearly less desirable than both going free. Thus apparently faultless reasoning leads to an apparently faulty conclusion.

Without interfering with the game's logic, the payoffs in Prisoner's Dilemma can be reduced to numerical point values, with 5 replacing $1,000, 3 replacing freedom, 1 replacing jail, and 0 replacing hanging. Replacing the drastic penalty of hanging with a point value means the game can be played more than once, and when it can, the logic changes too. If the numbers (5, 3, and so on) represent dollars, the goal of repeated games is to win as much as possible, and one can do that by cooperating with the other player (what was called "holding out" in the original game) more easily than by defecting from the other player (what was called "confessing"). Even an occasional defection (which might yield 5 points to the defector, with the opponent scoring 0 for that round) would not be a good strategy in the long run, because the opponent could retaliate and both scores would stay low.

Using repeated plays of Prisoner's Dilemma (about 200 games between each pair of opponents), Robert Axelrod organized a tourney conducted on a computer. Each entrant submitted a program telling the computer how to play. Points were awarded on a numerical system and the winner was the person whose program had the most points after it had played all rivals. Some astonishing and entirely unforeseen results emerged: One strategy was the undisputed winner. It won the preliminary round, it won the next round, and then, even after competitors knew the winning plan and had time to design strategies against it, it won the final round, against 62 competing strategies. Furthermore, it was the simplest of all the strategies submitted, requiring just five lines of computer code. The winning strategy was: Cooperate on the first move, then for each subsequent move do exactly what the other player did on the preceding move.

The strategy was submitted by an expert on game theory, Anatol Rapoport, and was called "Tit for Tat." Although it had a quality known as being "nice"—that is, it never sought advantage by being the first to defect—it was not a pacifist strategy. Tit for Tat called for instant retaliation—if the other player defected on one move, the player using Tit for Tat defected on the very next move, without fail. More charitable strategies entered in the tourney did not do well, because some "nasty" strategies were able to exploit them. Failing to retaliate instantly—for example, in a strategy with the self-explanatory title "A Tit for Two Tats," tempted opponents to exploit the strategy by repeated defections.

The tourney is described in Robert Axelrod's book *The Evolution of Cooperation*.[41] The book reports many other discoveries as well and has stimulated research to see how well the strategy applies to various real-life situations.[42] The book suggests that enemies can learn to cooperate under certain conditions, but following the correct strategy is a very important condition. Prescriptions such as "turn the other cheek" or "do unto others as you would have them do unto you" do not stand up as well as the simple rule, "first be nice, then reciprocate."

In several of the ongoing disputes in the world (Arab states and Israel or Pakistan and India, for example) the strategy explored by Axelrod may contain helpful lessons. But new problems arise when states consider the total elimination of the most fearsome weapons in their arsenal. It is often said that nuclear weapons have transformed warfare. They also have transformed attempts to achieve peace. They are so different that they deserve consideration in a separate chapter.

NOTES

1. Cited by Theodore Shabad, "An American Asks Cut in Arms Race," *The New York Times*, October 31, 1971.

2. Alton Frye, "Zero Ballistic Missiles," *Foreign Policy*, No. 88 (Fall 1992), pp. 3–20.

3. Merze Tate, *The Disarmament Illusion* (New York: Macmillan, 1942), pp. 66–67.

4. Francis P. Walters, *A History of the League of Nations*, Vol. I (London: Oxford University Press, 1952), p. 440.

5. "U.N. Bids the Big Five Cut Arms Budgets to Aid Poor Nations," *The New York Times*, December 8, 1973.

6. *The Economist*, January 28, 1989, p. 46.

7. Peter Grose, "$3.4 Billion Surplus Arms Given to Allies in 19 Years," *The New York Times*, March 30, 1970.

8. Tim Ahern, "Public Kept in the Dark on $25 Billion for Defense," *The Washington Post*, January 15, 1987, p. A19.

9. David Binder, "Eight Latin Nations Declare Intention to Limit Arms," *The New York Times*, December 13, 1974; Marvine Howe, "A Big Latin Arms Pact That May Signify Little," *The New York Times*, February 16, 1975; Alan Riding, "Mexicans Proposing Cuts in Latin Arms," *The New York Times*, December 27, 1978.

10. The better-known passage is Isaiah 2:4; it is reversed in Joel 3:10.

11. These conferences are described in Tate. (See note 2.)

12. James Eayrs, "Arms Control on the Great Lakes," *Disarmament and Arms Control*, Vol. 2, No. 4 (Autumn 1964), pp. 372–404; Trevor N. Dupuy and Gay M. Hammerman, eds., *A Documentary History of Arms Control and Disarmament* (New York: R. R. Bowker, 1973), p. 39.

13. Philip Noel-Baker, *The Arms Race* (New York: Oceana Publications, 1958), p. 86.

14. Hedley Bull, "Disarmament and the International System," (review of Philip Noel-Baker, *The Arms Race*), *Australian Journal of Politics and History*, Vol. 1, (May 1959).

15. Hedley Bull, *Strategic Arms Limitation: The Precedent of the Washington and London Naval Treaties*, Occasional Paper, Center for Policy Study (Chicago, 1971), p. 31.

16. Robert Shaplen, "From MacArthur to Miki," *The New Yorker*, August 4, 1975, p. 72.

17. Dupuy and Hammerman, eds., pp. 494ff. (See note 11.)

18. In an address December 10, 1987, after the Washington summit, Reagan referred to "our goal, first agreed to at Geneva to achieve deep, 50% cuts." United States Department of State, *Current Policy*, No. 1032.

19. R. W. Apple, Jr., "Bush and Gorbachev Sign Pact," *The New York Times*, August 1, 1991, p. A1.

20. R. H. S. Stolfi, "Equipment for Victory in France in 1940," *History*, Vol. 55, No. 183 (February 1970), pp. 1–20.

21. International Institute of Strategic Studies, *The Military Balance 1987–1988* (London: International Institute of Strategic Studies, Autumn 1987) "The Conventional Forces of NATO and the Warsaw Pact" (pp. 226–234); Malcolm Chalmers and Lutz Unterseher, "Is There a Tank Gap?" *International Security*, Vol. 13, No. 1 (Summer 1988) p. 8.

22. Daniel Yankelovich and Richard Smoke, "America's 'New Thinking,' " *Foreign Affairs*, Vol. 67, No. 1, (Fall 1988), p. 11.

23. Mikhail Gorbachev, *Perestroika: New Thinking for Our Country and the World* (New York: Harper & Row/A Cornelia & Michael Bessie Book, 1987), p. 203.

24. Angelo del Boca, *The Ethiopian War, 1935–1941* (Chicago: University of Chicago Press, 1965), pp. 80–81.

25. Allan Bullock, *Hitler*, rev. ed. (New York: Harper & Row, 1962), p. 447.

26. *The New York Times*, January 18, 1970.

27. Paul Lewis, "Iraq Approval Starts Peace Schedule," *The New York Times*, April 7, 1991, p. Y12.

28. Leslie H. Gelb, "Foreign Affairs: Mr. Bush's Nightmare," [Op-Ed], *The New York Times*, July 31, 1991, p. Z A17; *The Economist*, August 17, 1991, p. 37.

29. Mr. Trivedi, delegate of India to Geneva, quoted in *The Economist*, February 19, 1966, p. 687.

30. Tate, p. 21. (See note 2.)

31. See the summary in Bull, "Disarmament and the International System." (See note 13.)

32. *Verde Olivo*, October 6, 1968, quoted by Hugh Thomas, *Cuba* (New York: Harper & Row, 1971), p. 1,470.

33. Tate, p. 353. (See note 2.)

34. See the summary in Bull, "Disarmament and the International System." (See note 13.)

35. For example, John W. Spanier and Joseph L. Nogee, *The Politics of Disarmament: A Study in Soviet–American Gamesmanship* (New York: Frederick A. Praeger, 1962).

36. This fable has been attributed both to Salvadore de Madariga and to Winston Churchill.

37. John Mueller, "A New Concert of Europe," *Foreign Policy*, No. 77 (Winter 1989/90), pp. 5–9.

38. "Shortage of Warheads Means Subs Won't Be Fully Armed," *The New York Times*, May 19, 1991, p. Y11.

39. Alvin Z. Rubinstein, "After the Gulf War," *Foreign Affairs*, Vol. 70, No. 4 (Fall 1991), p. 64.

40. Robert Axelrod, *The Evolution of Cooperation* (New York: Basic Books, 1984).

41. Ibid.

42. For example, the entire issue of *World Politics*, Vol. 38. No. 1 (October 1985).

CHAPTER 11

NUCLEAR WEAPONS

The assumption behind armaments as an approach to peace is *si vis pacem para bellum*, "If you want peace, prepare for war." Potential aggressors will then not start wars because they would fear losing. Another approach to peace is to make war so horrible that states fear not simply losing a war but getting into one in the first place no matter how it turns out. Alfred Nobel, the inventor of dynamite, made this argument in the last century. In 1892 he told a leading organizer of disarmament conferences: "Perhaps my factories will put an end to war even sooner than your Congresses; on the day that two army corps may mutually annihilate each other in a second, probably all civilized nations will recoil with horror and disband their troops."[1] Alfred Nobel was speaking long before the advent of nuclear weapons. Such weapons make his arguments even more compelling.

THE NATURE OF NUCLEAR WEAPONS

We usually fix the beginning of the atomic age at July 16, 1945, when the first bomb was exploded at a test site near Alamogordo, New Mexico. There had been revolutionary innovations in military technology in the past, from gunpowder to the airplane. With each new development it took time before the effects of the new weapons were recognized and taken into account in strategic planning. Atomic weapons were assimilated more quickly. Within a few weeks after the first test they were used for all the world to see, with apparently decisive effects. Thinking and planning immediately began to take account of them.

The bomb exploded on July 16, 1945, was technically a *fission* weapon. It depended for its explosive force on a rapid chain reaction set off by splitting heavy elements, either a naturally occurring radioactive isotope of uranium (U-235) or an artificial element (plutonium) that is made by placing normal uranium in a reactor with an excess of neutrons. The theory of how to produce an atomic explosion was already clear in 1938 from work done by German scientists. The difficult part was producing enough fuel, either enriched uranium (U-235) or plutonium, to produce a bomb. It is estimated that by the closing years of World War II, 10 percent of the electrical capacity of the United States was going to produce material for the atomic bombs.[2]

The bombs were so powerful that a new measure of explosive power was needed to describe them. The standard used was the equivalent of 1 ton of TNT, the stuff of which World War II bombs were made. The big bombs of World War II, known as *blockbusters*, contained about a ton of TNT. In the 1970s the biggest TNT bomb was 7.5 tons, so large it had to be rolled out the door of a cargo plane. The atomic bombs were measured in terms of *thousands* of tons of TNT. The basic unit of measurement was called a *kiloton*, equal to 1,000 tons of TNT. The test bomb at Alamogordo had a force of 19,000 tons of TNT, or 19 kilotons; the Hiroshima bomb, 14 kilotons; the Nagasaki bomb, 20 kilotons.[3]

Powerful as these bombs were, they were nowhere close to the most powerful explosive that scientists could think of. The fission or splitting of heavy atoms releases only a fraction of the energy released by another process, the *fusion* or combining of light atoms. This process, similar to what goes on inside the sun, is clean. Unlike fission it produces no long-lasting radioactive particles. The major obstacle to achieving a fusion reaction is that starting it requires very high temperatures. The fusion bomb, originally called the "hydrogen bomb" because of the light elements used in it, is now usually referred to as a "thermonuclear weapon," because of the high temperatures needed to begin the fusion. So far, the only way we have to achieve these high temperatures is by a fission reaction. In other words, the fusion bomb needs an atomic bomb as a trigger, and this trigger will produce long-lasting radiation, called "fallout," even if the fusion reaction itself does not.

The first thermonuclear device tested by the United States, on November 1, 1952, vaporized the small Pacific island on which it was detonated and left in its place a crater 1 mile across. The great increase in power of this weapon over the atomic bomb called for still another measure of explosive power—the equivalent of 1 *million* tons of TNT, or 1 megaton. The test explosion of November 1952 had a force of 20 million tons of TNT, or 20 megatons. The biggest bomb ever tested was exploded by the Russians in 1961; it had a force of 58 megatons.

THE DIFFERENCE THAT NUCLEAR WEAPONS MADE

Politicians and commentators are tireless in telling us that nuclear weapons radically changed international politics. Undeniably they did, but it is important to be clear about exactly how they did it. The idea that first comes to mind is their destructive power. Without minimizing this destructive capacity, however, we must point out that the destruction caused by the atomic bombs was not so much greater than that of TNT weapons. Many people were killed by the atomic bombs—70,000 at Hiroshima, 35,000 at Nagasaki—but these attacks were not the most destructive air raids of World War II. The raid on Tokyo of May 1945 killed 84,000 with TNT bombs and fire bombs. It would have taken at least 400 atomic bombs to equal the amount of damage that TNT bombs did to Germany during World War II and between 800 and 1,200 atomic bombs to do as much damage to the Soviet Union as German forces did during World War II.[4] Granted that 400 bombs are far fewer than the number of TNT bombs actually dropped, it is at the same time a long way from saying that one atomic bomb equals all the bombs dropped during World War II.

It was the introduction of the fusion bomb in 1952 that brought a truly horrifying level of destruction. We think of a normal fusion bomb as being about 1 megaton. The radius of destruction of such a bomb is great; near misses are the same as direct hits. A 1-megaton bomb would destroy brick structures out to a distance of 3.5 miles; it would ignite most fabrics and paper out to 6 miles; it would cause second-degree burns out to 11 miles.[5] You can visualize this by picking a spot 11 miles from your home. If a 1-megaton thermonuclear bomb went off over your home and you were standing out in the open at that spot 11 miles away, you would suffer painful burns on your exposed skin.

But still, we must guard against exaggerating the power of these weapons. Because we express their power in terms of TNT, we can be misled by too close an analogy with TNT. Suppose we are trying to visualize a 20-megaton bomb (a large weapon, but one that can be carried by a single intercontinental missile). By "20 megatons" we mean the equivalent of 20 million tons of TNT. The average railroad boxcar holds 80,000 pounds of goods, or 40 tons. It would take 500,000 boxcars to hold the 20 million tons of TNT. Each boxcar is 40 feet long, so we would have a train 20 million feet long, or 3,788 miles. The rail distance from Los Angeles to New York is 3,082 miles. Thus we can say that a 20-megaton bomb would be more powerful than the TNT in a train stretching from one end of the country to the other.

Vivid as it is, this metaphor is misleading. In fact the damage from one 20-megaton bomb would be nowhere nearly equivalent to the damage our hypothetical freight train could do. A thermonuclear bomb would over-destroy a very small area: It would expend most of its energy in pulverizing and vaporizing the few thousand square feet directly beneath it. The amount of damage would rapidly diminish farther from the center of the explosion. Furthermore, because the explosive force is exerted in all directions (that is, the explosion is spherical), a lot of the power goes up and out into the atmosphere. The characteristic mushroom cloud represents wasted energy. For this reason, even though the bomb dropped on Hiroshima was one thousand times as big as a World War II blockbuster, the area it destroyed was only one hundred times as great.

Having all this power packed into one bomb is not as destructive as having it spread out, say among twenty bombs of 1 megaton each. Another important point is that having bombs of any size stored in a bunker is not the same as having useful military weapons. Without effective delivery systems, these nuclear bombs are useless. This important fact is often obscured by the misleading term "overkill." People who use the word seem to mean some-thing like this: The world has 3.5 billion people. If you add up the megaton-nage of all the strategic nuclear weapons the United States has, you get a total of perhaps 35,000 megatons. Therefore, we have the equivalent of 10 tons of TNT for every man, woman, and child in the world. Because 1 ton of TNT is more than enough to kill, we supposedly have an overkill capacity.

This sounds impressive, until you consider that in World War I the world had 1.8 billion people and the battling armies were equipped with at least 9 billion rifle bullets, or an overkill of five bullets for every man, woman, and child in the world. Put this way, overkill does not seem so useful a concept. Many steps intervene between the weapon stored in the arsenal (whether a bullet or a nuclear bomb) and actual destruction. The weapon must be loaded and fired. It must travel with enough power and accuracy to hit its target. It must penetrate active and passive defenses. It must not be wasted by hitting a target already destroyed. At any of these points a weapon can fail, and that is just as true of intercontinental ballistic missiles as of rifle bullets. Adding more missiles to a country's strategic arsenal is not necessarily more wasteful than adding an extra clip of rifle bullets to an infantry soldier's ammunition belt.

This is not to say that nuclear weapons make no difference at all. They certainly do, but the difference lies in areas other than sheer destructive power. One important difference is the speed with which the destruction can be accomplished. Even if it would have taken four hundred atomic bombs to equal the destruction inflicted on Germany in World War II, atomic weapons would have greatly speeded up the work. The conventional bombing of

Germany went on for five years; the four hundred atomic bombs could conceivably have been dropped in one night.

The overkill capacity in rifle bullets would have enabled the French to kill all the inhabitants of Germany once the German army quit fighting in 1918. As far as that goes, they could have killed them all with just one bayonet. But that would have taken a long time. It would have required deliberate planning. With nuclear weapons the population of Germany could be exterminated in a few minutes, even by accident, without any personal involvement by those doing the exterminating.[6]

We use the phrase "psychological distance" to describe our way of engaging in morally repugnant acts without feeling personally involved. Killing a rabbit with our natural weapons—teeth and fingernails—would be difficult for most people. Using a rifle makes it a lot easier because we can emotionally separate the squeezing of the trigger finger from the death of the rabbit. When the victim fades into total invisibility, killing becomes even easier. During the Vietnam War, helicopter pilots described strafing runs as shooting at little cloth dummies on the ground below. Yet a B-52 pilot, who normally bombed at a height so great that the plane was not visible from the ground, was horrified when he accompanied a friend on a helicopter gunship. "How can you stand to do this?" he asked. "You can actually see the people you are shooting!" Nuclear weapons, launched by an electronic signal given hundreds of miles from the missile silo and carried thousands of miles by intercontinental missiles, provide the ultimate in psychological distance.[7]

It is common to say that nuclear weapons add a new dimension to the strength of states, greatly increasing their power. In fact the overall effect is the opposite, making states as a group weaker, not stronger. States today are less able to do one of the important things that states are supposed to do: provide security for their inhabitants. The reason is that nuclear weapons give a great advantage to the offensive side.

It is sometimes said that for every offensive weapon, a defensive weapon is eventually developed. Actually, defensive weapons have never been very good. Defense was possible because offensive weapons weren't too good either. Armor could be penetrated by arrows, but arrows weren't always fatal even when they did penetrate. In 1940, during the Battle of Britain, the Royal Air Force defeated the German Luftwaffe by destroying only about 10 percent of the German planes in each raid. Because TNT bombs were not that destructive against cities, an attrition rate of 10 percent was enough to provide effective defense. Against nuclear weapons, however, an attrition rate of even 95 percent would be useless. Because defensive weapons can do so little, nuclear war cannot be kept away from cities and civilians. No longer would the outcome of a battlefield struggle among military specialists determine the fate of cities and civilians. The cities and civilians are available as targets for military operations from the inception of the war.

DETERRENCE

One result is that strategy today is not adequately described by the words "defense" and "offense." Strategic thinkers have had to develop new terms. A major distinction employed today is between "defense" and "deterrence." A practical example will show how they differ in meaning. Suppose I want to protect a sum of money. One way of doing it would be to make it physically impossible for someone else to take it. I could put it in a safe or I could stand over it with a pitchfork and jab at anyone who came near. The physical denial of some value to an opponent is what strategists mean by defense. Another way of protecting my money would be to stand over it with a cup of hot coffee in my hand, threatening to throw the coffee on anyone trying to take the money. In this case I am not making it physically impossible to take the money (the hot coffee would hurt but not disable); instead, I am trying to influence the mental calculations of a potential thief. If I am successful, then I have established a psychological relationship that strategists call deterrence.

Defense is *physical*. It goes into operation when war breaks out. For example, tanks move to the frontier, making it physically impossible for the enemy to advance. Deterrence is *psychological*, useful before war breaks out. It keeps the enemy from moving in the first place. In fact, once war has broken out, deterrence has failed; defense must take over.

In April 1969, the North Koreans shot down a US electronic intelligence plane flying off their coast. President Nixon wanted to protect planes on similar missions in the future. What deterrent measure could he have taken and what defensive measure? Keeping in mind that deterrence is psychological (working on the other side's mind), you might say that a deterrent measure would be some kind of warning, such as, "If you shoot down another plane, we will bomb Wonsan Harbor." If you remember that defense is a physical measure, you might suggest sending along fighter planes as escorts that can physically interpose themselves between intelligence planes and attacking North Korean fighters.

Measures designed for defense can also deter. The pitchfork that I wave over my pile of money, although a physical measure itself, will probably discourage anyone from trying to steal the bills. Fighter escorts for intelligence planes have a deterrent effect, often making it unnecessary for them to actually defend the planes they are escorting. This combination of defense and deterrence has been the rule throughout military history. Only recently have these two functions begun to separate. That is another important difference between the nuclear age and the nonnuclear age. Today we invest great sums in weapons that are designed for deterrence only; they have no value at all for defense. This condition is unlike anything we have had in the past.

In the past, a strong tank force might have had a deterrent effect, but if deterrence failed and an invasion began, that same tank force could defend the country. An ICBM force with nuclear warheads of megaton strength has only deterrent value; it can provide no defense. If war breaks out and an enemy attacks, will any American lives be saved if missiles are fired back? The answer is no. If war breaks out, deterrence has failed, and the sole reason for the existence of the missiles disappears.

If our missiles could in some way destroy enemy missiles on the ground before they were launched, that of course would be defense. When the enemy launches a massive attack and no targets are left, our missiles would lose their purpose. Or if we expect a war to last for years, then the destruction of the enemy's industrial capacity might physically impair the enemy's ability to attack us. But the kind of war in which we expect these missiles to be launched is the kind we expect to last at most a few days.

Once the capabilities and limitations of nuclear weapons became clear, it became necessary to work out new strategic doctrines, that is, guidelines on how to use the weapons. In the past, military strategy had been straightforward. Weapons deterred enemy aggression before war broke out and defended against that aggression if deterrence failed. In the nuclear age states had to choose between the two goals—deterrence or defense—and build weapons accordingly.

MINIMUM DETERRENCE

When both sides possess enormous means of destruction, the traditional fear of losing a war is joined by a second fear, that of ever getting into a war in the first place. Norman Cousins articulated this idea in 1961: "Nations no longer declare war or wage war, they declare or wage mutual suicide."[8] This unpleasant state of affairs has come to be known as the *balance of terror*.

With time, however, some people began to see positive aspects in such a balance. The balance of terror is maintained by deterrent weapons. If they fail to deter war, they are of no further use; they cannot be used for defense. Because they are not needed to fight enemy weapons, there is no need for superiority or even equality in numbers of weapons. All a strategist has to do is calculate the minimum level of force needed to deter.

Secretary of Defense McNamara suggested that the United States need only be able to inflict "unacceptable damage" on the Soviet Union to keep it from starting a war. Perhaps the Soviets themselves would find it hard to say exactly what theoretical level of damage they would find unacceptable, but McNamara estimated it conservatively at from 20 to 25 percent of the population and 50 percent of industrial capacity. In other words, any Soviet leaders mad enough to risk 25 percent of the Soviet population would be so mad that no further amount of damage could deter them, not 30 percent or 35 percent or whatever was attainable.

McNamara had his experts calculate the number of weapons needed to inflict various levels of damage on the Soviet Union (see Table 11.1). They found that with only 400 warheads the United States could be sure of destroying 30 percent of the Soviet population and 76 percent of its industrial capacity. Because the United States already had warheads far in excess of this number (by the 1960s, well over 10,000), no more were needed. A build-up in Soviet arms did not need to be matched by adding more US arms. If the Soviets persisted in adding more, it was only a waste of money. Once they had obtained the ability to inflict unacceptable damage on us, extra weapons did them no more good than they did us.

McNamara made it clear that the ability to inflict unacceptable damage has to be assured. If exactly 400 warheads were needed to inflict predicted levels of damage, then the United States would need more than 400 weapons in its arsenal to allow for failures in launching, weapons off course, and possible Soviet defensive measures. We even allowed for the number of weapons that could be destroyed if the Soviet Union fired first in an effort to wipe out as many of our weapons as it could. McNamara's doctrine of assured destruction called for adequate numbers of weapons landing on Soviet targets even after a disarming first strike.

McNamara's doctrine of assured destruction is one example of a type of strategic theory known as "finite deterrence." All such theories share the assumption that once a given level of deterrent weapons is reached, no more are necessary. Theorists differ on what the level should be. Secretary McNamara set it at from 20 to 30 percent of population and 50 percent of industry. McGeorge Bundy, former national security adviser, implied that it could be set much lower when he stated, "One bomb on a city would be a catastrophe without precedent."[9]

Table 11.1   WARHEADS AND CALCULATED LEVELS OF DAMAGE

1-Megaton Warhead (or Equivalent) Delivered to Target	Percentage of Population Killed	Percentage of Industry Destroyed
100	15	59
200	21	72
400	30	76
800	39	77
1,200	44	77
1,600	47	77

Source: Data from U.S. Congress, House, Committee on Armed Services, *Hearings on Military Posture*, 90th Cong., 2nd sess., April 3–27, 1968, p. 8507.

The theory implies that more than the minimum is actually bad, because excessive levels might suggest to the other side that we are not interested simply in deterring war. They might believe we are building toward a disarming first strike. This belief would impel them to engage in more building of their own and so fuel an arms race. Advocates of finite deterrence believe that the disarming first strike is an unattainable goal in any case and building arsenals with this aim, in addition to risking war, wastes money.

MAD AND ITS CRITICS

Advocates of finite deterrence hoped that both sides would adhere to their doctrine. They preferred *mutual assured destruction*, a term their opponents shortened to MAD. Proponents of MAD admitted that some of the implications of their basic premise contradicted customary ways of thinking and required some reflection before they could be accepted. What was mad, they argued, was not the doctrine but the situation into which nuclear weapons forced the world.

One implication was that any weapon that made it rational to strike first was a bad weapon. But this implication led to the belief that many defensive weapons were bad. For example, an effective defense against ICBM's, if possessed by only one side, would allow that side to attack an opponent without fear of retaliation. Because defensive weapons were believed to undermine deterrence, advocates of MAD opposed missile defense systems. For similar reasons they opposed efforts to improve civil defense. Logically, defensive systems would not make it rational to strike first if both sides possessed them, but advocates of MAD feared that one side might think it had gained a temporary advantage at some point and be tempted to use its brief invulnerability to strike first.

Another disturbing implication was that weapons intended to destroy other weapons are bad, but weapons intended to destroy people are good. The essence of finite deterrence was that populations must be exposed to retaliatory attack—in effect, held hostage. To hold them hostage, weapons must be aimed at them. Because cities are large and unprotected targets, missiles targeted on them need not be very big or very accurate. The sorts of missiles carried originally carried on submarines were quite sufficient for destroying cities even though they were small and inaccurate. On the other hand, any missile that was large or accurate could be used to disarm an opponent by striking first, and for this reason such weapons were opposed by advocates of MAD.

Finite deterrence was not without its critics. Their major objection to the doctrine was that the damage of an attack of cities was so great that it could only be threatened as a reprisal for the worst possibilities—a major attack on the United States itself. For any lesser attack the threat would not be credible.

But no one believed an all-out attack by the Soviet Union on the United States was very likely, even at the height of the Cold War. Much more likely were small threats to vital interests, such as seizure of oil fields in the North Sea, or piecemeal attacks, such as the takeover of West Berlin. A doctrine of finite deterrence could not deter such attacks. A country relying solely on finite deterrence would be at the mercy of another country with conventional superiority.

As the Soviet Union continued to add big and accurate missiles to its arsenal, some analysts even wondered if finite deterrence could deter an all-out attack on the United States. They worked out elaborate calculations showing how in certain circumstances the Soviet Union could strike first and do enough damage to US forces that the President might hesitate to order a retaliatory strike. One of the premises of finite deterrence was that the minimum force, whatever it was, had to be survivable, and in the 1980s some doubts were being raised about the ability of US forces to survive if attacked first.

Many critics of finite deterrence preferred a doctrine of damage limitation. Such a doctrine hoped to rely on a combination of measures. Active defenses, such as antiballistic missiles, would limit if not totally prevent damage to society if deterrence should fail. They would be supplemented by passive defense, such as blast and fallout shelters, hardening and dispersal of industry, and evacuation plans. In addition, a country should acquire offense weapons with warheads accurate enough to destroy enemy weapons without causing excessive damage to civilians. Under this doctrine, war would be fought in the way wars were fought in the past. The main targets would be enemy weapons (counterforce targeting), not enemy civilians (countercity or countervalue targeting).[10]

Advocates of damage limitation believed that their proposals would strengthen deterrence by making it credible. What good would the rival doctrine of finite deterrence do if the Soviet Army suddenly moved into Western Europe? Even when faced with a challenge this big, the United States would not use a handful of missiles to destroy Russian cities, knowing that all it would get in return would be the destruction of its own cities. In their view, their doctrine expanded the options from a simple choice between giving in or fighting an all-out war to a range that included limited war, perhaps confined to attacks on military bases or strategic resources.

Advocates of MAD came back with criticisms of damage limitation. One was cost. One advantage of finite deterrence was that once a state had enough weapons, it had no need to concern itself with the number its enemies had. If 400 missiles would do the job, it did not matter if a rival had 1,400 (provided, of course, those 400 could not be wiped out in a first strike). Damage limitation, by contrast had no limits. Every enemy move had to be met by a countermove. Every new enemy missile meant several new offensive missiles to take it out in a first strike or several new antimissile missiles to knock it down if the enemy used it in a first strike.

Another criticism was that it would not work. The idea of meaningful damage limitation would be an illusion. An ABM system would have to work perfectly, 24 hours a day, 365 days a year. A single ICBM warhead eluding an ABM system would cause unprecedented damage. Civil defense would not make much difference. American cities can barely cope with the daily commute on their highways. An attempt at total evacuation would be hopeless. Even after a successful evacuation, the small towns and rural areas could not hope to supply food for more than a brief period.

Finally, critics accepted the arguments of the advocates of damage limitation that it was more credible and precisely for that reason made war more likely. In times of crisis, one side or the other might be tempted to try to use nuclear weapons because their calculations told them they would emerge with less damage.

FINITE DETERRENCE'S LOGICAL EXTREME: NUCLEAR WINTER

During the 1980s each of these two strategic doctrines was pushed to its logical extreme, finite deterrence by the specter of *nuclear winter* and damage limitation by the fantasy of the Strategic Defense Initiative.

You recall that deterrence works to inhibit aggression by instilling fear; nuclear deterrence works by instilling fear of nuclear war. Believers in the strategic doctrine of finite deterrence postulate that a state can create that fear by arming to some fixed level of forces and then stopping. They concede that a state must still take some active steps to create a deterrence capability and must constantly look to its deterrent forces to make sure they remain invulnerable.

Theoretically, finite deterrence should be cheaper than damage limitation. In practice, we have experienced repeated requests for military spending in the name of "defending the deterrent"—for an ABM system, for multiple warheads, for a mobile ICBM, for longer-range submarine-launched missiles, and more. Some of these weapons have been acquired by the United States.

But at some level, weapons purchased in the name of finite deterrence begin to look like preparations for damage limitation. The original idea of a "balance of terror," in which each side was more afraid of nuclear war itself than of a potential aggressor, has faded. Even President Carter, an advocate of eliminating all nuclear weapons, approved a strategy that accepted nuclear weapons as usable in some circumstances and, despite his declared intentions, ended up increasing military spending.

This perpetual call for military expenditures drew fire from critics of the "mad momentum of the arms race."[11] They continued to argue that some minimum was adequate, and that minimum could be far below the numbers now in our possession. The 13,000 nuclear warheads in US hands and the 11,000 in Soviet hands were far in excess of the 100 or so that had been deemed adequate when the United States–Soviet rivalry began. The words of John Kennedy's national security adviser continued to be quoted: "One bomb on a city would be catastrophe without precedent."[12]

The logical conclusion of such thinking was the hope that a country would be deterred by the use of any nuclear weapons, even its own. In 1983, several scientists claimed to have found a reason for just such fear in the form of the effects of nuclear war on climate.[13] Pulling together existing studies in diverse fields, they concluded that nuclear weapons exploded during war would set massive fires, both in forests and urban areas. These fires would produce smoke and soot, which the intense heat of combustion would drive up into the stratosphere. Once the soot reached such altitudes, natural forces such as rain would not wash it down and it could be expected to stay for a year or more, drifting around the earth and blocking out sunlight. Loss of sunlight would produce a sudden and profound cooling of the earth's surface, with temperatures in the northern hemisphere in summer dropping an average of 25°C (equivalent to a drop from 75°F to 32°F).[14] Because this is the normal difference between summer and winter, nuclear war would thus produce a *nuclear winter*. Crops would fail, animals would die, rivers and lakes would freeze. Some even suggested life itself would be endangered.[15]

The argument, as scientists recognized at the time, rested on uncertainties. Most crucial was the chain of assumptions beginning with the amount of fuel that might burn, the amount of soot it would generate, the height to which it would be driven, and the length of time it would remain. The best-known popularizer of the theory of nuclear winter, Carl Sagan, was also among the most pessimistic. He wrote of a threshold as low as 500 nuclear explosions that could trigger a nuclear winter.[16] "A major first strike," he wrote, "may be an act of national suicide, even if no retaliation occurs."[17] Thus the concept of deterrence reached its limit—a state deterred by fear from using its own weapons.

The original study that produced the alarm relied on a very simplified model of climate, ignoring, for example, the great difference between climate over land and climate over oceans. In succeeding years other atmospheric scientists published papers refuting most of the claims of the first study.[18] Although most granted that given enough nuclear explosions, unforeseeable things would happen, they argued that the "idea of automatic suicide is now unsupportable."[19]

But even while natural scientists debated the theory, political scientists analyzed the consequences of nuclear winter for policy. For Sagan, the clear implication was that the world must reduce the total of nuclear warheads held by all countries to 500. Then each major power, possessing at most 250 warheads, would have too few weapons to follow any strategy but that of finite deterrence. States could not limit damage to themselves by aiming only at enemy weapons, because *all* nuclear explosions, even one's own, help trigger a nuclear winter. The concept of nuclear winter was the ultimate fantasy of those advocating finite deterrence—a virtually self-implementing concept.

But now political analysts pointed out that while nuclear winter might argue *against* the doctrine of damage limitation, it did nothing to strengthen the arguments *in favor of* finite deterrence. Even before the "discovery" of nuclear winter, critics had said finite deterrence was incredible. Striking back at enemy cities made no sense; it only guaranteed retaliatory strikes against our own. Nuclear winter made the argument even stronger, for cities were the targets most likely to produce the pernicious smoke and soot that would block the sun.

Some advocates of damage limitation tried to show that the prospect of a nuclear winter even strengthened their case. Albert Wohlstetter argued that nuclear winter could be avoided if nuclear weapons were targeted at limited numbers of military targets (as damage limitation prescribes) and not at cities (as finite deterrence prescribes).[20] The kinds of weapons and targets assumed by the original nuclear winter studies—big and inaccurate warheads aimed at cities and industry—were exactly what damage limitation theorists opposed. Although Wohlstetter's opponents would not be likely to concede the degree of rationality and tight control over weapons that he postulates, his argument showed that nuclear winter was not the clinching argument for finite deterrence that some had hoped.

DAMAGE LIMITATION'S LOGICAL EXTREME: THE STRATEGIC DEFENSE INITIATIVE

The same year that Sagan and his colleagues published their article, President Reagan introduced a proposal that carried the theory of damage limitation to its ultimate limit. In March 1983 he proposed that "we embark on a program to counter the awesome Soviet missile threat with measures that are defensive." He was, he said, ordering "a comprehensive and intensive effort to define a long-term research and development program to begin to achieve our ultimate goal of eliminating the threat posed by strategic nuclear missiles."[21]

The idea was not new. It had been voiced in the late 1960s in defense of the ABM program. Proponents argued that as long as we were spending large sums of money to be secure, it was better to spend them trying to save American lives than to take Russian ones. During the earlier debate, proponents of a missile defense were able to quote the Soviet premier Aleksei Kosygin, who had said, "Maybe an antimissile system is more expensive than an offensive system, but it is designed not to kill people but to preserve human lives."[22]

Reagan's speech was followed by more detailed Administration expositions of high-technology weaponry. Lasers orbiting on satellites would burn holes in enemy missiles as they were being boosted into space. Missiles not destroyed during the boost phase would be attacked by other devices as they traveled through space toward their targets. As the few surviving warheads re-entered the atmosphere, ground-based interceptor missiles would knock them out. Some proposals postulated several layers in all, creating something like a protective astrodome over the United States. Reagan himself seemed to conceive of SDI in this manner. Speaking in Glassboro, New Jersey (where Kosygin had made his remarks in favor of missile defense in 1967), he called SDI a "shield that could protect us from nuclear missiles just as a roof protects a family from rain."[23]

The consensus in the scientific community was that the technology for such a "leakproof" defensive system was not available and would not be for a long time.[24] To make clear that SDI existed only as an imaginative vision of the future, Reagan's political opponents gave it the name "Star Wars."[25] It was one thing, they argued, to produce cartoon animations for television news showing space stations shooting out flashes of light and destroying missiles; it was quite another thing to produce the hardware to do it. Someone commented that Reagan's asking for space-based lasers was like President Hayes asking for an air force. (Rutherford B. Hayes became president in 1877; the Wright brothers first flew in 1903.)[26] Even before Reagan left office, the agency set up to promote SDI had abandoned the original "astrodome" concept.

SDI carried the doctrine of damage limitation to its logical extreme. The critics of damage limitation found that their arguments still applied. The costs would be staggering (one estimate said $100 to $200 billion per year— or half of the entire defense budget).[27] In the end it would prove infeasible. And it would be destabilizing. No matter what the United States claimed, the Soviet Union would view SDI as a shield behind which the United States could prepare and launch a disarming first strike, hoping to escape with little or no retaliatory damage. Reagan promised to share the technology for SDI with the Soviet Union, but even American experts found this promise incredible.

Reagan personally intended the SDI to be a population defense. A National Security Council document issued in May 1985 made this clear: "The goal of our research is not, and cannot be, simply to protect our retaliatory forces from attack."[28] Nevertheless, some supporters of SDI were willing to consider a scaled-back version designed primarily to protect the deterrent, a view compatible with the contrasting doctrine of finite deterrence. In contrast to the fanciful orbiting lasers envisioned for a space-based system, supporters of a scaled-back version could point to proven technology that could be deployed in a reasonably short time, in particular a successor to ABM called LOADS (for low-altitude defense system). LOADS would provide terminal defense—that is, defense against the last stage of a ballistic missile's flight. Because such terminal defense might involve interceptors exploding close to earth and would never be 100 percent effective, it was considered more appropriate for the defense of missile silos than cities. Silos are typically located away from population centers and already protected by many feet of concrete. They are also numerous enough so that one or two incoming warheads passing through the LOADS screen would not do fatal damage to the entire deterrent force.

Advocates of this version of SDI also claimed that LOADS could meet the important criterion of a favorable cost-exchange ratio, that is, that the cost of a defensive weapon would be less than the cost of the offensive weapon it seeks to defeat. If this were not the case, a country building offensive weapons would soon drive a country building defensive weapons into bankruptcy. Those proposing LOADS conceded that the system was expensive, but that if it were made mobile, and if the ICBM's it defended were mobile, a potential enemy would need so many extra missiles for a first strike that the cost-exchange ratio would favor the defense.[29]

In this version, a strategic defense system might be attractive even to believers in finite deterrence, by helping assure the survival of the minimum numbers of retaliatory missiles that the strategy requires. Not everyone believed that such survival was assured for the coming decades. As missiles become increasingly accurate, they acquire an increasing capability to wipe out a rival's missiles in a first strike. A country relying on a limited missile force would then be forced to choose one of several options. It could choose to launch its missiles the instant it detected incoming warheads. The advantage of such a "launch on warning" strategy is that the incoming warheads would then hit only empty holes in the ground. The disadvantage is that malfunctions in the warning system, either response to false alarms or belated response, would lead to disaster.[30]

If it rejected launch on warning, a country could choose to build more missiles, or to put more warheads on existing missiles, or to add new types of delivery systems such as cruise missiles. In other words, a country could engage in an arms race. With more missiles in a force to start with, more would be likely to survive. But such a program would undermine one of the advantages of finite deterrence, that of keeping costs limited. Furthermore, more weapons would mean more opportunity for accidents or unauthorized launches. And an increase in numbers would blur the distinction between a limited retaliatory capability and a larger first-strike force. Those who favored the SDI pointed out that finite deterrence had not kept nuclear capabilities limited; so as long as states were adding new weapons anyway, it was preferable to add defensive ones.[31]

NUCLEAR WEAPONS AFTER THE COLD WAR

By the time of Reagan's "Star Wars" speech, the intellectual debate between finite deterrence (or assured destruction) and damage limitation (or flexible response) had exhausted itself. Neither side could develop a convincing case that its preferred strategy would make the country secure. The strongest arguments advanced were those pointing out the flaws of the opposing strategy. The inability of defense intellectuals to advance a convincing theory about how these weapons could be used suggests there may be no sensible way to use them at all.

A look over the past decades suggests that the theories of damage limitation or counterforce were seriously flawed. We now know that in 1961 the Kennedy Administration became aware of serious flaws in the Soviet air defense system. A disarming strike would almost certainly have been completely successful. But people in the Kennedy Administration recoiled in horror from the very possibility of using nuclear weapons.[32] Kennedy's counterpart Nikita Khrushchev, reflecting on the Cuban missile crisis, expressed the same sentiment. "What good," he said, "would it have done me in the last hour of my life to know that though our great nation and the United States were in complete ruins, the national honor of the Soviet Union was intact?"[33]

Several events at the beginning of the 1990s radically altered the way in which the world viewed nuclear weapons. Nuclear weapons, which all the permanent members of the Security Council possessed but Iraq did not, did not deter Saddam Hussein from his attempt to annex the neighboring country of Kuwait. And nuclear weapons played no role in rolling back Saddam Hussein's aggression. Precision-guided munitions and radar-evading aircraft were the decisive weapons.

Meanwhile radical changes in the Soviet Union made the possibility of any kind of Soviet military action outside its borders remote. The Soviet Union still possessed nuclear weapons, but so did France and Britain and China. If it was difficult to think of a rational way to use nuclear weapons during the Cold War, it was almost impossible to think of one after it ended.

But it was unlikely that weapons would disappear. If nuclear weapons were abolished by treaty, one or more states might cheat. Iraq had already demonstrated the possibilities of deception before it fully acquired a nuclear capability. In a nuclear-free world, the possession of a handful of weapons might, in some circumstances, confer an advantage.

Furthermore, the knowledge of how to construct nuclear weapons would not disappear, and in times of tension there might be a "rearmament race," with two or more countries trying to build nuclear weapons as quickly as possible. Such a race would probably be far more unstable than the original arms race because now each state would know when it had built a workable weapon and be tempted to use it first before its rival caught up.

The likelihood was for a move toward finite deterrence. Specialists in defense questions believed that it would be easy for the United States and its former Soviet rival to reduce down to the level of 6,000 to 12,000 weapons per country. Below that level, other nuclear countries would have to be drawn in. Some advocates thought that eventually states could possess no more than 100 nuclear weapons apiece.

In the changed conditions of the world, deliberate use of nuclear weapons, at least by major powers, seems unlikely. But as long as weapons exist, accidental or unauthorized use is still possible. The concept of arms control seeks to deal with this problem.

NOTES

1. Bertha von Suttner, *Memoirs*, Vol. I (New York: Garland, 1972), p. 437; originally published in 1910.

2. Robert M. Lawrence and Joel Larus, eds., *Nuclear Proliferation: Phase II* (Lawrence, Kan.: University Press of Kansas for the National Security Education Program, 1974), p. 49.

3. The size of the Hiroshima explosion is often but incorrectly given as 20 kilotons. See Bernard Brodie, *War and Politics* (New York: Macmillan, 1973), p. 53 fn.

4. P. M. S. Blackett, "Is the Atomic Bomb an Absolute Weapon?" *Scientific American*, Vol. 180, No. 3 (March 1949), p. 15.

5. Samuel Glasstone, ed., *The Effects of Nuclear Weapons*, rev. ed., prepared by United States Department of Defense for the Atomic Energy Commission (Washington, D.C.: U.S. Government Printing Office, 1964).

6. Thomas C. Schelling, *Arms and Influence* (New Haven: Yale University Press, 1966), Chapter 1.

7. Konrad Lorenz, *On Aggression*, trans. Marjorie Kerr Wilson (New York: Bantam Books, 1967), p. 234; Frank Harvey, *Air War—Vietnam* (New York: Bantam Books, 1967), p. 2. The incident of the B-52 pilot was related by a student in a political science class at Western Washington State College in 1969.

8. Norman Cousins, *In Place of Folly* (New York: Harper, 1961), pp. 107–108.

9. McGeorge Bundy, "To Cap the Volcano," *Foreign Affairs*, Vol. 48, No. 1 (October 1969), p. 10.

10. A typical advocate of such a view was Paul Nitze, "Assuring Strategic Stability in an Era of Déntente," *Foreign Affairs*, Vol. 54, No. 2 (January 1976), pp. 207–232.

11. For example, Spurgeon M. Keeny, Jr., and Wolfgang K. H. Panofsy, "MAD versus NUTS: Can Doctrine or Weaponry Remedy the Mutual Hostage Relationship of the Superpowers?" *Foreign Affairs*, Vol. 60 (Winter 1981/82), pp. 287–304.

12. McGeorge Bundy. (See note 9.)

13. R. P. Turco et al., "Nuclear Winter: Global Consequences of Multiple Nuclear Explosions," *Science* Vol. 222, No. 4630 (December 23, 1983), pp. 1283–1292.

14. Conway Leovy, "The Effects of the Atmosphere of a Major Nuclear Exchange," paper presented at the 18th meeting of the Pacific Northwest Colloquium on International Security, University of Washington, January 11, 1985.

15. Paul R. Ehrlich et al., "Long-Term Biological Consequences of Nuclear War" *Science* Vol. 222, No. 4630 (December 23, 1983), pp. 1293–1300.

16. Carl Sagan, "Nuclear Winter and Climatic Catastrophe," *Foreign Affairs*, Vol. 63, No. 2 (Winter 1984/85), pp. 275.

17. Ibid., p. 292.

18. Starley L. Thompson and Stephen H. Schneider, "Nuclear Winter Reappraised" *Foreign Affairs* Vol. 64 No. 5 (Summer 1986), pp. 981–1005.

19. Ibid., p. 999.

20. Albert Wohlstetter, "Between a Free World and None," *Foreign Affairs*, Vol. 63, No. 5 (Summer 1985), pp. 962–994.

21. Speech on March 23, 1983, *Vital Speeches*, April 15, 1983, pp. 389–390.

22. Donald G. Brennan, "The Case for Missile Defense," *Foreign Affairs* Vol. 47, No. 3 (April 1969), p. 445.

23. Speech at Glassboro, June 19, 1986, cited by Strobe Talbott, *The Master of the Game* (New York: Knopf, 1988), p. 305.

24. Ashton D. Carter, *Directed Energy Missile Defense in Space* (Washington, D.C.: Office of Technology Assessment, April 1984), p. 81; also more recent studies

25. A favorable account of such a system is Robert Jastrow, *How to Make Nuclear Weapons Obsolete* (Boston: Little, Brown, 1985); a critical view is Union of Concerned Scientists, *The Fallacy of Star Wars* (New York: Vintage, 1984).

26. The originator of this simile deserves credit, but I have been unable to track it to its source. I heard it on the radio and the original transmission has long ago disappeared into thin air.

27. Testimony of former Secretary of Defense Harold Brown before the Defense Subcommittee of the Senate Committee on Appropriations, *Department of Defense Appropriations for Fiscal Year 1987. Hearings*, Part 2, 99th Cong., 2nd sess., April 10, 1986, pp. 175–176.

28. Richard Halloran, *To Arm a Nation* (New York: Macmillan, 1986), p. 311.

29. Carter, *Directed Energy Missile Defense*, p. 81.

30. Richard Garwin, "Launch Under Attack to Redress Minuteman Vulnerability?", *International Security* Vol. 4, No. 3 (Winter 1979–80), pp. 117–139.

31. Keith B. Payne and Colin S. Gray, "Nuclear Policy and the Defensive Transition," *Foreign Affairs*, Vol. 62, No. 4 (Spring 1984), p. 839.

32. Fred Kaplan, *The Wizards of Armageddon* (New York: Simon & Schuster, 1983), pp. 294ff.

33. Interview with Norman Cousins, *Saturday Review*, October 10, 1977, p. 4.

CHAPTER 12

ARMS CONTROL

Any attempt to maintain peace by building weapons, either in a traditional arms race or in an effort to maintain a balance of terror, entails hazards. We could eliminate some of these hazards while leaving intact the basic idea of peace by mutual deterrence if we regulated the acquisition, maintenance, and use of armaments so that the decision to use them stayed under the control of a state's top decision-makers. Such an approach to peace is known as *arms control*. The definition does not specify eliminating weapons or even limiting their numbers. Eliminating a particularly destabilizing type of weapon could be a form of arms control, of course, but in another situation arms control might call for building more weapons. Later in the chapter, we will explain why this could happen. But first let us define arms control in a different way.

Arms control as an approach to peace was first put forward in the early 1960s with the paradoxical definition that it was a form of military cooperation among enemies or potential enemies.[1] It may seem puzzling to suggest that enemies cooperate militarily but even the bitterest enemies have some interests in common and it is on the basis of these shared interests that cooperation can occur. Consider two belligerent countries, each secretly preparing to wage unremitting war against the other, a hated enemy. No matter how aggressive the leaders of each state are, each wants the war to begin when he or she gives the order and not earlier because of accident or because some low-ranking officer jumps the gun. Even bitter enemies have a common interest in preventing actions that start unintended wars.

Even when rivalry is less intense, war might come about in unintended ways. In 1977 Egyptian President Anwar Sadat surprised the world by announcing that he was willing to make a state visit to Egypt's bitter rival Israel and address the Israeli parliament. The announcement caught Israeli intelligence by surprise, in large part because it was an entirely personal decision by Sadat, not evolving from a decision-making machinery within the Egyptian government or even from discussion with others, and certainly not a response to Egyptian popular opinion. The announcement was such a surprise that Israeli military intelligence thought it might be the cover for a ruse of some kind. The Israeli chief of staff placed the Israeli defense forces on alert and sent a drone aircraft to check on movements of Egyptian Army. The drone got lost, depriving the Israelis of information, but the Egyptians noticed the drone and put their own defensive network on alert. The Israelis immediately picked up signals of the increased alert. By now both sides had units on a high state of alert, all in response to a peace initiative.[2]

Leaders share an interest in preventing unintended war. They also share an interest in protecting their own populations as much as possible should war break out. Some weapons cause extensive damage not related to military goals; some, such as biological weapons, may even endanger the population of the country using the weapon. Even rivals have an interest in controlling such weapons. Finally, although rival leaders may not like to think about it, they have a shared interest in bringing a war to an end, once they decide it would be prudent to do so. Wars that perpetuate senseless destruction only because neither side has the ability to order a halt benefit no one.

Arms control as conceived in the early 1960s thus focussed not on the political causes of conflict but on the potentially harmful consequences of having weapons. This emphasis led to several concrete achievements and made the label "arms control" politically appealing—to military leaders because it did not appear to weaken deterrence through strength, and to the general population because it seemed to be doing something about the growing numbers and destructiveness of weapons. As a result of its political utility, the label came to be applied to a wide variety of activities, including some that would in the past have been called "disarmament." Both SALT I and SALT II were essentially quantitative limits on arms and the essence of proposals in START was reductions in arms. In some instances, of course, disarmament can serve the purposes of arms control, but "arms control" was applied to so many proposals more for political expediency than for analytic clarity. We will here limit use of the term to its earlier, more limited meaning.

ACCIDENTAL AND UNAUTHORIZED ATTACKS: THE HOT LINE, RECONNAISSANCE

No one, not even a reckless aggressor, wants an all-out nuclear war to start because of a technical accident. Perhaps a mouse chews the insulation from a wire and the short circuit launches a missile. It's not entirely a science-fiction writer's fantasy. Nikita Khrushchev indicated that a Soviet ICBM was accidentally fired toward Alaska and had to be destroyed. The United States has not revealed whether that stray missile showed up on its warning network, but on one occasion a flock of geese showed up and for a while was interpreted as a Soviet attack.[3]

Another type of unwanted trigger for all-out war is an unauthorized attack by, for example, a mad colonel who steals a plane and a bomb and takes off to start a war all by himself. A third type of trigger is a catalyst, a third country that starts a war between two others without becoming involved itself. In the early 1960s, people used the example of the Chinese, who had an atomic bomb but no modern means of delivery, smuggling the bomb into New York Harbor on a freighter. They would explode it, preferably at a time of tension between the United States and the USSR. The United States would assume that the Russians had begun an attack. We would launch our bombers and missiles against the Russians, the Russians would retaliate with any forces that survived, and China would emerge as the strongest country in the world. The likelihood of this scenario has faded, not only because of the passing of the Cold War but also because of repeated warnings from arms controllers. But catalytic war, even if unlikely, is still possible. One can imagine a dramatic rise in tension between potential nuclear powers such as Iraq and Iran or Pakistan and India. In a confrontation between such states, the victim of a surprise nuclear attack might not pause to ascertain that the weapon really had come from its rival and not from a third state seeking to make trouble.

A number of arms control measures are designed to prevent war resulting from accidental or unauthorized or catalytic use of weapons. Some measures improve command and control systems. An electronic lock, called the permissive action link (PAL), makes it impossible for one person acting alone to prepare a nuclear device for detonation. The United States developed the system after one of our bombers accidentally crashed in South Carolina in 1961 while carrying thermonuclear bombs and five of the six switches on the system we were using at that time were activated by the crash. We felt our system needed improvement. We found that the Russian system apparently had more problems than ours. The Russians couldn't trust themselves enough to put their missiles on full alert during the Cuban missile crisis in 1962. We passed on to them information on how to protect their weapons from unauthorized use.[4] You could call this giving the Russians our secrets—military cooperation with our potential opponents—but it is in our interest to avoid wars started by mad Russian colonels or by mad American colonels.

Avoiding accidents is important, but it is not the accident itself so much as the reaction to it that could set off a full-scale nuclear war. One way of keeping the leaders in each country from pushing the panic button is to eliminate the kinds of weapons that might make them panicky. Liquid-fueled missiles, sitting unprotected on the surface of the earth, are that kind of weapon. The Russians put such a missile, a type we called SS-4, into Cuba in 1962. Because a missile such as this would have been so easy to destroy if the United States struck first, American planners assumed the Russians, if they were rational, could use them only if *they* fired first. Knowing how vulnerable the missiles were, the Russians would have been tempted to fire them immediately if they had even suspected we were getting ready to strike at them. Fortunately the crisis was resolved before either side acted in accord with this complicated logic. Vulnerable missiles such as the SS-4 have now been replaced by storable liquid- or solid-fueled missiles protected in concrete silos underground. These newer missiles are more expensive, and both sides have many more of them, but we feel more secure now (especially now that *both* sides have them) than we did in the early 1960s.

But types of weapons continue to be a problem in the debate on the antiballistic missile. If an ABM system really works, and a nation's population is entirely protected, then that nation could start a war and wipe out its opponents without risking its own population. The possibility that this might happen is small, but the destruction such a war would cause is so great we must at least think about that possibility. Arms control advocates argue that any weapon that makes it rational to strike first in war is bad. The ABM is such a weapon; therefore, they argue, we should severely restrict it. And that is what the first major treaty resulting from the Strategic Arms Limitation Talks (SALT) did. The ABM Treaty of May 1972 limits each country to two missile sites with only 100 missiles for each site, not enough to provide a meaningful defense for a country's population.[5]

Another way of keeping leaders from starting wars as the result of accidents or unauthorized attacks is to increase the amount of information available to them when they make their decisions. An example of this technique is found in a story from World War II. Neither the Germans nor the Americans wanted to use poison gas, but each produced a stockpile of poison gas to have ready for retaliation in case the other side used it first. During the Allied invasion of Italy at Anzio, a German shell hit an American ammunition dump that had some of these poison gas shells stockpiled for retaliatory use. The gas that was released began drifting toward German lines. The American commander made a great effort to get a warning to his German opponent that poison gas was coming his way, that the German troops should take precautions, and that it certainly was not a deliberate attack. His efforts were successful, and the accident at Anzio did not lead to all-out use of poison gas in World War II.[6]

In recent times, one of the best-known techniques for increasing information available to Soviet and American leaders was the Hot Line. "Hot" meant that the line was always open. The Hot Line was not a telephone (which would have done little good, as American presidents have not been fluent in Russian nor have Soviet leaders been fluent in English) but a set of teletype machines, one printing in the Cyrillic alphabet, the other in the Latin. They were originally connected by land and sea cable and later by the more secure method of communications satellites. (On one occasion the original Hot Line cable is said to have been cut by a Finnish farmer plowing a field.)[7]

The Hot Line was established by an agreement signed in June 1963, six months after the Cuban missile crisis had revealed how unsatisfactory traditional diplomatic means of sending notes were. Messages from foreign office to ambassador to foreign office were taking more than six hours in an era when missiles could cover the same distance in forty minutes.

After its installation, the Hot Line was put to use on several occasions. Perhaps its most significant use as an arms control measure was during the 1967 war in the Middle East. On the third day of that war, Israeli torpedo boats and planes attacked an American intelligence-gathering ship in the area, the *Liberty*. A message to the *Liberty* from the Pentagon to pull back from the area of conflict had been misrouted and ended up in the Philippines. The US Navy assumed that the ship had withdrawn and had reason to think the Israelis had been told it had withdrawn. The attack came as a surprise and the United States wanted to send a task force to investigate. But the United States knew that Soviet vessels were closely shadowing the movements of the American fleet in the Mediterranean. It also was aware that the Egyptians had already charged that US forces had assisted the Israelis in the war. Thus, before moving ships into the area, the United States used the Hot Line to signal the Soviets that the purpose of the move was to rescue a US ship that had been attacked and that the United States had hostile intentions toward neither the Soviets nor their Egyptian allies.[8]

In September of 1971, the Hot Line was strengthened by the Agreement on Nuclear Accidents, by which the United States and the Soviet Union agreed to use the Hot Line in the event of an accident or the discovery of an unidentified object on their early warning systems. They also agreed to give each other advance notice of missile tests extending beyond their own borders in the direction of the other country.[9]

The Hot Line was not foolproof. There was no way to guarantee that messages transmitted over it were true. Certainly any plans for a first strike would have included false assurances over the Hot Line to lead the other side to believe that it had detected only test firings or perhaps accidents. Still, in the event of a real accident, it would have been vital to learn about it as quickly as possible, and it would have been reassuring to learn about it from the side responsible.

By the end of the Cold War, more elaborate plans for sharing information were under consideration. In 1988 the Soviet and American foreign ministers opened a Nuclear Risk Reduction Center in the US State Department, intended to pass the along the information required for verification of the growing number of treaties. But further developments along this line—such as crisis centers in both countries staffed jointly by Soviet and American citizens—were outdated by two developments. The growing trust between the two countries reduced the amount of secrecy, and the improvement of communications technology made available even to average citizens the ability to communicate rapidly with any point on the surface of the earth, in effect creating thousands of "hot lines."

Another technique that can increase information available to the decision-maker is espionage. Espionage is information gathering that the other side objects to. When it occurs (or, more precisely, when it is discovered), it usually increases tension. In 1960, a high-flying American spy plane, the U-2, was shot down over the Soviet Union just as a summit conference in Paris was about to begin. The Russians used the incident as a reason for canceling the summit. However, a good case can be made *for* such information gathering.

During the 1950s, the US strategic force consisted of the bombers of the Strategic Air Command. Bombers are comparatively fragile. Fighter aircraft can shoot them down with machine guns. The vast increase of explosive power in nuclear weapons meant that even warheads striking at some distance from an airfield could put the bombers stationed there out of commission. In the late 1950s the USSR began developing an ICBM. American planners began to worry that, if the Russians built enough of them, a surprise attack might eliminate most of our bombers. The problem was that we didn't know how many of the ICBM's the USSR had developed and we had no way of finding out. We did know that they had tested them. In October 1957 they used one of these rockets to launch the first artificial earth satellite, the Sputnik. Khrushchev boasted that Russian factories were turning out rockets on assembly lines.

The United States had developed an airplane, the U-2, which could fly over the Soviet Union at an altitude of 14 miles and take photographs that could be studied for signs of missile deployment. These flights were violations of the Soviets' sovereignty, and they protested, though privately, because they didn't want to publicize the fact that they couldn't stop the flights. But even though the United States was willing to risk running these flights, the intelligence they gathered wasn't very satisfactory. The U-2 had to be launched from countries near the USSR such as Pakistan and Norway, and these countries were apprehensive about Soviet reaction if something should go wrong. The flights therefore could not be frequent.

Only thirty were made, and as each covered only a small portion of European USSR, we never could be sure if we had spotted all the Soviet ICBM's.[10] The result was that the military services took a prudent approach and estimated that the Russians had a large number of missiles, enough to cause a missile gap between their strength and ours. The services urged the United States to build missiles that would be less vulnerable than bombers to a Russian surprise attack. The extent of the missile gap became a foreign policy issue in the 1960 presidential election, and immediately upon taking office, the Kennedy Administration speeded up the production of US missiles.[11]

Then the United States began using a new means of ascertaining Soviet capabilities: reconnaissance or spy satellites. These have many advantages over the U-2. They can be launched from the United States, eliminating dependence on allies. In the first decades of their use, they traveled too high above the earth to be shot down, and because they travel far above the atmosphere they do not violate the air space of other countries. They make repeated orbits, as many as one every ninety minutes, and thus have an improved chance of finding clear weather over their targets. Those in operation by the 1980s were monsters, as long as a six-story building and capable of staying aloft two years or more. They were coordinated with weather observation satellites, which told them when to photograph. They could change their altitudes and orbits to get the best pictures and could use a variety of films to produce stereo or multispectral photographs. Photo interpreters claim a satellite once photographed a man on a street in a northern Russian town reading *Pravda;* they knew it was *Pravda* because they could read the name on the masthead.[12]

The first US reconnaissance satellite was launched at the very end of 1960. In the early 1960s, for lack of information, the United States needlessly accelerated the arms race by building many missiles to catch up with a Soviet force that did not exist. It was an honest mistake, but it was a mistake nevertheless. When the Russians did begin building large numbers of missiles, they could claim that *they* were trying to close the missile gap. By the early 1970s, when the spy satellites were supplying us with detailed information (reportedly they could pick out objects less than 12 inches wide), we were totally confident about entering into arms limitation agreements with the USSR—not only because we knew how many missiles they had but also because we were sure we would know if they cheated.[13]

Photographic reconnaissance by satellites is no longer considered espionage (even though the information they acquire is much better than that collected by the U-2 flights), for now we have the Soviets' agreement on it. A provision included in both SALT I and SALT II (including the fully ratified

ABM Treaty of 1972) states that each party shall use "national technical means of verification." That phrase is understood to include, among other methods, photographic or imagery satellites.

EXCESSIVE COLLATERAL DAMAGE AND THRESHOLDS

So far we have been talking about military cooperation between potential opponents for just one purpose: to prevent all-out war from beginning in specified ways. But arms control can extend *into* a war, even if one should break out. A shared interest among opponents (not just potential opponents but those actually fighting each other) is to make the fighting less unpleasant. One way is to eliminate weapons that may cause excessive collateral damage, that is, harm to bystanders or the environment that serves no military purpose. Biological agents would be of this type—for example, bacteria that cause diseases such as the plague or anthrax. They would affect not only enemy troops but civilians, perhaps one's own troops and perhaps even people in the home territory of the country that first used them. Chemical agents such as poison gas and herbicides also cause excessive collateral damage.[14]

Weapons such as these present a problem. Most experts agree that all-out use of the most deadly of them would serve no useful military purpose. But the limited use of some of them, such as tear gas, might be very useful in some circumstances. If a guerrilla band used a group of women and children as a defensive shield behind which they launched an attack, who would not agree that it would be better to use tear gas than machine-gun fire?

Still, arms control advocates argue against *any* use of gas, even nonlethal gas. They call their argument "maintaining the threshold."[15] A *threshold* is a clear dividing line between one weapon and another, or between one way of using weapons and another. Gas is very different from high explosives, and thus there is a clear threshold between them. A .38-caliber bullet is not very different from a .45-caliber bullet, and thus no threshold separates them. A threshold helps prevent violence from escalating by accident. In the confusion of combat, an attack with nonlethal gas might be mistaken for an attack with lethal gas. If many of the troops being gassed were already suffering from respiratory infection, the attack might result in many fatalities. The commander of the troops who were gassed might then order what he thought was retaliation, but with lethal gas. "No gas" is unambiguously distinct from "gas"; "a little nonlethal gas" is not so unambiguously distinct from "a lot of nonlethal gas" or "a little lethal gas."

For this reason, stockpiling gas in ammunition dumps near the battlefield, as the Americans did at Anzio, was very risky. The German policy during World War II, by contrast, is an example of arms control: "The transport of German gases or any chemical warfare agent or spraying containers filled with agents, gas candles or gas munitions or airplane gas bombs to any points beyond the borders of the German Reich, or their storage at any such point . . . was strictly prohibited."[16]

A case in which the United States did take a step that could be described as maintaining a threshold was the announcement in May 1974 that the United States would unilaterally renounce the development of miniaturized nuclear weapons—those with an explosive power of less than 1 kiloton, which could be used interchangeably with conventional weapons on the battlefield for tactical operations such as knocking out tanks.[17] By denying ourselves even the possibility of using nuclear weapons in tactical operations, we keep the decision to use them (if we ever do use nuclear weapons) more firmly in the hands of the top leaders.

Another form of nuclear weapon poses much more difficult problems for arms control. This is the enhanced-radiation warhead, also called the neutron bomb. Most of the destructive power of such a weapon is in the form of prompt radiation—radiation from fast-moving neutrons that quickly lose their force—as opposed to either explosive power or lingering radiation in the form of fallout. Because the prompt radiation would be directed mainly at enemy soldiers, it would not cause excessive collateral damage to nearby civilian structures (or to distant civilian targets in the form of fallout), and thus it fulfills one of the aims of arms control. On the other hand, precisely because of this effect it would tempt political and military leaders to use it, and thus it lowers the nuclear threshold. A leader who might be terrified of unleashing a cataclysmic war with blast and fallout threatening the entire world might employ an enhanced-radiation weapon, thereby taking the first step up the escalation ladder. Thus although the weapon might be desirable according to one line of reasoning, it is undesirable from another.[18]

WAR TERMINATION AND COST REDUCTION

Besides preventing wars from starting and controlling the violence if they do, arms control, can serve a third purpose. It can make ending wars easier. Wars are not always easy to end. The side that wishes to de-escalate a conflict or withdraw at least partially may find that this action only encourages the other side to press harder and perhaps to increase its demands. In international politics there was an example during the Korean War. The original, stated purpose of the United States was to restore the territorial integrity of South Korea, but after the startling success of the amphibious landing at Inchon and the retreat of the North Korean troops, we changed our policy to reunification of the entire Korean peninsula.

One arms control measure that might facilitate war termination is to help the enemy retain its command and control structure. The United States did not eliminate the Japanese emperor at the close of World War II, and the emperor was able to call on Japanese soldiers to surrender. If he had not been there to do so, Japanese survivors in jungles around the Pacific would not have been just an occasional news curiosity but a major security problem.[19] More recently, the ABM Treaty of May 1972 states that one of the two ABM sites that is permitted should be around the "National Command Authority," that is, the capital. Even without this treaty provision, one can doubt the wisdom of trying to destroy the Kremlin or the Pentagon as part of the first blow in a war. After the Germans destroyed the French government with their stunning military victory in the Franco-Prussian War of 1870, they had to spend six months looking around for someone who could surrender (see Chapter 2).

Finally, we come to a purpose that people often advance for arms control: to reduce the costs of the arms race. Sometimes this happens. The ABM Treaty saved the United States what the government very conservatively estimated to be $40 billion. But saving money is more often an accidental than an intentional result of arms control. In some cases it may not be an area in which interests overlap. A very rich country competing against a poor country has no interest in reducing costs because the ability to meet these costs is one of its advantages.

In other cases, an arms control measure might actually increase costs. One of the proposals discussed in the early 1980s was a new, small ICBM with a single warhead, referred to as "Midgetman." Unlike the latest version of the Minuteman with three MIRV's or its proposed successor MX with as many as ten MIRV's, Midgetman would reduce the advantages of going first and thus make a preemptive strike less likely. A program to install large numbers of Midgetmen would be expensive, yet contribute to arms control.

DIFFICULTIES WITH ARMS CONTROL

Advocates of arms control do not claim that it can prevent all wars, and we cannot fairly criticize the approach for something that was never claimed. Still, we should realize that arms control cannot prevent a war that results from a rational calculation. In December 1971, India went to war according to a carefully prepared plan in order to accomplish specific foreign policy objectives, most important of which was the return to Pakistan of millions of Bengali refugees who were straining the Indian economy. It is hard to think of an arms control measure that could have prevented the India–Pakistan War of 1971.[20]

A more serious criticism is that arms control may not even be able to achieve the limited objectives it does have. The basic and mutual distrust that characterizes all states in the international condition of anarchy and makes complete disarmament seem impossible affects even the comparatively modest measures of arms control (see Chapter 7). Herman Kahn offers a vivid parable.[21] Suppose, he writes, two men are fighting a duel to the death with blowtorches, and they are fighting inside a dynamite factory. Then surely an arms control measure would be having the lights on. But, Kahn continues, it is not at all clear that this could be negotiated. Each would distrust the other. "Exactly which lights are to be left on?" "Does the other guy have sunglasses that will give him a temporary advantage the instant the lights go on?" And so an eminently rational agreement might never be reached.

The end of the Cold War has reduced but not eliminated this distrust. States continue to see issues through the narrow perspective of national interest. Consider the case of chemical weapons. Chemical weapons have for a long time been a logical candidate for arms control measures. The consensus is that they cause extensive collateral damage without providing for quick, decisive outcomes on the battlefield. In addition, the militarily superior states worry that weaker states might be able to use them to offset their inferiority in conventional weapons. The phrase "poor man's atom bomb" was coined to express this fear.

For years the states of the world have attempted to negotiate a treaty outlawing chemical weapons. Because the processes used to make poison gas are similar to those used for many other chemicals, it would be easy to conceal chemical munitions production; for this reason the United States has insisted that agreements include the right for inspectors to conduct unannounced, on-site inspections. Traditionally the Soviet Union opposed such inspections, on the grounds that they could be cover for broader espionage. But in the summer of 1991 it was the United States that abruptly reversed its position, asking that an agreement provide for the delay of a week between when inspections were demanded and when they were carried out.

Behind this apparent inconsistency was a American fear that unannounced on-site inspections might be used for espionage against industrial secrets the United States wanted to protect, in particular radar. In the Persian Gulf War, the stealthy aircraft of the United States had proved a much more potent weapon than the reported chemical capabilities of Iraq, and the United States was adjusting its negotiating position accordingly.

Thus the fundamental assumption of arms control, that even rival states have shared interests, runs into the obstacle of distrust. Other aspects of arms control run into obstacles as well. One of the premises of arms control, as we have seen, is that increasing the information available to decision-makers often provides more stability and less uncontrolled outbreak of war. But more knowledge is not always better. During World War II the Germans achieved a technological breakthrough and acquired a weapon no one else had. That weapon was a gas that could attack the body anywhere through the skin and paralyze the nervous system. Because no one else had it, no one had a defense against it. But the Germans never used their nerve gas, because they did not know they were the only ones who had it. The disarmament provisions of the Versailles Treaty had delayed their research for ten years, and they assumed that countries such as the United States had nerve gas and even more deadly types.[22] Not knowledge but ignorance restricted the violence in this case.

A reconnaissance satellite puts to rest doubts about missile gaps and helps prevent overreaction to ill-defined threats. But those same satellites also provide excellent information for targeting. The same satellites that told us the Soviets were far behind us in numbers of ICBM's deployed also told us exactly where those few ICBM's were. Perhaps that is what scared the Russians into trying to put their SS-4's into Cuba in the fall of 1962 in an effort to close their own missile gap.[23]

Advocates of arms control tell us not to count on saving money.[24] Nevertheless, saving money is often advanced as a reason for arms control. We might look at the cost of one small item: The electronic locks of a permissive action link for one nuclear warhead cost about $50,000.[25] Assuming that each of our 6,000 nuclear warheads in Europe is so protected, we are spending $300 million just to control one part of one system in our arsenal.[26]

NEW ISSUES IN ARMS CONTROL

Following the war against Iraq in the Persian Gulf, Secretary of Defense Dick Cheney testified before the House Foreign Affairs committee that for the United States the principal arms control interest had become preventing the spread of sophisticated technologies, particularly the capability to produce ballistic missiles, chemical weapons, nuclear weapons, and biological weapons. This spread is generally called "proliferation" and attention to it marks a shift from the actual rivalry between superpowers to a potential danger from the third world.

Cynics would point out that there is an element of national self-interest in Cheney's statements. Chemical and biological weapons could help equalize the great differences in power between states. Certainly Iraq's chemical capabilities got much more attention in the month before the Gulf War than did the capabilities of its tanks and artillery pieces.

Nevertheless, Cheney's point is taken seriously by many people. Wars have been spread evenly around the globe in the decades since World War II, but only a few have been "high-tech" wars, that is, ones using the advanced weapons. Examples of such wars are the Middle East war of 1973 and the war between Iraq and Iran from 1980 to 1988. Even though there have been few of these high-tech wars, they have been very destructive, much more so than the many other conflicts fought during the same decades. Thus attention to the weapons that made them destructive is warranted.

Until now regional wars have not threatened states in distant parts of the world because they were not fought with high-technology weapons. In Africa over the last decade, Libya fought Chad, Morocco fought Algeria, and Somalia fought Ethiopia, but the conflicts remained contained. The acquisition of the high-technology weapons mentioned by Secretary Cheney could turn regional powers into threats not just to their neighbors but to all states. The global threat posed by the possession of chemical and possibly biological and nuclear weapons by Iraq was one of the arguments used for taking action against Saddam Hussein in 1990.

We might separate potential targets for arms control agreements into two types. First would come weapons of mass destruction, to which even advanced states have stated opposition. These would include nuclear, radiological, chemical, and biological weapons. Advocates of arms control would oppose such weapons because they cause collateral damage.

In a second category would fall precision-guided weapons (such as smart bombs and cruise missiles) and radar-eluding "stealth" technology. Industrially advanced states would be reluctant to give these weapons up because they give these states a military edge. Rather than seek abolition, they might try merely to contain the spread of these weapons. But politically it is hard to get international agreement that applies only to some states but not others, particularly when the ones that are exempt are rich and powerful.

Still, one could argue that fairness is not the only consideration. The world might be better off with a double standard than no standards at all. If the United States knows it can defeat a lesser power such as Iraq in 100 hours because it deploys high-tech weapons, it will feel secure about cutting its military budget. On the other hand, if Iraq is permitted to have high-tech weapons, then same pressures for arming that characterized the Cold War will return, both for the United States and for its allies in the region.

Arms control will require several components that make up what are called "regimes." Looking at the existing arrangements to prevent the spread of nuclear weapons, we see typical components of a regime. First, there is a treaty or convention whereby states pledge not to acquire a certain category of weapons. Second, there is a second agreement whereby states already in possession agree not to give or sell or lend either the weapons themselves or materials or equipment or technology that could be used to produce the weapons. Third, an international agency must provide some form of inspection to assure compliance. In the case of nuclear weapons, inspectors of the International Atomic Energy Agency could visit the reactors, production sites, and research facilities of signatory states to make sure that all nuclear material was accounted for.

But the nuclear nonproliferation regime also demonstrates the difficulties. Some states may be reluctant to sign and invoke sovereignty to justify any refusal. The Nuclear Non-Proliferation Treaty was not signed by some of the states most likely to acquire nuclear weapons, including India, Pakistan, Israel, and South Africa.

Even among those countries which had signed the agreement, cheating occurred. Nuclear material was transferred from possessing states to non-possessing states, either deliberately by a government for national advantage (as in the case of France and Iraq), or illegally by private interests (as in the case of Pakistan and various supplies in Europe).[27] Even in cases where a government is not itself directly involved in cheating, it may not have an interest in aggressive action against smuggling if it is dependent on exports. Germany, for example, was the source of much material for nuclear and chemical warfare programs for Pakistan, Iraq, and Libya. The Germans believed that the amount of time required to investigate each requested permit to export high-technology equipment inhibited their foreign trade.

A more foolproof regime would require more intrusive inspection, leading to charges of infringement of national sovereignty. Furthermore, the burden would fall unequally. Technologically backward states would argue that they were being prevented from acquiring even innocent technology. States heavily dependent on foreign trade would argue that the regulations crippled their economy. The experience with the International Atomic Energy Agency suggests that inspection would be difficult under an international agency because of the diverse interests of representative states, because no military power exists to back it up, and because of the lack of incentives for competent people to become inspectors.[28]

The difficulties encountered by international inspectors is a reminder that international politics differs from domestic politics. Only when the world begins to resemble states will inspectors be able to perform like state inspectors. But how likely is this?

NOTES

1. This definition comes from an important early work on the subject, Thomas C. Schelling and Morton Halperin, *Strategy and Arms Control* (New York: Twentieth Century Fund, 1961), p. 2.

2. Ze'ev Schiff, *A History of the Israeli Army* (New York: Macmillan, 1985), pp. 204–205.

3. For some of these accidents, see Edward Klein and Robert Littell, "Shh! Let's Tell the Russians," *Newsweek*, May 5, 1969, pp. 46–47. Geese on the radar screen are mentioned by Oskar Morgenstern, *The Question of National Defense* (New York: Random House, 1959), p. 65.

4. Klein and Littell (note 3); Lewis A. Dunn, *Controlling the Bomb* (New Haven: Yale University Press, 1982), pp. 22–23, 184 n. 45.

5. The treaty was amended by a protocol signed in Moscow in 1974 limiting the number of sites in each country to one with one hundred missiles. A good source for the texts of treaties is *Keesing's Contemporary Archives*, published in London every two weeks.

6. The incident is reported by Lord Ritchie-Calder in the Introduction to Steven Rose, ed., *CBW: Chemical and Biological Warfare* (Boston: Beacon Press, 1968). No mention of it is made, however, in the official United States Army history of Anzio, Martin Blumensen, *The*

United States Army in World War II: Salerno to Cassino (Washington, D.C.: Office of the Chief of Military History, 1969).

7. *The New York Times*, July 21, 1968; see also Richard Hudson, "Molink Is Always Ready," *The New York Times Magazine*, August 26, 1973.

8. Lyndon Johnson recounts this event in his memoirs, *The Vantage Point* (New York: Holt, Rinehart and Winston, 1971), p. 301.

9. *The New York Times*, October 1, 1971.

10. Charles J. V. Murphy, "Khrushchev's Paper Bear," *Fortune*, Vol. 70, No. 6 (December 1964), pp. 114, 224–230.

11. For an account of the missile gap, see George H. Quester, *Nuclear Diplomacy* (New York: Dunellen, 1970), Chapter 4.

12. Jeffrey Richelson, *The U.S. Intelligence Community* (Cambridge, Mass.: Ballinger, 1985), pp. 114–115; Drew Middleton, "Satellites Main Source of Photo Data for U.S.," *The New York Times*, September 11, 1983, p. Y6.

13. For a fascinating description of satellites, see Ted Greenwood, "Reconnaissance and Arms Control," *Scientific American*, Vol. 228, No. 2 (February 1973), pp. 14–25.

14. For a description of some of these agents, see Seymour Hersh, *Chemical and Biological Warfare* (Indianapolis: Bobbs-Merrill, 1968).

15. A good statement of this argument is in Thomas Schelling, "Bargaining, Communication and Limited War," *The Journal of Conflict Resolution*, Vol. 1, No. 1 (March 1957), pp. 19–36.

16. Frederic J. Brown, *Chemical Warfare* (Princeton: Princeton University Press, 1968), p. 244 n.

17. *The New York Times*, May 24, 1974.

18. Fred M. Kaplan, "Enhanced-Radiation Weapons," *Scientific American*, Vol. 238, No. 5 (May 1978), pp. 44–51.

19. Actually, this reason was not a major factor considered by American decisionmakers. See Herbert Feis, *The Atomic Bomb and the End of World War II* (Princeton: Princeton University Press, 1966).

20. For an account of this war, see International Institute of Strategic Studies, *Strategic Survey, 1971* (London, 1972).

21. Herman Kahn, *On Escalation*, rev. ed. (Baltimore: Penguin Books, 1968), p. 16 n.

22. Brown, pp. 232–233. (See note 16.)

23. For an argument along this line, see J. David Singer, "Disarmament: The Domestic and Global Context," in *The New Era in American Foreign Policy*, ed. John H. Gilbert (New York: St. Martin's Press, 1973).

24. Thomas C. Schelling, "Arms Control Will Not Cut Defense Costs," *Harvard Business Review* (March–April 1961).

25. Thomas B. Cochran et al., *Nuclear Weapons Databook* (Cambridge, Mass.: Ballinger, 1984), Vol. 1, p. 30.

26. In 1983 the Defense Department told Congress in a secret report (leaked to the press) that it had 5,845 nuclear warheads in Europe. See Richard Halloran, "Report to Congress Provides Figures for Nuclear Arsenal," *The New York Times*, November 15, 1983, p. Y7.

27. See various examples in Steven Weissman and Herbert Krosney, *The Islamic Bomb* (New York: Times Books, 1981).

28. See testimony of Roger Richter, former inspector for IAEA, before subcommittees of the House Committee on Foreign Affairs, *Israeli Attack on Iraqi Nuclear Facilities*, June 25, 1981, pp. 51–59.

PART IV

ALTERNATIVES TO ARMS

CHAPTER 13

WORLD GOVERNMENT

World government is the most obvious solution to the problem of war. Our own national government controls fighting between groups with conflicting interests: white supremacists versus black militants, farm laborers versus farm owners, even feuding Appalachian families such as the fabled Hatfields versus the McCoys. Why not, then, a world government to control fighting on a world scale?

World government is more difficult to discuss than other approaches to peace because we lack actual cases to study. There have been historical examples of disarmament agreements, peace-keeping forces, and other proposed methods of bringing peace, but never a world state. The closest approximation to a world state was the ancient Roman Empire with its *pax Romana*. Most of our discussion therefore will be theoretical. We can draw analogies from experiences in the past and in the present, but they will be nothing more than analogies—that is, comparisons of situations that are alike in only some respects.

WORLD GOVERNMENT THEORY

Historical experience of world government may be lacking, but plans for it are not. Even as the modern state system was beginning to take form, writers were putting forth plans for transcending it. The Italian Dante, known for his long poem *The Divine Comedy*, advocated a universal kingdom including all the states of Europe. In his book *De Monarchia*, which appeared in 1313, Dante uses a style of argument that may seem strange to a modern reader. Nevertheless, his fundamental argument for world government survives unchanged among modern advocates: Peace is impossible without a single supreme authority that can settle quarrels among those beneath it. Only universal empire will bring universal peace.[1]

Modern advocates of world government do not often refer to *De Monarchia* when arguing their case, but they start with the same fundamental assumption. Today, however, in addition to many competing sovereign states, we must come to terms with nuclear weapons, intercontinental missiles, and global economic interdependence. Consequently, the most carefully worked-out proposals for world government consist of many components: a world legislature, a world police force, abolition of existing armies, machinery for peaceful settlement of disputes, and rule of law. Disarmament, peaceful settlement, and law can be advanced as approaches to peace on their own, and we will examine them later in separate chapters. In this chapter we will concentrate on the fundamental problems of a world government and look in detail at its most distinctive feature, a world police force.

Wars occur, we have seen, because no higher authority exists to prevent them. We call this condition international anarchy. If a world state existed, it would provide that missing higher authority and thus bring an end to anarchy. By disarming existing states, it not only would take away the means of fighting, it would also take away the governments that decide to build armies in the first place. The present system, with authority widely scattered, would be replaced by one in which authority would be concentrated in one center. Resorting to war as a means of settling disputes would no more be allowed than is resorting to duels in society. The private use of violence is known as taking the law into one's own hands, and it is universally condemned. Under our national government, the Hatfields are not allowed to take revenge on the McCoys. Under a world government, the Greeks would not be allowed to carry on their feud with the Turks in the Aegean Sea.

This description of world government relies on analogy. We must remember that analogies don't prove anything; they only illustrate. By drawing an analogy to domestic society, we haven't proved that a world state would prevent war or even that a world state would be possible. At most, we've given a vivid picture of what we are talking about. Argument by analogy is listed as a fallacy in textbooks on logic. We must be especially wary of this fallacy in thinking about something such as world government, which has never existed in reality.

We are all familiar with our own domestic society. If you have a quarrel with your neighbor about where your property line runs, you don't settle the quarrel by invading your neighbor's property with an armor-plated lawn mower; you go to court. Domestic disputes are settled, ideally and most often in practice as well, without force or threat of force. In international politics, that is not always the case. If a national oil shortage develops, the president may drop hints about landing the Marines to take over another country's oil fields. Domestic political problems are supposed to be handled differently. Motorists waiting in line for gasoline don't talk about seizing the corner gas station.

One problem with this analogy is that it is not a very complete description of how domestic politics works. Some kinds of violence are in fact beyond the control of national governments. If you're a little short of cash one month and walk into your local bank to demand all the cash in the drawer, it won't be long before the local police come around to pick you up. But if firefighters go out on strike in direct violation of a law forbidding strikes by city employees, the mayor does not always send a constable around to arrest the head of the firefighters' union. Government leaders realize that using force, no matter how legitimate, would only make the firefighters more determined and possibly win them sympathy from the other groups. In most cities strikes by public employees are illegal, but that has not prevented them.

Government leaders may decide that they cannot satisfy the grievances of some group; instead of negotiating they try to employ force. But the use of force fails. In Northern Ireland the government decided that giving in to the demands of the Irish Republican Army (IRA) would be unacceptable to the Protestant majority of Northern Ireland, but the use of force has failed to suppress the IRA. There is no question that the British government legally governs the territory of Northern Ireland. It meets all the normal criteria—government machinery on place, recognition by the inhabitants as well as foreign countries that it is the government, collection of taxes, issuance of authoritative laws. But it cannot maintain order.

When people talk about the ability of world government to control aggression, the analogy they use is the police versus the lone bank robber. But the analogy with the firefighters' union or the IRA would be more appropriate. Individual criminal acts are easy to deal with, organized political acts much harder. The threat to peace in the world comes not from individuals but from organized groups such as revisionist states, military factions, and revolutionary parties.[2]

The argument for world government is that war will be eliminated when the whole world is run like a single nation. But in fact many international conflicts arise from the failures of national governments to keep the peace.[3] The government in Pakistan could not control the Bengalis in East Pakistan either by meeting their demands or by suppressing them. The failure of governmental power within the state of Pakistan led to international war with India. If the prescription "government" doesn't always work at the national level, why should we be certain that it will work at the international level?

Another problem with analogies is that we naturally draw them from our own experience. Americans think world government will be like American government, that violators of world law will be punished as violators of domestic laws are. But the US experience is not necessarily typical. When the Supreme Court of the United States ruled that Richard Nixon had to turn over tapes of his White House conversations to the special prosecutor, he did so even though the tapes damaged him irreparably. When a court in India ruled that Prime Minister Indira Gandhi had to relinquish her office because she had violated campaign laws, she refused and threw the opposition leaders into jail. Why should we think that a violator of world law would follow the US model (and resign like Nixon) instead of the Indian model (and counterattack like Gandhi)?

Argument by analogy is one fallacy. A second fallacy to watch for is peace by definition.[4] Someone using this fallacy makes peace part of the definition of the proposal that is supposed to achieve peace. For example, someone might argue that diplomacy is the best approach to peace and define diplomacy as "negotiations instead of war." Well, we say, what about the Cyprus conflict of 1974? Diplomacy wasn't able to prevent that war. "Oh, no," replies the advocate of diplomacy, "the negotiations before fighting broke out were not really a substitute for war, so they weren't really diplomacy." In other words, success in preventing war is built right into the definition of diplomacy. If that's what someone insists diplomacy must mean, of course it will prevent war.

We should begin to suspect attempts to achieve peace by definition when we encounter forceful adjectives attached to proposals. For example, followers of the Baha'i religion believe in world government and describe how a "world tribunal will adjudicate and deliver its compulsory and final verdict in all and any disputes that may arise between the various elements constituting this universal system."[5] Simply adding the words "compulsory" and "final" does not make the argument more convincing.

When we are defining world government, we must take care not to do so in a way that produces peace by definition. Government is often said to be "legitimate monopoly of armed force." But this definition should not blind us to the frequent existence of armed force, even though illegitimate, that rivals the government monopoly. An obvious case of such rivalry is a civil war.

If we use "government" in the commonly accepted way, we can say that during the nineteenth century the states of the United States formed a single government, but the states making up Europe did not; Europe was in a condition of international anarchy. But because of the American Civil War, deaths from military action in the United States in the nineteenth century nearly equaled military deaths in the European countries.[6] Clearly government alone is no guarantee of peace and order. In Quincy Wright's list of 278 wars fought from 1480 to 1941, seventy-eight of them (28 percent) were civil wars.[7] It seems likely that a world state would continue to have wars, though they might be called rebellions or insurrections.

Some advocates of world government idealize it to such an extent that it resembles no government on earth. Although they rarely spell out their views in detail, they give the impression that in this new order decision-making will be immaculate. Representatives of the states of the world will gather in a room. When serious questions arise, from the Iraqi invasion of Kuwait to global warming, the answer will immediately be evident. There will be unanimous approval of a rational and ethical course of action. The solutions will be complete and consistent with each other, without loose ends. States will be disarmed, and troublemakers such as terrorists and criminal gangs will present much less of a problem to domestic tranquility than they do now. Laws will be obeyed, quite unlike what happens in our present society, where officers of savings and loans institutions betray the trust of people who invest their money with them.

But of course there is no reason to think that decision-making on the global level will be any different from political decision-making on any other level, from local water boards to state and federal legislatures. During the crisis over the Iraqi seizure of Kuwait, Representative Henry B. Gonzalez introduced House Resolution 34, impeaching (that is, accusing) George Bush. According to Gonzalez, Bush's offense was that he "violated . . . the U.N. Charter by bribing, intimidating and threatening others, including the members of the U.N. Security Council to support belligerent acts against Iraq." But surely, as a representative in Congress, Gonzalez must know that bribing and intimidating is how American presidents get passed the legislation they want. Perhaps he remembers the remark that President Lyndon Johnson made to Senator Frank Church, when Church opposed Johnson's policy on Vietnam. Church told Johnson that he was persuaded by the arguments of the newspaper columnist Walter Lippmann, whereupon Johnson said, "All right, Frank, next time you want a dam for Idaho, you go talk to Walter Lippmann."[8]

Politics, whether lawmaking by legislatures or policy-making by executives, is contentions. Rarely is there complete agreement. Indeed, if there were, there would be no need for political forums to argue and bargain. Usually more than one solution will be offered, and for each solution one person or group will take the lead. In the 1970s tobacco advertising was banned from the airwaves, not because members of Congress suddenly all realized that cigarettes cause cancer but because Senator Frank Moss of Utah introduced a bill, marshalled support for it, and engaged in bargaining (for example, agreeing to let the ban take effect several weeks into the new year, after the Super Bowl game had been played, to allow the networks to run cigarette ads one more time).

The politics of a world government are unlikely to be different. For given issues, one state is likely to take the lead, and that state is likely to be a powerful one. The organization of a coalition against Iraq by George Bush does not differ in its essentials from the organization of a coalition against cigarettes by Senator Moss.

ARGUMENTS IN FAVOR OF WORLD GOVERNMENT

Some defenders of world government may use fallacious arguments, but that doesn't make the idea itself wrong. Critics of world government sometimes employ a fallacy themselves, the fallacy of perfectionism. They argue that unless a system functions perfectly it is of no use at all. However, many systems function imperfectly yet are useful. Some people cheat with their checkbooks. They write checks when they have no money in their accounts or when they don't even have an account. But this misuse does not make checks useless devices. Merchants find the honest use of checks worthwhile enough to put up with occasional abuse. Only if the system were grossly abused would it make sense to do without it.

Even though world government would have flaws, it wouldn't need to function perfectly to be an improvement over what we have now. Wars in the form of rebellions or insurrections might indeed occur, but we could expect that there would be fewer of these civil wars. In Quincy Wright's list only 28 percent of all wars were civil wars. One could hypothesize that under a world government civil wars would continue to occur only one-third as frequently as international wars. Thus, even if world government did not eliminate war, it might reduce it by two-thirds. These figures do not constitute conclusive proof, of course, but they do give what lawyers call a *prima facie* case; that is, upon first looking at them they seem to argue in favor of world government and not against it.

It is true that, despite a central government, the United States experienced a severe war in the nineteenth century. But without such a government, war between the states might have come sooner and been fought repeatedly, and total military casualties might have been far greater than those in Europe.

Nor is the analogy with domestic politics totally worthless. One thousand years ago the area known today as France consisted of separate states—Burgundy, Lorraine, Normandy, and many others—usually at war with each other. Over a period of five centuries, the separate provinces were brought together in a unified state. Two facts about this unification could discourage advocates of world government. One is that it took many years. Another is that these years were full of wars fought to resist unification. Both of these are drawbacks for those who want instant peace. But, on the positive side, we can say that a unitary state was finally created, that war between the formerly sovereign units disappeared, and that reversion to anarchy has become less and less likely.

The development of peace and order within France was helped by the creative role of the state. War between Burgundy and Provence is unlikely today, not just because the central authority in Paris prevents it but also because a French state fosters a sense of community between Burgundy and Provence. Children in school learn the same history; radio and television broadcast the same news and entertainment; a single code of laws makes it easy for people in one region to travel, change jobs, or engage in business in another region.

Even if we have reservations about world government, we should not underestimate how important a central authority can be in prohibiting violence. International politics differs from other kinds of politics because large-scale murder (which we call war) is still legitimate. This type of murder is not totally unregulated. Ordinarily, individuals are not entitled to cross the border with Mexico and gun down people at will. But if a few conditions are fulfilled—making a declaration of war, joining the armed forces, and being ordered to attack—they could receive medals for gunning down Mexicans. This kind of behavior is approved at no other level of politics. World government would abolish legalized mass killing. Deaths would still occur, just as they do when a state's police force resorts to violence. Such deaths would no longer be considered a normal way of doing business, however, and we would not make especially violent police officers into folk heroes.

World government would thus contribute to an enlargement of people's moral horizons. At one time morality extended only as far as one's family; it was considered moral to cheat, rob, or kill outsiders in the defense of family interests. Gradually moral horizons were extended to the village and region and tribe. Killing members of one's own tribe was considered murder, but killing members of other tribes was not. In many tribal languages, the word for "human being" was often the same as the name of the tribe. Members of other tribes were by definition not human beings, and killing them was no more murder than was killing a wolf. Today our moral horizons have extended as far as our own nation-state. The bombardier who released the atomic bomb on Hiroshima would likely have had grave scruples about releasing it on Milwaukee.[9] Advocates of world government are asking us to take one last step and extend our moral horizons to encompass all human beings.

ADVOCATES OF WORLD GOVERNMENT

Interest in world government waxes and wanes. It wanes when national states seem to be doing well, providing security and prosperity for their citizens. When they do not provide these things, interest in replacing them with larger units begins to grow. The thirteen American colonies federated after a period of revolution. The countries of Europe began to move toward a European community after the disruptions of World War II. Even in the United States interest in a world government grew after World War II. Some polls at that time showed almost two-thirds of the respondents willing to support at least the abstract principle of a world body able to settle disputes between states and enforce its decisions.[10]

Such sentiments were cultivated by writers such as Norman Cousins, for years editor of the *Saturday Review*. You can read his arguments in editorials appearing in that magazine or in his influential book *In Place of Folly*.[11] According to Cousins, there is no alternative to world government. In the past we could afford to hesitate, bicker, and procrastinate because the consequences of failure were not the total destruction of humanity. No more, Cousins argues, in what might be labeled the *in extremis* position. The situation has changed so radically because of nuclear weapons and their delivery systems that equally radical departures in thinking are required. We face the possibility that all human life will be destroyed within a few days as the result of actions by a handful of military leaders. In this extreme situation all the old hesitations about taking radical steps are no longer valid.

Cousins and others with similar views clearly were writing under the impact of the then-new atomic weapon. Today it is easy for us to say that these fears were exaggerated. World government was not instituted, but the world did not come to an end. We were not in the extreme situation Cousins thought we were in. Perhaps his problem was that he was neither a scientist nor a military expert and lacked the competence to judge the new weapons. However, before we dismiss the in extremis argument, we should look at the version of it offered by Herman Kahn, a thinker with a background very different from Cousins'. Kahn made his reputation with his book *On Thermonuclear War*.[12] In it he looked in great detail and with great detachment at the consequences of nuclear weapons that Cousins warned about. What would happen in atomic war? Would all humanity be destroyed? Would the survivors envy the dead?

Kahn outraged many people by his answer. No, the survivors would not envy the dead. Thermonuclear war would be bad but not nearly so bad as many people expected. Kahn himself had a background in physics, and he used techniques of analysis developed at the Rand Corporation. These credentials did not impress some people, to whom he became a symbol of bloodthirsty irrationality. A reviewer in *Scientific American* asked, "Is there really a Herman Kahn," or is this a "staff hoax in poor taste?"[13]

Although Kahn warned against exaggerating the effects of nuclear war, he never advocated nuclear war—a distinction that was lost on some people because of their emotional reaction to his book. In fact, Kahn devoted much effort to devising ways to keep the initial stages of an international crisis from escalating to all-out war. His writings deal only with short-run measures to prevent escalation. In the long run, he wrote, the only plausible alternative is some variant of world government.[14]

Like Cousins, Kahn uses the in extremis argument. Suppose, he suggested, a few missiles are launched accidentally. Faced with the awesome prospect of escalation to total destruction, the United States and the Soviet Union might quickly conclude that deterrence and anarchy are no way to run the world and sign an agreement in a matter of days. Whatever theoretical proposal was available might be implemented almost overnight.

PRACTICAL DETAILS OF THE WORLD STATE

If world opinion suddenly shifts in favor of world government, what kind of blueprint do we want to have waiting? We should be clear that we are talking about a *government*, not a technocracy or rule by nonpolitical experts. A plan for world government is not like a plan for an automated telephone switchboard. It cannot operate without human judgment and political decisions. The constitution of a world state may read, "Arms are prohibited; violators will be automatically punished," but words alone tell very little about what a world government will be like in practice. The Soviet Union had a constitution with written guarantees of civil liberties; the United Kingdom, in contrast, has had no written constitution at all. Clearly anyone who relies on words alone to guarantee the protection of civil liberties could be seriously deceived.

Obviously a police force cannot be employed against a violator without a decision to do so. Someone must tell the police to arrest conspirators arming in secret, and the decision to arrest depends on other decisions. An official must decide to "see" a violation in the first place. Suppose a constable on duty at midnight in Bliggens City stops a car for weaving over the center line on Main Street and discovers that the car is driven by W. W. Bliggens, Chairman of the Board of Bliggens Textile Mills. Does the constable see a case of drunken driving and make the required arrest, or does he see a motorist fatigued by a hard day's work and in obvious need of a lift home? Blacks in the United States have charged that standards of law and order differ within the black and white communities. Murders in which both attacker and victim are black have been tolerated in a way that other murders have not been. Law enforcement officers, it is claimed, do not "see" crimes committed by blacks against blacks. Similarly some forms of world government could lead to toleration of certain kinds of collective violence—acts that did not threaten the interests of the world rulers or acts that were allowed because the world rulers were intimidated by the perpetrators. We have no right to be more naive about world government than we are about our own.

The question of "seeing" a violation is only one matter to be resolved. There are many others. Suppose a violation is clearly identified. How much force is to be employed against it? If an alleged violator promises to stop before enforcement has begun, is punishment then called for? Matters of judgment always come up. Who will make these judgments? Questions about who will run a world state, how they will be selected, and how they will be held accountable are very important.

Governments may range from very loose associations to very tightly controlled totalitarian states. The distinguishing characteristic is the amount of behavior they control. The government that governs least may control very little behavior; it may do little more than catch thieves and repel invaders. A totalitarian government strives for total control, over leisure activities, family life, and even private thoughts. Again we must avoid the pitfall of analogy. When Americans use the term "government," they naturally think first of the United States government and focus on two of its prominent features— its democracy and its federalism.

"Democracy" is an elastic term, and we need define it only loosely. *Democracy* is a form of government in which fairly large numbers of people participate in decision-making and even larger numbers are consulted before the decisions are made. At the opposite pole is *autocracy*, a system in which decisions are made by a very few and the decisions are not challenged. Whatever one's reservations about the present American system, one will probably admit that all decision-making is not concentrated in the hands of a very few. The president, members of Congress, and most other officials agree that something must be done to conserve energy, but no one official or group can decree that its solution be implemented.

Not all governments operate under such restraints. Although no government is entirely free of restraint, some are a lot freer than others. When the revolutionary government took over South Vietnam, it decided to stop crime on the streets by shooting thieves and looters and letting their bodies lie at the scene of the crime. Some Americans have proposed the same solution, but they have little chance of implementing it because too many groups would oppose it.

Americans generally agree that they pay a price for these restraints, the price of relative inefficiency. The United States has responded very slowly to a shortage of energy because so many groups need to be consulted. In contrast, the revolutionary Cambodian government in 1975 decided to reduce dependence on imported oil quickly by destroying motor vehicles and then just as quickly did so.

This line of thought suggests that a world government, if it were to be efficient, might be less democratic than the government we are used to. It might consult fewer people and pay less heed to objections to policies. The kind of opposition to registering firearms expressed by some Americans could not be tolerated on a world scale if a world government were to achieve the goal of preventing war. If a world government did have the power to compel people to surrender firearms (stop and think how much power the United States government would have to use just to have firearms registered), what else would it be able to do? Perhaps control the content of books, newspapers, and television programs? After all, this sort of regulation could be justified as helping to prevent war because books, newspapers, and television shape attitudes toward war and peace.

The firearms example is enlightening in another way. It is difficult to imagine the registration, much less the abolition, of private firearms in the United States, yet opinion polls have repeatedly demonstrated that only a minority of Americans opposes such control.[15] But this minority is well organized and politically active. The majority is confronting not isolated individuals but political groups. As we pointed out earlier, it is the political group that gives government the most trouble. We do not anticipate that a world government will encounter problems from solitary lawbreakers building atom bombs in their hobby rooms. Trouble will come from organized groups—the IRA, the PLO, or whatever may be active. Considering recent history, we do not have much reason for confidence that world government will be able to control them. In a few countries terrorists are controlled, but these countries can hardly be used as an argument in favor of world government, for they have enormous repressive forces. Neither Paraguay nor the Soviet Union had terrorists blowing up buildings, but most of us would not have liked to have lived there.

Most of us would oppose a government with extensive repressive power, preferring to take our chances with the present risk of war instead. For this reason most of the serious proposals for world government advanced in the West envisage the relatively weak control associated with the central government in a federal state. The federalism of the United States is often used as an example.

Unfortunately for the advocates of a weak world government, American federalism looks more attractive in its historical version than in its present-day form. Almost universal complaints about big government have not stopped the enormous growth of central government in recent decades. Behavior is now regulated in a way never imagined by writers of the Constitution. Government has a say in what kinds of workers are employed, how packages are labeled, and even where children are sent to school. This development is not unique to the United States. Governments around the world are growing bigger, not smaller.

Unsuccessful attempts to limit the scope of national governments have not discouraged proponents of a world federal system with limited powers. The best known of these proposals is described in *World Peace Through World Law*, by Grenville Clark and Louis Sohn.[16] The Clark and Sohn proposal is so modest that it hardly deserves the name "world government." Governmental authority would extend only to preventing war. In conformity with this limited aim, Clark and Sohn propose not to create a new organization but merely to revise the existing United Nations organization. The major parts of the revamped UN would be a General Assembly, an Executive Council, an Inspection Commission, and a World Police Force.

1. *The General Assembly*. Today the General Assembly of the UN has only limited advisory powers. Under the revision it would have no more power except in one area—maintaining peace. Because it would have real legislative powers for this purpose, Clark and Sohn propose a new voting system, weighted according to population. But they propose that the weighting be done by steps. The four largest countries would have thirty representatives each; the eight next-largest countries would have fifteen representatives each; and so on. The four largest countries are China, India, what was then the USSR, and the United States. A system of direct proportionality would mean that China, with three or four times the population of the United States, would have three or four times the representation. The system proposed by Clark and Sohn makes America's representation equal to China's (and also makes that of major communist countries equal to that of major noncommunist ones).

2. *Executive Council*. This body would be essentially the same as the Security Council of the UN, having the power to intervene and prevent war. However, in the current Security Council each of the five major states has the power to block action by voting against it. Clark and Sohn wish to eliminate this veto power. A qualified majority (twelve votes out of a total seventeen) would still be required for action. These twelve votes would have to include a majority of the four biggest countries, but a country could no longer prevent action against itself.

3. *Inspection Commission*. This commission, along with its staff, the Inspection Service, is entirely new. It would supervise disarmament. Because states, by agreeing to the Clark–Sohn plan, would be agreeing to disarm, the Inspection Commission would have to do no persuading. Its function would be to see that disarmament is carried out. During the first two years, it would take an arms census, counting the weapons each country has; over the next ten years it would supervise the reduction of the weapons at a rate of 10 percent a year.

4. *World Police Force*. This is another addition to the existing system. The World Police Force would enforce disarmament and prevent attacks by any remaining armed forces. In a disarmed world, the municipal police force of a

large state could threaten a small neighbor. A small Caribbean island, for example, might hesitate to host a convention of American sheriffs if they came armed. The World Police Force would be large enough to reassure any small country. It would consist of a regular force of about half a million and reserves up to twice that number. The police would be recruited from many countries and would be stationed around the world.

Clark and Sohn put forth many other specific proposals. They have considered many issues and provided many answers. If we do not now have a world government, the reason is not because no thinking has been done about it. What is needed is not further elaboration of schemes but the approval of states.

Clark and Sohn suggest ratification by five-sixths of the countries of the world (provided that these countries constitute five-sixths of the world's population) before the plan goes into effect. Approval of that magnitude— 83.3 percent—would reduce fear that the system would never work. The question is how to get that much approval. Perhaps Herman Kahn's prognostication is the best: After a big scare resulting from a close brush with war, people will suddenly find themselves ready to change their thinking; then the Clark–Sohn proposals, being the best at hand, will be adopted in a few days.

RESISTANCE TO WORLD GOVERNMENT

Proponents of world government do not rely solely on catastrophe to implement their plans. Traditionally they have used analogy not only to explain how world government would prevent war but also to show how such a government would come about. And again the analogy is frequently drawn from the United States. In 1783 the thirteen colonies were separate, sovereign states, loosely bound by the Articles of Confederation. By 1787 they had agreed to form a strong federal union and central government. The motto they chose, *E pluribus unum*, "out of many, one," summarizes what happened. One historian of these years titled his book *The Great Rehearsal*, suggesting that other parts of the world might later follow the American example.[17]

Opponents of world government likewise have traditional arguments. Their basic argument is that the American situation was unique. Those thirteen colonies had just completed a revolutionary war; the shift of political loyalties from small units to a larger one occurs only when other political and social habits are changing as well—in other words, in a revolutionary situation.[18] The revolutionary war was fought against a common enemy under one commander, who went on to become head of the new state. This cooperation in waging a war was facilitated by many things the colonists already had in common—language, culture, political tradition. It was not accidental that the part of North America where a different language was spoken, Quebec, was not included in the new state, or that those who did not share the political values of the revolution were often forced to emigrate to Canada. Whatever petty jealousies separated the thirteen colonies, there were no traditional barriers to movement or trade, certainly nothing comparable to what years of independent sovereign existence had created in Europe.

No one should deny, of course, that a union of small units is possible. The United States was formed of small units; so too was modern Switzerland. But we should not ignore the enormous barriers that vested interests normally put in the way of amalgamation. A "Greater New York" joining the parts of New Jersey, Pennsylvania, Connecticut, and New York State that are economically and in other ways tied to New York City is a rational solution to many of New York's problems, but such a solution is not likely because of set patterns and vested interests.

Similarly, countries resist amalgamation. In fact, such resistance is given the highest priority in a state's policy and is termed "national security." It is a basic policy of Pakistan to resist amalgamation with India, of Mexico to resist amalgamation with the United States, and so on. Four reasons are usually given.

1. People are attached to their culture, language, and traditions. They fear that these will be changed by amalgamation. The Protestants in Northern Ireland, for example, fear the effects of incorporation into an Irish state that is mostly Catholic.

2. People fear disruption of their economic system. Although all Koreans would like to live in one country, the difference between North Korea's state-controlled economy and South Korea's free-enterprise economy is a major reason the halves have not yet reunited.

3. People fear that a large political unit will be less responsive to their wishes. The Norwegians rejected membership in the European Communities in September 1972, in part out of fear that this loose union of states could eventually acquire too much authority and their own control over that authority would be diluted.

4. People who benefit from existing arrangements, such as those with jobs in government, fear they will lose income or power. It might be logical to have a single prairie state called Dakota, but we would expect any such proposal to be resisted by the existing governments in North Dakota and South Dakota.

Resistance to amalgamation appears to be very ingrained. This is clear if we look at a situation in which the four factors just listed do not apply, or at least do not apply with the force they normally have. Canada and the United States share a language (although both have a sizable minority speaking another language—French in one case, Spanish in the other). Canadians and Americans have a common political tradition. The economies of Canada and the United States work according to the same principles. The fourth factor, vested interests, is present, but both countries have a federal system, which would minimize the disruptions caused by any kind of union.

In spite of these similarities, these two neighbors have trouble taking even small steps toward political union. At the extreme western end of the United States–Canada boundary is the peninsula of Point Roberts, an area of the United States that can be reached on land only by traveling through Canada. A joint Canadian–US commission tries to deal with special problems that this enclave causes, such as the need to bus children through Canada to get them to school in the United States. In 1973 the Point Roberts Board presented a modest proposal to make the enclave the headquarters of an international park that would encompass much of the surrounding waters. The proposal was greeted with fury by the local residents. One called the Americans on the board "Benedict Arnolds." A sexton at the Point Roberts cemetery said he would gladly dig two graves free if the two major American proponents of the plan would drop dread.[19] If good neighbors sharing an unarmed border with a common language, tradition, culture, and economy react so strongly to the mildest proposal for cooperation, how will traditional enemies react to proposed amalgamation?

Feelings run just as high on the other side of the border. A 1988 agreement to institute a free trade regime between the United States and Canada, viewed by many economists as a necessary step toward economic survival in the face of European moves toward integration, provoked shrill opposition from Canada's two opposition parties. The leader of one party told a newspaper interviewer that "the word integration is one that implies to me the gradual surrendering of sovereignty. Canada has never needed that type of integration."[20]

Presumably Canadian opposition leaders feared loss of their sovereignty to Americans, or at least to such international bodies as might be set up to settle economic disagreements arising out of the treaty. Ironically, even as the leader of the opposition in Canada was defending Canada's sovereignty, the American vice president was speaking in similar terms. George Bush, campaigning for president, declared: "A president can't subordinate his decision-making to a multinational body. He can't sacrifice one ounce of our sovereignty to any organization."[21] An experienced observer would chalk both of these statements up to the heated rhetoric of an election campaign, but politicians say what they expect will resonate with their audiences.

In the end, the Canadian opposition did not prevail and Prime Minister Brian Mulroony won enough seats to pass the free trade bill. But his total number of seats in Parliament was reduced and the opposition attacks on the issue of free trade were credited with dropping his massive pre-election lead in public opinion polls to a slim plurality. The lesson was clear: Any Canadian politician daring to espouse any integration with the United States that went beyond the modest free trade proposal would be defeated by a tide of Canadian nationalism.

CONSENSUS VERSUS COERCION

Behavior in both the Point Roberts case and the free trade debate illustrate a basic proposition about government: It depends as much on subjective feelings as on objective institutions. If many people are opposed to cooperation with a group they view as outsiders, then objective factors such as a common language make little difference. The subjective element in government is termed *shared values* or *consensus*. All successful states depend at least in part on consensus. States also use force or coercion, but the amount of coercion needed depends on the amount of consensus already present—the greater the consensus, the less coercion is needed. This is why small, homogeneous, well-integrated states like Denmark and Costa Rica have both small police forces and low crime rates. They enjoy a wide consensus. On the other hand, in countries where different groups hold very different values—South Africa or Chile—large repressive forces have been needed.

It seems clear that in the world today there is little consensus on values important to a community. Differences are wide on such issues as the way to organize an economy and distribute wealth, the right to hold religious beliefs different from those of others, and the morality of divorce, birth control, and abortion. Any attempt to create a world state without consensus to build on will have to rely on coercion—in fact, a great deal of coercion. A world state that would include the Irish Republican Army and the British, the Palestinians and the Israelis, and the Greeks and the Turks would require a great deal of centralized power just to stay in existence.

This dependence on coercion undermines the claim that a world state would be limited. If the central authority could prevent the United States from having a cache of arms, could it not also prevent the United States from have a cache of surplus grain? Grain could be taken away from productive countries as a legitimate way to prevent war, on the argument that starvation is a cause of violence. Drastic changes in diet might follow. Would Americans accept world government if it meant an end to backyard barbecues? Or the central authority might decree that cattle in India should be slaughtered to save the grain they would otherwise consume. Fears of such action would provoke widespread resistance in India. Resistance to this kind of governmental control would generate new conflict, possibly more than the world has right now.

The need to rely on coercion when consensus is absent is supported by the little historical evidence about world government that we have. The closest humanity has ever come to a world state was the Roman Empire. It brought together the formerly separate states bordering the Mediterranean. Although there were areas of civilization elsewhere in the world, they had such little contact with the Mediterranean that in the minds of the Romans they did not exist. For all practical purposes, the Roman Empire did what world states are supposed to do. It abolished individual sovereignties and replaced them with a centralized authority.

The Roman Empire was created by force. Order was maintained by the famous Roman legions. The phrase *pax Romana*, the peace of Rome, stands for peace maintained by force. The peace was constantly tested by wars in the form of revolts against Roman rule, similar to national liberation movements today, and the revolts were brutally suppressed. The defeat of the Jewish Zealots, with the destruction of the Temple and the dispersal of the inhabitants of Judea, is the best-known.

A WORLD POLICE FORCE

The need for coercion in any world government that might come into existence in the foreseeable future means that we must pay special attention to the World Police Force proposed by Clark and Sohn. Where would this force of up to half a million young people come from? Obviously they would have to come from many countries to keep the force from being too lenient with any one country. Therefore most members would need the intellectual ability to learn a second language, yet be willing to take orders, live a regimented barracks life, and put their lives at risk. In an age when military service in all countries is increasingly unpopular, why would talented young people join? One author suggests high salaries and an appeal to idealism.[22] Perhaps such incentives would work, but the force would serve mainly garrison duty in enclaves scattered around the world. Garrison duty has always been considered tedious and has no obvious attraction for idealists. For the Allied Control Commission in charge of enforcing the disarmament of Germany after World War I, such duty led to laxness and unwillingness to investigate complaints. A study of the UN peace-keeping force on Cyprus found that the overriding feature of peace-keeping duty was "tedium and monotony."[23]

What about occasions when enforcement action must be taken? The kind of idealism called for is a new one—willingness to act against one's own country. One wonders if those willing to do this would make the best soldiers.[24] Traditionally, military duty has not been incompatible with other attachments; sacrificing for one's own country did not mean going against one's family. The same qualities that made Robert E. Lee an admired soldier led him to leave the US Army and fight along with the rebellious forces in his own section of the country. In a future state, it is hard to imagine a Bengali contingent on a World Police Force willing to use force against armed Bengalis trying to save themselves from extermination by Punjabis.

The attraction of high salaries is not clear either. One could hardly enjoy them while on garrison duty. Moreover, if the police force took part in unpopular acts, its members might have difficulty finding a place back home to enjoy their savings after retirement. The historical record is not encouraging. Going off to die for a patriotic cause has produced better soldiers than going off for monetary reward. Mercenary armies were possible only when the alternative was unbearable poverty, and even then they did not fare well against idealistic armies.

The source of high salaries is another problem. Police forces are not just men and women; they are also supplies, bases, and the finances to run them. The financial burden might be less than the present arms burden, but it would not be negligible any more than the police force is a negligible item in the budget of New York City. In the development of modern nation-states, monarchs started out with their own power base—royal lands and royal retainers. Louis XI of France relied on the area around Paris known as the Ile de France; the kings of Prussia relied on the Mark of Brandenburg. Proponents of a World Police Force, by contrast, propose that the force be dependent on charity. It is not difficult to imagine cases in which this would cause grave difficulties.

Suppose, in a disarmed world, Mexico gets massive US investment to develop oil fields near the US border but refuses to share their output with the United States. A force consisting of Texas Rangers and oil company security guards moves into Mexico to take over the oil fields. The World Police Force is sent in against them, but the United States, in self-righteous anger, cuts off its share of financing for the force and stops delivery of equipment such as helicopters that would be vital to enforcement action. It is easy to see that the success of a World Police Force will depend on its possessing an independent power base.

But once it gets such a power base, how can a police force be controlled by anyone for any purpose? How could demands for incredibly large salaries be resisted? How could protests against even the grossest violations of neutrality be effective? Even if the force did not become corrupt, it would have to be strong enough to prevent change, and a system that prevents change is for all practical purposes a tyranny.

One of the dangers of a name such as "World Police Force" is that again we draw an analogy to our own experience. We think of President Truman dismissing General MacArthur, with General MacArthur quietly fading away. We don't think of the more typical case, in which the attempt to dismiss the head of the armed forces leads to the overthrow of the government. The latter possibility is far more likely. In recent years about two-thirds of the countries in the world have experienced military coups. America's experience with a totally housebroken military is unusual and misleading as a model of what a world army would be like. Instead of politicians controlling their police, it is more likely that the police would control politics.

World government is a frontal attack on the problem of state sovereignty. Advocates of world government identify state sovereignty as a major cause of war. They wish to deprive the individual states of both the ability and the excuse to use force in their own behalf to settle disputes. Under world government, force would be centralized under one authority. But much of the case for world government rests on an analogy with domestic society, and analogies, though helpful in illustrating proposals, are not convincing proof. The differences between domestic society and international society are large—one of the most important being that people within states (at least within stable ones) have a lot more in common with each other than they have with outsiders. In the absence of consensus, great amounts of power would be needed to institute and maintain a world government. But concentrating all this power in one place would create a temptation to seize it. For this reason, too much reliance on force to solve the problem of war among states raises serious doubts about world government.

Even if you might find an enforced peace, a *pax Romana*, preferable to present international anarchy, the power to bring it about does not seem available in the world today. The Roman legions, however undemocratic, could govern an empire. Modern political leaders have difficulty governing New York City, not to mention Cyprus, Northern Ireland, or Lebanon. Those who wish to resist authority have many more weapons at their disposal than the Jewish Zealots did. From cars you can siphon gasoline to make Molotov cocktails; from construction sites you can steal dynamite to make bombs; and from nuclear reactors you can make off with enough plutonium to build a nuclear device. In the face of such developments, the amount of power needed to create and administer a world state simply is not available.

A global consensus that would serve as a foundation for world government does not yet exist. But we still have to consider the question of whether a limited consensus exists. If world government does not work on a global level, perhaps it will work on the regional level. After all, states themselves grew by the integration of local units. Perhaps world government will emerge from the integration of states. Perhaps there are lessons in current moves toward regional integration.

NOTES

1. For a discussion of Dante's style of argument and conclusion, see George H. Sabine and Thomas L. Thorson, *A History of Political Theory*, 4th ed. (Hinsdale, Ill.: Dryden Press, 1973), pp. 243–248.

2. Inis L. Claude, Jr., discusses this point at length in his excellent chapters on world government in *Power and International Relations* (New York: Random House, 1962), especially pp. 243–255.

3. Inis L. Claude, Jr., *Swords into Plowshares*, 4th ed. (New York: Random House, 1971), p. 424.

4. Claude, *Power and International Relations*, p. 218; he calls it "solution by definition."

5. Shoghi Effendi, *The World Order of Bah'u'llah*, rev. ed. (Wilmette, Ill.: Baha'i Publishing Trust, 1955), pp. 203–204.

6. Consult J. David Singer and Melvin Small, *The Wages of War, 1816–1965* (New York: John Wiley, 1972) for statistics on war. Using the list of European wars on page 297 and the battle deaths for these wars on pages 60–75, one arrives at a total of 648,180 battle deaths for Europe in the nineteenth century, excluding the period of the Napoleonic Wars. The American Civil War caused about 630,000 deaths in battle.

7. Quincy Wright, *A Study of War*, 2nd ed. (Chicago: University of Chicago Press, 1965), p. 651.

8. Stanley Karnow, *Vietnam: A History* (New York: Viking Press, 1983), p. 421.

9. This point was made by Kenneth Boulding in *The World Community*, ed. Quincy Wright (Chicago: University of Chicago Press, 1948), pp. 101–102.

10. *Newsweek*, October 14, 1946, pp. 44–45.

11. Norman Cousins, *In Place of Folly* (New York: Harper, 1961).

12. Herman Kahn, *On Thermonuclear War* (Princeton, N.J.: Princeton University Press, 1959).

13. James R. Newman, "Books: Six Discussions of Thermonuclear War," *Scientific American*, Vol. 204, No. 3 (March 1961), p. 197.

14. Herman Kahn, "The Arms Race and World Order," in *The Revolution in World Politics*, ed. Morton A. Kaplan (New York: John Wiley, 1962).

15. For example, see the *Gallup Report*, No. 187 (Princeton, N.J.: The Gallup Poll, April 1981), p. 14; see also *The New York Times*, June 20, 1983, p. Y9.

16. Grenville Clark and Louis Sohn, *World Peace Through World Law* (Cambridge, Mass.: Harvard University Press, 1958). See especially the Introduction.

17. Carl Van Doren, *The Great Rehearsal* (New York: Viking Press, 1948).

18. Karl W. Deutsch et al., *Political Community and the North Atlantic Area* (Princeton N.J.: Princeton University Press, 1957), p. 48.

19. *Bellingham* (Washington) *Herald*, December 4, 1973.

20. John F. Burns, Toronto correspondent of *The New York Times*, interview with John N. Turner of the Liberal Party, *The New York Times*, August 7, 1988, p. E3.

21. Richard N. Gardener "One Mainstream Dukakis . . . ," *The New York Times*, August 11, 1988, [Op-Ed], p. Y27.

22. See the discussion very much in the vein of Clark and Sohn by Arthur Larson, "Arms Control Through World Law," in *Arms Control, Disarmament, and National Security*, ed. Donald G. Brennan (New York: George Braziller, 1961), pp. 432–436.

23. Charles C. Moskos, Jr., *Peace Soldiers* (Chicago: University of Chicago Press, 1976), p. 84.

24. This point has been made by a number of commentators, among them Thomas C. Schelling in "Strategy: A World Force in Operation," in *International Military Forces*, ed. Lincoln P. Bloomfield (Boston: Little, Brown, 1964), p. 230.

CHAPTER 14

REGIONAL INTEGRATION

It is safe to say that the world is not ready for a single government, based on any mix of consensus and coercion. But what is now impossible on a global scale might succeed on a regional scale. Regional integration occurred when the United States of America was created out of thirteen separate colonies. True, North America still experienced wars in the following centuries—a war with Canada (and England) in 1812, a war with Mexico in 1846, and a war with Cuba (or rather, with its Spanish rulers) in 1898. Yet within the system created by union of the thirteen colonies, only one war was fought, and although it was a very bloody one, the possibility of another civil war seems remote indeed. During the same two hundred years, almost a dozen wars occurred in Central and South America. It seems likely that without the creation of the United States, more wars would have occurred on the North American continent.

In retrospect, the factors pushing the thirteen colonies toward unification seem obvious—shared traditions, language, culture, and economic system. Yet despite these similarities, creation of a unified state was not automatic. Ratification of the Constitution after the Convention in 1787 was by no means assured. Had the union failed, we might be emphasizing "obvious" reasons for failure—the differences between Catholics in Maryland and Protestants in New England, or between a plantation economy based on slavery in South Carolina and independent small farmers in Pennsylvania. These obstacles are in fact a cause for hope. The fact that the

United States of America was created despite differences among its constituent parts suggests we should not dismiss the integration of states into larger units too quickly. Nor is the process to be confined to history books. Two hundred years after the American experiment, another experiment in integration is taking place in Europe. What has happened so far gives us insights into steps toward curbing sovereignty by regional integration.

THE ROAD TO WORLD GOVERNMENT: THE EXAMPLE OF EUROPE

Some writers have called World War I and World War II a two-part "European Civil War." Perhaps it is going too far to imply that a unified Europe existed when the first of these wars began in 1914, but certainly the shared suffering during these wars did much to drive the Europeans toward unity.

The two wars did much to weaken several of the frequently cited barriers to integration, in particular breaking down economic systems and destroying vested interests. And although there remained strong barriers in the form of distinct languages, cultures, and traditions, the wars made Europeans realize they also had much in common. This was especially true of members of pre–World War II Christian parties. These parties, which had existed in all the continental countries and drew a large number but never a majority of voters, had acted mainly to protect the narrowly defined interests of the Catholic Church, such as the right to run parochial schools. The temporary ascendancy of enemies of the Church—Nazis in Germany, Fascists in Italy, German occupiers in France—deprived these parties of any responsibility for governing during the war. Some of the more thoughtful leaders drew several conclusions from their enforced exclusion.

One was the need to be concerned with broader social issues, such as a more equal distribution of wealth. Another, important in countries such as Germany with sizable Protestant populations, was the need to transcend the narrow Catholic interests of the prewar period. The movement that emerged from the wartime experience was known as Christian Democracy. Although only loosely organized at the international level, within each major country it led to the creation of important parties with leaders committed to European cooperation: the Christian Democratic Union in Germany, the Christian Democracy in Italy, and the Popular Republic Movement in France. Two of these leaders, Konrad Adenauer in Germany and Alcide de Gasperi in Italy, became prime ministers, and one, Robert Schuman in France, served as foreign minister. Perhaps coincidentally, each also came not from the central core, but a border area of his country—in fact, Schuman and de Gasperi both spoke German, while the German leader, Adenauer, came from the French-influenced Rhineland.

The Christian Democratic movement was only part of a more general change in the attitude of many Europeans. There had been a widespread reaction to nationalism. Extreme nationalism had been at the heart of both Nazism and Fascism, and these two movements were not only discredited by defeat but blamed for the desolate conditions Europeans found themselves in after the war.

The change in attitude resulting from the war was reinforced by external pressures. Some of these came from the Soviet Union, which was absorbing the East European countries into its sphere of influence. In the part of Germany under Soviet occupation, the popular Social Democratic Party was forced to merge with the unpopular Communist Party, to profit from the combined votes at the polls while keeping control in the hands of the Communist leadership. In Czechoslovakia a coalition government, made up of progressives, socialists, and communists, came to an end in 1948 when the Communists expelled all others by force. Non-Communist party leaders in Western Europe feared that the same thing would happen to their parties if they were weak and divided in the face of Soviet pressure.

Another external force was the United States, which encouraged a movement toward an integrated "United States of Europe." Americans wanted a strong Europe, both as a trading partner and as a bulwark against the kind of disorder that led to fascist governments after World War I. Americans did not seem to have given much thought at the time to the possibility that a United States of Europe could eventually be a formidable economic rival. Americans saw only a benign analogy with the creation of their own country.

The United States was able to add a material incentive to integration in the form of economic aid for European recovery. Commonly called the Marshall Plan, after Secretary of State George C. Marshall, who announced it in 1947, the massive infusion of funds (an amount equal in its first year to 10 percent of the United States federal budget) enabled the Europeans to recover from the destruction of six years of war. The aid was not granted on a bilateral basis but coordinated through an organization, the Organization of European Cooperation.

THE EUROPE OF THE SIX

Marshall Plan aid, going to former allies and enemies alike, raised the question of the recovery of German heavy industry, something the French viewed with alarm. In May 1950 French Foreign Minister Robert Schuman proposed a European Coal and Steel Community (ECSC) as a way of retaining some external control over Germany without outright occupation. It was a deal that made sense to all parties. The Germans got their industry restored; their neighbors got some say in how it could be used. The ECSC proposal was accepted by six states (France, Germany, Italy, Netherlands, Belgium, and Luxemburg) and went into effect in 1952. Members of the ECSC set up a High Authority of nine members, two from each of the larger states, one from each of the smaller ones. This High Authority could make *binding decisions* on the production and marketing of coal, steel, and related products. We usually think of the ability to make binding decisions as a hallmark of government. Yet here was an international body, the Higher Authority, empowered to set production levels, fix price ceilings, and prohibit marketing cartels. It could and did levy fines against companies that violated its regulations. Companies within a member state could not appeal to sovereignty as a reason for disregarding the rules. Such a company would find its own national courts enforcing the international rule.

Furthermore, this Higher Authority made its decisions by a simple majority. The ECSC dispensed with the unanimity rule or veto usually found in international bodies. The member states had surrendered a part of their sovereignty, although only in one area of economic life, to the supranational Higher Authority.

The ECSC came into existence because it was supported by a number of groups, even though each was supporting the community for its own reasons. The functionalists supported it as the first step toward total European integration. But the ECSC was not as inclusive as Schuman had hoped. The British refused requests to join, out of a traditional distrust for permanent ties with continental countries and out of fear that it would jeopardize British ties with the Commonwealth countries. European neutral countries such as Switzerland and Sweden were reluctant to join and European countries still ruled by dictators, such as Portugal and Spain, were not invited.

The success of the European Coal and Steel Community led to the creation of two additional communities among the same six countries. These were agreed to in 1955 and put into effect in January 1958. One of these was the European Atomic Energy Community (Euratom), the main concern of which was helping its member states forestall an energy shortage by using nuclear reactors to generate power. Euratom provided, among other things, common safety standards, shared research facilities, and community control of fissionable materials. The other new community was commonly called the Common Market; its formal title was the European Economic Community (EEC). By the EEC treaty the six countries agreed to establish a customs union over a period of twelve years, reducing to zero their tariffs on goods produced in the community and adjusting the tariffs on goods produced outside until they were all at the same level. The EEC also included provisions to encourage economic cooperation among its members in other ways. It facilitated the free movement of laborers from one country to another by allowing them to transfer social security benefits earned in one country to another.

Both Euratom and the EEC were patterned on the ECSC. Each consisted of a higher authority (called a commission in the new communities), controlled by an assembly and council and supported by a court. In 1967 the structures of all three communities were merged into one. A single commission in Brussels administers all three, answerable to a council of foreign ministers and an assembly called "the European Parliament."

THE ENLARGEMENT OF THE EUROPEAN COMMUNITY

Europe prospered in the 1960s. In part the Europeans were simply sharing in worldwide economic growth, but whatever its cause, prosperity worked to the benefit of European cooperation. The formal EEC goal of abolishing internal tariffs was reached eighteen months ahead of schedule and supporters of European integration then began to talk of more ambitious projects. All the cooperative programs (the Common Market, Euratom, and the Coal and Steel Community) were brought together as part of the single "European Community" and Europeans began to speak of "the EC" in the same way that Americans speak of "the USA."

An important milestone in the development of Europe was the enlargement of the European Community beyond the original six members. The deterioration of Britain's position in the world, in contrast to the success of the Community, led the British to reconsider their earlier refusal to join; in the 1960s they made several requests for membership. After several rebuffs, most coming from French President Charles de Gaulle, Britain was accepted as a member in January 1973, along with Denmark and Ireland. Membership had also been offered to Norway but the Norwegians rejected it in a referendum in September 1972. Mcmbership was extended to Greece in 1981, and Spain and Portugal in 1986, creating a "Europe of the Twelve."

It was not clear that the enlargement of the Community strengthened it. More members meant greater diversity—more economic differences, more national disagreements, even more official languages. With nine official languages, about one-third of the Community budget was going to interpretation and translation. New members undermined the consensus on some existing policies. In particular, British membership caused problems with the Common Agricultural Policy (CAP), a program that subsidized prices of farm products well above world market levels. The British found they were paying large amounts to finance the CAP, yet their own farmers were receiving few benefits and their consumers paying more for food.

The CAP was the single most expensive European program. Yet it was hardly an economic success. Surpluses grew—a "butter mountain" of more than one million metric tons, a "wine lake," and similar large stockpiles of cereals and beef.[1] In noneconomic areas, Europe had no common policy at all. Some states boycotted the Moscow Olympics of 1980 as a response to the

Soviet invasion of Afghanistan, others did not. Some supported a Palestinian state, others were lukewarm. Prime Minister Margaret Thatcher allowed US planes to take off from bases in Britain for an air raid on Libya in 1986, while other members would not allow the planes to fly over their territory.

Thirty years is the traditional length of a generation, and a generation after its founding in 1955, the European Economic Community was still not truly united. Indeed, it was not even truly a customs union. Outright tariffs had been abolished, but they were replaced by other technical barriers, such as testing and certification requirements, that were just as bothersome. It was estimated that the costs resulting from such rules, plus the border delays created by enforcing them, added 20 percent to the cost of goods in intra-European trade. Europeans still looked enviously at the United States, where an entrepreneur had instant and almost unrestricted access to a continent-wide market. In Europe, by contrast, business still had difficulty reaching beyond national borders.

To illustrate how hard it still was to do business in a divided Europe, Europeans frequently cite the case of telephones, an important component of modern business. European governments consider telephone communications analogous to mail and run the telephone system as part of their post offices. This had yielded ten different switching systems. As a result, the European companies that manufacture switching equipment had to spend $10 billion in development costs, compared to only $3 billion spent by the major US companies.[2] Such inefficiency meant that a business in the EC wishing to install telephone lines had to pay between $225 and $500, compared with $100 in the United States.[3]

PROJECT 1992

Thirty years after its hopeful start, the European Community was stagnating. Editorial writers coined the word "Eurosclerosis" to describe what was happening. But then the move toward integration started again in 1985, when Jacques Delors became president of the European Commission. Delors asked the EC's commissioner for the Internal Market, Lord Cockfield, to examine remaining barriers to a truly common market. Cockfield identified three hundred and drew up a timetable to eliminate them by December 31, 1992. The EC's Project 1992 was readily accepted because Europeans felt under pressure from their economic rivals, the United States and Japan. The European growth rate for the first half of the 1980s was lower (in 1984, the year before Delors took office, only 2.7 percent, compared with 6.8 percent for the United States and 5 percent for Japan[4]) and its unemployment rate was higher (10 percent compared with under 6 percent for the United States). Project 1992 also fit the climate of deregulation being nourished by markedly conservative governments in Britain and the United States, a climate given credit in some quarters for the strong economic performance of the United States under Reagan.

Project 1992's aims were modest—the creation of a barrier-free European trading area such as was envisioned, but not achieved, by the original agreement in 1955. In 1985 the logic of such a goal seemed even more compelling. The biggest country in Europe, West Germany, had a population of only 60 million, while Europe's economic rivals Japan and the United States had over 120 million and over 240 million, respectively. A united Europe, by contrast, would have over 320 million—a market one-third bigger than the American one. Europeans hoped to begin enjoying the same benefits as their rivals from large domestic markets.

Only the most optimistic Europeans expected Project 1992 to eliminate all barriers. In theory, by January 1993 there would be no delay at any internal European border, because there would no border controls. Traffic would move freely from Italy to France and from France to England. In practice, issues such as terrorism, drugs, and illegal immigration would likely make some states continue with border inspections. The Italian government and others fear that economic integration will benefit the Mafia, who will find it easier to move both contraband and cash profits. In 1989 the governor of the Bank of Italy told a parliamentary committee that in his estimation the Mafia had billions ready for laundering.[5]

The British feared an Irish terrorist might move from Italy to France to Britain. Indeed, even as the British EC commissioner Lord Cockfield was laying out Project 1992, the British government was planning a new $27 million customs hall at the terminus of the tunnel being dug under the English Channel to link France and Britain—hardly an indication that it expected controls to disappear.[6]

In theory, by January 1993 Europeans would enjoy total freedom in services as well as in shipping merchandise. Thus a British accountant who hated fog could freely set up business in Spain. In practice, cultural and language barriers were expected to remain, and double-entry bookkeeping in the sun would be available only to British accountants fluent in Spanish.

Optimists argued that if enough barriers were dismantled, Europe would benefit from 1.8 million new jobs, an extra 4.5 percent in growth and 6 points lower inflation over what would otherwise be expected over the next six years. If this happened (and if the increased prosperity was attributed to integration and not other factors), then it was thought that Project 1992 might lead to common economic policies and even a common currency. But others argued that the common currency must come first, a condition and not a consequence of success.[7] Surrendering power over currency is a major surrender of sovereignty and lacked universal support. Nevertheless, the members of the EC came together in a summit meeting at Maastricht in December 1991 and agreed to create a monetary union by 1997 if a minimum of seven EC members met a set of conditions on inflation rate, deficits, and interest rates. Even if conditions were not met, a common currency, to be known as the "ecu," for European Currency Unit, would go into effect by 1999. However, to win British approval, the Maastricht agreement included an "opt out" clause permitting Britain to exempt itself from the currency union. Although the agreement was less than the French and Germans had hoped for, it was a commitment to move forward.

In future decades it may be possible to look back to these years and see a slow growth toward political integration, but for people living in these years progress is barely perceptible. By the Europeans' own admission, they were confused in their response to Saddam Hussein's takeover of Kuwait in August 1990. They could agree on neither a political nor a military response and ended up participating on an individual basis in the coalition formed and led by the United States. In the debate preceding the war, the Dutch minister (Hans Van den Broek) argued vigorously against acting independently of the Americans. The French Foreign Minister (Roland Dumas) replied to him, "If the EC had majority voting on foreign policy, you would be outvoted." Whereupon the British Foreign Secretary (Douglas Hurd) exclaimed, "That is exactly why Britain wants to maintain unanimity."[8]

Far from a multipolar world, with Europe as one of the poles, the Persian Gulf War represented what one columnist called "the unipolar moment" for the United States. The Persian Gulf was a major source of oil for Europe, more important for Europeans than Americans, but many argued that Kuwait was not a European concern.

In the summer of 1991 civil conflict broke out in Yugoslavia, and again the EC states were unable to agree on a uniform political or military response. All agreed that the conflict should be settled peaceably, but stating a pious wish is not a policy. The real test of policy, in Yugoslavia as much as in the Persian Gulf, is what states do when others do not voluntarily do as they wish. When EC mediation efforts in Yugoslavia failed, the Europeans had no further policies. Repeated calls for cease-fires led at best to temporary cessations of hostilities that were soon broken. The sending of observers and relief convoys brought only risk to EC representatives without stopping the conflict. Instead of dealing with the conflict at the EC level, member states either pushed it up to the Europe-wide level of the Conference on Security and Cooperation in Europe (a 35-member body including even the United States) or pushed it down to the state level, with countries such as Germany taking unilateral initiatives.

By contrast, the EC acquitted itself well during the attempted coup against the Soviet government in August of 1990. The EC foreign ministers met within 36 hours and agreed to cut back on aid. But before any further steps were taken, the coup collapsed on its own. Had the Soviet hardliners remained in office, it is not clear what, if anything, the EC would have done.

This brief and limited test of cooperation did not disprove the words of the Belgian foreign minister, Mark Eyskens, uttered a few days before the Persian Gulf War: "Europe is an economic giant, a political dwarf, and a military worm."[9]

A PARTIAL SUCCESS

The history of the progress toward European integration tells us a lot about what the road to world government would be like. But a short-term perspective that concentrates on frustrations and failures should not distract us from one point. Europe has traveled astoundingly far. It has gone from being the most war-prone region of the world, by any measure—number of wars, number of battle deaths, number of civilian deaths—to being the most peaceful. Of the eighty or so conflicts since 1945, only one (the Russians' suppression of the Hungarian revolution in 1956) occurred in Europe. European armed forces exist today only to cooperate with each other (in NATO, or in the Persian Gulf), not to fight each other. War among European states has become almost unthinkable.

The states of the EC have surrendered some of their sovereignty. They allow some of their behavior to be controlled by supranational authority. The CAP has decreed that British consumers pay more for food so that inefficient French farmers might stay in business; the British complain but they comply. The European court has decreed that Italians do not have the exclusive right to define what kind of wheat goes into pasta, nor Germans the right to determine what may go into products labeled sausage. The traditional rights of sovereignty are disappearing in the countries that invented the concept three hundred and fifty years ago.

But if Europe has come far down the road, it has come slowly. The pace of integration is ponderous, marked by promises that turn out to be false starts. The Common Market of 1957, ballyhooed as the first step on the road to a return to the Europe of Charlemagne, turned out not even to be a truly barrier-free trade zone. And Project 1992, even at its most optimistic, will not create a regional government. If a small number of homogeneous states, all democracies, all paying lip service to a common heritage, all agreeing on the rationality of integration, can only make such modest progress, a world state of many more heterogeneous entitles is far in the future.

OTHER EXAMPLES

Europe is the best, if not the only, contemporary example of regional integration. The small European states of Belgium, Netherlands, and Luxemburg pioneered some forms of integration in a union they called "Benelux," but their efforts have been folded into the European Community.

The Scandinavian countries have taken some tentative steps toward a "Nordic Union" but have been stymied by political differences.

Regional integration has been tried and has failed on other continents—an East African Common Market, various unions in West Africa and Central America. In Asia, the Association of South East Asian Nations (ASEAN) has made some modest beginnings at cooperation. If Europe succeeds, its example will encourage groups such as ASEAN to attempt more.

Yet, in a way, the European example is also discouraging, because it took so long to travel such a short distance. It had the advantage of building on a common heritage. The countries that now make up Europe were united in the past, at least in a fashion, under the Holy Roman Empire. In modern times, they have maintained a high level of interdependence and communication with each other. Yet despite all these factors it took two very destructive wars to drive them together. It is a price that many would judge too costly to pay.

Regional integration at best promises only a partial solution. Although it eliminates war within regions, by itself it does nothing to eliminate war between major blocs. But the states of Europe have been able to regulate their conduct even before they have achieved complete integration. Perhaps a limited consensus among states would enable them to avoid war by relying on the rule of law. Regulating state behavior through the internalized constraints of international law is our next subject.

NOTES

1. Carlisle Ford Runge, "Assault on Agriculture Protectionism," *Foreign Affairs* Vol. 67, No. 1 (Fall 1988), p. 140, citing *Financial Times* (London), November 24, 1987, p. 3.

2. Steven Greenhouse, "Making Europe a Mighty Market," *The New York Times*, May 22, 1988, p. F6.

3. Nicholas Colchester "Survey: Europe's Internal Market" *The Economist*, July 9, 1988, p. 33.

4. International Monetary Fund, *Annual Report 1988* (Washington D.C.: IMF, 1988), p. 10.

5. Clyde Haberman, "Europeans Fear '92 Economic Unity May Benefit Mafia," *The New York Times*, July 23, 1989, pp. Y1, Y4.

6. *The Economist*, December 24, 1988, p. 57.

7. "More Nonsense About Monetary Union," *The Economist*, November 18, 1988, p. 77.

8. *The Economist*, January 19, 1991, p. 48.

9. Craig R. Whitney, "Gulf Fighting Shatters Europeans' Fragile Unity," *The New York Times*, January 25, 1991, p. Z A7.

CHAPTER 15

WORLD LAW

If might made right, we would expect legislators and judges to come from the ranks of professional wrestlers. But in our society might doesn't necessarily make right. On the contrary, the comparatively small, weak wife of a professional football player is able to take her husband to court for mistreating her. In our country, we have the rule of law, and this rule contrasts sharply with the anarchy of international politics. If law can prevent serious disorder within a state, can it also prevent violence between states?

WHAT LAW IS

We make a distinction between *is* and *ought* statements. "Eating a dozen green apples at one sitting is bad for your digestion" is an *is* statement, or *description*. "You should not steal green apples from Mr. McGuffy's tree" is an *ought* statement, or *prescription*. We normally think of law as a prescription backed up by a state-imposed sanction, or penalty: "You shouldn't steal green apples, and if you do you will be fined ten dollars."

There are many kinds of prescriptions—folkways, mores, ethical imperatives, laws. A *folkway* may prescribe some aspect of daily conduct. Penalties for ignoring folkways are often no more severe than mild disapproval. Rules governing the proper kind of footwear for formal occasions might be called folkways. Before Piere Elliot Trudeau became prime minister of Canada, he was known for violating this folkway by wearing sandals in the House of

Commons. The sanctions against him were not serious—raised eyebrows, a few jokes, nothing more. *Mores* prescribe more important behavior. In 1991 the relatively youthful and robustly healthy captain of a cruise ship carrying mostly elderly passengers was nevertheless one of the first ones off the ship before it sank in a storm. Even though no one could point to a specific law that he had broken, many people expressed outrage for what one expert on marine history called "betraying the responsibilities of a ship's master that date from the earliest days of navigation."[1] *Ethical imperatives* such as "It is wrong to steal even if you're sure you won't get caught" are enforced by conscience. Finally, *laws* are enforced by penalties imposed by governments.

Obviously, laws do not require a continuously visible threat of sanction to be effective. Compliance is usually automatic; people have internalized the prescriptions. Most drivers stop at stop signs even when no police car is behind them. The police need pay attention to only the few who do run stop signs. Laws that have not been internalized, such as prohibitions on the use of alcohol or marijuana, are not effective despite the best efforts of police. Still, at the back of every law is a sanction imposed by government. It is the sanction that makes law different from other kinds of prescription.

With no equivalent of a sovereign or a police force in international politics, it is hard to imagine what kind of sanctions could back up prescriptions on interstate behavior. And who would apply sanctions even if they did exist? Yet we do talk about international law, and when we do we are talking about something real. There are indeed prescriptions about how states should behave. States know what they are and follow them. They are *ought* statements, not *is* statements, and states usually do what these laws say they ought to do even if it is not always in their immediate interest. These prescriptions are occasionally violated, but that only proves they are significant. A law prohibiting what people have no desire to do would not be a very significant law.

EXAMPLES OF INTERNATIONAL LAW

International law regulates several kinds of activity. Diplomacy is one. One of the oldest rules of international law observed today came out of the Congress of Vienna in 1815, which met to make peace in Europe after the Napoleonic Wars. One minor difficulty at the Vienna Congress was deciding which representatives were most important. Some countries called their delegates ambassador; others called theirs minister plenipotentiary, envoy, or nuncio. Confusion about rank disrupted the formal receptions and balls, which were as important a part of the Vienna Congress as the bargaining sessions. To put each other at ease, the delegates agreed on an order of precedence, which continues to this day. Highest in rank is ambassador, followed by minister, minister resident, and chargé d'affaires. Thus assigning a minister instead of an ambassador to a country—as the United States did to Hungary after the 1956 revolution—is a sign of less than cordial relations.

In 1818, at the Congress of Aix-la-Chapelle, the diplomats solved another issue of precedence: the matter of which country would be given the highest honors. At a banquet, seats at the table vary in importance, depending on how close they are to the host. Diplomats from major countries had been known to walk out of banquets because they weren't given the seats they thought their countries deserved. The clever solution was to rank countries according to the individual ambassador's seniority. The person who had been accredited to a country longest would be first in rank. If he or she retired, the representative of another country (the one who had been there next longest) would fill the place. This system continues to this day, with the ranking ambassador known as the dean of the diplomatic corps. A variety of ceremonial duties fall to the dean, and a capable diplomat filling the post is often left in place by the sending state for many years. For example, for more than two decades the dean of the large Washington diplomatic corps was the ambassador to the United States from the small state of Nicaragua, who, when he retired in 1979, had served thirty-six years. His acceptance as dean was not deference to the power and prestige of Nicaragua but rather an orderly and, we might say, diplomatic solution to a once troubling problem.

A universally known prescription is "Don't shoot an envoy who comes under a white flag." The age-old practice of immunity for diplomats has been codified in a convention drawn up in Vienna in 1961. It lays down basic rules for diplomacy. One is that ambassadors and other embassy officials are immune from criminal prosecution. If they commit crimes, they may be expelled, but they cannot be hauled into court, even as witnesses. Another rule is that embassy premises are immune from search; they may not be entered even in wartime without permission. At the same time, the embassy may not be used in a manner inconsistent with diplomatic practices. If you rob a bank while you are traveling abroad, don't head for the nearest embassy; the staff will turn you right over to the police. Another rule is that embassies must have the freedom to communicate in secret with their home country. Usually they do so through the diplomatic bag or pouch, which is immune to search by customs officials. By mutual consent, communication may also be carried out by radio transmission.

All states acknowledge these international laws protecting diplomats. Most of the time, states respect these laws, despite strong temptations to violate them. The diplomatic bag is often suspected of being used for purposes other than communication with the home country. It has been strongly hinted that the United States diplomatic bag was used to smuggle manuscripts of Aleksandr Solzhenitsyn out of the Soviet Union, yet Soviet authorities did not violate the law by searching the bag.[2] The British suspected some Arab countries, particularly Libya, of using their bag to smuggle arms for terrorists, yet the British did not violate international law by searching Libya's diplomatic bag.[3] In fact, the only recent case of violating the diplomatic bag occurred when the prerevolutionary government of Cambodia searched the Chinese diplomatic bag for counterfeit currency that the Chinese were smuggling in to undermine the Cambodian economy, and it was Cambodia, not China, that was universally condemned.[4] There is often an advantage to be gained by doing something prohibited, such as searching the diplomatic bag. When states refrain, it is because they do not wish to break the law.

A second kind of law deals with intercourse among nations. It has long been agreed that sovereignty gives a government the right to require all foreigners to stop at the border and submit to inspection before entering a country. In the days of ship travel this search presented little problem; officials could inspect a ship before the passengers disembarked at dock. But with the invention of the airplane a new problem arose. Sovereignty extends upward into a country's airspace. How do you stop an airplane as it enters your airspace and ask it to submit to inspection? In Paris in 1919 and then at Chicago in 1944, procedures were worked out by which aircraft could at times enter another country's airspace without having to wait for specific permission. The frequent entry into other countries' airspace by international airlines is regulated by a series of bilateral treaties between the countries involved.

The complex of international laws dealing with air travel is termed "the regime of the air." Likewise there are regimes of the sea and outer space. The regime of the sea includes the provision for freedom of the high seas. Although states have not been able to agree precisely how far from shore the high seas begin, without question they include all waters more than 200 miles from land. Any state may sail in the high seas or fly aircraft over them. This right was reaffirmed in the Convention on the High Seas drawn up at Geneva in 1958. In recent years the states of the world have been negotiating to restrict economic exploitation of the high seas, by regulating the hunting of whales and by licensing enterprises mining the deep sea bed. These negotiations have not yet produced a new set of laws and in any case do not restrict the legal right to freedom to navigate the high seas.

A third kind of international law deals with war. Some laws regulate warfare itself. The rules of land warfare, agreed on in conferences at The Hague in 1899 and 1907, are intended to limit violence in war. One rule requires combatants to wear a distinctive uniform or emblem, recognizable at a distance, and to carry arms openly. The purpose is to demarcate clearly those fighting from those not, to minimize the shooting of civilians by mistake. Another rule of warfare, adopted by the 1907 Hague Conference, is the requirement that wars first be declared before fighting commences, to enable noncombatants to get out of the way.

One of the best-known rules on war is the 1929 Geneva Convention on Prisoners of War. They may not be made to do war-related work for the enemy; they must be fed at the same level of nutrition as the captor's troops; they need only tell their name, birth date, rank, and serial number. The Convention was revised at Geneva in 1949 to include wars other than declared ones, such as a war in which one side is a rebel movement not yet internationally recognized as a government. An additional Convention in 1949 provided for the protection of civilians in time of war.

Other international law deals with kinds of weapons. One outlawed weapon is poison gas. The Hague Conference of 1899 issued the Hague Gas Declaration prohibiting the use of projectiles that spread "asphyxiating or deleterious gases." The declaration did not stop gas use in World War I, and as a result many of the treaties imposed on the defeated countries after that war had special provisions prohibiting them from arming with poison gas. In the interest of fairness, all the major states declared in 1925 at Geneva that if they were not already bound by one of these treaties, they would be from that point on. Their agreement, known as the Geneva Gas Protocol of 1925, outlaws "the use in war of asphyxiating, poisonous or other gases." Compliance with the Geneva Protocol has been, until recently, better than with its predecessor, the Hague Gas Declaration. Poison gas was not used by major combatants against each other during World War II. There were several reported cases of use by the Japanese against the Chinese in 1941 and 1942, but China was not considered a major combatant and Japan had not signed the Geneva Protocol. Extensive use by Iraq against Iran in the Gulf War marks the first major breach of the Geneva Gas Protocol.

Despite this recent setback, laws regulating warfare have continued to expand in recent years. A series of treaties has attempted to regulate several aspects of arms competition. The first of these to be signed was the *Antarctica Treaty* of 1959. It provides that there will be no military activity or nuclear activity anywhere on that continent. Facilities built there by one country will be open for inspection by others. In 1967, many of the same features were incorporated in the *Outer Space Treaty*. It prohibits nuclear weapons in orbit or on celestial bodies and provides that space installations will be open on a reciprocal basis.

Other treaties of this type are:

Partial Test Ban Treaty of 1963, outlawing nuclear tests in the atmosphere, above the atmosphere, or under water;

Non-Proliferation Treaty of 1968, prohibiting countries that already had nuclear weapons from giving them away and countries that did not yet have them from acquiring them;

Seabed Treaty of 1971, prohibiting military emplacements on the ocean
floor;

Biological Weapons Treaty of 1972, outlawing the use or production of germ
weapons;

Environmental Modification Treaty of 1977, prohibiting attempts to tamper
with natural phenomena for military advantage (for example, seeding
rain clouds to cause floods).

Other attempts to regulate warfare have failed. In 1936, a convention
was signed at London regulating submarine warfare; it provided that merchant ships should not be sunk without warning and without making
provision for survivors. As you can see from late-night movies on television,
the London Convention on Submarine Warfare was not observed during
World War II. Recent treaties on arms control may not stand up well over
time. Not all states have agreed to all of them.

Unsuccessful treaties, however, cannot detract from the substantial body
of successful international law. It is clear that when we talk about international law, we are talking about something real. Even without a world police
force, some regulation of behavior among states is possible.

SOURCES OF LAW

Law is not just another name for something we do anyway. Much
observance of law is habitual, but something special attaches to law and
makes it more than just habit. The prescriptions known as law include an
authoritative element. Part of this authority comes from the way in which
law originates. Law has clearly recognized sources. In domestic society the
most obvious of these sources are the decrees of the sovereign power—the
king or queen in early modern times, the parliament or congress today. But
monarchs and legislatures are not the only sources of law. The customary
division of government into lawmaking and law-adjudicating branches
should not mislead us. Judicial decisions can also be sources of law. The
1954 Supreme Court decision in *Brown* v. *Board of Education* made segre-
gated schools as illegal as a statute of Congress would have done.

Another source of law recognized in our society is custom. If you own a
vacant lot and don't fence it, people may begin to use it as a short cut
between a public road and their own property. If you take no steps to stop
this trespass and it continues long enough, you may then lose your right to
fence off the lot. In this case customary usage gradually acquires the force of
law.

These cases demonstrate the need for community assent to a source of
law. Judicial decisions are binding because people accept them as binding.
Custom is binding because people accept it as binding. A source of law that

was once viewed as binding, but in our society is no longer so viewed, is the Bible. Even though some people still accept Biblical prescriptions, our society as a whole does not consider the Bible a source of law.

In international politics, three sources of law are generally recognized. One is, as in our own society, custom. A good illustration of custom is the case known as the *Paquette Habana*. In 1900 the United States Supreme Court ruled that even though the United States had been at war with Spain in 1898 and had blockaded Cuba, its possession, it was illegal for the United States to have captured Cuban fishing boats as prizes of war because ancient usage exempted coastal fishing vessels from capture.[5]

A second source of international law is "general principles of law recognized among civilized nations."[6] In practice this means teachings of legal scholars and previous decisions of judicial bodies (such as courts of arbitration). But court decisions are not as important in international law as they are in our society because the principle of *stare decisis*, "precedent must be followed," is not always accepted.

The third and most important source of international law is the treaty. Sometimes it is bilateral; sometimes it includes additional parties as guarantors; and sometimes it is open-ended, intended to be signed by as many states as possible. It may be called a convention, a protocol, or an agreement. Whatever the name, a treaty is like a contract. It must be agreed to voluntarily, and it is valid only for those who agree to it. For this reason we say that much of international law is consensual: It must have the consent of a state before the law applies to the state. For years France and China refused to adhere to the Partial Test Ban Treaty of 1963, and for them the treaty was not valid law.

The examples of international laws regulating diplomacy, the regimes of sea and air, warfare, and arms control were in the form of treaties. Let's take one of them, the Non-Proliferation Treaty of 1968, to illustrate how a treaty becomes binding law. There are three steps. First is the *signature*, which means nothing more than agreement on wording. This is not unimportant, of course, because signing a treaty typically follows months of negotiations in which the wording was the main issue. But signature alone does not bind a state. The Geneva Gas Protocol of 1925 was signed by the United States; in fact, the United States was responsible for the original draft. But the next two steps by which a treaty becomes a law were not taken for fifty years; thus the United States in all that time was not legally bound by the agreement.

The next stage is *ratification*, which means the treaty is accepted as binding by the state. Each state has its own procedures for ratifying treaties. The constitution of the Fifth Republic of France provides that the French president alone will ratify treaties; the president therefore could sign a treaty and, by the next stroke of the pen, ratify it. Technically, this is done by signing another document called the article of ratification.

In the United States we commonly say that the Senate ratifies treaties, but this is not precisely correct. The Senate gives its approval for ratification, but the president does the actual ratifying. Normally, approval by the Senate is tantamount to ratification. Because the executive branch had to sign the treaty to bring it to the Senate in the first place, one would not expect the president to refuse to ratify it.

In the case of the Geneva Gas Protocol, it was the Senate that blocked the ratification; the president wanted the treaty very much. The Non-Proliferation Treaty was one case in which the distinction between approval of ratification and ratification was important. The Senate approved ratification on March 13, 1969, but the treaty was not ratified by the president until November 24, 1969. It was even considered possible that the president would not ratify it at all. Part of the reason for the delay was that between the signing and the ratifying a new president was elected. President Johnson's Administration negotiated and signed the treaty, but President Nixon was not enthusiastic about it. He waited to sign it until his staff completed an overall assessment of relations with the USSR.

Even after ratification a treaty does not go into effect until states exchange articles of ratification or (more commonly) until the treaty is deposited. This third step, *deposition*, means that the treaty is stored in designated archives from which it can be retrieved for examination if a question arises about its exact wording. Even then the treaty may have a provision that it will not enter into force until a specified time has elapsed or a set number of states have ratified it. One article of the Non-Proliferation Treaty specified that forty countries plus the United States, the United Kingdom, and the Soviet Union had to sign it before it took effect. It finally became binding law on March 5, 1970, when the three countries in whose capitals it was originally signed—the United States, the United Kingdom, and the USSR—by agreement all deposited it at once. Each of these three countries was designated to provide archives for an authentic copy of the treaty.

Deposition is usually accompanied by publication. A treaty is more likely to be respected by those it affects if its contents are widely known. But sometimes treaties are secret, and these treaties are just as valid as published ones.

REASONS FOR OBSERVING TREATIES

We have shown what international law is and how it comes into being, but we still have to show why it is obeyed. All laws, domestic as well as international, are obeyed for many reasons. Because the definition of law includes the idea of sanctions or punishment, it is natural to think first of obedience out of fear of punishment. But this is not the only reason or even the most important. Much law is obeyed because we think it rational to do so. Take the law that says you should drive your car on the right side of the road.

This is a prescription, not a description of what people would do in any case (British visitors to the United States might prefer to drive on the left side, as they do back home). Imagine what would happen if there were no law: Each time you saw a car approaching, you would have to stop, get out, and negotiate with the driver about which side to pass on. Traffic law makes life a lot easier for drivers by providing predictability, and therefore it is rational to obey it.

Law provides predictability in many areas. A check written today will be honored by the bank tomorrow; a rental agreement signed this month will still apply six months from now. Such predictability makes much of social and economic life possible, and we have little hesitation about obeying most of these laws.

Driving on the right side of the road is an obvious case in which it is rational to obey the law. But what about a case in which obedience is not so obviously rational, such as not cheating on an examination? Is honesty the best policy, or is cheating?

There are a number of possible situations:

1. I alone cheat; everyone else is honest.
2. I and a few others cheat; no one else does.
3. Nobody cheats.
4. Quite a few cheat, including me.
5. Everyone cheats.
6. Almost everyone cheats, but not me.
7. Everyone cheats but me.

These situations are listed in the rational (although not ethical) order of preference. I do best when the number of cheaters is so small (either case 1 or case 2) that the risk of detection by the proctors is minimal. The reason for ranking 4 and 5 lower is that the risk of discovery and penalization becomes too great. Better to pick 3, which avoids the risk. As a practical matter it may be impossible to act on the basis of case 1 or case 2. If everyone else in the class has a copy of this list, the minute it becomes obvious that I am cheating, they will start cheating too. For this reason it may, practically speaking, be most rational to act on case 3. You could say, "All things considered, honesty is often the best policy."[7]

The same logic applies to many international laws. There may be a rational advantage to breaking them ("cheating") if you are the only one doing it; but if the chances are great that your violation will be followed by others' violations, you obey the law. Thus one reason for obedience is rational self-interest.

Another reason becomes clear when we compare the fate of two laws regulating weapons, the Geneva Gas Protocol of 1925 and the London Convention on Submarine Warfare of 1936. During World War II, almost all sides observed the gas prohibition, mostly because each side had gas shells and bombs ready to use in retaliation if the other side initiated the use of gas. Because of mutual deterrence, gas was not used; international law simply reflected this underlying condition. But with submarines the conditions were very different. In the Atlantic the Germans had no surface fleet to speak of; they had only submarines. The Allies were heavily dependent on surface ships. The situation was asymmetrical. Obeying the London Convention by giving advance warning would have put German submarines at great risk. Therefore the Germans sank surface vessels without warning. In the Pacific the situation was reversed. There the Japanese had the surface ships and the Americans the submarines. Again there was no mutual deterrence because the situation was asymmetrical, and this time the Americans broke the London Convention.

We have then a second reason for obeying law: sanctions. That is, breaking a law will result in some kind of penalty for the lawbreaker. A major sanction in international politics is retaliation. The practice of retaliation has been so common that it is considered legal, if it is conducted within guidelines: Peaceful effort should be made first; a reprisal should be proportional to the offense; and retaliation should cease when the violation does. In its simplest form, this means that if one side breaks a treaty, the other side no longer feels itself bound by the treaty. When Germany used poison gas against the French and British in World War I, the French and British declared themselves no longer bound by the Hague Gas Declaration and used gas against the Germans.

Other cases of sanctions are more complex. In 1960 Cuba nationalized all large industrial and commercial enterprises, including those owned by Americans. The United States protested that this was a violation of international law because the Cuban government did not offer adequate and prompt compensation. There were no sizable Cuban investments in the United States to seize in retaliation, so the United States embargoed exports to Cuba. Was that form of retaliation proportionate to the offense? That kind of question is difficult to decide.

Other costs are incurred by a country breaking a treaty, and these may be considered forms of punishment. Other countries will think twice before signing another agreement with a lawbreaker. Even friendly states may be less inclined to show trust or support. One may even come under pressure from domestic sources (if one's governmental system is the kind that allows domestic criticism).

DIFFICULTIES WITH INTERNATIONAL LAW

International society lacks an authority capable of imposing sanctions on lawbreakers. Although several types of courts with impartial judges exist, they lack the ability to impose penalties and the police force to carry them out. Sanctions in international law must be imposed by the aggrieved party, not by a third party. Such self-help raises difficult questions.

A frequent question, which occurs in domestic society as well, is, "Was the law actually violated?" When American investments abroad are nationalized, the law is broken only if compensation is not prompt and adequate. It is not always easy to tell whether such compensation has been made. When Peru nationalized the International Petroleum Company in 1969, it offered compensation but first subtracted from it the $690 million it said the company owed in back taxes. Standard Oil of New Jersey (which owned International Petroleum) resisted this interpretation, and the Peruvians resisted the American claim for more compensation. Neither side said it was disregarding international law, but the dispute could not be settled.

Then one must decide whether a response to a violation is appropriate. In 1914, during revolutionary upheaval in Mexico, some American soldiers were temporarily jailed by one of the factions. The United States demanded both their release and an apology. It got the release but did not get the apology, so United States troops seized and held the Mexican city of Veracruz until the apology was given. It is hard to imagine a domestic system of law in which a neutral judge would allow such severe sanction for such a trivial offense.

Assuming that a violation is unambiguous and a proportionate sanction can be found, such a sanction may turn out to be ineffective. Retaliation seems to work best if the situation is perfectly symmetrical. The law protecting diplomats is usually respected, even when war breaks out, because each country's diplomats serve as hostages to the other country. When the situation is not symmetrical, it is often difficult to find an effective sanction. The United States embargoed trade with Cuba, but Cuba did not pay the $2 billion of claims against it, perhaps because by the time the embargo was imposed annual trade with Cuba amounted to only $14 million.[8] Other countries have nationalized foreign investments and no embargo has been applied, sometimes in the belief that an embargo would have no effect, sometimes because the embargo would hurt the country applying it more than it would hurt the alleged culprit. Sometimes no sanction is available short of military action. If the violator is militarily stronger than the aggrieved country, then this kind of sanction is ruled out. The application of military sanctions more often reflects relative military power than relative legal merit. The United States could safely seize Veracruz, but when the United States refused in 1911 to abide by a decision of an arbitration court ordering it to return 600 acres of land to Mexico, the Mexicans did not seize El Paso to enforce the law.

International law must rely more than domestic law on internalization of norms, or self-restraint. But self-restraint is a weak restraint. If an issue is not considered vital to national security, law will often be effective. The bulk of valid international law deals with matters such as currency transfers, rules for navigation at sea, and public health measures. But even with nonvital interests, the law runs into occasional difficulty, as the problems with compensation for nationalized investments illustrate. In questions of vital interest, self-restraint is no restraint at all.

One area of international law that has been deeply eroded in this century is the law protecting neutral states in time of war. Warring states claim that vital interests require them to violate neutral countries' rights. The Germans began sinking neutral ships carrying goods to Britain during World War I, on the very sound argument that those goods were giving Britain the ability to carry on the war. In 1939 the British planned to put mines in the neutral waters of Norway to prevent Swedish iron ore from reaching Germany. Churchill defended this plan by saying, "The letter of the law must not in supreme emergency obstruct those who are charged with its preservation and enforcement."[9] Similarly former Secretary of State Dean Acheson argued that the propriety of US actions against Cuba during the 1962 missile crisis was not a legal issue. He argued, "The power, position, and prestige of the United States had been challenged by another state; and law simply does not deal with such questions of ultimate power. . . . No law can destroy the state creating the law. The survival of states is not a matter of law."[10] If the leaders of states noted for their respect for law can argue in this way, who cannot?

International law is often disregarded in the name of self-defense. This sometimes happens in domestic society as well: Specific kinds of normally illegal behavior, even killing, are considered justifiable if done in self-defense. But in domestic law, cases of self-defense are considered exceptional, and someone wishing to use self-defense as an excuse must show that a variety of special conditions were met. In international law, by contrast, self-defense is neither unusual nor hard to justify. In fact, the right to plead self-defense is built into the structure of treaties. We assume that when a state signs a treaty, it does so in good faith. We expect the state to abide by the provisions of the treaty. *Pacta sunt servanda*, "treaties are to be observed," is the legal name we give to this principle. But with each treaty is a clause, understood if not always written out, known as *rebus sic stantibus*, "if things remain the same." That is, the treaty is valid only for as long as the conditions under which it was ratified continue.

For example, the United States and the Soviet Union agreed in 1963 not to test nuclear weapons in space. But suppose a country that did not sign the treaty (such as China) develops a stunning new nuclear weapon for use in space. The USSR (or the United States or even both) might then argue that conditions had changed and, invoking Article IV of the treaty that "extraordinary events" had "jeopardized the supreme interest of its country," withdraw from the treaty. We may agree that some sort of escape clause is reasonable; contracts in domestic law often have them. But this escape clause is so elastic that almost any act can be justified by it.

In 1919 the Germans signed the Versailles Treaty and promised to disarm. But they did so only because they were weak, isolated, and occupied after a defeat in war. Fifteen years later conditions had changed, and the Germans began to rearm. To the charge that they were violating law, the Germans could reply, *rebus sic stantibus.*[11]

For a while, in the late nineteenth and early twentieth centuries, such clauses were not actually written into treaties, and some scholars argued that the doctrine was obsolete. But recently states have gone back to making the clause explicit. You can see from the wording how big a loophole it provides. Here is Article X from the Non-Proliferation Treaty:

> Each Party shall in exercising its national sovereignty have the right to withdraw from the Treaty if it decides that extraordinary events, related to the subject matter of this Treaty, have jeopardized the supreme interests of its country.[12]

Notice who does the deciding. Each country is judge in its own case, and no other country has the right, legally, to stop it. The only safeguard in this treaty is a requirement to give three months' notice before withdrawing.

The idea of *rebus sic stantibus* appears to contradict the argument that law provides predictability; in fact the two are related. By predictability we mean that things will work tomorrow the way they work today. Law extends the present into the future. It is by nature conservative, for it freezes the status quo. But what if some group doesn't like the status quo? If they can bring about a change in the status quo and then in the accompanying law, there is no problem. But if there is no mechanism for changing the law, then it is only realistic to expect such a group to disregard the law if they are at all able to.

Suppose the law says, "Colored people will sit at the back of the bus." This law reflects a relationship in society: white superiority and black inferiority. But what if conditions change? What if whites are no longer so sure of their superiority and blacks don't accept inferiority? Using the metaphor of law as frozen political relationships, we might say that the old law must be unfrozen. In a system that functions well, the time required to thaw it will be kept to a minimum. There will be recognized ways of unfreezing the old law and bringing it into line with the new relationship. The city council will pass a new ordinance, and the signs in the buses will come down.

International politics lacks the institutionalized ways of changing laws that we have in domestic society. The only recourse for a state that believes it is suffering under a particular treaty obligation is to go to the other parties to the treaty and ask them to change it. But often there is no incentive for other states to agree to a change. Thus the gap between the law (reflecting past political conditions) and new political conditions can be very great.

The fate of the Versailles Treaty illustrates such a gap. The treaty reflected the political conditions of 1919—Germany defeated and France victorious. In subsequent years the relationship changed, but there was no way for Germany to get its increasing power translated into a new treaty. In fact, as German power grew, the French clung more stubbornly to the provisions of the Versailles Treaty, giving the Germans little choice but to break the treaty.

From this argument you can deduce that law will be stronger in a system in which relationships are changing slowly if at all. In such a conservative system, law will grow in extent and in force. We see such growth of law in the international politics of the nineteenth century. The nineteenth-century system was conservative, and international law flourished. One example from this period will show how close international law came to working in the same way as domestic law does. In 1899 a revolutionary government took over in Venezuela and refused to pay debts that its predecessor government owed to Britain, Germany, and Italy. This was a clear violation of law, which states that new states or regimes are responsible for obligations incurred by the states or regimes they succeed. When the new Venezuelan government refused to comply with the law, British, German, and Italian gunboats blockaded Venezuelan ports until the government did obey, in the same way a loan company would reclaim a car if payments were not made on it.

TWO REVOLUTIONS AND THEIR EFFECTS

An enforcement action such as the blockade of Venezuelan ports would be impossible in the world today. We live no longer in the conservative system of the nineteenth century but in a revolutionary time. Two revolutions are going on simultaneously, making it difficult to arrive at an effective system of international law. We might call them the "anticolonial" and the "technological" revolutions. We will discuss the anticolonial revolution first.

Most third world countries are former colonies and do not want to be bound by rules drawn up by their former masters. It seems clear to them that the international law of the nineteenth century reflected European superiority and Asian, African, and Latin American inferiority.

In 1961 India used military force to occupy and annex an enclave on its coast that had for 450 years been the Portuguese colony of Goa. Portugal claimed that the invasion was a clear violation of international law. If the crossing of a frontier by 40,000 troops—without provocation, with no calls for liberation from the inhabitants, and with no previous attempt to negotiate—was not aggression, what was? But the Indians argued, with the support of the majority in the United Nations General Assembly, that any international law that could be twisted to such conclusions was unacceptable. The Indian delegate dismissed the existing body of international law with a sentence: "If any narrow-minded, legalistic considerations—considerations arising from international law as written by European law writers—should arise, those writers were, after all, brought up in the atmosphere of colonialism."[13] The new version of international law, argued by the Indians, was that because there could be no legitimacy in colonial possession, aggression in this case was not aggression.

Because of the anticolonial revolution, some of the oldest doctrines in international law are under attack. In November 1979, Iranian revolutionaries seized the United States embassy in Tehran and held diplomatic personnel hostage with the connivance if not the approval of the Iranian government. Such a flagrant violation of one of the oldest international laws was justified as an attack on American imperialism and espionage. Despite the obvious self-interest of all governments in guaranteeing the immunity of their own diplomats, the violation of international law by Iran was not universally condemned in the Third World. The governments of Pakistan and Libya failed to live up to their obligations to protect embassy premises and allowed mobs sympathetic to the Iranian cause to burn American embassies in their capitals. There were even people in the academic field willing to defend the Iranian violation of international law. They referred to "the one-sidedness of the old international law" that among other things extended protection only to diplomats but not to resistance fighters.[14] According to this line of reasoning, if a system of law has any flaws, then even individual parts of it lack validity. The implication is that as long as fundamental disagreements exist among states, even legal agreements limited to such traditional practices as protecting diplomats should not be considered binding.

The doctrine of the freedom of the high seas is also under attack. The countries of the west coast of South America—Chile, Peru, and Ecuador—were among the first to claim a zone of economic control 200 miles out into the ocean and to patrol it to keep out fishing boats from states that once dominated the region economically. Their argument was that because the cultivable land between the Pacific Ocean and the Andes Mountains was so limited, they needed exclusive access to the fisheries to feed their people. They would no longer allow these fisheries to be exploited by distant countries that were already rich and well fed. Freedom of the high seas, they claimed, was only an excuse for developed countries with large fishing fleets to exploit resources needed by underdeveloped countries. Even Hugo Grotius in 1625, argued a Chilean diplomat, supported the freedom of the high seas not simply as an intellectual concept but to defend the trading interests of the Dutch East India Company.[15]

The second revolution in the world today is in technology, and we can use the law of the sea again to see how these changes undermine international law. For centuries it was generally agreed that sovereignty extended out to sea in "territorial" waters to a distance of 3 miles. Not that countries would not have been happy to claim more, but 3 miles was as far as the military technology of the time would allow them to patrol. Territorial waters were in effect determined by technology. A decision on territorial waters made by Dutch jurists in 1737 is known as the "cannon-shot rule" because the range of cannon was about 3 miles.

Because of changes in technology there is now almost no limit to how far out a state can patrol. But with the technological limits removed, states have found it difficult to agree on a new guideline for the extent of territorial waters. Conferences in 1958, 1960, 1974, and 1975 failed to come up with any agreement at all. States were claiming anywhere from 3 miles to 200 miles. Countries (such as Japan and Great Britain) with extensive ocean-going fishing fleets argued for narrow territorial waters. Countries (such as Burma and Iceland) that wanted to protect their own fishing industries from foreign fishing fleets argued for wider territorial waters. Unlike the Dutch in 1737, states could no longer let technology answer the question. In 1982, the Third United Nations Conference on the Law of the Sea finally produced a treaty that, among many other provisions, defined territorial waters as 12 miles. Even then, not all states—most prominent among them the United States—signed it immediately. It was only in December 1988, as one of his last acts in office, that President Reagan by executive proclamation extended the territorial waters of the United States to 12 miles.

WORLD PEACE THROUGH WORLD LAW?

Proposals for replacing the rule of force with the rule of law run the danger of trying to achieve peace by definition. Of course rule of law will bring peace, if rule means "effective settlement of disputes." By the same logic, rule of poets or rule of political scientists would also bring peace, but only because the desired end is already built into the definition of the means.

Unlike the hypothetical world state, international law already exists. We can see that it does not provide an effective restraint on the behavior of states in the crucial area of war and peace. We must reject the argument that law has not yet been tried so that one can know whether it would prevent war or not. It has been tried, and it has not prevented war.

The problem is not in any technical deficiency in the law itself—failure to word treaties in ironclad language, for example—but in the refusal of states to accept law when vital interests are at stake. The confusion that we sometimes find on this point is evident in a statement made by American Secretary of State Christian Herter. He proposed "to create certain universally accepted rules of law which if followed, would prevent all nations from attacking other nations."[16] Mr. Herter's statement is confused. One cannot create universally accepted rules of law. Either one discovers which norms are already accepted and codifies them, or one prescribes norms and then tries to create acceptance for them.

International law today follows mainly the first alternative. For the most part it is a codification of what states would do anyway. Poison gas was not a militarily decisive weapon. Because gas required so much protective equipment for the side that used it, the material was awkward to train with, to transport to and store in the battle area, and to employ in battle. Without much incentive to use gas in the first place, states found it easy to agree on outlawing it. Submarines, on the other hand, proved useful and have not been outlawed.

This is not to say that law can make no contribution at all to controlling international violence. It is useful for states to acknowledge that they agree on the few things they do. It is useful to set off areas of agreement from areas of disagreement. It is useful to conclude agreements in the relatively calm atmosphere of peacetime; during war, agreement may be desired but hard to achieve. Despite the violence of World War II, the Geneva Convention on Prisoners of War was largely observed by the Germans and the Americans in relation to each other. It was easier to observe it because the agreement had been ratified before the war began. Had no such agreement existed, it is easy to see how midwar negotiations on treating prisoners could have gotten bogged down on issues such as the rights of the prisoners to have Coca-Cola or a lager beer, with each side accusing the other of trying to write the rules to its own advantage.

We have some reason to believe that neither side in World War II originally intended to engage in large-scale bombing of civilian targets.[17] But the desires of the two sides were not reinforced by a treaty as they were in the case of poison gas. It is at least possible that a convention limiting aerial bombardment to, for example, the zone of military operations could have prevented escalation into massive raids of the type that destroyed Dresden.

International law can be useful in cases in which basic agreement among states seems to exist and can be strengthened by being made more explicit. But often there is no basic agreement. It is one thing to rule out a weapon considered marginally effective by military experts; it is something very different to renounce a technique considered basic to self-defense.

Advocates of world law seek not to create accepted laws but to win acceptance for laws already created. One way to win acceptance would be enlightened self-interest. The same motivation would lead all students to be honest on examinations. But this incentive has not been effective over past centuries, and it is hard to imagine what kind of radical change would suddenly make it effective now. Another possibility is to change the nature of international law. But doing away altogether with the consensual basis of international law and replacing it with the kind of law we have in domestic society is another way of saying world government. In a state, people are bound by laws even if they do not explicitly agree to them, provided the laws are arrived at by the proper procedures. But these laws have the sanction of the state behind them. The more controversial the law and the more powerful the group resisting it, the more force is needed to impose the sanction.

We are back where we ended Chapter 13, lamenting a lack of consensus yet fearing coercion. Fear of the coercive power of a world state is a powerful force for the retention of sovereignty. Yet even when states remain sovereign, they can work together on occasions when they feel threatened by war or the threat of war. Such arrangements have existed in the past, under the name of "balance of power" systems. With changing conditions in international politics, it is possible such arrangements could come into being again.

NOTES

1. Frank Braynard, curator of Merchant Marine Museum, Kings Point L.I., quoted by Josh Kurtz, "Captain Faulted for Leaving Ship First," *The New York Times*, August 6, 1991, p. Z A4.

2. David K. Shipler, *The New York Times*, December 14, 1978.

3. "When the Diplomatic Bag Goes Off in the Streets of London," *The Economist*, August 26, 1978, p. 17.

4. Henry Kamm, "Cambodia Scans Diplomatic Mail," *The New York Times*, February 23, 1970, pp. 1, 11.

5. An excellent textbook describing this case among others is Gerhard von Glahn, *Law Among Nations*, 3rd ed. (New York: Macmillan, 1976).

6. This is part of the Statute of the International Court of Justice (see Chapter 17). The Statute lists teachings of scholars as a separate source, but it seems to me only an operational definition of general principles. How else could we know what they are?

7. This is a modified version of material presented by Herman Kahn in *On Escalation* (Baltimore: Penguin Books, 1968), p. 19.

8. *The Economist*, August 27, 1977, p. 38.

9. Winston S. Churchill, *The Gathering Storm* (Boston: Houghton Mifflin, 1948), p. 547.

10. Dean Acheson, *Proceedings of the American Society of International Law* (Washington, D.C., 1963), pp. 13–15.

11. This argument is developed by E. H. Carr in *The Twenty Years' Crisis* (London: Macmillan, 1961), Chapter 11.

12. *United States Treaties and Other International Agreements* (Washington, D.C.: U.S. Government Printing Office, 1971), Vol. 21, Part 1, p. 483.

13. Quoted by Rupert Emerson, "The New Higher Law of Anticolonialism," in *The Relevance of International Law*, eds. Karl W. Deutsch and Stanley Hoffman (Garden City, N.Y.: Doubleday, 1971), p. 224.

14. Statement of concerned scholars at Lisbon Conference of World Order Models Project, July 13–20, 1980, in *Macroscope*, No. 8 (Fall 1980), p. 12.

15. Robert L. Friedheim, "The 'Satisfied' and 'Dissatisfied' States Negotiate International Law," *World Politics*, Vol. 18, No. 1 (October 1965), pp. 20–41.

16. Christian Herter, speech to the National Press Club, Washington, D.C., February 18, 1960, in *Vital Speeches*, Vol. 26, No. 1 (March 15, 1960), p. 327.

17. See George Quester, *Deterrence Before Hiroshima* (New York: John Wiley, 1966).

CHAPTER 16

BALANCE OF POWER

For extended periods in history, international politics has operated in a way that is at the opposite pole from world government. Instead of one sovereign authority, there have been many sovereign states, each jealously guarding its autonomy. Instead of being concentrated in a central police force, power has been distributed among all the states, and each state has kept total control of its own army. This absence of central authority and centralized force has been considered desirable. Leaders have tried to keep power distributed among many states in such a way that each state would be too weak to threaten any of the others. In theory, if any state did try to increase its power enough to pose a threat, all the other states would unite to stop it. In practice, however, a state would unite with others to control an aggressor only when it felt threatened itself. To draw an analogy with the Wild West, there was no world police force, only a world posse.

THE BALANCE OF POWER AS INTERNATIONAL SYSTEM

The policy followed in these periods was generally called "the balance of power." This term has been applied to so many situations and policies (one author has counted eight usages)[1] that it is not useful without an accompanying definition. Here the expression refers to a proposal to prevent or limit war by distributing power among many states. The proposal rests on the assumption that as long as power is not abolished (as it might be, for example, under a proposal for peace by disarmament), then it must be met by countervailing power. It is not safe for a state to rely on only the good will of powerful neighbors; only matching power can provide adequate protection in all circumstances. To put it differently, this proposal depends on mutual deterrence. Any potential aggressor is deterred by the potential combined power of all the other states in the system.

But here confusion sets in. If this is all balance of power means, many arrangements could be called by that name. A bipolar system of the type we had during the Cold War years would fit the definition. After all, was not the United States just trying to keep a balance with the USSR (and vice versa)? An accelerating arms race would also fit. Yet these situations are clearly different from the classic balance of power systems that operated in the eighteenth and nineteenth centuries.

A balance of power system differs from other approaches to peace not by its goal, deterrence, but by its means of achieving that goal. The emphasis in the eighteenth and nineteenth centuries was on matching a rival's power, not by building up one's own armed forces but by forming a coalition of one or more other states also threatened by the growing power of the rival. Deterrence was achieved by alliances, not by arms races, and that is what sets this proposal off from the international system of today. In historical balance of power systems there was no increase in the power of a single state or even in the system as a whole; rather, power was rearranged to counter aggression. Most of the time states pursued independent policies and were not bound to each other by permanent alliances. Only when one state threatened the independence of another did a group begin to coalesce to oppose the belligerent. If the aggressor state was smart, it quit right then. If not, it faced a war in which it was outnumbered. If not deterred from pursuing its disruptive aims, it was defeated by preponderance. But once the war was over, the alliance of victors broke up, and the newly defeated aggressor was returned to its former place and size, ready to serve as an ally if some other country threatened the system.

For the political leaders of the time, the primary reason for maintaining a balance of power system was to prevent not war but hegemony, that is, the domination of the entire system by one powerful state. As we shall see, willingness to go to war was an essential part of the policy. Nevertheless, we may consider the balance of power as a possible approach to peace. For one thing, if it works as it is supposed to, it does prevent all war by deterrence. Participants in a balance of power system are willing to go to war but hope their willingness will make war unnecessary. For another, even if such a system does not deter all war, the resulting wars are likely to be shorter and less destructive than those that would occur under any other kind of system. Small wars fought to regulate the balance might be the closest to peace the world can come. Certainly small wars are preferable to the massive violence of World War I and World War II.

The principles of the balance of power were applied to a concrete political situation in March 1936 when Winston Churchill urged that England take the lead in organizing an "armed League of all Nations" to take action against Nazi Germany. This policy was not popular in England at the time (Churchill was widely considered a warmonger), and to win adherents Churchill used this version of history:

> For four hundred years the foreign policy of England has been to oppose the strongest, most aggressive, most dominating Power on the Continent. . . . We always took the harder course, joined with the less strong Powers, made a combination among them, and thus defeated and frustrated the Continental military tyrant whoever he was, whatever nation he led.[2]

In the past, the strongest power had been France under Louis XIV or Napoleon. In 1936, it was Germany under Hitler, but that didn't really matter, argued Churchill. England's policy should be to oppose any country that tried to dominate the continent of Europe. Concentration of power was dangerous in any hands. Safety for England lay in the distribution of power among several countries.

The principles of the balance of power were also applied to the Persian Gulf in recent times. When the war between Iraq and Iran began in 1980, many countries hoped that neither would win. If Iraq won, it would become the dominant power in the Arab world, threatening the independent existence of its weak Arab neighbors and posing a serious threat to Israel. If Iran won, its radical version of Islam would become more attractive, winning adherents and causing instability throughout the Middle East. When it appeared that Iran was prevailing, the United States began to give assistance to Iraq, primarily in the form of military intelligence obtained from satellite reconnaissance.

Once the war ended in stalemate, the United States continued limited support of Iraq, including large amounts of technical aid. Only when Iraq itself became a greater threat than Iran, by invading and annexing Kuwait in August of 1990, did the United States shift away, organizing a coalition to force Iraq to withdraw from Kuwait. But after a sharp but short war in early 1991, the United States stopped short of destroying Iraq's military power. Like Bismarck's treatment of his former enemies in the nineteenth century, President Bush kept *his* former enemy in existence to provide a balance against Iran.

RULES OF THE BALANCE OF POWER

Although this way of arranging international relations is usually termed the balance of power, it would be more precise to call it a multistate, shifting alliance system. The system rests on the assumption that a state's own interests are served by having a number of other states around. If power is to be distributed (as opposed to being centralized in a world government), then it is best distributed uniformly. If a state wants to preserve its own independence, it must support the independence of others.

Ideally, the system should operate according to a set of informal but widely understood principles or rules:

1. Be suspicious of an increase in power by another country—any country. When assessing other countries, be concerned with their capabilities, not their intentions. (Realistically, state leaders do pay attention to intentions. Winston Churchill had to admit in his anti-German speech in 1936 that France still had a bigger army than did Germany. But he pointed out that the German army was growing rapidly.)

2. Always ally with the weaker side. Ignore considerations such as friendship or morality. (As Churchill said, "If Hitler invaded Hell, I would make at least a favorable reference to the Devil in the House of Commons."[3])

3. Support a state or group of states only until it is out of danger. Remember that no alliance is permanent.

4. Show moderation toward the aggressor after it is defeated. Because no alliance is permanent, today's enemy may be tomorrow's ally.

These four principles deal directly with the issue of aggression by creating a situation which deters aggression. In addition to the negative mechanism of deterrence, the traditional balance of power system worked in a more active way to control violence. Leaders acted according to a fifth rule, which we may add to the four already listed:

5. Settle nonessential quarrels in peripheral areas in a way that does not disturb the central balance.

Historically, one method of settling outside quarrels was to partition any piece of land that might be in dispute, regardless of the wishes of its inhabitants. A famous example from the eighteenth century involved Poland. Although officially a recognized country under a king, it had too little power to play a significant part in international politics. Instead it was a source of temptation to its larger neighbors, Austria, Russia, and Prussia. To prevent Poland from becoming the stake in a war, the major powers agreed to divide Poland among themselves. The partition was done in three stages, in 1772, 1793, and 1795. At each stage each of the three big countries took another slice. By 1795 nothing was left of Poland; it ceased to exist as a country. An attempted uprising by the Poles in 1794 was easily suppressed by the cooperative efforts of the big countries and only paved the way for the country's final division.

Partition was one device used to preserve the balance. Neutralization was another. A century later, in the international system created by Bismarck, colonial disputes in Africa threatened to lead to war between European countries. One focus of conflict was the Congo River Basin. When Henry Stanley began exploring it for King Leopold of Belgium, the French hurried to send in an explorer of their own. Then the British tried to secure a foothold by backing up the Portuguese in an old claim that had never been followed up by occupation. Competition for this area, considered a rich source of trade, could have led to war. Instead Bismarck convened a conference on problems in Africa at Berlin in 1884. One result of the conference was to declare the Congo Basin neutral and open to navigation by all countries, thereby taking it out of the European power struggle.

BALANCE OF POWER AND THE CONTROL OF INTERNATIONAL VIOLENCE

Seen from the twentieth century, the balance of power systems of the eighteenth and nineteenth centuries have some attraction. There were wars, but they were less destructive than the major wars of the twentieth century. They were fought for limited objectives, not for universal goals such as converting whole populations to a superior way of life. Major states were assured of survival even if they were defeated in war. They were not subjected to division into parts and reform of their social system as happened to Germany in 1945. In the balance of power system, each state had an interest in preserving all the other states.

But on closer examination, it is not clear that the balance of power system actually had all those advantages. Let us take the points one by one. One scholar, Michael Haas, did a careful study of systems with many states (multipolar or balance of power) and systems with only two states (bipolar).[4] He concluded that in multipolar systems wars were on the whole shorter but more numerous than in a bipolar system, and in multipolar systems wars were relatively more violent and involved more countries.

Wars waged to preserve the balance of power system were fought for limited objectives (to restore the balance, not to create something new), but new wars kept occurring because not all states shared the limited objectives. The system would not keep aggressive new countries such as Prussia from appearing on the scene, trying to expand their power, and at times succeeding. But even if the system had contained Prussia, the wars necessary to do it would illustrate the basic point that the balance of power system depends on war as an essential instrument to keep functioning. It requires limited wars to avoid unlimited ones. In the end, balance of power systems of the eighteenth and nineteenth centuries failed to avoid big wars too. The eighteenth-century system ended in the ideological wars of the French revolution and the expansionist wars of Napoleon. The nineteenth-century system ended in World War I.

It is true that major states had a reasonable chance of survival under the balance of power system, but minor states such as Poland did not fare so well. They might be neutralized or even partitioned against their will. Each state had an interest in preserving a multistate system, but the exact composition of that system might change over time.

A RETURN TO THE BALANCE OF POWER?

With all these arguments against the balance of power system, you may wonder why we bother to mention it. The reason is that serious thought has been given to a return to such a system. We must remember that the only time in the history of the world that we have had any extended period of peace is when there has been a balance of power.

> I think it will be a safer world and a better world if we have a strong, healthy United States, Europe, Soviet Union, China, Japan, each balancing the other, not playing one against the other, an even balance.[5]

These were the words of President Nixon in 1972. They were echoed in 1978 by President Carter's national security adviser, Zbigniew Brzezinski:

> The accommodation with China opens up the possibility of a genuine framework for wide-ranging international cooperation involving the United States and Europe, the United States and Japan, the United States and China, and I would also hope, eventually, the United States and the Soviet Union.[6]

The notion was echoed yet again in 1987 in the popular book, *The Rise and Fall of the Great Powers*, by Paul Kennedy. Despite the boastful claim of the Reagan Administration to have restored America to its position as "number one," many Americans were drawn to Kennedy's notion of US decline and attentive to his discussion of "the problems and opportunities facing today's five large politico-economic 'power centers,'" which were the familiar countries mentioned by Nixon and Brzezinski.[7]

Interest in the balance of power system grew as the bipolar system of the Cold War faded into history. That system was dominated by two countries known as superpowers, a term which meant that each had power greater than the power of all the lesser powers combined. Against such a superpower, a coalition would not be effective. The other superpower could perhaps equal it, but certainly could not present it with overwhelming power. Thus a balance of power system would not work.

In the minds of the superpowers, all issues became Cold War issues. Conflict was always interpreted by the way it affected the superpowers. Events in Korea and Vietnam that could have been described as civil wars became global wars instead. Each superpower defined its own interests mainly in military terms and mainly in response to what its rival was doing. Foreign aid was usually in the form of military assistance. If the Soviet Union offered foreign aid to one country, the United States offered foreign aid as well, if not to the country then to a regional rival.

Each superpower gathered around it a group of client states. Each insisted that these countries define, or at least pretend to define, their own national interests in terms of the superpower rivalry. The Soviet Union prevented Czechoslovakia from accepting Marshall Plan aid. The United States tried to stop Britain from selling buses to Cuba.

In fact, this description of bipolarity exaggerated its importance. The bipolar system was never perfect and it began to decline quite early. Yugoslavia split with the Soviet Union in 1948 and showed the world that there could be an independent form of communism not controlled by the Soviet Union. A decade later France under Charles de Gaulle withdrew from formal membership in the NATO alliance. A few years later China split with the Soviet Union. Japan remained a military ally of the United States but grew economically at such a rapid rate that it was seen as an economic power in its own right.

END OF BIPOLARITY

As the new players in world politics—Europe, China, Japan—were increasing in power, the superpowers were declining. At the Houston meeting of the seven leading economic powers in July 1990 an aide to President Bush announced, "the age of the superpowers is obviously over."[8] One obvious reason was the fracturing of the Soviet Union. Even as he spoke, the Communist Party of the Soviet Union was holding its last party conference as a monolith. In the months that followed component republics broke away and the economy collapsed.

But there were other reasons as well. It was their vast nuclear arsenals that set the superpowers off from all the others. Since World War II ended in 1945, these had not been used; their use had not even reasonably been threatened. By 1990 they had come to be seen as unusable. They represented only an expensive drain on the treasury (and the environment). Military power was still employed, but it was in the nature of quick assaults on Grenada and Panama, and countries such as Israel (in 1967) or India (in 1971) had shown themselves just as proficient.

It was by military measures above all that the superpowers were distinguished from all others, but by 1990 many wondered if economic power were not more important. By economic measures the Soviet Union did not qualify even as one of the world's leaders. Even the United States' economic problems had crippled its ability to play the role it once had. In 1948

Marshall Plan aid from the United States had rebuilt Western Europe. In 1990, most of the money for rebuilding Eastern Europe was expected to come from the EC and possibly Japan. The US had none to spare.

THE BALANCE OF POWER IN THE CONTEMPORARY WORLD

But would the bipolar world necessarily be replaced by a balance of power system? Writers on the balance of power have listed conditions needed before such a system can function. Let us look at some of them.

1. *Minimum number of states.* Because the system's essence is in shifting alliances, three is the logical minimum. With two there can be no shift. Even three may be too few, because presumably two states could always ally against and defeat the third. (George Orwell does create such a three-state balance of power system in *1984,* but then *1984* is fiction.) A practical minimum would be five or six, which is in fact the number of major states active in the systems of the eighteenth and nineteenth centuries.

One can identify a handful of states that might be major actors in international politics in the coming years—the United States, a united Europe, a successor state to the USSR built around Russia, Japan, China, and perhaps India. Thus the requirement for a minimum number of states would be met.

2. *Equality of power.* When we speak of five or six states, we assume that these states are roughly equal in power. Power is defined as the ability to win war. If two states are equal in power, then the outcome of a war between them is not obvious beforehand.

If we look at our list of potential members of a balance of power system, we do not find a rough equality of power. At the one extreme, the United States is capable of what is often called "projecting power." It can send military forces and supplies far beyond its own borders. But the United States is so superior to others that some call it a unipolar world. The former Soviet Union is likely to be self-absorbed for along time. China is strictly a regional power, lacking planes and ships to operate far from home.

Europe and Japan cannot yet even be called regional powers. Europe is still far from political unity, and although individual states control considerable military forces they have never acted in a coordinated fashion. Japan has a sizable military force but scrupulously keeps it a "self-defense" force, refraining from building the typical weapons of "power projection" such as aircraft carriers and long-distance aircraft. Japan is showing only the beginnings of interest in acting in world affairs.

The dependence of Europe and Japan on outside sources of energy illustrates how difficult it is to assess the power of countries today. Measured by industrial output, Japan is a major power. Measured by energy resources, some states in the Middle East are powerful.

3. *Commensurability of power*. What this phrase means is that power can be measured by some common standard, so that the power of one state can be compared with that of another. In the eighteenth and nineteenth centuries, power was directly related to territory and its accompanying population and resources. Acquisition of territory (such as Silesia by Frederick the Great) was alarming because it meant an increase of power. A case in which power is not commensurable is that of David and Goliath. By traditional measures David was weak, but his secret weapon—the slingshot—upset traditional calculations.

Power today is less related to such permanent factors as territory. A country like Japan, with little territory and few resources, can nevertheless show great economic strength. But at the same time such a country has a great vulnerability, because it depends on resources, such as oil, that are not under its control. A country that is powerful when oil is plentiful and cheap might suddenly weaken if oil becomes hard to obtain.

4. *Usefulness of war*. In the eighteenth and nineteenth centuries, the technology of warfare—basically foot soldiers armed with rifles and short-range artillery—made a balance of power system possible. On the one hand, war was a serious enough business to work as a threat: The consequences of having states at war with you were potentially disastrous. On the other hand, war was not so destructive that it scared states from even making the threat to use it. War was a credible instrument of policy. It cost something to wage war, but the cost was bearable.

Modern weapons have changed the nature of warfare. In the eighteenth and nineteenth centuries, battles were fought by professional soldiers in sparsely inhabited areas, with open spaces big enough to maneuver the thousands of troops. Civilians and cities were generally spared. The soldiers themselves were often the poorest in a society, people for whom the hardships of campaigning did not differ much from the hardships of daily life.

Long-range bombers and missiles have made civilians as likely to be killed as soldiers, and modern armies are composed of a fair cross section of society. States must find provocation very severe indeed before they risk the lives of their citizen-soldiers or their soldiers' families back home.

5. *Neutrality of alignment*. Another essential condition of the balance system was that states changed alignment without regard to emotional issues such as friendship or ideology. During the years of Cold War rivalry, ideological differences between communist and noncommunist (or even between Russian and Chinese versions of communism) seemed to rule out such maneuvering. In this regard, the reduced importance of ideology, particularly in Russia and China, seems to facilitate a return to the balance of power. But even as this is happening, the growth of international trade

introduces a new obstacle to changing alignments. It would be difficult for Japan and some European countries whose economies are so dependent on trade to join an alliance against major trade partners. A balance of power system calls for total freedom on alignment, yet one cannot imagine the Japanese risking the loss of the huge American market by joining an alliance to stop some US action.

6. *Willingness to participate.* States had to take enough interest in what was happening in world politics to care if aggression occurred and to organize against it when it did.

In some of the recent cases of aggression—for example, Iraq's attack on Iran in 1980—the world did not seem to care. The Iraqi attack on Kuwait was followed by a global response more in keeping with the attitudes that kept the balance of power system working. But Kuwait was an exceptional case. As everyone knew, Kuwait had oil. Critics remarked that the United States would hardly have exerted itself if the main export of Kuwait had been broccoli.

More typical are the conflicts in the contemporary world that have nationalism at their root, and nationalism makes states less likely to intervene in world conflicts than they were in the past. Most of us share the basic premise of nationalism, that members of the same national group should live together in one state. This has meant that we are not alarmed by a conflict fought to consolidate a national group into a state. Such conflicts are thought to be entirely understandable. When critics of US involvement in the Vietnam war said, "North Vietnam's leader Ho Chi Minh is really a nationalist," they were making an argument that many Americans found effective. Few Americans took seriously the idea that the North Vietnamese, after taking over the South, would move on to the Philippines, much less the Hawaiian Islands. Nationalism seemed to put a definite limit on how far they would expand. By contrast, back in the eighteenth century Austrians were threatened by the actions of Prussia's ruler Frederick the Great because national considerations were almost unknown in those days and there was no obvious limit to a state's expansion. Times had changed by the early twentieth century. Many people did not feel alarmed when Hitler annexed German-speaking Austria and German-speaking Sudetenland. Many were ready to appease him at the Munich conference in 1938. It was only when he moved to incorporate the obviously non-German populations of Czechoslovakia and Poland in 1939 that the rest of the world became convinced his ambitions were limitless.

Because most contemporary conflicts are rooted in nationalism, they seem self-limiting, and the constant vigilance and suspicion of every other country's moves that was characteristic of the balance of power system are not justified. Indeed, in the decade after the Vietnam war most Americans seemed to embrace the opposite preference, a desire to withdraw from world affairs. Thus in 1974 the United States did not apply pressure on Turkey (as it had in 1964 and 1967) to head off an invasion of Cyprus, nor did it counter Soviet moves into Angola in 1975. This withdrawal from world affairs seemed to abate somewhat after Ronald Reagan assumed the presidency in 1981, and the United States became more assertive. In 1983 American troops landed on the small Caribbean island of Grenada, ostensibly to rescue American medical students, but in a larger sense to limit the spread of Cuban influence. Also under Reagan, American Marines were deployed to Lebanon and American naval forces to the Persian Gulf. Under Bush, American forces took the leading role in a coalition war to liberate Kuwait.

Yet the willingness of the American public to tolerate military involvement for such vague purposes as "maintaining an equilibrium" still was very limited. American casualties were negligible in Grenada, Panama, and the Persian Gulf. When American forces in Lebanon did suffer casualties, the troops were withdrawn. Fear of public opposition kept the Reagan Administration from ever committing forces to Central America, despite its own conviction that the triumph of left-wing insurrections threatened US security.

In the end, the operation of a balance of power system depends entirely on the decisions of individual states. If states agree to act, the system goes into operation. If states do not agree, nothing happens. In the years after World War I, steps were taken to build on the principles behind the balance of power system by making the rules more explicit and the membership more nearly universal. The new arrangement was known as collective security.

NOTES

1. Ernst B. Haas, "The Balance of Power: Prescription, Concept, or Propaganda?" *World Politics*, Vol. 5, No. 4 (July 1953), pp. 442–477.
2. Winston S. Churchill, *The Gathering Storm* (Boston: Houghton Mifflin, 1948), pp. 207–208.
3. Winston S. Churchill, *The Grand Alliance* (Boston: Houghton Mifflin, 1950), p. 370.
4. Michael Haas, "International Subsystems: Stability and Polarity," *American Political Science Review*, Vol. 64, No. 1 (March 1970), pp. 98–121.
5. Interview with the staff of *Time*, January 3, 1972, p. 15.
6. James Reston, "The World According to Brzezinski," *The New York Times Magazine*, December 31, 1978, p. 9.
7. (New York: Random House, 1987), p. xxi.
8. R. W. Apple, Jr., "A New Balance of Power," *The New York Times*, July 12, 1990, p. Z A11.

CHAPTER 17

COLLECTIVE SECURITY

World government and the balance of power system are in many ways opposites. World government means one central authority, a permanent standing world police force, and clearly defined conditions under which this force will go into action. A balance of power system has many sovereign authorities, each controlling its own army, combining only when they feel like it to control aggression. To most people world government now seems unattainable. Balance of power systems have existed but are not trustworthy ways to prevent war. Some people have proposed something in between the two, whereby states would give up some but not all of their authority. This proposal is known as collective security.

WHAT COLLECTIVE SECURITY IS

One must take care in using the phrase "collective security." It is a technical term, with a specific meaning, but it is often loosely used or even misused. Part of the trouble is that it looks as though you should be able to figure out the meaning just by looking at the words. Another part of the trouble comes from deliberate misuse by people trying to win acceptance for other schemes that have nothing to do with collective security but look more attractive packaged under that label. Things such as military aid and peacetime alliances have been given this label to win acceptance from a reluctant American public.

In its technical meaning collective security is a system of states that join together, usually by signing a treaty, and make an explicit commitment to do two things: (1) They renounce the use of force to settle disputes with each other, and (2) they promise to use force against any of their number who break rule 1. Notice that collective security shares with the balance of power the principle "meet force with opposing force," or "gang up on the aggressor." The aggressor should be deterred by the prospect of an overwhelming coalition. If deterrence fails, then the aggressor will be defeated by military action undertaken by this coalition.

Collective security applies only to what goes on inside the system; its purpose is to keep peace among its members, not to protect them against outsiders. For this reason, it was not proper to call a Cold War alliance such as NATO a *collective security* system. It was not the main purpose of NATO to defend Iceland from aggression by Britain (which would have been collective security, because they were both members of NATO), but to defend both Iceland and England against aggression by non-NATO countries.

NATO, the Warsaw Pact, and similar organizations were more properly called *collective defense* organizations or simply alliances. Competing alliances are specifically ruled out between any members of a collective security system. In such a system a state has no need to designate a few other states as especially trustworthy in case of need. According to collective security all other states in the system will automatically become allies in case of aggression. Alliances at any other time would only arouse suspicion.

Collective security makes it possible for states to renounce the use of force by assuring them that they will not be helpless if another state illegally uses force against them. At the same time, it requires that all states participate in sanctions against an aggressor. A policy of neutrality or isolation is not allowed.

Thus in two ways collective security is a move from the unrestricted state sovereignty of the balance of power to the abolition of state sovereignty of world government. It forbids its members to resort to force to settle disputes and it requires them to use force to punish any member state that does. In these two ways it infringes on the traditional rights of sovereign states. But in all other respects states remain independent and sovereign. They are free to pursue other national interests, to enrich themselves, to compete for trade, and to run their domestic affairs as they see fit.

THE ADVANTAGES OF COLLECTIVE SECURITY

A collective security system offers advantages over the balance of power system. It offers security to all states in the system, not just the big ones. Because it does guarantee protection for all states, all have an incentive to join it. No state knows when it might become a victim of aggression and need the backing of all the others.

Collective security also avoids the biggest weakness of a balance of power system—its uncertainty. The balance operated haphazardly because it was never clear when states should move to shift alliances. They preferred to wait and see if a small addition of territory by a member state would make any difference in the overall balance. If it made no difference, they would not act. Collective security, by its explicit commitments to all states in the form of a treaty, eliminates doubt about what will happen to any state that resorts to force for any reason whatsoever: It will be met by opposition from all the other states. The balance of power system allowed one state to make a move, if other states did not like it, they could fight a "war of adjustment." Because aggression will be countered immediately, there will be no need for subsequent wars of adjustment in collective security.

Another advantage of collective security is its simplicity. Use of force in interstate relations is simply outlawed. Disputes between states will undoubtedly continue to arise, but states will have to find peaceful ways of resolving them. The principle of collective security has nothing to do with the reasons for using force, the background of the quarrel, or the probable consequences of defeat for one side or the other. All these calculations were very important in a balance of power system, as each great power tried to calculate the possible effects of a given war on the equilibrium of the entire system. In collective security there is no need for these calculations; all countries act against the one that first resorts to force.

A collective security system is set up by a treaty or other agreement that identifies the members and describes the conditions under which it goes into operation. A typical formulation for the aggression that triggers a collective response is "violation of territorial integrity and political independence," although an agreement could be more limited than that. For example, in March 1935, Britain proposed a regional pact to prevent aerial warfare. According to this proposal (which in the end was not agreed to), Britain, France, Germany, Italy, and Belgium would all agree that an unprovoked air attack by one on any other would trigger automatic massive retaliation against the violator by all the other countries.

This British plan lacked a feature that probably would have been added if it had come anywhere close to adoption—an organization to supervise it. Collective security systems need some kind of machinery to identify violations and coordinate efforts for defense. The most elaborate system of this kind was the League of Nations, which was set up after World War I. It was the first global organization whose primary task was preventing war. Its effective life ran from 1920 to 1936 and provides us with a case study of collective security in practice.

AN ATTEMPT TO IMPLEMENT COLLECTIVE SECURITY: THE LEAGUE OF NATIONS

In many ways the League of Nations was only a logical extension of practices that had developed before World War I. Conference diplomacy, by which all countries' delegates met in public assembly instead of in secret bilateral talks, had been used at the Hague Conferences in 1899 and 1907 to draw up rules for warfare. An international civil service, with bureaucrats owing loyalty to the world community rather than to a single country, was already running organizations such as the Universal Postal Union and the International Labor Organization. Even the essential feature of the League, the surrender of sovereignty in questions of war and peace, had been at least foreshadowed by the many alliances that committed states to go to war to aid others in specified circumstances. What made the League different was its universality. It was theoretically open to all states that would accept its obligations. In practice some states were rejected, in the beginning at least, on the argument that their governments were not democratic and therefore not subject to the effects of outraged public opinion if they chose to disregard collective security obligations. Germany was not yet considered rehabilitated in the eyes of the victors and was not allowed to join the League until 1926. Russia did not join until 1934. The majority of countries in Asia and Africa were not admitted because most were some kind of colonial dependents of European powers; even Ethiopia had a hard time getting accepted because the ruler was not able to govern his country effectively enough to abolish slavery. A major omission was the United States, not because it wasn't welcome but because the United States refused to approve ratification.

The founders of the League designed it according to what they thought were the lessons of World War I. Chief among these was the failure of the balance of power to prevent war. Instead of allowing themselves flexibility to realign against an aggressor, the great powers had let themselves be locked into two competing blocs. The remedy was collective security, which would rule out any alliance bloc until aggression was committed, at which time the aggressor would be automatically confronted by all other states. This principle of collective security was embodied in Article 16 of the Covenant of the League of Nations:

> Article 16. 1. Should any Member of the League resort to war in disregard of its covenants . . . it shall, *ipso facto*, be deemed to have committed an act of war against other Members of the League.

The Latin phrase *ipso facto* means "by that fact"; in other words, the resort to force is considered an act of war no matter what the explanation.

Another lesson of World War I was that secret diplomacy and secret treaties made every country uncertain about what would happen if any country did use force. Therefore, founders of the League spoke of "open covenants openly arrived at." Any business that needed discussing could be discussed openly in the Assembly of the League of Nations. There was no need for secret treaties because a state could have only one alliance obligation in any case, to its collective security partners.

Another apparent lesson of World War I was the decisive importance of economic power. It was evident that the British and French had finally won the war when the Americans joined not because the Americans were superior fighters but because they were backed by industrial might. The Covenant therefore stressed economic sanctions against an aggressor. Article 16 goes on to state that if a country resorts to force, other members of the League would

> ... undertake immediately to subject it to the severance of all trade or financial relations ... and the prevention of all financial, commercial or personal intercourse between the nationals of the Covenant-breaking State and the nationals of any other State, whether a Member of the League or not.

It would take time to coordinate other sanctions, such as military ones, but in the meantime economic sanctions would be taking effect. It was widely expected that those alone would be enough to make an aggressor stop.

As conceived by Wilson, collective security was to be the opposite of balance of power politics, relying instead on moral pressure, and if that failed, economic sanctions.[1] Sanctions were seen as a humane alternative to war. But only to the nearsighted are economic sanctions humane. A total embargo affects an entire society, and within a society a bellicose leadership and a military establishment can protect itself from the effects of an embargo better than innocent civilians. Aggressor states already have their arms and armies. Only years of embargo will render them useless through wear and lack of spare parts. Food and fuel will run out first, and dwindling supplies will be allocated to "national security," not maternity hospitals and kindergartens.

The authors of the Covenant were vaguely aware of the effect on civilians of the blockade of Germany during World War I but tried to put it out of their minds, preferring to emphasize that their victory over Germany came on the battlefield. Direct attacks on uniformed soldiers were more valorous than the slow starvation of civilians. The Germans, however, had they been listened to, would have described the inhumane effects of the blockade.

In 1990 the world returned to the approach recommended by Wilson and the League, applying economic sanctions to Iraq. The policy won wide support, being seen as a reasonable alternative to the "quagmire" of Vietnam (for the Americans) or Afghanistan (for the Russians) or to the "butcher bill" of previous wars. But only a month into the embargo a UN relief agency official in Amman warned: "How long will the Americans be able to hold to the embargo when the television news begins to show shots of hungry children?''[2] And indeed, even as Iraq continued to break its own word and deny UN inspection teams the right to investigate chemical, biological, and nuclear warfare installations, American newspapers were running photographs of malnourished Iraqi children.

HISTORY OF THE LEAGUE

But the weaknesses of collective security were not yet apparent when the organization began to function in 1920. The first decade of the League passed without a decisive test of collective security. Some minor disputes were settled inside the League and some were ignored or settled outside the League.[3] But the League was not confronted with a major international crisis that would test the theory and practice of collective security until the Manchurian crisis of 1931 (see Figure 17.1). Manchuria at this time, although nominally still part of China, was being exploited (in the economic sense) by its more powerful neighbors, chief of which was Japan. Japan already

Figure 17.1   Manchuria in 1931

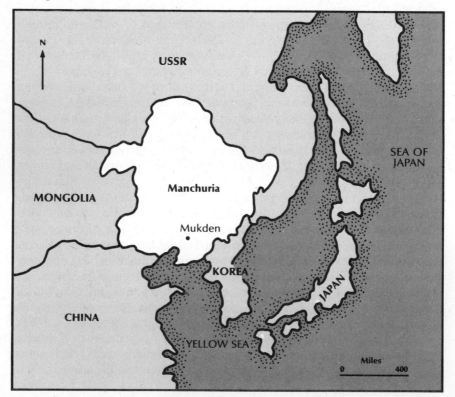

occupied the neighboring territory of Korea and had leases on factories, mines, and railroads in Manchuria. The military party in Japan wanted to occupy all of Manchuria outright, annex it, exclude the growing number of Chinese emigrating from the southern part of China, and develop its industrial potential for Japan's benefit. This expansionist faction was well represented among the Japanese troops stationed in Manchuria to guard Japanese investments.

On September 18, 1931, a minor explosion occurred on a railroad line administered by the Japanese. Japanese troops stationed in the railroad zone blamed Chinese troops and immediately staged a suspiciously well-planned takeover of Chinese arsenals and garrisons in the area. Civilians in the Japanese government tried to control the military party while explaining to the world that this was only a local incident. At first the world was unaware of what was happening, because communications from such a distant area were slow and not very accurate and because the Japanese diplomats at the League headquarters in Geneva were themselves opposed to imperial expansion. But on October 8, 1931, a hopelessly outclassed Chinese garrison decided to resist anyway, and the Japanese in angry retaliation bombed the city of Chinchow. Events in Manchuria had become impossible for the League to ignore. In response to Chinese protests, the League passed resolutions requesting that the Japanese withdraw, but the Japanese ignored them, continuing to expand their control until, on February 18, 1932, they set up a puppet state to govern all of Manchuria, ostensibly a national liberation movement but obviously controlled by the Japanese.

The League reacted cautiously. It appointed a Commission of Inquiry in December 1931, which made a thorough investigation and issued a report of 100,000 words that was adopted by the League on February 24, 1933, that is, seventeen months after the Japanese troops began their takeover. For all its length, the report's conclusions were quite simple. It concluded that "without any declaration of war, a large part of Chinese territory has been forcibly seized and occupied by Japanese troops."[4] It would seem that China had been the victim of aggression and the League would come to China's aid. But, no, the League decided that because Japan had not declared war, Article 16 did not apply. All the League did was accept a suggestion by the commission that changes in territory made by armed force would not be recognized. In other words, the only penalty applied to Japan would be that the postage stamps and currency of the puppet state would not be accepted by other countries. This moral condemnation of the Japanese merely angered them without in any way making them change their behavior. The next month they announced their withdrawal from the League.

The Manchurian crisis revealed a basic feature of the League's collective security system. Theoretically all states would participate in sanctions against an aggressor. In practice, some states would have to bear a bigger burden than others. Japan was an island nation in the Pacific, part of the "Far East" in European eyes. Enforcing an embargo (or stronger action) would require considerable power. Of the League members, only Britain had the kind of power—naval power—that could be projected into this region, and British leaders agreed that an expedition in Asia would distract attention and divert energy from Europe, where the real danger to their security would come from. The United States, also a naval power and with more direct interests in this area, was not a member of the League, and the isolationist mood that had kept it from joining the League continued strong. The only other state capable of acting in this area was Russia, but it was not yet a League member and was in any case preoccupied with domestic disorder brought on by the forced collectivization of the peasantry. Russia chose instead to pursue an appeasement policy with Japan, granting de facto recognition to the puppet state in March 1935. Manchuria was in Japan's sphere of influence and no major power chose to challenge it.

The next major crisis to confront the League came from Latin America. Conflict between Bolivia and Paraguay over 100,000 square miles of an uninhabited river basin known as the Chaco turned into full-scale war in 1932 (see Figure 17.2). The League tried to impose sanctions in the form of an arms embargo but did not succeed in stopping shipments of arms until August 1934. Rapid action by the US Congress at this time suddenly made an arms embargo possible. American opinion had been aroused by advertisements of US armaments companies in a Bolivian newspaper, and Congress unanimously gave the president power to prohibit sales of arms and munitions to Bolivia and Paraguay. By this time the two countries were coming to realize that neither of them could win in any case, and in June 1935 they allowed other American states to work out a peace. As in the case of Manchuria, the dispute occurred in the sphere of influence of one power and only if that power chose to act was the League able to act. The United States was not the aggressor, as Japan was, but the inability of outsiders to intrude in a great power's sphere of influence was similar.

The third major crisis that the League confronted was too much for it and led to its collapse. The crisis involved Abyssinia, or, as it is called today, Ethiopia. (See Figure 17.3.) Italy, which already controlled a colony in the neighboring territory of Eritrea, had wanted for decades to extend its control to Ethiopia, one of the few remaining territories in Africa not controlled by Europeans. The Italians had tried to take over Ethiopia at the end of the nineteenth century but failed, suffering a humiliating defeat at the battle of Adowa in 1896. Forty years later Mussolini wanted to avenge that defeat and demonstrate the new Italian renaissance under Fascism. Italy's ambitions in the 1930s were not different from France's and Britain's in the preceding century when they had occupied territory in Africa. The Italians just came too late in history. Ethiopia was no longer "unoccupied" territory but a fully recognized sovereign state and a member of the League of Nations.

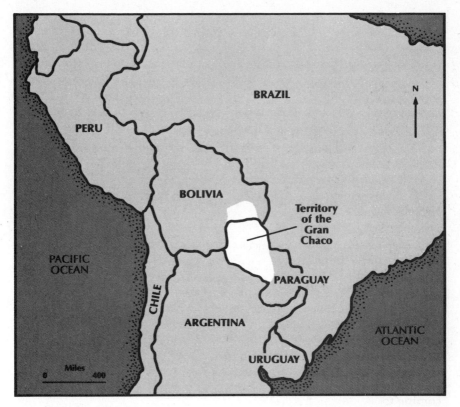

Figure 17.2   The Gran Chaco

But Italy was not ashamed to be pursuing nineteenth-century aims in the twentieth century and made no effort to hide its intentions. Preparations for invasion in Eritrea were obvious. Italy employed thousands of laborers to build roads, docks, and airfields. Several million tons of equipment were stockpiled. Natives of Eritrea were mobilized for military training. Reserves in Italy were called up.

In December 1934, Italian troops clashed with Ethiopians. According to the Italians the clash was a border dispute, although even according to the Italians' military maps the Italians were 80 miles inside Ethiopia. In January 1935, Emperor Haile Selassie of Ethiopia appealed to the League for support. But because the 1934 clash was only a military engagement, not an attempt to seize territory, League members felt there were no grounds for action under the doctrine of collective security. Even though Ethiopia felt threatened by 500,000 Italian troops massing across its border, the Italians had committed no overt aggression.

Having prepared without hindrance, Italy launched its attack in Octo-

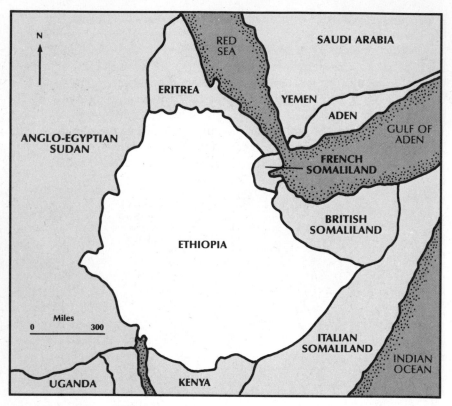

Figure 17.3   Ethiopia in 1935

ber, 1935. The League within a week found that Italy had resorted to war and ten days later voted to apply sanctions against Italy. These were to include an embargo on arms, new loans and bank credits, and all imports from Italy. But the League could not bring itself to embargo the one commodity essential to Italy's invasion, oil. Furthermore, the League did not insist on the closure of the Suez Canal, which would have cut Italy's supply line. No one even breathed the possibility of military action against Italy in defense of Ethiopia.

This failure to take decisive steps against Italy was grounded in the belief of the other major powers in the League that Germany posed a bigger threat to their own security and Italy might be needed at some future point as an ally. Thus, to avoid alienating Italy, the British Foreign Minister Samuel Hoare and the French Premier Pierre Laval had even worked out a solution whereby Italy could keep control of half of Ethiopia, under the pretext of administering for the League. Even when the Hoare–Laval plan leaked to the public in December, 1935, it did not generate enough outrage to force the

League to take sterner measures. The limited sanctions that had been applied were not enough to make Italy stop. In fact, they had the unintended effect of uniting the majority of the Italian people behind Mussolini for the first time since he took office. Italy went on to win the war against Ethiopia, using airplanes and poison gas among other modern weapons. Emperor Haile Selassie fled the country and appeared before the League in May 1936, a living reproach to its cowardice and passivity. "God and history will remember your judgement," he told them.[5] In July 1936 the League acknowledged its own moral bankruptcy by lifting even the limited sanctions. Later it even recognized Italian sovereignty over Ethiopia.

REASONS FOR THE FAILURE OF THE LEAGUE

The Ethiopian crisis marked the death of collective security as practiced by the League of Nations. The League's failures in this crisis illustrate some of its structural weaknesses. One problem was that nobody quite trusted it. The great powers gave lip service to the new idea of collective security but secretly they still believed in the old idea of the balance of power. Britain and France did not want to push Italy too hard because they thought they might need Italy as an ally in a future conflict with Germany. With the benefit of hindsight we know that this hope was vain and that Italy and Germany fought on the same side in World War II, but it was not obvious to diplomats in 1935 that this "Berlin–Rome Axis" was going to come into being. The issue of the South Tyrol, inhabited by Germans and ruled by Italians, was widely believed to be an insurmountable obstacle to German–Italian cooperation. The same sort of calculation paralyzed the League in the Manchurian crisis. Preparing a defense against Germany in Europe was more important to Britain and France than the abstract principle of opposing aggression no matter where it occurred. In the abstract, perhaps, peace was "indivisible," but when their own peace was threatened, states reverted to old-fashioned calculations of balance of power.

The behavior of the smaller members of the League was no more virtuous. Those states in favor of applying sanctions against Italy in the Ethiopian crisis were mostly countries close to Italy that feared an expansion of its power—Czechoslovakia, Rumania, Yugoslavia, Greece, and Turkey. But other countries in this area supported Italy, not because they thought Italy was in the right in Ethiopia but for reasons of self-interest. Austria shared with Italy a fear of Germany. Albania and to some extent Hungary were client states dependent on Italy. Other states in more distant parts of the world (Scandinavia, Latin America) saw little of direct interest to themselves in the crisis.

Perhaps the attitude of the smaller members would have been less important if all the major states had been members. But Japan had by this time quit the League as a result of the Manchurian crisis and Germany had left the League over the issue of rearmament. (Germany felt it would benefit no matter how the Ethiopian crisis was resolved. Either Italy would be defeated and a potential rival cut down, enabling Hitler to recover the South Tyrol, or the Western democracies would demonstrate their impotence and Germany could make gains elsewhere.) But the most serious omission was the absence of the United States. Even if oil products had been included in the League embargo, profit-seeking companies in the United States would have been glad to send its oil to Italy to make up what they were being denied from League members. League members probably would not have risked interference with US ships to enforce an embargo.

The ability of a single country effectively to undermine the embargo of all the others reveals the weakness of the belief in the automatic success of economic sanctions. In the absence of unanimous support for an embargo, some kind of force must be used to make it work. An embargo must be turned into a blockade, and because so much of world trade moves by sea (three-quarters in the case of Italy in 1936), a blockade means reliance on naval power. Only a navy could deny supplies to Italy, and in 1936 only Britain had a navy capable of doing the job. But the British admiralty was justifiably worried about the consequences of modern military technology for their navy. In 1924 a US advocate of air power, General Billy Mitchell, had demonstrated the vulnerability of ships by sinking old battleships off Cape Hatteras. The British did not want their navy to confirm these experimental results in actual combat.

THE PROBLEMS OF COLLECTIVE SECURITY

The failure of the League of Nations can be seen as the result of the historical situation in which it had to operate, particularly the failure of the United States to join and the harsh Versailles peace settlement that encouraged the rise of Hitler. But troublesome as these problems were, the League also suffered fundamental difficulties with any collective security system.

One problem is the definition of "aggression." A collective security system needs explicit and unambiguous criteria on which to act. The existence of such criteria is one way in which it contrasts with the balance of power. Under the balance of power mere suspicion of another country's intentions might be enough to justify a preventive war. But the need for a legal definition leads collective security to concentrate on overt acts, such as sending troops in uniform over a demarcated frontier. Thus when Haile Selassie became alarmed at Italian preparations for invasion in January 1935, he could not get the League to act, not only because its members were reluctant to oppose Italy but also because Italy had not yet done anything to violate the Covenant of the League. Likewise, the best way to have headed off World War II would have been to have done something about German rearmament, beginning in 1935. But any League action would have been interference in the internal affairs of a sovereign state. As a result of the need to adhere to legal definitions, when wars did break out, they were much bigger and the aggressor was much harder to defeat.

States have found it impossible to arrive at an unambiguous definition of aggression. The classic formulation of "violation of territorial integrity and political independence" is not always adequate. Hitler's occupation of the demilitarized zone along the Rhineland in 1936 violated both the Versailles treaty and the Locarno treaty, but the Rhineland was German territory. Hitler's annexation of Austria in 1938 extinguished the political independence of Austria, but it was supposedly at the request of the Austrian government.

More recent cases are even more ambiguous. In May 1967, Egypt closed the Strait of Tiran to ships going to the Israeli port of Elat, thereby cutting off Israel's trade (including oil) with Asia. (See Figure 17.4.) In response, Israel

Figure 17.4   The Strait of Tiran

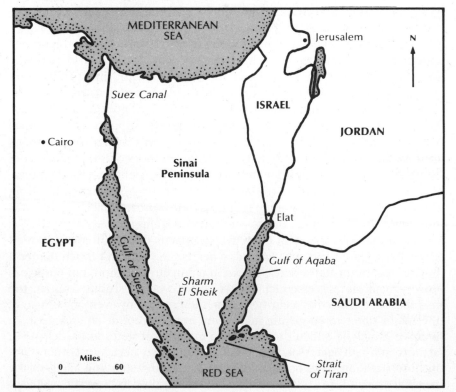

Fiaure 12.4 The Strait of Tiran

attacked Egypt. Which country was the aggressor? Egypt was blocking an Israeli port, and a blockade has traditionally been considered an act of war. By this criterion Egypt started the 1967 war. But Egypt claimed it was merely excluding ships from its own territorial waters, and such action was not an act of war. States do not agree on the legal issue. The Strait of Tiran is a place where ships must pass through the territorial waters of a state (Egypt) to get from one international body of water (the Red Sea) to another (the Gulf of Aqaba). A rule of international law called the "right of innocent passage" was included in a convention on the law of the sea drawn up at Geneva in 1958. That convention has been accepted by many states, but not by Egypt.

After years of trying to define aggression, in 1974 the United Nations issued a definition covering many kinds of behavior—invasion, bombardment of territory, blockade of ports, attack on armed forces, and sending terrorists. But the usefulness of definition was badly weakened by two loopholes. One was that "acts enumerated above are not exhaustive and the Security Council may determine that other acts constitute aggression under the provision of the Charter."[6] In other words, aggression is whatever the Security Council says it is. Given a Council with the right political composition, Egypt could find support for Gamal Abdel Nasser's statement that the very existence of the state of Israel is an act of aggression.

This loophole expands the definition of aggression. A second loophole contracts it. It states that "nothing in this definition could in any way prejudice the right to self-determination, freedom and independence of peoples forcibly deprived of that right, particularly peoples under colonial and racist regimes or other forms of alien domination; nor the right of these people to struggle to that end and to seek and receive support, in accordance with the principles of the Charter." In other words, when Indian troops crossed the frontier into Goa in 1961, they were not committing an act of aggression, because people forcibly deprived of the right of self-determination were seeking and receiving support in their struggle to that end. Using this definition, one might argue that the North Korean attack of 1950 was not aggression but an act of national self-determination.

A second problem with collective security is the requirement that all states participate in actions against an aggressor. It doesn't much matter if one or two minor states refuse to join in enforcement action, but participation by major states is essential. If power is not evenly distributed among the members of a collective security system, then refusal by even one or two of the major states to cooperate may doom any attempt at enforcement. In practice it may be difficult to get even a majority of states to participate in action against an aggressor. States will be reluctant to act against other states if those states are very powerful neighbors, or long-standing allies, or the perceived victims. In 1935, Albania would not oppose its powerful protector

Italy; in 1950 the Soviet Union would not oppose its ideological ally North Korea; in 1967 many states would not blame Israel for initiating hostilities.

Furthermore, states will be reluctant to make sacrifices for quarrels that seem remote. In September 1948, Indian troops invaded the state of Hyderabad to force it to join the Republic of India (see Figure 17.5). Hyderabad appealed to the United Nations but its appeal was ignored. No member of the UN felt threatened because no member saw itself as another candidate for incorporation into the new Indian state. Hyderabad had been part of the British colonial possession of India and was totally surrounded by states that had joined the new Republic of India. No other state was in a similar position and thus no other state felt itself threatened by this precedent.

The UN did come to the defense of South Korea in 1950. At first glance this appears to be collective security in action, with states from many parts of the world coming to the aid of a small, remote country under attack. But in fact the North Korean invasion aroused the United States not so much because of concern for the abstract principle of collective security (after all,

Figure 17.5   Hyderabad in 1947

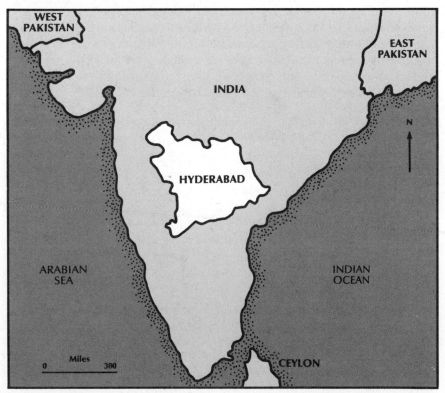

the United States had not reacted to the Indian invasion of Hyderabad two years earlier) as because of interest in neighboring Japan, which was then under American occupation. European countries supported action in Korea because they saw an analogy with Germany, where the Communist half of a divided country was also preparing for reunification by force. They believed that by showing resolve in Korea they might deter a Communist attack in Europe.

The theoretical requirement of collective security that all states take part in actions against an aggressor is often justified by the claim that "peace is indivisible." That is, peace in each country is threatened by war anywhere. Conflict in distant parts of the world cannot be walled off and ignored. The indivisibility of the peace is often contrasted favorably with the appeasement policy of Britain before World War II, when Chamberlain argued against helping Czechoslovakia because the Sudetenland crisis was a "quarrel in a faraway country between people of whom we know nothing."[7] The British of course found themselves shortly thereafter at war, and Chamberlain's statement has been ridiculed ever since.

Traumatic as the Munich experience was for Europeans and Americans, it may be an error to make too much of this single example. In fact not all small disputes lead to larger ones. India's annexation of Goa in 1961 was not a prelude to Indian world conquest. Whatever the justice of the settlement, to either the Portuguese, who were deprived of their territory by armed force, or the native Goans, who were never consulted on their preferences but seemed in fact to prefer Portuguese rule, that conflict did not bring the world to the brink of war.

In recent years the belief in the "indivisible peace" has taken the form of the Domino Theory. US intervention in Vietnam was originally defended as necessary to prevent neighboring countries from going communist. Dwight D. Eisenhower had noted in his diary, even before becoming president, that it was important for the French to maintain control in Vietnam, for "if they quit and Indochina falls to Commies, it is easily possible that the countries of Southeast Asia and Indonesia would go, soon to be followed by India."[8] At a press conference in April 1954 Eisenhower said, "You have a row of dominoes set up, you knock over the first one, and what will happen to the last one is the certainty that it will go over very quickly. So you could have a beginning of a disintegration that would have profound consequences."[9]

In fact Eisenhower's worst fears came true and the Communists did take over in 1975, yet only Vietnam's small weak neighbors of Laos and Cambodia followed it into the Communist bloc. Furthermore, fifteen years later that bloc itself had dissolved and the Communist victory in Cambodia was undone by a UN-negotiated agreement. The long, costly Vietnam war to keep dominos from falling had been unnecessary.

One might ask whether the solution offered by the balance of power system wasn't better: Instead of trying to prevent all conflicts, isolate them when they occur in remote parts of the world. The South Americans fought a number of destructive wars in the nineteenth and twentieth centuries (the Chaco War, the War of the Pacific, the War of La Plata) but these are almost unknown to North Americans because the conflicts were isolated by the Monroe Doctrine, which kept Europeans out, and did not become world wars. They were nobody's Vietnams.

Another difficulty with collective security is that organizations by their very nature react slowly to crises. First it must be determined who is at fault. War is a serious matter and states must be sure of the facts before they engage in belligerent acts against aggressors. It is easy to criticize the League for its ponderous efforts in the Manchurian crisis, but communications were poor and information spotty. Even the Japanese government was not sure of what was happening. Critics always have the benefit of hindsight. The aggression of Iraq against Kuwait in 1990 was exceptional in its clarity. Ten years earlier in the same part of the world the origins of the war between Iraq and Iran were shrouded in obscurity. In that war Iraqi troops crossed the border first but claimed that Iranian artillery had been shelling them. The 1980 situation is more typical than the 1990 one.

Because under collective security action may be taken only when actual acts of aggression occur, no advance planning is possible merely on the basis of suspicion. This means that an aggressor has an enormous advantage. An aggressor can plan for months or even years, carry through a move with lightning speed, and then present the world with a fait accompli. The collective security organization then has the unpleasant choice of accepting the results of aggression or mounting a massive campaign that will cause destruction all out of proportion to the violation. The example of Kuwait is instructive. Had the country not been one of the richest in the world, the destruction caused by the Gulf War would have been all out of proportion to any possible gain from being liberated. Even with their high per capita income the Kuwaiti's recovery was slow and painful.

The fait accompli is an effective tactic. Because modern means of warfare such as missiles and airplanes threaten civilian as well as military targets, states are reluctant to expose their own populations to attack to undo the results of aggression elsewhere. They are tempted to redefine aggression to exclude such acts and let the results stand. Had Iraqi Scuds carried nuclear warheads, more than one state within their range might have been willing to give serious consideration to Iraq's claim that it was merely reclaiming a historic province when it annexed Kuwait.

Other recent wars in the Middle East in 1967, on the Indian subcontinent in 1971, and on the island of Cyprus in 1974 illustrate this problem as well. Israel, India, and Turkey each carried out rapid military operations, which were completed before the world could react. The task of reversing the results of these operations was so massive that the results were allowed to stand. One or more countries continued to protest against the results of these quick operations, but no one expected countries of the world to combine in military operations to undo them. One can argue that the UN is not a true collective security organization, so its members had no legal obligation to act in any of these three cases. But even if there had been such an organization, you can see the difficulties its members would have confronted when faced with such faits accomplis, and this was true even though none of these states at the time had nuclear forces.

Only rarely is an act of aggression so blatant as Iraq's annexation of Kuwait in August, 1990. At the time many observers expected Saddam Hussein to seek to divide the coalition against him by a conciliatory gesture, such as withdrawing from much of Kuwait but retaining portions of Kuwait's oil fields. Had he done so, it is unlikely a war against him would have found much support. Even with his uncompromising stand, many observers doubted that the coalition could maintain sanctions for long, an important factor in President Bush's decision to press for war.

Finally, like so many plans for peace, collective security preserves the status quo and thus works to the advantage of states that benefit most from the status quo. An ironclad collective security agreement would be like a poker game interrupted in the middle when one player is far ahead. Gambling is suddenly declared illegal but the player who is ahead is allowed to keep his or her winnings.

Furthermore, so long as the principle of noninterference in internal affairs is observed, groups such as the Bengalis will have to suffer whatever a dominant ethnic group subjects them to. Going to their aid would be interference in internal affairs and thus aggression. For this reason, the UN definition of aggression, even with its enormous loopholes, is more realistic than a rigid one would be, for it reflects the need to have ways of changing the status quo. But one problem with such elastic definitions is that they provide no assurance to any state that it will receive support if another state uses force against it. The same African states that opposed the use of force to aid the Ibo people of Nigeria in their war to set up an independent state in 1967 encouraged the use of force against the Portuguese colonies in Mozambique and Angola. Winning support as a victim of aggression is more the result of having enough political supporters than of any objective conditions such as having enemy troops cross your frontier.

REGIONAL COLLECTIVE SECURITY

Both theory and practice suggest that collective security will not work on the global level. But it might have a chance in more limited areas, where differences between states are not so great. Some people have advocated more emphasis on organizations that limit their membership to states in a geographic region of the world. We call this approach to peace regional collective security.

Like all collective security systems, a regional one would try to preserve peace only among its members. It would create an island of peace in a world where great power rivalry, ideological struggles, and competition for resources might continue to cause conflict elsewhere. In this way regionalism reverses a basic tenet of supporters of the League of Nations that peace was indivisible, because the idea rests on the assumption that one region of the world can be sealed off from the rest of the world.[10]

By this argument, regional organizations will have more success in maintaining peace among their numbers because these members are more likely to have common interests. They may have similar resources (such as oil or coffee) or similar problems (such as tribal divisions). These similarities will enable them to understand regional disputes better and come up with appropriate solutions, and such solutions are more likely to be heeded coming from sympathetic sources.

In many parts of the world numerous state boundaries are the result of artificial divisions between imperialist powers. Syria and Jordan are separate countries mainly because France administered one and Britain the other. A world organization is too big and unwieldy to deal with problems arising from such divisions; individual states by themselves cannot handle them either. Only at the regional level can realistic solutions be found, argue the regionalists. Also, confining the business of maintaining peace to the regional level provides a good excuse for excluding major powers. Even Asian states fearful of expansionist neighbors might not want outside assistance if they would have to pay the price of massive destruction that Vietnam did.

Although no regional organizations exist strictly for collective security, a number have the potential and have taken some actions in the name of preserving peace. Typical of these is the Organization of African Unity (OAU). It was founded in 1963 and is open to all independent states on the continent of Africa. Outsiders are excluded from membership, and its primary goal is solving problems within the region, not providing protection for members against external enemies. Other organizations in this category are the Arab League, formed in 1945 and gradually increasing its membership as more Arab states became independent, and the Organization of American States (OAS), formed in 1948.

The role once foreseen for regional organizations is illustrated by a conflict three decades ago between two former British possessions in the Middle East, Iraq and Kuwait (see Figure 17.6). Iraq became independent in 1936, but the British retained Kuwait as a protectorate until 1961. As independence for Kuwait approached, the Iraqis laid claim to it as a former

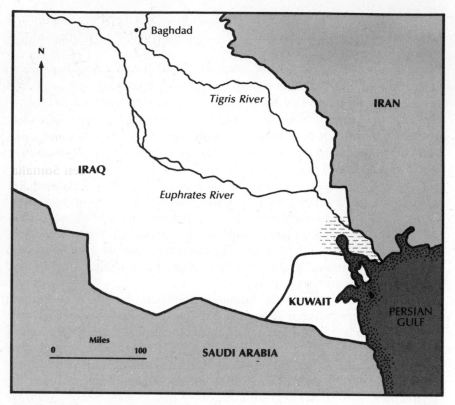

Figure 17.6   Iraq and Kuwait

province. Unwilling to be absorbed, Kuwait asked the British to station troops. After several meetings the Arab League decided to admit Kuwait as a member, thereby giving increased legitimacy to its claim to exist as a sovereign, independent state. Iraq alone resisted. Meanwhile the Arabs, eager to be rid of a British military presence, sent troops of their own to replace the British in Kuwait. A force of 3,300 from five Arab countries backed up the Arab League's decision to recognize Kuwait's sovereignty by giving it protection against Iraq. Iraq appeared to give up its opposition to an independent Kuwait in 1963, although events three decades later showed how powerful even long dormant irredentist claims can be.

Part of the reason regionalism was viewed optimistically was that it conformed nicely with a widespread desire in the United States to reduce American responsibility in other parts of the world. If regional organizations worked better anyhow, then we could do what we wanted and be virtuous at the same time. President Nixon expressed this view in his "State of the World" message of 1971: "It is no longer possible to . . . argue that security or development around the globe is primarily America's concern. The defense and progress of other countries must be first their responsibility and second a regional responsibility.''[11]

Events during the decade following Nixon's speech struck severe blows to the hopes of regionalism. The most important regional organizations suffered major setbacks in their attempts to keep peace. The organization that many considered the most promising, the OAU, suffered the most. The African continent experienced many serious conflicts, several of them coming to their own violent conclusions with the OAU standing helplessly by.

The most serious conflict was the prolonged quarrel between Somalia and Ethiopia. During the decade or so that it continued it claimed an estimated 50,000 lives. The underlying cause was Somalia's irredentist claim to the Ogaden desert region of Ethiopia, inhabited mostly by Somali nomads but under Ethiopian jurisdiction since it was forcibly seized in 1897 (see Figure 17.7). Ethiopia for its part argued that it was only trying to assert its

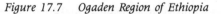

Figure 17.7   Ogaden Region of Ethiopia

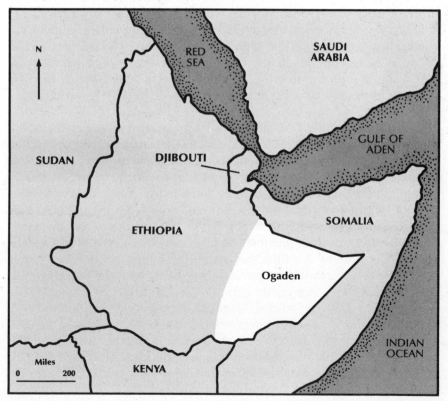

authority in its sovereign territory. Somalia pretended the conflict was being waged mostly by local guerrillas fighting for national liberation with only incidental help from Somalia, although in fact the conflict was a deliberate Somali campaign. At the 1977 conference of the heads of state of OAU members, the two states exchanged bitter accusations over the fighting in the Ogaden. The OAU did no more than refer the conflict to a special committee. The conflict ended in the following months, not because of this OAU committee but because of a successful offensive in which Ethiopia was assisted by Cuban troops and Soviet equipment. Yet such outside military assistance was the very thing regionalism was supposed to prevent.

Another failure of the OAU was its inability to solve the conflict between Zaïre and its southern neighbor Angola. President Mobutu of Zaïre charged in 1978 that the province of Shaba was being invaded by forces from Angola. Here the level of violence was much lower than in the Ogaden war, but even so the OAU had little to do with its resolution. An outside intervention force, organized primarily by France and consisting largely of French and Belgian troops, restored Zaïre's control over Shaba.

Likewise the OAU was unable to prevent an attack on Tanzania by its northern neighbor Uganda in the fall of 1978, and a much larger retaliatory attack by Tanzania in the spring of 1979. At another end of the continent, the conflict between Morocco and Algeria over the status of the former Spanish colony of Sahara continued into the late 1980s despite repeated efforts at OAU summit meetings to bring the sides to negotiations. When they did agree to talk in 1988, it was in response to a request by the UN, not a regional organization.

Only once did the OAU attempt a major peace-keeping effort, and it ended in failure. In late 1980, Libya sent 14,000 troops to assist one faction in a civil war in its southern neighbor Chad. After a year of indecisive fighting, the Libyans pulled out, supposedly to be replaced by an OAU peace-keeping force. But the peace-keeping force failed—only three of the six African countries that had promised to send troops did so, and even they required subsidies from outside powers, the United States and France in particular. By April 1982 the force had run out of money, and in June the commander ordered it withdrawn, citing the failure of the Chadians to accept the OAU proposals for political settlement. With the peace-keeping force gone, the civil war continued.

But Libya continued to give diplomatic support to one faction in Chad. Libya's support included using its position during its turn as host to the OAU summit meeting to grant a seat to the faction it favored. Because of this behavior, enough states stayed away to deny a quorum. Thus the weakness of the OAU had progressed beyond an inability to settle conflicts; it was now so divided it could not even convene meetings.

The OAU did resume meeting in 1983, although still quarreling about leadership and membership, but did nothing to move the various conflicts in Africa toward solution. After the failure of the peace-keeping venture in Chad, the forces in the northern part of the country were increasingly under the control of Libya and once again included Libyan troops. The forces in the south turned to the French for support. In 1987, with the help of American and French military aid, the southern faction was able to defeat Libyan forces in the north and drive them out of Chad. Thus, repeating the pattern set earlier in Ethiopia and Zaïre, the conflict was settled not by the regional organization but by outside powers.

By many measures the most serious and longest-running conflict in Africa was a complex dispute involving guerrilla war in Angola (the UNITA insurgents supported by South Africa) and guerrilla war in the former German colony of South-West Africa (ruled by South Africa and contested by insurgents supported by Angola). South-West Africa became the independent state of Namibia, and UNITA insurgents made peace with the Angolan government as the result of mediation in which the United States played a major role. The OAU played no role at all.

Another regional organization, the Arab League, suffered a similar failure in the conflict between South Yemen and North Yemen. Attempts at mediation by Syria and Iraq were unsuccessful in resolving the dispute. To the dismay of regionalists, stability was finally restored when the United States sent arms to North Yemen, helping to balance the arms that South Yemen was receiving from the Soviet Union.

Whatever little authority the Arab League retained was totally shattered by its paralysis following Iraq's invasion of Kuwait. Despite rhetoric about the need to find "an Arab solution," the organization was sharply divided into two camps. In the end, several of the Arab states joined with outsiders such as the United States, Britain, and France in war against a fellow League member.

Some modest success might be claimed for the Organization of American States in containing the 1979 civil war in Nicaragua. Although the OAS did little to limit the violence of the war itself, which caused over 20,000 deaths, just its existence may have inhibited the Nicaraguan government from retaliating against its unarmed neighbor, Costa Rica, for providing sanctuary for guerrillas. (When Nicaraguan planes did strafe targets over the border, Panama and Venezuela provided military assistance to Costa Rica—although on their own, not as the result of an OAS decision.)

In the subsequent violence in Central America, the OAS played almost no role at all. El Salvador fought a civil war, charging that the insurgents were armed by neighboring Nicaragua. Nicaragua in turn charged that forces based in Honduras were conducting operations designed to overthrow its government. The initiatives that were put forward to settle these conflicts came from individuals (President Arias of Costa Rica), single countries (Mexico), or at best small groupings of countries (the Contadora group). The regional organization to which they all belonged was hardly ever mentioned.

Following this series of disappointments, it is difficult to accept the claim that regional organizations can succeed where global organizations have failed. Likewise, the hope expressed in the Nixon Doctrine has proved illusory. The problems of agreeing on what constitutes aggression, organizing a timely response, and getting states to participate in collective action when it is not clearly in their self-interest have been too serious for collective security to overcome. The coalition against Iraq that forced the restoration of independence to Kuwait was the result of exceptional circumstances and not a part of a trend toward a new world order. Solutions to the problem of aggression are less likely to be arranged by global or regional organizations than by two states working directly through diplomacy or indirectly with the help of third parties.

NOTES

1. Robert Osgood, "Woodrow Wilson, Collective Security, and the Lessons of History," in Earl Latham, ed., *The Philosophy and Politics of Woodrow Wilson* (Chicago: University of Chicago Press, 1958).

2. John F. Burns, "On the Road to Baghdad with Powdered Milk, but No Exemptions," *The New York Times*, September 25, 1990, p. Z A7.

3. The standard history of the League is F. P. Walters, *A History of the League of Nations*, 2 vols. (London: Oxford University Press, 1952).

4. Westel W. Willoughby, *The Sino-Japanese Controversy and the League of Nations* (Baltimore: Johns Hopkins Press, 1935).

5. Elmer Bendiner, *A Time for Angels* (New York: Alfred A. Knopf, 1975), p. 375

6. *The New York Times*, April 13, 1974. The abbreviated version of the text is in the accompanying news story.

7. Winston S. Churchill, *The Gathering Storm* (Boston: Houghton Mifflin, 1948), p. 315.

8. Diary entry of March 17, 1951, cited by John Prados, *The Sky Would Fall* (New York: The Dial Press, 1983), p. 10.

9. *Public Papers of the Presidents: Dwight D. Eisenhower, 1954*, pp. 381–390.

10. Joseph S. Nye, *Peace in Parts* (Boston: Little, Brown, 1971), pp. 3, 129.

11. *U.S. Foreign Policy for the 1970s: Building for Peace: A Report to the Congress* by Richard Nixon (Washington, D.C.: U.S. Government Printing Office, February 25, 1971), p. 14.

CHAPTER 18

DIPLOMACY

Balance of power, collective security, and disarmament all deal with the *instrument* of war, not with the *reasons* states have for fighting in the first place. If we could eliminate the quarrels that lead to war, we would wipe out war as surely as if we had total disarmament. Few times in history have the objectives that a war was fought for been worth the price that was paid. Suppose the French government in 1914 had been confronted with this simple proposition: "If you will take 1,363,000 of your strongest and healthiest young men, stand them against walls, and shoot them, you will be allowed to put the provinces of Alsace and Lorraine back under your administration." No government would have dared accept such an exchange, yet in the end, that is the price France paid in World War I for exactly that gain.

One of the problems in World War I was that no country was sure of the war aims of the others. Consequently, each imagined the worst and so fought more stubbornly. Clarification of aims would have alleviated if not eliminated much of the suffering that war caused.

The process of talking over differences, clarifying aims, and exploring adjustments short of fighting is called *diplomacy*. It has many aspects. The one we want to concentrate on might be defined as the art of resolving disputes between states by highly skilled communication among the trained representatives of governments. The emphasis in diplomacy is on communication; everything connected with diplomacy—special representatives, high training, and formal procedures—is designed to enhance such communication.

THE STRUCTURE OF DIPLOMACY

There are two parts to diplomacy—the apparatus that conducts it and the forms that it follows. The apparatus consists of two parts—officials inside one's own country and officials overseas. We usually reserve the name "diplomat" for the ambassadorial staff serving abroad, but its counterparts at home are also part of the diplomatic service. The branch of the government responsible for sending representatives to other states is typically called the "foreign ministry," although for historical reasons it is called the Department of External Affairs in Canada, the Foreign Office in Great Britain, and the State Department in the United States. Most of the important officials in diplomacy are members of a professional service (called the Foreign Service in the United States) similar to the officer corps of an army. They are selected on a competitive basis, given special training, and promoted through the ranks. Members of the Foreign Service serve both at foreign posts and at home.

Officials in the State Department are essential to diplomacy, but attention is usually focussed on embassy officials posted abroad. The most important of these is the ambassador, who is the official personal representative from one head of state to another. The idea that an ambassador is a personal representative goes back to monarchic times, when all kings considered themselves brothers and sent representatives more as a family obligation than as a government service. The notion that a diplomat is a personal representative is still taken seriously. Ambassadors must present their credentials in person to the head of state, and when a head of state is changed, the ambassadors must be reaccredited.

An ambassador must actually reside in the country to which he or she is accredited. But the ambassador and the ambassadorial staff have special privileges and immunities in their host country, such as freedom from taxes, from prosecution for criminal offenses, and even from "insults to diplomatic dignity." (One practical meaning of that phrase is that suitable housing must be made available.) The embassy itself must have freedom from search and seizure, and it must have the right to secret communication with the home country. All this is designed to facilitate communication among states. In time of crisis it is not necessary to go looking for ways to get messages to another state. One merely summons the ambassador. On more than one occasion ambassadors have been summoned in the middle of the night.

Below the ambassador come a number of other embassy officials—counsellors, secretaries, and attachés. If the embassy is very large, as it often is for a major country, these ranks are further divided into first counsellor, second counsellor, first secretary, second secretary, and so on. When the ambassador is absent from the country, one of these high-ranking officials will be appointed chargé d'affaires, to run the embassy until the ambassador returns. Attachés are embassy personnel with technical specialties, often drawn from outside the ranks of the Foreign Service. There can be agricultural attachés, aviation attachés, cultural attachés, military attachés, and others depending on the kinds of business conducted between the two states involved. California citrus growers want to protect their groves from insects found in Asian citrus groves; an American agricultural attaché in Japan can help with the negotiation of necessary safeguards for importing Japanese produce to the United States.

Another type of diplomatic official, dealing exclusively with administrative matters, is the consul. Although each country has only one embassy in any other country, it may have a number of consulates, located in the cities that do most business with that country. West Coast port cities frequently have consulates from Asian countries. Cities in the northern United States frequently have Canadian consulates. It is to a consulate that you go for visas or for help on shipping and business regulations. If you are abroad, the consulates of your own country can provide help with legal matters—marriage, taxes, and sometimes even trouble with the local police.

The number of embassy personnel can be quite high; United States embassies in Germany and Italy have had from 400 to 500 officials in recent years. (When the Khomeini regime took over in Iran, President Carter ordered 1,100 United States diplomatic personnel home—and there were still 63 left to take as hostages.) Such countries are assigned not just a military attaché but an army attaché, an air force attaché, a naval attaché, and corresponding staffs. The number of officials is sometimes criticized as excessive, but there is often a justification for each one. An example of how they might be useful comes from the 1967 War in the Middle East.

On June 8, Israeli jets spotted an unidentified vessel 15 miles off their coast. According to one version, they then approached both the United States military attaché and the Soviet military attaché, asking each whether the ship was from either of their countries. When told it was not, they assumed it was a hostile ship. An error was made, as it turned out, because the ship belonged to the United States. Some sources now argue that the story was no more than a fiction to cover a deliberate attack.[1] But the story remains an example of how diplomats *could* be useful.

MODERN TECHNOLOGY AND DIPLOMACY

The large size (and the large expense) of embassies and the increasing number of them, as the number of countries in the world increases, have led people to ask whether all this apparatus is necessary. Norway has considered abolishing all embassies. In their place it would create teams of experts who would fly to other countries when a matter arose in which Norway's interests needed representing. All other contacts with states would be maintained through the UN.[2]

The assumption that underlies this proposal is that in the modern world the traditional diplomat is obsolete. The modern world is too complex for one representative to deal with, no matter how well trained. If the American ambassador to Japan wants to negotiate an agreement to prevent the spread of citrus grove pests, he or she must rely on agricultural experts. If the ambassador wants to negotiate monetary matters, he or she must rely on financial experts. Furthermore, with improved transportation and communications, it is easy to fly in the relevant experts, even the secretary of state. The days are long past when travel time to a diplomatic post was measured in weeks and consequently the ambassador was the authoritative voice of the United States abroad.

In the conduct of a state's foreign policy the ambassador is often bypassed. During the long American engagement in Vietnam, there were times when the US ambassador in Saigon appeared to be little more than a briefing officer for visiting officials from Washington. When the president wanted more information, he did not call home the ambassador; he sent out members of his cabinet. In 1986, when the United States was pressuring Ferdinand Marcos of the Philippines to leave office after a dishonest election, Marcos did not trust messages transmitted by the US ambassador. He thought these messages originated with low-level bureaucrats in the State Department. Despite the presence in Manila of the ambassador, defined as "the personal representative of one head of state to another," Marcos chose instead to telephone in the middle of the night a US Senator in Washington known to be a personal friend of President Reagan. Only after receiving a message from this unofficial representative to "cut and cut cleanly" did he decide to leave office.[3]

Professional diplomats are bypassed only at a cost, however. When the trained ambassador is neglected, so too are the virtues we associate with diplomats: first-hand knowledge of a country, discretion in communications, caution in making commitments or public statements. When the conduct of foreign policy is in the hands of untrained politicians, mistakes and embarrassment are more likely.

Presidents at the beginning of their term are likely to complicate American foreign policy. In 1969, President Nixon made a tour of Asia. Speaking about the United States possession of Guam, he proclaimed the Nixon Doctrine, that Asians would be left to take care of their own affairs. "Peace in Asia cannot come from the United States," he said. "It must come from Asia." Yet shortly afterward, in Thailand, he seemed to reverse himself: "The United States will stand proudly with Thailand against those who might threaten it from abroad or from within."[4] Foreign observers were understandably puzzled. Which was the *real* United States policy? It is typical for politicians to promise different things to different audiences—high grain prices to farmers, low bread prices to homemakers. This is understood, even expected, and because few campaign promises are taken seriously, little harm is done. But diplomats pride themselves on precision. Contradictory statements breed confusion and make foreign relations difficult.

President Ford made a similar error at the beginning of his presidency. In response to a question at a news conference following the fall of Saigon, he reaffirmed American commitments to Asian countries, naming South Korea, Indonesia, the Philippines, and Taiwan. Yet ever since President Nixon's visit to China the United States had worked assiduously to convey the impression that the Taiwan issue was different from all the others. President Ford's spontaneous remark, like President Nixon's spontaneous remark in Thailand, required weeks of "clarification" and "amplification."[5]

At the beginning of his term of office, President Carter welcomed Israeli Prime Minister Yitzhak Rabin to the United States and spoke of US support for "defensible borders" for Israel. Through years of usage in Mideast diplomacy, "defensible borders" has become a shorthand expression for the Israeli policy of not returning all the territory it occupied in the 1967 war. Evidently without realizing what he was doing, President Carter was committing the United States to a policy position he did not intend. The next week President Carter referred to the US goal of a "homeland" for Palestinians, using another shorthand expression, this time one meaning Palestinian control of all disputed territory, with no room for a state of Israel. Both statements created confusion and alarm in Arab states and Israel, effects that would have been averted if the president had left diplomacy in the hands of professional diplomats.[6]

The growth of electronic communications has meant greater public attention to foreign policy. Satellite reports on television have made available to millions of Americans the sort of information about foreign countries once available only to officials of the State Department. Greater public involvement in diplomacy restricts the freedom of the diplomat; what were once almost purely foreign policy questions became domestic questions as well. The hostile demonstrations in front of the US embassy in Tehran in 1979 made it impossible for President Carter to pursue quiet accommodation, even if he had been so inclined. The one outstanding success of recent diplomacy, the 1979 peace treaty between Egypt and Israel, was possible in part because of the unusual step of excluding the press from the negotiations at Camp David in September 1978. Politicians in Israel, Egypt, and the United States, unable to learn of offers and concessions as they were made, were unable to voice opposition piecemeal. When the final balanced package was announced, opposition was more difficult.

Increased public attention to foreign affairs creates a temptation for political leaders to sacrifice foreign policy for domestic advantage. Someone in the government opposed to Kissinger's pro-Pakistan policy in the 1971 war between India and Pakistan leaked secret memoranda to the press, making relations with India even worse. Israeli leaders in 1975, desperate to win domestic support for concessions to Egypt in the Sinai, leaked secret US commitments to them. Someone in the State Department who favored the Greeks in the Cyprus dispute leaked a confidential memorandum suggesting how aid might be used to improve US relations with the Turks.[7] The cumulative effect of such leaks is the inhibition of free discussion or even free thought inside the government. No one will suggest for discussion any policy that might later prove to be unpopular. The foreign policy interests of the country become secondary to protecting one's own career.

DUTIES OF DIPLOMATS

Contemporary conditions make life more difficult for the diplomat, yet it is not clear that the traditional services of the diplomat can be provided by anyone else. Let us turn to the list of duties of diplomats as defined by the Vienna Convention of 1961 to see exactly what diplomats should do.[8]

The first duty of a diplomat is to represent his or her state. This means doing such things as attending the celebrations of other states' national holidays or expressing condolences upon the death of other states' high officials. This is a symbolic function and leads to some symbolic behavior. When Germany was divided into two states, the West German state at first refused to recognize East Germany. Yet West German ambassadors at times would find themselves in countries where the East Germans had trade missions or consulates. The West German ambassador always left receptions or parties whenever an East German representative arrived, thereby making a symbolic contribution to the claim that only one Germany existed.

The Soviet Union would often show displeasure at some US policy by boycotting the Fourth of July celebration. Thus US diplomats were relieved that Soviet officials attended a July 4 celebration in 1988 even though an American naval vessel had shot down an Iranian civilian airliner only a day before. Five years earlier the United States had vigorously condemned the Soviet Union for shooting down a South Korean airliner, but the new Soviet regime under Gorbachev chose to forgo the chance for revenge.

A diplomat is also charged with promoting friendly relations between the sending country and the receiving country. The ambassador is the chief interpreter of his or her country's policy abroad. When you think about it, where else can you go to find out another country's side of a story? Why does Ecuador seize American tuna boats? Our news agencies are staffed by Americans, and even if they strive for objectivity they cannot always attain it. In such a case you can write the Ecuadorian embassy. Probably you will receive copious amounts of information supporting the Ecuadorian side of the controversy.

With increased popular participation in government, states have made an effort to promote friendly relations not just with the members of the governing elite but with the broad masses of population. In 1953, the United States Information Agency (for several years called the International Communications Agency) was set up as a separate agency, although working with the State Department, to make information about America available abroad. Among other things, it runs libraries in foreign cities, making available books and periodicals on America, education programs, films, and speakers. Other countries provide similar services.

One of the most important duties of diplomats is ascertaining conditions in the host state. The periodic reports (known as diplomatic cables) sent back from embassies are an important source of information for the government, even though they now compete with both foreign correspondents and intelligence reports. These cables cover all aspects of relations with another country. They may cover purely domestic developments. For example, it is the job of ambassadors in Washington to predict for their home governments who is most likely to win an American election. A candidate for president will be received more warmly on a foreign fact-finding tour if his or her chances of winning are evaluated by the ambassador as very high.

In recent years this function of diplomats has been a source of friction with unstable or revolutionary countries. During the Cultural Revolution in China, the Red Guards showed great sensitivity to foreign diplomats who tried to read the wall newspapers that recorded their debates. After the overthrow of the shah, Iranian militants accused the US embassy of being a "nest of espionage." Yet when diplomats attempt to ascertain political conditions within a host state—including possible strife and discontent—they are only doing their job.

Of course a diplomat is not entitled to all information. States may keep secrets, and diplomats are restricted to legitimate methods for learning them. The tension between a state's attempts to keep secrets and a diplomat's attempts to discover them is most acute in the case of the military attaché. The military attaché is part of the ambassadorial staff and, because of special interest and expertise in military affairs, is most likely to be interested in what the host state is most likely to consider secret—types or numbers of weapons, states of readiness of armed forces, new weapons under development. Some channels of information, such as items in the newspapers, are obviously open even to a military attaché. Other kinds of information are clearly prohibited. Between what is clearly allowed and what is clearly prohibited is a gray area. Photographs of a military airfield may be forbidden. But what about a snapshot of friends at a picnic that just happens to include in the background a plane taking off from an airfield? Occasionally an attaché is caught in this gray area and is expelled. Such expulsion is usually accompanied by the simultaneous expulsion of a military attaché by the sending state (that is, when the Poles expel a Canadian military attaché, the Canadians expel a Polish one), often making it impossible for outsiders to determine who got caught spying and who is only the victim of retaliation.

It is useful for one state to obtain from its diplomats specific bits of information. In addition, diplomats convey a general impression, the climate of relations. It could be argued that if, during most of the 1960s and late 1970s, the president of the United States had picked up his red telephone and ordered an all-out attack on the Soviet Union, nothing would have happened, at least not for a long time. The order most probably would not have been believed. "What is this—some kind of joke?" would have been the first response. Attempts would have been made to verify first the order and then the president's sanity. The climate of relations between the United States and the Soviet Union during the past decades was not compatible with nuclear attack. Even so simple a matter as the number of Americans in the USSR at any time (diplomats, tourists, musicians, business representatives) would have made an attack difficult. By contrast, when the Germans were preparing to attack the Russians in 1941, they gradually recalled as many Germans as they could. Workers on loan to Russian shipyards were sent home on vacation and never returned. Diplomats were recalled and never replaced. When the German attack came in June 1941, only a handful of Germans were left in Moscow.[9] The mere presence of diplomatic personnel is reassuring; their departure, cause for alarm.

When there are no diplomatic relations at all, one state may have very distorted views of another's policies. It is generally agreed that the United States exaggerated the threat of China in the 1960s, in part because we were accepting a Soviet version of what the Chinese were saying. Lacking official representatives of our own in China, we found it difficult to disprove Russian charges such as the one that the Chinese would welcome a nuclear war.

Ascertaining conditions is a duty of a diplomat that ranks in importance with another duty, protecting a state's interest. This protection includes the interest of a state's citizens. Some of the forms this takes are well known: efforts to promote trade, protests against the seizure of property, responsibility for evacuating Americans in the event of hostilities. Protection also extends to simple matters. A man in my town had once been hospitalized in Morocco. When a local hospital wanted his records, they found the Moroccan hospital unresponsive. They then applied to the State Department, which through a consul in Morocco was able to facilitate transferral of the records.

The duty of the diplomat that is probably of least importance today is negotiation. Increasingly, the resident ambassador has been bypassed in major negotiations between two countries. But this does not mean a downgrading of diplomacy as a means of resolving disputes. Officials of the State Department are as much diplomats (in our meaning of the term) as are ambassadors. When the secretary of state negotiates, a diplomat is at work. And even on those occasions when the secretary of state comes from a background devoid of training in diplomacy, his deputies and assistants are from the Foreign Service.

DIPLOMATIC PROCEDURE

Diplomats are quick to point out that there is no substitute for personal contact, even in the day of transoceanic television. Even allowing for their bias on the subject, we may grant that they have a point, as a story from World War II illustrates. By June 1945 it was clear that the Japanese were defeated. Confidential reports from the general staff to the Japanese cabinet indicated that their industry could no longer produce even ammunition. But Japanese leaders were reluctant to surrender because they thought doing so would mean the removal and perhaps even execution of the emperor. Some Americans in the State Department were aware that this was the main obstacle to a Japanese surrender, but they were hampered both by promises to the Russians of unconditional surrender and by domestic propaganda against the Japanese. At the Potsdam Conference at the end of July 1945, the Allies drew up a declaration hinting, without actually coming out and saying it, that the emperor might be retained even after surrender. The Japanese received this declaration by radio because, in accordance with normal practice, diplomatic relations had been broken when the war began. Some members of the Japanese cabinet wished to study the declaration and see whether there was some way they could use it to justify a surrender. Before this study took place, they wished to reserve comment on the declaration. But the word used by the Japanese premier to describe this wish to reserve comment was *mokusatsu*, which is best translated "to treat with silent contempt." One of the premier's advisers later commented:

> To interpret *mokusatsu* as "ignore" was a great mistake. Really, we meant "no comment." During the war, the Japanese people were urged not to use the English language—to forget English. Therefore, I could not recall the English term "no comment." I thought that the Japanese expression which was most close to "no comment" was *mokusatsu.*[10]

The Japanese reply to the declaration was communicated, again by radio, and the Americans interpreted it as a rejection of their offer. The president then ordered the chief of the air force to drop the atomic bomb at the first opportunity.

But imagine this exchange taking place not through radio waves but face to face. The Japanese foreign minister says, "We wish to treat your offer with silent contempt." The face of the American ambassador clouds over, his jaw drops, he begins to turn away in sorrow. The Japanese foreign minister says, "Wait, perhaps you misunderstand. If you comprehend what I am saying you would not have that look on your face. Let me rephrase it. Perhaps 'no comment' is the phrase I want." The American ambassador smiles with relief and rushes to the embassy to cable Washington to hold off any vigorous military moves.

Perhaps the historical case was not so simple. The quotation comes from a man who had a great deal of self-interest in his interpretation of events. There is in fact reason to believe that the Japanese cabinet would ultimately have rejected the Potsdam Declaration in any case. But by seeing a concrete illustration of how personal contact could make a crucial difference, we can see why political leaders continue to affirm the importance of diplomacy. Henry Kissinger, after discussing his contacts over the years with Soviet Ambassador Dobrynin, describes the role of the professional diplomat as "crucial in crises when judgments affecting matters of life and death depend on a subtle and rapid understanding of intangibles."[11]

Diplomats, when performing their official duties, follow codified procedure known as *diplomatic protocol*. Much of the behavior this regulates is ceremonial—spelling out, for example, who greets an official arriving at the airport. Because contemporary American society has become so informal, such details may strike us as comical, but they are still taken seriously by many people. Protocol prescribes that a departing head of government be seen off at the airport by the ambassador of the country he or she is going to visit. When the head of the Indian government left for the United States in 1970, the American ambassador was not present at the airport. His excuse was that the switchboard operator had failed to wake him on time. One member of the Indian Parliament, in a fitting gesture, made him a present of a musical alarm clock.[12]

A more important purpose of protocol is to allow governments great precision in their communication with each other. A government may decide to deliver a formal *Note*, a less formal *Note Verbale*, or an even less formal *Aide-Mémoire*. By its choice of means, a government indicates how serious it considers a matter. In 1968 the United States sent two destroyers into the Black Sea. According to the Montreux Convention of 1936, which regulates traffic into the Black Sea, ships from states not bordering the Black Sea may enter it only if their guns are less than 203 millimeters (8 inches). The destroyers had guns of only 127 millimeters, but one had missile-launchers of 305 millimeters. The Russians issued a protest to Turkey, which, as the country controlling the straits into the Black Sea, was given the responsibility by the Montreux Convention for enforcing the convention's terms. The Russians delivered their protest in a Note, which was addressed to the foreign minister and signed by the ambassador. The Turks replied with the less formal Note Verbale or "oral note," which despite its name is written but addressed more impersonally to the foreign ministry and never signed.

The Turks not only rejected the Russian claim but indicated by this means that they did not wish to treat the question as a serious matter.[13]

Although protocol permits precision, it does not guarantee it. Defenders of traditional diplomacy, such as Harold Nicolson, neglect an important part of diplomacy: lying. Indeed, a famous definition describes a diplomat as an honest man sent abroad to lie for his country.[14] Often, a diplomat tries to be at least ambiguous or equivocal if not downright deceptive. In the years after the Communist accession to power, China frequently used the phrase "not stand idly by" to suggest support for various threatened neighbors such as Korea or Vietnam. But the precise nature of the commitment of China to these neighbors was never made clear, which was in fact China's intention.

In 1950, when China used diplomatic channels to send a warning to the United States not to cross the 38th parallel and carry the Korean War into North Korea, the major problem for the United States was not lack of clarity. The United States knew the meaning of the words conveyed by intermediaries from the Chinese. The major problem was the truth of the words. Did China truly intend to enter the war if US troops crossed the 38th parallel or were they only bluffing? Even the presence of a Chinese diplomatic mission in Washington staffed by the most highly trained diplomats would not have solved the problem.[15]

The language of diplomatic notes is extremely formal, but this formality serves a useful purpose. Here is an example from the height of the Cold War. In April 1950 the Soviet Union shot down a US Navy plane over the Baltic Sea. The United States delivered a written note of protest, part of which read:

> The Ambassador of the United States has been instructed to protest in the most solemn manner against this violation of international law and of the most elementary rules of peaceful conduct between nations. . . . The United States Government confidently expects that, when its investigation is completed, the Soviet Government will express its regret for the unlawful behavior of its aviators, will see to it that those responsible for this action are promptly and severely punished, and will, in accordance with established custom among peace loving nations, pay appropriate indemnity for the unprovoked destruction of American lives and property.[16]

Notice the characteristics of diplomatic language. The ambassador does not take personal responsibility; rather he "has been instructed to protest." Nor does he blame the foreign minister to whom he is protesting; rather it is "those responsible for this action." The Soviet Union is given time to make up its mind how to respond; this is described as time to complete "its investigation." Finally, the United States is telling the Soviet Union what its demands are: expression of regret, disclaimer of responsibility (which is what punishment of "those responsible" means), and indemnity.

THE VALUE OF DIPLOMACY

The 1950 incident, while providing an example of diplomatic formality and correctness even under provocation, is not a case in which diplomacy succeeded. The Soviet Union did not comply with US demands. The Cold War did not abate. Although the number of incidents of this sort did not escalate, that may have been as much the result of American attempts to avoid them as of diplomatic warnings.

A better illustration of the value of diplomacy occurred almost twenty years later. On June 30, 1968, Soviet fighters forced down on Soviet territory in the Kurile Islands a US plane taking soldiers to Vietnam (see Figure 18.1). The next day, July 1, was scheduled for signing the Non-Proliferation Treaty. We have some reason to think that the plane incident was an effort by someone in the Soviet military forces opposed to arms control to provoke an incident with the United States that would lead to cancellation of the ceremony. A few days before, Foreign Minister Andrei Gromyko had referred to such opponents: "To the good-for-nothing

Figure 18.1   The Kurile Islands in 1968

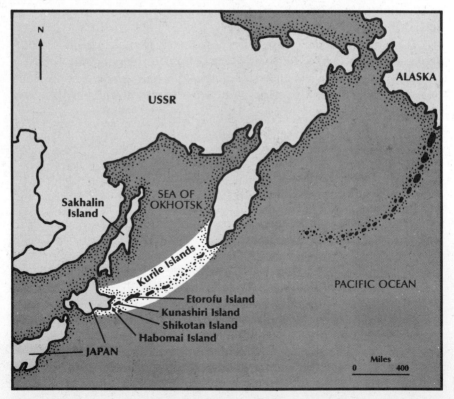

theoreticians who try to tell us . . . that disarmament is an illusion, we reply: by taking such a stand you fall into step with the most dyed-in-the-wool imperialist reaction."[17]

But the US government did not let itself be drawn into a crisis. It immediately got in touch with Soviet officials to clarify the incident. Secretary of State Dean Rusk telephoned Soviet Ambassador Anatoly Dobrynin. United States Ambassador to the Soviet Union Llewellyn Thompson discussed the matter with Soviet Premier Kosygin the next day during the signing ceremonies for the Non-Proliferation Treaty, which went ahead as planned. The United States expressed regret over a violation of Soviet airspace, even though the radar records of the Japanese Air Self-Defense Force indicated that the plane was first approached by other aircraft and only then changed course. The next day, July 2, the plane and passengers were released, to continue on to Vietnam. Neither the Soviet press nor the official *Department of State Bulletin* reported the incident. Diplomacy had turned a possible conflagration into cold and scattered ashes.[18]

Here is a second example of a dispute solved by diplomacy. In November 1969 the foreign ministers of Italy and Austria (meeting in a neutral third country, Denmark) signed a 120-point agreement on South Tyrol, putting to an end a dispute going back fifty years. Though it had a German-speaking majority, South Tyrol (see Figure 18.2) had been transferred to Italy as part of the spoils of World War I. For decades the Italians had tried to assimilate the province, but even in 1969 the German-speaking population still outnumbered the Italian-speaking, 230,000 to 130,000. In the mid-1960s terrorists based in the northern part of Tyrol, on the Austrian side of the border, began attacks on border guards and customs houses to call attention to their demands for greater autonomy if not return to Austria. The Italians warned the Austrians that they would close the border if the attacks were not stopped. Negotiations between diplomats of the two countries finally led to the 1969 agreement. The Italians promised greater autonomy for the region of South Tyrol (although nothing close to the unification with Austria that the extremists wanted). They also promised the Austrians that they would support the Austrian request to associate with the Common Market. These concessions enabled the Austrians to overcome domestic opposition and to crack down on terrorists operating out of Austria.[19]

The first example, the settlement of the Kurile incident of 1968, illustrates how diplomacy can avert conflict. The two countries involved were quick to communicate to each other what the issue was, how seriously they viewed it, and what they intended to do about it. Presumably the United States received assurance that this was an "unauthorized" act and those responsible would be punished. Presumably the Russians made it clear that such acts were not part of Soviet policy and would not stop the signing of

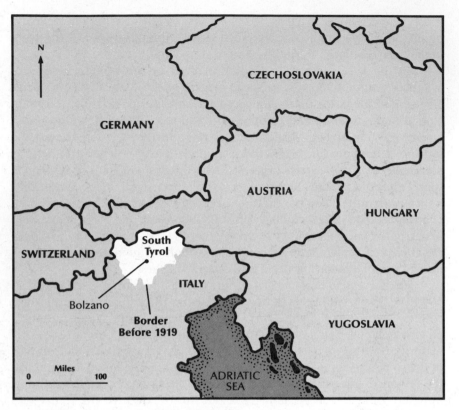

Figure 18.2   The South Tyrol in 1969

arms control agreements. A more violent response, perhaps even escalating to war, was averted. Diplomacy is also helpful to governments that want to avoid a conflict being forced on them by domestic pressure. Austrian government leaders in 1969 ranked many foreign policy objectives higher than the recovery of South Tyrol, but a strong nationalist minority that could awaken widespread sympathy made it difficult for them to avoid the issue. The Italians, aware of the pressures the Austrians were subjected to, were able to offer some small concessions to their German-speaking minority, enabling the Austrian government to claim that it had won some gains and justifying their actions against nationalist extremists. Furthermore, by offering a concession in an unrelated area—support for association with the Common Market, to which Italy belonged and which Austria wanted to join—the Italians enabled the Austrian government to turn attention away from the nationalist issue. Good diplomacy can make it easier for a government to take a course of action that it knows is for the best even if it is unpopular.

THE NEW DIPLOMACY AND ITS PROBLEMS

Diplomats operate, but wars still occur. Negotiations between Greeks and Turks over Cyprus in 1974 could not prevent war from breaking out. This is not because diplomats weren't doing their job but because there are limits to what even the best diplomats can do.

Some writers have blamed conditions of the modern world for the inability of diplomacy to resolve more disputes.[20] They contrast the "new diplomacy" of the twentieth century unfavorably with the "old diplomacy" of the nineteenth century and earlier. In the nineteenth century diplomats spoke the same language, both literally and figuratively. Not only were they all fluent in French; they also came from the same social class, attended the same schools, and lived in the same style, no matter which country they represented. The result was a shared set of values: discretion, face-saving, compromise, above all avoidance of personal rudeness. A diplomat never called another a liar; the proper locution was "Your Excellency appears to be misinformed." This was a far cry from the Russian coal miner calling for attention by pounding his shoe on the table at the UN.

And yet, we may ask, is this objection so serious? Khrushchev, the Russian coal miner, has been replaced by more polished leaders. Henry Kissinger was able to negotiate with the North Vietnamese and the Chinese despite their public attacks on the United States. Anwar Sadat and Menachem Begin were able to overcome decades of invective against each other and agree on a peace treaty within eighteen months. On the other hand, even the stiff formality of the nineteenth century was not successful in avoiding all war. The wars for German unification were as serious as war in the modern world and were not averted because Prussians, Austrians, and French all spoke French. Henry Kissinger has pointed out that resident diplomats, who acquire a "feel for the complexities of other capitals and leaders," may be all the more necessary today precisely because political leaders do not come from similar backgrounds and communicate within the same cultural framework.[21]

Another criticism of the new diplomacy is the loss of confidentiality. A keystone of the new diplomacy, as promoted by President Woodrow Wilson, was "open covenants openly arrived at." President Wilson himself found this impossible to put into practice. He negotiated crucial parts of the Versailles Treaty behind closed doors with the French and British prime ministers while Marine guards patrolled the corridors.[22] But in recent years technological and political changes have brought us closer to Wilson's ideal. Reporters pursue important diplomatic figures, making secret contact with other diplomats difficult. Television crews on motorcycles waited outside Henry Kissinger's residence in Paris to record any meeting with North Vietnamese diplomats. Since the invention of the xerographic copying machine, it is difficult to preserve the secrecy of documents; in only a short time they can be reproduced in massive quantities.

An even more serious obstacle to confidentiality comes from politicians. Members of Congress increasingly demand to learn the details of negotiations. The diplomat must heed these demands. Failure to inform Congress ensures that blame for failure will rest solely with the executive branch. It may also lead to failure to provide the necessary appropriations to make good on promises. But the need to explain and justify in public decisions made during private negotiations places a constraint on the negotiators. Politicians are interested more in domestic opinion than in reaching an agreement with a foreign country. They may see more political advantage in crying, "Sellout!"

The attempts of American diplomats to negotiate an end to the war with the Japanese in 1945 met with protests from Congress. Senator Richard Russell of Georgia, upon reading the Potsdam Declaration in the newspaper, telegraphed a protest to the White House. He wrote that Americans "believe that we should continue to strike the Japanese until they are brought groveling to their knees. We should cease our appeals to Japan to sue for peace. The next plea for peace should come from an utterly destroyed Tokyo."[23] Public pressure of this sort appears to have weighed more heavily on the president than the advice of professional diplomats, such as Joseph Grew, who were urging that we induce the Japanese to surrender not by dropping the atomic bomb but by promising that we would allow them to retain their emperor.

Similarly, the Cyprus dispute was intractable in 1974, even following a clear-cut Turkish military victory, because neither Turkey nor Greece had a government strong enough to make a concession. Each was afraid that the charge of selling out would be enough to topple it. The diplomats could have devised a solution; the politicians would have been afraid to implement it.

Democratic leaders are presumed to be the representatives of their people, and it is seen as undemocratic for representatives not to tell these people what they have been doing on their behalf. Furthermore, promises made in negotiation often require extensive domestic support for their fulfillment. Henry Kissinger's negotiations with Middle Eastern countries involved extensive promises of aid, but this money could not come out of his own pocket. Knowledge by foreign countries that Congress might not make good on such promises undermines the secretary of state's effectiveness. Yet when the Congress comes to consider the issue, it brings its own priorities. Proposals to deal with the Cyprus problem were viewed differently by the secretary of state and the Congress because many members of Congress had vocal constituents of Greek origin but few constituents of Turkish origin. The argument by the secretary of state that one-sided measures (such as cutting off aid to Turkey) by themselves would not resolve the dispute was less persuasive to representatives seeking reelection than the votes of Greek Americans.

Increased popular participation in politics is a characteristic not only of the United States but of the entire world. This has meant that some solutions to disputes available to diplomats in the nineteenth century are no longer available in the twentieth century. One traditional solution was neutralizing an area. After Belgium declared its independence from France in 1830, there was concern among European countries about how the new country would affect the balance of power. This concern was alleviated by declaring it neutral—permanently out of the balance of power. Another traditional solution was partition. European countries avoided war in Africa by simply dividing up the continent, ignoring in the process any political units or ethnic boundaries already established. Where partition was not applied, spheres of influence often were. By the Monroe Doctrine, the United States reserved for itself special rights in the western hemisphere. Russia, Britain, and other European countries did the same in parts of China.

Increased participation in politics makes such solutions difficult to the point of impossibility. The people living in these countries do not want to submit to partition, foreign influences, or even neutralization. The wars in Korea in 1950 and in Vietnam from 1946 to 1975 were fundamentally wars in opposition to partition. Cuba's foreign policy under Castro is a repudiation of the Monroe Doctrine. Even pledges of neutralization are seen as conflicting with the sovereign rights of a nation. Austria, bound to neutrality by the peace treaty of 1955, has declared its right to join the Common Market, even though the Soviet Union has claimed this move would violate Austrian neutrality.

The role of diplomats is changing in other ways. Domestic constituents are increasingly important in foreign policy. The president embargoes grain sales to Russia because of the invasion of Afghanistan and farmers protest. The United States tries to maintain normal relations with South Africa and protesters harass South African diplomats. More ambassadors accredited to the US government in Washington show up on Capitol Hill, the Japanese to lobby against bills aimed at forcing them to open their markets to American goods, the Turks to make the case for more aid.[24] Under these new conditions, diplomats are beginning to see part of their job as mollifying subnational groups or even mediating among them. Diplomats are losing their unique status as agents of a unified and coherent state and are becoming instead political operators.[25]

But we should not spend too much time lamenting the passing of the old aristocratic world. In 1661 France came close to declaring war on Spain because the Spanish ambassador's coach had cut in front of the French ambassador's coach in London.[26] Although diplomatic slights are not likely to result in war today, a whiff of aristocratic decadence still attaches to the diplomatic profession. In 1965 President Lyndon Johnson received news of conflict in the Dominican Republic. He chose to ignore the Organization of American States, even though it had its headquarters in Washington. Part of the reason was that the OAS had a reputation for "endless deliberation and a fascination with legalistic quibbling." Another part was that the telegram alerting Johnson to the crisis arrived in the late afternoon. One White House aide said later, "It was getting close to cocktail time, which is not the best moment for rounding up OAS ambassadors."[27]

Even if all diplomats were chosen for their competence, they could not do the impossible. Diplomacy cannot bring about negotiated settlements when neither side has any desire to concede. Some wars are not the result of a failure in communication. In some cases the sides may understand all too well what is at stake.

In 1967 the United States urged restraint on Israel, to give diplomacy time to work. We had little reason to think it would. Nasser believed he had the upper hand militarily and had no reason to compromise. Even when the Israelis had demonstrated their military superiority in their attack on June 5, he could not accept it, believing instead that the attack had been made with British and American help. If an actual demonstration of military power is not effective, it is hard to see how the words of diplomats would be.

Sometimes people advocate diplomacy on the grounds that "if we're talking, we're not fighting."[28] This is a strange argument. No factory manager would say, "We should bargain with the union, because if they're talking, they're not striking." Strikes go on during negotiations and so do wars. The Vietnam negotiations were finally brought to a conclusion after the bombing of North Vietnamese cities. Critics have argued that this bombing was unnecessary, but they can hardly argue that it was incompatible with diplomacy. The agreement was signed shortly thereafter. Fighting can enhance bargaining power, so we might expect, on some occasions at least, diplomacy to be accompanied by an increase in conflict. This is more likely to be true of negotiations to end fighting in progress than of those to head fighting off, and it may not be true even then. But clearly negotiations do not make war disappear.

LIMITATIONS OF DIPLOMACY

Advocates of diplomacy as an approach to peace assume an underlying harmony of interests among states. Even when states differ in philosophy and national characteristics, they can still find overlapping interests. Iran, whatever the character of the regime in power, has oil; the United States, whatever policies it may be following, has grain. Both countries would benefit from trade with each other, even though domestic politicians in each may temporarily obscure that basic interest in appeals to passion. Professional diplomats try to emphasize common interests and reduce the importance of passion in the relations among states. To the extent that political leaders heed them, diplomats make relations among states more rational.[29]

If states' interests are fundamentally in harmony, then reasoned discussion will serve to make this harmony apparent. The more states communicate with each other, the more rational their policies toward each other will become. Over the centuries diplomacy has developed into a highly formal system of communication. But the importance of the traditional practitioners of this art, the professional diplomats, in preventing war has been diminished by the modern technology of transportation and communication and by increased popular participation in policymaking. The cool reason of the diplomatic elite is being replaced by the more emotional demands of the less-well-informed masses.

Without question the world of diplomats on many occasions has helped prevent small incidents from becoming the occasion for war. On the other hand, there have been enough cases to demonstrate that diplomacy alone is not enough to prevent war. Perhaps the assumption of a basic harmony of interests is mistaken; perhaps political leaders are not yet rational enough to recognize such basic harmony. Whatever the reason, historical experience should not make us optimistic about the ability of diplomats alone to prevent all wars.

But unlike some proposals for achieving peace, one could not argue that diplomacy in some ways makes the world more dangerous. World government or balance of power systems may increase violence in the world; arms races increase violence if they fail to deter war. Increased reliance on diplomacy may not bring peace, but it is unlikely to increase the risk of war.

In one particular way, diplomatic contact needs to be increased. Because of the symbolic function of a diplomat, it has been customary to break diplomatic relations in time of war. The ambassadors go home and embassies are turned over to the custody of third states. This also happens in crises short of war. The United States broke relations with Cuba in 1961 over the expropriation of American investments. Such behavior reduces communication at the time it is needed most. It demonstrates that two states are not always the best judges of their own interests or able to conduct business with each other in rational fashion. Sometimes neutral outsiders, third parties, can provide valuable assistance. This assistance can take various forms: mediation, arbitration, adjudication. A number of means and institutions are designed for these purposes, and we will look at them next.

NOTES

1. Joseph Goulden, *Truth Is the First Casualty* (Chicago: Rand McNally, 1969), p. 103; see also James Bamford, *The Puzzle Palace* (New York: Penguin, 1983), pp. 279–293.
2. C. L. Sulzberger, "Sent to Lie Abroad No More," *The New York Times*, January 28, 1972.

3. Bernard Gwertzman, "For Marcos, a Restless Night of Calls to U.S.," *The New York Times*, February 26, 1986, p. Y8.

4. *Newsweek*, August 4, 1969, p. 38; *Newsweek*, August 11, 1969, p. 17.

5. News conference on May 6, 1975; transcript reprinted in *The New York Times*, May 7, 1975.

6. Nadav Safran, *Israel: The Embattled Ally* (Cambridge, Mass.: Harvard University Press, 1978), pp. 567–568.

7. Leslie H. Gelb, "Senate Unit Charges U.S. with Using Relief to Help Turkey," *The New York Times*, October 14, 1974, p. 3.

8. United Nations, *Conference on Diplomatic Intercourse and Immunities*, Vienna, March 2–April 14, 1961, 2 vols. (Geneva, 1962).

9. Barton Whaley, *Codeword BARBAROSSA* (Cambridge, Mass.: MIT Press, 1973), pp. 110–111.

10. Len Giovannitti and Fred Freed, *The Decision to Drop the Bomb* (New York: Coward-McCann, 1965), p. 231.

11. Henry Kissinger, *White House Years* (Boston: Little, Brown, 1979), p. 139.

12. *The New York Times*, October 23, 1970; *The New York Times*, October 25, 1970.

13. *The New York Times*, December 7, 1968; Charles W. Thayer, *Diplomat* (New York: Harper & Brothers, 1959), p. 99.

14. Henry Wotton, 1651, "An ambassador is an honest man sent to lie abroad for the commonwealth."

15. This point is developed in detail in Robert Jervis, *The Logic of Images in International Relations* (Princeton: Princeton University Press, 1970), pp. 24–25.

16. *Department of State Bulletin*, Vol. 22, No. 565 (May 1, 1950), pp. 667–68.

17. John Newhouse, *Cold Dawn: The Story of SALT* (New York: Holt, Rinehart and Winston, 1973), p. 104 (quoting *Pravda*).

18. *The New York Times*, July 1–3, 1968.

19. *The New York Times*, December 1, 1969.

20. Hans J. Morgenthau, in "The Decline of Diplomacy," *Politics Among Nations*, 4th ed. (New York: Alfred A. Knopf, 1967), pp. 525–531; Harold Nicolson, *Diplomacy*, 3rd ed. (London: Oxford University Press, 1963).

21. Kissinger, p. 139. (See note 11.)

22. Nicolson, p. 43. (See note 20.)

23. Paul Kecskemeti, *Strategic Surrender* (New York: Atheneum, 1964), p. 165.

24. Stephen V. Robert, "Foreign Policy: Lot of Table Thumping Going On," *The New York Times*, May 29, 1985, p. Y10.

25. Gilbert R. Winham, "Practitioners' Views of International Negotiation," *World Politics*, Vol. 32, No. 1 (October 1979), pp. 111–135.

26. Nicolson, p. 99. (See note 20.)

27. Philip Geyelin, *Lyndon B. Johnson and the World* (New York: Praeger, 1966), p. 251.

28. Vice-Admiral J. Victor Smith to *Pueblo* court of inquiry, *Christian Science Monitor*, March 13, 1969, p. 3.

29. Hedley Bull, *The Anarchical Society* (New York: Columbia University Press, 1977), pp. 170–183.

CHAPTER 19

THIRD PARTIES

Diplomacy cannot always prevent war. If there are no diplomatic relations between states, then diplomats have no opportunity to exercise their skills. Sometimes domestic forces keep states from maintaining diplomatic contact. The United States initially broke off relations with the new Communist Chinese regime in 1949 for the legitimate reason that the Communists were refusing to respect the diplomatic immunity of American diplomats. But long after the dispute had occurred the United States was inhibited from renewing diplomatic ties by powerful domestic pressures from the "China Lobby." As President Eisenhower and Vice-President Nixon left office in 1960, they both warned incoming President Kennedy that although they would support the new administration on most foreign policy issues, they would publicly oppose any conciliatory moves toward China.[1] Similarly, in the Middle East the governments of Arab states have encountered strong opposition in establishing diplomatic relations with Israel.

At other times, diplomatic contact may be present but the communication between two states may be seriously distorted by the stress of crisis. Communication among states during the weeks of crisis preceding World War I has been intensively studied by scholars from Stanford University. They conclude that during periods of high tension between states the communication channels are overloaded, with the result that messages become shorter, with less detail and less discussion of alternatives. Decision-makers tend to "suture off" part of the communications apparatus, relying on fewer and fewer sources of information. Along with this they show a tendency to make decisions on the basis of feelings and emotions rather than rational calculations.[2] This distortion of communication is the result of crisis. But even when there is no crisis, religious and national feelings distort communication. It is difficult for a Turk to react dispassionately to a report that Greek Cypriots are murdering Turkish Cypriots, or for Arabs to examine critically a report that Israelis are desecrating Moslem holy places.

Communication often breaks down so thoroughly that it is impossible even to agree on the facts of a case. Border disputes typically involve different interpretations of matters that should be factual. Another case that is often a dispute over facts is the accusation by one country that another country is arming against it. In 1967 Egypt accused Israel of mobilizing forces on its northern border for an attack on Syria. Lacking diplomatic representatives in Israel, it was difficult for the Egyptians to verify this act or for the Israelis to prove to them that these fears were unfounded.

Even when communication among states is not greatly distorted, diplomacy may reach an impasse because each has its prestige committed to a publicly stated position. Compromise is then difficult because the original contest is replaced by one over prestige. All disputes have two aspects: the dispute itself and the bigger question of what the solution to the dispute is going to reveal about the relative power of the disputants. When the child asks the baby sitter for permission to watch half an hour more of television, the question is primarily a test of power. Baby sitters, like states, hesitate to give in because they know that one request will be followed by many more. But if both sides are determined not to appear to be appeasers, even reasonable compromises are ruled out.

THE VALUE OF THIRD PARTIES

Third parties can help alleviate these difficulties. For one thing, they can facilitate communication. One common form of this is what we call providing *good offices*. Good offices are the services of a neutral agent, trusted by both sides, who transmits messages. Children have to provide good offices when parents aren't talking to each other and mother says, "You tell your father that his dinner is ready." Back in 1968, before airplane hijackings had become commonplace, a Palestinian group, the Popular Front for the Liberation of Palestine (PFLP), hijacked an Israeli airliner as it flew over Italy and diverted it to Algeria. The Algerians, embarrassed by this unexpected landing, held on to the plane, crew, and passengers, not knowing what to do with them. Israel, having no diplomatic relations with Algeria, went to United Nations Secretary General U Thant and asked him to use his good offices to arrange for return of plane, crew, and passengers. The Algerians hesitated, and two weeks later the International Association of Air Line Pilots threatened a boycott of Algeria unless the crew was released. Now it was Algeria that turned to the Secretary General for his good offices.

Neutral third parties can also facilitate settlement through a method known as *inquiry*, or establishing the facts of a case. Many quarrels are ostensibly over issues of fact—such as the exact location of a border—but when tension is high, it is difficult for rivals to agree on facts. In 1974 a clash on the border between Iran and Iraq resulted in the deaths of sixty-five soldiers. The United Nations Secretary General appointed a Mexican diplomat to help the two countries find a solution. One of his first discoveries was that the two countries were using entirely different maps of the border.[3] In 1975 Iran and Iraq signed a treaty specifying with precision just where their common border ran. (Charges of Iranian failure to abide by this treaty were part of Iraq's justification for going to war in 1980—an illustration of the limits of the third-party methods.)

Another contribution to peaceful settlement that can be provided by third parties is to delay any action until tempers have cooled down a bit. This contribution was described by a former American ambassador to the UN in this way:

> I see some things that you cannot solve, now. Maybe in 10 years you can, but you can't do it now, and the best thing you can do is to sort of spin it out and drag it along and temporize and pettifog, and that way they don't shoot each other, and that is that much clear gain.[4]

If you suspect that diplomats are trying to bore countries to the point at which they accept a solution, you might be right. There are cases in which inaction and delay seem to have contributed to a solution. After World War II both Italy and Yugoslavia claimed Trieste and the area around it (see Figure 19.1). As part of the possessions of Mussolini's Italy it was occupied by the victors of World War II. Because Italian and Yugoslav populations were interspersed, no solution was acceptable to both sides. Diplomatic protests were accompanied by violent demonstrations, reaching their climax in September 1947, when only a US roadblock stopped invading Yugoslav troops. The issue was put before the United Nations, but no country moved to impose a solution. Periodic resorts to violence continued, with riots in 1948, 1952, and 1953, but by 1955 tempers had calmed down enough for the countries involved to sign an agreement providing for a compromise settlement. Final agreement was not reached until 1975.

The Trieste case illustrates another contribution of third parties: providing a neutral place for disputants to meet. The discussions leading to the 1955 agreement on Trieste were held in London. Not only did this avoid suggestions of inequality between the two sides (for the Yugoslavs to negotiate in Italy would indicate Yugoslav subservience to Italy, and vice versa) but it also helped shield the diplomats from inquiring reporters and noisy

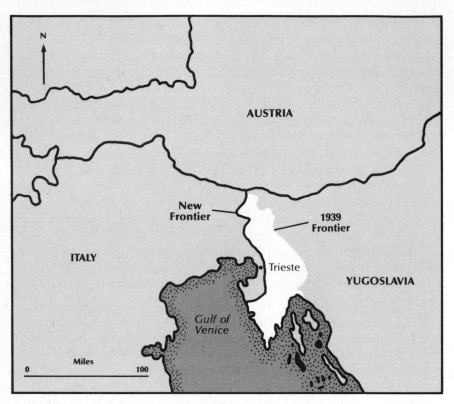

Figure 19.1   Trieste in 1955

demonstrators from one side or the other. The US ambassador to Austria, Llewellyn E. Thompson, was sent to London to facilitate the Trieste talks. To keep his purpose secret, he pretended that he was going to London to buy clothes. He was ordered to London the day his youngest child was born; when the agreement was finally signed, his fictitious wardrobe had assumed incredible proportions and his daughter was eight months old. But, in the early phases, neither the Italian nor Yugoslav press had an inkling that the volatile Trieste issue was under discussion, a fact to which Thompson later attributed much of the success of the conference.[5]

MEDIATION: CYPRUS, INDOCHINA, THE MIDDLE EAST

Of course a third party may go considerably further in helping to settle a dispute. Two recognized methods are mediation and conciliation. In *mediation*, the third party not only carries messages but also adds to them suggestions for settlement. In *conciliation*, a person or commission studies the problem and issues a report. Both methods are nonbinding; their success depends on the basic desire of each side to reach a settlement.

The record of these methods is mixed, as the recent history of the Middle East shows. The United Nations appointed Count Bernadotte as official mediator between Israel and the Arabs in spring of 1948, but he failed to head off war. During the fighting, his proposals were considered so favorable to the Arabs that he was assassinated by Zionist extremists. His successor, Ralph Bunche, fared much better and won the Nobel Peace Prize for arranging the armistices that ended the war. Following the 1967 war, the UN mediator Gunnar Jarring failed to move the sides toward settlement. After the 1973 war, Henry Kissinger, acting for the United States, arranged a cease-fire in 1973 and disengagements in 1974 and 1975.

An episode from the 1974 "shuttle diplomacy" of Kissinger illustrates the way in which mediators can facilitate settlement. The Israelis had made a proposal that Kissinger thought the Syrians would find so unacceptable that they would break off negotiations. They proposed that they withdraw their troops to allow the UN to set up a buffer zone, but only from territory they had recently captured from Syria. In the next stage of his shuttle, Kissinger did not give the Syrians the details of the Israeli plan; he concentrated instead on the concept of a buffer zone. After winning adherence to this concept from both sides, he was then able to get agreement on the location of the zone as part of "working out the details."[6]

Mediation makes it possible for a state with prestige committed to a publicly stated position to back down. The value of a third party was demonstrated in the Cyprus dispute of 1967. Cyprus has been a perennial problem because of its strategic location and its ethnic diversity. Slightly more than 80 percent of the population are Greeks, and most of them would prefer union with Greece; slightly less than 20 percent are Turks and would prefer partition of the island. In 1967 the central government of Cyprus, which was dominated by the Greek Cypriots, attempted to extend governmental control into Turkish villages. The Turks resisted, firing on Greek Cypriot police patrols. The violence quickly escalated. Thousands of troops from the Greek mainland, far in excess of the 950 troops permitted by treaty, were sent to reinforce the Greek Cypriot National Guard. Demonstrations in Turkish cities by students and young men called for war with Greece; the Turkish government mobilized an invasion force and invasion fleet.

Several organizations sent mediators to the area—the UN, NATO, and the US government. The most effective of them was the one sent by President Johnson, Cyrus Vance. He made half a dozen trips between the Greek and Turkish capitals, as well as several trips to the Cypriot capital, and got an agreement. Although it was never announced publicly, the Turks demobilized their invasion force, the Greeks recalled their troops, the National Guard was downgraded, and the UN peace-keeping force already on Cyprus was expanded. Neither side really wanted war. The Greeks, in the assessment of experts, would have lost any war with Turkey. The Turks wished to avoid a conflict with the United States, which might mean loss of US aid and support. But both governments were under domestic pressure not to give in. It helped them to be able to say that they were acceding to American wishes. Furthermore, because the suggestions for concessions came from Cyrus Vance, neither side could interpret the other's move as a sign of weakness. Vance provided each of them a ladder to climb down, while keeping the other side from kicking the ladder over.[7]

Unfortunately not all mediation attempts end with success. Even Cyrus Vance's efforts on Cyprus in 1967 did not achieve a permanent solution. The invasion averted in 1967 took place in 1974, over the same issue. Unlike the case of Trieste, delay did not make the solution easier.

Two other conflicts have also seen mediation efforts fail to cool off violence. Vietnam was the major conflict of the 1960s; the Middle East was the major conflict of the 1970s. In each case mediation played a part in a settlement, but in each case the settlement failed. The war in Vietnam between the forces of Ho Chi Minh, at that time called the Viet Minh, and the French was brought to an end by the Geneva Conference of 1954. At that conference the British, the Russians, and the Chinese all mediated between the French and the Viet Minh.[8] As a result of the conference, the French withdrew from all of Indochina, but the Viet Minh got control of only the northern half of the country. Article Seven of the Final Declaration of the Geneva Conference called for elections in all of Vietnam within two years, provided "all necessary conditions obtain." But the declaration is totally ambiguous on this point. It doesn't say what kind of elections. A vote on whether to reunify? A vote for a government for the entire country? And the meaning of the qualification "all necessary conditions" is never spelled out. One commentator described his meeting a member of the delegation to the 1954 Geneva Conference six years later and commenting on the vagueness of Article Seven, whereupon the Frenchman seized his hand and said, "Thank you for the compliment, for such was our intention; we stayed up all night phrasing and rephrasing Article Seven."[9] The diplomats provided a formula that could be interpreted in different ways by different parties, enabling each side to describe the conference as a victory. The diplomats of course knew what they were doing; they were not solving the problem, they were buying time, hoping that the problem would solve itself. In Vietnam it did not.

In the Middle East the war in 1967 came to an end after only six days, but it was not until five months later that the Security Council endorsed Resolution 242, which was intended to provide a basis for negotiations to end the conflict. The months of delay were devoted to an attempt by third parties to word a resolution in a way that both sides could accept. The mediation was successful to the extent that wording was agreed on. Both Israel and several Arab states (Egypt and Jordan) accepted Resolution 242, but only because it could be read in different ways. Different readings were possible in part because of slight variations in the text from one language to another. The English version stated that Israel would withdraw from "territories of recent conflict"—implying from some territory but perhaps not all. The equally official French version said Israel would withdraw from "the territories of recent conflict," implying from every inch. Nor was this the only problem. The Arab states stressed the portion of the resolution calling for Israeli withdrawal. Israel gave priority to the call for respect for the right of every state in the area "to live in peace within secure and recognized boundaries." As in the case of Indochina in 1954, the time gained by this measure did not lead to peace. By 1970 Egypt and Israel were engaged in the "War of Attrition," and by 1973 they were fighting a full-scale war.

ARBITRATION: THE RANN OF CUTCH, THE ALABAMA CLAIMS

It is debatable whether clarity or vagueness is more conducive to settling disputes. Those who prefer clarity advocate arbitration and adjudication. *Arbitration* is settlement by a third party, where each side agrees in advance to accept the decision of the third party. Unlike mediation, where the third party merely makes suggestions, arbitration gives the final say to the arbitrator. Arbitration has been used to settle hundreds of international disputes in the nineteenth century, thousands in the twentieth century. Almost all have been minor or peripheral, but occasionally a major one has been settled in this way. One case is a dispute between India and Pakistan. There were armed clashes between India and Pakistan in the spring of 1965 in the Rann of Cutch. A rann is a salt marsh; this one is 35,000 square miles. The boundary had been undefined since the former British possession was partitioned into the two states, India and Pakistan, in 1947. Following these clashes Britain mediated the dispute and got India and Pakistan to agree to arbitration. An arbitration panel of three members was set up, one member nominated by India, one by Pakistan, and one by the secretary general of the UN. The panel made its award in February 1968: 350 square miles to Pakistan, the rest to India, with the 275-mile border to be demarcated by stone pillars. The decision appears to be unfair to Pakistan, but in fact the 350 square miles they received was the highest ground in the Rann, suitable for grazing. The territory awarded to India, though not useful for grazing, was of course much larger, and the Indian government could also suggest that gas and oil might be found beneath it. The award was implemented by June 1969.[10] India and Pakistan did subsequently go to war but not over the Rann of Cutch. The question of the border in this area appears to have been solved.

International arbitration became popular in the nineteenth century after the first major success of the procedure in resolving a dispute between two countries in 1872. The case, known as the *Alabama* claims, grew out of the American Civil War. The United States claimed that warships purchased illegally in the then neutral country of Britain by Confederate agents had damaged US interests. One of them, the cruiser *Alabama*, had sunk sixty-five Union ships. By the Washington Treaty of 1871 both countries agreed to arbitration. The next year the arbitration panel found Britain liable for the damage and awarded $15.5 million to the United States. The British accepted this decision and possible hostilities between the two countries were averted.

The success of the *Alabama* claims case led to a number of proposals for applying arbitration to all cases of international conflict. The Hague Conference of 1899 set up the "Permanent Court of International Arbitration," although it was not a court at all but rather a list of names from which states could choose arbitrators. It was not extensively used, however. Undaunted, President William H. Taft in 1909 proposed setting up an international tribunal to settle international disputes, in the beginning among the United States, Great Britain, and France, and later among all states. President Taft indicated in speeches to the public that he thought this would be the first step toward a world court that would eventually solve the problem of war, eliminate the burden of armament, and bring international harmony.[11]

ADJUDICATION: THE "LOBSTER WAR," THE CORFU CHANNEL

Settling disputes in already existing courts is called *adjudication* and differs somewhat from arbitration. In arbitrating disputes, the arbitrators have some freedom in making their award. They can compromise, make concessions to both sides, and in general make their award as much on the basis of its acceptability as on the basis of fairness. Adjudication, on the other hand, is thought of as depending on the legal rights and wrongs of the case, which President Taft called "a clean judgment of the facts and the law on its merits."[12] Under adjudication the likelihood is greater that one party will come out a clear winner and the other a clear loser, because the judges are deciding on the legal merits of the case, not the acceptability of their judgment.

Progress toward a world court was interrupted by World War I, but in 1920 a Permanent Court of International Justice was set up under the League of Nations. In 1946 its official name was changed to the International Court of Justice; it is commonly called the World Court. With the demise of the League of Nations, its affiliation was transferred to the United Nations. Any member of the United Nations is automatically a party to it. It consists of fifteen judges, sitting in The Hague. It provides what President Taft advocated, a way for states to settle disputes peacefully.

Consider this war that did *not* take place between France and Brazil in 1963. The two states were quarreling over lobsters. The Geneva Convention of 1958 on the Continental Shelf gives states the rights on anything of value on or under their continental shelves (such as oysters or oil) out to the limits of exploitability or to where the water is about 200 meters (650 feet) deep. In 1962 France began sending lobster boats to South American waters, over the continental shelf of Brazil. The Brazilians ordered the French to move out to deeper waters, leaving the continental shelf to smaller Brazilian vessels. The French rejected this demand and sent a destroyer to accompany the lobster boats. Brazil then put its navy on the alert. By this time (April 1963), both states were asking themselves if they really wanted to go to war over lobsters. Deciding that they didn't, they agreed to send the dispute to adjudication. France claimed that lobsters are like fish—they swim about; therefore they are not part of the continental shelf. Brazil claimed that lobsters are like oysters—they cling to the bottom; therefore they are part of the continental shelf. The court had an essentially zoological question on its hands—are lobsters swimmers or crawlers?

It sounds like the story of the "Lobster War" would be a perfect illustration of the value of international adjudication. Sad to say for the advocates of the World Court, is it not. The dispute was settled without violence, but not by adjudication. Agreement was worked out in private by diplomats from the two countries and ratified by an exchange of letters between presidents in December 1964. Both the negotiations and the content of the letters were kept secret, so it is difficult to say more about them. The agreement by the two countries to send the dispute for adjudication seems to have been a diplomatic ploy. At first Brazil wanted the dispute adjudication but France did not. Then there was a legal dispute about which procedure was appropriate under a treaty between the two countries signed in 1909. Finally France submitted the dispute not to the World Court but to the International Bureau of the Permanent Court of Arbitration in The Hague. Before that body could act, the dispute was settled by diplomacy.[13]

The "Lobster War" is thus a case where the World Court could have been used but was not. In this way it is typical of international disputes, which rarely wind up before the World Court. From 1945 to 1975, according to a detailed study by one scholar, there were 310 significant conflicts between states.[14] In approximately the same period only twenty-six disputes were brought before the World Court (along with an additional fourteen requests for advisory opinions). Of the twenty-six, seven went unsettled and eight were settled independent of the Court; in only eleven cases was the Court partially or entirely responsible for the settlement.[15]

The major reason for the poor record of the World Court is clear from an examination of one of the first cases to come before it, the Corfu Channel case (see Figure 19.2). This resulted from an incident in October 1946, when British destroyers were heavily damaged by mines in the waters of the channel between the island of Corfu (owned by Greece) and Albania. The British claimed that at the very least the Albanians knew that the mines were there, even if they hadn't put them there, and had failed to give warning. The case was brought before the Court in May 1947; judgment was rendered in April 1949. (Like all other courts, the World Court moves slowly.) The Court found that Albania was guilty of failing to notify the world in general and the approaching British naval units in particular of the minefield in an international channel. The Court then awarded damages to Great Britain for the damage to the ships and the loss of life of forty-four sailors. All this was strictly in accordance with prescribed procedures. Expert testimony backed up the decision of the Court. The law on the matter was very clear. But Albania disregarded the decision. No compensation was ever paid.[16]

Figure 19.2   Corfu Channel

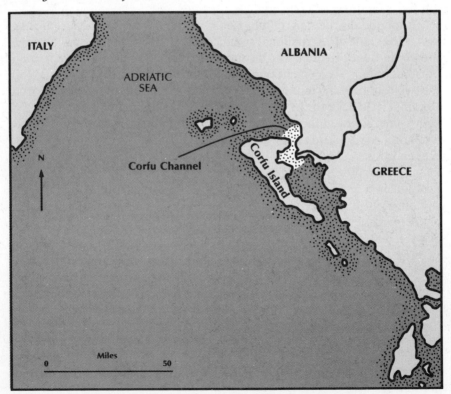

The Court had no means of enforcing its judgment. In domestic political systems, a court calls on members of the executive branch—sheriffs or marshals—to see that its decisions are carried out. The World Court is part of a much less well developed political system. The Court has no agents of its own to enforce its judgments. At best, the losing party can invoke article 94 of the United Nations Charter, which states: "If any party to a case fails to perform the obligations incumbent upon it under a judgment rendered by the Court, the other Party may have recourse to the Security Council, which may, if it deems necessary make recommendations or decide upon measures to be taken to give effect to the judgment." Repeated use of the word "may" indicates that even in theory the Council offers no ironclad guarantee of implementing a Court's decision. In practice, the Security Council has had a case referred to it only once. (We will look at the weaknesses of the Security Council in the next chapter.)

The lack of a dependable enforcement mechanism is one weakness of the Court. Another weakness was also revealed by the Corfu Channel case. The Court consists of fifteen members, each from a different country. In this case, because there was a British judge but no Albanian, Albania was allowed to pick an additional judge for the case. (It picked a judge from Czechoslovakia, a country that presumably would be sympathetic.) The final vote of the court was eleven to five against Albania. Those voting in the minority were the Soviet Union, Poland, Czechoslovakia, Egypt, and Brazil. Three of these dissenters were Communist, as was Albania, and a fourth, Egypt had an interest in upholding the principle of control of international channels by neighboring states because of a similar situation in the Middle East, where Egypt bordered on the Strait of Tiran. On the other hand, the judges who voted for Britain came from "free world" states. In other words, there did not seem to be much difference between the way a judge on the Court voted and the way the foreign minister of the same country would vote in a strictly political conference, where there was no pretense of judicial impartiality. From this it is a short step to predicting how a case will be decided by examining the foreign policies of the states represented on the Court. That is, in fact, a good guide to how the World Court has decided. But knowing in advance how the Court will decide, the side that will lose has no incentive to submit its case. We often guess what the decision of the United States Supreme Court will be, but these guesses sometimes turn out to be wrong: The Nixon Administration was surprised by decisions of a supposedly "conservative" Supreme Court on more than one occasion. But it is this unpredictability that makes the Supreme Court effective. It reinforces the belief that the Supreme Court does decide issues on their merits and not the political preferences of the judges. The World Court enjoys no such confidence.

As a contrast to the Corfu Channel case we might look at one of the eight cases successfully resolved by the World Court, the Arbitral Awards case, which settled a border dispute between Nicaragua and Honduras. These two countries engaged in limited hostilities in 1957 before agreeing to a suggestion by the Organization of American States (OAS) to submit their dispute to the World Court in 1958. Both accepted the decision of the Court when it was issued in 1960. But these two states are exceptional. They are among only eight states in the world that accept the jurisdiction of the Court without reservation. The dispute involved neither ideological differences nor vital interests. Both states were under pressure from their neighbors in the OAS to accept the decision. In no way did the dispute begin to match the complexity and intractability of the issues that trouble the Middle East or those that have led to conflict between the East and West.

The inability of the World Court to settle disputes with ideological components is evident from the record of states that have used the Court. In the three decades following its creation in 1945, thirty-four states appeared before it; of them, half (seventeen) were either Western European or English-speaking democracies. Only eight states appeared more than once, and almost all of them (seven) also were Western European or English-speaking democracies. By contrast, no Communist state had ever initiated a case. In fact, Czechoslovakia, Hungary, and the Soviet Union all refused to submit to the Court's jurisdiction, and cases in which they were involved were discontinued without settlement.[17]

AN EVALUATION: EL CHAMIZAL, SPANISH SAHARA

One political scientist, K. J. Holsti, has made a systematic attempt to compare various forms of settlement.[18] He first identified seventy-seven conflicts over a forty-year period (1919–1939 and 1945–1965, excluding the years of World War I and World War II). He defined "conflict" as limited to serious disputes between states where force or threat of force was used. After finding seven disputes of this type, he identified 131 attempts to settle them (obviously, more than one attempt was made to solve some of the conflicts). Table 19.1 shows what Holsti found about these various forms of settlement. Notice that none of these methods was successful as much as half of the time; the best rate of success achieved was only 47 percent. Of course even that rate of success justifies the efforts of diplomats and third parties. We probably would be willing to undergo an operation for terminal cancer even if the success rate was only 47 percent. But the findings suggest that as practiced today diplomacy and third-party settlement do not guarantee an end to war.

A more recent study by Ernst Haas shows that things have not changed much in recent years. Haas looked at the role played by international organizations (United Nations, Arab League, Organization for African Unity, Organization of American States) in settling disputes. An international organization is only one of several possible third parties but is probably the most important in the contemporary world. In the period 1945 to 1981, Haas identified 217 disputed involving military operations and fighting. Of these, 79 (or about 36 percent) were not even referred to one of the organizations. Of those that were referred, only 31 cases met with "great success" and 32 more with "limited success." In other words, third parties were able to produce success only in 63 out of 217 cases, for a rate of about 30 percent.[19]

A major obstacle to any peaceful settlement is the still universally accepted principle of sovereignty. Sovereignty means supreme power, unrestrained by anything, and, as Albania demonstrated in the Corfu Channel case, that means unrestrained by a decision of the World Court. A dramatic illustration of the pervasiveness of sovereignty comes from the United States. For a long time the boundary between the United States and Mexico has been the Rio Grande. In 1864 a flood on the river in the neighborhood of El Paso led to a relocation of the river bed, with the result that 630 acres that had been on the Mexican side of the river were now on the American side. This piece of land is known as the Chamizal Tract. Almost half a century passed before the United States and Mexico agreed to resolve the dispute by arbitration. An arbitration commission consisting of one US citizen, one Mexican, and one Canadian was set up in 1910. In 1911 it awarded the tract to Mexico. Even though arbitration means that states bind themselves in advance to the decision of the arbitrators, when the decision was announced, the United States refused to accept it; not until 1967 was the land returned to Mexico. Yet the president of the United States at this time was William H. Taft, the same one who was trying to introduce treaties that would require arbitration of disputes between states. Speaking in 1914 to the New York Peace Society in favor of his plan, President Taft said:

Table 19.1   SUCCESS IN SETTLING DISPUTES

Method Used	Number of Times Used	Percentage of Success
Mediation	9	22
International tribunal	11	45
Multilateral conference	16	44
Bilateral negotiations	47	47
International organization	48	37

Source: Compiled from K. J. Holsti, "Resolving International Conflicts," *The Journal of Conflict Resolution*, Vol. 10, No. 3 (September 1966), pp. 285–289

But the query is made: "How will judgments of such a court be enforced; what will be the sanction of their execution?" I am very little concerned about that. After we have gotten the cases into court and decided and the judgments embodied in a solemn declaration of a court thus established, few nations will care to face the condemnation of international public opinion and disobey the judgment.[20]

One wonders what other states he had in mind by that phrase "few nations."

Outright defiance of judicial or arbitral decisions is an extreme manifestation of sovereignty. It is more common for states to place restrictions on techniques of peaceful settlement before submitting to them. The United States agreed in 1946 to the compulsory jurisdiction of the World Court for international disputes, but it did so only with a reservation. When the Senate was debating acceptance of compulsory jurisdiction, Senator Tom Connally of Texas attached an amendment stating that "this declaration shall not apply to . . . disputes with regard to matters which are essentially within the domestic jurisdiction of the United States of America as determined by the United States of America. . . . "[21] The Connally Reservation shielded the United States from many potential cases. In 1984, however, the government of Nicaragua brought before the World Court a complaint that the United States was violating its sovereignty by such acts as mining Nicaraguan harbors in support of guerrillas opposed to Nicaragua's Sandinista regime. The United States first argued that the Court did not have jurisdiction in a "political dispute." When the Court ruled that it did, the United States then said it would no longer take part in the case and finally, in October of 1985, withdrew from the compulsory jurisdiction of the Court.[22]

The United States was not alone in applying a reservation to its acceptance of the Court's jurisdiction. Canada declared in 1974 that it would not be bound by the World Court in matters relating to its marine environment—hence, a possible dispute arising from a US supertanker carrying oil along the British Columbia coast from Alaska would not go to the Court.[23] Nor was the United States alone in retracting its acceptance of compulsory jurisdiction. France did the same in 1974, after the Court refused to accept its argument in a dispute with Australia and New Zealand that French nuclear tests on French possessions in the Pacific were domestic matters outside the jurisdiction of the Court.[24] At the time when the United States withdrew from compulsory jurisdiction, out of 160 parties to the Statute of the International Court of Justice, only 44 accepted its compulsory jurisdiction.[25]

Even in the unlikely event that states would willingly renounce their sovereignty and allow a World Court to settle quarrels between them, and in the equally unlikely event that a truly neutral, widely respected Court could be set up, there is reason to doubt that the problem of war would be solved. One feature of adjudication that its advocates point to is what President Taft called its "clear judgment of the facts and the law on the merits." But such judgments may not be the wisest solutions or the most just. A decision based on law can only be as just as the law and, as we have seen, much of international law today derives from the imperialist age of the nineteenth century and is perceived by many countries as anything but just. Courts can only restate established rights and duties. But sometimes it is a change in these rights and duties that is called for. Sometimes a state may resort to the law precisely to avoid a more just solution. In the mid-twentieth century most people accept the right of self-determination—that people living in an area should decide themselves to which state they want to belong and what form of government they want to have. Yet King Hassan of Morocco in 1974 tried to take his dispute with Spain over the Spanish colony of Spanish Sahara to the World Court to head off a referendum by Spain that would have given the inhabitants of Spanish Sahara self-determination. He seems to have calculated that the inhabitants might not have voted to join Morocco, as he wished, but that with the right political combination on the World Court he could obtain a ruling that Spanish Sahara legally belonged to Morocco, regardless of what its inhabitants wanted.

Third parties can make a contribution to settling disputes without war. They can help ascertain the facts of a case. Mediators can restore broken communication and reduce distortion in messages. All these services cut down the number of wars that might otherwise start from misunderstanding. When parties to a dispute recognize that it is not in their best interest to fight, arbitration panels and courts can provide face-saving ways of accepting compromise. The rate of compliance with judgments in disputes that do get submitted for arbitration and adjudication is fairly high. The problem is that not all disputes get submitted and, because of sovereignty, it is difficult to force a state to agree to allow a third party to intervene. The difficulty of getting such an agreement, however, is a little less when the third party is an international organization to which the disputing states belong. Within the context of third-party settlement we turn to the major international organization of our time, the United Nations.

NOTES

1. Morton Halperin, *Bureaucratic Politics and Foreign Policy* (Washington, D.C.: Brookings Institution, 1974), pp. 73–74.

2. Robert North et al., *Content Analysis* (Evanston, Ill.: Northwestern University Press, 1963); Ole R. Holsti, "The 1914 Case," *American Political Science Review*, Vol. 49, No. 2 (June 1965), pp. 365–378.

3. Kathleen Teltsch, "Iraq and Iran Agree to Discuss Border Under U.N. Auspices," *The New York Times*, May 22, 1974.

4. Henry Cabot Lodge, Jr., testimony before Charter Review Hearing, quoted by Inis L. Claude, Jr., *Swords into Plowshares*, 4th ed. (New York: Random House, 1971), p. 238.

5. Charles W. Thayer, *Diplomat* (New York: Harper & Brothers, 1959), pp. 96–97.

6. William B. Quandt, *Decade of Decisions* (Berkeley: University of California Press, 1977), p. 233.

7. *The Economist*, December 9, 1967.

8. Philippe Devillers and Jean Lacourture, *End of a War* (New York: Frederick A. Praeger, 1969), for example, pp. 292–293.

9. Douglas Pike, *War, Peace, and the Viet Cong* (Cambridge, Mass.: MIT Press, 1969), p. 160.

10. Thomas J. Hamilton, "Court Awards Pakistanis Portions of Rann of Cutch," *The New York Times*, February 20, 1968; Qutubuddin Aziz, "India and Pakistan Complete Rann of Cutch Demarcation," *Christian Science Monitor*, June 11, 1969.

11. William H. Taft, *The United States and Peace* (New York: Charles Scribner's Sons, 1914).

12. Ibid., p. 169

13. *Keesing's Contemporary Archives*, June 15–22, 1963, pp. 19, 474.

14. Robert Lyle Butterworth, *Managing Interstate Conflict, 1945–74* (Pittsburgh: Center for International Studies, University of Pittsburgh, 1976).

15. John King Gamble and Dana Fischer, *The International Court of Justice: Analysis of a Failure* (Lexington, Mass.: Lexington Books, 1976), pp. 110–111.

16. Gerhard von Glahn, *Law Among Nations*, 2nd ed. (London: Macmillan, 1970), pp. 292–295.

17. Gamble and Fischer. (See note 15.)

18. K. J. Holsti, "Resolving International Conflicts," *The Journal of Conflict Resolution*, Vol. 10, No. 3 (September 1966), pp. 272–296; with some additions in K. J. Holsti, *International Politics*, 2nd ed. (Englewood Cliffs, N.J.: Prentice-Hall, 1972), p. 476.

19. Ernst B. Haas, "Regime Decay: Conflict Management and International Organizations, 1945–1981," *International Organization*, Vol. 37, No. 2 (Spring 1983), p. 195 fn. and pp. 242–256. Haas errs on the side of optimism, attributing success to an international organization far too readily.

20. Taft, pp. 179–180. (See note 11.)

21. *Department of State Bulletin*, Vol. 15, No. 375 (September 8, 1946), p. 453.

22. Text of Nicaragua's complaint, *The New York Times*, April 11, 1984, p. Y8.

23. *International Legal Materials*, Vol. 9, No. 3 (May 1970), pp. 598–599.

24. *The Economist*, May 22, 1973, p. 33.

25. *U.S. Decision to Withdraw from the International Court of Justice*. Hearing before the Subcommittee on Human Rights and International Organizations of the Committee on Foreign Affairs, House of Representatives, 99th Congress, 1st session, 30 October 1985; printed statement by Abraham Sofaer, p. 22.

CHAPTER 20

THE UNITED NATIONS

It has been common for political leaders to borrow a phrase from Abraham Lincoln and refer to the United Nations as "the last, best hope of earth." Any discussion of a world order that excludes war must include the United Nations because, for all its imperfections, it does exist and is the only global organization dedicated to peace and security.

THE UNITED NATIONS SYSTEM

The United Nations Charter, signed in 1945, set up a system with seven main parts. Two have passed into obscurity—the Economic and Social Council, intended to promote issues of welfare, and the Trusteeship Council, intended to facilitate the transfer of territories from colonial status to statehood. Two others are thought of more often as independent bodies—the International Court of Justice, and functional agencies such as the World Health Organization. A fifth component, the Secretariat, is concerned primarily with administration, although its head, the Secretary General, often plays an important role in issues of war and peace.

The remaining two components are what we normally think of when we hear references to the "United Nations"—the General Assembly and the Security Council. The General Assembly of all members who meet regularly each September often receives more publicity, but it is the smaller Security

Council that is charged, according to Article 24 of the Charter, with "primary responsibility for the maintenance of international peace and security."

To meet its responsibility, the Security Council has been given the most far-reaching authority of any existing international body. Article 39 states that the Security Council "shall determine the existence of any threat to the peace, breach of the peace, or act of aggression and shall make recommendations, or decide what measure shall be taken . . . to maintain or restore international peace and security." That is a very comprehensive mandate. There is no need to wait for overt acts of aggression, such as tanks crossing borders; a "threat to peace" is enough. Article 41 authorizes the Security Council to call on members to apply nonviolent sanctions against offenders. Article 42 authorizes the Security Council to call for military operations against offenders. And Article 43 calls on member states to make available to the Security Council military forces for operations.

On paper at least, the UN clearly limits the sovereignty of its members in two ways: It decides when they are to employ armed force, thereby taking away from states their traditional power to decide when to declare war; and it has the power to send troops against a sovereign state for some violation of international peace or threat to peace, even though the state in question might view this as a purely internal matter. The election of an extreme nationalist leader to head of state (another Hitler) might be considered by other states a "threat to peace" and be used to justify international action to nullify such an election. Nothing in the UN Charter rules out such a possibility.

But what is written down on paper does not always turn into practice. Articles 42 and 43 of the Charter became dead letters. They were never employed and no one expected them to be employed. An illustration of what happened to the section as whole is the fate of the Military Staff Committee, which, according to Article 46, was to prepare the UN military forced called for in Article 43. For years the Military Staff Committee did indeed meet quite regularly, every other Thursday, in a basement conference room. Its members were military attachés from the United States, Britain, France, the Soviet Union, and China. They would assemble for a business meeting that lasted five minutes, including time for translation into all four languages. The only item of business was to fix the time of the next meeting, which was always set for Thursday in two weeks. The only time meetings were longer was when one member was being assigned to new duties by his government; on those occasions the others gave speeches praising the contributions of the departing attaché to the work of the committee.[1]

Perhaps at some point life will be breathed back into these articles, but even in the crisis over Iraq's seizure of Kuwait the UN did not officially revive them. The crucial Security Council resolution of November 29, 1990, was worded ambiguously, merely authorizing "member states cooperating with the Government of Kuwait" to "use all necessary means to uphold and implement" the earlier Security Council resolutions. It referred only to Chapter VII of the Charter, but not to any specific Article (such as 42 or 43) found within that chapter. The Soviet Union demanded that the Military Staff Committee be revived as a price of its support, but it was revived in a very diluted fashion, not convening at the UN headquarters itself but at the missions of the member states and attended by political as well as military advisers. Its handful of meetings were used only to exchange information and not for planning, much less directing, the military operations against Iraq.

Those who saw the UN as a first step toward world government were clearly mistaken. The unity among the victors of World War II did not last long; such unity rarely does. If the UN was to survive, it had to make only minimal demands on its members. The nation-state is still the sovereign unit of international politics. The name taken for the organization, the United Nations, reveals who has the real power in the world. States have joined the UN because they believe it will further their national interests. They may put up with some small inconveniences that membership in it causes, but if UN action seems to harm an important national interest, they will simply withdraw from it. One state has already done so. Indonesia protested the creation of the state of Malaysia in Southeast Asia. Malaysia included not only the former British colonies of Malaya and Singapore but also some territory claimed by Indonesia. In early 1965 President Sukarno of Indonesia took his country out of the UN rather than share membership with a country that he claimed had no right to exist. (President Sukarno was overthrown shortly thereafter and Indonesia then returned to the UN.)

THE UNITED NATIONS AND COLLECTIVE SECURITY

The UN does not even go so far as to outlaw all war. Article 51 states that "nothing in the present Charter shall impair the inherent right of individual or collective self-defense if an armed attack occurs against a Member of the United Nations, until the Security Council has taken the measures necessary to maintain international peace and security." The difficulty of determining when an action is self-defense makes the qualification of this article next to useless. In 1971 there was a war between India and Pakistan. Pakistan claimed that it was defending itself against all-out attack from India. India claimed that it was engaged in "protective reaction" against attacks from Pakistan. Because violence between the two countries had escalated gradually, it was difficult for a neutral outsider to determine exactly when aggressive action began.

This article also qualifies the right of self-defense by limiting it to the period before the Security Council can act. But the Security Council often does not act, indeed cannot act, and for this reason the UN cannot be called a collective security organization. The essence of collective security is "all for one." If one state is attacked, all the others must come to the victim's aid. It is especially important that the major states participate in collective security; their absence was a major reason for the failure of the League of Nations. Yet the United Nations Charter provides an explicit escape clause for major states. This is the "unanimity rule," more commonly called "the veto." The Security Council was set up with eleven members. Five of them were permanent members, and these five were actual or potential great powers—United States, USSR, Britain, France, and China. (It was not such a bad selection. These were the first five countries to acquire nuclear weapons.) The other six members of the Security Council were elected for two-year terms. Action by the Security Council on matters affecting peace and security (including the employment of military force) required a vote of seven out of eleven, but that seven had to include "the concurring votes of the permanent members." In other words, unanimity by the five major powers was required; any one of them, by refusing to give its concurrence, could in effect veto any proposal. (The membership of the Security Council was enlarged in 1965 to include ten nonpermanent members. Now nine votes are required for action, but the unanimity rule still holds.)

This was not an oversight. It was a deliberate plan to keep the organization from destroying itself on the opposition of the major states. There is little point in trying to mount collective action against a state that is a threat to peace if the major states are not giving that action their support. The League of Nations discovered this in Manchuria, the Chaco, and Ethiopia. There is also no point in trying to mount collective action against a major state. Even before the power of nuclear weapons was evident, states were aware that such an attempt could end only in a major war. The unanimity principle acts as a fuse for the UN machinery—when too great a load is placed on the machine, the fuse blows out and keeps the overload from destroying the machine. Like the League of Nations before it, the UN has failed to solve some major international conflicts; unlike the League, the UN was not itself destroyed by this failure.

THE UNITED NATIONS AND THE KOREAN WAR

For a brief time in 1950, it looked as though the UN might transform itself into a collective security organization after all, regardless of the wishes of its founders or even of all its members. The occasion was the North Korean attack on South Korea. The United States had said that it did not consider South Korea within its defensive perimeter and that seemed to mean that the United States would not resist a North Korean attack, inside the UN or out. But then US leaders acted contrary to their own publicly stated policy and decided to use military force against North Korea. Following the decision to deploy American forces, the United States went to the UN for an endorsement of this action. At this time the Russians were boycotting meetings of the Security Council to protest against its failure to allow the newly victorious Chinese Communists to take the Chinese seat, so the Russians were not present to veto the US move in Korea. (By this time, the unanimity rule had come to be interpreted to mean "no negative vote by a permanent member of the Security Council." In other words, action could be taken if a permanent member was absent or abstained.)

The Russians quickly abandoned their boycott and returned to their place on the Security Council. They could not retract UN support already given, but they could prevent any further Security Council action. In September 1950 a successful American landing at Inchon turned the war around. For the first time the Americans saw the possibility not just of driving the North Koreans back across the 38th parallel but of actually defeating them altogether so that Korea could be reunited under South Korean leadership. Russian presence in the Security Council guaranteed that such a change in goal for the UN forces in Korea would be vetoed, and the United States devised what it called the "Uniting for Peace" resolution. This was passed by the General Assembly on November 3, 1950. It stated that if the Security Council failed to act because of the great power veto, the item could then be transferred to the General Assembly. The General Assembly could not *require* action (as the Security Council could, under the Charter), but by a two-thirds majority it could *recommend* collective action. (Participation in the Korean effort was voluntary in any case, even though the Security Council had approved it—only sixteen countries of the membership of sixty were contributing to the UN force.) The Uniting for Peace resolution reveals its American parentage by its obvious parallels to the American constitutional system for overriding presidential vetoes. Unfortunately other parts of the UN system are not at all analogous to the American system. If the unanimity rule was the fuse to protect the UN, then the Uniting for Peace resolution was the penny in the fuse box. It kept the organization functioning despite the opposition of one of its most powerful members and increased the risk of total breakdown.

The Korean action was for many years the closest the UN came to acting like a collective security organization. In succeeding years it began backing away for several reasons. One was the acquisition of a nuclear arsenal by the Soviet Union—not just a single atomic "device," such as had been tested as early as 1949, but quantities of usable weapons of the thermonuclear type. If collective security seemed risky in 1945, it had become foolhardy by 1955. Another reason was a shift in the composition of the UN. In 1950 the UN consisted of so many dependable allies of the United States that critics could justifiably speak of an "automatic majority" for US policies. Getting an item transferred to the General Assembly, as the "Uniting for Peace" procedure called for, was a guarantee that the US position would prevail. But in 1955 the UN began to grow. Of sixteen countries admitted that year, six were allies of neither the United States nor the Soviet Union. This shift continued, as Table 20.1 shows. This table does not try to summarize actual voting behavior. In fact, some countries formally allied with the United States often voted against the United States. But the table makes clear the trend. The UN expanded in size, and most of the members were not allied with either of the superpowers. Many called themselves nonaligned and formed their own bloc. Cold War issues and even fundamental questions of war and peace were often of less importance to the nonaligned states than colonialism and the distribution of the world's resources. Furthermore, the willingness of the Soviet Union and its allies to support the nonaligned states on many of these issues meant that, if anything, the General Assembly was more likely to produce a two-thirds majority opposed to the interests of the United States.

The Cold War thus paralyzed the two major organs of the UN. The Security Council was paralyzed by the veto power of the permanent members. There was almost no issue of war and peace that did not involve either one of the superpowers or one or more of its allies. The General Assembly had turned into an auction, in which the Soviet Union generally was more successful than the United States in bidding for the votes of the nonaligned bloc.

THE UNITED NATIONS AND PREVENTION OF WAR

If you accept the argument that the UN was never intended to be a collective security organization, you are less likely to be disappointed by its failures to maintain international peace and security. It has not prevented wars because it is not capable of doing so without going beyond the guidelines that its members have agreed to. Attempts to use it to prevent war would mean not success but massive defections.

Table 20.1   UN MEMBERSHIP

Year	Total UN Membership	US and Allies	Communist Bloc	Others
1945	51	34	5	12
1950	60	37	5	18
1955	76	39	9	28
1960	100	40	9	51
1965	118	41	11	66
1970	132	42	11	79
1975	141	42	13	86
1980	152	35	12	105

The inability of the UN to prevent war was evident in 1967 in the Middle East. It seemed to be the ideal place for the organization to be effective. Two previous wars in the area, in 1948 to 1949 and in 1956, had been ended by UN cease-fires; a UN Truce Supervisory Organization was still in operation from the 1948 to 1949 war; a UN Emergency Force (UNEF) of several thousand men was patrolling an area that Israel had evacuated after the 1956 war. United Nations attention was focussed on the Middle East when the crisis began in May 1967. The Security Council considered the issue; the Secretary General urged caution. Then the Egyptians ordered the expulsion of the UNEF. It left in a matter of hours, and Egypt moved troops into the Sinai area it vacated. President Nasser stated privately that his intention was to provoke Israel into an attack, in order to put the blame for starting the war on Israel.[2] Israel did what Nasser wanted, although with greater success than he had predicted.

The UN in general, and the Secretary General (as the one responsible for the UNEF) in particular, have been criticized for this rapid withdrawal. Yet the UN had no alternative. The UNEF was stationed on only the Egyptian side of the armistice line; Israel had refused to allow the UNEF on its soil. The conditions under which such UN forces were dispatched clearly included the provision that they would not violate the host state's sovereignty, that they were present only with the host state's permission, and that they could be removed at any time. In any case, Egypt had already arranged through diplomacy with India and Yugoslavia for withdrawing their contingents of UNEF and, with their departure, the smaller remaining contingents had no wish to remain. An international force could have prevented the war in 1967, but one operating under the conditions imposed by UN members on the UNEF could not.

The war in 1971 between India and Pakistan also illustrates the fundamental inability of the UN to prevent war. The crisis between the two countries began building up in February 1971, long before full-scale war broke out in December. Yet no country would even put the matter on the agenda of the Security Council. Perhaps this refusal came from recognition of how futile such a move would be—with one permanent member (the USSR) backing India and another permanent member (China) backing Pakistan, any proposal not acceptable to both would have been vetoed. Faced with this potential Council deadlock, Secretary General U Thant tried quiet diplomacy, but three months of secret negotiations were fruitless. Even the Secretary General's suggestion for a modest force of a hundred civilian observers on the border was not accepted.[3] Pakistan for its part claimed that there was no threat to peace, because events inside East Pakistan were a purely internal matter. India was already giving military aid to the rebels and planning large-scale military action and wanted no UN interference.

In some ways a greater tragedy was the failure of the UN to do anything about the civil war in Nigeria. In 1967 one tribal group, the Ibos, attempted to set up their own state in the southeastern third of the country, which they named Biafra. From then until early 1969 they fought a war with the central Nigerian government that caused about 2 million deaths. Compared with the Vietnam War, which drew much more attention, this was a vastly more destructive conflict. Yet no effort was made in the UN to stop it. Unlike the Vietnam War, the Middle East conflict, or even the India–Pakistan dispute, this was in no way a Cold War issue. The major powers had no stakes in the conflict. Yet the UN was unable to act. Too many members feared secessionist movements in their own countries. Any move that would have given legitimacy to the secessionist movement of Biafra, even engaging in negotiations with them, might have encouraged movement elsewhere. When a large number of the UN's members are reluctant to act, the UN can do nothing.

The inability of the UN to prevent war is built into its very structure. Thus we should not be surprised to see the pattern of inaction established in past decades repeated again and again. In the 1970s the regimes of Pol Pot in Cambodia and Idi Amin in Uganda murdered large numbers of their own citizens (perhaps one-quarter of the population in Cambodia). These murderous regimes were eventually removed by wars waged by neighboring states, yet in these wars, as in the case of the India–Pakistan War and the Nigerian civil war, the UN did not act. China on its own launched a retaliatory attack on Vietnam in early 1979 in response to the Vietnamese attack against its client state Cambodia. The UN Security Council did no more than debate the attack for two weeks; in the end no resolution was even brought to a vote. After Iraq attacked Iran in 1980, the Security Council did go a step further, passing resolutions requesting the withdrawal of foreign troops, but never mentioning Iraq by name. Not until 1987 did a Security Council resolution mandate a cease-fire in the Gulf War, a mandate that was ignored for almost a year.

The failure of the UN to act on obvious questions of international peace has been accompanied by an all-too-great willingness to act on other issues. Action is the wrong word, because what the UN does is pass resolutions that have no chance of being implemented. These are usually directed against one or more of the major powers. They may be supported by large majorities in the General Assembly, but all these votes may represent very little in the way of total and economic strength. As critics of the UN like to point out, one could put together in the General Assembly a two-thirds majority of states whose contribution to the UN budget is only 2.75 percent of the total budget. Because dues are assessed according to a country's ability to pay, budget contribution is a fair if rough estimate of a state's power. Another way of illustrating the same point is to consider that a two-thirds majority can consist of states whose combined total population is only 10 percent that of the world's; again, such a vote is hardly a reflection of actual power.

Many of these resolutions, far from aiming at the pacific settlement of disputes, are meant to increase tension. The countries sponsoring the resolutions are using the UN as a tool of their foreign policy; they want to bring pressure on their enemies and force a capitulation instead of seeking a compromise solution. It is generally agreed that the United States was not wise to attempt to use the UN in this way in the first decade of the organization's existence (keeping China out of the UN while condemning it for aggression in Korea), and it does not seem wise for others to do so today.

An example of a resolution used for combat rather than conciliation was the 1975 General Assembly resolution declaring "Zionism is a form of racism." The resolution was directed at Israel, which considered Zionism no more than its version of national liberation. To Israelis, the desire for Jews to live together in a country that observes Jewish holidays and bases its legal code on Jewish religious precepts is no more racist than Saudi Arabian laws prohibiting Christmas trees or Swiss restrictions on Greek and Turkish immigrants. The purpose of the Arab sponsors of the resolution was not of course to settle a philosophic question but to further the process of isolating Israel in the world and to embarrass Egypt, which had been moving toward independent peace initiatives. Thus, far from promoting peaceful settlement of a dispute, the resolution was intended to thwart it.[4] (The resolution was revoked in December 1991, at the insistence of the United States, but even the revocation did little to promote peace. The United States was able to win votes because of the collapse of the Soviet Union, the disunity of the Arab world following the war with Iraq over Kuwait, and the weakened influence of oil-rich states in a world where oil was no longer scarce. But neither the United States nor the United Nations were then able to take advantage of changed conditions in the world to prevail on Israel to make serious moves toward a settlement with the Palestinians.)

The judgment that the United Nations has served more often to heighten tension than to abate it is reinforced by the observation that states with fundamentally friendly relations do not turn to the UN for help in settling disputes. The United States settled disputes with Mexico on water from the Colorado River and with Canada on fishing rights entirely outside the UN system. Even with Cuba, the United States was able to negotiate an agreement on extraditing airplane hijackers outside the UN. Only when states do not seriously expect agreement do they turn to the UN—as illustrated by Cuban resolutions asking for an end to "colonialism" in Puerto Rico.[5]

United Nations resolutions reflect not a world community but the sum of selfish interests of the states that can put together a majority. These states may claim to be acting on principle, but when their interests change, the principle they claim to espouse changes. In October 1973, when Egypt attacked Israel, the Arab oil-producing states imposed an embargo of oil products on states that did not support the Arab side. Yet three years earlier, the UN had passed a resolution proposed by Third World countries declaring that "no state may use or encourage the use of economic, political or any other type of measures to coerce another state in order to obtain from it the subordination of the exercise of its sovereign rights and to secure from it advantages of any kind."[6] States threatened with the loss of oil were reluctant to point out the inconsistency between the oil embargo and this resolution, but the Russians and Chinese went so far as to praise the Arab states for using oil as a political weapon.

Recently states have seized on the weapon of expulsion from the UN as a way to punish their enemies. Targets of campaigns for expulsion have been Taiwan, Cambodia, South Africa, and Israel. Although no state has been formally expelled, the same effect has been achieved by the refusal to recognize the credentials of a state's delegates. This device was used in 1981 to exclude South Africa from a special session of the General Assembly on Namibia, a former German colony under South African control and whose future South Africa considered a matter of vital national interest. However much emotional satisfaction a state may derive from seeing an enemy banished by a majority of the General Assembly, it is hard to see how this behavior increases the possibilities for world peace. Expulsion both reduces the likelihood that the expelled state will comply with UN requests and cuts down on the communication that is the prime purpose of diplomacy.

CONTRIBUTIONS OF THE UNITED NATIONS TO PEACE

It is clear that the UN, as it is now constituted and as it now functions, is not a world government. It is not even a collective security organization. In some cases it is more likely to increase than decrease international conflicts. But this is not to say that it is totally without value. The UN's contributions to peace are similar to those of third parties in disputes. Its advantages are that it is permanently available and, in some cases, more dependably neutral than other third parties.

One thing a third party can do is provide good offices, and the UN has done this. The Secretary General, officially the head of the Secretariat and in practice spokesman for the entire organization, has frequently been called on to provide good offices. A notable success for Secretary General Dag Hammarskjöld came when eleven American fliers, held in Chinese prisons after coming down on Chinese territory during the Korean War, were released by the Chinese. The United States, having no diplomatic relations with China, asked the Secretary General to use his good offices to secure their release. Hammarskjöld was an exceedingly discreet diplomat and never took credit for the release of the fliers, but their release followed a trip of his to Peking and it took place on the occasion of his birthday.[7]

Another contribution the UN makes to peaceful relations between states is providing a neutral place where diplomats can meet. A survey in 1960 of randomly selected delegates revealed that 86 percent believed they had more contact with other diplomats at the UN than at a post in a national capital. Moreover, 91 percent said that they had more contact with delegates from unfriendly countries. Some reported that they had been instructed to stay away from the foreign ministry when posted to an unfriendly country. A visit by the Ethiopian ambassador to the Foreign Ministry of Somalia (when those two countries were quarreling over the boundary between them) might have given rise to speculation about secret deals or concessions by one country or the other. The UN headquarters in New York provides greater anonymity. If tentative contact toward an unfriendly country is fruitless, it can always be denied.[8]

The UN can also be used as a fact-finding body, although not much use has been made of this potential. The immediate cause of the Middle East war of 1967 was a report Egypt received that Israel was mobilizing troops against Syria. Israel denied this and invited the Russian ambassador to inspect the area himself. He declined but the UN Truce Supervisory Organization reported that the charges were unfounded. Unfortunately events were out of control by that time and the finding came too late to prevent the war.[9]

Another area in which the UN has been employed without complete success is truce supervision and observation. A UN Truce Supervisory Organization has kept a record of violations in the Middle East since the 1949 armistices but that has not prevented additional wars. In 1958 the UN was called into Lebanon during a civil war. The Lebanese Christians charged that the Lebanese Muslims were getting arms from across the border in Syria (which at that time was joined to Egypt in the United Arab Republic). Anthony Nutting, a pro-Arab British diplomat who was friendly with President Nasser, revealed in his biography of Nasser that weapons were indeed being smuggled and the UN teams were unable to discover them. He wrote:

> A team of United Nations observers, led by representatives of India, Norway and Ecuador, was sent to Lebanon to investigate these complaints. But since they were unable to operate at night when the main traffic in arms from Syria took place, the observers reported to Hammarskjöld that they had found no evidence of any large-scale gun-running.[10]

The UN has also supplied mediators, again not always with success. In the Arab–Israeli conflict, the UN has appointed a number of mediators, with mixed results. Count Folke Bernadotte was appointed at the time the first war broke out in 1948. He was assassinated by Jewish extremists in September but even in the period before that his efforts were of no avail. The Israelis noticed that his peace proposals always reflected the actual military situation and so broke several cease-fires to improve their military situation before returning to bargain with him.[11] United Nations efforts also failed after the 1967 war. Gunnar Jarring, Swedish ambassador to the Soviet Union, was appointed mediator in the same Security Council resolution that was to lay a basis for settlement. Despite praise from all sides for the professional competence with which he handled his job, he had no success.

Secretary General Hammarskjöld had some limited success in working out arrangements between Israel and Egypt to de-escalate violence along the border in 1956. But the greatest success for a UN mediator was the series of armistice agreements ending the 1948–1949 war, mediated by a deputy to the secretary general, Ralph Bunche. Under what became known as the "Rhodes formula," Bunche met with Arab and Israeli delegations in a hotel on the Greek island of Rhodes. Because the Arabs did not recognize Israel, Bunche had to carry messages from one floor of the hotel to another. His efforts resulted in signed agreements that are the closest to recognized international frontiers that Israel has come.

We have compiled quite a list of contributions the UN can make to world peace. But notice something about every item on this list. Each contribution could be (and often is) made equally effectively by some other agency. Take "good offices." They can be provided by any neutral party. In the chapter on third parties we used as an example the 1968 hijacking of an Israeli airliner to Algeria. First Israel and then Algeria requested the UN Secretary General to use his good offices to secure the release of the plane, passengers, and crew. Although the hostages were eventually let go, the release was arranged through the good offices not of the UN but of Italy, in whose airspace the Palestinian guerrilla group had initially hijacked the plane. In 1985, in a well-publicized hijacking of a TWA airliner, the passengers of which eventually were held hostage in Beirut by Shiite Muslims, the UN Secretary General had to ask if he could be of help. But both sides virtually ignored him and it was the International Committee of the Red Cross that played the major role in arranging a settlement.[12]

The UN may provide a better meeting place for diplomats than national capitals, on the whole, but before the UN existed the capital of a major power (Paris or London or Washington) provided neutral meeting places for diplomats; even with the UN in New York City these other cities still function as "diplomatic capitals," where ambassadors from quarreling countries can meet unobtrusively to sound each other out. Fact finding and truce observation can also be performed by other groups, as in one of the minor diplomatic exchanges during the Cuban missile crisis of 1962. The United States asked that the UN verify that Soviet missiles had indeed been removed from Cuba; the Russians suggested representatives of the International Committee of the Red Cross instead. (In the end, no group verified the removal of missiles.)[13] Finally, mediators have as often come from outside the UN as within. United

Nations officials Ralph Bunche and Dag Hammarskjöld had successes in the Middle East but so did US officials Cyrus Vance and Henry Kissinger.

In one way the UN is unique, and that is as a world forum for speech-making. If the UN were to disappear, such activity would diminish. It is not clear that speeches always further the cause of peace. You could make a good case that often they do the opposite. One may doubt that the Israelis were made more willing to make concessions to Arabs after repeatedly hearing themselves compared to Nazis. Those who argue that virulent rhetoric is a substitute for war would have to argue that the Czechs should have been reassured by Hitler's rhetorical attacks on them in 1938—shortly before he took over their country.[14]

Still, there have been occasions when the purely rhetorical function of the UN may have made a contribution to peace. In 1956 the Hungarians rose in revolt against Russian control of their country. The Russians, judging a pro-Russian government in Hungary to be of vital interest, sent large numbers of troops into Hungary to put down the revolt. The Republicans, who then controlled the executive branch in the United States, had for years been talking about liberating Eastern Europe. The Hungarian revolt provided an excuse. But by this time the Republicans wished to avoid an armed confrontation with the Russians, especially with President Eisenhower seeking reelection that year on the theme of peace and prosperity. Instead of sending troops to Hungary, the United States sent debaters to the UN, where they roundly condemned the Russians. The Russians ignored the UN but great publicity was given to its debates in the United States, conveying the impression to the American people that their government was doing something to aid the cause of the Hungarians.

The UN provided the same service for the Russians in 1967. Israel attacked Egypt and destroyed most of its aircraft, which had been supplied by the USSR; it overran the Egyptian armies, which had been equipped and trained by the Russians. Thus Russian prestige was called into question by the war. But instead of committing troops to aid the Egyptians, they chose to go to the UN and attack the Israelis verbally. As a world forum, the UN provides a way of meeting obligations to give support without going to war.

A REVIVAL OF THE UNITED NATIONS

As the UN approached the end of its fourth decade, its influence was at an all-time low. The recently named Secretary General Javier Pérez de Cuéllar referred in his first annual report in 1982 to "the erosion of the authority and status" of the organization and warned, "We are perilously near to a new international anarchy."[15] In the long list of violent conflicts between states during that preceding year—the Falkland Islands, Lebanon, Iraq and Iran, Afghanistan, Southeast Asia, Africa, and Central America—

the Secretary General admitted his organization had played no significant role at all.

In 1985 the UN celebrated its fortieth anniversary. That year the General Assembly passed 259 resolutions during its annual session, but time ran out before it could consider such issues as the war between Iran and Iraq or conflict in Central America. The only action taken by the UN on the most serious conflicts facing the world during its anniversary year was to put them on the agenda for the coming year.[16]

Then several events contributed to a change in UN fortunes. In the same year the UN celebrated its fortieth anniversary, Mikhail Gorbachev became party leader in the Soviet Union. The next year the Soviet Union signaled a renewed interest in the UN by agreeing to start paying its share of a special UN operation it had previously opposed. This signal was followed by a major announcement in September 1987 of an entirely new orientation. In an extended article, run in both *Pravda* and *Izvestia*, Gorbachev argued for strengthening the UN in a host of ways: to give it expanded authority to regulate military conflicts, economic relations, and the environment; to verify compliance with arms control and peace treaties; even to set up a tribunal to investigate acts of international terrorism.[17] Nor were these mere hollow words. The declaratory policy was soon followed by concrete acts. The next month the Soviet Union announced it would pay all outstanding debts, including $197 million for peace-keeping operations.[18] Several months later, in a move all the more significant because it was made without fanfare, the Soviet Union changed its policy toward Soviet citizens assigned to the UN headquarters staff, meeting a long-standing US demand by allowing them to serve longer terms and, by implication, making them less subject to Soviet control.[19]

This shift in Soviet interest toward the UN coincided with the stalemate in the Iraq–Iran war. The usefulness of a neutral third party is clearly illustrated by its role in this war. When large numbers of Iraqi troops crossed the border into Iran in 1980, the UN could not bring itself to even name Iraq as an aggressor. Although fighting raged for years, UN efforts to stop it were feeble. The spiritual leader of Iran, Ruhollah Khomeini, defiantly proclaimed, "Even if the Security Council orders, we will not make peace." Until 1987 Khomeini's boast was not even challenged. Only in that year did the UN Security Council pass a resolution that explicitly ordered a cease-fire. Iraq, for whom the war was going badly, agreed immediately. But not until a year later did Iran agree as well.

Only the most naïve would claim that the UN resolution, devoid of any enforcement action, had produced the cease-fire. Iran agreed to it because by 1988 it was too exhausted to continue fighting. The role of the UN lay elsewhere. When the two sides were ready to make peace, they had a third party to turn to. Not only did the Security Council resolution provide a basis for a settlement, the UN could also provide machinery to help implement it. Shortly after the acceptance of the resolution by both sides, the Secretary General dispatched a team of military observers to monitor the armistice.

In the same year the UN provided help to the Soviet Union in withdrawing from Afghanistan. Although the UN had begun mediation efforts in 1981, a little over a year after the Soviet invasion, only after seven years of talks did the parties to the conflict sign an agreement. The *fact* of the agreement resulted not from mediation but from high-technology anti-aircraft missiles supplied by the United States to the anti-Soviet guerrillas.[20] But the *shape* of the agreement resulted from the mediation of the UN under Secretary General Diego Cordovez. The Soviets could argue that they had negotiated a settlement and hence achieved their objectives in Afghanistan. Pakistan and the United States for their part promised to wind down assistance to the rebels. A UN force of fifty observers was put into place to monitor compliance. In fact the agreement was mostly cosmetic. The Soviets were prepared to evacuate Afghanistan no matter what happened, and the UN observers contributed almost nothing.

The UN had not by itself brought these conflicts to an end. Only when the parties themselves decided they were ready to end the conflict was the UN able to provide its services to facilitate agreement. But having participated in the settlements in Afghanistan and the Iraq–Iran War, the UN was emboldened to try new initiatives in old conflicts it had previously ignored. The Secretary General turned to the thirteen-year-old conflict between Morocco and the Polisario guerrillas over the former Spanish Sahara. In August 1988 he proposed a cease-fire, to be patrolled by a UN peace-keeping force, followed by a UN-supervised referendum to see if inhabitants would prefer to live under Polisario or Morocco. Within two weeks, the Moroccan Foreign Minister and a senior Polisario official told him they were ready to accept the peace plan.[21] Again, the war ended not because the UN ordered it to, but because both sides were exhausted by the stalemate. Still, they had not taken a step toward peace until the Secretary General pushed them, and once they agreed, the UN could provide machinery to implement the solution.

A RETURN TO COLLECTIVE SECURITY?

Conflicts in Afghanistan, Iraq and Iran, and Morocco were already moving toward resolution with the help of the UN when, on August 2, 1990, Iraqi forces seized the small neighboring country of Kuwait. The UN Security Council met and condemned the move, as it had condemned similar aggression many times in the past. One observer noted that Saddam Hussein obviously expected such condemnation and obviously discounted it in advance.[22]

But then, contrary to past experience, the UN did not content itself with resolutions. The condemnation was followed by a resolution calling for a mandatory boycott of all sales from Iraq and an embargo on all sales to Iraq. Although the UN had asked for economic sanctions on a few occasions in the past (against Rhodesia and South Africa), on August 25 it took the unprecedented step of endorsing the use of naval power to enforce the sanctions. Finally, on November 29, 1990, the UN Security Council endorsed the use of military force to reverse the results of the August invasion.

The UN resolution of November 29 was worded in an ambiguous fashion, merely permitting states to come to the aid of Kuwait but not requiring them to do so. Without the lead of the United States in organizing and leading a military coalition, it is unlikely that military force would have been used.

Some people drew a parallel with the action in Korea in 1950. As had been the case in Korea, the UN was following the lead of the United States. Actual UN involvement in the war with Iraq was minimal, even less than in the war in Korea. The UN resolutions were valuable mainly for getting the US Congress to lend its support. Once the fighting started, the UN did little. The UN did not even go as far as it had in Korea, where the American commander General Douglas MacArthur had also been designated the head of UN forces. In the Persian Gulf, General Norman Schwarzkopf was never anything but commander of the coalition forces, with no official UN role and not even the pretense of reporting to the UN. President Bush tried to argue that he did not need Congressional authorization because he was acting under a UN resolution, but not even the use of the UN flag was authorized.

As time passed and Iraq continued to occupy Kuwait, support in the Security Council waned. Even the initial vote, merely calling for withdrawal, did not have unanimous approval—the Arab state of Yemen hesitated to antagonize another Arab state. When mandatory sanctions and then enforcement for the embargo were called for, both Yemen and Cuba were opposed. On the crucial vote permitting use of force, Yemen and Cuba continued to oppose and China abstained. India, a major force in the Third World, announced it would cancel refuelling rights for American military transports flying from the Pacific into the Gulf.

Even that minimal UN action was possible only because of the highly unusual circumstances surrounding events. Like Korea in 1950, it was a clear-cut case of aggression—masses of troops in uniform crossing a clearly demarcated frontier. In the case of Kuwait, the victim was a full-fledged UN member. Saddam Hussein for his part refused all effort to make a reasonable compromise or to submit to arbitration. Only such clearly delineated aggression galvanizes the UN into action. Leaders such as Saddam Hussein are unusual and after the example of the Persian Gulf War are less likely to imitate his tactics.

After hostilities ceased, the UN did almost nothing about Hussein's mistreatment of his own people. The Kurds, guaranteed rights as a minority in Iraq in 1925 by the League of Nations and hence, by extension, by its successor, the United Nations, rose up to claim those rights against the weakened regime of Saddam Hussein. By early April, military action by the Iraqi armed forces who had survived the war turned many Kurds into refugees—110,000 into Iran, 100,000 into Turkey, and 600,000 along the border. The UN did little to help them. Reverting to its old practices, it merely passed one of the hollow resolutions, similar to ones it had passed so often in the past. Cuba, Yemen, and Zimbabwe were opposed, with China and India abstaining. The resolution did not call even call for trade sanctions, although in fact sanctions were still in effect under the earlier resolutions. The situation demonstrated the impotence of economic sanctions alone. They did nothing to prevent Iraq from continuing to persecute its Kurdish minority.[23]

Fear of violating the principle of sovereignty kept most states from supporting the idea of a protected zone for Kurds. As so often in the past, the UN was paralyzed by sovereignty issue. Many member states had discontented ethnic minorities of their own and did not want to establish a precedent of international intervention to resolve minority grievances. As one representative said, who among us is without sin? Action was taken by the United States and Britain without even the minimal UN backing that the Kuwait liberation had. Only after US and British forces had provided protection from the Turkish side of the border did the UN send unarmed observers to help with the distribution of aid to the refugees.

UNITED NATIONS PEACE-KEEPING FORCES

During the years when the Security Council did little because of the Cold War, there was one area in which the UN did make a visible contribution to peace—by providing "peace-keeping forces" to areas of conflict. These forces had their beginnings in the truce supervisory organizations of the UN's first years. In 1961 Secretary General Dag Hammarskjöld called the dispatch of such forces "preventive diplomacy." *Peace-keeping*, it should be emphasized, is a specialized term with a precise meaning. It is not equivalent to "collective security" or "enforcement action" or "settling disputes." It means only the use of UN troops physically to separate two sides after an armed conflict.

At first glance, the dispatch of UN troops to a crisis area may seem to be collective security. The similarity seems to have confused George McGovern, who said during his 1972 campaign for the presidency, "We need to strengthen the peacekeeping forces until they truly can keep the peace whenever war threatens and whenever conflict begins."[24] But peace-keeping operations, as now conducted by the UN, are in important ways the opposite of traditional collective security. Collective security emphasizes drawing in all states against the aggressor; in practice this means relying primarily on the major powers. But a main purpose of peace-keeping is to keep the major powers *out*. This fundamental justification for UN operations was outlined by Secretary General Hammarskjöld in a report in 1961. He said that the preceding years had demonstrated that the UN could not be effective in areas of big power rivalry. The UN did not act on Cold War issues such as the status of Berlin and no one expected it to. But there were, Hammarskjöld said, many conflicts in the world not directly related to big power rivalry. He recommended that the UN work to localize these disputes; he recommended keeping the big powers out by bringing the little powers in. If an external force was needed to restore order, it should come from the small powers, under the direction of the UN, rather than from a big power. It was called "preventive diplomacy" because it would prevent small conflicts from being drawn into the great power rivalry. Of course what Hammarskjöld had in mind went beyond what we normally think of as diplomacy. Armed soldiers were an essential component.

The UN made use of military personnel as early as 1948 in the Middle East but the members of the original Truce Supervisory Organization were guards from UN headquarters. Not until 1956 did we get the first UN deployment of force of the kind we now refer to as peace-keeping. That force, known as UNEF, for United Nations Emergency Force, consisted of regular soldiers made available to the UN by their governments. It was set up in a great hurry, without months of committee work and endless debate, in response to the Suez war of 1956. At the end of October Israel invaded Egypt and then France and England sent troops into the Suez Canal zone—in order, they said, to protect the canal during the fighting. In fact, the invasion had been arranged ahead of time by the three states to give the French and British an excuse to reclaim the canal, which Nasser had nationalized in July. The British and French were counting on the passive acceptance of their move by the United States. They didn't get it and found themselves under diplomatic attack by Americans as well as by the Soviets and third world countries. Because of extreme caution, their military operations were not going well either and the British were soon looking for a face-saving way to retreat. Lester Pearson of Canada then proposed a solution that satisfied everyone.

Pearson recommended creating a UN military force to replace the British and French and provide whatever protection the Suez Canal might need. (By this time, the Egyptians had already sunk block ships—worthless hulks—and had closed the canal, depriving the British and French of a major excuse for intervening.) The British were happy to have an excuse for an otherwise humiliating retreat; the French were not happy but had no choice once the British accepted the UN cease-fire. The United States was happy to see its NATO allies terminate an unpopular adventure. The Egyptians were happy to be rid of the British and French and have some protection against further Israeli advances.

Dag Hammarskjöld acted with great dispatch and put together a force of six thousand drawn from twenty-five countries. To keep Americans and Russians out, as well as French and British, the UN specified that no permanent members of the Security Council could participate. The members of UNEF came from middle-level powers such as Finland, Canada, Brazil, and India. The UNEF, created on November 6, began arriving November 15; by December 22 it had completely replaced the French and British forces. At the beginning of the next year Hammarskjöld negotiated an agreement with the Israelis for a withdrawal from the Sinai in return for stationing UNEF between Egypt and Israel.

The success of UNEF encouraged the UN to apply the solution of a peace-keeping force to a crisis in 1960. At the end of June 1960, Belgium granted independence to its colony of the Congo, but before the end of July it was clear that the new government could not maintain order. One province seceded, the army mutinied, and Europeans who had stayed in the Congo came under attack. The Belgians were planning to use force to rescue their nationals. The Russians accused them of using this as a front behind which they would restore colonial control. The Russians in turn were accused of taking sides in the Congolese civil war for their own purposes. In the midst of accusation and counteraccusation, the UN voted for a force known as ONUC (from its French title: *Opération des Nations Unies—Congo*). It was justified as an effort to keep outside powers from interfering in the domestic affairs of the country. In fact, ONUC had to interfere in domestic affairs in order to restore order. The force grew very large—20,000—and very costly. At its maximum it cost $120 million a year, larger than the UN's regular budget. At one time or another almost every country found something to complain about in ONUC, but in the end a central government was restored without interference by the major powers.

A third important peace-keeping force was the one of 6,500 sent to Cyprus in 1964 to patrol the lines between the hostile Greek and Turkish communities. This force, known as the UN force in Cyprus, UNFICYP, was still in place when the war broke out in the Middle East in 1973. When a cease-fire there was arranged, the UN Security Council authorized the Secretary General to raise a peace-keeping force to administer it. A contingent of 645 troops from Cyprus was immediately transferred to become the basis for the fourth peace-keeping force, the United Nations Emergency Force in the Sinai Peninsula. A short time later a second group, known as the UN Disengagement Observer Force, was sent to the Golan Heights. Together they eventually numbered 6,000.

A close look at these cases will clarify exactly what a peace-keeping force is. Notice that it does not bring about agreement between two sides that are fighting; rather, it assists in implementing agreements already reached. In the Middle East and in Cyprus, cease-fires had already been arranged before the peace-keeping force was dispatched. A cease-fire, particularly in its first hours, is not always very firm. The presence of a neutral party patrolling a buffer zone between two enemy forces will not prevent one or the other from resuming hostilities but will complicate efforts to mount a surprise attack. Either one side gives a warning to the peace-keeping force (and thus to the other side) or it doesn't, and then has a lot of apologies to make to the Austrians and Finns and Canadians whose soldiers it has killed.

A peace-keeping force can investigate reported violations of the cease-fire and prevent accidents from escalating into renewed fighting. The effect of an unexplained gunshot can be disastrous when two tense armies face each other. In July 1975, Air France sent its new plane, the Concorde, on a test flight over the Mediterranean. Because it travels faster than sound, it creates a sonic boom. When it passed south of Beirut, gunmen in two hostile Lebanese communities started shooting at each other, each thinking the other had taken a shot at them.[25] Peace-keeping forces can avert that kind of accident. In addition to investigating and reporting to both sides on the origins of such unexplained noise, a peace-keeping force by its physical presence inhibits each side from resorting too quickly to violence, each knowing that if it does, the peace-keepers will be the first to be hit.

Finally, peace-keeping forces can provide local police functions, including such simple matters as directing traffic in frontier areas. In the Congo the demands on the ONUC grew to such proportions that for a while the UN was running the country.

Notice that these activities are not the kind of enforcement of Security Council directives envisaged by Articles 41 and 42 of the Charter. Nor are they attempts to bring two sides together in pacific settlement. The peace-keeping forces make no efforts to settle the conflict or even to bring the two sides together for talks. In both the Middle East and Cyprus there have been mediation efforts by the UN, but these came not from the peace-keeping forces (UNEF and UNFICYP) but from a separate agency.

LIMITATIONS OF PEACE-KEEPING

Let us return to George McGovern's hope that peace-keeping forces can be strengthened until "they truly can keep the peace whenever war threatens and whenever conflict begins." Peace-keeping, as it is practiced now, operates under such stringent conditions that not much expansion is possible. Dag Hammarskjöld, in elaborating the "preventive diplomacy" role of the UN, laid down conditions that he thought were essential for UN peace-keeping. The basic one is that a force cannot be stationed on the territory of a state without that state's consent. Far from being able to send a force in whenever conflict breaks out, the UN must wait for a request from the state or states involved. This condition implies that the state also has the right to revoke its invitation and expel a force any time, although beginning in 1973 the Security Council authorized forces for minimum periods of six months. The authorization must be renewed every six months, and if a state decides to exercise its sovereignty and deny entry to a peace-keeping force, the United Nations will comply.

Another condition is that troops in the force must be neutral—in two senses. They must not be directly involved in big power rivalries and they must not be involved in the dispute at hand. Typically this requirement excludes permanent members of the Security Council (although in Cyprus, because British forces were already stationed at bases on the island, they were included in UNFICYP). It also implies that each party to a dispute gets a veto over the contingents that make up the peace-keeping force.

Furthermore, the UN force does not become a party to the dispute in any way. Finally, the UN force never initiates the use of armed force. This rule had to be modified somewhat in the Congo, to permit the UN to disarm some of the rebel forces, but in other cases of peace-keeping the rule has been followed. The UN forces rely on their blue UN flag and blue helmets, not on the light weapons they carry, to protect themselves.

It was Hammarskjöld's view that only if these conditions were imposed would a majority of states, and particularly the big powers, support peace-keeping forces. He was probably right, but the practical effect is that only certain disputes lend themselves to the services of a peace-keeping force. These must be disputes in which neither party by itself is capable of imposing a settlement. If one country is strong enough (and determined enough) it will presumably have its way. Unless the conflict was stalemated there would be no incentive to call in the UN. Thus the India–Pakistan dispute of 1971 was settled purely by India's military superiority. Another kind of dispute that precludes the use of a UN force is one involving a major power or even one in an area considered vital by a major power. During the height of the Cold War we did not expect a UN force to be called in to patrol the border between Czechoslovakia and the USSR. More recently, as long as the United States was supporting guerrillas based in Honduras attempting to overthrow the Sandinista government in Nicaragua, we would not have expected the UN to be asked to patrol the border between Nicaragua and Honduras.

The deployment of a UN force also depends on a decision by the appropriate international body. Which body is appropriate has been a subject of controversy. The position of some states—most notably the Soviet Union but also France—has been that only the Security Council can authorize and control peace-keeping forces. Back in 1956, when the first such force was being proposed, essentially for use against France and Britain, the presence of both countries on the Security Council guaranteed a veto. Under the Uniting for Peace Resolution the matter was transferred to the General Assembly. Thus it was the General Assembly that authorized the first major UN peace-keeping force, the UNEF. The Russians had objections but were willing to go along because Egypt favored such a force. At the beginning of the next dispute, over the Congo, the Soviet Union at first was willing to back UNEF because it interpreted the force as an anti-Belgian, therefore anti-imperialist, move. But when ONUC did not perform as the Soviet Union had expected, it withdrew support, especially in the vital area of financing. Because ONUC was so expensive, this withdrawal created a crisis for the UN organization. In 1964, when the UN decided to send a force to Cyprus, contributions to it were voluntary and the force itself was modest in size and scope of activity. It was only after the 1973 war in the Middle East, when a force was dispatched to the buffer zones created there, that the Soviet Union's condition of authorization by the Security Council was met. But by this time agreement in the Security Council was complicated by a new factor: Communist Chinese membership on the Security Council. China had a veto and China favored continued war by the Arabs. In the end, when the war began to go badly for the Arabs, China did not veto the peace-keeping force, choosing instead to abstain. But in future conflict it may be harder to deploy a UN force, because the interests of China and the Soviet Union and the United States (not to mention Britain and France) are more likely than not to diverge.

Even if a peace-keeping force is authorized, troops must be forthcoming and so must financing. The General Assembly can only recommend action, and even the Security Council is unlikely to go beyond a polite request for troops. Until now, the United States has financed a large part of these forces (25 percent of those in the Sinai, for example), and some of the middle-level powers have been willing to supply troops. The Scandinavian countries, along with Canada and Austria, have made notable contributions, their soldiers volunteering for hazardous duty at a time when young men in other countries generally enjoy freedom from military service. But these are volunteers, and there is no guarantee that they will be available in all situations.

Along with other UN activity, peace-keeping hit a low point in the 1980s. After a major Palestinian guerrilla raid into Israel in 1978, Israel mounted a retaliatory attack and occupied territory in southern Lebanon. The Israelis withdrew after the creation of the United Nations Interim Force in Lebanon (UNIFIL). But UNIFIL turned out to be the least successful of UN forces. The Arab states expected it to stop Israeli interference in southern Lebanon; the Israelis expected it to stop Palestinian attacks across the border. It did neither very well, and, unlike previous UN peace-keeping forces, suffered considerable casualties among its members. When large Israeli forces swept into Lebanon again in 1982, UNIFIL was unable even to slow them down. At the conclusion of the fighting, PLO forces agreed to evacuate Beirut, but the influence of the UN had sunk so low that it was not asked to provide troops to supervise. Instead an ad hoc force composed of French, Italian, and American troops protected the Palestinians during their withdrawal.

The use of troops from these three countries suggested that peace-keeping duties could be handled just as readily outside the UN. Once the PLO had evacuated Beirut, the American troops were withdrawn but then quickly reintroduced following a massacre of Palestinian civilians in refugee camps. The peace-keeping duties of these Marines gradually expanded through 1983. Then over 240 were killed in a single bomb attack on their barracks in October. This attack reduced American enthusiasm for unilateral peace-keeping, and the Marines were withdrawn early the next year.

With the revival of UN activity in 1988 came a new interest in peace-keeping forces. The observers sent to Afghanistan did little more than help the Russians save face. The larger force sent to Iran and Iraq was more useful, although it was not crucial because the front was stabilized more or less along a natural barrier, the water of the Shatt el Arab. More important were the forces set up to administer settlements following internal conflicts in Namibia and in Spanish Sahara. In these cases, the peace-keeping forces had the responsibility both to keep the peace after the withdrawal of foreign military forces' armies and to supervise elections. The sizes contemplated were much larger—two thousand for Spanish Sahara, nine thousand in Namibia (although later the number was cut in half).

Again it is important to keep recent events in perspective. Even with a revival of the UN's fortunes, we have only moved back to the modest realities of 1960, not to the bold dreams of 1945. The UN is a useful place to turn once a stalemate is reached. It still has to demonstrate that it can be a choice of first resort, to which states with grievances can turn with a realistic expectation of a solution.

NOTES

1. *The New York Times*, January 19, 1969.
2. Nadav Safran, *From War to War* (New York: Pegasus, 1969), pp. 300–301; see also Nasser's speech at Cairo University, July 23, 1967 in *The Israel–Arab Reader*, rev. ed., ed. Walter Laqueur (New York: Bantam, 1971), especially p. 203.
3. Kathleen Teltsch, "Effort to Get U.N. Presence in Pakistan Deadlocked," *The New York Times*, October 14, 1971.
4. Bernard Lewis, "The Anti-Zionist Resolution," *Foreign Affairs*, Vol. 55, No. 1 (October 1976), pp. 54–64.
5. Abraham Yeselson and Anthony Gaglione, *A Dangerous Place: The United Nations as a Weapon in World Politics* (New York: Grossman, 1974), pp. 193–195.

6. United Nations, General Assembly, Official Records, Twenty-Fifth Session, Supplement No. 28 (A/8028), "Resolutions Adopted by the General Assembly During Its Twenty-Fifth Session," p. 123.

7. Kathleen Teltsch, *Crosscurrents at Turtle Bay* (Chicago: Quadrangle Books, 1970), pp. 52–53.

8. C. F. Alger, "Personal Contact in International Exchanges," in *International Behavior*, ed. H. C. Kelman (New York: Holt, Rinehart and Winston, 1965), p. 527.

9. Safran, p. 274. (See note 2.)

10. Anthony Nutting, *Nasser* (New York: E. P. Dutton, 1972), p. 233.

11. Safran, p. 32. (See note 2.)

12. *The New York Times*, June 22, 1985, p. Y4.

13. *The New York Times*, November 3, 1962, p. 7.

14. Yeselson and Gaglione, pp. 166–167. (See note 5.)

15. Javier Pérez de Cuéllar, "Report on the Work of the Organization," *UN Chronicle*, Vol. 19, No. 9 (October 1982), p. 12.

16. Elaine Sciolino, "259 Edicts and Many Festivities Later, U.N. Ends Historic Session," *The New York Times*, December 22, 1985, p. Y4.

17. Marshall Shulman, "The Superpowers," *Foreign Affairs*, Vol. 66, No. 3 (Winter 1987/88), p. 502; Bill Keller, "Soviet Says U.N. Should Be Given Greater Powers," *The New York Times*, October 8, 1987, pp. Y1, Y4.

18. This included $172 million for the force in Lebanon and $25 million for forces in the Sinai and Golan Heights. Rita Houser, "When the Kremlin Says Yes," *The New York Times*, November 3, 1988, [Op-Ed], p. Y27.

19. Evidence that this was a serious move and not grandstanding is that the shift was made in May, but only made public in June. Paul Lewis, "Soviet Announces Shift on U.N. Staff Demanded by U.S.," *The New York Times*, June 4, 1988, pp. Y1, Y4.

20. The Swedish Committee for Afghanistan conducted a survey of agriculture by sending in guerrillas trained to gather data. The charts they produced show things getting worse on all measures until 1985—villages bombed, livestock shot, irrigation systems destroyed, grain stores destroyed. The next year, when the Stingers arrived, destruction went back to the 1980 level. (*The Economist*, June 4, 1988, p. 30.)

21. Paul Lewis "Foes in Saharan War Accept U.N. Plan for Truce and Referendum," *The New York Times*, August 31, 1988, p. Y4.

22. Gary Sick, quoted by R. W. Apple, Jr., "Invading Iraqis Seize Kuwait and Its Oil," *The New York Times*, August 3, 1990, p. Z A4.

23. Douglas E. Kneeland, "Senator Proposes a Greater Reliance on United Nations to Keep the Peace," *The New York Times*, October 29, 1972.

24. Paul Lewis, "U.N. Votes to Condemn Handling of Iraq Rebels," *The New York Times*, April 6, 1991, p. Y5

25. *The New York Times*, July 19, 1975, p. 2.

CHAPTER 21

FUNCTIONALISM

The United Nations is best thought of as a system with several components. Some parts of this system receive extensive publicity—the Security Council, which meets during international crises; the General Assembly, which often features speeches by heads of state during its annual plenary session in the autumn; and the Secretary General, who often speaks for the United Nations, or provides good offices between quarreling states, or attempts to mediate disputes. Other parts have withered away—the Trusteeship Council, which was set up to oversee the transformation of colonial empires to independent states, and the Economic and Social Council, which never moved beyond meetings in which welfare issues were discussed but not acted on.

Another part of the system has operated successfully but with little publicity. These are the twenty-nine specialized agencies, funds, or programs, under the Secretariat or loosely associated with it. They are sometimes called "functional" agencies or programs because each deals with a practical activity or program, as their names illustrate—the World Health Organization (WHO), the Food and Agriculture Organization (FAO), the International Atomic Energy Agency (IAEA).

For one school of thought, these functional agencies are the most important part of the United Nations. Adherents to this school, who call themselves functionalists, believe that WHO and FAO, not the Security Council or the General Assembly, are more likely to bring about world peace.

This theory requires some elaboration. It does not seem to be the stated purpose of these agencies to solve disputes among states. Take the World Health Organization. Article 1 of its constitution states, "The object of the WHO shall be the attainment by all peoples of the highest possible levels of health." It then goes on to list some specific tasks: control of communicable diseases (such as smallpox and malaria), improvement of maternal and child care, and of environment health (through pure drinking water and sewage disposal). The membership of the WHO is practically the same as the membership of the UN. Its members come together for a yearly assembly; the rest of the time its affairs are run by an executive board. But at its yearly assemblies it does not discuss world peace or abolishing war; it discusses world health. In 1967 the WHO assembly embarked on a ten-year campaign to eradicate smallpox. It mobilized two thousand epidemic experts from fifty countries, plus hundreds of thousands of local public health workers. The Soviet Union supplied large amounts of vaccine; the United States contributed many of the medical experts. At one point China gave up some funds due to it from the WHO so they could be spent to check a recently discovered epidemic of smallpox in India. The cooperative effort by countries that are often rivals succeeded. In 1968, smallpox was still found in thirty-two countries and caused thousands of deaths. By 1975 the number of cases was down to 125, in two countries, and in October 1977 the last case of the disease was identified and treated. After more than two years of searching for further cases in remote regions of the world, the WHO at its assembly in May 1980 declared the disease eradicated.

FUNCTIONALISM'S THREE-PRONGED ATTACK

It is heartening to learn of such successes in health, but their connection with world peace needs some explanation. Functionalists see this kind of activity as promoting peace in three ways.[1] First, it solves basic human problems and so reduces the tensions that lead to war. Hunger is a basic human problem in many parts of the world. Functional organizations develop new strains of wheat and rice, which enable countries to feed their populations by producing more food instead of by going to war. (Notice the assumption of the functionalists: War is caused, in part at least, by human misery.)

Second, activities such as the WHO's attack on smallpox subvert the sovereignty of the nation-state. Subversion is not an activity that governments approve of, at least not when they are the governments being subverted. But with widespread agreement that the sovereignty of many separate states is a major obstacle to world peace, attempts to erode that sovereignty are welcomed by many advocates of world peace. Most often they are not so blunt as to call it subversion; they might refer to "limitations on unbridled sovereignty" instead. To illustrate why functionalism is subversive, let us look at smallpox eradication. One of the last states to have a number of cases was Bangladesh, and the WHO was concentrating much of its efforts there. The vaccine and many of the health workers working to eradicate smallpox were not coming from the sovereign state of Bangladesh but from the world as a whole, so the citizens of Bangladesh would feel less cause to give undivided loyalty to Bangladesh. If the world community (in the form of the WHO) assisted them when they needed help, citizens of Bangladesh might be inclined to offer assistance to others in the world when it is needed elsewhere. They might be less inclined to support policies of their own government that were hostile to countries that contributed to helping them.

Functional activities go even beyond that. They create within a country, even within a government, groups whose interests are closely tied with international interests. The minister of health is charged, among other things, with controlling communicable diseases. If the best way for him or her to fulfill this responsibility is by making use of the WHO, then the minister becomes an advocate of world cooperation. A village doctor needs smallpox vaccine to carry out his or her duties. If that vaccine comes from the WHO, then the village doctor has a vested interest in seeing that the WHO continues to function inside that country. Functional activities thus give some people inside a country vested interests in international activity.

We sometimes use the expression "social contract" as an imaginative way of saying that people are loyal to government because government provides benefits for them. Functionalism undermines the "social contract" of the nation-state. We need not be blindly loyal to our country's government because the government is not the only source of benefits. Little by little, the national "social contract" is replaced by an international one—if it is international organizations that provide benefits, it is to them we feel loyalty. (Notice the assumption of the functionalists that underlies this second aspect of their proposals: Wars are caused, at least in part, because the world is broken into separate sovereign units, and these units create vested interests in keeping states apart instead of cooperating.)

The third way in which functional activities promote peace is to bring together people from different countries in face-to-face contact. Foreigners seem less "foreign" and more human when they are living right in your midst. It is harder to accept generalizations about other national groups ("all Germans are militarists," "all Americans are greedy") when German and American doctors are living in your village or town, vaccinating your neighbors against smallpox, and offering living proof that all the generalizations are wrong. (Notice, finally, the assumption underlying this aspect of functionalism: War is caused, in part, by one country's distorted image of another.)

Functionalism is a very attractive theory. It is difficult to voice opposition to activities such as wiping out smallpox, increasing grain production, and sending students to study abroad. We should be doing these things anyway, for their own sake, and if we get world peace as a bonus, so much the better. A state might resist direct attempts to limit its authority, say by setting up a world police force; it would be more difficult for a state to turn down an offer of international assistance in introducing new, more productive strains of rice. But in the long run, say the functionalists, these techniques will be just as destructive of national sovereignty as any world police force.

Another attractive feature of functionalism is that it appears to involve a lot less effort than many other plans for world peace. The rapid pace of technological change is doing a lot of the work for us. Writings by people associated with the World Order Models Project have emphasized this feature. A book devoted entirely to this theme is *World Without Borders* by Lester R. Brown.[2] One example from the book will illustrate his argument. Brown discusses the impact of communications satellites, which make possible direct communication between any two points on earth. Before they went into operation, direct communication between Argentina and Chile was next to impossible, even though they had a 1,000-mile border in common; the Andes Mountains (which delineate that border) were an insuperable barrier to telephone lines. Now these two countries lease fifty-six satellite circuits and can enjoy direct telephone contact and even simultaneous television broadcasts.[3] National differences will not disappear overnight, but the national boundaries between the two countries will become less firm and contacts between people will depend less on permission of the governments.

ROBBERS' CAVE AND MIDDLE EAST WATER

Of course we can't say yet where technological changes and technical cooperation will lead. But perhaps we can get an idea by looking at the evidence we do have—historical and experimental. The historical evidence comes from a widely held view of how ancient civilizations began. This theory, advanced by Karl Wittfogel, might be called the "hydraulic theory" of society: Civilization developed along large rivers such as the Nile and the Yellow River because flood control and irrigation projects require central planning and collective action. This gave rise to a specific type of political system, which Wittfogel calls "oriental despotism." If Wittfogel's theory is correct, then it supports the functionalists' claim that technical cooperation gives rise to political cooperation. World cooperation today, the functionalists believe, would create something very different from oriental despotism, but the connection between technical activity and political structure would be the same.[4]

Experimental confirmation of the functionalist theses comes from the "Robbers' Cave" experiment, named after a boys' summer camp in Oklahoma. At this camp, the boys were arbitrarily divided into two groups, then rivalry between the two was promoted by such means as competitive sports. With rivalry well entrenched, the counsellors tried to maneuver the groups into cooperative activities. The water supply was cut and cooperation from both groups was necessary to restore it. A desirable movie was available only if both groups pooled their treasuries. Throughout the summer the counsellors interviewed the boys to find the amount of trust they showed toward members of the other group. They found that after the two groups were forced to cooperate there was more trust and less hostility.[5]

It is hard to say how valid it is to apply experimental evidence of this kind to international relations. You are more likely to find it convincing proof that functionalism could work if you are already favorably disposed toward functionalist proposals. If you are skeptical of functionalist claims, you will find it easy to list reasons why the Robbers' Cave was not at all like international relations. All the participants were from the same society—white, middle-class, Protestant Americans. They were all young (eleven years old). Their groups had been in existence for a very short time. The stakes in their rivalry were trivial. And the counsellors were always in control and in the end could always make binding decisions. Nevertheless, I cite it because it is one of the few bits of evidence we have. There are no comparable experiments on the international level.

But there have been a number of proposals that, if enacted, would do what the Robbers' Cave experiment was trying to do. Consider this plan proposed by President Eisenhower to bring peace to the Middle East. After the war in 1956, and again in 1967, he proposed that an international corporation build three large nuclear power plants in the Middle East, to be operated under the International Atomic Energy Agency. They were to do two things—generate 1.4 million kilowatts of electricity and produce 1 billion gallons of fresh water every day. The power and water thus produced would be made available to Israel, Jordan, Egypt, and Syria. In the words of President Eisenhower, this "would bring a more abundant life to some millions of people and reduce the tensions from which wars are generated."[6]

A CRITIQUE OF FUNCTIONALISM

The Eisenhower plan was never accepted by the Middle Eastern countries, but if it had been, would it have achieved the results Eisenhower expected? Let us look first at his assumption that misery is a cause of war, so that by alleviating misery you eliminate war. You will remember that this was the assumption underlying the first prong of the three-pronged functionalist attack on war. One of the first systematic attempts to examine the relationship between economic conditions and violence was made in the mid-nineteenth century by a French sociologist, Alexis de Tocqueville. In 1856 in a book called *The Old Regime and the French Revolution*, Tocqueville made a startling discovery. The years preceding the outbreak of revolutionary violence in France in 1789 had not brought a falling standard of living but rather increasing prosperity. This prosperity, however, did not lead to greater contentment. On the contrary, Tocqueville wrote, "It is a singular fact that this steadily increasing prosperity, far from tranquilizing the population, everywhere promoted a spirit of unrest." Further confirming this idea, he discovered, "those parts of France in which the improvement in the standard of living was most pronounced were the chief centers of the revolutionary movement."[7]

Since Tocqueville first pointed out that the evidence does not support the common-sense view that misery causes violence, the relationship between economic conditions and violence has become a major subject for research. Scholars have produced a number of theories but have not arrived at any agreement, beyond agreeing that the common-sense view is wrong. That which is true within a society seems also to be true between societies. War is not likely to occur when people are most miserable. Life in Germany was very difficult during the great inflation of 1923, when even a wheelbarrowful of paper money would buy little. But it was not in 1923 that Germany went to war; that came in 1914, after a period of steady economic growth at a rate unparalleled by any other country. In 1914 the Germans were enjoying the highest standard of living they had ever experienced. Again, it was not in the depths of the great depression in 1932 and 1933 that Germany went to war, but in 1939, when conditions had improved.

There is a lot of evidence to support the claim that prosperity will not prevent violence. This is not to say that we should not try to alleviate human misery and improve living standards around the world. But we should be clear that the best reason for doing so is moral obligation and not political expediency.

The failure of Eisenhower's Middle East plan even to win acceptance reveals another weakness of functionalist theory: Governments will resist subversion. Governments will say "no" to plans that would provide them with economic benefits if they feel their own power is threatened. This was clearly shown in a case where the government was not even in power yet. Algerian nationalists began a war for independence from France in 1954. By 1958 they were doing so well that the regime of the Fourth Republic could no longer survive and was replaced by the Fifth Republic under Charles de Gaulle. In an effort to end the Algerian rebellion, General de Gaulle went to the Algerian city of Constantine in 1958 and offered the Algerian nationalists increased prosperity if they would stop fighting. French technicians, he said, would develop newly found deposits of natural gas and oil in the

Sahara and the economic benefits would be shared with the Algerians, raising their standard of living. The Algerian nationalists rejected the offer. The standard of living in Algeria went down after Algeria became independent in 1962, but it would have been hard to find an Algerian to argue that prosperity was preferable to national sovereignty.

Unfortunately for functionalists, there are many more cases demonstrating that states frequently put political goals ahead of economic ones. East Africa is periodically troubled by plagues of locusts, as destructive today as they were in Biblical times. They appear in swarms that cover from 10 to 40 square miles; each square mile of locusts devours 14 tons of vegetation a day. To control them seven states in East Africa cooperate in the Desert Locust Control Organization. They maintain aircraft to locate swarms, a radio network for tracking them, and planes and trucks for spraying. In 1978 locust swarms threatened severe destruction to crops and grazing land because the program had failed. War between two member states, Ethiopia and Somalia, prevented cooperation. Even though all countries stood to suffer, this war for nationalist objectives had priority over preventing famine. Such cases call into question a basic fundamentalist tenet, that technical cooperation leads to political cooperation. In East Africa, political conflict destroyed technical cooperation.[8]

Again we encounter one of the chief villains in our story, state sovereignty. State governments will invoke this principle to justify breaking off cooperation if they feel a vital interest is threatened, and the state alone is judge of its vital interests. In a head-on contest between sovereignty and functionalism, sovereignty wins. Here is an actual case. Cholera is a highly contagious disease. In centuries past it was fatal to millions of people. Today it can be controlled, but an essential part of control is quarantine. The WHO requires countries discovering cases of cholera to report them so that restrictions can be imposed on the area where it is found. But these restrictions damage a country's economy; the state has difficulty exporting food products, attracting tourists, even maintaining normal business contacts. In 1970 the West African country of Guinea had 2,000 cases of cholera but refused to report them, calling them "summer diarrhea" instead. Finally, the WHO, on its own, reported that there was cholera in Guinea. Guinea's reaction was a threat to quit the WHO.[9] Instead of producing international cooperation, the incident created tension. If pushed too far, a state can always invoke the principle of sovereignty and refuse to accept international help by calling it interference in domestic affairs.

States do of course often accept international assistance. Despite some resistance, the smallpox campaign was successful in the end. But the chances of a program's being welcomed seem to be inversely proportional to the degree that it threatens a country's sovereignty: The more subversive the program, the less likely it is to be accepted. The Universal Postal Union is one of the oldest international organizations, founded in 1875. It arranges for delivery of foreign mail and equalizes the cost of delivery between countries. But in its hundred years of existence it has not created a political superstructure. The hydraulic civilizations of the past may have required a centralized political structure to work, as Karl Wittfogel theorized; the same has not been true of postal services.[10]

There was one more way in which Eisenhower's Middle East plan was supposed to promote peace—by facilitating personal contact between Arabs and Israelis. Engineers from each of the countries, under the supervision of the International Atomic Energy Agency, would have had some task in the operation of the plants. We must be careful to avoid proof by definition. If we postulate lack of personal contact as one element of hostility, then the minute we have put citizens from hostile states side by side we have reduced hostilities. The question is whether this initial contact produces any wider effects.

It is clear that at times hostile states can cooperate on limited measures to meet a common threat. What is less clear is that such limited cooperation will spill over into other areas. The United States, the Soviet Union, and China all played a major part in the eradication of smallpox, but relations among them seemed worse by the time the campaign ended. The states bordering the Mediterranean faced a common threat from the pollution of that sea. Meeting in Barcelona in 1976, they signed a convention prohibiting the dumping of harmful substances, including crude oil, mercury, and DDT. Despite serious conflicts in the region, the convention was signed by Greece, Turkey, and Cyprus, and by Israel, Egypt, Syria, and Libya. The states have continued to cooperate in follow-up meetings held several times a year under the auspices of the United Nations Environmental Program. Yet this limited cooperation did not even extend so far as to promote cooperation in another functional organization. At the 1979 meeting of the WHO assembly, the Arab states (with the sole exception of Egypt) tried to suspend Israel's rights as a member of WHO.

One recent researcher has argued that the Mediterranean Plan has been successful. Although the Mediterranean has not been restored to its earlier condition (20 percent of its beaches are still deemed unsafe for swimming), at least it has not gotten worse. Furthermore, several regimes (such as Algeria) that had adamantly opposed any cleanup efforts that would harm their industrial development have changed their policies.[11] But even if this is true, the major hope of functionalists has not been realized. Cooperation on technical issues has not led to cooperation on other issues. The conflict between Israel and its Arab neighbors is just as intractable. Turks and Greeks still disagree on Cyprus.

It would be discouraging enough to learn that limited technical cooperation has no spillover effect, but there is evidence to suggest that such cooperation may even have harmful effects. Researchers have looked at what happens to people's attitudes when they come in contact with people from other countries. Some of the findings seem to support the hopes of the functionalists. There is support for the proposition that as a result of foreign contact people acquire a more differentiated view of other societies—that is, they see the societies as complex and the people as individuals. But some of the research suggests that personal contact will not have a particularly powerful effect in eliminating misunderstandings that may lead to war. Studying the effect of foreign travel, one researcher concluded that people who travel abroad become more committed to their own country and its policies. An American who may be critical of America upon leaving the country becomes more pro-American and identifies more closely with American policies as the result of being abroad. The same is true in reverse for foreign visitors to America.[12] This research finding does not invalidate the entire functionalist premise but it does suggest that the result of personal contact will not be immediate acceptance of opposing points of view.

More evidence against the functionalist position comes from studies conducted in Israel. Researchers there studying Arab workers in Israel found that despite years of working side by side with Israelis, the Arabs showed no significant decrease in hostility. Researchers questioned Arabs who had worked alongside Israelis for at least a year, showing them pictures and asking them to provide captions. A typical example was a picture showing Israelis bringing electric power lines to an Arab village. All Arab comments were negative, stressing Israel's political and economic motives and not the economic benefits to the villagers. Furthermore, the research found the highest incidence of negative attitudes among Arabs who had worked in Israeli industry for the longest periods.[13]

Finally, we turn to the claim that technological change is doing the functionalists' work for them, creating a global society whether governments are in favor of it or not. Without question technology is changing world politics, but the changes are not necessarily all in the direction of more cooperation. Technology can create new conflicts, as the following example shows.

Because the number of frequencies at which radio stations can broadcast is limited, some regulation is needed; the alternative would be so much interference that no one could be heard. Within the United States, regulation is the responsibility of the Federal Communications Commission. In international politics, regulation is done through a functional agency, the International Telecommunications Union (ITU). The ITU sponsors conferences every twenty years to discuss the allocation of frequencies. A major problem at the World Administrative Radio Conference of 1979 was the assignment of short-wave bands.

At the preceding conference in 1959 there were only 300 short-wave transmitters; by 1979 there were 1,500, and many of the new ones were in developing countries that had not been members of the ITU in 1959. The ITU, like the United Nations, operates on the principle of one state, one vote. Because 90 percent of the short-wave frequencies were used by only 10 percent of all countries, the developing countries could argue that fairness required redistribution of the assignments. But such a straightforward political solution ignores the disparities in population size, geographic extent, and sheer technical ability to make use of the reserved bands.[14]

In addition, many of the developing countries use short-wave radio for what are called "fixed services"—business and military communication that is handled by telephone services in more advanced countries. Using short-wave for fixed services, for which alternatives are available, deprives others of the same short-wave frequencies for use in broadcasting, for which no alternatives are available. The problem is further complicated by the desire of many governments to prevent broadcasts into their countries that might undermine their monopolies on news. Reducing the short-wave frequencies available to advanced countries would enhance political control. What were formerly technical issues have become political ones. Instead of the area of political conflict being narrowed as technical cooperation grows, technology is bringing new areas of conflict.

Functionalist proposals are worthy of support. No one is going to argue in favor of smallpox. But to expect these activities to lead to world peace may be expecting too much. As they begin to encroach on deeply held values, they encounter more and more resistance. The WHO has had success with its malaria and smallpox campaigns; it has not been able to do anything about population control because of conflicting political, moral, and religious views on that question. Sovereignty is a value deeply held by many people in many countries today. Many wars have been waged in the twentieth century to achieve it or preserve it. And sovereignty is invoked to resist roundabout attempts to subvert the nation-state as much as to resist direct attacks. The advocates of world government have correctly identified the major obstacle to world peace: division of the world into sovereign nation-states. The solution they propose, a head-on assault on the principle of sovereignty, in the end may be no more difficult than any other.

NOTES

1. David Mitrany is generally considered the leading exponent of this point of view. See his *A Working Peace System* (Chicago: Quadrangle Books, 1966). A more readable introduction is found in Inis L. Claude, Jr., *Swords into Plowshares*, 4th ed. (New York: Random House, 1971), Chapter 17.
2. New York: Vintage Books, 1973.
3. Ibid., p. 266.
4. Karl A. Wittfogel, *Oriental Despotism* (New Haven: Yale University Press, 1957).

5.   M. Sherif et al., *Intergroup Conflict and Cooperation* (Norman, Okla.: University Book Exchange, 1961).

6.   John W. Finney, "G.O.P. Pushes Plan on Mideast Water," *The New York Times*, October 20, 1967.

7.   Alexis de Tocqueville, *The Old Regime and the French Revolution* (Garden City, N.Y.: Doubleday Anchor Books, 1955), p. 175.

8.   "The Year of the Locust," *The Economist*, June 17, 1978.

9.   *The Economist*, September 12, 1970, p. 34.

10.   This point is made by George H. Quester, *The Continuing Problem of International Politics* (Hinsdale, Ill.: Dryden Press, 1974), p. 11.

11.   Peter M. Haas, "Do Regimes Matter?" *International Organization* Vol. 43, No. 3 (Summer 1989) pp. 377–404.

12.   Ithiel de Sola Pool, "Effects of Cross-National Contact on National and International Images," in *International Behavior*, ed. Herbert C. Kelman (New York: Holt, Rinehart and Winston, 1965).

13.   "Israeli Jobs Failing to Win Arabs," *The New York Times*, November 1, 1977; Yehuda Amir et al., "Contact Between Israelis and Arabs and Its Effects," mimeographed (Tel Aviv: Barllan University, n.d.), p. 17.

14.   "Scramble for the Waves," *The Economist*, September 1, 1979, p. 37.

PART V

ECONOMIC ISSUES

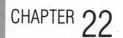

TRADE AND
TRADE WARS

During the decades of the Cold War, political leaders typically distinguished between core issues and marginal issues. The core issues were sometimes called "high policy," presumably because they were decided at the highest level of government, and included issues deemed vital to national security— spending for weapons, military alliances, and overseas bases. The marginal or peripheral issues, known as "low policy," were often handled in a routine fashion by low-level bureaucrats, and included economic matters such as trade, overseas investment, and international monetary policy. Politicians acted as if they were obeying unwritten rules. One was to keep the low policy economic issues out of high policy. For example, when Americans promoted a united Europe after World War II, they ignored the possibility that they were creating a major economic rival; instead they emphasized that a united Europe would be better able to withstand Communist subversion and would be a stronger military ally. In negotiations, economic concessions were traded only for economic concessions and political concessions only for political concessions. Thus the United States did not make a favorable balance of trade a condition for basing troops in Germany or Japan.

In fact, economic issues were high policy, that is, vital to national well-being, but given the massive size of the US economy, it was possible for the United States to act as if they were not. By the early 1970s it had become clear to most people that the distinction was artificial. Indeed, as Soviet military power began to fade, economic issues became the new high policy, more important than military issues. As early as 1989, the first public opinion polls began to show that more Americans feared Japanese economic power than feared Soviet military power.[1]

NEW ECONOMIC CONDITIONS

By the time the American–Soviet military rivalry ended and economic issues moved to the fore, the world differed in several important ways from the early days of the Cold War. One of the new economic conditions is the rise of the welfare state. People now demand that their governments provide prosperity. Governments that do not provide prosperity are turned out of office in the next election. It was not always so. People once thought that economic fluctuations such as "the business cycle" were natural phenomena and governments were no more to blame for recessions than for the eruption of Mount St. Helens. No more. Economic welfare is believed to be within the power of governments to produce. By the Full Employment Act of 1946 the United States Congress declared itself responsible for maintaining full employment. In the rich countries of the world governments now control high percentages of gross national product as they provide unemployment insurance, health care, and many other forms of social security. In 1961 public expenditures in the richest countries of the world averaged a little under 30 percent of their gross national products; by 1984 the percentage had jumped to 45 percent.[2]

At the same time that people began to demand more of their governments, states were becoming more democratic, in the sense that governments must take into account what people want. Elections are obviously more important today in Western Europe than they were in the nineteenth century and even (for some countries) than they were in the 1930s and 1940s. Even when the countries of Eastern Europe were dominated by communist parties subservient to Moscow, they could not ignore the standard of living of the population without disastrous consequences. The lot of the Polish peasant in the nineteenth century was not crucial to the survival of the Polish government; the lot of the Polish farmer and worker became the dominant issue in Poland in 1980. The overthrow of communism had more to do with governments' failure to produce prosperity than it did with their failure to provide liberty.

People demand prosperity of their governments because they have come to expect it. Before World War II economic performance went up and down; sometimes economies declined by as much as 7 percent a year. But once states recovered from World War II, they entered a "golden age" of sustained economic growth. From 1951 to 1973, the advanced economies of the world grew by an average of 5 percent a year in real terms.[3] People came to expect continued economic growth. The United Nations went so far as to declare it a human right. The International Covenant on Economic, Social, and Cultural Rights, approved by the General Assembly in 1966, declared that everyone had the right to "the continuous improvement of living conditions."[4]

The most important changed condition for Americans has been the decline of the United States' relative position in the world economy from the position of clear superiority held from 1945 to 1965. In that period, nine of the ten biggest banks in the world were American. By 1990 none were. In 1987 the National Academy of Engineering concluded that the Japanese were superior to the Americans in 25 out of 34 key technologies.[5] By the end of the 1980s the United States had virtually been driven from the market for the most important kind of electronic component, the D-RAM (dynamic random access memory chip). Japan held 70 percent of the world market for 1-megabit chips, 90 percent for 4-megabit.[6]

In the view of at least some analysts, America's superior position did not result from superior intelligence, industry, or organization as much as from the fact that our competitors were disabled by the war. In fact, before World War II, the Europeans were superior in many aspects of basic science, as well as engineering. The United States coasted from 1945 on; by 1965 the free ride was ending.[7]

The decline came as the importance of world trade grew. By the 1980s it had become commonplace to recite figures illustrating the importance of world trade to the United States economy. Government officials frequently repeated that one out of every six US manufacturing jobs depended on markets abroad, one out of every three acres of US farmland produced for export, and one out of every three dollars of US corporate profits derived from international activity.[8]

It is in this context that the persistent trade deficit seems so serious. If, as the Department of Commerce estimated, each $1 billion of US exports creates 25,200 jobs,[9] then a decline in US exports would produce unemployment. If, as the Secretary of Commerce claimed, about half of the US economic growth for 1988 resulted from a 28 percent surge in exports,[10] then a decline in exports would mean a decline in growth.

The most celebrated deficit has been in trade with Japan. In the mid-1980s it was running at over $50 billion out of a total of about $150 billion, or over one-third of the entire merchandise trade deficit.[11] Other figures showed that while the total volume of merchandise trade between the two countries grew by $61 billion from 1980 to 1986, $53 billion of that growth was in Japanese exports to the United States and only $8 billion was in American exports to Japan.[12] Even with the US economy in recession, the dollar at a record low (making exported goods very cheap), and the Japanese government promoting imports, the deficit was still running at about $40 billion (out of a total of $100 billion) in 1990.

Japan is not America's only trading partner (not even its major one—Canada is more important) but because it has received so much attention it is worthwhile looking at Japan in detail. One starting point we can all agree on: Japan is obviously a successful economy. One economist pointed out at the beginning of the 1990s that over the preceding six years the Japanese economy had grown the equivalent of a full South Korean economy every year.[13] Even more revealing is how they responded to crisis. In the 1973 oil crisis, they responded by increasing exports 50 percent in a year. From 1975 to 1985, Japan reduced its dependence on oil by 25 percent.[14] In the 1982 recession, industrial production in the United States dropped to a negative 9.5 percent; in Japan it dropped, but to 2.4 percent. In the late 1980s the "Four Tigers" of Asia (Korea, Taiwan, Hong Kong, and Singapore) began to compete in electronics. Korean VCR sales in the United States grew from 3.5 percent in 1985 to 20 percent in 1988. Yet in 1988 the Japanese electronics industry grew at its fastest rate in 4 years.

Arguments about the trade deficit with Japan can be divided into two groups: those that concentrate on objectionable Japanese practices and those that concentrate on Japanese virtues. It is sometimes difficult to talk about what is objectionable in Japan, because the Japanese have discovered they can immunize themselves against criticism by a semantic vaccine. The moment someone raises a criticism against a Japanese practice, they shout "Japan basher" and all but the most philistine shrink back, like a vampire confronted with a crucifix.

Of course name-calling is not a substitute for reasoned argument. Sensitive readers may be comforted to learn Americans are not alone in their criticism of Japan. In an interview before she became French prime minister, Edith Cresson told a French newspaper, "Japan is an adversary who does not respect the rules of the game and whose overwhelming desire is to conquer the world. Those who can't see that must be blind. Japanese investments are not like others. They destroy jobs."[15] Although exceptionally outspoken, she articulates a widely held European view.

OUTRIGHT PROTECTIONISM

After being named prime minister, Cresson continued her attacks. In a television interview, she articulated a major accusation against Japan. "I'm against the clear imbalance that exists," she said, "between the European Community, which is not at all protectionist, and the Japanese system, which is hermetically sealed."[16] In a massive report issued in 1985, the US Department of Commerce found that Japan had more barriers to trade than any other country in the world.

The most blatant form of protection is the tariff, that is, a tax on imports. The Japanese claim that the *average* tariff on *manufactured* imports is 4.9

percent, as opposed to 5.7 percent for the United States. To this counter-charge the critics make two replies. Some *nonmanufactured* goods are important for the United States—certain foods, such as peanut butter (on which the Japanese have a 33 percent tariff), and many forest products, such as paper and plywood (4.5 to 20 percent tariffs).[17] But more important, *average* tariff is not as important as *specific* tariffs. The Japanese target very specific products, such as color film, to keep out competitors while they build up their own industry. Once the industry has been built up, they are willing to relax protection, although usually only after much bargaining.

Another protectionist device is the import quota. States simply limit the quantity of a good that can be imported. Quotas often are applied to agricultural products. One study found that the Japanese applied import quotas to 22 categories of agricultural products, more than any other OECD country. Specific products that have troubled Americans have been oranges, rice, and beef.

RESTRICTIVE PRACTICES

In addition to measures of outright protectionism, trade with Japan is kept limited by many restrictive practices. An example is the retail distribution system in Japan. Store size is limited by law. The Large-Scale Retailers Law requires merchants to get the permission of neighbors and local shop-keepers if they want to build a shop bigger than 5,000 square feet. (A typical American grocery store runs to 50,000 square feet.) In a nation with 1.2 million small shopkeepers, such permission is seldom granted. Indeed, the law was passed to keep the small shops in business. In consequence, the biggest 200 retailers in Japan still account for only 27 percent of retail sales.

Consider how this would affect a business. If Kodak film wanted to sell its product in Japan, many sales representatives would have to visit a multitude of small stores, each one of which would buy at best a small amount. By contrast, Fuji film trying to sell its product in the United States can deal with big American chains and let them worry about the distribution to retail locations. The system is so cumbersome that even the Japanese find their market difficult to break into. The bankruptcy rate for new business is six times that in the United States. In the words of one economist, "The system doesn't discriminate against foreigners—it discriminates against newcomers."[18] In fact, Japanese newcomers find the American market easier to penetrate than their own, one more factor leading to trade deficits.

A good example of a restrictive practice is the use of product specifications to exclude foreign goods. When a company or government agency seeks to buy some product, let us say, writing paper, it specifies what characteristics that product must have. It could say the paper must be relatively heavy (e.g., "20 pound") or that it be made at least 75 percent from recycled paper. It is normal for all companies to do this. What is charged to the Japanese is that they write specifications in ways that have no bearing on the product but simply to exclude foreign producers. For example, the Central Sprinkler Corporation of Lansdale, Pennsylvania, a leader in the United States in fire protection equipment, sold its automatic sprinklers to Japan beginning in 1965. Then in 1976 the Japan Fire Board rewrote standards so that US sprinklers no longer qualified. Central Sprinkler tried but failed to get the Japanese standards revised. It even prepared a videotape showing its sprinkler putting out a fire that Japanese sprinklers could not. Yet the Japan Fire Board did not budge, offering one weak reason after another—for example, that the America company had not used metric measures in its applications.[19]

Related to product specification is the use of licensing requirements to exclude foreign goods. In all countries products that might pose a health risk often require government certification before they can be sold. Governments examine such aspects as the shelf life—making sure, for example, that after six months on the shelf a type of eye make-up does not decompose into chemicals that can cause blindness. The complaint brought against the Japanese is that they require all products to be retested, even if they have been proven safe elsewhere. The tests for the shelf life of cosmetics must begin when the product enters Japan. Clinical data on body scanners collected in the United States is not acceptable, presumably on the argument that Japanese bodies are somehow different.[20] (The Japanese even tried to exclude European skis, on the argument that Japanese snow is different.)

New products may also need patent protection. In the United States new products or processes typically receive patents eighteen months after application; until the patent is granted the application is kept secret. But in Japan the process typically takes six or seven years; yet the applications, with all technical specifications, are made public after eighteen months. The system serves to legalize piracy. The Corning Glass Works had a fiber-optics patent pending in Japan for 12 years; during that period, the Japanese learned to make fiber-optics and even sold their product to America. It took Texas Instruments even longer. It applied for a patent on its original semiconductor on February 6, 1960; the patent was granted by the Japanese Patent Office on October 30, 1989. By that time Japanese chip makers were selling 90 percent of all computer chips sold in Japan and even 80 percent of those sold in the United States. Furthermore, the Japanese patent agreement covered only semiconductors sold by Japanese firms in Japan (not in the United States) and none sold before October 30, 1989.

One more example of restrictive practices is the use of customs inspection for harassment. Most international trade is carried in large containers, and in the United States and other industrialized countries these containers are merely sampled by customs inspectors to see that they contain what the cargo manifest claims they contain. In Japan the practice has been to inspect every item in a crate individually—bowling balls to make sure they all have three holes, roller skates to make sure they all have wheels that spin, and so on.[21] (The French, in retaliation for this practice, required in 1982 that all Japanese videotape recorders enter France through the customs house at Poitiers, where each machine would be inspected individually. The tiny customs station, located in the middle of the country hundreds of miles from the nearest port, was deliberately understaffed, and the number of machines clearing French customs dropped from 64,000 to 10,000 a month.[22])

BALANCE ON PROTECTED TRADE

There is no question that such restricted practices exist, nor are they confined to Japan. Even the United States engages in such behavior. Although it has regularly complained about the Japanese quota on oranges, the United States since 1930 has had a 44 percent tariff on imported orange juice, a measure designed to protect American jobs in the orange juice industry. (At an estimated cost to consumers of $500 million a year, it protects those jobs at a cost of $200,000 per job.)[23]

The question is first, how significant are these barriers? Perhaps the Japanese success is due to such practices. But it could also be that they succeed in spite of barriers. Or perhaps barriers are irrelevant. Second, what should the United States do about them—imitate them, expend political capital to end them, or ignore them?

There is surprising unanimity on the significance of these barriers. Estimates from both the US government and private institutes agree that at best trade barriers account for only about a quarter of the trade deficit.[24] For example, the United States Department of Commerce estimated in 1985 that if Japan eliminated all unfair business practices, US exports to Japan might rise by $10 billion, at a time when the total deficit was about 37 billion.[25] Balanced against the Japanese barriers are various US barriers against Japan (including limits on textiles and automobiles), which may work out to roughly the same amount.[26]

VIRTUES

Whatever the Japanese did to keep foreign products out of Japan had nothing to do with the ready acceptance of their own products abroad. It was indeed true that Japanese customs inspectors were insisting on looking at not just a sample but every single bowling ball and rollerskate and frying pan, but that was not the reason people around the world were buying Japanese cars and stereos. If changing what is objectionable in Japan will not significantly influence the trade balance, other countries might turn their attention to imitating the good Japan.

Japan is sometimes referred to negatively as "Japan Inc.," implying that it is not a state like other states but a business corporation. But one might interpret this label in a positive way. In Japan, government and business are in a mutually supportive relationship, not an adversarial one, as in the United States. When Congress passed the Clean Air Act in 1974, American automobile manufacturers were not permitted to collaborate in meeting pollution standards. Such behavior would have been a violation of antitrust laws. Instead American companies had to engage in costly duplication of each other's efforts to meet the standards.

The Japanese government goes beyond merely not interfering with Japanese business. Through its agency, the Ministry of International Trade and Industry (MITI), it provides information and advice and sometimes concrete incentives in the form of subsidies to steer Japanese industry in directions it thinks will be profitable in the future. In the 1970s, for example, MITI encouraged the creation of a semiconductor industry made up of big firms. In the 1980s this industry was able to undercut smaller American firms, in part because the large size of the parent companies enabled them to ride out fluctuations in the market.

Underlying these successes are more fundamental strengths in Japanese society. Eighty-five percent of Japanese children attend kindergarten, and, by age 6, can read and add (compared to 65 percent in the United States). This is followed by 9 years of compulsory schooling. Ninety-four percent go on to high schools (which charge fees). Students who complete high school are competent to take jobs, with the consequence that the Japanese spend almost nothing for remedial programs for their employees while US firms spend about $25 billion a year.

Some of the Japanese success in education may be the result of an attitude observed by William J. Bennett, the former secretary of education, that "the Japanese generally seem to expect a level of performance that is closer to children's true intellectual capacities than Americans ordinarily do." For example, the Japanese assume that anyone can learn math by working hard enough; Americans accept the excuse, "I can't do math."

As a result, the average seventeen-year-old American knows half as much mathematics as the average seventeen-year-old Japanese. It is thus no surprise that a Japanese semiconductor company, opening a plant in the United States, had to seek out graduate students to perform quality control work done by high school students in Japan.[27] A better-educated work force enabled the Japanese to establish a reputation for high-quality products, or "error-free" performance. American companies are happy with two defects per hundred; the Japanese strive for one per one million.[28] Consequently, American products failed in the marketplace because of their low quality.

Commenting on the General Motors closure of eleven plants, one financial analyst said, "Their cars are too expensive . . . and the quality of their vehicles is not up to international standards."[29]

In October 1990, a representative of Toyota lectured 200 North American executives of automobile parts manufacturers. He pointed out that the defect rate on parts was 100 times higher for 75 US (and European) companies than for 147 Japanese companies.[30] In the same issue of the newspaper was another story with the headline, "G.M. Plans to Shut up to 9 Factories; Loses $1.98 Billion."

Japanese culture as a whole appears to be more oriented to problem-solving and less litigious than US culture. One way of demonstrating this difference is to look at the product of higher education. Japan produces twice as many engineers per capita as the United States. One economist remarked that with twice as many engineers on the payroll, it was not surprising that Japanese products are better engineered than US ones.[31] The United States by contrast, turns out lawyers. Vice President Quayle pointed out in a speech to American Bar Association, August 13, 1991, that the United States had 281 lawyers for every 100,000 people, while Japan had only 11.[32]

Thus, Japan's education system turns out dedicated problem-solvers, while America turns out those who benefit financially from the continuation of problems. Admiral Hyman Rickover, the head of the atomic submarine program, said in his farewell testimony to Congress in 1982 that instead of solving problems, American corporations hire lawyers to evade contractual responsibilities. The same point is made by the often-told joke about the only lawyer in a small town, about to go bankrupt for lack of business, until he persuaded another lawyer to move to town—then they both prospered.

The economic consequences of this cultural difference are illustrated by the disputes between the United States and Japan in the mid-1980s over computer chips. The United States complained about the low price for which Japanese computer chips were selling and chose a legal rather than engineering remedy, forcing the Japanese to agree to a market-limiting agreement. But the fundamental reason for the disparity in prices lay in different business strategies. In the period from 1975 to 1985, Japanese firms had spent 12 to 15 percent of sales on research and development while US firms had let research and development expenditures slip to 6 to 7 percent of sales. While the Americans were trying to stave off collapse by using political remedies, the Japanese were developing new technology for creating energy-efficient chips.[33]

Chief among the Japanese virtues is a commitment to international trade. Japanese businesses scan global technology to keep abreast of the latest developments. The Japanese are often mocked for being copiers. It is frequently pointed out that only 5 Nobel Prize–winners have been born in Japan, as opposed to 188 in the United States (as of April 1989). But one could as easily see borrowing as a virtue, based on having enough humility to believe there is something to learn. By contrast, when in 1988 the American Electronics Association set up a newsletter on Japanese electronics, only 21 of 17,000 members subscribed. (The newsletter folded.)

Unwillingness to invest in a newsletter illustrates another fundamental difference between America and Japan, known as "time horizons." The Japanese are more willing to wait for results. Companies do not demand to see immediate profits. It is often said that Japanese firms are willing to invest for a decade before showing a return. Americans by contrast are under pressure to show gains as rapidly as every three months, when reports on performance are due to the Securities and Exchange Commission. Because these reports affect a company's stock prices, managers are under pressure to produce quick results. One consequence was that between 1950 and 1980, American business sold advanced technology to the Japanese in over 30,000 contracts, license agreements, and other arrangements, for the paltry sum of $10 billion. One business analyst called it "the greatest fire sale in history."[34] Selling technology brought a small short-term return but caused long-term losses of business. In 1988 the International Trade Commission (an agency of the United States government) estimated that inadequate protection of "intellectual property" had cost American firms an estimated $24 billion in lost sales in 1986.[35]

In part the ability of Japanese businesses to invest depends on the willingness of Japanese citizens to save. For years after World War II many Japanese had a "postwar mentality," similar to American attitudes after the Great Depression. After surviving a dreadful period, people were willing to work hard to keep it from happening again. In addition the Japanese had experienced military defeat and the leveling of their cities and felt a need to sacrifice personal comforts to rebuild the nation. Instead of consuming all they earned, they saved at a rate estimated to be as high as 25 percent, or three times that of Americans. Because the money they were earning was being reinvested, their standard of living remained low. The "average standard" of housing for a Japanese family of four in 1985 was 818 square feet. The average size of a new house in Japan in 1983 was 932 square feet; in the United States, it was 1,450 square feet.[36] Japanese workers are reluctant to take holidays. Japanese Ministry of Labor statistics show that although the average Japanese business provides fifteen paid holidays, on average Japanese take only half of them.[37]

It was only in the late 1980s that there were signs that the Japanese were ceasing to conceive of themselves as poor. The government was encouraging the process, trying to reduce the workweek from forty-eight hours to forty and urging the Japanese to take vacations.

One problem in simply adopting Japanese practices is their close relationship to Japanese culture. The persistent "postwar mentality" helps explain the very high savings rate. In 1988 a professor at Harvard estimated the United States savings rate had dropped to only 2 percent, compared to the average savings rate of 10 percent in the leading industrial countries (that is, five times as much) and of 16 percent in Japan (or eight times as much). Yet one cannot simply will a "postwar mentality" on the American people.

Another reason for high savings reflects another characteristic of Japanese society. The Japanese have determined that they wish to be self-sufficient in a food they consider basic, rice, and therefore have chosen to use scarce land to grow rice. But because land is scarce, housing prices are high. In the greater Tokyo area, 90,000 acres are classified as farmland, enough to build 3 million condominiums. But because the Japanese chose to subsidize rice, that housing is not built. For this reason, over half the Japanese live in houses below the "average standard" of 818 square feet for a family of 4. For this reason, the average Japanese spends 10 times annual family income for housing (compared to 4 times in the United States).[38] And for this reason, Japanese savings are high. The Japanese are saving up to buy a house. These savings are then available to firms for investment.

SOLUTION: PROTECTIONISM?

Imitating Japanese culture would be difficult. Instituting protectionist measures would be easier, and politically more acceptable because of the widespread belief that Japan is protectionist. A major advocate of protectionist measures has been Lee Iacocca, president of Chrysler. At the dedication of new technology center for Chrysler, he remarked that the Big Three should consider promoting federal legislation to limit the Japanese car industry to a fixed percentage of the American market. We are "out of the electronics business, the VCR business and soon we could be out of the car business."[39]

THE CASE AGAINST PROTECTIONISM

Economists for over 200 years have argued that, over the long run, free trade is the best guarantor of economic growth. Free trade encourages each country to make what it can make most efficiently. For the same amount of resources and effort, more goods are produced. If a country tries to keep out "cheap foreign imports" (and it is almost always the cheap ones that people object to) by adding a tax called a "tariff," then it only raises the prices of those goods to its own citizens. Its own workers may manufacture these goods instead, but because they cost more, fewer of them will be made and fewer will be bought. The country as a whole will suffer a decline in living standards. In the telling words of one critic, "Soviet industry has enjoyed a level of protectionism unthought of in the non-communist world. . . . It is no coincidence that the negative features of the Soviet economy are precisely those that any textbook on free trade would predict."[40]

What is protected by tariffs and other barriers to imports is the economic interest of the few in the industries involved; everybody else in the country is penalized. The way this happens is illustrated by the case of automobiles. In the face of rising imports from Japan, the United States pressured the Japanese to agree to a "voluntary export restraint" (VER), holding the number of cars exported from Japan to 1.68 million from 1981 through 1983 (down 7 percent from the level of 1980) and then to 1.85 million in 1984. One economist estimated that this protectionist measure represented a subsidy by the American consumer of $13 billion. Cars in the United States were more expensive (by $1,500 on the average) because consumers could buy fewer less-expensive imports. The Japanese, limited to a fixed number, exported only their more expensive models. The $13 billion subsidy, as calculated by this economist, broke down as follows: $4 billion to the Japanese automobile manufacturers (and American dealers of Japanese cars); $3 billion to autoworkers, mostly in the form of overtime benefits to those still working (as opposed to the creation of new jobs); and $6 billion to American automobile manufacturers.[41] In 1983, Ford paid 6,035 of its managers an average bonus of $13,000 on top of their regular salaries; General Motors paid 5,807 of its managers an average bonus of $31,000. And autoworkers earned an average of $23 an hour (or $48,000 a year).[42]

The voluntary export restraints continued, at slightly different levels, throughout the 1980s, yet they did not stop the erosion of the American car industry, as indicated by Iacocca's remarks in 1991. Yet at the time he spoke, the median cost of new American car has moved up to $16,600, equal to half the median family income. Iacocca's own salary continued to be astronomical and the workers at the new Saturn plants, designed directly to compete with the Japanese, were preparing to abandon their willingness to share profits from the car for a straight wage package of about $20 an hour, at a time when hourly compensation in manufacturing was averaging $11.28.[43]

Because a country with a protective wall of tariffs will spend more of its resources on its own products, it will have less to spend on imports. But this means that other countries will earn less and so have less money to buy exports. If Americans buy fewer Japanese cars, the Japanese will have less income to spend on American airliners.

If other countries respond to protective tariffs by raising tariffs of their own, world trade quickly declines and everyone's income falls. Such a downward spiral is what followed when in the 1930s the United States introduced the Smoot-Hawley tariffs. Within a few months other countries introduced similar tariffs. Within a year and a half, twenty-six countries had quantitative restrictions. Monthly imports, worldwide, dropped from almost $3 billion in January 1929 to less than $1 billion in January 1933.

Protective tariffs helped turn the recession of 1929 into the Great Depression of 1931–1934.

THE CASE FOR PROTECTIONISM

The persistence of the trade deficit with Japan has given rise to analysts who challenge the free trade ideology. They argue that free trade is like many other ideals. It works better in theory than in practice. A truly free market is theoretically most efficient in domestic society too, yet in practice the government regulates the market in all kinds of ways. Recently the Food and Drug Administration decided that manufacturers must tell the truth in labels on food, because even the head of the FDA had trouble deciphering "lite" and "70 percent fat free," despite the fact that he had advanced degrees in both medicine and law. These critics of unrestrained free trade point out that other countries manage their trade, yet manage to prosper. Japan is an example, but so are European countries such as France.

Free trade may bring only short-term advantages to a country's citizens. Suppose that, as has been alleged, 21 Japanese companies conspired to sell color television sets below cost on the American market. (It was alleged that they could afford to do this by keeping out imports in their home market and forcing Japanese consumers to pay high prices for their TV sets.) According to the theory of free trade, Americans would be foolish not to take advantage of the cheap TV sets. But, say the critics, suppose this tactic of "dumping" (selling below cost) drives American manufacturers out of business? Then the Japanese can charge anything they want. "Dumping" is replaced by "gouging." Viewed from the long term, it is economically rational to protect one's own industry, even if it means temporarily higher prices.

The VER in automobiles is a bad example that not even advocates of managed trade would defend. But they would cite another voluntary restraint, the Multi-Fiber Agreement. According to this agreement, concluded in 1974, imports of textiles into the United States were allowed to grow at a limited rate—6 percent a year. Enough growth was allowed to spur American manufacturers to become more efficient but not so much that they were faced with the prospect of bankruptcy. Had American manufacturers expected to go out of business, they never would have invested to save their businesses. But, protected by the MFA, they invested $1.6 billion a year, making their business one of America's most modern. Furthermore, the cost of textiles lagged behind the general inflation rate—27.5 percent behind during the second decade the agreement was in effect.[44] The solution, these analysts say, is not just blanket protection but carefully thought out and carefully managed agreements for specific problems.

Advocates of managed trade are themselves criticized by advocates of free trade. The MFA is a favorite target of criticism, in part because it hurts poorer countries. Yet it is a goal of the United States to build up the economies of poorer countries so that they can pay off debts they owe us and generate foreign exchange with which to buy American products. The MFA may help textile factories but it hurts Caterpillar.[45]

SOLUTION: NEGOTIATIONS?

Assuming that unfair trade practices account for much of America's troubles, one way of attacking them would be through negotiations. The General Agreement on Trade and Tariffs, signed after World War II, has led to a series of eight rounds that have collectively lowered tariffs from a world average of about 40 percent at the close of World War II to about 5 percent in the 1980s. During the same period, the volume of world trade expanded by 500 percent. Many economists see a connection between the growth of world trade and world prosperity.

The most recent GATT round began in 1985 in Uruguay and formally ended in failure five years later. Although discussions covered trade in services and "intellectual property rights" (e.g., computer software), the biggest single obstacle was farm products.

The problem begins with subsidies to and price supports for farmers in wealthy countries in order to keep prices high and keep their farms in business. When both the costs of subsidies and the higher food prices that result are considered, the cost to the wealthy countries of agricultural protection is about $250 billion a year. It also produces great surpluses of food. For years, the United States has had grain elevators filled with corn; the European Community has had a "butter mountain" and a "wine lake."

Because of overproduction, these countries want to export farm products. Because farmers are subsidized, states find it makes sense to sell below cost to get rid of surplus. But selling below cost is an unfair trade practice and causes rancor. The United States began the Uruguay round by asking for an almost total reduction of special protection for agricultural products. The United States, although an industrial leader, has traditionally been a big producer and exporter of food, typically about 25 percent. Europe was at one time a market, although as European surpluses have grown, Europe has turned instead into a competitor.

Eliminating restrictions on agricultural trade would bring obvious benefits. It would reduce government spending to subsidize farmers, it would lower prices to consumers, and it would help the United States with its balance of payments. But restrictions could be eliminated only at the price of antagonizing farmers. Although not numerous, they form a cohesive lobby. Because of population distribution, they often can return a substantial bloc to legislatures. Furthermore, they find emotional support among their fellow citizens when they argue for "food security" and even for preserving the national identity. Thus the Japanese, although often willing to make purely economic decisions (such as phasing out inefficient industries), have chosen to subsidize weekend rice farmers and thereby have forced consumers to pay as much as eight times the world price for rice. Rice is closely identified with Japanese identity and the knowledge that they grow their own is psychologically satisfying, even if it does not make economic sense. It is similar to repeated appeals in America to preserve "the family farm."

The power of these domestic constituencies was enough to stalemate the Uruguay round of GATT. This power also frustrated another attempt to negotiate trade obstacles, known as the Structural Impediments Initiative. Recognizing that the most serious obstacles to trade with Japan were not traditional barriers such as tariffs but rather the innumerable restrictive practices, the United States and the Japanese met in late 1989 and 1990 for a series of talks. Each country brought a list of complaints to the bargaining table (the Americans listed 240 items, the Japanese 80). The United States talked about the retail distribution system. The Japanese talked about the low American savings rate.

Although innovative, the SII's were unsuccessful because each side ended up asking the other to change its culture. The Japanese, for example, suggested that each American be limited to just a couple of credit cards. They suggested that Americans end low-interest car loans, impose a high gasoline tax, and get gas-guzzling cars off the road. The Americans for their part suggested that the traditionally secretive Japanese business conglomerates make public the minutes of their monthly meetings. It is not surprising that negotiations did not work.

SOLUTION: TRADE BLOCS?

Another approach to intensified economic competition would be large regional trading blocs, each permitting free trade among its members but excluding outsiders with protectionist measures. The European push toward a single market by 1992 did much to stimulate these fears. Although the avowed purpose of the European 1992 project was to create freer trade, it was also motivated by fear of economic competition from the United States and Japan. There is no treaty agreement among the Europeans to keep the demolition of their internal barriers from being accompanied by the erection of external ones. EC leaders talked of "reciprocity" in trade with other countries, which can only mean specific, bilateral trade deals, as opposed to multilateral free trade under GATT.

European legislatures talk of "domestic content," which would require that goods manufactured in Europe be assembled from parts also manufactured in Europe. In some people's minds, such laws would be directed against the Japanese practice of evading trade restrictions by setting up what are called "screwdriver plants," that is, plants which merely screw together parts manufactured in Japan or elsewhere. Long before the 1992 deadline, business corporations began taking the threat seriously. Despite the fall in the value of the dollar, American investment overseas almost doubled in 1987, to $22.6 billion. Much of that investment was in Europe (for example, Apple Computer in Ireland, Cummins Engine in Britain) and one reason frequently cited by these companies was fear of greater protection after 1992.

The United States and Canada concluded a free trade agreement in 1988, again not explicitly intended to be protectionist but with the potential to move in that direction. For example, the agreement removed a 19 percent duty on fine paper from Canadian suppliers. Having made concessions to the Canadians (presumably in return for benefits to other segments of the economy), the American paper mills could in the future be even more reluctant to make similar concessions to Europeans. At the same time, Canadian suppliers now have an interest in excluding Europeans from the North American market.

The Reagan Administration hoped to extend the free trade area south to include Mexico in a "North American Free Trade Agreement" (NAFTA). President Reagan spoke of a Common Market "from the Yukon to the Yucatan." Initially the idea was not well received by the Mexicans. Carlos Salinas de Gortari, before he was inaugurated as President of Mexico in 1988, expressed opposition to such an idea, citing the difference in economic levels between his country and the other partners. But during a visit to Europe in the first half of 1990, President Salinas was surprised by the West European fascination with economic possibilities in East Europe and dismayed at how little attention they paid to Mexican economic progress since 1985. He came back with a changed view on a free trade zone.[46] He began pressing to conclude an agreement in even less time than the three years needed to negotiate the US–Canada agreement.

Other candidates for trading blocs are less clear. Japan is the target of much of the bloc organizing but could organize Asians into a bloc it dominated. It was reported in 1988 that "some senior Western officials are seriously concerned at how far the Japanese have gone toward preparing a bloc of their own."[47] Such a bloc would presumably include the "Four Tigers" of Asia and members of the Association of South East Asian Nations (ASEAN) such as Thailand and Malaysia. But the Japanese are the major beneficiaries of worldwide free trade and would organize an Asian bloc only as a last resort.

Some economists have expressed alarm at the trend. Countries not included in a trading bloc would suffer. Many of these countries must trade to free themselves from their burden of debt and would not benefit from a closed system. If Latin America is left outside the NAFTA, it would be a great sufferer, finding economic growth even more difficult than it now does. On the other hand, if it is brought in, its problems with debt, inflation, slow growth, and unstable governments would make it a dubious asset to the other members. The Europeans confront the same problem with the economies of Eastern Europe, weakened by decades of Communist mismanagement.

Beyond the hardships that trading blocs would impose on individual countries is the fear that they would lead to a drop in overall world trade, with everyone losing. Yet other economists see regional blocs as a way of controlling Japanese competition. Paul Krugman, a well-known economist at MIT, told a conference in 1991 that in the real world, regional trading blocs is "as good as we are going to get."[48]

PUZZLES OF TRADE

Trade issues are difficult for beginning students to grasp because they are difficult for experts. One cannot simply learn what experts are saying, because experts do not agree. One is almost required to become an expert oneself in order to judge the validity of the experts' arguments.

Trade Composition. Traditionally, trade figures have been presented as numbers representing total exports or imports. But some economists argue that much more is involved. In 1987 Japan's deficit with the United States hit a record high of $56.3 billion. In 1990 it had fallen to $41.1 billion. Yet many found the 1990 figure worrying. The trade gap in relatively advanced technologies such as computers, office machinery, and power-generating equipment had actually gotten worse, by $2.3 billion. But the over-all trade balance looked better because the loss in advanced technologies was more than offset by an improvement of $3.6 billion in breakfast cereals, meat, fish, logs, and scrap metal.[49] High-tech industries add more value and have greater potential for growth. Logging merely depletes a natural resource and turns natural beauty into eroded clearcuts. The picture that emerged from a breakdown of gross statistics led one analyst to ask, "Are we really a nation of scrap metal collectors and lumberjacks?"[50]

Direct Investment. In 1990 there was a good deal of attention given to the fact that the best-selling car in America was not American at all but Japanese—the Honda Accord. But on closer examination it turns out that most of these cars are assembled in the United States. They are built in so called "transplant" factories—Japanese-owned plants operating in places such as Tennessee and Kentucky. About half of the 2 1/2 million cars with Japanese nameplates sold in America are manufactured in such factories.

The problem only gets more complex. On the one hand, these factories employ American workers and buy some of their supplies from American manufacturers. According to a detailed study, a 1989 Honda Civic derived 20 percent of its value from American labor and 16 percent from parts supplied by American suppliers, or a total of 36 percent. On the other hand, these factories continued to rely on Japan for crucial parts and for services such as engineering. The 1989 Honda Civic derived 38 percent of its value from parts imported from Japan by Honda.

The remaining percentage of value of the Honda (26 percent) came from parts supplied by Japanese firms based in the United States. Because Honda was a part-owner of many of these suppliers, it was in a position to dictate the prices they charged, and the US Customs Service accused them of selling at a loss, as a way of understating US profits and thus minimizing liability for US taxes.[51] These profits, of course, return to the parent company in Japan. The manager of Honda of American Manufacturing is an American citizen but his salary is counted as an expense by the parent company in Tokyo.

As a final complication, when these cars assembled in Japanese-owned plants in America are exported to other countries, they count as American exports. The traditional way of drawing up trade balances is inadequate, since the output of such factories is obviously neither totally American nor totally Japanese.

The Japanese have greatly expanded direct overseas investment in recent years, from $20 billion in 1987 to $50 billion in 1990. By no means does all of this investment occur in the United States. Much goes to low-wage countries in Southeast Asia. Over 46 Japanese electronics firms have set up operations in Thailand. In 1990, the deficit in US–Japanese trade in consumer electronics fell by $400 million, but US imports from Thailand rose to $310 million. Trade shifted from Japan to Thailand because Japanese firms shifted production from Japan to Thailand. Again traditional ways of describing trade balances, in this case suggesting that the US trade picture with Japan is improving, are inadequate.[52]

OUTLOOK

Economic competition with Japan sometimes took on the language of warfare. The Japanese were accused of aggressive tactics. America was said to be on the defensive. The nation was said to be at risk. One former trade negotiator criticized the US tactics at the bargaining table in language similar to that used by earlier critics of arms talks with the Soviet Union. Where once it was the Russians who placated us on issues such as missile size or intermediate-range bombers, now it was the Japanese who were duping us with meaningless "side letters" or "letters of understanding" in place of concrete language in the treaty.[53] But talk of trade "wars" is only metaphorical. Such "wars" are unlike the deadly conflicts that have troubled states for centuries and are more like the competition that occurs continually in domestic society, regulated by courts and legislatures. No one is killed. In any case it is not accurate to describe the Japan–America relationship as a trade war, at least not yet. The more radical legislative proposals failed to gain the needed support and their advocates are temporarily quiet.

Still, the danger remains that economic rivalry could slip into bitter conflict, where one state would take steps that would harm itself, just to inflict harm on another. One political commentator noted, "It is worth recalling that during the 1920's—the last 'threatless' era—commercial competition quickly deteriorated into economic warfare."[54] It is widely believed that strict tariffs to protect domestic industry will be met by retaliation, leading to a world where every state protects its own industries, production becomes less efficient, prices are higher for everyone, and so everyone's standard of living declines. It is a prospect less grim than a repetition of World War II, but not a pleasant one for all that.

Finding a solution to the problem of world prosperity is becoming as difficult as finding a solution to the problem of world security. The problems may seem daunting and the conflicting solutions discouraging. One should remember a question once posed to Albert Einstein. "Why," he was asked, "are there so many geniuses in physics and so few, if any, in political and social sciences?" Einstein replied, "I guess physicists work on easier problems."

NOTES

1. *Washington Post*–ABC News Poll, February 1989, Richard Morin, "Americans Rate Japan No. 1 Economic Power," *The Washington Post*, February 21, 1989, p. A19.

2. Survey, *The Economist*, September 24, 1983, p. 29; "The Gorging Leviathan," June 14, 1986, p. 15.

3. Samuel Brittan, "A Very Painful World Adjustment," *Foreign Affairs*, Vol. 61, No. 3 (America and the World, 1982), p. 563.

4. Article II, published in *The International Bill of Human Rights* (Glen Ellen, Calif.: Entwhistle Books, 1981).

5. Clyde V. Prestowitz, Jr., *Trading Places* (New York: Basic Books, 1988), p. 100, citing National Academy of Engineering, *Strengthening U.S. Engineering Through International Cooperation* (Washington, D.C.: National Academy Press, 1987).

6. Peter Passell, "Economic Scene: U.S. Memories: Who Is the Loser?" *The New York Times*, January 24, 1990, p. Z C2.

7. Lester Thurow, "Other Countries Are As Smart As We Are," *The New York Times*, April 5, 1981, p. F2.

8. C. Fred Bergsten, "The Costs of Reaganomics," *Foreign Policy* No. 44 (Fall 1981), p. 36.

9. Ibid.

10. C. William Verity, Secretary of Commerce, cited in Robert D. Hershey, Jr., "U.S. Trade Gap Narrows Again As Imports Fall," *The New York Times*, December 15, 1988, p. Y34.

11. Mike Mansfield, "The U.S. and Japan: Sharing Our Destinies," *Foreign Affairs*, Vol. 68, No. 2 (Spring 1989), p. 5.

12. Ronald A. Morse, "Japan's Drive to Pre-eminence," *Foreign Policy*, No. 69, (Winter 1987–1988), p. 20.

13. Kenneth Courtis, senior economist, Deutsche Bank, Tokyo, quoted by James Sterngold, "Leaders Come and Go, But the Japanese Boom Seems to Last Forever," *The New York Times*, October 6, 1991, p. E3.

14. Clyde Haberman, "Japan's Emphasis on Stability," *The New York Times*, April 28, 1986, pp. Y21, Y26.

15. *The Economist*, May 18, 1991, p. 52.

16. Steven Greenhouse, "French Leader Firm on Japanese," *The New York Times*, May 20, 1991, p. Z C2.

17. *The New York Times*, February 26, 1985, p. Y29.

18. Jon K. T. Choy, economist, Japan Economic Institute, Washington, D.C., cited by Nicholas D. Kristof, "Japan Trade Barriers Called Mainly Cultural," *The New York Times*, April 4, 1985, p. Y1.

19. Susan Chiba, "Can U.S. Goods Succeed in Japan?" *The New York Times*, April 7, 1985, p. F29.

20. *The Economist*, April 13, 1985, p. 69.

21. *The New York Times*, November 21, 1982, p. E3.

22. Paul Lewis, "The Latest Battle of Poitiers," *The New York Times*, January 14, 1983, pp. D1, D3.

23. *The Economist*, April 30, 1988, p. 20.

24. US trade negotiators estimate that trade barriers accounted for only 25% ($5 to 10 billion) of the $37 billion trade deficit in 1984. See *The New York Times* April 7, 1985, p. F1.

25. Clyde H. Farnsworth, "200 Foreign Barriers to U.S. Exports Listed," *The New York Times*, October 31, 1985, p. Y36.

26. Institute of International Economics, quoted by Yoshi Tsurumi, "The U.S. Trade Deficit With Japan," *World Policy Journal*, Spring 1987, p. 208.

27. Edward B. Fiske, "Lessons: Behind Americans' Problems with Math a Question of Social Attitudes," *The New York Times*, June 15, 1988, p. Y27.

28. Yoshi Tsurumi, "The U.S. Trade Deficit with Japan," *World Policy Journal*, Spring 1987, p. 213.

29. Maryann N. Keller, analyst, Furman, Selz, Mager, Deitz & Birney, cited by Steven Prokesch, "General Motors to Shut 11 Plants; 29,000 Workers Will Be Affected," *The New York Times*, November 7, 1986, p. Y38.

30. David E. Sanger, "U.S. Suppliers Get a Toyota Lecture," *The New York Times*, November 1, 1990, pp. C1, C5.

31. Lester Thurow, *The Economist*, November 9, 1985, p. 22.

32. Figures from "Agenda for Civil Justice Reform in America, a Report from the President's Council on Competitiveness"; Quayle's speech in *The New York Times*, August 14, 1991, pp. Z A10.

33. "Lightning Strikes Semiconductors," *The Economist*, June 11, 1988, p. 65.

34. James Ableggen and Thomas M. Trout, "Facing Up to the Trade Gap with Japan," *Foreign Affairs*, Vol. 57, No. 1 (Fall 1978), p. 160.

35. "The Sun Also Rises Over Japan's Technology" *The Economist*, April 1, 1988, p. 57.

36. Susan Chira, "Wealthy Japan's Spartan Style," *The New York Times*, October 30, 1985, p. Y1, Y41.

37. Susan Chira, "It's Official! Vacations Really Aren't Un-Japanese," *The New York Times*, August 6, 1988, p. Y4.

38. "Who Will Lead Japan?" (leader) *The Economist* August 22, 1987, p. 13.

39. Doron P. Levin, "Iacocca Talks of Seeking Quota on Japanese Cars," *The New York Times*, October 16, 1991, p. Z C10.

40. Jerry F. Hough, "Gorbachev's Strategy," *Foreign Affairs*, Vol. 64, No. 1 (Fall 1985) p. 41.

41. Yoshi Tsurumi, "They're Merely a Subsidy for Detroit," *The New York Times*, December 16, 1984, p. F3.

42. John Holusha, "Detroit Brings Back the Bonus," *The New York Times*, April 14, 1984, p. 31.

43. Doron P. Levin, "Reality Comes to G.M.'s Saturn Plant," *The New York Times*, November 14, 1991, p. Z C1, C5; Hourly Pay of Nonsupervisory and Production Workers, August 1991, Bureau of Labor Statistics, Sylvia Nasar, "Life Support for the Recovery," *The New York Times*, October 1, 1991, p. Z C1.

44. Robert Kuttner, *End to Laissez Faire* (New York: Alfred A. Knopf, 1991), pp. 140–144.

45. A persistent advocate of free trade is Jagdish Bhagwati. See his "Jumpstarting GATT," *Foreign Policy* No. 83 (Summer 1991), pp. 105–118, or *Protectionism* (Cambridge, Mass.: The MIT Press, 1988).

46.   *The Economist*, June 16, 1990, p. 21.

47.   Flora Lewis, "Foreign Affairs: The Menace of Trade Blocs," *The New York Times*, October 23, 1988, p. E23.

48.   Louis Uchitelle, "Blocs Seen Replacing Free Trade," *The New York Times*, August 26, 1991, pp. C1, C4.

49.   Clyde H. Farnsworth, "U.S. Is Asked to Review Japan Trade," *The New York Times*, March 25, 1991, p. Z C1.

50.   Kevin L. Kearns, "Japan's Sleight of Hand in Trade," *The New York Times*, April 7, 1991, p. F11.

51.   Paul Magnusson, James B. Treece, and William C. Symonds, "Honda: Is It an American Car?" *Business Week*, November 18, 1991, pp. 106–107.

52.   Clyde H. Farnsworth, "U.S. Is Asked to Review Japan Trade," *The New York Times*, March 25, 1991, p. Z C1; James Sterngold, "Japan's Importing More, but Who's Benefiting?" *The New York Times*, February 25, 1991, p. Z C4.

53.   Clyde V. Prestowitz, "Secret Letters—Japanese Dodge," *The New York Times*, [Op Ed], April 14, 1989, p. Y23; see also his book, *Trading Places (note 5). 1988.*

54.   Edward N. Luttwak, "The Alliance, Without an Enemy," *The New York Times*, [Op-Ed], February 3, 1989, p. Y21.

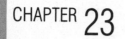

GLOBAL ISSUES

"The circumstances that endanger the safety of nations are infinite . . . ," argued Alexander Hamilton in Federalist No. 23. What Hamilton and the authors of the Constitution had in mind were external attacks, but Hamilton argued that "it is impossible to foresee or define the extent and variety of national exigencies. . . . " In 1787 the danger of such attacks on North America was small, but expanding commercial ties and advancing military technologies soon forced America to play a greater role in world politics. The oceans provided a moat protecting Fortress America in the age of sailing ships, but in the age of steam power that moat diminished. For Americans World War II began with ship-borne airplanes appearing out of the waters of the northern Pacific over Pearl Harbor.

Concern with military threats led the United States in the 1980s to spend about $300 billion dollars for military preparations, or approaching 7 percent of its gross national product. There was some argument about the proper percentage—some saw 7 percent as too high, others thought it was not high enough. But there was no argument about the basic need for some kind of defense establishment. The wars of the preceding decades, some of which involved America directly, some American allies, seemed to show that Alexander Hamilton's fears were still justified.

More recently economic prosperity has become a major American concern. The safety of the nation was now endangered by poor economic performance and fiercely competitive trading partners. Some of the language of warfare began to be used to describe international economics—trade wars,

But it is possible that both these traditional threats to the safety of the nation will be eclipsed by a newer one. The new threat to survival comes not from the deliberate policies of specific countries but from the spontaneous actions of millions of individuals. Each action taken by itself is not harmful, indeed may be considered desirable, but when all these actions are taken together they threaten us all. For centuries young couples have produced children, to the pleasure of their families and the welcoming approval of their societies. The birth of an individual child still brings joy, yet the simultaneous births of hundreds of thousands of children might doom the human race. For centuries people have built fires to warm themselves, to cook their food, and to help fabricate manufactured goods. Warm stoves are still symbols of cheer and welcome, yet if enough fuel is burned, the carbon dioxide produced may warm the globe to a point at which catastrophic climate changes occur.

In war we put a face on the enemy. Threats to peace come from the actions of specific countries. In 1974 Turkey felt its compatriots on Cyprus were being mistreated and so it went to war. For the Turks, the Greek Cypriots were the enemy; for the Greek Cypriots, the Turks. Even in economic competition we often put a face on an enemy. America's economic troubles have produced talk about "Fortress Europe" and "economic Pearl Harbors." But global problems are faceless. They do not originate in one country alone, nor do they result from deliberate policies of specific governments. As the four following examples illustrate, this faceless quality is part of what makes them so hard to deal with.

POPULATION

The number of people in the world is large and growing rapidly. There are more human beings than any other type of vertebrate in the world (human beings having recently pulled ahead of rats). What alarms observers is that the number of people is increasing at an accelerating rate. One way to express this rate is to calculate the number of years it takes to add one billion people to the earth's population. We estimate that it took until about the year 1800 before total population reached one billion, that is, from two to five million years. Another billion people were added between 1800 and 1930, a period of 130 years. A third billion were added between 1930 and 1960, a period of 30 years. The four billion mark was passed about 1975, so that the time required to add a billion has been cut to 15 years. Another billion were added by 1987 and the six billion mark is expected to be passed about 1998. If the population of the earth continues to increase at this accelerating rate, we will indeed soon have a planet on which there is "standing room only."[1]

But will population continue to increase at an increasing rate? Some people dismiss these predictions as just more in a series of warnings and alarms. They frequently refer to the gloomy predictions of the Reverend Thomas Robert Malthus, an English clergyman who published similar predictions as far back as 1798.[2] In a pamphlet titled "An Essay on the Principle of Population," Malthus correctly identified the basic principle that causes population growth to accelerate. This is simply that a couple can give birth to many more children than the two needed to replace them when they die. Even if a couple gives birth to only four children (and in the days of Malthus the average number of children was greater than that), and those children reach adulthood, the couple is reproducing at a rate that will double the population. If each couple in the second generation (usually reckoned as coming thirty years later) gives birth to four children, the population doubles again, making a fourfold increase over sixty years. In another generation at the same rate, population is eight times what it was. Today we call this type of growth "exponential."

At the same time, Malthus wrote, the sources of food for these people (such as arable land) are fixed. As a consequence of his analysis, Malthus predicted great human misery for his country as starvation, disease, and war cut down excessive population.

Today we know that Malthus' prediction was wrong. For one thing, the size of the families in England began to drop until it was closer to what population experts call a "replacement rate." For another, providing food and other resources for a much larger population was not as difficult as Malthus had thought. It was not necessary to bring large amounts of new land into cultivation because the amount of food produced on existing farms was increased through machinery, fertilizer, and improved breeds of plants and animals.

But perhaps Malthus was not wrong, only premature. Even with spectacular advances in food yields per acre, sooner or later a population increasing at an exponential rate will outstrip the food supply, simply because land cannot reproduce itself. And though the birthrate has declined in some parts of the world, overall it is still large enough to cause alarm.

When in the 1960s some writers tried to resurrect Malthus' views, others refused to join in the alarm. In nature, these skeptics pointed out, exponential rates of growth never last long. Thus, they predicted, within a decade or so the world would enter "a new phase of history, one with declining rates of growth."[3] And indeed in 1982 the United Nations Fund for Population reported a drop in the rate of growth, from 1.99 percent (1960 to 1965) down to 1.72 percent (1975 to 1980).[4] By the end of the 1980s it had dropped slightly more, to 1.70 percent.[5]

Yet these world figures are only an average. They mask still very high growth rates in some regions. Furthermore, they indicate only that the rate of growth is slowing down. In absolute numbers the world's population continues to grow. Because the population is already so high, even a small percentage increase adds billions of people, and it is these billions that create the problems that states will be forced to address.

CONSEQUENCES OF POPULATION GROWTH

Uncontrolled population growth is a source of human misery, as the often-cited case of Bangladesh illustrates. Bangladesh is a country the size of Iowa, but whereas Iowa has a population of about 3 million, Bangladesh has a population of over 100 million. Each year the population of Bangladesh increases by the equivalent of Iowa's total population. Although the growth rate has been slowly falling in Bangladesh, at the present rate of change the population will not stabilize until it reaches 245 million, or 4,358 people per square mile.[6]

Population growth dilutes the per capita wealth of society. Such dilution might be tolerable in a society as rich as the United States—fewer snowmobiles or hot tubs, perhaps. But the consequences are serious for a society where most people are already at the edge of sustenance. A 1983 study indicated that in Bangladesh people were consuming less rice than they did twenty years earlier, despite large amounts of foreign aid. Eighty percent of children under age five were found to be malnourished. In 1983 an Indian nutritionist told a meeting of a World Bank committee that in that year 23 million babies would be born in India. Of that number, 4 million would die in childhood and 9 million would suffer serious physical and mental disabilities as a result of severe malnutrition. A further 7 million would suffer fewer disabilities from less severe but still serious malnutrition. Only 3 million, or 15 percent, would grow up to be healthy adults.[7]

At the same time, population growth reduces a society's ability to cope with its problems. People have to live somewhere, and so land goes out of cultivation to provide space for housing. In Egypt officials estimate that 1,500 acres of agricultural land are lost to "informal" (that is, unlicensed) housing each year. An Egyptian agronomist estimated that Egypt loses 60,000 acres of soil a year just to provide the mud for bricks for buildings.[8] People use fuel for cooking, and in most countries the fuel is wood. People in Kenya burn 27 million tons of wood a year. The population of Kenya is expected to double by the end of the century. At the present rate of consumption there will be no wood left by then, and dependence on expensive imported petroleum will be a major drain on Kenya's resources.

In their early years, children are consumers. Money spent to feed and clothe them is money that is not invested in permanent improvements. When the children reach adulthood, they find there are no jobs because there was no investment to provide jobs. In Mexico in 1978 (before the surge in oil prices), it was estimated that 800,000 young people entered the job market each year, but the Mexican economy created only 400,000 new jobs each year.[9]

An obvious consequence for domestic politics in the United States is massive immigration of unemployed Mexicans. But the possibility of war between Mexico and the United States seems remote. This absence of international tension between the two countries seems to contradict the position of some writers, who suggest that crowding by itself is a source of tension. For example, one student of human aggression writes that "to reduce world population, or at least to stem the flood of its increase, is the most important single step which can be taken by mankind to reduce hostile tension."[10] The German expression *Lebensraum* ("living space") is often used in English with sinister implications, in part because it was used by Hitler as a justification for wars of expansion. As the earth becomes more crowded, it is said, there will be wars for *Lebensraum*.

Perhaps people who use this argument prefer using a term from a foreign language because it gives the appearance of substance to an otherwise very thin argument. There isn't much evidence to back it up. Careful studies of the relationship between population density and interstate aggressiveness have found no significant correlation between the two. For example, a study that was part of the Correlates of War Project, covering the period from 1815 to 1965, found no significant relationship between population density and external wars. Studies of other periods have confirmed this finding.[11]

But it would be premature to dismiss population as having no effect at all on international politics. Population growth or population density might cause conflict in association with other factors. A more technical way of saying it is that there might be an intervening variable between population and war. Consider Japan. In the 1930s the foreign policy of Japan could fairly be described as expansionist, imperialistic, and militaristic. The population density was often given as the explanation for this policy. In the 1950s and 1960s the population of Japan was even denser than it was in the 1930s, yet the Japanese were strongly antimilitaristic. There is a major difference between the two periods: In the 1930s Japanese access to resources was hindered by the United States and other countries. In the 1960s, the Japanese were able to invest, buy, and sell around the world. Although the Japanese case shows that population density alone does not lead to aggression, it suggests that population density will lead to violence if access to resources is hindered. Some confirmation of this hypothesis is found in an analysis of several European states during the forty-five years before World War I. Though the correlation between density and interstate violence was low, the correlation between density and colonial expansion was extremely high.[12] This shifts our attention from the issue of population to that of resources.

FOOD

The first resource that comes to mind when discussing the effects of a rapidly growing population is food. War among the starving over shrinking food supplies is one of the grim visions of the future often held up to us. Many of these predictions (like those of Malthus almost two centuries ago) assert that disaster will occur within a very short time. In 1967 a book appeared with the title *Famine–1975!*[13] In 1974 the United Nations sponsored a World Food Conference, a forum at which speaker after speaker warned of impending world disaster.

The year 1975 came and went without world famine. In fact, ten years later the most serious problem facing world agriculture was a surplus of grain. Farmers in the United States were being driven into bankruptcy. Fully one-third of the United States wheat harvest each year was going into storage. The attention given to starvation in African countries such as Ethiopia distracted from the fundamental reality that the world had in storage 190 million tons of grain. The famine in Africa was cause by a shortfall of 3 or 4 million tons. Making up the shortfall made no noticeable dent in that enormous reserve.[14]

Countries traditionally thought of as starving showed great gains in food production. From 1982 to 1985 China showed a 15 percent increase in corn production, 20 percent in rice, and 40 percent in wheat; by 1984 China had become the largest producer of wheat in the world, with higher yields per acre than those in the United States. India began harvesting record crops in 1976, the last year it had to import grain. By the 1980s it was looking for export markets, one of the factors driving down the price of grain and devastating the American farmer.[15]

Pessimists argued that such surpluses were temporary. Some of the gains were one-time only, from introducing new strains of rice or wheat. Once yields had increased three or four times, there was little prospect for continued increases. Other gains came from unusually favorable weather. When India experienced a drought in the early 1980s, grain production stagnated. When the United States experienced a drought in 1988, world stocks dropped. Most alarming, many of the gains in production resulted from bringing into cultivation marginal land where the soil would quickly erode or from introducing irrigation from unsustainable water supplies, in effect "mining" water that could never be replaced.[16]

Even if the world continued to produce two and one-half times the amount of food grain needed to sustain the world's population (assuming it was consumed in direct form as grain and not converted to meat), there would still be a food supply problem. It is estimated that out of a total world population of 5 billion, 1 billion people suffer from malnutrition. A person living in southern Asia is likely to consume on the average 1,900 calories a day; an American is likely to consume on the average 3,300 calories a day.[17] The problem is not one of absolute scarcity; it is one of distribution.

The figures show that the world produces two and one-half times as much grain as would be necessary if grain were consumed directly, as cereal, bread, and so on. One problem is that in more affluent societies grain is usually not consumed directly; instead it goes to feed animals and the animals are then slaughtered for meat. But this is a relatively inefficient way to use grain. It takes five times as much in the way of agricultural resources to feed an American on a typical diet of animal protein as it does to feed an Asian subsisting mostly on rice or wheat. In 1974 an average Asian consumed about 400 pounds of grain a year, almost all of it directly. An American by contrast consumed almost 2,000 pounds of grain a year, but only 150 pounds directly; the rest was converted to other forms first (including 100 pounds of alcohol).[18]

An obvious solution would be for Americans to eat less meat and more cereal—in other words, for American eating habits to become more like those of Asians. But the trend in world food consumption has been in the opposite direction, with others adopting the American pattern. In America itself during the three decades of increasing prosperity after World War II, consumption of meat increased as per capita income rose. Steak on the table was part of the good life. Similarly rises in income in the countries of Europe, in the Soviet Union, and in Japan were accompanied by increased consumption of meat.

Thus there are two sources of pressure on food resources: rising population and rising affluence. At the same time, land is being lost to agricultural use. Prime agricultural land that lies close to cities is being taken out of cultivation to house expanding populations. Overgrazing of livestock and other poor land management practices have led to the loss of large amounts of once cultivatable land to desert. Shifting rainfall patterns have led to the gradual movement southward of the Sahara Desert by several miles each year. Significant additions to agricultural land through irrigation seem unlikely because most sources of irrigation water have already been tapped. Finally, most of the oceans are being fished at what experts consider the maximum level for a continuously sustained yield.[19]

These trends suggest that the outlook for the future is grim. But agricultural optimists argue that gains are still possible—for example, from genetic engineering of new strains of plants or from raising yields in those parts of the world where they are still low.[20] But the case of the optimist seems weaker as time goes on.[21] Gains in productivity leveled off in 1984, yet population continued to grow.[22] In 1989 the UN's Food and Agricultural Organization expressed alarm that world grain reserves had fallen below the 17 percent of world consumption that it considers necessary as a buffer against crop failures.

It might appear that the debate on resources has not changed much since the days of Thomas Malthus. Someone makes a prediction of impending disaster based on a logical projection of a present trend. The prediction turns out to be wrong because of human ability to come up with a technical solution. A France that would have been considered overpopulated with only 40 million people in the 1700s was considered underpopulated with only 40 million people in the 1900s.

But the current debate is different because it emphasizes the connections between factors that in the past were thought of separately: The food supply may be increased by technical improvements but these improvements in turn have direct consequences in such areas as energy supplies, mineral resources, and pollution. The solution of one problem may only make other problems more severe.

Here is a dramatic illustration of this point. Scientists point out that primitive agricultural methods rely mostly on human labor. The yields of primitive farmers may not be very high but these techniques supply from five to fifty calories of food energy for every calorie of energy expended in producing the food. In other words, primitive agriculture produces a *net gain* of calories. The highly industrialized agriculture practiced in countries such as the United States requires five to ten calories of energy just to produce one calorie of food energy. In other words, industrialized agriculture results in a *net loss* of calories. If energy supplies were unlimited, this would not be of great concern. But awareness is increasing that the fossil fuels used to run tractors or even to convert into fertilizer are a nonrenewable resource and supplies will not last indefinitely.[23]

Nor is strain on resources the only harmful consequence of increasing yields per acre. Nitrogen fertilizer is one of the keys to increased yields; the "miracle" strains of grain that have produced the "green revolution" are entirely dependent on high doses of nitrogen. But not all the nitrogen applied to a field can be absorbed by the plants. Some is carried off by rainfall or irrigation water and finds its way into streams or lakes where it becomes food for microorganisms. The resulting growth of these microorganisms rapidly deprives the water of oxygen, making it uninhabitable for other forms of life such as fish. The dead and dying fish in turn make the water unfit for human consumption. Even when this sequence of events does not occur, large amounts of nitrogen in drinking water can be a health hazard to human beings.[24]

NONRENEWABLE RESOURCES

The argument, then, is not simply that we are running out of food but that we are simultaneously approaching limits in many areas—arable land, fresh water, ocean fisheries, fossil fuels, and strategic minerals.[25] Shortages in only one of these areas would have serious consequences in each of the others. This style of analysis first became popular as the result of efforts of an international group of thirty scholars who met in Rome in 1968. The Club of Rome, as they came to call themselves, sponsored a project on "the predicament of mankind." The first report for the Club of Rome's project, published in 1972, was called *The Limits to Growth*.[26]

The Limits to Growth focussed attention on a number of issues, especially *nonrenewable resources*. These are substances, unlike food, that cannot be replenished by human effort. The report estimated that if the present trend of steadily increasing rates of use continued, reserves of such basic industrial minerals as copper, lead, mercury, petroleum, silver, tin, and zinc would be exhausted in as little as twenty years.[27] It further calculated that to attain an equilibrium that could be sustained for many years into the future, consumption of these resources would have to be reduced to one-fourth of the 1970 level by the year 1975.[28]

The report of the Club of Rome was successful in stimulating debate on the issue, although less successful in winning unanimous support for the group's position among politicians or academics. Politicians did not inaugurate measures to cut consumption of resources to one-fourth of the 1970 level. Although some academics accepted the conclusions of the report and added studies of their own, others published counterarguments. These critics pointed out that the projections in *The Limits to Growth* are so pessimistic because they depend on *known reserves*, yet known reserves are always relatively low because no rationally run business corporation has any incentive to locate more than a ten- or twenty-year supply. Anaconda Copper will not spend money in the 1980s to locate all the copper ore it will need from 1995 to 2095.[29] Even assuming that reserves are exhausted, these critics argue, prices will rise and this will have three effects. First, companies will then have an incentive to hunt for more reserves (or to use lower-grade ore than was economical before, or to use recycled material). Second, demand will decrease and so the rate of consumption will decrease. Third, people will start hunting for less-expensive substitutes. For example, the telephone industry can use glass fibers instead of copper wires to transmit messages.[30] These effects were demonstrated when oil prices rose dramatically in 1973— exploration increased and new sources were found, prices went up and people used less, and because prices were high manufacturers built more-fuel-efficient cars and better-insulated houses. By the mid-1980s oil prices were dropping.[31]

This failure to take into account the possibility of substituting one product for another, the critics say, results from a static definition of "resource." *The Limits to Growth* assumed that the resources needed in 1972 would be the ones needed for all time in the future. Using such assumptions, a similar book two hundred years earlier would have predicted a shortage of wood for fuel (ignorant of the uses of petroleum) and iron for making pots and pans (ignorant of aluminum). The man for whom the Mercedes automobile is named believed in 1903 that there would never be a total world market for more than one million automobiles because not more than one million artisans in the world were trainable as chauffeurs.[32] The neo-Malthusians make projections about the rate of consumption but do not make similar projections about the rate of technological innovation. One 700-page report devoted 220 pages to the environment but only 15 pages to technology.[33]

Events since the publication of the first Club of Rome report have not born out the group's predictions. Yet issues raised by the report have not gone away. The debate between the neo-Malthusian pessimists and the optimists continues. In 1980, a special commission organized by the United States Department of State and the Council on Environmental Quality submitted a report to President Carter entitled *Entering the Twenty-First Century*. Known informally as the *Global 2000 Report*, it claimed that in some areas of the world the population was already exceeding the "carrying capacity" of the earth. Borrowing a concept from biology, they argued that just as too many deer will destroy all vegetation and then starve to death, human beings in some areas were eroding the land's ability to support human life.[34]

The *Global 2000 Report* went quite far in making specific predictions. At present and projected growth rates, its authors predicted that the carrying capacity of the entire globe would be reached during the next century. They predicted that arable land per person would decline to 0.6 acres by the year 2000, that growing population would cause a 35 percent decline in water supply, and that nearly 1,000 billion barrels of the world's original petroleum endowment of 2,000 billion barrels would have been consumed by 2000.[35]

The entire enterprise was discredited by the failure of some specific predictions, making it easy for people to dismiss the entire report as the work of Chicken Littles ("The sky is falling! The sky is falling!"). For example, the predictions of an oil shortage that they relied on had already led President Carter to invest billions of dollars in plants to produce a "synthetic" oil from coal. But the following decade saw a slump in oil prices as supplies glutted the market. The "synfuel" plants were shut down and people went back to big cars without concern for miles per gallon.

Nevertheless neo-Malthusian thinking continues, for example in the work of the Worldwatch Institute. In their yearbooks, they repeatedly make the case that in one area after another the world is reaching the limits of sustainable growth.[36] Chastened by the experience of Chicken Littles of the past, they avoid specifying dates for particular shortages or disasters, but point out that if we wait until disasters actually arrive, it will be too late to reverse the damage.

ENVIRONMENTAL POLLUTION

The *Global 2000 Report* gave even more of its attention to renewable resources, such as wood and food crops, and the irreversible changes caused by growing numbers of people trying to meet their basic needs from finite cropland, pasture, forests, and water supplies. One kind of change is environmental pollution. Loss of cropland to desert in South Asia and sub-Saharan Africa will lead to increased misery for people living in those areas, but some forms of pollution could have swift, catastrophic consequences for all people, rich and poor alike.

Once again we encounter predictions of impending doom that are difficult to prove. For example, we have heard much about the ozone layer, which is believed to protect the earth's surface from harmful ultraviolet rays of the sun. At times people have come forward with predictions that this layer will be dangerously depleted by such diverse phenomena as supersonic jetliners and the propellant in spray cans, and that loss of the protection that ozone provides against ultraviolet (UV) rays would cause an increase in skin cancer. Such predictions have been followed by others to show that these fears are exaggerated. In both cases the more serious analysts admitted that we know very little about the ozone layer. In fact, we didn't even know it existed until space exploration began.[37]

Fear of the exhaust from supersonic airlines turned out to be an exaggeration. In fact, few such airliners entered into commercial service. But concern about aerosol sprays grew. The propellant in such cans was typically a chlorofluorocarbon, or CFC. CFC's are also used as coolants in air conditioners and in making insulating foam. A related chemical, a halon, is used in fire extinguishers. After much study, scientists concluded that these chemicals were responsible for depleting the ozone layer, particularly around the poles, at an alarming rate. It is difficult for laypeople to evaluate such findings, but the research convinced a crucial group, the research chemists at Du Pont, a company selling $600 million worth of CFC's a year.[38] Most people would conclude that if professional scientists whose economic interest is affected still agree that depletion of the ozone layer is a problem, then nonscientists have a strong reason to go along.

Still, not all alarms turn out to be so well founded. One of the early arguments about the ozone layer assumed a continual rise in the rate at which jet exhausts and aerosols were used. Critics of neo-Malthusians attack such straight-line projections, pointing out that if such methods had been used in England in the 1850s, people studying the increases in both population and amount of travel would have concluded that by the end of the nineteenth century London would be buried under several hundred feet of horse manure.[39]

But people who are alarmed about environmental pollution claim that their concern is better founded. They point out that we are confronted today by entirely new circumstances. Many of the products that cause us concern are new, artificial substances that do not occur in nature. Having never existed in the past, they have no natural enemies in the form of microorganisms waiting to consume them once they are discarded. A traditional fishing net made of plant fiber disintegrates and decays; a net made of nylon floats in the ocean for a long time, trapping fish and mammals long after it has broken away from a fishing boat.[40]

The problem of the ozone layer illustrates the problem with these durable artificial substances. It was precisely the durability of CFC's and halons that made them so valuable. Because they would not combine readily with other substances, they were not poisonous or explosive. They could be used to extinguish fires on valuable items such as machines without causing more damage than the fire already had. But it is this fact that they do not disintegrate that also makes them dangerous. Not subject to decay, they persist for years and gradually drift up miles above the surface of the earth, where they finally do encounter a dangerous enemy—the very ultraviolet radiation the ozone layer helps filter out. At these high elevations, UV rays have not yet been filtered out, and they are strong enough to break down the CFC's. The component parts then combine chemically with the ozone, destroying it and thus exposing people on the ground to dangerous levels of UV radiation.

The case of the ozone layer illustrates another point: Many of the effects of these products are not felt until years later. The pesticide DDT was introduced about the time of World War II, yet only twenty-five years later did it begin to kill off brown pelicans in the Gulf of Mexico. Asbestos fibers are now known to cause a painful and invariably fatal cancer of the chest lining, yet death occurs only twenty-five or thirty years after exposure; people who worked with asbestos years ago, even for periods as short as six months, are now finding they were subjecting themselves to a grave risk that was totally unknown.[41] Finally, the rate at which these new products are being introduced has greatly accelerated, and even if all of them are first carefully tested, there is no way of testing how they will react with the thousands of other artificial substances already in circulation. For example, adding chlorine gas to water has long been accepted as a safe way of purifying it. Like CFC's, chlorine in water has been viewed as a chemical product that saves people from typhoid and cholera without harmful effects. Yet when traces of acetone get into water through industrial discharge, the chlorine reacts with it to produce toxic or cancer-causing agents such as chloroform.[42] Thus with each new product the risk of some unforeseen and catastrophic combination increases.

The basic point of the environmentalist is the interrelatedness of many aspects of life. It was one of the contributions of the study for the Club of Rome to include calculations of the environmental cost of overcoming scarcity. But estimating the cost in money is only part of the problem. If fossil fuels are exhausted, energy may come from nuclear reactors. But nuclear reactors produce highly poisonous waste that may persist for 22,000 years or more. Nuclear reactors may cause an excessive rise in temperature in bodies of water or air used for cooling, changing local weather in radical ways. The waste products of nuclear reactors can be diverted for bombs. These are all undesirable effects but their exact cost is hard to quantify.

We may be able to overcome shortages in food, energy, and resources, but only at considerable cost because of the interrelatedness of all these components of the environment. Yet it is this very interrelatedness that makes the environmental crisis as much a cause for hope as for despair. Because most of the problems of pollution are global, the solution must be global. The acid rain that poisons lakes in Canada appears to come from coal-burning plants in the United States—Canada alone cannot solve the problem. The burning of fossil fuels in all countries appears to be putting large quantities of carbon dioxide into the upper levels of the atmosphere, where it allows rays of the sun to pass through on their way to earth but keeps them from being reflected back into space. The carbon dioxide thus acts like the glass in a greenhouse, with the same potential effect of raising the earth's temperature enough to alter rainfall patterns, make some areas too warm for raising crops, and perhaps even melt the polar icecap. Because this "greenhouse effect" seems to be the result of human activity, it could conceivably be controlled by human activity, but only on a global scale.[43]

It has sometimes been said, half-jokingly, that the only thing that would get the states of the earth to cooperate would be an invasion from Mars. Might environmental pollution become a functional equivalent of invaders from Mars? There are reasons to doubt it. Although it is true that sometimes societies suffering from internal dissension put aside their conflicts in the face of a common enemy, this is not universally so. The German threat to France in 1940, for example, was not enough to bring about unity among the French. But even granting that groups will unite in the face of an outside invader, we cannot be sure that environmental pollution will appear as such a threat. An obvious difference is that pollution presents no readily identifiable person or group of persons on whom we can focus our hatred. As the content of wartime propaganda makes clear, it is the emotion of hatred that pulls groups together in times of conflict. But pollution is not a person or even a force that can be personified into a focus for hatred. The enemy, as Walt Kelly had Pogo declare, is us. Furthermore, the threat to our existence would not come suddenly, as the appearance of Martians would. The threat to life from pollution would be incremental, with only marginal changes from day to day. There is abundant evidence to show that human beings adjust readily to incremental changes. It takes abrupt changes to make people change in a radical way.[44]

The world has begun to take some small steps in the direction of confronting environmental problems. Part of Gorbachev's new thinking in foreign policy was a repeated call for cooperation on ecological issues. The academies of sciences in the two superpowers set up a joint committee on the environment. At a more practical level, the United States sent medical experts on radiation to the Soviet Union after the Chernobyl reactor exploded and burned. Several years later, the Soviet Union sent a large oil skimming vessel to help Americans clean up an oil spill from a grounded Exxon tanker near Valdez, Alaska.

Such steps were symbolically important but did little to solve the fundamental environmental issues facing the world. More significantly, the industrial states of the world were able to agree to curtail production of the most harmful types of CFC's believed to be depleting the ozone layer. By a treaty signed in Montreal in 1987, signatories agreed to cut production of CFC's in half. When new scientific evidence showed that the layer was depleting faster than believed, the states met again only a year later and drew up plans to phase out production altogether.

While a hopeful sign, this cooperation is still not a compelling argument for optimism. CFC's are a small item in world trade. The companies that manufacture them will lose billions in revenue in the short run but can expect to come up with substitutes that they will market. Some of the products for which CFC's are used are mainly luxuries—automobile air conditioning, for example. Others, such as home refrigerators, although viewed as necessities by Americans, are still uncommon in much of the world.

A more difficult issue to resolve will be global warming. Rich countries have focussed on the loss of tropical rainforests to timber-cutting, inundation by dams, and burning to clear land for agriculture. The poor countries where these forests are located protest that they need to use these lands for their own development. They in turn point to the gases released into the atmosphere by the 400,000,000 automobiles in the world, mostly in the wealthy countries. To emphasize this point, one conference on global warming proposed that motorists in rich countries be taxed to plant forests in poor countries.[45]

Such suggestions only begin to address the problem. One can imagine a reduction in the use of air-conditioners, which have become common only in the last decades. It is almost impossible to imagine human beings giving up the more universal use of fossil fuels, whether in coal-fired electric generating plants or in trucks and buses. Furthermore, even if production of warming gases is restrained, so long as the world's population continues to grow, use of fossil fuel will grow as well. Indeed, if the poor states of the world are to develop, their per capita use will have to increase even in the highly unlikely event that their population does not.

PREDICTED CONSEQUENCES FOR INTERNATIONAL POLITICS

Failure to solve the problem of pollution will mean a deterioration of the conditions of life for people all over the globe. Oceans will be too polluted for swimming and beaches too littered for sunbathing. An increase in UV radiation will make sunbathing unwise in any case. Changing climate patterns brought on by global warming may mean sweltering summers.

But such changes may be gradual and hard to blame on some one enemy. Other global issues, however, may lead to conflict between states. The problem of scarce resources has led one writer to warn that "'wars of redistribution' may be the only way by which the poor nations can hope to remedy their condition."[46] Another writer warns that the uneven effects of global warming, weakening some economies more than others, can exacerbate the risk of war or generate regional conflicts.[47] Although these writers go farther than others in making their warning explicit, the idea is implicit with many writers on questions of resources. Although such wars are possible, there are good reasons for thinking they are not likely.

Even a brief look at past cases shows that states are less likely to go to war when their populations are most miserable. An obvious case is Germany, which was not belligerent during the great inflation of 1923 but rather back in 1914, a period of unparalleled prosperity. The depression of the early 1930s may have helped Hitler come to power but it was not until the late 1930s, with prosperity returning, that Germany went to war again. More recently, Guatemala was threatening its neighbor Belize in the fall of 1975. The threats were forgotten following a devastating earthquake in Guatemala City in early 1976, even though the Guatemalans were clearly more miserable after the earthquake than before.

There are logical reasons for this behavior. During famine and other periods of hardship, people are too weak and too preoccupied with immediate survival to undertake military expeditions. A war between states is not the equivalent of a ghetto riot that ends with the looting of a supermarket. A war requires planning, preparation, training, and resources. Despite the recent emphasis on transnational ties, there are still borders between states and borders (at least those of advanced states) are still effective barriers, particularly against destitute and starving people. Furthermore, famine or other disaster does not come overnight and presumably a government capable of going to war (not all are) would have diverted as many resources as possible to coping with the emergency—factories would build tractors instead of tanks, fuel would go to irrigation pumps instead of jet aircraft, foreign exchange would buy grain instead of missiles. By the time these measures proved inadequate, the ability of the government to solve its problems by military means would be greatly reduced.

The emphasis on the large number of people living in the poor countries of the world creates a misleading impression of the military options available to them. A war of "redistribution" is unlikely and it is even more unlikely that such a war would involve a united front of all the poor countries in the world. Despite the convenience of labels such as "North" and "South," there are great differences among the Group of 77. Some members, such as Brazil, are approaching the industrialized states of the North in per capita income. (Brazil's most severe shortage is oil.) Other countries, such as Iran, are rich in oil, yet short in arable land, water, and minerals. Finally, some countries, such as Bangladesh, are deficient in all respects. It is difficult to imagine a single issue that could lead Brazil, Iran, and Bangladesh to cooperate in a military venture.

This does not exclude the possibility of political instability in a poor country or war between one poor state and another. Large-scale migration by starving people is possible over borders that are today poorly protected or not even well defined, as in much of central Africa. But such migration, which has already occurred along the southern edge of the Sahara Desert, has not been accompanied by violence. Even if it should be, it would be far from the war of South against North that predictions allude to.

A more likely possibility is that some poor states, perhaps only one, will resort not to war but to extortion to solve the problem of scarce resources. India has already exploded a nuclear device and a number of other states have the potential to do so. Once in the hands of the poor states, nuclear weapons may, as one writer suggests, "be used as an instrument to force the developed world to undertake a massive transfer of wealth to the poverty-stricken world"[48]

This is a possibility that must be taken more seriously than that of a head-on collision in war between rich and poor states. There have been cases in which such tactics have been employed within states. Radical groups in Argentina have forced business corporations to make large donations to hospitals in return for the release of kidnapped executives. In the United States the Symbionese Liberation Army succeeded in extorting a large donation of food from the Hearst family.

Nevertheless, there are reasons for thinking that this course of events is unlikely. Practically, though it may be possible for a poor state to fabricate a weapon, it would be difficult for it to come up with an accurate and reliable delivery system. To achieve its goal of forcing a redistribution of wealth, such a state would have to make an overt threat to use the weapon. But the threat would be a warning and with such a warning, a wealthy state could prepare to defend itself against whatever crude delivery systems (such as converted airliners) might be available. Of course there is a chance that such defensive preparations would fail, but the chance of failure might be small enough that a wealthy state would be willing to take it. Once such a device was used (or even only threatened), the likelihood that the threatened state would then agree to a transfer of wealth would virtually disappear. The citizens of such a state, obviously opposed already to such a transfer (otherwise the threat would not have been made) would self-righteously argue that the "barba-rous" conduct of the poor state making the threat was reason enough for refusing to comply. Instead of sending food or other resources, they would be more likely to send bombs.

In the world today a state confronted with massive poverty and starva-tion would appear to have a better chance of improving the life of its citizens by appealing to the moral responsibility of the rich states rather than trying to stir up their fears. The religious and political values widely shared in the rich countries recognize an obligation to relieve human suffering. Often in the past these countries have been able to avoid acting in accordance with their values because they were able to ignore the problems facing the rest of the world, but such developments as demands for the New International Economic Order have made that less and less probable.

However, although it might be prudent for the leader of a poor state to rely on moral appeals rather than nuclear threats, there is no guarantee that such appeals would meet with success. Indeed, some people have suggested that it will be the rich states that will resort to military force to maintain "the present stratified international system."[49] In this view, the threat to world peace occasioned by diminishing resources will come not from the poor states but the rich.

Asking people to give up what they already have is more difficult than denying them something they never had. A person can think of all kinds of justifications for maintaining an accustomed standard of living. Consider the remarks of President Johnson to American soldiers in Korea, made in 1966: "We don't ask for much, but what we ask for we are going to get, we are going to keep, we are going to hold."[50] Not all Americans agreed with President Johnson's assessment that "we don't ask for much" at a time when the "we" represented only 6 percent of the world's population but con-sumed 30 percent of the world's energy and 50 percent of the world's manufactured goods; but we cannot dismiss his remarks as coming from an unrepresentative minority. Indeed, President Johnson considered himself, and was considered by others, to be a humane man, genuinely interested in improving the condition of life of poor people. But clearly for him the poor people of his own country had a prior claim on wealth and resources. As the United States' share of world consumption has contracted in the 1980s from 50 percent to under 25 percent, Americans are even less willing to put global issues ahead of domestic ones.

AN EVALUATION

Whatever the final judgment of the experts, the belief is widespread that resources are going to be a major source of problems in coming years. There is a fear that resources will become more scarce and an expectation that demands for a fairer distribution of what resources there are will increase.

Whatever else, these beliefs about resources will create some new conflicts in international politics. Unresolved but unnoticed questions of boundaries will become sources of conflict if territory is suddenly suspected of containing oil or other minerals. For example, the group of Spratly Islands in the South China Sea became a potential source of conflict among the Philippines, Vietnam, and China because of the possibility of oil fields nearby.[51] The harmonious sharing of resources, possible in the past because there was plenty for all, may become less common as each state tries to guarantee its share of a diminishing resource. For example, the reduction of fish catches led Iceland to lay exclusive claim to the fishing grounds within 50 miles of Iceland, bringing Iceland's coast guard into conflict with British fishing boats and the British naval vessels sent to protect them.[52]

So far the attempts to solve problems of resources cooperatively have had little success. After years of effort the states of the world still have not agreed on laws to govern the use of the sea. In the past the waters called "the high seas" were open to all because their resources were not considered especially valuable and the means to exploit them were limited. Now that both of these factors have changed, interest in the outcome of international attempts to regulate the high seas is intense. Successful cooperation in this area could lead the way to global cooperation on the other issues of concern—population, food, resources, and pollution.[53]

It is difficult for a writer to avoid being caught up in the temper of the time. But it does appear that the issues discussed in this chapter are new and unprecedented. It does appear that they offer unprecedented opportunities and incentives for a kind of global cooperation never seen in the past. The record of human behavior does not support optimism; it is just as possible that the dire predictions of war or environmental catastrophe will be correct. But perhaps the belief that both the dangers and the opportunities are unprecedented will spur us to unprecedented efforts and we will achieve unprecedented results.

NOTES

1. Carl T. Rowan and David M. Mazie, "Is Population Control Impossible?" in *Politics and Environment*, 2nd ed. (Pacific Palisades, Calif.: Goodyear, 1975), p. 26. Another set of predictions using "doubling time" is found in Paul R. Ehrlich, *The Population Bomb* (New York: Balantine Books, 1968).

2. For a discussion of Malthus' ideas, see Robert L. Heilbroner, *The Worldly Philosophers* (New York: Simon & Schuster, 1953), Chapter 4.

3. Herman Kahn and William Brown, "A World Turning Point," in *The Next 25 Years*, ed. Andrew A. Sprekke (Washington, D.C.: The World Future Society, 1975), p. 25.

4. *The New York Times*, June 13, 1982, p. Y4.

5. Figures from Population Reference Bureau, Washington, D.C., *1988 World Population Data Sheet* for mid-1988.

6. Iowa's population is actually declining, from 2,914,000 in the 1980 census to about 2,850,000 in 1987. In 1987, Bangladesh had a population of 107,000,000 and a growth rate of 2.7 percent a year, or 2,890,000. Projections for future growth are from a World Bank study.

7. *The Economist*, March 19, 1983, p. 64.

8. Ali Abdul Walid, agronomist; *The Economist*, July 2, 1988, p. 38.

9. *Business Week*, July 3, 1978, p. 44.

10. Anthony Storr, *Human Aggression* (New York: Bantam, 1970), p. 135.

11. Stuart Bremer et al., "The Population Density and War Proneness of European Nations, 1816–1965," *Comparative Political Studies*, Vol. 6, No. 3 (October 1973), pp. 329–348; John A. Vasquez, "Statistical Findings in International Politics: A Data-Based Assessment," *International Studies Quarterly*, Vol. 20, No. 2 (June 1976), p. 200.

12. Nazli Choucri, *Population Dynamics and International Violence* (Lexington, Mass.: Lexington Books, 1974), p. 60.

13. William Paddock and Paul Paddock, *Famine—1975!* (Boston: Little, Brown, 1967).

14. Barbara Insel, "A World Awash in Grain," *Foreign Affairs*, Vol. 63, No. 4 (Spring 1985), p. 904.

15. Ibid., pp. 893, 904.

16. Lester R. Brown, "Reexamining the World Food Prospect," in Lester R. Brown et al., *State of the World 1989: A Worldwatch Institute Report* (New York: Norton, 1989), pp. 49–51.

17. "How to Feed the Third World," *The Economist*, March 22, 1975, p. 72.

18. Ibid.; Lester R. Brown, "The Next Crisis? Food," *Foreign Policy*, No. 13 (Winter 1973/74), pp. 3–33; James Reston, "How to MIRV a Cow," *The New York Times*, July 7, 1974.

19. Lester R. Brown, "The Next Crisis? Food," *Foreign Policy*, No. 13 (Winter 1973/74), p. 9.

20. Ibid., p. 31.

21. "How to Feed the Third World," *The Economist*, March 22, 1975, p. 72.

22. Lester R. Brown, Christopher Flavin, and Sandra Postel, "A World at Risk," in *State of the World 1989*, p. 12. (See note 16.)

23. John S. Steinhart and Carol E. Steinhart, "Energy Use in the U.S. Food System," *Science*, Vol. 184 (April 10, 1974), pp. 307–316.

24. Barry Commoner, *The Closing Circle* (New York: Bantam Books, 1971), Chapter 5.

25. Willis W. Harman, "Notes on the Coming Transformation," in *The Next 25 Years*, p. 14.

26. Donella H. Meadows et al., *The Limits to Growth* (New York: Universe Books, 1972).

27. Ibid., pp. 56–59.

28. Ibid., p. 163.

29. Wildred Beckerman, *In Defense of Economic Growth* (London: Jonathan Cape, 1974), pp. 218–224.

30. Ibid., p. 224.

31. Barry Hughes, *World Futures* (Baltimore: Johns Hopkins University Press, 1985), pp. 105–106.

32. Norman Macrae, "Survey: The Next Ages of Man," *The Economist*, December 24, 1988, p. 18.

33. Hughes, p. 166, referring to the *Global 2000 Report*.

34. *The Global 2000 Report to the President: Entering the Twenty-First Century*, Gerald O. Barney, study director, Vol. 1 (Washington, D.C.: U.S. Government Printing Office, 1980, p. 3).

35. Ibid., p. 39.

36. See, for example, Lester R. Brown and Sandra Postel, "Thresholds of Change," *State of the World 1987* (New York: W. W. Norton, 1987), pp. 3–19.

37. "Ozone Damage Overestimated?" *Chemistry*, Vol. 49, No. 4 (May 1976), p. 24.

38. Cynthia Pollock Shea, "Why Du Pont Gave Up $600 Million," *The New York Times*, April 10, 1988, p. F2.

39. Ibid.

40. Commoner, pp. 156–163. (See note 24.)

41. Robert Sherill, "Asbestos, the Saver of Lives, Has a Deadly Side," *The New York Times Magazine*, January 21, 1973, pp. 12ff.

42. "Drinking Water: Another Source of Carcinogens?" *Science*, Vol. 186, No. 4166 (November 29, 1974), pp. 809–811.

43. See the report by 150 scientists from eleven countries, coordinated by NASA, described by Philip Shabecoff, "Altered Atmosphere a Threat to Earth, New Study Warns," *The New York Times*, January 13, 1986, pp. Y1, Y6.

44. For specific application of this observation to international politics, see Robert Jervis, "Hypotheses on Misperception," *World Politics*, Vol. 20, No. 3 (April 1968), pp. 465–466.

45. New Delhi, India, February 1989, sponsored by International Union for Conservation of Nature and Natural Resources and Tata Energy Research Institute. Sanjoy Hazarika, "Global-Warming Panel Urges Gas Tax in West," *The New York Times*, February 26, 1989, p. Y6.

46. Robert L. Heilbroner, *An Inquiry into the Human Prospect* (New York: W. W. Norton, 1974), p. 43.

47. David A. Wirth, "Climate Chaos," *Foreign Policy*, No. 71 (Spring 1989), pp. 10, 13.

48. Heilbroner, p. 43. (See note 46.)

49. Dennis C. Pirages and Paul R. Ehrlich, *Ark II: Social Responses to Environmental Imperatives* (San Francisco: W. H. Freeman, 1974).

50. *The New York Times*, November 2, 1966.

51. Fox Butterfield, "Spratly Islands Causing Concern," *The New York Times*, January 25, 1976.

52. Robert Alden, "Cod War: High Seas Fishing Is No Sport," *The New York Times*, June 3, 1973, Section IV, P. E6.

53. John Temple Swing, "Who Will Own the Oceans?" *Foreign Affairs*, Vol. 54, No. 3 (April 1976), pp. 527–546.

THE UNITED STATES IN THE WORLD: THE FUTURE

Most fields of study, no matter how "academic," sooner or later involve real-life choices. English majors become editors who accept or reject manuscripts for publication. Psychology majors become clinicians who testify in child custody cases.

Political science in general, and international politics in particular, is no different. You have choices, from the personal ones of what to study and what career to pursue to the more social ones of whether or not to vote, for whom to vote, and what policy to advocate. If you believe military threats are still great, you may pursue a career in the military. If you think military threats have disappeared, you may work on the campaign of a candidate pledged to further defense cuts. If global warming alarms you, you may protest the clearing of rain forests.

The decisions you make will be better ones if they are based on an understanding of general principles and an acquaintance with facts. But the decisions do not follow inevitably from the principles and facts. People can be well versed in international politics and still advocate very different policies. Even most of the generalizations about international politics can be challenged. Perhaps this is to be expected. The more vital an issue is, the more it invites controversy.

THE PERSISTENCE OF SOVEREIGNTY

Consider the concept of sovereignty. Jacques Delors, the executive head of the European Community, said recently, "national sovereignty no longer means very much in the modern world economy."[1] Yet even as the EC was eroding the sovereignty of its members, new claims for sovereignty were being made in the other half of Europe. As the Soviet Union was breaking up, its last president, Mikhail Gorbachev, suggested that the name for its successor be the "Union of Sovereign States."

As Delors was speaking, a war was raging in Yugoslavia between members of constituent republics. The United Nations did not act to stop it and was extremely reluctant even to offer a peace-keeping force to monitor a cease-fire, once the parties had agreed to stop it themselves. The reason was sovereignty. Most members of the United Nations feared that any interference in Yugoslavia, however justified, could then be used as a precedent to intervene elsewhere. For them, the jealous preservation of sovereignty was worth the cost of lives lost by Croatians and Serbs and the destruction of historic monuments like Dubrovnik. The inaction of the world on Yugoslavia was a powerful rebuke to Delors' optimism.

Or consider this. At its annual meeting in 1991, the United Nations General Assembly debated a European proposal that the UN appoint a senior official, to be provided with $50 million in readily available funds, to coordinate disaster relief. Over the preceding two decades, over 3 million people had died and 800 million had been rendered homeless by disasters such as drought and floods. Aid from the rich countries to areas such as the Horn of Africa and the Middle East was often poorly handled, often because of political intervention. Governments in countries such as Sudan and Iraq tried to channel foreign aid toward supporters and away from opponents.

The proposal was endorsed by the major aid donors as well as by the Secretary General. Yet it was greeted by many members with hostility and suspicion. They opposed any automatic right to intervene, even to save lives: Disaster relief should come only at the invitation of governments. Speaking for the two-thirds of the members who consider themselves nonaligned, the representative from Ghana declared that "respect for sovereignty is not an idle stipulation which can be rejected outright in the name of even the most noble gestures."[2]

The persistence of sovereignty means the persistence of international anarchy. If an issue attracts international attention, as did Saddam Hussein's invasion of Kuwait in 1990, perhaps collective action may take place. But such attention is rare. Chances are the following issues will force you to consult a newspaper index: Indonesia's takeover of East Timor, Libya's annexation of part of Chad, or India's economic boycott of Nepal. In each of these cases world organizations such as the United Nations did not concern themselves, reinforcing the lesson that in the end each state must be responsible for its own security.

THE WORLD IS A DANGEROUS PLACE

Recently a political scientist, John Mueller, has advanced the proposition that war has become "rationally unthinkable."[3] He argues that war no longer makes economic sense and that leaders of states have come to realize that it does not. In fact, it has all but disappeared from their minds as an instrument of policy and become "subrationally unthinkable" as well.

The frequency of war over the past century will make many readers cautious in accepting Mueller's argument. Perhaps war has disappeared, yet it will take time for the memories to disappear. All the conditions that are commonly identified as causes of war remain: human nature, international anarchy, states with grievances, leaders willing to take risks, armaments.

Furthermore, the unexpectedness with which war has arisen in the past makes it hard to be comfortable with the end of the Cold War. Once the Napoleonic Wars had ended in 1815, the rest of the nineteenth century was seen as an era of peace. The wars in the 1860s and 1870s involving German unification were localized and short. The world entered the twentieth century expecting continued peace. Norman Angell had published a popular book, *The Great Illusion*, declaring war obsolete. This expectation made the shock of World War I all the greater. In more recent times wars have continued to come up unexpectedly. At the beginning of 1967 no one foresaw a war in the Middle East. Again in the Middle East, in 1973 no one outside of the leadership in Egypt and Syria expected a war. In 1990 American intelligence satellites recorded Saddam Hussein's military build-up along the border with Kuwait, yet the intelligence agencies were surprised that an invasion took place. War may be "subrationally unthinkable" for many people, but certainly not for all.

War remains a problem because of the weakness of other means of resolving conflict. Solutions that deal with arms are fraught with difficulty. Measures that focus on balancing arms are filled with risk of accident and misperception. Measures that call for restricting arms require trust and cooperation that is difficult to achieve among rivals.

Solutions that attack the problem of international anarchy run up against the obstacle of sovereignty. The United Nations has failed to deal with most of the conflicts that occurred during its existence because it could not override the sovereignty of its members. Collective action against aggression in Korea in 1950 and Kuwait in 1990 and 1991 was exceptional, the results of special circumstances not likely to be repeated often.

Because the possibility of war has not disappeared and because international mechanisms are so weak, states must still look to their own defenses.

Consider nuclear weapons. Despite a universally expressed horror of such weapons, the world has not been able to stop their spread. For years states as diverse as India, Israel, and Brazil invoked the concept of sovereignty to justify their refusal to sign the Nuclear Non-Proliferation Treaty. While formally denying nuclear programs, they also informally let it be understood that only the possession of their own nuclear arsenal let them feel secure against their enemies (India against China, Israel against Arab states, Brazil against Argentina). The nuclear potential of small states has then been used by the United States as a justification for continuing to spend for expensive missile defense programs.

But as the cost of such programs spirals out of control, traditional rhetoric about no price being too high for defense has begun to ring hollow. Today many people believe that defense burdens can easily be too high. The collapse of the Soviet economy, staggering under the burden of maintaining a fearsome arsenal, has provided vivid proof.

In the new economic conditions, a state must pay attention as much to its economy as to its defenses. In the summer of 1988, Henry Kissinger (who had been secretary of state under Nixon) and Cyrus Vance (who had been secretary of state under Carter) wrote, "When we served as secretaries of state [1973–1981], only a relatively small portion of our time was spent on international economic issues. Our successors do not have this luxury."[4]

Economic issues differ in important ways from military issues, yet the conditions of world politics remain the same—competition under international anarchy. Some states may find it possible to cooperate in economic matters such as free trade zones, just as states find it possible to cooperate in military alliances. But even as they cooperate, the fundamental problem of competing interests remains. America's prosperity will not come from an international decision. It will result only from actions by the United States itself.

AMERICAN INSTITUTIONS

As laid out in the first chapter in this book, there is a strong case that America is in decline. One can seek to arrest this decline by changing institutions and changing policies.

In a trenchant article in 1980, the head of a foreign policy institute delivered a harsh judgment on the inadequacy of American institutions. He wrote: "The growing inability of the U.S. system to deliver reliable policy adds to the worldwide impression of America as a foreign policy problem."[5] One example he could cite was America's reaction to the oil supply crisis of the 1970s. During the 1970s, oil prices rose rapidly, in part because of actions by the cartel of oil-producing states. The major developed states tried to lessen the cartel's power by reducing consumption. Despite repeated promises to do so at economic summits, the United States government did not deliver. In 1977 President Carter boldly announced an energy policy to reduce dependence on foreign sources, a policy which he called "the moral equivalent of war." But only one year, six months, and nineteen days later was an energy bill signed into law, and it was a watered-down, much-compromised version of Carter's original proposals. In subsequent years the United States did reduce both consumption and imports of oil, but the great amount of time it took, particularly compared with other industrialized states, does not encourage optimism about meeting future challenges.

President Reagan convinced many voters that it was "morning again" in America but did little to improve America's ability to deliver reliable policy. The country under Reagan again demonstrated its sclerosis, failing to deal with the large federal budget deficit, again despite repeated promises to allies at economic summits. To make up the deficit, the federal government had to borrow, and to attract borrowers it had to keep interest rates high, thereby forcing other countries to keep their interest rates high if they wanted to attract investors. The American budget deficit was a burden carried by other states. The President refused to propose new taxes; Congress lacked the courage to raise taxes itself but also refused to cut spending. Only the ability of the Federal Reserve system to raise and lower interest rates kept the system in balance without severe inflation or recession, prompting the British journal *The Economist* to describe the chairman of the Federal Reserve as "the only moving part" in America's policymaking machinery, otherwise clogged by the checks and balances of separation of powers and pressure group politics.[6]

Even members of the United States government agreed with such criticism. In a 1987 sample of 114 members of Congress, 95 percent found the legislative process too chaotic—for example, far too much time was taken up with an ineffectual budget process.[7]

In 1987, in behavior unusual for a people priding itself on being modern and progressive, Americans lavished time and money congratulating themselves on having one of the oldest constitutions in the world. Yet states that have drawn up constitutions more recently (Japan, 1947; Germany, 1949; France, 1958) seem to be performing better—responding quickly to changes, managing resources, and planning for the future. Today Americans might well ask themselves, "Is an eighteenth-century document compatible with the twentieth century?"

An example of the problem is the "division of powers," designed to keep tyrants like King George III from assuming despotic power. In normal circumstances, both houses of Congress and the president must agree in order for a law to come into effect. In the first 150 years of the American republic, the president and the majority in two houses of Congress came from the same political party. Only 25 percent of the time were they split. But from President Truman through Reagan, our government has been "divided" 60 percent of the time; in the last 20 years, 80 percent.[8] Typically Congress refuses to pass legislation requested by the president and the president vetoes legislation passed by Congress.

AMERICAN POLICIES

A discussion of policies for America is more difficult. Policies are associated with the political positions taken by parties or factions within parties. In order to sidestep the issue of partisanship, it is useful to look at advice coming from abroad.

During the Structural Impediment Initiative talks with the Japanese in 1989 and 1990, the Japanese made many suggestions. Among the ones most emphasized were:

Increase the savings rate.

One can argue that the American economy began to decline in the early 1970s, yet Americans did not notice because their family incomes did not drop. In part this was true because more members of a family worked. In 1960, fewer than one-third of women with children under 18 held jobs outside the home; by 1987 almost two-thirds did. Indeed, by 1988 over half of new mothers held jobs, despite the difficulty of caring for an infant while working outside the home.

But another reason family income did not decline was borrowing. Consumer debt, as a percentage of after-tax personal income, rose from 62.7 percent in 1970 to 74.9 percent in 1980 to 96.9 percent in 1990.[9] It is not surprising that the savings rate for Americans is as low as 2 or 3 percent of income. Admittedly one can find economists who are not alarmed by the low savings rate,[10] and one can hear pleas from politicians to spend more, not less. Yet countries that are doing well economically have high savings rates. In 1989 Japan's saving rate was 15.3 percent and Germany's was 12.2 percent. By contrast, America's was 5.6 percent.[11]

Various policies have been suggested to accomplish this goal. Consumption could be taxed more. Income from savings could be taxed less. Going into debt in order to consume could be made more difficult.

Invest more.

Americans are urged to save so that they will have money to invest. Economists disagree over the precise importance of investment, but comparing figures for different countries suggests that investment is important.

From 1964 to 1985, both German and Japanese labor productivity grew at around 5 percent per year. That means that each German or Japanese worker on average produced 5 percent more goods each year—a very great improvement indeed, and noticeable in the economic booms associated with both economies. American labor productivity in the same period was growing at less than 1 percent a year.

One clue to the reason that German and Japanese productivity was growing so rapidly is in the rate at which their economies were devoting resources to capital investment. In those years, German capital was growing at a rate per worker of better than 4 percent; Japanese capital was growing at a rate of more than 8 percent. In the same period American capital was growing at less than 2 percent per worker.[12]

The American economy was so much larger at the beginning of that time period that no one paid much attention to the difference in investment rates. But over time the German and Japanese economies began to approach the American. Lagging rates of labor productivity and investment received new attention.

Increase support for education and worker training.

One might argue that money in American industry is going to the wrong place. In 1960, the average salary of the chief executives of America's 100 largest nonfinancial corporations was $190,000, which was equivalent to 40 times the earnings of an average factory worker (or 12 times after taxes). In the late 1980s, the average salary had risen to $2,000,000, which was equivalent to 93 times the earnings of an average factory worker (or 70 times after taxes).[13]

At the same time, little was being do to train or educate workers. In 1988, Roger Smith, the head of General Motors, got a bonus of $3.7 million. Production workers at General Motors each got $254 in a profit-sharing scheme.[14] One finds it hard to imagine workers straining for excellence in performance for a bonus that amounts to an extra $4.88 a week.

A work force that is not well cared for will, over time, not perform well. Some years ago Ezra Vogel outlined sources of Japanese strength—Japanese businesses make constant surveys of their work-force needs. In cooperation with the government, they work out new training requirements and use retraining programs to provide new jobs for those workers who are displaced by a changing economy. The result of these policies is the maintenance of a social fabric in which the majority share the national goals.[15]

When the Japanese opened a Toyota plant in Tennessee, they deliberately kept it a low-tech clone of an existing plant in Japan. Yet they spent far more time training workers than GM did at its new high-tech plant in Hamtramck. A study of performance in the automobile industry found the Japanese "transplant" factories more efficient than any American company.[16]

Much is made of the greater emphasis the Japanese education system places on engineers, yet there is also a difference in the way engineers are treated. One study found that on the average, Japanese engineers spend twice as much time designing products and half as much time in meetings as their American counterparts. The study also found that American production engineers were treated contemptuously in such ways as not being shown a design until manufacturing begins, or being asked to draw every component, whether standard or not.[17]

Abandon the short-term mentality.

One can lay off workers, and if the remaining workers produce the same number of goods, worker productivity goes up. Some of the gain in worker productivity in the United States over the past decade can be attributed to such layoffs. But the loss of jobs does society no good and, in the absence of other measures to improve economic performance, offer only a short-term solution and reflect a mentality that some foreign observers believe is a source of America's economic troubles. Akio Morita, the president of Sony, said, comparing Japan with America, "We are focusing on business ten years in advance, while you seem to be concerned only with profits ten minutes from now. At that rate, you may well never been [*sic*] able to compete with us."[18]

Specific policies that would lead to a change in attitude may be more difficult to devise. The Japanese suggested that the Americans change the requirement that companies issue quarterly reports. The Securities and Exchange Commission requires this of companies that trade stock, and because the stock market is the major way in which American companies raise capital, they must comply. But a short-term fall in profits shows up in the quarterly report, leading to a fall in the value of a stock. Thus managers pay more attention to performance over a three-month period than they do to the long term. Under these conditions it makes sense to sell off a patented product or process for short-term gain, even if it enables another company to compete successfully over time.

Many other factors in contemporary American culture contribute to an emphasis on the short-run. The most common form of television and radio presentation about politics is the 30 second "spot." Newspapers and magazines run "briefs" instead of stories; even those stories that are run are shorter than in the past. Books with titles like *The One Minute Manager* do well. Reversing such cultural trends is difficult.

CONCLUSION

Underlying all these recommendations is the need for a shift in fundamental attitudes. Those making this recommendations suggest that America must first take international competitiveness seriously. Military threats from Pearl Harbor to Saddam Hussein, have been taken seriously. By contrast, economic threats are less immediate and arouse less emotion. The task of policymakers is to get them taken seriously without turning them into military threats. Phrases like "an economic Pearl Harbor" are not only overworked but in major senses misleading. Military conflict is not the same thing as economic competition. But both must be taken seriously.

A great many issues compete for America's attention. To judge from the rhetoric on university campuses, AIDS, cultural diversity, and feminism are the major concerns of the day. But to one degree or another the solutions to such problems will depend on economic health. A shrinking economy will make it more difficult for women and other underrepresented groups to obtain a fair share, or for the expected increase in people with AIDS to receive medical treatment. The issues are connected. Concern with any domestic issue only heightens concern for the fundamental health of the American polity in a changing world.

NOTES

1. John Ardagh, "Will the New Europe Please Sit Down," [profile of Jacques Delors], *The New York Times Magazine*, November 10, 1991, pp. 42, 44, 46.
2. Paul Lewis, "Disaster Aid Plan Upsets Third World," *The New York Times*, November 13, 1991, p. Z A4.
3. *Retreat from Doomsday* (New York: Basic Books, 1989), e.g., p. 240.
4. Henry Kissinger and Cyrus Vance, "Bipartisan Objectives for Foreign Policy," *Foreign Affairs*, Vol. 66, No. 5 (Summer 1988), p. 910.
5. Thomas L. Hughes, "The Crack-Up," *Foreign Policy*, No. 40 (Fall 1980), p. 43.
6. Leader, January 7, 1989, p. 13.
7. Julie Johnson, "Harried Lawmakers Find Congress 'Too Chaotic,' " *The New York Times*, January 13, 1988, p. Y9.
8. Lloyd Cutler, "The Cost of Divided Government," *The New York Times*, November 22, 1987, p. E27.
9. Leonard Silk, "Economic Scene: Behind the Gloom of Consumers," *The New York Times*, November 29, 1991, p. Z C2.
10. For example, Robert Eisner, "Low U.S. Savings Rate: A Myth," *The New York Times*, March 11, 1990, p. Z A23.
11. Central Intelligence Agency, *Handbook of Economic Statistics 1990*, "Personal Savings Rates."
12. Ralph Landau, "Capital Investment: Key to Competitiveness and Growth," *Brookings Review*, Vol. 8, No. 3 (Summer 1990), pp. 52–56.
13. Robert B. Reich, *The Work of Nations*, (New York: Alfred A. Knopf, 1991) p. 7.
14. Maryann Keller, *Rude Awakening* (New York: Morrow, 1989), p. 256.
15. Ezra Vogel, "Pax Nipponica?" *Foreign Affairs*, Vol. 64, No. 4 (Spring, 1986), p. 763.
16. Keller, p. 210 (see note 14); study of performance in US auto industry since 1979 by Harbour & Associates Inc., Troy, Mich., cited in Doron P. Levin, "Study Says Ford Is a Leader in Efficiency," *The New York Times*, January 3, 1990, p. Z C4.
17. Study by Leif Soderberg, partner with McKinsey (consultancy firm), in *The Economist*, February 18, 1988, p. 68.
18. Quotation from an unauthorized translation of the book *A Japan That Can Say No*, cited by James Fallows, "Wake Up, America!" *The New York Review of Books*, March 1, 1990, p. 14.

INDEX

Abel, Theodore, 157
ABM (antiballistic missile)
  Treaty, 226, 230, 232
  weapons, 174, 175, 176, 214–215, 217, 219, 226
Accidental war, 225–226, 227–228, 380
Acheson, Dean G., 62–63, 198, 282
Action–reaction (in arms races), 173–175
Adjudication, 352–256
Afghanistan, 71, 124–125, 266, 341, 375, 383
Aggression, definition of, 148, 312–314, 318
Air, regime of, 274
Aix-la-Chapelle, Congress of, 273
Alabama case, 352
Albania, 354–355
Algeria, 235, 322, 346–347, 372, 390–391
Alsace and Lorraine, 27–28, 36, 39, 41, 161, 325
Ambassador, 272–273, 326
Amin, Idi, 142
Anarchy, 146–150, 242
Anderson, Jack, 4–5
Angell, Norman, 32, 443
Angola, 299, 322, 323

Antarctica, 137, 188, 275
Anticolonialism, 284–285
Appeasement, 45–46, 135
Aqaba, Gulf of, 81
Arab League, 319–320, 323, 357
Arab nationalism, 77
Arafat, Yasir, 89, 90
Arbitration, 351–352, 357
Argentina, 122, 175–176, 178, 188, 388
Aristotle, 153, 157, 160
Arms control, 223–236
Arms race
  causes of, 173–177
  costs of, 178–180
  definition of, 169–170
  quantitative, 170–172
  technological, 173–175, 179
  US–USSR, 170, 173, 174–175, 178
  and war, 135, 168–170, 177–178
ASEAN (Association of South East Asian Nations), 270, 414
Assured destruction, 213–217
Atom bomb, 48–49, 68–69. *See also* Nuclear weapons.
Attaché, 326–327, 331–332

Austria
  Habsburg Empire, 18–28, 40, 45, 136,
    157, 161, 171
  modern, 60, 313, 337–338, 341
Axelrod, Robert, 202–203
Ayacucho Pact, 188
Azerbaijan, 54–55

Balance of power, 289–299, 301, 302–303
Bangladesh, 11, 98–101, 142, 158, 161,
    258, 387, 424
Baruch plan, 198
Beck, James, 36
Begin, Menachem, 89, 339
Belgium, 163, 184, 341
Belize, 435
Bell, Coral, 70
Bennett, William J., 406
Ben-Gurion, David, 79
Berlin, 59, 62, 293
Bernadotte, Count Folke, 349, 371
Biafra, 161, 368
Biological weapons, 186, 191, 224, 230,
    234, 235, 275
Bipolarity, 60–61, 290
Bismarck, Otto von, 18–30, 197
Black Sea, 334
Bodin, Jean, 139–140
Bolivia, 308
Bombing, strategic, 47–48, 206, 207
Bradley, Omar, 63
Brazil, 353
Britain. *See under subject headings.*
Brown, Lester, 388
Brzezinski, Zbigniew, 294
Bullock, Alan, 157
Bunche, Ralph, 349, 372, 373
Bundy, McGeorge, 212, 216
Bush George, 6, 191, 200, 245, 246, 291,
    299, 318

Cambodia, 250, 274, 368, 370
Canada, 189, 199, 254, 255–256, 261,
    326, 332, 358, 414
Cannon shot rule, 286
CAP (Common Agricultural Policy), 265,
    269
Carter, Jimmy, 17, 177, 215, 327, 329,
    430, 444, 445
Castro, Fidel, 121, 130, 341
Catalytic war, 225
CFCs (chlorofluorocarbons), 431–432, 434

Chaco war, 308, 364
Chad, 235, 322–323, 442
Chamberlain, Neville, 17, 45, 147, 316
Chamizal tract, 357
Chemical warfare. *See* Poison gas.
Cheney, Dick, 234
Chile, 285, 388
China, 66–69, 99–100, 122, 141, 143,
    146, 160, 175, 197, 220, 225, 275,
    277, 307, 331, 332, 335, 345, 376,
    386, 426
Cholera, 391
Christian Democrats, 262–263
Christian view of war, 151, 153–154
Church, Frank, 245
Churchill, Winston, 55, 282, 291, 292
Clark, Grenville, 252–253, 257
Clausewitz, Carl von, 18, 22, 28, 29, 90,
    95, 112
Club of Rome, 423, 429–430
Cockfield, Lord, 266, 267
Cold War, 53–61, 69–72, 366, 378
Collective security, 301–324, 377–378
Common Market. *See* Europe, EEC.
Conciliation, 348
Congo, 293, 379. *See also* Zaïre.
Connally Reservation, 358
Constantine Plan, 390
Conventional Forces in Europe,
    Treaty on, 200
Corfu Channel, 354–355, 357
Correlates of War, 425
Costa Rica, 168, 256, 323
Cousins, Norman, 211, 248–249
Cresson, Edith, 402
Cruise missiles, 199, 235
Cuba, 226, 234, 261, 277, 280, 281, 341,
    343, 369, 372, 376
Cuius regio euius religio, 136
Cutch, Rann of, 351
Cyprus, 101–106, 158, 161, 244, 259, 299,
    330, 339, 340, 346, 349, 379–380,
    381, 422
Czechoslovakia, 40, 44–46, 49, 59, 142,
    147, 162, 194–195, 263, 316

Damage limitation strategy, 214–215
Dante, 241–242
Dayan, Moshe, 85, 88
Defense
  concept of, 210–211
  weapons, 217–220

Defense budget, 8, 187–188, 200
Deficit, trade, 401
de Gaulle, Charles, 142, 265, 295, 390
Delors, Jacques, 442
Deng Xiaoping, 2
Denmark, 22–23, 163, 256, 265, 337
Deterrence, 119–120, 210–217, 220
Diplomacy, 244, 272–274, 285, 304, 325,
   343, 371
Disarmament, 40, 183–203, 257
Dobrynin, Antoli, 334, 337
Dominica, 140–141
Dominican Republic, 342
Domino theory, 316
Dreadnought, 172, 198
Dulles, John Foster, 61, 64, 82

Ecuador, 285, 330
Egypt, 80–88, 90, 224, 330, 346, 355,
   367, 369, 378, 389, 424
Eisenhower, Dwight D., 82, 178, 195, 198,
   316, 345, 373, 389, 392
El Salvador, 126
Enhanced radiation warhead, 231
Espionage, 228–230
Ethiopia, 194, 235, 304, 308–311,
   321–322, 364, 391, 426
Europe
   ECSC (European Coal and Steel Commu-
      nity), 263, 264
   EEC (European Economic Community),
      144, 254, 265–266, 337
   integration of, 263–269
   Project 1992, 266–269, 413
Eyskens, Mark, 269

Fait accompli, 69, 317–318
Fay, Sidney B., 36, 42
Finite deterrence, 211–215, 221
Fisher, Sir John, 168, 172
Food, 426–428
Ford, Gerald, 329
France, 24, 26–28, 140, 142, 161, 169,
   170–172, 184, 185, 187, 190, 193,
   197, 220, 232, 236, 246, 247, 258,
   277, 353, 405
Franz Ferdinand, Archduke, 33, 34, 36
Functionalism, 385–394

Gaddis, John Lewis, 70, 71
Gandhi, Indira, 99, 244
Gas. *See* Poison gas.

GATT (General Agreement on Trade and
   Tariffs), 412–413
Geneva
   Conference on Continental Shelf (1958),
      353
   Conference on Disarmament (1922), 185,
      187, 190
   Conference on the High Seas (1958), 274
   Conference on Indochina (1954), 350
   Convention on Prisoners of War (1929),
      275, 287
   Gas Protocol (1925), 111, 275, 277, 278,
      279
Germany, 1, 8–9, 10, 18–30, 163, 175,
   184, 185, 190, 193, 194, 196, 208,
   209, 230, 232, 233–234, 236, 257,
   258, 267, 310–312, 390
Ghana, 442
Global 200 Report, 430
Goa, 284, 314, 316
Golan Heights, 85, 87
Gonzalez, Henry B., 245
Good offices, 346–347, 372
Gorbachev, Mikhail, 2, 11, 95, 191, 192,
   193, 330, 374, 434, 442
Greece, 56–58, 101–106, 242, 256, 265
Greenhouse effect, 433
Grenada, 295, 299
Grew, Joseph, 158
Grotius, Hugo, 140, 285
Group of 77, 436
Groves, Leslie, 48
Guatemala, 435
Guevara, Ché, 197
Guinea, 391
Gulf War 1980–1988. *See* Iraq, war with
   Iran.
Gulf War 1991. *See* Iraq, war with US-led
   coalition.

Haas, Ernst, 356–357
Haas, Michael, 293
Hague conferences, 187, 188, 274–275,
   280, 304, 352
Haile Selassie, 309, 311, 312
Haiti, 11
Hamilton, Alexander, 2, 23
Hammarskjöld, Dag, 370, 372, 373,
   377–379, 380, 381
Hayes, Rutherford, 218
Herter, Christian, 286
Herzl, Theodor, 76

Hijacking, 372
Hitler, Adolf, 17, 43–46, 135, 157, 158, 159, 161, 162, 168, 298, 312, 313, 425
Hoare, Samuel, 310
Hobbes, Thomas, 137
Hollings, Thomas, 3
Holsti, K. J., 356
Home, Douglas, 95
Honda, 415–416
Honduras, 356
Hot Line, 227–228
Human rights, 401
Hungary, 119, 269, 373
Huntington, Samuel, 177–178
Hussein, King (Jordan), 88, 91
Hyderabad, 315

Iacocca, Lee, 409, 410
IAEA (International Atomic Energy Agency), 235, 236, 392
ICBM (*intercontinental ballistic missiles*), 173, 225, 228–229, 234
Iceland, 168
Idealism, 17–18
IGO (intergovernmental organization), 144–146
IMF (International Monetary Fund), 2
India, 96, 197, 225, 232, 236, 243, 244, 254, 256, 284, 315, 334, 367, 376, 386, 424, 426, 442
  war with Pakistan, 98–101, 295, 329, 351, 363
Indonesia, 442
INF (Intermediate Nuclear Forces) agreement, 191, 192, 199
Inquiry, 347
Integration, regional, 261–270
International Court of Justice, 352–356
Intifada, 91–92
Iran, 54–55, 107–113, 225, 234, 285, 298, 327, 331, 342, 347. *See also* Azerbaijan.
Iraq, 195, 196, 197, 220, 225, 233, 234–236, 245, 246, 275, 305–306, 318, 319–320, 323, 347, 377
  war with Iran, 107–113, 121, 186, 291, 298
  war with US-led coalition, 6–7, 291, 298, 317, 362–363, 369, 375, 442
Ireland, 243, 254, 256, 259, 265

Israel, 80–92, 122, 123, 126, 197, 224, 227, 256, 295, 313–314, 327, 329, 330, 342, 346, 370, 378, 393
Italy, 187, 194, 308–311, 337–338, 346, 347–348
ITU (International Telecommunications Union), 393–394

Japan, 64, 158, 187, 190, 195, 196, 231–232, 275, 307, 311, 333–334, 340, 401–411, 425
Jarring, Gunnar, 349, 372
Jenkins, Brian, 126
Johnson, Lyndon B., 245, 342, 437
Jordan, 80, 84–85, 88, 91

Kahn, Herman, 232–233, 248–249, 253
Kennedy, John F., 61, 220, 345
Kennedy, Paul, 294
Kenya, 424
Khomeini, Ruhollah, 108, 112, 327, 374
Khrushchev, Nikita, S., 220, 225, 228
Kim Il Sung, 64, 121
Kissinger, Henry, 7, 87–88, 329, 334, 339, 340, 349, 373, 444
Korea, 119, 122, 144, 162, 185, 210, 231, 254, 314, 315, 335, 341, 364, 402
  war in 61–69
Kosygin, Aleksei, 217, 218, 337
Krugman, Paul, 415
Kurds, 124, 377
Kurile Islands, 336–337
Kurth, James, 176
Kuwait, 122, 123, 220, 245, 268, 291, 298, 317, 318, 319–320, 323, 369, 375, 442, 443

Laval, Pierre, 310
Law, international, 271–288
League of Nations, 43, 57, 149, 162, 303–312, 364, 377
Lebanon, 126, 259, 299, 380, 382
Leibnitz, Gottfried Wilhelm, 141
Lenin, V. I., 35–36, 159–160
Liberty, 227
Libya, 235, 266, 274, 322–323, 442
Lilienthal, David, 298
Lippmann, Walter, 245
LOADS (low-altitude defense system), 219
Lobster War, 353
Locust control, 391
Lorenz, Konrad, 154–156

Lorraine. *See* Alsace and Lorraine.
Luce, Henry, 1

Maastricht, 267
MacArthur, Douglas, 64, 65, 67, 190, 258, 376
McGovern, George, 377, 380
McNamara, Robert, 9, 174, 211–212
MAD (*mutual assured destruction*). *See* Assured destruction.
Makarios, Archbishop, 103
Malthus, Thomas Robert, 423, 426, 428
Manchuria, 306–307, 364
Marcos, Ferdinand, 328
Marshall, George C., 7, 58, 59, 263, 295
Marx, Karl, 159
Mazzini, Giuseppe, 161
Mediation, 348–351, 375
Mediterranean, pollution in, 392
Meese, Edwin, 128
Melman, Seymour, 9, 186
"Merchants of death," 157–158
Mexico, 247, 254, 258, 261, 281, 357, 369, 424
Midgetman, 232
Military planning, 33
MIRV (*multiple, independently targetable re-entry vehicle*), 173–174
Missile gap, 229
MITI (Ministry of International Trade and Industry), 406
Mobilization, 34–35
Mobuto Sesu Seko, 322
Moltke, Helmuth von, 25
Monroe Doctrine, 341
Montreal Protocol on Ozone Layer (1987), 434
Montreux Convention, 334–335
Morgenthau, Hans J., 154
Morita, Akio, 448
Morocco, 235, 322, 332, 359
Moss, Frank, 245–246
Moynihan, Daniel Patrick, 5, 7–8
Mozambique, 129
Mueller, John, 199, 200, 443
Mujibur Rahman, 98
Mulroony, Brian, 255
Multi-Fiber Agreement, 411
Multinational corporation, 145
Multipolar. *See* Balance of power.
Munich (conference), 45–46, 298, 316
Mussolini, Benito, 42, 308

NAFTA (North American Free Trade Area), 414
Namibia, 323, 370, 383
Nasser, Abdul Gamel, 81–86, 122, 314, 342, 371
Nation, 138–139
Nationalism, 101–106, 263
NATO (North Atlantic Treaty Organization), 8, 60, 101, 103, 193, 200, 302
Nauru, 140
Neo-Malthusians, 430, 431
Nepal, 442
NGO (nongovernmental organization), 145
Nicaragua, 7, 126, 128, 131, 273, 323, 356, 381
Nicolson, Harold, 335
Nigeria, 318, 368
Nixon, Richard M., 60, 158, 179, 210, 244, 294, 320, 328, 345
Nobel, Alfred, 205
Non-Proliferation Treaty, 197, 199, 235–236, 276, 277, 278, 283, 337, 444
North–South conflict, 436
Norway, 228, 254, 265, 282, 327
Nuclear weapons
   characteristics of, 206–207
   disarmament of, 185, 186–187
   effects on peace, 207–210
   proliferation of, 122–124
Nuclear winter, 215–217
Nutting, Anthony, 371
Nye, Gerald, 157, 159
Nye, Joseph, 5

OAS (Organization of American States), 319, 342, 357
OAU (Organization of African Unity), 319, 321–323, 357
Ogaden, 321–322
Oil, 3, 111–112, 243
ONUC (*Opération des Nations Unies—Congo*), 379
OPEC (Organization of Petroleum Exporting Countries), 3, 108
"Open skies," 195, 198
Oppenheimer, J. Robert, 48
Overkill, 208
Ozone, 11, 431–432, 434

Pacta sunt servanda, 282
Pakistan, 96–101, 122, 225, 228, 232, 243, 254, 329, 351, 363, 367

Palestinians, 88–92, 127, 128, 129, 144, 251, 266, 329, 346, 372, 383
Pannikar, K. M., 67
Paquette Habana, 277
Paraguay, 251, 308
Paris, Pact of (Renunciation of War), 149
Partial Test Ban Treaty (1963), 197, 275, 277
Patriot missile, 6
Pax romana, 247, 257
Pearson, Drew, 4
Pearson, Lester, 378
Péréz de Cuéllar, Javier, 373
Permissive Action Link (PAL), 225, 234
Peru, 281, 285
PFLP. *See* Palestinians.
Philippines, 160, 328
PLO. *See* Palestinians.
Poison gas, 37–38, 42, 47, 111, 123, 186, 194, 197, 226–227, 230–231, 233–234, 275, 287
Poland, 7, 39, 43, 49, 54, 149, 162, 185, 292, 332
Pollution, 392
Population, 422–425
Portugal, 265
Poseidon, 176
Powell, Colin, 121
Preventive diplomacy, 377
Prisoners' dilemma, 201–202
Proliferation, nuclear, 234
Prussia. *See* Germany.

Quayle, Dan, 407

Rabi, Isador, 48
Rann of Cutch. *See* Cutch, Rann of.
Rapoport, Anatol, 202
Reagan, Ronald, 167, 179, 188, 191, 192, 217–218, 270, 286, 299, 328, 445
Realism, 18
Rebus sic stantibus, 282–293
Recognition, 141–144
Red Cross, International Committee of, 372
Regimes, 235
Regionalism, 261–270, 318–324
Reich, Robert, 11
Renamo (Mozambique National Resistance), 129
Reparations, 27, 40–41
Resources, 428–430
Revisionists, 36

Rhineland (demilitarized zone), 40, 44, 313
Rhodes formula, 372
Rhodesia, 129
Richardson, Lewis F., 169
Rickover, Hyman, 407
Robbers' Cave, 389
Rousseau, Jean-Jacques, 146, 200
Ruhr, 42
Rumania, 54, 59, 129
Rush–Bagot Agreement, 189, 199
Rusk, Dean, 158, 337
Russell, Richard, 340
Russia, 171, 187

Saar, 39, 41, 43
Sadat, Anwar, 86, 90, 224, 339
Saddam Hussein, 5, 108, 109, 121, 122, 123, 131, 196, 197, 200, 220, 235, 268, 318, 375, 376, 442, 443
Sagan, Carl, 216
Sahara, Spanish, 322, 359, 375, 383
Salinas de Gortari, Carlos, 414
SALT (Strategic Arms Limitation Talks), 193, 224, 226, 229
Satellite, artificial earth, 229–230, 234, 291
Schleswig-Holstein, 22–23
Schlieffen Plan, 33, 34
Schuman, Robert, 262, 263
Schwarzkopf, Norman, 376
Scud (missile), 110, 121, 122, 196, 317
SDI (Strategic Defense Initiative), 217–220
Sea, law of, 274, 286
Seabed, 276
Security dilemma, 149
Self-help, 148
Serbia, 34, 36, 37, 40, 45, 157
Seven Weeks' War, 24–26, 28
Shaba, 322
Si vis pacem para bellum, 168–169, 175, 205
Smallpox, 386–388, 392
Social contract, 137–138, 387
Sohn, Louis, 252–253, 257
Somalia, 235, 321–322, 391
Sources of law, 276–277
South Africa, 122, 236, 341, 370
South Tyrol. *See* Tyrol.
Sovereignty, 139–141, 149–150, 274, 309, 386, 391, 394, 442, 443
Spain, 143, 265
Spanish Sahara. *See* Sahara.

Spending, defense. *See* Defense budget.
Spratly Islands, 438
Sri Lanka, 125
Star wars. *See* SDI.
START (Strategic Arms Reduction Talks), 192, 199, 224
State
  definition of, 137–139
  state-centric system, 136–144
Stinger missile, 132
Structural Impediments Initiative, 413
Submarines, 38–39, 276, 279–280, 287
Sudetenland, 40, 44, 45, 194, 298, 316
Suez, 81–83, 85–88, 310, 378
Switzerland, 60, 140, 162, 168, 185
Syria, 85, 87, 89, 323, 346, 349

Taft, William Howard, 352, 357, 358
Taiwan, 64, 122, 370, 402
Tallinn line, 174
Tanzania, 322
Technology, 24–26, 33, 37–39, 47–49, 173–175, 176, 179
Terrorism, 81, 83, 125–132, 267
Test ban. *See* Partial Test Ban Treaty.
Thatcher, Margaret, 266
Third parties, 345–359, 370
Third World, 60–61
Thompson, Llewellyn E., 348
Threshold, 230–231
Thucydides, 18
Timor, East, 442
Tiran, Strait of, 81–83, 84, 313–314, 355
Tocqueville, Alexis de, 390
Toyota, 447
Trade. *See* World trade.
Treaties, 175–177
Trieste, 347–348, 350
Truman, Doctrine, 56–58
Truman, Harry S., 59, 63
Turkey, 56–58, 101–106, 149, 242, 256, 299, 334–335
Tyrol, 40, 41, 45, 311, 312, 337–338

Uganda, 142, 322, 368
UNEF (United Nations Emergency Force), 367, 378–379
UNFICYP (United Nations Force in Cyprus), 379–380, 381
UNFIL (United Nations Interim Force in Lebanon), 392

Union of Soviet Socialist Republics (USSR). *See under subject headings.*
United Nations
  Charter, 361, 364
  and collective security, 318, 363–364, 375–377
  Fund for Population Activities, 423
  General Assembly, 100–101, 365, 368, 382, 442
  in international politics, 138, 142, 162, 168, 195, 252–253, 327, 357, 361–383, 443
  in Korea, 64, 69, 158
  and Middle East, 79, 350–351, 369
  peacekeeping, 371, 377–383
  Resolution 242, 91–92, 350–351
  Secretary-General, 346–347
  Security Council, 55, 350
United States. *See under subject headings.*
United States Information Agency, 331
Uniting for Peace Resolution, 365, 382
Universal Postal Union, 304, 391
U Thant, 346, 367
U-2 aircraft, 228–229

Vance, Cyrus, 350, 373, 444
Vattel, Emerich de, 140
Venezuela, 175, 284, 323
VER (voluntary export restraint), 410, 411
Veracruz, 281
Versailles, Treaty of, 39–41, 42, 44, 142, 184, 187, 190, 234, 283, 284, 313, 339
Vienna Congress (1815), 272–273
Vienna Convention (1961), 273, 330–332
Vietnam, 71, 124–125, 147, 158, 209, 245, 250, 298, 316, 328, 335, 339, 341, 342, 350
Vogel, Ezra, 447
Vuono, Carol, 120, 125

War. *See also name of participant.*
  casualties, 29, 53
  causes of, 151–163
  laws governing, 148–149, 188, 274–276, 363
  limited, 68–69
  role in international politics, 148–149, 443
  termination of, 28, 106, 231–232
  threat of, 117–124
Warming, global, 245, 433, 435
Warsaw Pact, 60, 200, 302

Wars for German Unification, 18–30
  causes of, 18–22
  destructiveness of, 29, 50, 53
  lessons of, 28–30, 232
Washington Naval Conference (1922), 187,
  189, 195
Weinberger, Caspar, 124
Westphalia, Peace of, 136, 137, 140
WHO (World Health Organization),
  385–387, 391, 392
Wilson, Woodrow, 57, 160, 184, 305, 339
Wittfogel, Karl, 388, 392
Wohlstetter, Albert, 174, 217
World Administrative Radio Conference,
  393–394
World Court. *See* International Court of
  Justice.
World government, 241–270, 301
World Peace Through World Law, 252–253

World police force, 257–259
World trade, 399–417
World War I
  causes of, 33–37, 135, 170–171
  destructiveness of, 31, 38, 50, 325
  lessons of, 43, 44, 45, 304–305
World War II
  causes of, 41–46, 135
  destructiveness of, 49, 50
  lessons of, 49–50, 333–334
Worst-case estimation, 171, 174
Wright, Quincy, 245, 246

Yemen, 83, 85, 323, 376
Yugoslavia, 40, 268, 347–348, 367, 442

Zaïre, 322
Zionism, 75–78, 79, 369